ACE Group Fitness Instructor Manual
A Guide for Fitness Professionals

Third Edition

American Council on Exercise®

Editors

Cedric X. Bryant, Ph.D., FACSM

Daniel J. Green

Sabrena Merrill, M.S.

AMERICAN COUNCIL ON EXERCISE

Library of Congress Catalog Card Number 2011904383

ISBN 978-1-890720-37-7
Copyright © 2011 American Council on Exercise® (ACE®)

F G H I

Distributed by:
American Council on Exercise
4851 Paramount Drive
San Diego, CA 92123
(858) 576-6500
FAX: (858) 576-6564
ACEfitness.org

Project Editor: Daniel J. Green

Technical Editors: Cedric X. Bryant, Ph.D., FACSM, & Sabrena Merrill, M.S.

Cover Design & Art Direction: Karen McGuire

Production: Nancy Garcia

Photography: Dennis Dal Covey

Index: Kathi Unger

Chapter Models: Opal Bruce, Angel Chelik, Chris Gagliardi, Jessica Matthews, Giselle Pineda

Acknowledgments: Thanks to the entire American Council on Exercise staff for their support and guidance through the process of creating this manual.

NOTICE

The fitness industry is ever-changing. As new research and clinical experience broaden our knowledge, changes in programming and standards are required. The authors and the publisher of this work have checked with sources believed to be reliable in their efforts to provide information that is complete and generally in accord with the standards accepted at the time of publication. However, in view of the possibility of human error or changes in industry standards, neither the authors nor the publisher nor any other party who has been involved in the preparation or publication of this work warrants that the information contained herein is in every respect accurate or complete, and they are not responsible for any errors or omissions or the results obtained from the use of such information. Readers are encouraged to confirm the information contained herein with other sources.

P16-009

Table of Contents

Reviewers

Barbara A. Brehm, Ed.D., is a professor of exercise and sport studies at Smith College, Northampton, Mass., where she teaches courses in stress management, nutrition, and health. She is also the director of the Smith Fitness Program for Faculty and Staff. Dr. Brehm writes extensively for fitness professionals and has received widespread recognition for the regular columns she wrote as a contributing editor for *Fitness Management* magazine. She is the co-author of *Applied Sports Medicine for Coaches,* and author of several other books, including *Successful Fitness Motivation Strategies.*

Kristin Fischer, M.S., is a continuing education provider and educator for ACE, as well as a Master Trainer for BOSU® and Gliding™. She is the president of KristinFischerFitness, serving as a personal trainer, group fitness instructor, and health educator. Fischer is an ACE subject matter expert and an exam development committee member. An ACE-certified group fitness instructor and personal trainer, Fischer has a master's of science degree in kinesiology from the University of Illinois and holds several specialty certifications.

Chris Freytag holds three ACE certifications and serves as Chairman of the Board of Directors for ACE. She received her bachelor's degree in journalism from the University of Wisconsin, Madison, and currently works as a practicing fitness professional as well as a health and fitness expert to many fitness, TV, and print-related companies. She has authored four books and created dozens of fitness workouts available on DVD and digital download. Freytag also writes for *ACE Certified News* and other fitness-industry publications.

Stephanie Harris, M.D., is a neurologist practicing in Eugene, Ore. She has been a group fitness instructor since 1992 and is an adjunct instructor in the Department of Physical Education and Recreation at the University of Oregon. Dr. Harris has participated on the ACE group fitness instructor role delineation and exam development committees and was awarded the ACE Group Fitness Instructor of the Year Award in 2004.

Fred Hoffman, M.ED., is the director of international services for the Club & Spa Synergy Group. He holds a master's degree in health education and is certified by ACSM and ACE. A consultant and master trainer for companies such as Batuka®, Reebok®, TRX®, and BOSU®, Hoffman has presented at conventions and trained instructors in nearly 50 countries on six continents. He is the recipient of the 2007 IDEA Fitness Instructor of the Year Award.

Reviewers

Karen B. Merrill, M.S., ATC, LMT, is a nationally certified athletic trainer, personal trainer, and massage therapist. She is the chairman of the board for Ho'ola Cancer Exercise Wellness Program, a charitable non-profit corporation, and the president of Body Resolve, Inc., a multifaceted fitness and wellness organization.

Jack Raglin, Ph.D., FACSM, is a professor and director of graduate studies in the department of kinesiology at Indiana University. He is a Fellow in the American Psychological Association, the American College of Sports Medicine, and the American Academy of Kinesiology.

Kimberly Spreen is the director of group fitness for Life Time Fitness and director of yoga for LifePower Yoga. She is a member of the IDEA Program Director Committee, one of Exercise TV's Star Trainers, as well as star of several exercise videos and co-creator/co-producer of EMPOWER! Fitness Events. Known for her passion, enthusiasm, and humor, Spreen travels the world as a presenter, motivational speaker, and continuing education provider.

Anne Irwin Tillinghast, M.A., C.S.C.S., ACSM-HFS, directs the fitness programs at Johns Hopkins University in Baltimore, Md., where she serves as the assistant director of athletics and recreation. She is a subject matter expert and faculty member for the American Council on Exercise, a member of the exam development committee, and certified as a group fitness instructor and personal trainer through ACE. Tillinghast holds a bachelor's degree in biological anthropology from SUNY Geneseo, and a master's degree in dance from UCLA.

Nancey Trevanian Tsai, M.D., is assistant professor of neurosurgery at the Medical University of South Carolina and serves on ACE's Board of Directors. She has been an ACE-certified personal trainer since 1996 and works with high-performance athletes as well as special populations.

Andi Wardinsky, M.S., is the group fitness manager for PRO Sports Club, a private health club with three locations based out of Bellevue, Wash. She has a bachelor's degree in sport science as well as a master's degree in physical education from the University of Idaho, and holds numerous fitness certifications. Wardinsky, an ACE-certified group fitness instructor and personal trainer, educates fitness professionals about the business of the fitness industry through local establishments, conferences, colleges, and universities. She is also an ACE exam development committee member.

Foreword

In the more than 25 years that the American Council on Exercise has been championing education and professionalism in the fitness industry, much has changed about the industry and, more specifically, group exercise instruction. What began as a means of improving health through the use of traditional dance and aerobic movements now includes classes ranging from such traditional fare as step training and kickboxing to boot-camp and sport-specific classes, not to mention the countless fusions and emerging modalities. Through it all, dance movements—and all the fun and benefits they yield—have remained a constant.

Another constant in this ever-changing field is the American Council on Exercise's core mission of enriching quality of life through safe and effective physical activity. ACE has established its vision for the future of the fitness industry and overall outlook for America's focus on healthy living. This vision involves inspiring, motivating, and encouraging people to make physical activity an integral part of their everyday lives. Group fitness instructors (GFIs) are in a perfect position to take action in support of the organization's goal to combat the obesity epidemic. Specifically, ACE is advocating greater collaboration with community leaders to develop and enhance exercise programs, encouraging neighbors to get more involved with each other and their communities, and rallying with other industry partners to create greater public access to fitness resources and federal funding to help support fitness initiatives on a local level all across the country.

In addition to teaching the basics of exercise programming and class leadership, this manual takes a more holistic approach to group fitness instruction, enabling GFIs to take advantage of the fact that they interact with so many fitness facility members each and every day. Knowing how the human body functions is not enough; modern fitness professionals must know how to motivate individuals by incorporating aspects of behavioral psychology into their classes, lead groups of exercisers by using teaching techniques suitable for multiple learning styles simultaneously, and modify workouts based on the specific needs of individuals ranging from pregnant women to older adults with osteoporosis.

Clearly, group exercise instruction is far more complex than it once was, but the goal of contemporary Body Pump™ routines is the same as it was during those early Jazzercise™ classes—to positively influence people to have an enriching relationship with physical activity and develop a lifelong fitness habit. The overall goal of combating obesity may seem daunting, but GFIs can work toward that ideal one participant at a time.

Scott Goudeseune
President & CEO
American Council on Exercise

Introduction

The American Council on Exercise is proud to introduce the Third Edition of its *ACE Group Fitness Instructor Manual.* This textbook, which was written by 16 industry experts specializing in everything from health behavior psychology to business and law, will help group fitness instructors (GFIs) design safe and effective exercise classes for a variety of populations performing any of a number of types of exercise.

As with all ACE manuals, this new manual offers the most current, complete picture of the instructional techniques and professional responsibilities group fitness instructors need to teach safe and effective exercise. Designed to serve as a study aid for the Group Fitness Instructor Certification Exam, it is also a comprehensive resource for both new and veteran instructors. It is important to note that this manual assumes an understanding of the material presented in *ACE's Essentials of Exercise Science for Fitness Professionals.*

The manual begins by defining the ACE-certified GFI, including the scope of practice and possible avenues of career development. **Chapter 1: Who Is the ACE-certified Group Fitness Instructor?** also covers the unique place that GFIs hold in the allied healthcare continuum and the recognition that the ACE certification has received from the fitness, health, and education communities, as well as the Department of Labor.

Chapter 2: Principles of Pre-class Preparation and Participant Monitoring and Evaluation represents a new approach to these topics. The author has narrowed the focus of this content to feature only those assessment and monitoring techniques that are truly practical in a group setting and are commonplace in the industry. Adhering to the concepts presented in this chapter will help limit potential areas of liability and allow the GFI to provide outstanding and safe exercise experiences for all participants.

The next two chapters discuss the topics of programming and leading group exercise classes. **Chapter 3: Group Exercise Program Design** divides a class into its various segments— warm-up, cardiorespiratory, muscular strength and endurance, and flexibility—and presents guidelines and practical tips for each. **Chapter 4: Teaching a Group Exercise Class** will help GFIs meet their participants' individual needs through effective program implementation and teaching techniques and strategies. Cueing and musicality are also discussed.

Programming a balanced class and teaching it well certainly has a positive impact on participant adherence, but **Chapter 5: Principles of Adherence and Motivation** takes things further by defining the traits of an ideal GFI and offering specific strategies that will build adherence. Behavioral change theories are also presented that will arm GFIs with user-friendly tips to help participants make lifelong behavior modifications.

The next two chapters address the challenge of teaching classes with participants with special needs. **Chapter 6: Exercise and Special Populations** covers everything from asthma to arthritis, and diabetes to multiple sclerosis. Guidelines and teaching tips are offered for special populations, as well as for older adults and youth. The complexities of pregnancy's impact on health and a woman's ability to safely exercise warrant extended coverage. **Chapter 7: Exercise and Pregnancy** discusses the physiological adaptations that occur during pregnancy as well as the risks associated with certain movements and postures. Very specific programming recommendations are offered as well.

Chapter 8: The Prevention and Management of Common Injuries teaches GFIs how to manage both pre-existing injuries and those that occur during the course of an exercise class. While diagnosis and treatment is outside the scope of practice for most fitness professionals, GFIs will often lead classes with individuals who are recovering from injury, and therefore must be able to modify movements accordingly. **Chapter 9: Emergency Procedures** covers medical emergencies and injuries that a GFI may encounter during a career in the fitness industry, from asthma attacks and hypoglycemia to seizures and head injuries.

Chapter 10: The Business of Group Fitness is an all-new topic in this edition. By introducing the "group fitness trifecta"—education, teamwork, and class value—this chapter enables GFIs to define and enhance their value and overall standing in a fitness facility by teaching them how facility management measures the value of their employees. In addition, improving teamwork among the group fitness staff will enhance the experience of facility members.

Chapter 11: Legal and Professional Responsibilities explains basic legal concepts that concern GFIs and shows how these concepts can be applied to reduce injuries to program participants. It is important to remember that taking proper action can reduce the likelihood that a lawsuit will be filed, and can mitigate potential damages.

Finally, the appendices present ACE's Code of Ethics, the Group Fitness Instructor Certification Exam Content Outline, and the ACE Position Statement on Nutritional Supplements. In addition, the appendices include an introduction to some of the group fitness specialty areas available in the ever-changing fitness industry—traditional aerobics, step training, kickboxing fitness, group indoor cycling, aquatic exercise, fitness yoga, Pilates, stability ball training, group strength training, and fitness boot camp and sports conditioning.

Cedric X. Bryant, Ph.D., FACSM
Chief Science Officer

Daniel J. Green
Project Editor

Sabrena Merrill, M.S.
Exercise Scientist

Studying for the ACE Group Fitness Instructor Exam

ACE has put together a comprehensive package of study tools that should serve as your core materials while preparing for the ACE Certification Exam. Using the following study tips will optimize your chances of success.

Begin by studying *ACE's Essentials of Exercise Science for Fitness Professionals.* This book covers the foundational knowledge that you will need to take full advantage of the information presented in the *ACE Group Fitness Instructor Manual,* Third Edition. The authors of the *ACE Group Fitness Instructor Manual* wrote with the assumption that readers had already mastered the content presented in the *Essentials* book. For example, the exercise analyses presented in **Chapter 4: Teaching a Group Exercise Class** assume an understanding of human anatomy and the physiology of training, both of which are presented in the *Essentials* book. If at any point in your reading you come across a topic that you are not entirely confident with, revisit the *Essentials* book to sharpen your understanding.

Each chapter of *ACE's Essentials of Exercise Science for Fitness Professionals* includes a Study Guide that will help you identify areas that require additional study time and more focused attention. In addition, multiple-choice questions are included that mirror the style and types of questions that are included on the ACE certification exams.

Review the Exam Content Outline, which is presented in Appendix B of this book. This document was created by active members of the fitness industry and is the basis from which the ACE Group Fitness Instructor Exam is written. Using this document to target your studies and identify areas of weakness will be a powerful study tool.

Use the *Master the Manual* to focus your studies as you work your way through the *ACE Group Fitness Instructor Manual.* The *Master the Manual* uses the same format as the Study Guides in the *Essentials* book, with the addition of chapter summaries that point out key topics, and will be an invaluable tool as you prepare for the ACE Exam.

Other ACE study materials include the following:

- *Flashcards:* ACE's flashcards focus on foundational anatomy and physiology topics and feature detailed illustrations that will help strengthen your understanding of these essential topics.
- *Companion DVD for the ACE Group Fitness Instructor Manual:* This DVD, which is entitled *Essentials of Group Fitness Instruction* and features well-respected group fitness expert and international presenter Lawrence Biscontini, presents many of the critical elements covered in the manual in a user-friendly, practical format. This will be a valuable tool throughout your career in the fitness industry.

- *Glossary and Index:* Keep an eye out for boldface terms as you read. Each of these important terms is included in the book's glossary as a quick reference whenever a new concept is introduced. If you need more in-depth information on the topic, check the indexes of both the *ACE Group Fitness Instructor Manual* and the *Essentials* book.

- *www.acefitness.org:* The ACE website offers everything from calculators using equations commonly utilized in the fitness setting to online continuing education courses—which means that it will remain a valuable resource for tools and information throughout your fitness career.

- *Online Group Fitness Instructor Certification Exam Study Assistance:* Sign up at www.acefitness.org/getcertified/studyassistanceprogram-gfi.aspx to take advantage of ACE's free Study Coach Program, which offers a study timeline and weekly email reminders and tips that will guide you in your studies, as well as an ongoing Exam Preparation blog.

- *ACE Resource Center:* ACE's Resource Center specialists are available to answer your questions as you prepare for the exam. The Resource Center can be reached at (800) 825-3636, ext. 796.

Sabrena Merrill, M.S., has been actively involved in the fitness industry since 1987, successfully operating her own personal-training business and teaching group exercise classes. Merrill is a former full-time faculty member in the Kinesiology and Physical Education Department at California State University, Long Beach. She has a bachelor's degree in exercise science as well as a master's degree in physical education/biomechanics from the University of Kansas. Merrill, an ACE-certified Personal Trainer and Group Fitness Instructor, is an author, educator, and fitness consultant who remains very active within the industry.

CHAPTER ONE

Who Is the ACE-certified Group Fitness Instructor?

By Sabrena Merrill

Since the 1980s, group fitness programs have been a standard amenity offered at most commercial fitness facilities. While the equipment, choreography, and modalities of group exercise continue to change and evolve, the attraction of these programs has remained constant, as new and veteran exercisers alike seek refreshing and motivating approaches to physical activity. As group fitness programs have evolved, so too has the group fitness instructor. Once a pastime for exercise enthusiasts, group fitness instruction has become an important profession that provides elements of social interaction and fun to large numbers of participants who might not otherwise become engaged in physical activity.

Often a group fitness instructor (GFI) migrates into teaching because of his or her passion for exercise and for helping others. To be successful, a GFI must have the desire and ability to educate and motivate participants. Clearly, GFIs have to possess characteristics of extroversion and leadership as well as the knowledge to safely and effectively teach and modify exercise for a variety of participants.

Decades ago, when the traditional form of group fitness (called dance exercise or "aerobics") became popular, the cultural value placed on the benefits of regular exercise was just beginning to take hold in the United States. Due to ongoing research on the health advantages of engaging in consistent physical activity, there have been several published recommendations on the topic. After a comprehensive review of the research linking physical activity to health, the U.S. Department of Health & Human Services released the *2008 Physical Activity Guidelines for Americans,* the first comprehensive guidelines on physical activity to be issued by the U.S. government. These guidelines list the following major research findings regarding physical activity and its associated health benefits:

- Regular physical activity reduces the risk of many adverse health outcomes.
- Some physical activity is better than none.
- For most health outcomes, additional benefits occur as the amount of physical activity increases through higher intensity, greater frequency, and/or longer duration.
- Most health benefits occur with at least 150 minutes a week of moderate-intensity physical activity, such as brisk walk-

ing. Additional benefits occur with more physical activity.
- Both **aerobic** (endurance) and muscle-strengthening (resistance) physical activity are beneficial.
- Health benefits occur for children and adolescents, young and middle-aged adults, older adults, and those in every studied racial and ethnic group.
- The health benefits of physical activity occur for people with disabilities.
- The benefits of physical activity far outweigh the possibility of adverse outcomes.

An increased public awareness of regular exercise as a component of a healthy lifestyle, as well as the proliferation of a savvier, more educated fitness consumer, has led to the need for competent exercise leaders. The ACE-certified GFI provides safe and effective group fitness leadership to participants ranging in age from youth to older adults, and ranging in health and fitness status from **overweight** and **sedentary** to athletic.

A GFI has various employment scenarios from which to choose. Most GFIs opt to teach classes on a part-time basis. Typically, a GFI leads by showing the participants how to perform the exercises, which exacts a physical toll on the instructor. Thus, teaching numerous classes each day is probably not the most healthful practice. Instead of exposing the body to daily hours of exercise instruction, many GFIs choose to teach one or two classes several days per week. Since fitness facilities often schedule group fitness classes during times when a majority of the general population is off work (such as early mornings, lunch time, and evenings), teaching part-time classes is a viable option for GFIs who also have other, non-fitness related occupations. It is also becoming more commonplace for clubs to offer more robust schedules during the day to accommodate stay-at-home moms and those who work at home and have flexibility in their schedules. In this respect, GFIs who have other occupations and do not work traditional daytime hours also have an opportunity to teach part-time.

The prospect of becoming a professional group fitness instructor can be very appealing, especially to those who are eager to help others become healthier and achieve their fitness goals. Leading groups of people with safe and effective exercise instruction requires knowledge of exercise science along with the ability to effectively demonstrate and communicate how to perform specific movements. In addition, a GFI must also have a sincere desire to help each individual in class, regardless of the participant's fitness level, skills, or abilities. A GFI must always be cognizant of the various levels of the participants and take special care to avoid excluding anyone from the group activities.

It is not uncommon for a first-time attendee to join a class and have no idea of the intensity level or complexity of the exercise format. In these situations, a GFI must take measures to treat the new person fairly, demonstrate ample modifications, and make him or her feel successful about completing the class while effectively challenging the other class participants. Successful GFIs are leaders who genuinely act to teach and motivate their class participants instead of simply performing in front of a captive audience.

Full-time GFIs are uncommon. The reasons for this have to do with the physicality of the profession and the unique aspects of managing a group fitness program schedule. First, the volume of exercise required for an instructor to teach full-time (e.g., more than four to five classes per day, every day) is extremely taxing on the body. Second, a group fitness program would essentially be devastated if an instructor who taught full-time became injured or requested time off. Individuals who claim group fitness to be their full-time occupation typically manage a group fitness department in a commercial facility. It is common for group fitness coordinators to share in the responsibility of substitute teaching classes that need to be covered, as well as teach their own classes, while simultaneously managing the group fitness program.

Many GFIs who want to make a full-time commitment to helping people create health and wellness through exercise have successfully combined the roles of the group fitness instructor and personal trainer. This increasingly popular career path is emerging as fitness professionals perform both one-on-one fitness training and group instruction. This scenario has numerous benefits in that it allows fitness instructors to develop relationships with more potential clients/participants, is an effective cross-promotion tactic whereby group fitness participants can be informed by their instructor about personal training and personal-training clients can be educated about the benefits of group fitness by their trainer, and provides the fitness professional with an option for full-time employment that offers variety and a good income. Lastly, the combination of group fitness instruction and personal training allows the fitness professional to devote eight or more hours a day to working in an exercise environment without experiencing the potential for overtraining that often comes with teaching too many group fitness classes in succession.

The Future of Group Fitness

The U.S. Department of Labor (DOL), Bureau of Labor Statistics (2010), refers to the professionals in the fitness industry as Fitness Workers, with Group Exercise Instructors classified as a primary profession within the industry. The DOL defines the nature of the job of group exercise instructors as working to "conduct group exercise sessions that usually include aerobic exercise, stretching, and muscle conditioning. Cardiovascular conditioning classes often are set to music. Instructors select the music and choreograph a corresponding exercise sequence." The DOL goes on to state that "group exercise instructors are responsible for ensuring that their classes are motivating, safe, and challenging, yet not too difficult for the participants."

Expected Growth in Fitness Worker Jobs

According to the DOL, employment of fitness workers is projected to increase by 29% between 2008 and 2018. This expected increase is much faster than the average for all occupations, and is attributed to a number of factors, including the following:

- Increasing numbers of baby boomers who want to stay healthy, physically fit, and independent
- Reduction in the number of physical-education programs in schools
- Growing concerns about childhood obesity
- Increasing club memberships among young adults concerned about physical fitness
- An aging population seeking relief from arthritis and other ailments through individualized exercise, **yoga,** and **Pilates**
- A need to replace workers who leave fitness occupations each year

Group Fitness Instructor Qualifications

See "Recognition From the Department of Labor" on page 15 for the DOL's statement regarding the importance of obtaining a quality group fitness instructor certification.

The Allied Healthcare Continuum

The allied healthcare continuum is composed of health professionals who are credentialed through certifications, registrations, and/or licensure and provide services to identify, prevent, and treat diseases and disorders (Figure 1-1). Physicians are at the top of the allied healthcare pyramid, evaluating patients to diagnose ailments and implement treatment plans that can include medication, surgery, rehabilitation, or other actions. Physicians are assisted in their efforts by nurses, physician assistants, and a number of other credentialed technicians. When ailments or treatment plans fall outside their areas of expertise, physicians refer patients to specialists for specific medical evaluations, physical or occupational therapy, psychological counseling, dietary planning, and/or exercise programming.

Physicians and nurses teach patients the importance of implementing their treatment plans. **Physical therapists** and **occupational therapists** lead patients through therapeutic exercise and teach them to perform additional exercises at home to facilitate rehabilitation. **Athletic trainers** teach athletes exercises to prevent injury and take them through therapeutic exercises following injury. **Registered dietitians** teach clients proper nutrition through recipes, meal plans, food-preparation methods, and implementation of specialized diets. While these professionals might also give patients or clients guidelines for general exercise (e.g., "try to walk up to 30 minutes per day, most days of the week"), few of them actually teach clients how to exercise effectively. This is where fitness professionals, including GFIs, hold a unique position in the allied healthcare continuum.

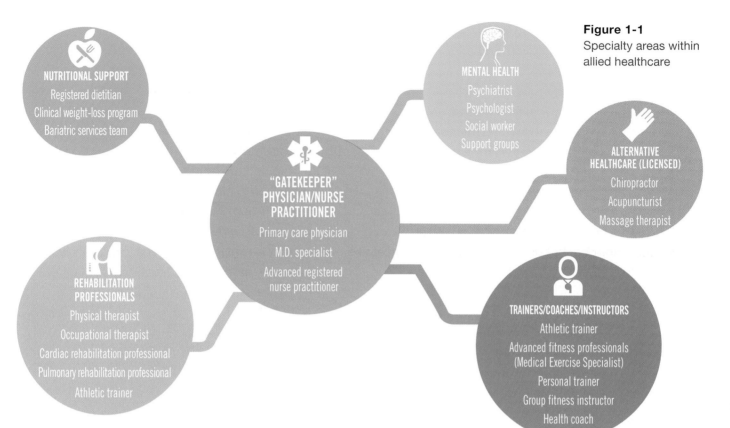

Figure 1-1
Specialty areas within allied healthcare

NUTRITIONAL SUPPORT
Registered dietitian
Clinical weight-loss program
Bariatric services team

MENTAL HEALTH
Psychiatrist
Psychologist
Social worker
Support groups

ALTERNATIVE HEALTHCARE (LICENSED)
Chiropractor
Acupuncturist
Massage therapist

"GATEKEEPER" PHYSICIAN/NURSE PRACTITIONER
Primary care physician
M.D. specialist
Advanced registered nurse practitioner

REHABILITATION PROFESSIONALS
Physical therapist
Occupational therapist
Cardiac rehabilitation professional
Pulmonary rehabilitation professional
Athletic trainer

TRAINERS/COACHES/INSTRUCTORS
Athletic trainer
Advanced fitness professionals (Medical Exercise Specialist)
Personal trainer
Group fitness instructor
Health coach

The majority of GFIs will work with apparently healthy participants, helping them improve fitness and health. In all cases, it is crucial for the fitness professional to stay within the boundaries of his or her education, certification, and legal **scope of practice.**

The ACE Group Fitness Instructor Certification

The decision to pursue certification as a group fitness instructor is an important step in being recognized as a competent professional. The ACE Group Fitness Instructor Certification Program was developed to assess candidate competency in planning and leading group exercise sessions to enhance the general well-being and exercise skills of participants. Candidates who achieve a passing score on the ACE Group Fitness Instructor Certification Exam meet or exceed the level of competency required to

work as a professional group fitness instructor with minimum supervision. In the credentialing world, this threshold of professional competence is referred to as the "minimum competency" required for a person to work in the profession. The primary purpose of a certification is always to protect the public from harm by assessing if the professional meets established levels of competence in the knowledge, skills, and abilities necessary to perform the job in a safe and effective manner. For the professional, a certification can separate him or her from others who have not proven themselves to be at the same level of competence.

Fitness professionals who earn the ACE Group Fitness Instructor Certification are competent to work as professional group fitness instructors performing exercise leadership for healthy individuals in group settings.

By earning an ACE Group Fitness Instructor Certification, the professional has proven his or her competence in applying knowledge to make safe and effective exercise-programming decisions in a variety of class situations, while minimizing exercise participant risk and exposure to harm (e.g., physical, emotional, psychological, financial, or other harm).

Defining "Scope of Practice"

A scope of practice defines the legal range of services that professionals in a given field can provide, the settings in which those services can be provided, and the guidelines or parameters that must be followed. Many factors go into defining a scope of practice, including the education, training, and certifications or licenses required to work in a given field, the laws and organizations governing the specific profession, and the laws and organizations governing complementary professions within the same field. Most laws defining a profession are determined and regulated by state regulatory agencies, including licensure. As a result, the scope of practice for licensed practitioners can vary from state to state in a given profession. In addition, most professions have organizations that serve as governing bodies within the profession that set eligibility requirements to enter educational programs or sit for certification exams, and that establish codes for professional conduct and disciplinary procedures for professionals who break these codes.

The laws, rules, and regulations that govern a profession are established for the protection of the public. The laws governing a GFI's scope of practice and the ramifications faced by instructors who provide services that fall outside the defined scope are detailed in Chapter 11. The eligibility and certification requirements to work within this legal scope of practice are defined by the professional organizations that offer group fitness instructor certifications. These organizations also establish codes of ethical conduct and mandate that they are upheld by certified professionals and applicants in all actions related to group fitness instruction. It is crucial for practitioners in every industry to be aware of the scope of practice for their given profession to ensure that they practice within the realm of the specific education, experience, and demonstrated competency of their credential.

Scope of Practice for ACE-certified Group Fitness Instructors

The ACE-certified Group Fitness Instructor scope of practice is presented on page 7. ACE-certified Group Fitness Instructors must work within this defined scope of practice to provide effective exercise leadership for their class participants, gain and maintain support from the healthcare community, and avoid the legal ramifications of providing services outside their professional scope.

GFIs should never provide services that are outside their defined scope of practice. For example, a GFI may be asked nutrition questions by participants wanting to reduce weight and/or **body fat.** GFIs can help participants with their weight-loss goals by leading effective exercise classes that bring about positive **body composition** changes and helping them to adopt more healthful behaviors. This can include showing participants how to utilize the tools available at www.ChooseMyPlate.gov or educating them about the recommendations in the *Dietary Guidelines for Americans* to help them gain a better understanding of healthful foods and

ACE-certified Group Fitness Instructor Scope of Practice

The ACE-certified Group Fitness Instructor is a fitness professional who has met all requirements of the American Council on Exercise to develop and implement fitness programs for individuals who have no apparent physical limitations or special medical needs. The ACE-certified Group Fitness Instructor realizes that group fitness instruction is a service industry focused on helping people enhance fitness and modify risk factors for disease to improve health. As members of the allied healthcare continuum with a primary focus on prevention, ACE-certified Group Fitness Instructors have a scope of practice that includes:

- Developing and implementing exercise programs that are safe, effective, and appropriate for individuals who are apparently healthy or have medical clearance to exercise
- Conducting pre-exercise health screenings and stratifying risk for cardiovascular disease with participants in order to determine the need for referral and identify contraindications for exercise
- Administering appropriate fitness assessments based on the participant's health screening, current fitness, lifestyle factors, and goals utilizing research-proven and published protocols
- Assisting participants in setting and achieving realistic fitness goals
- Teaching correct exercise methods and progressions through demonstration, explanation, and proper cueing and exercise leadership techniques
- Instructing class participants in how to properly monitor exercise intensity using heart rate, perceived exertion, and/or ventilatory response
- Empowering individuals to begin and adhere to their exercise programs using guidance, support, motivation, lapse-prevention strategies, and effective feedback
- Assessing the class environment by evaluating/monitoring the room and equipment before and during each class session
- Educating participants about fitness- and health-related topics to help them in adopting healthful behaviors that facilitate long-term success
- Protecting participant confidentiality according to the Health Insurance Portability and Accountability Act (HIPAA) and related regional and national laws
- Always acting with professionalism, respect, and integrity
- Recognizing what is within the scope of practice and always referring participants to other healthcare professionals when appropriate
- Being prepared for emergency situations and responding appropriately when they occur

and make better choices (U.S. Department of Agriculture, 2010). Participants who are looking for more detailed nutritional programming, such as specific meal plans, recipes, or recommendations for nutritional supplements, should be referred to a registered dietitian, as these services are beyond the scope of practice of GFIs and are in the legal domain of services provided by registered dietitians in most states.

Knowledge, Skills, and Abilities of the ACE-certified Group Fitness Instructor

The ACE Group Fitness Instructor Certification is designed for fitness professionals wanting to provide general exercise leadership to apparently healthy individuals in a group setting. The certification program is continually evaluated to ensure that it is consistent with the most current research and industry standards. In addition, every five years a group of industry experts analyzes the specific job requirements for GFIs to update the outline of tasks, knowledge, and skills required to perform the job of group fitness instruction effectively. After being validated by several thousand ACE-certified Group Fitness Instructors, this outline is published as the ACE Group Fitness Instructor Exam Content Outline (Appendix B), which serves as the blueprint for the ACE Group Fitness Instructor Certification Exam and provides a template for candidates preparing for the exam. It is also a written job description of the knowledge, skills, and abilities required to be an effective ACE-certified Group Fitness Instructor.

Education and Experience

There is no single course of study for individuals looking to enter the profession of group fitness instruction. To become an ACE-certified Group Fitness Instructor, a candidate must show that he or she is able to apply the knowledge required to be a safe and effective GFI by passing the ACE Group Fitness Instructor Certification Exam. There are many paths to reaching this goal, including self-study using preparatory materials from ACE or other sources that cover the ACE Group Fitness Instructor Certification Exam Content Outline, preparatory courses or workshops delivered live or online, educational internships, professional experience, and college courses. Each candidate must select his or her own path based on time, financial resources, learning styles, and personal factors. As a general rule, ACE recommends that candidates allow three to six months of study time to adequately prepare for the ACE Group Fitness Instructor Certification Exam.

The growth in the fitness industry has led numerous colleges and universities to offer programs to help students prepare to become qualified fitness professionals. These programs help students prepare for certification exams by offering courses that teach the specific knowledge and skills required to become personal trainers or group fitness instructors, or to work with individuals who have special needs. ACE has an Educational Partnership Program that provides colleges, universities, and technical/professional schools with curricula, instructor materials, and discounts to students preparing for ACE certification programs. These programs are not required to earn an ACE certification, but they provide students with helpful instruction from people with advanced degrees and experience in the field. For more information on educational institutions participating in the ACE Educational Partnership Program, visit www.acefitness. org/university/default.aspx.

Preparation and Testing

The knowledge, skills, and abilities tested include developing and enhancing **rapport** with participants, providing appropriate class programming and design, developing and applying appropriate and effective group instructional methods, and always acting in a professional manner within the GFI's scope of practice.

Fitness professionals interested in sitting for the ACE Group Fitness Instructor Certification Exam should download the *ACE Certification Candidate Handbook* from the ACE website (www.acefitness.org/getcertified/pdfs/ Certification-Exam-Candidate-Handbook. pdf). This complimentary handbook explains how ACE certification exams are developed, what the candidate should expect, and the procedures for earning and maintaining an ACE certification. The handbook also includes explanations about the multiple-choice and scenario-based questions found on the ACE certification exams, along with sample questions to help candidates understand the difference between questions that assess recall knowledge and those that assess applied knowledge. In addition, the handbook provides candidates with test-taking strategies and a list of available study resources.

Professional Responsibilities and Ethics

The primary purpose of professional certification programs is to protect the public from harm (e.g., physical, emotional, psychological, and financial). Professionals who earn an ACE Group Fitness Instructor Certification validate their capabilities and enhance their value to employers, class participants, and other healthcare providers. This does not happen simply because the individual has a new title. This recognition is given because the ACE credential itself upholds rigorous standards established for assessing an individual's competence in making safe and effective exercise-programming decisions. ACE has established a professional ethical code of conduct and disciplinary procedures, and ACE certifications have all received third-party accreditation from the **National Commission for Certifying Agencies (NCCA).**

To help ACE-certified Professionals understand the conduct expected from them as healthcare professionals in protecting the public from harm, ACE has developed the ACE Code of Ethics (Appendix A). This code of conduct serves as a guide for ethical and professional practices for all ACE-certified Professionals. This code is enforced through the ACE Professional Practices and Disciplinary Procedures (www.acefitness.org/getcertified/certified-code.aspx). All ACE-certified Professionals and candidates for ACE certification must be familiar with, and

comply with, the ACE Code of Ethics and ACE Professional Practices and Disciplinary Procedures.

ACE Code of Ethics

The ACE Code of Ethics governs the ethical and professional conduct of ACE-certified Professionals when working with clients/participants, the public, or other health and fitness professionals.

Every individual who registers for an ACE certification exam must agree to uphold the ACE Code of Ethics throughout the exam process and as a professional, should he or she earn an ACE certification. Exam candidates and ACE-certified Group Fitness Instructors must have a comprehensive understanding of the code and the consequences and public harm that can come from violating each of its principles.

ACE Professional Practices and Disciplinary Procedures

The ACE Professional Practices and Disciplinary Procedures are intended to inform ACE-certified Professionals, candidates for ACE certification, and the public about the ACE application and certification standards relative to professional conduct and disciplinary procedures. ACE may revoke or otherwise take action with regard to the application or certification of an individual in the case of:

- Ineligibility for certification
- Irregularity in connection with any certification examination
- Unauthorized possession, use, access, or distribution of certification examinations, score reports, trademarks, logos, written materials, answer sheets, certificates, certificant or applicant files, or other confidential or proprietary ACE documents or materials (registered or otherwise)

- Material misrepresentation or fraud in any statement to ACE or to the public, including but not limited to statements made to assist the applicant, certificant, or another to apply for, obtain, or retain certification
- Any physical, mental, or emotional condition of either temporary or permanent nature, including, but not limited to, substance abuse, which impairs or has the potential to impair competent and objective professional performance
- Negligent and/or intentional misconduct in professional work, including, but not limited to, physical or emotional abuse, disregard for safety, or the unauthorized release of confidential information
- The timely conviction, plea of guilty, or plea of *nolo contendere* ("no contest") in connection with a felony or misdemeanor that is directly related to public health and/or fitness instruction or education, and that impairs competent and objective professional performance. These include, but are not limited to, rape, sexual abuse of a participant, actual or threatened use of a weapon of violence, or the prohibited sale, distribution, or possession with intent to distribute of a controlled substance.
- Failure to meet the requirements for certification or recertification

ACE has developed a three-tiered disciplinary process of review, hearing, and appeals to ensure fair and unbiased examination of alleged violation(s) of the Application and Certification Standards in order to (1) determine the merit of allegations and (2) impose appropriate sanctions as necessary to protect the public and the integrity of the certification process.

Certification Period and Renewal

ACE certifications are valid for two years from the date earned, expiring on the last day of the month. To renew certification for a new two-year cycle, ACE-certified Professionals must complete a minimum of 20 hours of continuing education credits (2.0 CECs) and maintain a current certificate in **cardiopulmonary resuscitation (CPR)** and, if living in North America, **automated external defibrillation (AED)**.

Continuing education is a standard requirement in healthcare to help ensure that professionals stay up to date with the latest research in their respective fields for the protection of the public. Given the dynamic nature of the fitness industry and the rapidly advancing research in exercise science, it is imperative for fitness professionals to complete continuing education on a regular basis. By completing continuing education, ACE-certified professionals can stay current with the latest findings in exercise science and keep their services in line with the most recent guidelines for fitness and healthcare.

ACE encourages its certified professionals to complete additional continuing education as necessary to help advance their careers and enhance the services they provide. Each year, the ACE Academy approves thousands of continuing education courses, providing ACE-certified Professionals with many options for maintaining their credentials and advancing their careers. ACE-certified Professionals holding more than one ACE certification can apply the CECs they earn to each of their current certifications.

ACE-certified Professionals are encouraged to renew their certifications before they expire. ACE offers a six-month extension of the renewal period for professionals who go beyond the deadline, but it is merely a grace period for certification renewal, not an extension of the actual certification. During this grace period, the certification is expired and will only become current again once renewed. The ramifications for ACE-certified Professionals that allow their certifications to expire can include not being able to advertise the fact that they hold the ACE certification until it is renewed, discontinued professional liability insurance, and loss of employment. Once the grace period expires, the only way to "renew" a certification is to retake and pass the exam.

Participant Privacy

It is not uncommon for class participants to share confidential information, such as medical conditions or health concerns, with a GFI through conversation. In addition, some GFIs collect health-history information prior to the start of specific programs, such as a six-week boot-camp class. GFIs should maintain a level of security for each participant's personal information. Failure to do so could prove detrimental for the participant and the participant–instructor relationship, and may violate the ACE Code of Ethics and state or federal privacy laws.

To help prevent violations of participant privacy, ACE-certified Professionals should become familiar with, and adhere to, the **Health Insurance Portability and Accountability Act (HIPAA),** which addresses the use and disclosure of individuals' protected health information. By following HIPAA regulations, GFIs can maintain the confidentiality of each participant's protected health information according to the same rules that govern most healthcare professions. More details about participant privacy and keeping participants' protected health information secure can be found in Chapter 11 and Appendix A.

Referral

It is important for healthcare professionals, including GFIs, to understand their profes-sional qualifications and boundaries, and to always refer participants who require services outside their scope of practice to the appropriate qualified healthcare professionals. Doing so ensures that participants are provided with appropriate care from qualified providers and prevents healthcare professionals from offering services that they do not have the education, training, credentials, and/or legal right to offer.

Sometimes a GFI will need to investigate a bit further to determine if referral is warranted. For example, if a participant wants to lose more weight than would be advisable based on his or her current body composition, the GFI can first explain healthy body-fat ranges, point out that the participant's body composition is within the normal range, and work with him or her to determine a safe and achievable weight-loss goal. However, if the participant feels that he or she still wants to aim for the original weight-loss goal, the group fitness instructor should refer him or her to a registered dietitian who has experience with body image and related issues.

Developing a Referral Network

It is important for a GFI to develop a network of referral sources to meet the varying needs of his or her participants. Instructors should identify allied health professionals who are reputable and aspire to the same professional standards as an ACE-certified Group Fitness Instructor. Potential referral sources include the following:

- Instructors of classes outside a GFI's expertise (e.g., yoga, **tai chi, qigong,** and aquatic exercise)
- Personal trainers
- Support groups (e.g., cardiac rehabilitation, cancer survivors, and Overeaters Anonymous)
- Massage therapists
- Registered dietitians
- Smoking-cessation programs

As the group fitness instructor develops a referral network, it is important to research instructors, programs, or organizations before recommending any programs or services to a participant. Do they have the proper licensure or certification? Can they provide a list of references? How many years of experience do they have? The GFI does not want to jeopardize his or her reputation by referring participants to substandard health and fitness "professionals." With proper networking, the GFI may also gain referrals from the other health and fitness professionals within the network.

Safety

All fitness professionals should do what they can to minimize risk for everyone in the fitness facility. This includes having equipment that is properly spaced and in good working order; having racks, shelves, hooks, or other storage spots for portable equipment, including stability balls and dumbbells; and ensuring that floors and equipment are cleaned, maintained, and free from clutter and moisture. GFIs should also pay attention to the cleanliness of the facility, including the availability of wipes or other sanitizers for cleaning equipment following usage. An emergency plan, AED, and appropriate first-aid supplies are essential in case an injury or incident occurs.

Even with the best risk-management program, injuries and incidents can still occur. As such, ACE recommends that all ACE-certified Professionals carry professional liability insurance for protection in the event a participant is injured during a class (see Chapter 11).

Supplements

Supplements are not regulated by the U.S. Food and Drug Administration (FDA), so their strength, purity, safety, and effects are not guaranteed. Some supplements can cause adverse interactions and complications with other prescribed medications or congenital problems. Still, the supplement market constitutes a multimillion-dollar industry. The lure of this profitable revenue stream, coupled with consumer interest for a quick fix, leads some fitness facilities to sell nutritional supplements as a profit center. It is not illegal for fitness facilities to sell commercial nutritional supplements, but it is irresponsible for them to provide supplement recommendations without staff that have the expertise and legal qualifications required to give such advice (e.g., registered dietitians and medical doctors). Facilities selling dietary supplements are assuming a huge liability risk in the event that a member has a negative reaction to a supplement recommended by a staff member who is not legally qualified to do so (see Chapter 11).

Some fitness professionals amass substantial knowledge about dietary supplements. However, they are no more qualified to recommend these supplements to clients or class participants than they are to recommend or prescribe medications. Unless a GFI is also a registered dietitian or a physician, he or she does not have the expertise or legal qualifications necessary to recommend supplements. The ACE Position Statement on Nutrition Scope of Practice for Fitness Professionals can be found in Appendix E.

GFIs should, however, educate themselves about supplements. Class participants often ask GFIs about supplements, thinking that supplements are necessary to achieve fitness, weight loss, or other goals. The GFI can help the participant understand that fitness goals can be reached without supplements and that supplements can have negative and potentially harmful side effects.

Ramifications of Offering Services Outside the Scope of Practice

To achieve their fitness goals, individuals must adopt healthful behaviors that can include a regular exercise program, eating a more healthful diet, and initiating lifestyle changes to decrease stress. An ACE-certified Group Fitness Instructor is qualified to help participants with general exercise programming needs and basic nutrition information based on the USDA's *Dietary Guidelines for Americans* (2010).

ACE-certified Professionals offering services that are within the legal realm of another healthcare profession are in violation of the ACE Code of Ethics and are at risk for potential legal prosecution. For example, if a participant tells an instructor that he or she experiences muscle soreness following group strength classes, the instructor can provide education about the benefits of massage, but cannot perform hands-on massage therapy for the participant, as this would constitute the practice of massage without a license.

Accreditation of Allied Healthcare Credentials Through the NCCA

Healthcare professionals recognize the important role that physical activity plays in improving and maintaining good health. Unfortunately, the lack of professional credentials held by some individuals working in fitness has slowed the acceptance of fitness professionals as legitimate members of the allied healthcare team by some healthcare providers. As a result, ACE and other leading professional fitness organizations have earned third-party accreditation from the NCCA for their fitness certification programs. For a complete list of NCCA-accredited fitness certification organizations, visit www.credentialingexcellence.org.

The NCCA is the accreditation body of the Institute for Credentialing Excellence (ICE) [formerly known as the National Organization

for Competency Assurance (NOCA)] a nonprofit, 501(c)(3) organization. Formed in 1977, ICE originated as the National Commission for Health Certifying Agencies (NCHCA). Originally funded through the U.S. Department of Health & Human Services, the NCHCA had a mission to develop standards for quality certification in allied health fields and to accredit organizations that met those standards. The NCHCA evolved into NOCA (in 1987) and then ICE (in 2009) to expand accreditation globally to certification programs outside healthcare that met the rigorous standards of the NCCA.

The NCCA has reviewed and accredited the certification programs for most professions within allied healthcare. This includes the credentials for registered dietitians, occupational therapists, athletic trainers, podiatrists, nurses, nurse practitioners, massage therapists, personal trainers, group fitness instructors, and advanced fitness professionals. By earning NCCA accreditation for all four of its certification programs, the American Council on Exercise has taken the professional and responsible steps necessary for ACE-certified Professionals to be accepted as legitimate members of the allied healthcare continuum.

Recognition From the Fitness and Health Industry

In the fitness industry, NCCA accreditation has become recognized as the third-party standard for accreditation of certifications for group fitness instructors and other fitness professionals, as seen in the following professional standards, guidelines, and recommendations:

- The Medical Fitness Association (MFA), the professional membership organization for medically integrated health and fitness facilities, has made it a standard that medical fitness facilities hire only fitness professionals who hold NCCA-accredited certifications.

- *ACSM's Health/Fitness Facility Standards and Guidelines* recommends that clubs hire only fitness directors, group exercise directors, fitness instructors (including personal trainers), and group fitness instructors who hold a "certification from a nationally recognized and accredited certifying organization" [American College of Sports Medicine (ACSM), 2007]. It then states that "In this instance, the term accredited refers to certification programs that have received third-party approval of its certification procedures and practices from an appropriate agency, such as the National Commission for Certifying Agencies (NCCA)."

- The International Health, Racquet, and Sportsclub Association (IHRSA) recommends that club owners only hire personal trainers with certifications from agencies accredited by the NCCA or an equivalent accrediting organization.

There are other professional organizations currently in the process of developing voluntary fitness facility standards that will include requirements for hiring fitness professionals holding certifications from NCCA-accredited fitness organizations. In reference to the ACSM and IHRSA recommendations, the only other organization for possible consideration as a credible accreditation organization for certifying agencies is the American National Standards Institute (ANSI), which focuses primarily on third-party accreditation of industrial and workplace safety and quality standards.

Recognition From the Education Community

The ACE Educational Partnership Program offers four separate college curricula that instructors can use to teach courses in personal training, group exercise, exercise for weight management, and exercise for special populations, and to help students prepare for the corresponding ACE certification exam. The ACE Personal Trainer curriculum is the most widely utilized of the four, with more than 200 ACE Educational Partners using this curriculum in their regular course offerings. The ACE curricula help instructors with course design, provide discounts for students, and help exercise science departments meet one of the primary outcome assessments stated in the *Standards and Guidelines for the Accreditation of Educational Programs for Personal Fitness Training* from the Commission on Accreditation of Allied Health Education Programs (CAAHEP, 2007).

The CAAHEP is the largest programmatic accreditor in the health sciences field. The Committee on the Accreditation for the Exercise Sciences (CoAES) was formed under the guidance and sponsorship of CAAHEP to establish standards that academic programs in kinesiology, physical education, and exercise science must meet to become accredited by CAAHEP (2007).

One of the primary outcomes assessed by the CAAHEP *Standards and Guidelines for the Accreditation of Educational Programs for Personal Fitness Training* is the students' performance on a national credentialing examination accredited by the NCCA. This recognition of NCCA-accredited group fitness instructor certifications as the standard for this outcome assessment is an important endorsement of the NCCA accreditation by the educational community. The ACE Group Fitness Instructor

Certification Program, with its NCCA accreditation, helps universities and colleges meet this outcome assessment standard for exercise science departments to earn accreditation from CAAHEP.

Recognition From the Department of Labor

The Department of Labor (DOL) reports that while most group fitness instructors do not necessarily need to be certified to gain employment, "most organizations encourage their group instructors to become certified over time, and many require it." The DOL then goes on to state that, "One way to ensure that a certifying organization is reputable is to see that it is accredited by the National Commission for Certifying Agencies." The American Council on Exercise is one of the few organizations specifically identified by the DOL as offering quality certifications for group fitness instructors.

Other professions listed as fitness workers by the DOL include personal trainers and fitness directors.

Career Development

For a GFI who wants to become a full-time fitness professional, it is important to have a general idea of the career path that he or she wants to follow. Career paths can include becoming a fitness director, group exercise coordinator, or general manager of a larger club, opening a group exercise/personal-training studio, or opening a home-based fitness-training business. Even for GFIs who want to pursue and maintain part-time employment in the fitness industry, it is important to create a professional development plan that fulfills the continuing education and self-development requirements for being a good instructor.

Career goals are personal. They are based on the specific needs of the professional to meet his or her career objectives and are balanced with his or her other commitments.

Career paths should be viewed as guidelines to help the professional reach certain career goals, with the flexibility to be modified as needed based on new clientele, changes in family, industry recessions, and other important events. A career plan can help a professional determine if a new opportunity or continuing education offering is in line with his or her goals. After setting a career plan that spans one, three, five, or more years, a fitness professional can use this plan as a template for researching and selecting continuing education compatible with his or her goals.

Continuing Education

ACE-certified Professionals are encouraged to select continuing education based on personal areas of interest, client or participant needs, and desired career path. By completing continuing education in one or more areas of focus, a fitness professional can advance his or her career by becoming a specialist in areas such as weight management, youth fitness, sports conditioning, or older adult fitness. This can help the GFI become recognized as an expert in a given field, attracting specific clientele and advancing his or her career. Factors that should be considered when selecting continuing education courses include checking if the course will be at the appropriate level, seeing if the instructor has the appropriate qualifications to teach the course, learning if the course is ACE-approved or will have to be petitioned for CECs, and determining if the education provided is within the scope of practice.

Advanced Knowledge

ACE-certified Professionals should select continuing education that will help advance their current knowledge, skills, and abilities, without being too advanced. The continuing education needs for a newly certified fitness professional and a fitness professional with 10 years of experience will be different. If these two professionals attend the same conference together, it would be beneficial for them to independently select sessions that meet their individual career paths and needs, rather than going to the same sessions and having the new instructor be overwhelmed by the advanced subject matter, or the veteran bored by information that he or she already knows.

Continuing education should help the GFI work toward one or more career goals. For a management-focused fitness professional, this could include taking management courses, while an instructor who teaches older adult classes and is looking for new programming ideas would have a different course of study entirely. It is also important for ACE-certified Professionals to stay current, as standards and guidelines are released based on new findings in exercise science and related healthcare research. A GFI can do this through continuing education courses or through his or her own research of the published scientific literature.

Specialization

Specialization is a great way for a fitness professional to become recognized as an "expert" for a particular type of training or population. By gaining advanced knowledge and skills in a specialized area, a GFI can enhance the services provided to participants with special needs—and hopefully attract more participants seeking these specialty services. For example, a GFI who is interested in working with older adults might go on to do extensive continuing education in teaching this population, possibly earning a specialty certificate in exercise for older adults. Once the instructor is recognized for providing safe and effective classes for older adults, he or she should more readily attract senior participants, and should be able to earn more per class when providing these advanced lessons.

Areas of specialization should be selected by the GFI based on his or her desired career path, interests, and participant base. The area of specialization should also fall within the scope of practice, or provide the instructor with knowledge that is complementary to what he or she does within the scope of practice. For example, a course teaching techniques for manual manipulations of the shoulder would be educational, but would provide the instructor with techniques that he or she could not use within the defined scope of practice.

Certification vs. Certificates

There are numerous opportunities for fitness professionals to gain further knowledge in their chosen area of expertise. These opportunities are available as continuing education in the form of workshops, lectures, online programs, and published materials. Often, the industry's tendency to mislabel continuing education programs as "certifications" rather than "certificates" or "specialty certificate programs" has led to confusion among certified fitness professionals. Certifications provide an assessment of professional competence, whereas certificates show that an individual has completed a course on a particular topic. For example, a GFI who completes a weekend workshop and receives a certificate of completion for advanced sport stretching techniques is not advanced sport stretching techniques is not certified in advanced sport stretching instruction. Instead, the GFI has advanced his or her knowledge in the area of sport stretching techniques and can now provide a new training component in his or her classes.

Continuing education workshops, such as those that offer specialty certificates, provide the GFI with new knowledge and skills, as well as the ability to offer new class modalities. Participation in these types of programs is essential for the continued career development of a certified fitness professional. However, certificate programs are not certifications and the difference between the two is an important distinction to understand.

Additional Fitness Certifications

Another way for a GFI to earn continuing education and advance his or her career is to earn additional certifications. ACE encourages professionals to earn certifications that provide them with new areas of expertise. ACE offers four certifications, each providing a different area of expertise for fitness professionals. For a GFI looking to become better at interpersonal communication and exercise program design and application, or to simply supplement his or her group-fitness income, ACE offers its Personal Trainer certification. To meet the needs of the growing number of individuals who are trying to change lifestyle behaviors and lose weight, ACE offers an advanced credential titled the Health Coach certification. And, for advanced fitness professionals who want to work with clients who have special needs or are post-rehabilitation for cardiovascular, respiratory,

metabolic, or musculoskeletal diseases and disorders, ACE offers the Medical Exercise Specialist Certification.

New Areas of Expertise Within Allied Healthcare

A fitness professional who wants to expand the services that he or she provides into another area of allied healthcare must earn the appropriate credentials to ethically and legally provide those services. This could include becoming a licensed massage therapist, earning a nutrition degree and becoming a registered dietitian, earning a master's degree in physical therapy and becoming a licensed physical therapist, or going to medical school and becoming a medical doctor. In all of these situations, the fitness professional earning the new credential will advance his or her career and the services that he or she can provide, becoming an advocate for exercise and fitness training in his or her new professional arena.

Summary

GFIs play an important role within the fitness industry in that they are responsible for leading new and veteran participants through exercise classes, usually with a frequency of several times each week. Exposing groups of individuals to the fun and social elements of regular exercise increases the likelihood that those participants will be motivated to adopt and maintain physical activity as part of a healthy lifestyle. Most GFIs work part-time, but there is an increasing trend of instructors working as full-time fitness professionals by taking on the combined roles of GFI and personal trainer or fitness department manager.

References

American College of Sports Medicine (2007). *ACSM's Health/Fitness Facility Standards and Guidelines* (3rd ed.). Champaign, Ill.: Human Kinetics.

Commission on Accreditation of Allied Health Education Programs (2007). *Standards and Guidelines for the Accreditation of Educational Programs for Personal Fitness Training.* www.caahep.org/documents/Personal%20Fitness%20Standards%20January%202007.pdf

U.S. Department of Agriculture (2010). *Dietary Guidelines for Americans 2010.* www.health.gov/dietaryguidelines/

U.S. Department of Health & Human Services (2008). *2008 Physical Activity Guidelines for Americans: Be Active, Healthy and Happy.* www.health.gov/paguidelines/pdf/paguide.pdf

U.S. Department of Labor, Bureau of Labor Statistics (2010). *Occupational Outlook Handbook 2010–11 ed. Fitness Workers.* www.bls.gov/oco/ocos296.htm. Retrieved October 10, 2010.

Suggested Reading

American College of Sports Medicine (2014). *ACSM's Guidelines for Exercise Testing and Prescription* (9th ed.). Philadelphia: Wolters Kluwer/Lippincott Williams & Wilkins.

American Council on Exercise (2010). *ACE Personal Trainer Manual* (4th ed.). San Diego, Calif.: American Council on Exercise.

American Dietetic Association, Dietitians of Canada & American College of Sports Medicine (2007). *Joint Position Statement: Nutrition and Athletic Performance.* www.ms-se.com/pt/pt-core/templatejournal/msse/media/0309nutrition.pdf

Eickhoff-Shemek, J.M., Herbert, D.L., & Connaughton, D.P. (2009). *Risk Management for Health/Fitness Professionals: Legal Issues and Strategies.* Philadelphia: Wolters Kluwer/Lippincott Williams & Wilkins.

Janot, J. (2004). Do you know your scope of practice? *IDEA Fitness Journal,* 1, 1, 44–45.

Riley, S. (2005). Respecting your boundaries. *IDEA Trainer Success,* 2, 4, 12–13.

U.S. Department of Health & Human Services (2003). *Summary of the HIPAA Privacy Rule.* www.hhs.gov/ocr/privacy/hipaa/understanding/summary/privacysummary.pdf

Additional Resources

Ethics Resource Center: www.ethics.org

Institute for Credentialing Excellence (ICE): www.credentialingexcellence.org

International Health, Racquet, and Sportsclub Association: www.cms.ihrsa.org

Medical Fitness Association: www.medicalfitness.org

Medline Plus Reference on Drugs and Supplements (A service of the National Library of Medicine and National Institutes of Health): www.medlineplus.gov

Sabrena Merrill, M.S., has been actively involved in the fitness industry since 1987, successfully operating her own personal-training business and teaching group exercise classes. Merrill is a former full-time faculty member in the Kinesiology and Physical Education Department at California State University, Long Beach. She has a bachelor's degree in exercise science as well as a master's degree in physical education/biomechanics from the University of Kansas. Merrill, an ACE-certified Personal Trainer and Group Fitness Instructor, is an author, educator, and fitness consultant who remains very active within the industry.

CHAPTER TWO

Principles of Pre-class Preparation and Participant Monitoring and Evaluation

By Sabrena Merrill

Health Screening

Participation in regular physical activity, such as group exercise, is an important component of a healthy lifestyle. The numerous health benefits associated with being physically active provide compelling motivation for healthcare professionals to promote regular exercise. The health advantages of being regularly active include, but are not limited to, an improvement in cardiovascular and respiratory function, a reduction in **coronary artery disease (CAD)** risk factors, and decreased morbidity and mortality [American College of Sports Medicine (ACSM), 2014].

For most individuals, becoming more physically active is a safe and effective means to improve health-related fitness measures (i.e., body composition, cardiorespiratory endurance, muscular strength and endurance, and flexibility) as well as skill-related fitness components (i.e., agility, coordination, **balance,** power, reaction time, and speed).

However, there are certain instances when embarking on a new physical-activity program is contraindicated without a prior medical examination and an exercise stress test. A person with cardiac disease has an increased risk of experiencing a cardiovascular event, such as **myocardial infarction**, during exercise compared to an otherwise healthy person (Balady et al., 1998). To prevent dangerous cardiovascular events from occurring, appropriate screening and evaluation are necessary to identify and counsel those with underlying cardiac disease before they start moderate or vigorous exercise programs.

In a typical commercial fitness center setting, a group fitness instructor (GFI) teaches participants of various conditioning levels, skills, and abilities. Often, members who have just joined the facility will sample the different types of group fitness classes, which means that not only are these participants new to the gym, but they are also experiencing a variety of exercise modalities to which their bodies are unaccustomed. How can a GFI in this situation be sure that his or her class participants have been appropriately screened for safe participation in an exercise program? It is common practice for commercial fitness centers to require new members to complete a self-guided minimal preparticipation screen that instructs those who have indicated that they have **cardiovascular disease (CVD)** risk factors to visit their physicians before engaging in vigorous-intensity exercise. Thus, GFIs can reasonably assume that their participants have been screened for low-to-moderate intensity exercise. All GFIs should investigate their employer's preparticipation screening policies to ensure that a minimal health appraisal assessment is being conducted on each member.

The Pre-exercise Health Appraisal Questionnaire

Two examples of self-guided screenings for physical activity are the Canadian Society for Exercise Physiology's **Physical Activity Readiness Questionnaire (PAR-Q)** (Figure 2-1) and the AHA/ACSM Health/Fitness Facility Preparticipation Screening Questionnaire (Figure 2-2). The PAR-Q is recognized as a minimal, yet safe pre-exercise screening measure for low-to-moderate intensity (but not vigorous) exercise training. Participants are directed to contact their personal physician if they answer "yes" to one or more questions. The AHA/ACSM Health/Fitness Facility Preparticipation Screening Questionnaire directs those with elevated CVD risk to consult a physician, or other qualified healthcare professional, before participation (Balady et al., 1998). As a minimum level of protection, all individuals considering starting a new exercise program on their own without the specific attention of a health and/or fitness professional (including those planning on starting a group exercise program) should complete a self-guided health screening questionnaire.

There are certain situations in which a GFI should require his or her participants to complete a more in-depth health-risk appraisal. If a GFI is an independent business owner who provides group fitness instruction on a contract basis or who runs outdoor fitness classes, such as boot-camp sessions, he or she should have each participant complete a detailed medical/health

Physical Activity Readiness
Questionnaire - PAR-Q
(revised 2002)

PAR-Q & YOU

(A Questionnaire for People Aged 15 to 69)

Regular physical activity is fun and healthy, and increasingly more people are starting to become more active every day. Being more active is very safe for most people. However, some people should check with their doctor before they start becoming much more physically active.

If you are planning to become much more physically active than you are now, start by answering the seven questions in the box below. If you are between the ages of 15 and 69, the PAR-Q will tell you if you should check with your doctor before you start. If you are over 69 years of age, and you are not used to being very active, check with your doctor.

Common sense is your best guide when you answer these questions. Please read the questions carefully and answer each one honestly: check YES or NO.

YES	NO		
☐	☐	1.	Has your doctor ever said that you have a heart condition **and** that you should only do physical activity recommended by a doctor?
☐	☐	2.	Do you feel pain in your chest when you do physical activity?
☐	☐	3.	In the past month, have you had chest pain when you were not doing physical activity?
☐	☐	4.	Do you lose your balance because of dizziness or do you ever lose consciousness?
☐	☐	5.	Do you have a bone or joint problem (for example, back, knee or hip) that could be made worse by a change in your physical activity?
☐	☐	6.	Is your doctor currently prescribing drugs (for example, water pills) for your blood pressure or heart condition?
☐	☐	7.	Do you know of **any other reason** why you should not do physical activity?

If

you

answered

YES to one or more questions

Talk with your doctor by phone or in person BEFORE you start becoming much more physically active or BEFORE you have a fitness appraisal. Tell your doctor about the PAR-Q and which questions you answered YES.

- You may be able to do any activity you want — as long as you start slowly and build up gradually. Or, you may need to restrict your activities to those which are safe for you. Talk with your doctor about the kinds of activities you wish to participate in and follow his/her advice.
- Find out which community programs are safe and helpful for you.

NO to all questions

If you answered NO honestly to all PAR-Q questions, you can be reasonably sure that you can:
- start becoming much more physically active — begin slowly and build up gradually. This is the safest and easiest way to go.
- take part in a fitness appraisal — this is an excellent way to determine your basic fitness so that you can plan the best way for you to live actively. It is also highly recommended that you have your blood pressure evaluated. If your reading is over 144/94, talk with your doctor before you start becoming much more physically active.

DELAY BECOMING MUCH MORE ACTIVE:
- if you are not feeling well because of a temporary illness such as a cold or a fever — wait until you feel better; or
- if you are or may be pregnant — talk to your doctor before you start becoming more active.

PLEASE NOTE: If your health changes so that you then answer YES to any of the above questions, tell your fitness or health professional. Ask whether you should change your physical activity plan.

Informed Use of the PAR-Q: The Canadian Society for Exercise Physiology, Health Canada, and their agents assume no liability for persons who undertake physical activity, and if in doubt after completing this questionnaire, consult your doctor prior to physical activity.

No changes permitted. You are encouraged to photocopy the PAR-Q but only if you use the entire form.

NOTE: If the PAR-Q is being given to a person before he or she participates in a physical activity program or a fitness appraisal, this section may be used for legal or administrative purposes.

"I have read, understood and completed this questionnaire. Any questions I had were answered to my full satisfaction."

NAME _____

SIGNATURE _____   DATE _____

SIGNATURE OF PARENT _____   WITNESS _____
or GUARDIAN (for participants under the age of majority)

Note: This physical activity clearance is valid for a maximum of 12 months from the date it is completed and becomes invalid if your condition changes so that you would answer YES to any of the seven questions.

CSEP
SCPE © Canadian Society for Exercise Physiology   Supported by: [🍁] Health   Santé
                                                                    Canada   Canada

Figure 2-1

The Physical Activity Readiness Questionnaire (PAR-Q)

©2002 Used with permission from the Canadian Society for Exercise Physiology. www.csep.ca

Assess your health needs by marking all *true* statements.

History
You have had:
☐ a heart attack
☐ heart surgery
☐ cardiac catheterization
☐ percutaneous transluminal coronary angioplasty (PTCA)
☐ pacemaker/implantable cardiac defibrillator/rhythm disturbance
☐ heart valve disease
☐ heart failure
☐ heart transplantation
☐ congenital heart disease

> **Recommendations**
> *If you marked any of the statements in this section, consult your physician or other healthcare provider before engaging in exercise. You may need to use a facility with a medically qualified staff.*

Symptoms
☐ You experience chest discomfort with exertion.
☐ You experience unreasonable breathlessness.
☐ You experience dizziness, fainting, or blackouts.
☐ You experience ankle swelling.
☐ You experience unpleasant awareness of a forceful or rapid heart rate.
☐ You take heart medications.

Other health issues
☐ You have diabetes.
☐ You have asthma or other lung disease.
☐ You have a burning or cramping sensation in your lower legs when walking short distance.
☐ You have musculoskeletal problems that limit your physical activity.
☐ You have concerns about the safety of exercise.
☐ You take prescription medications.
☐ You are pregnant.

Cardiovascular risk factors
☐ You are a man older than 45 years.
☐ You are a woman older than 55 years.
☐ You smoke, or quit smoking within the previous 6 months.
☐ Your blood pressure is ≥140/90 mmHg.
☐ You do not know your blood pressure.
☐ You take blood pressure medication.
☐ Your blood cholesterol level is ≥200 mg/dL.
☐ You do not know your cholesterol level.
☐ You have a blood relative who had a heart attack or heart surgery before age 55 (father/brother) or 65 (mother/sister).
☐ You are physically inactive (i.e., you get less than 30 minutes of physical activity on at least 3 days per week).
☐ You have a body mass index ≥30 kg/m².
☐ You have prediabetes.
☐ You do not know if you have prediabetes.

> *If you marked two or more of the statements in this section, you should consult your physician or other appropriate healthcare provider before engaging in exercise. You might benefit by using a facility with a professionally qualified exercise staff* to guide your exercise program.*

☐ None of the above is true.

> *You should be able to exercise safely without consulting your physician or other appropriate healthcare provider in a self-guided program or almost any facility that meets your exercise program needs.*

*Professionally qualified exercise staff refers to appropriately trained individuals who possess academic training, practical and clinical knowledge, skills, and abilities commensurate with the credentials defined by the American College of Sports Medicine.

Figure 2-2
American Heart Association/American College of Sports Medicine Health/Fitness Facility Preparticipation Screening Questionnaire
American College of Sports Medicine (2014). *ACSM's Guidelines for Exercise Testing and Prescription* (9th ed.). Philadelphia: Wolters Kluwer/Lippincott Williams & Wilkins.

history questionnaire. In cases where a GFI works exclusively with special populations (e.g., older adults, people with **diabetes,** or prenatal participants) or in a medical fitness setting (working with rehabilitation patients), it is essential that the participants fill out an appropriate professionally guided health screen. In this situation, *professionally guided* implies that a health/fitness professional, such as a qualified GFI, administers the screen to identify participants who would benefit from medical consultation prior to beginning exercise.

Professionally guided health-risk appraisals are more elaborate than self-guided screens. The process involves reviewing detailed health/medical history information, stratifying the participant's CVD risk, and offering specific recommendations for exercise, preparticipation medical examination, exercise testing, and physician supervision.

Disease Risk Stratification

ACSM has developed CVD risk-factor thresholds that can be used to determine a person's risk for experiencing a cardiovascular event during exercise (Table 2-1). After

Table 2-1

Atherosclerotic Cardiovascular Disease Risk Factor Thresholds for Use With ACSM Risk Stratification

Positive Risk Factors	Defining Criteria	Points
Age	Men ≥45 years Women ≥55 years	+1
Family history	Myocardial infarction, coronary revascularization, or sudden death before 55 years of age in father or other first-degree male relative, or before 65 years of age in mother or other first-degree female relative	+1
Cigarette smoking	Current cigarette smoker or those who quit within the previous six months, or exposure to environmental tobacco smoke (i.e., secondhand smoke)	+1
Sedentary lifestyle	Not participating in at least 30 minutes of moderate-intensity physical activity (40 to <60% $\dot{V}O_2R$) on at least three days/week for at least three months	+1
Obesity	Body mass index ≥30 kg/m² or waist girth >102 cm (40 inches) for men and >88 cm (35 inches) for women	+1
Hypertension	Systolic blood pressure ≥140 mmHg and/or diastolic blood pressure ≥90 mmHg, confirmed by measurements on at least two separate occasions, or currently on antihypertensive medications	+1
Dyslipidemia	Low-density lipoprotein (LDL) cholesterol ≥130 mg/dL (3.37 mmol/L) or high-density lipoprotein (HDL) cholesterol <40 mg/dL (1.04 mmol/L) or on lipid-lowering medication; If total serum cholesterol is all that is available, use serum cholesterol ≥200 mg/dL (5.18 mmol/L)	+1
Prediabetes*	Fasting plasma glucose ≥100 mg/dL (5.55 mmol/L), but ≤125 mg/dL (6.94 mmol/L) or impaired glucose tolerance (IGT) where a two-hour oral glucose tolerance test (OGTT) value is ≥140 mg/dL (7.77 mmol/L), but ≤199 mg/dL (11.04 mmol/L), confirmed by measurements on at least two separate occasions	+1
Negative Risk Factor	**Defining Criteria**	**Points**
HDL cholesterol[†]	≥60 mg/dL (1.55 mmol/L)	–1
	Total Score:	

*If the presence or absence of a CVD risk factor is not disclosed or is not available, that CVD risk factor should be counted as a risk factor except for prediabetes. If the prediabetes criteria are missing or unknown, prediabetes should be counted as a risk factor for those ≥45 years old, especially for those with a body mass index (BMI) ≥25 kg/m², and those <45 years old with a BMI ≥25 kg/m² and additional CVD risk factors for prediabetes. The number of positive risk factors is then summed.

[†]High HDL is considered a negative risk factor. For individuals having high HDL ≥60 mg/dL (1.55 mmol/L), one positive risk factor is subtracted from the sum of positive risk factors.

Note: $\dot{V}O_2R = \dot{V}O_2$ reserve

collecting detailed health and medical history information, a GFI who teaches specialty classes, or who works with special populations, can use this data to place participants in a specific category of risk. The risk stratification process designates individuals into one of three categories: low, moderate, or high risk.

Low-risk participants are those who have no signs or symptoms of cardiovascular, pulmonary, and/or metabolic disease and have no more than one CVD risk factor. Moderate-risk individuals have no signs or symptoms of the aforementioned diseases but have two or more CVD risk factors. Lastly, high-risk individuals have one or more signs or symptoms of, or have been diagnosed with, cardiovascular, pulmonary, and/or metabolic disease.

Figure 2-3 provides a flow chart for recommending exercise testing and testing supervision based on risk stratification. It also summarizes moderate and vigorous exercise intensities based on percent $\dot{V}O_2max$ and **metabolic equivalents (METs)**. A GFI can use the risk-stratification process to identify those in need of referral to a healthcare provider for more extensive medical evaluation, ensure the safety of exercise testing and participation, and determine the appropriate type of exercise test or program.

Signs or symptoms are also included in risk stratification, but given the need for specialized training to make a diagnosis, and respecting the **scope of practice** of GFIs, these signs and symptoms must only be interpreted by a qualified licensed professional within the clinical context in which they appear. These signs and symptoms include the following (ACSM, 2014):

- Pain (tightness) or discomfort (or other angina equivalent) in the chest, neck, jaw, arms, or other areas that may result from **ischemia**

- Shortness of breath or difficulty breathing at rest or with mild exertion **(dyspnea)**
- Orthopnea (dyspnea in a reclined position) or paroxysmal nocturnal dyspnea (onset is usually two to five hours after the beginning of sleep)
- Ankle **edema**
- Palpitations or **tachycardia**
- Intermittent **claudication** (pain sensations or cramping in the lower extremities associated with inadequate blood supply)
- Known heart murmur
- Unusual fatigue or difficulty breathing with usual activities
- Dizziness or **syncope,** most commonly caused by reduced **perfusion** to the brain

GFIs should be familiar with each of these conditions and document them in a client's file if (1) the client has a history of any of these symptoms; or (2) develops these signs of symptoms while under the trainer's supervision.

While GFIs cannot diagnose signs or symptoms, it is helpful to know that:

- These symptoms are more likely to be apparent in individuals with a greater number of positive risk factors.
- The stratification between low-, moderate-, and high-risk individuals only requires differentiation between zero, one, and two risk factors, and the medical diagnosis of diseases.

It is also evident from Figure 2-3 that a participant's risk stratification will determine a recommended intensity of exercise (unless a person is in the high-risk category, in which case it is recommended that he or she perform a medically supervised exercise test before engaging in moderate- or vigorous-intensity exercise). For example, if a GFI determines that a participant is

Figure 2-3

Medical examination, exercise testing, and supervision of exercise testing preparticipation recommendations based on classification of risk

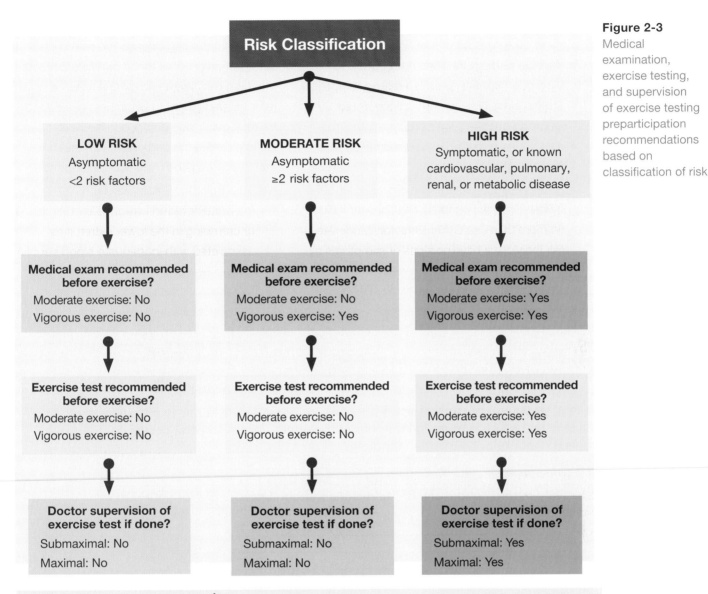

Risk Classification

LOW RISK
Asymptomatic
<2 risk factors

MODERATE RISK
Asymptomatic
≥2 risk factors

HIGH RISK
Symptomatic, or known cardiovascular, pulmonary, renal, or metabolic disease

Medical exam recommended before exercise?
Moderate exercise: No
Vigorous exercise: No

Medical exam recommended before exercise?
Moderate exercise: No
Vigorous exercise: Yes

Medical exam recommended before exercise?
Moderate exercise: Yes
Vigorous exercise: Yes

Exercise test recommended before exercise?
Moderate exercise: No
Vigorous exercise: No

Exercise test recommended before exercise?
Moderate exercise: No
Vigorous exercise: No

Exercise test recommended before exercise?
Moderate exercise: Yes
Vigorous exercise: Yes

Doctor supervision of exercise test if done?
Submaximal: No
Maximal: No

Doctor supervision of exercise test if done?
Submaximal: No
Maximal: No

Doctor supervision of exercise test if done?
Submaximal: Yes
Maximal: Yes

Moderate exercise: 40% to <60% $\dot{V}O_2R$; 3 to <6 METs; "An intensity that causes noticeable increases in heart rate and breathing"

Vigorous exercise: ≥60% $\dot{V}O_2R$; ≥6 METs; "An intensity that causes substantial increase in heart rate and breathing"

Not recommended: Reflects the notion that a medical examination, exercise test, and physician supervision of exercise testing are not recommended in the preparticipation screening; however, they may be considered when there are concerns about risk, more information is needed for the exercise test, and/or are requested by the patient or client.

Recommended: Reflects the notion that a medical examination, exercise test, and physician supervision are recommended in the preparticipation health screening process.

Note: $\dot{V}O_2R$ = $\dot{V}O_2$ reserve; METs = Metabolic equivalents; Cardiovascular disease = Cardiac, peripheral artery, or cerebrovascular disease; Pulmonary disease = Chronic obstructive pulmonary disease (COPD), cystic fibrosis, interstitial lung disease, or asthma; Metabolic disease = Diabetes mellitus (type 1 or 2) and thyroid disorders; Renal disease = Kidney disease

Reprinted with permission from the American College of Sports Medicine (2014). *ACSM's Guidelines for Exercise Testing and Prescription* (9th ed.). Philadelphia: Wolters Kluwer/Lippincott Williams & Wilkins.

categorized as "moderate risk," the GFI must take specific precautions to ensure that the participant does not engage in vigorous-intensity exercise during the group fitness class. These precautions could include educating the participant about monitoring his or her **heart rate (HR)** and feelings of exertion so that intensity can be reduced when necessary. Also, the GFI has a responsibility to teach modifications to exercise to ensure that the participant has a successful, enjoyable exercise experience.

Medical Referral

If it is determined through the risk-stratification process that a participant meets the "high risk" threshold for CVD, the GFI must refer the participant to his or her physician for medical evaluation and supervised exercise testing. Before the participant can return to the class, he or she must submit to the GFI a physician's medical release form, which explains the participant's physical-activity limitations and/or guidelines (Figure 2-4). Once they have been established, any deviation

---

Sample Medical Release Form

Date _____

Dear Doctor:

Your patient, _____, wishes to start a personalized training program. The activity will involve the following:

(type, frequency, duration, and intensity of activities)

If your patient is taking medications that will affect his or her exercise capacity or heart-rate response to exercise, please indicate the manner of the effect (raises, lowers, or has no effect on exercise capacity or heart-rate response):

Type of medication(s) _____

Effect(s) _____

Please identify any recommendations or restrictions that are appropriate for your patient in this exercise program:

_____

_____

_____

Please identify any medications that could increase your patient's risk for falls:

_____

_____

_____

Thank you.
Sincerely,
Fred Fitness
Personalized Gym, Address, Phone

_____ has my approval to begin an exercise program with the recommendations or restrictions stated above.

Signed_____ Date_____ Phone_____

Figure 2-4
Sample medical release form

Case Study Example

Amanda is a 59-year-old woman who stands 5'3" (1.6 m) and weighs 189 lb (86 kg). She currently smokes one pack of cigarettes a day and indicates no history of physical activity over the past 10 years. She also has a **sedentary** occupation and travels frequently for work. Her latest physical examination revealed the following information:

- **Blood pressure** (repeated twice): 136/88 mmHg
- Total **cholesterol:** 208 mg/dL
- **High-density lipoprotein (HDL)** cholesterol: 41 mg/dL

- **Low-density lipoprotein (LDL)** cholesterol: 134 mg/dL
- No medications
- Fasting blood glucose (last medical exam): 98 mg/dL

- Family history:
  - ✔ Father diagnosed with CAD at age 62
  - ✔ Mother diagnosed with **type 2 diabetes** at age 50

Questions:

- What are Amanda's positive risk factors for heart disease?
- What is her risk stratification according to ACSM's guidelines?
- What testing and programming guidelines should a GFI follow prior to working with Amanda?

Positive Risk Factor	Participant Information	Defining Criteria	Score
Age	59	>55-year-old threshold for women	1
Family history	Male: none (father diagnosed with CAD at age 62)	No myocardial infarction, coronary revascularization, or sudden death before 55 years of age in father or other first-degree relative, or before 65 years of age	0
	Female: none	in mother or other first-degree female relative	0
Cigarette smoking	1 pack a day	Current cigarette smoker	1
Physical activity	Sedentary	Performs less than 30 minutes of moderate-intensity physical activity at least three days per week	1
Hypertension	SBP = 136 mmHg	<140 mmHg threshold	0
	DBP = 88 mmHg	<90 mmHg threshold	0
Dyslipidemia	Total cholesterol = 208 mg/dL	Do not use, as HDL and LDL are available	N/A
	HDL = 41 mg/dL	>40 mg/dL threshold	0
	LDL = 135 mg/dL	>130 mg/dL threshold	1
	Medications	None reported	N/A
Prediabetes	Blood glucose = 98 mg/dL	<100 mg/dL threshold	0
Obesity	BMI = 33.6 kg/m²	>30 kg/m² threshold	1
	Waist circumference	No measurement at this time	N/A
	Body fat	No measurement at this time	N/A
Negative Risk Factor			
HDL	HDL = 41 mg/dL	<60 mg/dL threshold	0
		Total score:	5

Note: CAD = Coronary artery disease; SBP = Systolic blood pressure; DBP = Diastolic blood pressure; LDL = Low-density lipoprotein; HDL = High-density lipoprotein; BMI = Body mass index

What are Amanda's positive risk factors for heart disease? Age, current smoker, high LDL, high BMI, and sedentary lifestyle

What is her risk stratification according to ACSM's guidelines? Moderate, as she has no known diagnosis, although she has five positive risk factors

What testing and programming guidelines should a GFI follow prior to working with Amanda? Theoretically, she could participate in moderate-intensity activity and submaximal testing without a medical exam. However, given her number of risk factors, Amanda should consider getting a medical exam before starting an exercise program or participating in group exercise.

from the physical-activity limitations or guidelines must be approved by the participant's personal physician.

Pre-class Preparation

Preparing to teach a safe and effective group fitness class involves more than planning choreography, choosing appropriate exercises, and selecting motivating music. Pre-class preparation should also include an evaluation of the group fitness room and equipment before the start of each class. Also, prior to teaching his or her first class in a particular setting or facility, the GFI should assess the environment before, during, and after that time slot for any potential problems, such as room temperature that is too hot or too cold or a previous class infringing on the time slot of the next scheduled class.

Assess the Room

Once a GFI has been hired or contracted to begin teaching, he or she should assess the environment of the room or area chosen for the class. That is, an instructor should visit the group fitness space prior to designing the class so that he or she can account for the available equipment, square footage, and flow of traffic into and out of the area.

Evaluating the size and unique architecture of the room and/or space is essential before an instructor can determine proper exercise class programming. If the room is small, or if it has awkward structures, such as support columns in the center of the room, the format of the class should reflect these issues. For example, smaller rooms provide less space for participants to travel during choreography and architectural obstacles might require the instructor to teach from various locations throughout the space in order to see the participants and be seen by the participants.

Having access to, and permission to use, specific equipment during a group exercise class is another important consideration for the GFI. Many facilities store various types of equipment in their group fitness rooms, including equipment intended for other uses, such as personal training, or equipment that requires special advanced training to safely operate, such as **Pilates** reformer machines. A GFI should understand the equipment available for use during his or her class and adhere to the facility's policies regarding proper use and storage of that equipment. Also, it is not uncommon for clubs to securely store their group fitness equipment, so a GFI should check to be sure that he or she knows how to unlock any anti-theft devices securing the equipment before the first class.

Many fitness centers that offer group exercise programming aim to please the members by scheduling as many classes as possible during the times when the gym is busiest. While this practice is great for offering a high-volume, varied schedule to participants, it sometimes creates complications when the group fitness space is transitioning from one class to the next. For example, when an equipment-intensive class, such as group strength training, is scheduled to finish just before another class featuring a different type of equipment, such as group cycling or Pilates reformer training, it could result in the latter class always starting at a later-than-scheduled time. This is frustrating for both instructors and participants. This problem could be avoided by scheduling more time between the two classes so that participants can safely secure equipment and transition into and out of the room.

Another potential schedule-related issue is the safety of the group exercise area after participants leave perspiration on the floor. "Hot" **yoga** sessions and intense cycling classes promote heavy sweating, which could wreak havoc on the next class if it is a fast-moving, balance-dependent format, such as kickboxing or step training. If time is not allotted for the appropriate clean up of any moisture on the floor, participants could easily slip and fall on the wet surface, creating a potential safety and liability issue.

Room temperature can also be an issue in group exercise rooms. Fitness facilities often keep their group exercise rooms very cool to accommodate for aerobic-based classes attended by many people who contribute to the ambient air temperature by giving off their own body heat. However, hatha yoga or sport stretching classes held in a frigid room can be uncomfortable and counterproductive, as stretching should not be performed in a cold environment. In such cases, if there is only one group exercise room in the club, thus restricting the areas available to hold classes, it might be beneficial to schedule classes requiring warm temperatures at opposite ends of the day from classes that rely on cool temperatures. This allows the room ample time to warm up or cool down, depending on the needs of the particular class.

While it is usually not the role of the GFI to develop the group exercise schedule, it is a GFI's responsibility to observe the environment during the time slot of a class and report to the group fitness coordinator any potential problems. Addressing potential issues before a new class begins saves time and frustration later.

Prepare Equipment

Before each class, a GFI should enter the group exercise space a few minutes early to evaluate the status of the equipment. This includes both exercise equipment and technical equipment, such as a stereo and microphone. A quick assessment should be

adequate to reveal if the equipment needs to be replaced or repaired.

Any exercise equipment that does not appear to be functioning properly or that has obvious signs of deterioration should be removed from the group exercise space or locked in a secure location that is not accessible by participants. If removing the equipment is not an option because it is too large (e.g., group exercise cycle, Pilates reformer, or rebounder), a conspicuous sign should be placed on the equipment that alerts the participants that the piece is out of order and could result in injury if used in its present condition. The policies of each fitness facility typically dictate the responsibilities of the staff regarding placing signage on faulty equipment. The GFI must fully understand those policies and notify the appropriate staff person, if necessary, to place the signage on the equipment prior to the start of class. It is also the responsibility of the GFI to follow up with the appropriate staff person regarding the status of the malfunctioning equipment to find out if the piece will be repaired or replaced. **Rapport** among the participants and the GFI can be enhanced when the GFI keeps the participants informed of equipment status, as this shows a level of concern for the safety of the participants.

Other exercise equipment, such as dumbbells, barbells, stability balls, and elastic resistance should also be checked for signs of wear and tear. A GFI should pay extra attention to equipment made of rubber, such as stability balls and resistance bands, because these items are especially prone to breakdowns and tears after repeated use and exposure to heat and perspiration. As mentioned previously, if a GFI finds a piece of exercise equipment in a state of deterioration, he or she should remove it, making it inaccessible to class participants.

Lastly, any technical equipment required to effectively teach a class (e.g., microphone, sound system, or heart-rate monitor) should be checked for proper functioning prior to starting each class. Often, clubs will have backup technical equipment and batteries for situations when technical problems arise. The GFI should know if these backup items exist as well as how to access and use them when necessary.

Appropriate Attire and Equipment

The GFI should have a good understanding of the appropriate attire and equipment involved in instructing the specific modalities he or she has been hired or contracted to teach. Class attendees often look at the GFI's attire to determine an appropriate outfit for the class. Thus, a GFI must act as a role model for participants when it comes to proper exercise wear. Instructors should wear clothing that allows participants to clearly view the key movements of the body. For example, many Pilates and yoga exercises involve subtle adjustments of the joints to correctly perform a movement. Clothing that has excess material could block the participant's view of the instructor's form, thus limiting the effectiveness of the instruction. Layers of loose cotton material can trap heat and cause an exerciser's core body temperature to rise unnecessarily. Also, long, baggy shirts can become lodged under an exerciser's body during stability ball, BOSU™ trainer, or foam roller work and cause pulling of the material around the neck. These are just a couple of reasons why exercise attire is typically form-fitting and made of material that wicks away the moisture of perspiration from the skin. While it is important for the GFI to wear exercise apparel that allows clear viewing of exercise movements,

care must be taken to avoid wearing too little, and thus appearing unprofessional.

In a group indoor cycling class, a GFI should wear apparel that makes the exercise experience as effective as possible. Cycling shorts with built-in padding can make sitting on the saddle more comfortable. Cycling shoes can make the ride more effective. Educating participants about these types of cycling-specific clothing can enhance rapport and help the class attendees get the most from their workouts.

A GFI should have knowledge of any specific equipment or accessories that can make a class more effective and enjoyable for participants. Even if a particular fitness club does not own the equipment, the GFI can be an advocate for educating the club management and the class participants about adding the pieces. For example, yoga class participants can benefit from having accessories such as yoga blocks, towels, and stretching straps that allow them to achieve positions that otherwise would not be possible without those pieces. Certain mats are better for certain modalities than others. Yoga mats are thin and "sticky" and allow a better grip between the skin and the mat compared to traditional floor mats. Pilates mats are similar to yoga mats, but they are thicker, allowing for a more comfortable experience during rolling movements during which the joints need more cushioning than is provided by traditional mats or yoga mats. While the difference between yoga mats and Pilates mats might appear minimal, the use of the appropriate mat can make a significant difference in the enjoyment of the exercise.

Know the Participants

Understanding the general characteristics of the participants in the class can guide the GFI when designing the workout, which includes elements such as the complexity of exercise movements, intensity of the exercise, modifications that may be required, and even music selection. Prior to teaching a class, a GFI should know for whom the class is intended. Is the class a high-intensity cycling workout held at 4:00 in the afternoon that appeals to the young, college population, or is the class a senior stretch-and-tone session that starts at 10:00 in the morning and attracts older adults with flexible schedules? In addition to preparing for the specific type of class (e.g., low-impact aerobics class versus a group strength training workout), having knowledge of the general ages and ability levels of the participants attending the class will determine the appropriate exercise selection and modalities, as well as the type of music, to be used in the class.

Orient New Participants and Preview Class Format

One of the most important rapport-building actions that an instructor can perform is to make new participants feel welcome the first time they set foot in the group exercise space. A GFI should always make an effort to learn new participants' names and encourage them to continue trying the class, even if they are unable to master all of the exercises in the first few sessions. For most GFIs teaching in a commercial fitness setting, a continuous stream of new participants trying their classes is a common experience. For this reason, GFIs should always make a brief statement at the beginning of each class that includes an introduction (so that the participants can call the instructor by name) and a description of the objectives of the class. Even if the participants are not new to the class, this type of opening statement is always a good reminder to the attendees that the GFI is professional and committed to teaching a safe and effective class.

Acknowledge Class Participants

Successful GFIs who teach packed classes and who create a solid following have achieved this level of accomplishment through knowledge of safe and effective exercise programming and by developing rapport with their class participants. Rapport is the feeling of mutual trust and respect between people. When GFIs acknowledge their class participants through effective communication, they are building rapport. Strategies such as always greeting and addressing participants by name and giving specific, appropriate **feedback** during class through effective cueing are ways a GFI can establish and maintain good rapport with class attendees.

Sample Opening Statement to a Class With Participants of Various Skills and Abilities

"Good morning, everyone! Welcome to Step and Core. My name is Susie and I will be leading you through 45 minutes of step conditioning followed by 10 minutes of core training. We will begin with a warm-up to get the muscles, joints, and heart ready for action. At the end of class, we will finish with five minutes of stretching. I see a few new faces in the class today. To help everyone, regardless of fitness level, I will be showing modifications during class of various ways to make the exercise easier or harder. If you feel like you're working too hard, try lowering your step and keeping your arms lower than your heart. If you feel like you want more of a challenge, you can watch me perform the power moves in class and try those yourself. Also, if anyone has any specific injuries or health conditions that could affect your performance in class, now is a good time to let me know. If you have questions, please find me after class and we can address them at that time."

Methods of Monitoring Cardiorespiratory Intensity

To receive the beneficial health effects of **aerobic** exercise, all adults should accumulate at least 150 minutes of moderate-intensity physical activity per week (U.S. Department of Health & Human Services, 2008). This includes activities such as exercise in group fitness settings. While health improvements occur with moderate amounts of physical activity, it is also recognized that greater health benefits are obtained with greater amounts of physical activity. Low- to moderate-intensity activities are sufficient to improve fitness for many sedentary, **overweight,** or low-fit individuals. However, for those wanting to achieve higher levels of fitness, a more structured exercise routine is necessary.

For increases in aerobic fitness, ACSM recommends that individuals perform activities that work the large muscle groups of the body in a continuous, rhythmic fashion for a prolonged period of time (ACSM, 2010). In the group fitness setting, examples include low- or high-impact aerobics, step training, group cycling, rebounding, aquatic exercise, and hip-hop or other forms of dance exercise.

The appropriate intensity for aerobic exercise depends on several factors, including the exerciser's level of conditioning and his or her fitness goals. Beginners who have been sedentary or who are overweight should proceed with an exercise program that is low intensity for longer durations. Those who are more fit and are interested in maintaining or increasing their fitness levels can perform higher levels of intense aerobic exercise for shorter periods of time during each session.

Monitoring exercise intensity within the cardiorespiratory segment is important. Participants need to be given information

regarding the purpose of monitoring HR during exercise and instruction on how to obtain a **pulse rate.** Proper instruction on how to take the HR is the first step to monitoring intensity effectively. The following are a few recommended sites for taking the heart rate:

- *Carotid pulse:* This pulse is taken from the carotid artery just to the side of the larynx using light pressure from the fingertips of the first two fingers. Remember, never palpate both carotid arteries at the same time and always press lightly to prevent a drop in heart rate and/or decreased blood flow to the brain (Figure 2-5).
- *Radial pulse:* This pulse is taken from the radial artery at the wrist, in line with the thumb, using the fingertips of the first two fingers (Figure 2-6).
- *Temporal pulse:* This pulse can sometimes be obtained from the left or right temple with light pressure from the fingertips of the first two fingers (Figure 2-7).

Figure 2-5
Carotid heart rate monitoring

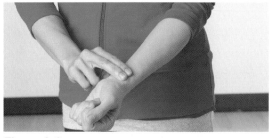

Figure 2-6
Radial heart rate monitoring

Figure 2-7
Temporal heart rate monitoring

Understanding the effective use of HR, **ratings of perceived exertion (RPE),** the **dyspnea scale,** and the **talk test** is the next step in effectively monitoring exercise intensity. Some methods are preferred depending on the format. Research on group exercise has determined that HR taken in high/low classes represents a lower relative exercise intensity than that of running (Parker et al., 1989). Other research on different forms of group exercise (step, interval high/low, and progressive treadmill training) concluded that HR may not be an appropriate predictor of exercise intensity and that RPE is the preferred method (Roach, Croisant, & Emmett, 1994).

Many HR research studies were performed on runners and cyclists rather than group exercise participants. In a treadmill class or an indoor cycling class, use of HR monitors can be effective. However, in a kickboxing class, where arms and legs are moving in many different directions and against gravity, RPE might be a better choice. Finally, there is research suggesting that utilizing HR is not appropriate in aquatic exercise in which the chest is submerged (Frangolias & Rhodes, 1995). There is no one method that works for all different types of group exercise ses-

sions or participants (Table 2-2). Many GFIs have stopped using manual HR monitoring because it disrupts the flow of the class. Using HR monitors is always an option as well. There are no hard-and-fast rules for monitoring intensity other than that it is an important responsibility of the GFI. Not monitoring intensity or failing to give constant intensity-monitoring gauges reflects an inadequate level of participant supervision and may compromise safety.

Table 2-2	
Recommended Methods of Intensity Monitoring	
Class Format	**Intensity-monitoring Method**
High-low, step training, kickboxing	HR, RPE, or talk test
Aquatic exercise	RPE or talk test
Group indoor cycling	HR or talk test
Equipment-based classes	HR, RPE, or talk test

Note: HR = Heart rate; RPE = Ratings of perceived exertion

Target Heart Rate

Aerobic exercise intensity can be determined and monitored by understanding how certain physiological variables correlate with increases in exertion during an exercise session (i.e., an exerciser experiences increases in heart rate and breathing rate as continuous aerobic activity is performed). ACSM recommends an exercise intensity range of 55 to 65% up to 90% of an individual's **maximum heart rate (MHR)** for improvements in aerobic fitness (ACSM, 2010). This range is called the **target heart rate (THR)** zone.

Using MHR as a method to recommend aerobic exercise intensity is fairly convenient. To figure out a participant's THR range, first estimate his or her MHR using the following formula: MHR = 208 – (0.7 x Age) (Tanaka, Monahan, & Seals, 2001). Using this formula, a 40-year-old participant's estimated MHR would be 180 beats per minute (bpm), which can be expressed as 208 – (0.7 x 40) = 208 – 28 = 180 bpm. Next, figure out THR, which is based on a percentage of MHR. For aerobic activity, the recommended range is between 55 and 90% of MHR. For example, the 40-year-old participant's THR range is 99 to 162 bpm (180 bpm x 0.55 = 99 bpm and 180 bpm x 0.90 = 162 bpm). Table 2-3 lists a sampling of MHR and THR based on different age groups using the 208 – (0.7 x Age) calculation.

Table 2-3		
Estimated Maximum and Target Heart Rates Based on the 208 – (0.7 x Age) Calculation (55 to 90% Maximum Heart Rate)		
Age	**Maximum Heart Rate (bpm)**	**Target Heart Rate (bpm)**
20	194	107 to 175
30	187	103 to 168
40	180	99 to 162
50	173	95 to 156
60	166	91 to 149
70	159	87 to 143

The percentage of maximal HR method is a very common and easy-to-calculate way to determine THR. To use this method, MHR must first be directly determined from a maximal stress test or estimated using a mathematical equation. Many estimation calculations are based on the traditional calculation of "220 – Age" for estimating MHR (Fox, Naughton, & Haskell, 1971). However, this formula is subject to a standard deviation of approximately ±12 beats per minute (bpm). This means that in a group of 100 40-year-old individuals, this standard MHR calculation would yield an MHR of 180 bpm. But because this formula is a prediction of the true MHR value, the actual MHR for about two-thirds of the class would range somewhere of between 168 and 192 bpm,

while the remaining 32% would fall further outside that range. ACSM suggests the use of formulas with standard deviations closer to 7 bpm, including the following (Gellish et al., 2007; Tanaka, Monahan, & Seals, 2001):

- Gellish et al. formula: 206.9 – (0.67 x Age)
- Tanaka, Monahan, and Seals formula: 208 – (0.7 x Age)

Sample Calculation: Using Percentage of MHR to Determine THR Range

A 38-year-old participant wants to exercise at 60–90% of his MHR.

Using the Tanaka, Monahan, and Seals formula: MHR = 208 – (0.7 x Age)

- MHR = 208 – (0.7 x 38) = 208 – 26.6 = ~181 bpm

181 bpm x 0.60 to 0.90 = THR range

- 181 x 0.60 = 109 bpm
- 181 x 0.90 = 163 bpm

THR range = 109 to 163 bpm

It is important to understand that the MHR estimation method of determining aerobic exercise intensity is an approximation and carries with it a certain amount of error. In fact, this method has a variability of up to plus or minus 10 to 20 bpm. The most accurate way to assess MHR is to directly measure it with a clinical monitoring device during a **graded exercise test.** Since most exercisers do not have access to this type of testing, the "220 – Age" formula was introduced. Due to lack of reliability, when the training heart rate is based on an estimated MHR—whether it is based on "220 – Age" or any of the other commonly used equations—it should be used in combination with the RPE scale, which is described later in this chapter.

Maximum Heart Rate: How Useful Is the Traditional Prediction Equation?

Two methods exist for determining MHR. The most accurate way is to directly measure the MHR with an **electrocardiogram (ECG)** monitoring device during a graded exercise test. The other way is to estimate MHR by using a simple prediction equation or formula. In 1971, the formula "220 – Age" was introduced and was widely accepted by the health and fitness community (Fox, Naughton, & Haskell, 1971). However, the validity of the formula has come under attack for several reasons. The subjects used in the study to determine the formula were not representative of the general population. In addition, even if the prediction equation did represent a reasonable average, a significant percentage of individuals will deviate substantially from the average value for any given age. In fact, standard deviations of plus or minus 10 to 20 beats per minute have been observed. Consequently, basing a participant's exercise intensity (i.e., training heart rate) on a potentially inaccurate estimation of MHR can be problematic. When the training heart rate is based on an estimated MHR, it should be used in conjunction with the ratings of perceived exertion scale (see Table 2-4 on page 39). Modify the intensity of the workout if a participant reports a high level of perceived exertion, even if his or her training heart rate has not been achieved.

During a group fitness class, participants can check their pulse rates from time to time to see if they are in their THR zone. This can be accomplished by finding a pulse on the thumb side of the wrist, in the neck to the side of the Adam's apple, or in the temple. Participants can be instructed to palpate their pulse points and count the number of heartbeats for 10 seconds. The GFI should time the duration of the pulse counting and instruct participants when to start and stop counting. The number of pulse beats can be multiplied by six to get the number of heartbeats per minute.

Percent of HR Reserve

Another method to determine THR range is to use a percentage of **heart-rate reserve (HRR),** which is found by using what is commonly known as the Karvonen formula (Figure 2-8). The recommended

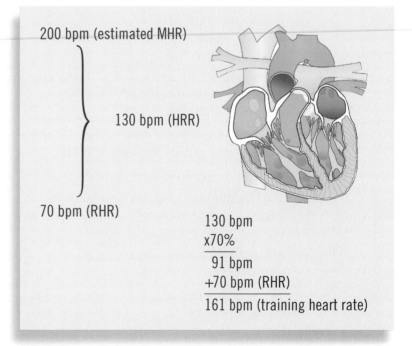

Figure 2-8

Use of the Karvonen formula for a 20-year-old man (average shape; resting heart rate = 70 bpm)

Note: bpm = Beats per minute; MHR = Maximum heart rate; HRR = Heart-rate reserve; RHR = Resting heart rate

percent of HRR (50 to 85%) corresponds to a similar percent of **maximal oxygen uptake** (50 to 85%). This method differs from the MHR method in that the **resting heart rate (RHR)** is taken into account when determining THR (see Figure 2-8). As in the MHR method, the measured heart-rate response and/or RPE must be used alongside this method when the participant is taking prescribed medications that alter HR.

The key to this method is to take a percentage of the difference between MHR and RHR (i.e., the HRR), then add the RHR to identify the THR. The reserve capacity of the heart reflects its ability to increase the heart rate and **cardiac output** above resting levels to maximal intensity. Current ACSM guidelines state that HRR is only a "guideline" used in setting exercise intensity (ACSM, 2014), which is why it is important to give participants an appropriate range of intensity within which to work.

Electronic Heart-rate Monitors

Another option to assist in determining exercise intensity is called heart-rate **telemetry.** In this method, the exerciser wears an electronic heart-rate monitor strapped to his or her chest during the workout that transmits heart rate to a wristwatch. Heart-rate telemetry is especially convenient in group fitness classes that rely heavily on the individual participant's heart rate as a measure of intensity and progression through the class. The use of heart-rate monitors is common in group cycling, but the devices can be used in most other aerobic-based group fitness classes as well.

If the heart rate is too fast (greater than 90% MHR) the participant should be coached to slow down. If the heart rate is below 55% MHR, and the participant is capable of more intensity, he or she should be encouraged to pick up the pace. It is important to keep in mind, however, that heart-rate monitoring devices can produce erratic readings. It is advisable to use RPE and physical observation along with electronic heart-rate monitoring technology to ensure the exerciser's intensity stays within an acceptable range.

Sample Calculation: Using HRR to Determine THR Range

A 38-year-old participant wants to exercise at 50 to 85% of his HRR; resting heart rate of 70 bpm.

Using the Tanaka, Monahan, and Seals formula:
MHR = 208 – (0.7 x Age)
- MHR = 208 – (0.7 x 38) = 208 – 26.6 = ~181 bpm

MHR – Resting heart rate (RHR)
- 181 bpm – 70 bpm = 111 bpm

Multiply by 0.50 and 0.85
- 111 bpm x 0.50 = 56 bpm
- 111 bpm x 0.85 = 94 bpm

Add RHR
- 56 bpm + 70 bpm = 126 bpm
- 94 bpm + 70 bpm = 164 bpm

THR range = 126 to 164 bpm

Overweight or deconditioned people reach their THR more quickly and with less effort. Athletic and very fit individuals reach their THR more slowly. People taking drugs that slow heart rate, such as beta-blockers taken to reduce **hypertension,** may not reach their THR despite intense exercise. Participants who are taking heart-rate altering medications should discuss with their doctors what THR is desirable and rely more on their feelings of exertion as an indicator of intensity.

Talk Test

Another technique, called the talk test, takes into account an exerciser's ability to breathe and talk during a workout. If a person can comfortably answer a question during exercise while still feeling like he or she is getting a good workout, it is likely that the activity being performed is appropriate for cardiorespiratory conditioning. The talk test is especially useful for beginners who are learning to pace themselves by monitoring their bodily responses to exercise. For those with higher fitness levels, the use of the talk test may not be appropriate.

A GFI can conduct the talk test on participants by simply asking them questions and listening for responses during the conditioning portion of class. Ideally, the responses of the participants should be in the form of sentences, rather than one-word statements, such as "fine" or "okay." For example, a GFI could ask a participant to describe how he or she is feeling and the participant could respond by saying, "I feel like I'm working pretty hard." If the exerciser can string those words together in a sentence without stopping and gasping for air, he or she is probably working at an appropriate intensity. Of course, this method is not always reliable, since many participants may feel uncomfortable speaking out and responding to the instructor in class. However, educating the class on the concept of the talk test might elicit more responses from participants if they know the GFI is using their vocal cues as a gauge for intensity.

Ratings of Perceived Exertion

Another method for measuring exercise intensity is by assigning a numerical value to subjective feelings of exercise exertion. Known as the RPE scale, this method, developed by Dr. Gunnar Borg, takes into account all that the exerciser is perceiving in terms of fatigue, including psychological, musculoskeletal, and environmental factors. RPE correlates well with physiological factors associated with exercise, such as heart rate, breathing rate, oxygen use, and overall fatigue. Table 2-4 lists two commonly used rating scales. For the RPE method of monitoring exercise intensity, the participant uses a scale to assign a rating to his or her physical effort.

When using the Borg 6–20 scale, an RPE of 12 to 13 (somewhat hard) corresponds to approximately 55 to 69% of MHR, whereas a rating of 15 to 16 (hard) corresponds to about 90% of MHR. Thus, individuals who train in the RPE range of 12 to 16 achieve the most efficient path to increased aerobic fitness.

In the group fitness class setting, explaining the Borg 6–20 RPE scale to participants is

Table 2-4	
Ratings of Perceived Exertion (RPE)	
RPE	**Category Ratio Scale**
6	0 Nothing at all
7 Very, very light	0.5 Very, very weak
8	1 Very weak
9 Very light	2 Weak
10	3 Moderate
11 Fairly light	4 Somewhat strong
12	5 Strong
13 Somewhat hard	6
14	7 Very strong
15 Hard	8
16	9
17 Very hard	10 Very, very strong
18	* Maximal
19 Very, very hard	
20	

Source: Adapted from American College of Sports Medicine (2014). *ACSM's Guidelines for Exercise Testing and Prescription* (9th ed.). Philadelphia: Wolters Kluwer/Lippincott Williams & Wilkins.

Using the First Ventilatory Threshold in the Group Exercise Setting

The talk test is based on the physiological principle of ventilation. As exercise intensity increases, ventilation increases in a somewhat linear manner. At certain intensities, metabolic changes occur that are associated with breathing. One point, called the "crossover" point, or the **first ventilatory threshold (VT1),** represents a level of intensity where **lactic acid** begins to accumulate within the blood (Figure 2-9). Prior to this intensity, fats are a major fuel and only small amounts of lactic acid are being produced. The body's need for oxygen is met primarily through an increase in **tidal volume** (or depth of breath) and not respiratory rate. Hence, the ability to talk should not be compromised and should not appear challenging or uncomfortable to the individual. Past the crossover point, however, ventilation rates begin to increase exponentially as oxygen demands outpace the oxygen-delivery system and lactic acid begins to accumulate in the blood. Consequently, respiratory rates increase and talking becomes difficult.

There are field tests that can be performed to determine a person's VT1 (the *ACE Personal Trainer Manual,* 4th Edition, has a detailed protocol for this process). However, performing an individual cardiorespiratory fitness assessment is not a common responsibility of the GFI. To make VT1 more applicable to group fitness participants, the GFI can teach them the talk test method and take it a step further by having participants find their HR while they are on the verge of VT1. The HR at VT1 can then be used as a target HR when determining exercise intensity. Those interested in sports conditioning and/or competition would benefit from training at higher intensities, but those interested in health and general fitness are well-served to stay at, or slightly below, this exercise intensity.

Another important metabolic marker is the **onset of blood lactic acid (OBLA),** the point at which lactic acid accumulates at rates faster than the body can buffer and remove it (blood lactate >4 mmol/L). This marker represents an exponential increase in the concentration of blood lactate, indicating an exercise intensity that can no longer be sustained. This point has historically been referred to as the **lactate threshold** or **anaerobic threshold,** and corresponds with a second noticeable increase in respiration called the **second ventilatory threshold (VT2)** (see Figure 2-9). This is an important marker, as it represents the highest sustainable level of exercise intensity, a strong marker of exercise performance.

Well-trained individuals can probably estimate their own HR response at VT2 during their training by identifying the highest sustainable intensity they can maintain for an extended duration (e.g., 15–20 minutes). The *ACE Personal Trainer Manual,* 4th Edition, has a detailed protocol for this process, but the role of the GFI typically does not include this type of high-intensity individual exercise testing. This test should only be performed by those who are deemed low- to moderate-risk and who have already attained an aerobic conditioning base through months of cardio-respiratory endurance exercise. Individuals who train near or at VT2 are usually competitive athletes. Many exercisers will never have the ability or desire to train at the intensities associated with VT2.

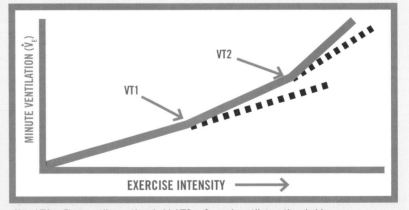

Note: VT1 = First ventilatory threshold; VT2 = Second ventilatory threshold

Figure 2-9
Ventilatory response to increasing exercise intensity

usually difficult. A GFI who uses the 0–10 category ratio scale, rather than the 6–20 scale, as a means to incorporate RPE into the class setting will probably fare better in educating the participants about the use of RPE. An appropriate range of intensity for increasing cardiorespiratory fitness within the 0–10 scale is between 3 (moderate) and 5 (strong).

Another, perhaps more practical, way to use RPE is to simply instruct the participants to use words instead of numbers to evaluate how hard they are working. For example, a GFI could explain prior to the conditioning portion of class that participants should gauge their intensities by feelings that correspond to the words "just noticeable," "light," "hard," and "maximal." An appropriate perception of intensity, using these words as indicators, would range somewhere between *light* and *hard*, whereas *just noticeable* and *maximal* are (depending on the class) intensities to avoid.

Dyspnea Scale

When an unconditioned person attempts to exercise vigorously, he or she can experience **dyspnea** (difficult and labored breathing). Individuals who have pulmonary conditions, such as **asthma** and **emphysema,** also can experience problems with breathing during exercise. GFIs should observe their class participants for signs of difficulty with breathing so that the participants can be coached to reduce their intensity if dyspnea occurs.

Participants can be taught the dyspnea scale to gauge the appropriateness of breathing performance during class. It is normal for participants engaging in cardiorespiratory exercise to experience mild and even moderate difficulty breathing, but those suffering from severe difficulty should be instructed to stop exercising and breathe deeply to recover from intense exercise.

Dyspnea Scale

The dyspnea scale is a subjective score that reflects the relative difficulty of breathing as perceived by the participant during physical activity.

+1 Mild, noticeable to the exerciser, but not to an observer

+2 Mild, some difficulty that is noticeable to an observer

+3 Moderate difficulty, participant can continue to exercise

+4 Severe difficulty, participant must stop exercising

Application of Intensity Monitoring to the Group Exercise Setting

Monitoring exercise intensity during group fitness classes is a skill that GFIs must be able to teach to their participants. Of course, a GFI must be able to recognize warning signs that indicate participants are in distress due to overexertion, but ultimately the responsibility for exercising within an appropriate range of intensity rests with the participant. This concept should be explained by the GFI at the beginning of each class. It is important for the class to understand that while the GFI will do his or her best to provide a safe and effective exercise experience, each individual participant must gauge the intensity of his or her true effort and adjust performance accordingly.

It is helpful to explain to the participants at the beginning of class the physical sensations that are normal with various intensities of exercise and how to adjust performance, if necessary. For example, a GFI could announce, "At different points during class, we will check the intensity of our effort. I will ask you to think about how hard you are working. You should reflect on how fast you are breathing and how fatigued you feel at the moment the question is asked. Those of you who are wearing heart-rate monitors and who are aware of your target heart rate range can check your monitor while simultaneously taking an inventory of how you feel. If you feel like you're working too hard (at a level that cannot be sustained), I will show you how to reduce the intensity of what we are doing at that time. If you feel as if you're not working hard enough, I'll show you how to increase the challenge."

It is advisable to perform intensity-monitoring checks several times during the workout. An intensity check can be as simple as taking 10 seconds to ask the participants how they feel. At the very least, an intensity check should be performed during a relatively high-intensity point of the cardiorespiratory conditioning portion of the class, and again after the cardiorespiratory cool-down portion of class. It is important for the GFI and each participant to acknowledge that the intensity of effort was elevated at the appropriate times during class and that it was decreased prior to the conclusion of class.

It is up to the GFI to choose an intensity-monitoring method that is most suitable for his or her skills and abilities, as well as one that is most practical for the class setting. Whether using THR, the talk test, RPE, or the dyspnea scale, a GFI must feel comfortable with the method so that its application is simple and easy for the participants to understand.

Looking for Warning Signs

Sometimes, even while using intensity-monitoring strategies, participants can over-exert themselves during a group exercise class. A competent GFI will be able to recognize cues or warning signs that necessitate the lowering of intensities for individual participants or the class as a whole.

The first, and perhaps most obvious, warning sign that a GFI is likely to observe

when a participant is working too vigorously is a breakdown in proper form and exercise execution. For example, an individual who is beginning to fatigue during a step training class might not be able set his or her foot completely on top of the bench, allowing the heel to hang off the platform. This increases the risk of tripping and poses a hazard to the participant and the classmates around him or her. Another situation that would illustrate compromised form due to overexertion is a participant getting fatigued while performing a bench press exercise in a group strength training class. Excessive arching of the back, shoulder elevation, and locking the elbows at the top of the repetition to rest would indicate that the exerciser has reached muscular fatigue of the chest, shoulders, and triceps, and is now using other muscles for compensation.

In either of these examples, it would be appropriate for the GFI to recommend a reduction in the intensity of the exercise. In most cases, it is adequate for a GFI to make a general statement to the entire class about proper execution of the exercise and how to reduce the intensity through modifications if the participants find themselves exhibiting poor form. Sometimes, however, it might be necessary for the GFI to approach a participant and use specific, corrective feedback if the exerciser continues to risk injury by performing movements incorrectly. A non-intimidating way of doing this in class would be for the GFI to walk over to the participant, mute the microphone, and give the participant a few cues to help correct form.

Other warning signs that could indicate a need for reducing exercise intensity include labored breathing, excessive sweating, and dizziness. A GFI should recommend to participants who are experiencing these symptoms to stop exercising and lightly march in place until the symptoms subside. As the heart rate lowers and the breathing becomes more normal, the participant can attempt to continue at a new lower intensity. However, it might be necessary to discontinue the exercise session if the symptoms do not improve. More severe signs, such as chest pain or discomfort, heart palpitations, **tachycardia,** intermittent **claudication,** or severe musculoskeletal pain, indicate the need for immediate cessation of exercise and possibly the activation of the emergency management system (EMS).

Observational Assessments

One of the most powerful instructional strategies that can be used by a GFI is to observe participants while they are performing a movement and then provide feedback based on those observations. A participant's **posture,** exercise form and technique, and tolerance to fatigue should be monitored by the GFI throughout the class.

Posture and Movement

Since all movement is based on a person's posture, a GFI should be able to recognize the important characteristics associated with proper spinal alignment and good overall posture. The following points represent what a GFI should look for when assessing a participant's standing posture.

- Lateral view (Figure 2-10a)
  - ✔ The head should be suspended (not pushed back or dropped forward) with the ears in line with the shoulders, shoulders over hips, hips over knees, and knees over ankles. An imaginary plumb line dropped from

overhead should pass through the cervical and lumbar vertebrae, hips, knees, and ankles.
  - ✔ Participants must maintain the three natural curves of the spine. A decrease or increase in the spinal curvature changes the amount of compression the spine can withstand. The hips can be tucked slightly, particularly for individuals with exaggerated lumbar **lordosis,** pregnant women, and participants with a large, protruding abdominal area.
  - ✔ The knees should be unlocked or soft. Hyperextended knees shift the pelvis, contributing to an increased low-back curve and back strain, along with decreased blood flow to and from the legs.
- Anterior and posterior views (Figures 2-10b and 2-10c)
  - ✔ The feet should be shoulder-width apart with the weight evenly distributed. Excessive **pronation** or **supination** could lead to musculoskeletal injuries if a participant performs high volumes of exercise with poor foot mechanics. Any individual who complains of joint pain in the ankles, knees, hips, or back should consult his or her healthcare provider, especially if he or she exhibits high arches (excessive supination) or flat feet (excessive pronation).
  - ✔ There should be overall symmetry between the two sides of the body with no visible lateral shifting or leaning to one side.
- Anterior view (Figure 2-10b)
  - ✔ The arms should hang with equal spaces between the arm and the torso and the hands should hang such that only the thumbs and index fingers are

Figure 2-10
Assessing a
participant's posture

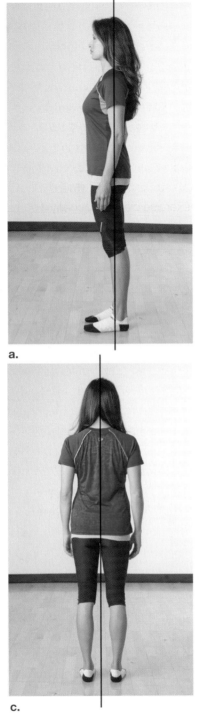

a.

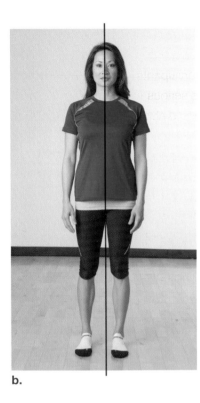

b.

c.

hang with the knuckles facing forward
indicate an imbalance of the muscles
of the shoulder and/or forearm.

✔ The kneecaps (patellae) should be oriented forward without deviation into
internal or external rotation. A patella
that appears rotated inward or outward
is an indication of a potential muscular
imbalance or structural deviation of the
hips and/or foot/ankle complex.

Form/Technique

While it certainly is not the responsibility of the GFI to conduct individual postural
assessments and design restorative exercise
programs for participants, knowledge of ideal
postural alignment is crucial for understanding
proper exercise technique. A GFI can cue participants to maintain correct posture throughout the exercise class with statements such
as, "Be sure to keep your shoulders set back
and down and your knees slightly bent while
we do the next exercise."

Muscular imbalances are often found
around the knees, hips, trunk, and shoulder
girdle due to the characteristics of occupational sitting. Giving participants in group
exercise classes an opportunity to work
those joints through their intended ranges
of motion, while simultaneously promoting
adequate strength and flexibility of the joints'
associated structures, is one way to help
them improve posture.

Generally, a participant's exercise technique
should adhere to a few basic guidelines:

• Controlled, purposeful movements require
more muscle involvement, and thus protect the joints better than quick, jerky
movements. This is true of both resistance
exercise and cardiorespiratory exercise.

• The availability of specific amounts of
weight in group strength training is often

visible (i.e., no knuckles should be
visible from the anterior view). A one-
sided, asymmetrical space between
the arm and the torso indicates a
muscular imbalance at the trunk or
shoulder girdle complex. Hands that

limited, resulting in some participants lifting loads that are too light for advancing muscular fitness. In these situations, it is important to cue the participant to focus even more on the muscular contraction being performed to move the weight rather than increasing the velocity of the lift. In classes that promote momentum training, such as in kettlebell classes, it is essential for a GFI to have the proper knowledge and training to correctly instruct the technique.

- In load-bearing cardiorespiratory classes, such as traditional aerobics and step training, participants should be cued to control the descent of the lower extremity as it makes contact with the ground (or step) surface by making as little noise as possible with the feet. This practice will ensure a thoughtful impact with the ground and result in muscular deceleration forces that attenuate much of the ground reaction forces that could affect the body's joints. Coaching a participant to "land quietly" or to "be light on your feet" are helpful cues.

- Regardless of the exercise being performed, participants should be coached to always demonstrate good posture. This typically means that the spine and pelvis should maintain their neutral, or ideal, positions through a mild contraction of the core musculature, the shoulders should be set back and down, and the knees should remain slightly bent.

Exercise Tolerance/Fatigue

A GFI must carefully observe each participant in class for signs of exercise intolerance and fatigue. In a class full of individuals with varying degrees of fitness, a GFI will probably have to devote more attention to beginning exercisers and special populations. This is why it is crucial for a GFI to be able to provide modifications to all exercises presented in class. The newer or less-fit attendees can be instructed on how to perform a safe and effective workout without exercising too vigorously by simply watching the GFI's modifications.

Recognizing the warning signs of overexertion mentioned earlier in this section is of paramount importance when leading any exercise class, especially if some participants have health limitations. While not as serious as overexertion, exercise fatigue should also be monitored by the GFI. Recall that the most obvious sign of fatigue is improper exercise technique. Participants should be taught that the inability to continue performing an exercise correctly is an indication that they need to stop what they are doing and modify the exercise. Executing any exercise with improper form will likely reinforce the poor technique so that it will occur again in the future.

Group fitness programs are typically scheduled with the intent to offer a variety of different exercise classes that might appeal to a large portion of the fitness center members. In this sense, most schedules are created for the general public and not for individuals with unique health concerns and needs. Therefore, a GFI must conduct a quick "screening" of participants that often comes in the form of asking them if they are aware of the type or intensity level of the class. Individuals with health limitations will often approach a GFI to inquire about the format of the class and to let the instructor know of their concerns. However, a GFI cannot rely on participants always informing them of their health issues. In addition to asking class attendees if they are aware of the physical requirements of the workout, and if they have any questions about modifications, the GFI should also intently watch for warning signs of exhaustion or injury throughout the class.

Physical-fitness Assessments

For most class situations, it is likely that GFIs will be teaching new participants or individuals who attend sporadically. These circumstances make it difficult to measure participants' fitness through physical assessments, because the instructor has no control over the exercise program and follow-up testing. Additionally, many instructors are unknowledgeable about physical-fitness testing because conducting assessments is not a common practice in the group setting. Furthermore, the format of a typical group fitness class does not allow instructors the freedom to use valuable class time for the performance of physical-fitness tests.

Despite the challenges facing instructors regarding the practice of conducting physical assessments in their classes, all fitness professionals should be aware of common exercise testing procedures and their role in a comprehensive exercise program. Developing skills in physical-fitness testing will be an overall advantage because it will help an instructor understand how to measure the important components of health-related fitness (i.e., cardiorespiratory endurance, flexibility, and muscular strength and endurance) and track participants' progress during a program. These skills will also become more useful as the trend of short-term group exercise programming takes hold. Many commercial fitness facilities and recreational community programs offer classes limited to timeframes lasting six to eight weeks. In these situations, it is very likely that the same group of participants who started the program will also finish the program. These short-term programs easily lend themselves to physical-fitness testing, as long as it is made clear to participants that

pre- and post-program fitness assessments will take place.

There are several good reasons to conduct physical-fitness assessments in the group fitness setting. First, performing pre-program baseline measurements, followed by reassessments using the same testing protocols, is one of the best ways to develop **motivation** in new exercise participants. Reports of high satisfaction levels are more likely when participants are able to look back to see how far they have come and see the extent of their fitness development. Second, fitness tests act as feedback. That is, what can be measured can also be managed. Performance feedback from periodic fitness assessments provides valuable data that let a participant know if he or she is on track to achieve the exercise-program goals. Third, fitness tests act as points of reference for program design. If the results of a battery of physical assessments reveal an area of fitness that is particularly lacking, the participant can work to improve the deficient area to enhance overall performance. Finally, being able to provide fitness-assessment services to participants sets an instructor apart from other GFIs who do not have this skill set and shows that the instructor is a professional concerned about the safety and effectiveness of the participants' exercise programs.

When administering a battery of physical-fitness tests within one class period, it is important to sequence the order of the tests so that the effects of the previous tests have minimal impact on the performance of the subsequent tests. For example, the appropriate ordering of tests for a group fitness class would be cardiorespiratory endurance, followed by muscular fitness, and lastly flexibility.

However, if it is not possible to perform all of these assessments, neuromuscular assessments such as **static balance** assessments are quick and easy to perform (refer to the *ACE Personal Trainer Manual,* 4th edition, for more information on sequencing assessments). Providing basic information to participants regarding their ability to establish and maintain balance will give them a framework they can build upon to improve their movement quality. Utilizing basic assessment tools and following up with exercises to address common balance concerns will provide education and give participants ownership of their exercise experience. For example, incorporating moves such as single-leg balance while performing alternating arm raises during the muscle conditioning segment and explaining how this will help improve balance as well as maintain core integrity will give the exerciser a sense of purpose and allow the movement to carry over into real life. The ACE Integrated Fitness Training™ (ACE IFT™) Model suggests performing static balance assessments first, as they are generally informative, the results are easy to interpret, and they provide the participant with useful information (see page 59) (ACE, 2010).

Health-related
Components of Fitness

The following selection of classic fitness assessments is commonly utilized in one-on-one settings. It is important to note that proper training is required to perform one-on-one assessments. This training is beyond the scope of this book and beyond what is commonly performed by most GFIs. However, being able to answer questions about these tests is important.

Body Composition

Hydrostatic weighing, also known as underwater weighing, is considered the "gold standard" of body-composition assessment. Body density is calculated from the relation-

ship of normal body weight to underwater weight, with percent fat being calculated from body density. Though hydrostatic weighing is more precise and the choice of many researchers, it is often impractical in terms of expense, time, and equipment.

Bioelectrical impedance analysis is another popular method for determining body composition. It is based on the principle that the conductivity of an electrical impulse is greater through lean tissue than through fatty tissue. Reliability using this method is problematic because environmental issues, such as hydration state, temperature, and humidity, can have an impact on the results and are hard to standardize. Assessing body composition via bioelectrical impedance requires minimal technical training with the analyzers, which range widely in price and quality.

For complete protocols of the assessments mentioned in this section, visit www.acefitness.org/fitnesstests.

Anthropometry is the science of measuring human physical dimensions, proportions, and body composition. **Anthropometric assessments** for measuring body composition include circumference measurements using a tape measure, waist-to-hip circumference ratio, and skinfold caliper measurements. Skinfold caliper measurements, which can be used to calculate body-fat percentages, require special training and are not practical for a group setting. They are therefore recommended for use in a one-on-one setting. It is important to keep in mind that there is a margin of error (plus or minus 3 to 4%) with each skinfold test, and all tests must be compared to identical tests performed by the same tester under identical testing situations for optimum results. General body-fat percentage categories are listed in Table 2-5.

Table 2-5

General Body-fat Percentage Categories

Classification	Women (% fat)	Men (% fat)
Essential fat	10–13%	2–5%
Athletes	14–20%	6–13%
Fitness	21–24%	14–17%
Average	25–31%	18–24%
Obese	32% and higher	25% and higher

Figure 2-12
Hip circumference

Table 2-6

Waist-to-hip Ratios and Associated Levels of Health Risk

Classification	Men	Women
High risk	>1.0	>0.85
Moderately high risk	0.90–1.0	0.80–0.85
Lower risk	<0.90	<0.80

Adapted from Van Itallie, T.B. (1988). Topography of body fat: Relationship to risk of cardiovascular and other diseases. In: *Anthropometric Standardization Reference Manual.* Champaign, Ill.: Human Kinetics.

Field tests for measuring body composition within a group exercise setting include waist-to-hip circumference and **body mass index (BMI).** Performing waist-to-hip measurements is an easy way to teach participants about the risks associated with body-fat distribution. The waist measurement is the smallest waist circumference below the rib cage and above the umbilicus, measured while standing with the abdominal muscles relaxed (not pulled in) (Figure 2-11). If there appears to be no "smallest area" around the waist, the measurement should be made at the level of the navel. Hip circumference is defined as the largest circumference of the buttocks-hip area taken while the person is standing (Figure 2-12). The waist-to-hip ratio illustrates where a person carries his or her body fat and whether this is a risk factor for diseases of the heart, diabetes, and some types of cancer (Table 2-6).

BMI is another way to estimate body composition that is quick, easy, and does not require equipment or training. Technically, BMI does not estimate body composition. Instead, it attempts to determine whether an individual is obese and how much his or her health risks are increased with increasing **obesity.** BMI is calculated as follows:

$$BMI = Weight\ (kg)\ /\ Height^2\ (m)$$

See Table 2-7 for a reference chart. Information on BMI is a good topic to include in a newsletter or handout for group exercise participants, as people can perform this assessment on their own. However, caution should be followed whenever using total body weight instead of taking into account fat and lean body weight. More muscular, athletic individuals may be calculated as overweight using the BMI method, when in fact they sim-

Figure 2-11
Waist circumference

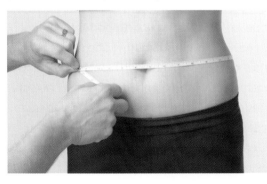

Body Mass Index Example

$$BMI = \frac{Weight\ (kg)}{Height^2\ (m)}$$

Convert weight from pounds (lb) to kilograms (kg) by dividing weight in lb by 2.2

Weight = 140 lb   140 ÷ 2.2 = 63.6 kg

Convert height from inches to centimeters (cm), and then to meters (m), by multiplying height in inches by 2.54 and then dividing by 100:

Height = 58 inches 58 x 2.54 = 147.3 cm
147.3 ÷ 100 = 1.47 m

$$BMI = \frac{63.6}{1.47^2} = 29.4$$

Table 2-7	
Body Mass Index Reference Chart	
Weight Category	**BMI Range**
Underweight	<18.5
Normal weight	18.5–24.9
Overweight	25.0–29.9
Grade I Obesity	30.0–34.9
Grade II Obesity	35.0–39.9
Grade III Obesity	>40

ply have a large portion of lean body weight. This is a major limitation of BMI testing.

Cardiorespiratory Endurance

Maximal and submaximal cardiorespiratory exercise tests using the treadmill or bicycle ergometer are not well-suited for measuring the cardiorespiratory fitness of groups. In the group fitness setting, field tests for measuring cardiorespiratory endurance, such as the YMCA submaximal **step test,** are more appropriate because they are easy to administer, practical, inexpensive, and less time-consuming than the treadmill and bicycle ergometer tests. One important consideration for administering a cardiorespiratory field test with a group of individuals is that participants must be taught how to accurately measure their heart rates, as discussed earlier in this chapter.

The YMCA submaximal step test is a three-minute step test that requires participants to step on and off of a 12-inch (30-cm) step bench at a standardized cadence. Although this test does not result in an estimation of **maximal oxygen consumption,** it gives an estimation of cardiorespiratory fitness in comparison to established norms based on post-exercise heart rate.

Muscular Strength and Endurance

GFIs can measure participants' muscular fitness using calisthenic-type strength and endurance tests. These tests are based on specific exercises, such as the half sit-up and the push-up, and require the participant to perform a maximum number of repetitions for each exercise during the assessment.

The push-up test is used to evaluate upper-body muscular strength and endurance in men and women. Men are required to perform the test in the standard position with the hands and toes in contact with the floor. Women are required to use the modified position with the hands and knees in contact with the floor. Women who choose the standard push-up position (i.e., with the hands and toes in contact with the floor) must be notified that their scores will not be comparable to the standardized norms because the data represented in the norm table were produced from research using only the modified position for women.

The half sit-up test is used to evaluate abdominal muscle strength and endurance in men and women. It was developed to replace the traditional full sit-up test so that potential low-back problems could be avoided. Additionally, full sit-ups call upon the hip flexors for a large portion of the

range of motion (ROM). Thus, half sit-ups minimize the involvement of the hip flexors during the movement and are a better assessment exercise for abdominal muscle function. To complete the test, the participant performs half sit-ups to a standardized cadence for one minute without pausing.

Neuromuscular Efficiency

Neuromuscular efficiency is the ability of the neuromuscular system to allow muscles that produce movement and muscles that provide stability to work synergistically as an integrated functional unit. This component can be assessed with static balance assessments and movement screens that identify muscle imbalances and postural deviations, which may be structural or related to poor movement quality or posture. Structural deviations are generally considered non-correctible, whereas muscle imbalances and most movement quality–related issues are correctible. For instance, someone with scoliosis has a structural deviation of the spine that cannot be corrected with exercise, whereas someone who has weak postural muscles, such as the muscles of the middle back, can improve his or her standing and sitting postures by performing strengthening exercises for the rhomboids and middle trapezius. Some common assessments include static postural assessments, functional movement screens, flexibility/muscle-length testing, shoulder mobility, and balance/core assessments.

Flexibility

Evaluating ROM using flexibility tests is a great way to determine areas of the body that may need an emphasis on stretching. Stiff, inflexible soft tissues pose a risk for injury and may adversely affect the performance of the simplest tasks. Inflexibility due to disuse, improper body alignment, or

repetitive-task exposure is commonly seen in the areas of the hamstrings, lower back, and shoulders. To address these areas, two easily administered tests can be used: the sit-and-reach test and the shoulder-flexibility test.

The sit-and-reach test is used to assess low-back and hip-joint flexibility. Just as the name implies, the test is completed when a participant reaches forward while sitting with the legs extended forward to see how much ROM the hamstrings and low-back will allow. Participants with a history of low-back dysfunction and/or pain should avoid performing this test. The test is scored based on how far past the feet the subject can reach.

The shoulder-flexibility test measures the multirotational components of the shoulder joints. The test is completed when the participant reaches behind the back with both hands (one hand reaches down from above, and the other hand reaches up from below). The participant attempts to bring the fingertips of both hands together behind the back. Scoring is based on the distance, if any, between the fingertips. Anyone with a history of shoulder dysfunction and/or pain should avoid performing this test.

Summary

Regular participation in group exercise can be an important component of a healthy lifestyle. It is common for a GFI to teach participants of various conditioning levels, skills, and abilities. Because of the various populations potentially present in each class, the GFI must have knowledge of the appropriate health screening procedures to ensure a safe and effective class for all individuals. Pre-class preparation also includes an evaluation of the group fitness room, equipment, and scheduling logistics. During class, a

GFI must have knowledge of how to properly monitor the group's intensity as well as have the practical application skills to educate the participants on self-monitoring strategies. While physical-fitness assessments are not the norm in group exercise, there are circumstances when conducting these tests could be beneficial. A GFI should have knowledge of appropriate fitness assessments that could be performed in the group setting.

References

American College of Sports Medicine (2014). *ACSM's Guidelines for Exercise Testing and Prescription* (9th ed.). Philadelphia: Wolters Kluwer/Lippincott Williams & Wilkins.

American Council on Exercise (2010). *ACE Personal Trainer Manual* (4th ed.). San Diego, Calif.: American Council on Exercise.

Balady, G.J. et al. (1998). Recommendations for cardiovascular screening, staffing and emergency policies at health/fitness facilities: A Joint Position Statement by the American College of Sports Medicine and the American Heart Association. *Medicine & Science in Sports & Exercise,* 30, 1009–1018.

Fox III, S.M., Naughton, J.P., & Haskell, W.L. (1971). Physical activity and the prevention of coronary heart disease. *Annals of Clinical Research,* 3, 404–432.

Frangolias, D. & Rhodes, E. (1995). Maximal and ventilatory threshold responses to treadmill and water immersion running. *Medicine & Science in Sports & Exercise,* 27, 7, 1007–1013.

Gellish, R.L. et al. (2007). Longitudinal modeling of the relationship between age and maximal heart rate. *Medicine & Science in Sports & Exercise,* 39, 5, 822–829.

Parker, S. et al. (1989). Failure of target heart rate to accurately monitor intensity during aerobic dance. *Medicine & Science in Sports & Exercise,* 21, 2, 230–234.

Roach, B., Croisant, P., & Emmett J. (1994). The appropriateness of heart rate and RPE measures of intensity during three variations of aerobic dance. *Medicine & Science in Sports & Exercise,* 26, 5, (Supplement).

Tanaka, H., Monahan, K.D., & Seals, D.R. (2001). Age-predicted maximal heart revisited. *Journal of the American College of Cardiology*, 37, 153–156.

United States Department of Health and Human Services (2008). *2008 Physical Activity Guidelines for Americans.* www.health.gov/paguidelines.

Van Itallie, T.B. (1988). Topography of body fat: Relationship to risk of cardiovascular and other diseases. In: *Anthropometric Standardization Reference Manual.* Champaign, Ill.: Human Kinetics.

Carol Kennedy-Armbruster, M.S., received her bachelor's degree in leisure studies from the University of Illinois and her master's degree in exercise and sport science from Colorado State University. She will soon complete her Ph.D. from Indiana University in Human Performance. For 20 years, she worked in health clubs and recreational facilities as a fitness instructor and manager. She is now a senior lecturer within the Department of Kinesiology's Health Fitness Specialist Undergraduate Curriculum at Indiana University. Kennedy-Armbruster teaches classes on group exercise leadership, one-on-one fitness training, living well, and fitness management. She has produced videos on aquatic exercise and functional exercise progression, and coauthored a research-based textbook, *Methods of Group Exercise Instruction.*

Kelly Jo Baute, M.S., received her bachelor's degree in exercise science and her master's degree in applied sport science from Indiana University and is completing her doctorate in Motor Control and Bio-Anthropology. She has worked as a group fitness instructor, group fitness coordinator, and director of fitness for a community wellness program and a fitness club facility. She is now a full-time lecturer within the Department of Kinesiology's Fitness Specialist Undergraduate Curriculum at Indiana University, where she instructs classes in group exercise leadership, one-on-one fitness training, and sport and exercise psychology.

Group Exercise
Program Design

By Carol Kennedy-Armbruster & Kelly Jo Baute

Historically, group exercise program design has been structured to enhance people's health-related components of fitness, such as cardiorespiratory endurance, **muscular strength** and **endurance, flexibility,** and **body composition** through movement. While this continues to be an essential focus, group exercise program design potentially involves much more; it is about empowering people with the ability to improve their quality of life as well as expanding their social engagement by connecting them with others. McNeill et al. (2006) found that individuals who participated in physical activity for enjoyment and to achieve goals were more likely to have better **self-efficacy** and that social support contributed to their **motivation** for continuing to participate in a physical-activity program.

Factors that can enhance motivation and self-efficacy are important because drop-out rates from physical-activity programs have averaged 50% for the past several decades, despite innovations in programming (Dishman, 2001). Individual factors (motivation and self-efficacy), as well as factors within the social (social support) and physical (access to facilities) environments, contribute to one's health behavior or participation in physical activity (McNeill et al., 2006) (see Chapter 5 for more information on exercise adherence and the many factors that contribute to continued participation in a group exercise program).

To move beyond the health-related components of fitness, it is essential to offer programs led by experienced group fitness instructors (GFIs). Edmunds, Ntoumanis, and Duda (2008) found that when a GFI gave participants the opportunity to select the exercises, was cognizant of participants' feelings, and demonstrated "concern for their well-being," exercise participants' behavioral, cognitive, and affective responses to exercise were positively influenced. The skills needed to provide this type of group exercise leadership stems from genuine concern for improving the health of the participants, the desire to continue to educate and increase knowledge, and a passion for creating and providing effective social support.

The evolution of group exercise programming can be traced back to aerobic dance–based classes developed by Jackie Sorenson in 1969. Sorenson worked with Dr. Kenneth Cooper and participated in Cooper's 12-minute running test. A non-runner, Sorenson scored well and attributed her performance to her experience and participation in dance (Kennedy &

Yoke, 2009). Hence, Sorenson's experience and passion for dance inspired her to create a group exercise program design that was able to reach many people and revolutionized the group exercise industry. Other similar programs soon followed. Jazzercise™, a choreographed, aerobic dance–based program was also founded in 1969 by Judy Sheppard Missett. Jazzercise became a worldwide phenomenon and is currently offered in more than 30 countries. From these pioneering programs, numerous others have been developed over the past 30 years. Today, group exercise programs include traditional high- and low-impact classes, step training, group indoor cycling, kickboxing, sports conditioning, dance, boot camp, aquatic exercise, strength and conditioning classes, mind/body classes such as **yoga** and **Pilates,** flexibility/stretching classes, abdominal/core classes, equipment-based classes, and more. Other growing trends include group exercise performed outdoors and branded programs such as Les Mills' Body Pump™ series. Outdoor settings have been especially successful for boot-camp classes, but also can be used for walking and aquatic exercise classes. For instance, the *2010 IDEA Fitness Programs and Equipment Trends Survey* lists outdoor boot-camp classes as growing by 69% among the survey respondents and branded choreography programs as growing by 23% (Schroeder & Dolan, 2010). As the fitness industry is driven by trends, programs are continuously being created by passionate and motivated fitness professionals. It is important that those in the fitness industry continue to be mindful of the safety and efficacy of these programs. The American College of Sports Medicine (ACSM) guidelines on exercise programming for healthy adults can serve as a template for exercise programming (ACSM, 2014). Driven by research findings, ACSM's guidelines are a reflection of the health and fitness needs of the apparently healthy population, as illustrated by the addition of neuromuscular exercise to the ACSM guidelines. Neuromuscular exercise such as **balance** and agility training may be effective in preventing falls in an increasingly older population (ACSM, 2014). See Table 3-1 for a summation of the 2014 ACSM exercise programming guidelines for appar-

ently healthy adults. The current guidelines include cardiorespiratory, muscular strength and endurance, flexibility, and neuromuscular exercise recommendations. How does one program for cardiorespiratory exercise? Cardiorespiratory duration includes 20 to 60 continuous minutes or discontinuous 10-minute bouts that add up to 20 to 60 minutes total. However, according to the *2010 IDEA Fitness Programs and Equipment Trends Survey* most group exercise classes are still one hour in duration (Schroeder & Dolan, 2010), even though

Table 3-1

General Exercise Recommendations for Healthy Adults

Training Component	Frequency (days per week)	Intensity	Time (Duration) or Repetitions	Type (Activity)
Cardiorespiratory	≥5 or ≥3 or 3–5	Moderate (40% to <60% $\dot{V}O_2R$/HRR) Vigorous (≥60% $\dot{V}O_2R$/HRR) Combination of moderate and vigorous (40% to <60% $\dot{V}O_2R$/HRR; or ≥60% $\dot{V}O_2R$/HRR)	>30 minutes* 20–25 minutes* 20–30 minutes*	Aerobic (cardiovascular endurance) activities and weightbearing exercise
Resistance	2–3	60–80% of 1 RM or RPE = 5 to 6 (0–10 scale) for older adults	2–4 sets of 8–25 repetitions (e.g., 8–12, 10–15, 15–25; depending upon goal)	8–10 exercises that include all major muscle groups (full-body or split routine); Muscular strength and endurance, calisthenics, and neuromuscular (balance and agility) exercise
Flexibility	≥2–3	Stretch to the limits of discomfort within the ROM, to the point of mild tightness without discomfort	>4 repetitions per muscle group Static: 15–60 seconds; PNF: hold 6 seconds, then a 10–30 second assisted stretch	All major muscle-tendon groups Static, PNF, or dynamic (ballistic may be fine for individuals who participate in ballistic activities)

*Continuous exercise or intermittent exercise in bouts of at least 10 minutes in duration to accumulate the minimum recommendation for the given intensity

Note: $\dot{V}O_2R = \dot{V}O_2$ reserve; HRR = Heart-rate reserve; 1 RM = One-repetition maximum; RPE = Ratings of perceived exertion; ROM = Range of motion; PNF = Proprioceptive neuromuscular facilitation

Source: American College of Sports Medicine (2014). *ACMS's Guidelines for Exercise Testing and Prescription* (9th ed.). Philadelphia: Wolters Kluwer/ Lippincott Williams & Wilkins.

perceived lack of time is a main reason for individuals not participating in exercise. Restructuring class schedules and offering a group exercise class schedule that includes convenient times and formats is important for a successful fitness program. It is important to note that the IDEA survey was completed by fitness program directors and not necessarily fitness participants. This could be a limitation of interpreting the survey information for use in program development.

As the prevalence of **obesity** continues to escalate, it is clear that the need to provide opportunities to get people moving is ever more important. In 2008, the *Physical Activity Guidelines for Americans,* a collaborative effort of health and fitness experts that is sponsored by the U.S. Department of Health and Human Services (HHS), were released (U.S. Department of Health & Human Services, 2008). These guidelines are the first physical-activity guidelines issued by the federal government and are an attempt to offer solutions to help Americans achieve better health (Table 3-2). While guidelines from organizations such as ACSM and HHS are important contributions in the effort to solve the inactivity crisis, guidelines alone do not change behavior. Creative group exercise program design that is offered at ideal times with a variety of class lengths and formats and led by certified and well-trained group exercise leaders provides participants the ideal environment to become more physically active and be successful in adhering to a regular exercise regimen. Seguin et al. (2008) suggest that "program-specific training or experience plays an important role in leader confidence as well as competence around the planning, organization and administration, and/or execution of implementing the program and sustaining it."

Table 3-2			
Classification of Total Weekly Amounts of Aerobic Physical Activity Into Four Categories			
Levels of Physical Activity	**Range of Moderate-intensity Minutes a Week**	**Summary of Overall Health Benefits**	**Comment**
Inactive	No activity beyond baseline	None	Being inactive is unhealthy.
Low	Activity beyond baseline but fewer than 150 minutes a week	Some	Low levels of activity are clearly preferable to an inactive lifestyle.
Medium	150 to 300 minutes a week	Substantial	Activity at the high end of this range has additional and more extensive health benefits than activity at the low end.
High	More than 300 minutes a week	Additional	Current science does not allow researchers to identify an upper limit of activity above which there are no additional health benefits.

U.S. Department of Health & Human Services (2008). *2008 Physical Activity Guidelines for Americans: Be Active, Healthy and Happy.* www.health.gov/paguidelines/pdf/paguide.pdf

The ACE Integrated Fitness Training™ Model

Fitness facilities around the world face the mounting challenges of an aging and increasingly overweight population and an overburdened healthcare system that is often unable to meet the need for preventive care. Fitness professionals are seeing an influx of clients and class participants with an increasingly long list of special needs, creating confusion as they attempt to develop exercise programs and group fitness classes that safely and effectively address their clients' and participants' needs.

To address these complex concerns, the ACE Integrated Fitness Training (ACE IFT™) Model was introduced in the 4th edition of the *ACE Personal Trainer Manual* (2010). The ACE IFT Model provides personal trainers with a systematic and comprehensive approach to exercise programming that integrates assessments and programming to facilitate behavior change, while also improving **posture,** movement, flexibility, balance, core function, cardiorespiratory fitness, muscular endurance, and muscular strength. While the ACE IFT Model was developed as a tool for personal trainers—and though GFIs typically will not conduct the formal assessments necessary to accurately classify their participants in terms of their health and fitness levels—its core concepts can be applied in a group fitness setting.

The ACE IFT Model consists of two components, each of which is then divided into four phases that run parallel to the health–fitness–performance continuum (Table 3-3 and Figure 3-1). Rapport is the foundation for success during all phases, whether the exerciser is a highly motivated fitness enthusiast or a sedentary adult looking to adopt more healthful habits. The primary focus of each of the four phases of the ACE IFT Model is as follows:

- Functional movement and resistance training
  - ✔ *Phase 1: Stability and mobility training:* Correcting imbalances through training to improve joint stability and mobility prior to training movement patterns
  - ✔ *Phase 2: Movement training:* Training movement patterns prior to loading those movements
  - ✔ *Phase 3: Load training*: Adding external resistance to various movement patterns
  - ✔ *Phase 4: Performance training:* Improving performance through training for power, speed, agility, and reactivity

Table 3-3				
ACE Integrated Fitness Training Model— Training Components and Phases				
Training Component	**Phase 1**	**Phase 2**	**Phase 3**	**Phase 4**
Functional Movement & Resistance Training	Stability and Mobility Training	Movement Training	Load Training	Performance Training
Cardiorespiratory Training	Aerobic-base Training	Aerobic-efficiency Training	Anaerobic-endurance Training	Anaerobic-power Training

Note: The phases of the ACE IFT Model are not necessarily discrete in terms of their connection to the function–health–fitness–performance continuum. Progression principles should be followed when transitioning from one phase to the next for each training component.

Figure 3-1
ACE IFT Model phases and the health–fitness–performance continuum

- Cardiorespiratory training
  - ✔ *Phase 1: Aerobic-base training:* Building an aerobic base to improve parameters of cardiorespiratory health
  - ✔ *Phase 2: Aerobic-efficiency training:* Progressing toward improved fitness by introducing aerobic intervals to improve aerobic efficiency
  - ✔ *Phase 3: Anaerobic-endurance training:* Progressing to higher levels of fitness by developing **anaerobic** endurance
  - ✔ *Phase 4: Anaerobic-power training:* Improving performance by developing anaerobic power

It is important that GFIs look at their classes and individual participants from multiple perspectives in order to keep people progressing and excited to continue exercising. Unlike personal trainers who specifically design an exercise program for a given client, GFIs must first program for the group before offering modifications for individual participants who may be in various phases of the ACE IFT Model. The core challenge for many GFIs—whether they are newcomers or experienced instructors—often involves finding a balance between leading a group and making sure individual members of that group progress appropriately and safely. For this reason, GFIs should always communicate to participants that it is their responsibility to manage their movements and work within their personal fitness levels.

One situation in which the ACE IFT Model may be applied more directly in a group setting involves the development of longer-term group programming for participants who begin a program together and progress as a group. For example, a GFI may lead a group of new mothers through the postpartum return to exercise, or help a group of skiers prepare for the upcoming season. In these cases, preparticipation screening can be used to classify each individual's health and fitness level, as a baseline against which to measure future success, and as a tool to improve motivation and adherence.

Group Exercise Professionalism and Attitude

Combining current research with participants' needs to design a safe and effective class requires a high level of effort and a positive attitude on the part of the instructor. These ingredients will subsequently contribute to a positive and healthy atmosphere that will establish and facilitate learning and help promote better adherence among participants. A comfortable environment can be influenced by a wide range of factors, from the quality of an instructor's communication skills to his or her attire. Each factor helps establish a professional and caring attitude. A GFI needs to be a motivator and an educator (Kennedy & Yoke, 2009). Sy and Cote (2005) found that leaders with a positive mood transferred their positive attitude to the group and led group members to "engage in agreeable and friendly behavior." Additionally, it has been found that participants experience less social anxiety when the class is instructed with a "socially enriched leadership style" and participants "had more positive perceptions" in this type of setting (Martin & Fox, 2001). Furthermore, participants' level of learning is ultimately facilitated by the instructor. Strong et al. (2006) found that people who exercise for extrinsic motives, such as appearance, are less likely to continue with an exercise program. These authors suggest that designing programs that deemphasize appearance- or image-related factors and instead focus on health- and enjoyment-related motives are more effective in promoting long-term adherence. This research is supportive of participants' needs for positive and rewarding experiences. Research supporting that regular physical activity improves health is well documented; however, this evidence has not been successful in getting and keeping people moving on a regular basis. Creating enjoyable, motivating, progressive, and positive environments for participants can help them adopt and adhere to physical activity.

Student-centered Instruction

The motivational and inspirational aspect of instructing includes having new choreography, new music, and state-of-the-art equipment. The educational part of instructing includes having the knowledge of *why* certain moves are selected, making sure current research and knowledge are incorporated into the group exercise session, and making educated choices and decisions about the information given to participants. Student-centered instruction is the art of facilitating learning, or creating an environment that allows for the dissemination of key facts that will enhance participants' interests and address their needs.

It is important to compare and contrast a teacher-centered instructor with a student-centered instructor. The teacher-centered instructor can often foster dependence, intimidation, unattainable goals, and quick fixes. The student-centered instructor, on the other hand, strives to establish an atmosphere of independence, encouragement, attainable goals, and realism (Table 3-4). Learning to take responsibility for the health and well-being of participants starts with understanding the importance of establish-

Table 3-4	
Teacher-centered Instruction versus Student-centered Instruction	
Teacher-centered Instruction	**Student-centered Instruction**
Dependence: You need me to be able to exercise. Here's a DVD of my class for when you go on vacation.	*Independence:* Remember to work at your own pace. I will show modifications, but it will be your responsibility to monitor your intensity level accordingly. Here's how to do that …
Intimidation: If you can't do 20 push-ups you don't belong in this class!	*Encouragement:* Awesome work! Remember, if there is pain, there will be little gain. Stay with it and you'll feel better.
Unattainable goals: You'll see changes instantaneously from this class!	*Attainable goals:* Learning to enjoy movement is a process that will take time. Try adding extra activity outside of class, like taking the stairs or mowing your yard. Those activities count as movement experiences also.
Quick fixes: 50 more outer-thigh leg lifts and you'll get rid of that extra "stored energy" on your thighs.	*Reality:* Outer-thigh leg lifts will strengthen your outer-thigh muscles, but there is no such thing as "spot reduction" of a specific area.

ing a positive attitude and atmosphere and finding appropriate teaching methods to reach participants. There is more than one form of learning (e.g., visual, auditory, and kinesthetic), and finding ways to teach to a group that includes more than one form is a challenge. GFIs need to utilize more than one form of teaching. Student- and teacher-centered learning are two forms of teaching or leadership styles. Goleman, Boyatzis, and McKee (2004) describe additional leadership styles that can be applied to group exercise leadership to enhance participants' learning and overall experience:

- *Visionary:* Inspires by articulating a heartfelt, shared goal; routinely gives performance **feedback** and suggestions for improvement in terms of that goal
- *Coaching:* Involves taking people aside for a talk to learn their personal

aspirations; routinely gives feedback in those terms and stretches assignments to move toward those goals

- *Democratic:* Involves knowing when to listen and ask for input, and get buy-in; draws on what others know to make better decisions
- *Affiliative:* Involves the realization that having fun together is not a waste of time, but builds emotional capital and harmony

Creating a Healthy Emotional Environment

Another major factor in creating a comfortable atmosphere for participants is establishing a healthy emotional environment. Education and motivation alone are not what keep participants coming back to group exercise. It is necessary to tap into the feelings and emotions of participants to impact adherence. One study concerning overweight women's perceptions of an exercise class revealed that the most powerful influences affecting their exercise behavior were concerns about embarrassment and judgment by others (Bain, Wilson, & Chaikind, 1989). Fox, Rejeski, and Gauvin (2000) found that enjoyment during physical activity is optimized when a positive and supportive leadership style is coupled with an enriched and supportive group environment. Goleman (2006) explains that the emotional centers of the brain replicate what is being experienced. If a GFI has a positive, upbeat, and happy attitude, the participants will "attune" themselves to the same emotions. Instructors spend many hours preparing music, organizing the class flow, and selecting equipment, when, in fact, working on establishing a comfortable atmosphere is just as important to participants, if not more so. To tap into the "emotional centers" of the

participants, GFIs should be certain to greet participants as they enter the class, learn their names, and use positive words and expressions to draw upon these emotional components to create a positive and fulfilling experience that will make them want to come back. A meaningful increase in physical activity will improve health; however, if the participants do not adopt the behavior, improvement will not take place. Additionally, as the various leadership styles described earlier imply, not all leadership takes place at the front of the room. Consider moving around, leading segments or demonstrating moves in areas other than the front of the class. This allows more interaction with the participants and gives individuals in the back or at the sides of the class the opportunity to see better and experience the workout differently. If mirrors are utilized during the workout, it is important to face the participants as much as possible throughout the class to make direct eye contact. Looking at people through a mirror throughout the duration of class does not promote true interaction. Refer to Chapter 4 for more information on teaching styles.

Instructors also need to realize that what they do and say has an impact on the class atmosphere. According to Goleman (2005), having "emotional intelligence" in any group setting dictates the success of the group experience. Goleman believes that "the emotional economy is the sum total of the exchanges of feeling among us. In subtle (or not so subtle) ways, we all make each other feel a bit better (or a lot worse) as part of any contact we have; every encounter can be weighted along a scale from emotionally toxic to nourishing." A specific example of this within a group exercise setting would be announcing before class how great it feels to be in a group exercise class to improve overall health and well-being. Contrast this message with telling an overeating indulgence story and stating specific intentions to "work it off" during the class. The first statement leaves participants with a health-related sense of purpose for the workout. The second statement can send a message that punishment through exercise is recommended after overindulging. Sending positive health messages throughout the group exercise experience is important for establishing the "emotional atmosphere" of the workout and utilizing the role-model aspect of teaching in a positive way.

An environment where instructors present a "body beautiful" image can also be rather intimidating. Crawford and Eklund (1994) compared similar video exercise routines, with the instructor wearing a thong in one and the same instructor wearing shorts and a T-shirt in another. "High physique-anxious" participants rated the thong video more unfavorably than the shorts and T-shirt video. Instructors can help participants become more comfortable with their own bodies and keep them exercising by wearing a variety of exercise clothing. A study of 148 female fitness instructors at an instructor conference found that 64% of instructors perceived an ideal body as one that was thinner than their own bodies (Nardini, Raglin, & Kennedy, 1999). The average percent **body fat** of the instructors was 20.5%; the national average for this age group is 23.1%. Instructors' body-image perceptions are just that—perceptions. Perceptions can be changed, and this begins with the fitness instructor's self-awareness (Evans & Kennedy, 1993). If instructors are to make an impact on the health and well-being of participants, it will be important to address this issue on a per-sonal level. Finally, be aware of the impact of the physical environment. Ginis, Jung, and Gauvin (2003) found that regardless of body-image concerns, women in mirrored environments felt worse after exercising than women in non-mirrored environments. Participants respond favorably when mirrors are used appropriately—that is, when participants are encouraged to watch and recognize form and movement. Remind the participants to use the mirrors to check their form and learn to recognize if their movement is correct. For instance, ask the participants to watch if their knees are aligned correctly or to check if their posture is correct. Try to refocus the mirror issue away from a body-image focus and instead emphasize form correction. Demonstrating to participants their ability to learn movements and become more successful at exercise will ultimately improve their self-efficacy and lead to further enjoyment and engagement with physical activity. Encouraging participants to use the mirrors as a form of feedback will help to reinforce their stages of learning, from novice to experienced exercise participants.

Class Format

The next step is to take the student-centered approach to group exercise instruction into the development of the overall class format. No single class format is appropriate for every type of group exercise class. In a step class it is appropriate to warm up by incorporating the step benches; however, in a kickboxing class it is preferable to practice kickboxing moves during the warm-up segment rather than to use a bench. It may be suitable to perform some static stretching in the warm-up segment of a low-impact class for seniors, but not necessarily for young children. A 15-minute abdominal class may not even contain stretching, since the purpose of the class is confined to abdominal strengthening.

Thermoregulation is an especially important consideration in aquatic exercise classes because water temperature that is either too low or too high can affect exercise performance and the participant's overall experience. For example, if the water temperature is too low, participants will need a longer warm-up and the cool-down will need to be shortened, as body temperature will drop quickly. As a consequence, performing static stretches to enhance flexibility at the end of a water workout may not be appropriate because participants can get cold. When water temperature is low, the cool-down will be shortened and stretching may need to be moved to the deck. Conversely, water temperature that is too high will make the exercise environment uncomfortable once participants begin to warm up. In this case, participants will not be able to dissipate heat and the exercise experience will be less pleasant. An appropriate response would be performing exercises that are more focused on muscle conditioning as opposed to cardiorespiratory exercises or an interval workout combining short periods of cardiorespiratory movement with muscle conditioning. These are just a few examples of why the same class format design may not be appropriate for all group exercise classes.

The previous examples are based on the general principles involved in each major segment of group exercise—**pre-class preparation,** warm-up, cardiorespiratory, muscular strength and endurance, and flexibility/cool-down. These general principles apply to all types of group exercise, including high/low impact, step training, aquatic

exercise, indoor cycling, kickboxing, dance, and sports conditioning or boot camp.

Typically, most group exercise classes begin with pre-class preparation followed by a warm-up, which includes using specific movements to prepare for the cardiorespiratory activity. These movements are performed at a low-to-moderate speed and ROM. They are also designed to specifically warm up the body for the activity to follow and to increase blood flow to the muscles. The **cardiorespiratory segment** that follows the warm-up is primarily aimed at improving cardiorespiratory endurance by keeping the **heart rate (HR)** elevated for 10 to 30 minutes. It can also help individuals with their weight-control efforts. Following the cardiorespiratory workout, a gradual cool-down slowly lowers the HR to near pre-exercise levels to help maintain circulation and reduce the risk of excessive pooling of blood in the lower extremities. A muscular strength and endurance segment can also be included either before or after the cardiorespiratory segment, depending on the class design or training emphasis. The class ends with a flexibility/cool-down component that includes stretching and relaxation exercises designed to further lower HR, help prevent muscle soreness, and enhance overall flexibility.

In "fusion" classes, the segments might include 30 minutes of indoor cycling followed by 30 minutes of strength work. These classes may be combined or offered individually. Regardless of format, focus on providing a safe and effective workout that addresses the health-related components of fitness (as appropriate for the participants) as well as social engagement, in order to increase participant enjoyment and ultimately increase long-term adherence.

Offering Options

Notice how the four components—warm-up, cardiorespiratory endurance, muscular strength and endurance, and flexibility—common to most group fitness classes are similar to the health-related components of fitness. It is important to note that the emphasis given to each component will vary depending on the objective of the class as well as the fitness level, age, health, and skill levels of its participants. It is difficult to design a specific type of group exercise class to meet everyone's needs. For example, leading a class with both beginners and advanced participants can be challenging for instructors. Therefore, calling a yoga class that features 30 minutes of activity "30-minute Yoga Light" is helpful for beginners, while another class called "Yoga Power Hour," which features 60 minutes of activity, will attract more advanced participants. The number-one reason people do not exercise is perceived lack of time, so it is a good idea to let participants know the duration of each session. Beginning classes should be shorter in duration and focus on less-intense movements; the skills needed to perform the cardiorespiratory segment also need to be basic. Using words like "complex movement patterns" to describe longer-duration sessions that require more skills for the cardiorespiratory segment would help the advanced exerciser locate an appropriate class. Keep in mind that participants may walk to work in the morning or perform other exercise on their own and only need a flexibility or muscular strength and conditioning class. Offering different options and not staying with the typical hour-long format that encompasses all components is likely to meet more people's health goals.

Warm-up

There are a few common principles guiding the warm-up for any group exercise class:

- The beginning segment includes an appropriate amount of dynamic movement.
- The warm-up focuses largely on rehearsal moves.
- All the major muscle groups (if appropriate) are addressed through dynamic range-of-motion movements; if they are included, static stretches are held briefly (five to 10 seconds).
- Verbal directions are clear and the volume, tempo, and atmosphere created by the music are appropriate.

Appropriate Dynamic Movement

The purpose of the warm-up is to prepare the body for the more rigorous demands of the cardiorespiratory and/or muscular strength and conditioning segments by raising the internal temperature. For each degree of temperature elevation, the metabolic rate of cells increases by about 13% (Astrand & Rodahl, 2003). In addition, at higher body temperatures, blood flow is shunted away from the internal organs and redirected to the working muscles, and the release of oxygen to the muscles begins to increase. Because these effects allow more efficient energy production to fuel muscle contraction, the goal of an effective warm-up should be to elevate internal temperatures 1 or 2° F, so that sweating occurs.

Increasing body temperature has other effects that are beneficial for exercisers as well. The potential physiological benefits of the warm-up include:

- Increased metabolic rate

- Gradual redistribution of blood flow to working muscles
- Decreased muscle-relaxation time following contraction
- Increased speed and force of muscle contraction
- Increased muscle, tendon, and ligament elasticity
- Gradual increase in energy production, which limits lactic-acid buildup
- Reduced risk of abnormal heart rhythms

Many of these physiological effects may reduce the risk of injury because they have the potential to increase neuromuscular coordination, delay fatigue, and make the tissues less susceptible to damage (Alter, 2004). Therefore, the overall focus of the warm-up period is to increase core body temperature, which can be accomplished by including appropriate dynamic movement.

Rehearsal Moves

Blahnik and Anderson (1996) define rehearsal moves as "movements that are identical to, but less intense than, the movements your students will execute during the workout phase." Anderson (2000) states that rehearsal moves should make up the majority of the warm-up, thus preparing participants mentally and physically for the challenges of the workout ahead. Examples of rehearsal moves include teaching participants how to hill climb briefly in an indoor cycling class, performing one interval segment during an aquatic exercise warm-up to prepare for a cardiorespiratory interval-training segment, or using light weights in the warm-up to prepare for a muscle-conditioning class. The whole concept of rehearsal moves relates to the principle of **specificity,** which states that the body adapts specifically to whatever demands are placed on it.

One of the main reasons participants become frustrated in a group exercise session is that they are unable to perform the movements effectively. Introducing new movement patterns in the warm-up will assist with activating associated **motor units.** In order to become successful at movements, participants need the opportunity to practice. Learning how to successfully complete a skill is a reflection of practice; the more practice, the better the skill will be performed. Giving participants the opportunity to practice a new move or skill will enhance their ability to perform and ultimately give them the sense of success and mastery, which can enhance overall adherence.

For example, in a high/low class where a **grapevine** half-turn movement is performed, use the warm-up to break down the move, identify the directional landmarks in the room, and name the specific move. Thus, when a grapevine half-turn is referred to in the cardiorespiratory segment, the class participants will know what to do. The same idea applies to a difficult skill in a kickboxing class such as a side kick movement pattern. Practice this side kick slowly, using the music at half tempo in the warm-up when maintaining a higher level of intensity is not the main focus. When the side kick comes up in the routine, it will have been "rehearsed," and this will make it easier for participants to maintain their cardiorespiratory intensity level. Rehearsal moves make up a large part of the warm-up, as their purpose is to warm up both physically and neuromuscularly.

Stretching/Flexibility

To stretch or not to stretch during the warm-up is a much-debated issue, and there is no consensus in the current scientific literature. Handrakis et al. (2010) found that pre-exercise stretching improved **dynamic balance** and had no effect on performance moves such as hops and jumps, and therefore recommend incorporating static stretching prior to exercise.

Taylor et al. (1990) found that gains in flexibility were most significant when a stretch was held for 12 to 18 seconds and repeated four times per muscle group. Another study found that stretching the hamstrings for 30 seconds produced significantly greater flexibility than stretching for 10 seconds (Walter, Figoni, & Andres, 1995). If these studies were the complete story, stretching in a group exercise warm-up would probably not occur, as it is impossible to stretch a muscle group four times and hold it for 30 seconds and still accomplish the goal of warming up. Additionally, static stretching can detract from the warming-up process. Therefore, dynamic stretching may be a better alternative.

Several prominent exercise-science textbooks (ACE, 2010; McArdle, Katch, & Katch, 2006; Neiman, 2003; Howley & Franks, 2003) and stretching books (Alter, 2004) recommend an active warm-up with rehearsal moves followed by brief stretching with a focus on the warm-up; enhancing flexibility should be reserved for the cool-down portion of the workout. With this in mind, the warm-up should contain mostly warm-up movements, but static stretches can be included if they are limited to brief periods (five to 10 seconds) intended to lengthen the muscle in preparation for activity. GFIs should also consider the ambient environment; cold weather should increase the amount of time spent warming up. In addition, older adults will require additional warm-up time compared to younger individuals.

In terms of organizing a group exercise class format for the warm-up segment, begin performing large-muscle, dynamic movements and incorporate rehearsal movements. If static stretches are included, be sure to maintain some movement. For example, while performing a standing hamstring stretch; keep the upper body moving with triceps extensions to continue warming up. In a cycling class, keep the legs pedaling and perform some upper-body stretches. When teaching a 30-minute session, it might be preferable to save the stretching for the end when it will be most beneficial in terms of enhancing flexibility. In this situation, it might not be appropriate to do static stretching. When teaching a 60-minute class that provides more time for the warm-up segment, actively contract the hamstrings and then stretch them briefly for optimum effectiveness.

A group of older adults might prefer warming up and then performing several minutes of static stretching. For older adults, balance is also an issue. This is an ideal time to include neuromuscular exercises. Have the participants use the wall for assistance and lead them through various balance exercises such as balancing on one foot and raising a heel off the floor. The instructor will need to assess the group and determine the amount of challenge the participants are able to perform with success. After the warm-up, perform static stretches for increased flexibility.

Although flexibility is a health-related component of fitness and should be included in the workout, the decision on how to go about warming up and stretching is an individual one. Whether it is at the end of the workout, in the middle, or during the warm-up should be a choice made by the instructor based on feedback from the participants until more definitive research on the topic has been conducted. It is known that optimum flexibility is achieved at the end of the workout, and dynamic movement should be performed before any static stretching in the warm-up.

Tempo of Music

Many group exercise classes utilize music during the warm-up as a way to motivate participants and create more overall enjoyment in the experience. Several research studies have validated the idea that music is beneficial from a motivational standpoint (Boutcher & Trenske, 1990; Gfeller, 1988). In terms of using music to create a beat to follow, research has found that external auditory cues, such as rhythmic music and percussion pulses, favorably affect coordinated walking and **proprioceptive** control (Staum, 1983). Kravitz (1994) found that subjects regularly report that they believe their performance is better with music accompaniment. Moving to the beat of the music is not always necessary in a group exercise setting. In fact, some yoga and outdoor group exercise sessions do not even use music. However, while using the beat is important throughout the duration of most kickboxing, step, and high/low classes, music is often used as background sound to help motivate or set a mood in classes such as cycling, boot camp, and aquatic exercise. Keep in mind that even in a "beat-driven" step class, participants may benefit by less beat-driven music during the strength and stretching segments. Also, in an indoor cycling class, the warm-up music might be something to sing along with that does not contain a lot of strong drumbeats or fast-paced tempos. The mood the music

establishes helps create and guide the individual segments of the class.

Cardiorespiratory Segment

There are a few common principles behind the cardiorespiratory segment of most group exercise classes. A group fitness instructor should:

- Promote independence/self-responsibility
- Gradually increase intensity
- Give impact and/or intensity options
- Build sequences logically and progressively
- Incorporate exercises that target a variety of muscle groups
- Use music to create a motivational atmosphere
- Monitor intensity using HR and/or **ratings of perceived exertion (RPE)** (see Chapter 2)
- Incorporate a post-cardio cool-down/ stretch segment

Promote Self-responsibility

Whether teaching a Pilates, group-treadmill, or boot-camp class, it is impossible to be everywhere or help everyone simultaneously. Each participant is working at a different fitness level and may also have his or her own set of goals. It would be ideal if all classes could be organized according to intensity and duration, but the reality is that many participants attend a particular class because the time is convenient, not necessarily because the duration, intensity, or content are optimal. If participants try to exercise at the instructor's level or another participant's level, they may work too hard and sustain an injury or not work hard enough to meet their goals. To help promote independence and self-responsibility, encourage participants to work at their own pace, use HR monitoring or RPE checks, and inform them how they should be feeling throughout the class. For example, during the peak portion of the cardiorespiratory segment, let them know that they should have an increased respiratory rate. During the post-cardio cool-down, tell them that they should feel their heart and respiratory rates slowing down. Be as descriptive as possible about perceived exertion throughout the workout. Also, it is important to demonstrate high-, medium-, and low-intensity options to teach the class at various levels. Help participants achieve the level of effort they want to reach and continually remind them that it is up to them to select intensity based on their needs, goals, and fitness levels—the instructor cannot be solely responsible for participants' exercise intensity levels. Edmunds, Ntoumanis, and Duda (2008) found that participants who were given autonomy had a more positive experience. Depending upon the dynamics and cohesiveness of the group, a GFI may identify participants who are working at higher or lower levels. It is recommended that the instructor maintain a moderate intensity most of the time, but also present other options and intensities as the need arises. Mastering this concept is the true "art" of group exercise instruction.

Gradually Increase Intensity

Even though the human body adapts to exercise very efficiently, gradually increasing intensity is necessary for the following physiological reasons:

- It allows blood flow to be redistributed from internal organs to the working muscles.
- It allows the heart muscle time to adapt to the change from a resting to a working level. One of the most difficult transitions for the rhythm of the heart is the period of time from resting to high-intensity activity or from high-intensity work back to resting levels. At rest, the cardiorespiratory system circulates about 5 liters (~1.5 gallons) of blood per minute. At maximal strenuous exercise, the increase in workload requires as much as 30 to 40 liters (~8–10 gallons) per minute to accommodate working muscles.

- It allows for an appropriate increase in respiratory rate. The major muscle involved in breathing, the diaphragm, is like any other muscle and needs time to adapt to increasing metabolic demands. Without time to warm up properly, a rapid increase in breathing can result, which may lead to side aches and shallow breathing. Some degree of hyperventilation typically accompanies the onset of exercise, but a sudden increase in breathing rate means that the transition into the cardiorespiratory segment may not have been gradual enough, which can lead the participant to feel as if he or she is not able to get enough air (i.e., **dyspnea**).

For example, to gradually increase intensity during a boot-camp class, begin the class with a light jog around the room, progress to performing simple drills such as skipping, and then progress to drills that incorporate ladders, hurdles, or cones. Gradually adding intensity and complexity will allow participants to warm up physiologically, neurologically, and psychologically, better preparing them for the overall exercise experience. In an aquatic exercise class, use moves that have a smaller **range of motion (ROM)** or shorter lever length. Finally, in an indoor cycling class, keep the flywheel tension set at a lower resistance for the first few minutes.

Impact and/or Intensity Options

In most group exercise classes, movement selection can increase impact and/or intensity. It is the GFI's job to make sure that this increase is balanced and appropriate for the participants. For example, in a boot-camp or sports-conditioning class, a GFI may elect to jump with both feet back and forth over lines on the floor. This is a high-impact movement. The next movement selection might be a more moderate-impact movement like a brisk walk around the room. Impact is not as much an issue in an indoor cycling class where intensity options become more important. For example, a hill climb out of the saddle at a high resistance that lasts longer than three minutes is considered a higher-intensity option. This might be followed by a lower-resistance seated movement. All group exercise modalities have movements that can vary impact and intensity. It is important to take this into consideration when choosing or choreographing movement **combinations** and segments.

Another option to consider for the cardiorespiratory segment is incorporating intervals. **Interval training** is a form of cardiorespiratory conditioning in which individuals alternate working at high and low intensities. True interval training consists of work and rest intervals of equal or varying durations (e.g., 30 seconds of high-intensity work followed by 30 seconds of rest or recovery, or 30 seconds of high-intensity work followed by one minute of rest or recovery). **Fartlek training** is a form of interval training that allows the exerciser to change the intensity based on how he or she is feeling, so that the duration of the intervals is not predetermined. Either form of interval training is a fun and viable addition to group exercise, especially in formats such as boot camp or step training. However, it is important to keep in mind that higher levels of intensity can be uncomfortable for some participants. Beginning or novice exercisers, as well as overweight or obese participants, will respond less favorably. Ekkekakis and Lind (2006) found that overweight individuals who were asked to perform treadmill exercise at a 10% faster speed than they would have self-selected reported a less "pleasurable" experience.

Building Sequences

Building sequences involves taking complex moves and breaking them down into smaller parts. Consider participant success when teaching movements. Practice develops successful performance; therefore, GFIs should break moves and combinations down into small, "chewable" parts so that participants are able to learn with better success. In a kickboxing class, for example, building sequences logically would include teaching a group how to perform a front kick with a front jab for the first time by breaking down the movement. First, have participants perform a knee lift, then turn this into a front kick by teaching them to extend from the knee without "snapping" or locking out the knee. Build onto this move by adding a front jab with the opposite arm. After the participants have mastered the front kick, add a front jab with the opposite arm. It is important in kickboxing to teach proper kicking and punching techniques, reminding participants not to snap or lock the joints. When choreography or movements are complex, it will be necessary to break down moves into segments of eight counts and then add on until a series of four groups of eight counts is completed. Progressing properly in an aquatic exercise class would mean marking or identifying a specific move by performing it, then progressively increasing intensity by speeding up the movement, then traveling with the move, and then resisting the movement by traveling against the water's current. If sequences are logically and progressively put together, participants are better able to learn and successfully perform moves. This also creates a certain "flow" to the class through logical progressions and organization. The class is easier to learn and follow, which ultimately sets up participants for success and increases the likelihood they will return. An observant GFI will know when participants are not experiencing this flow, by noticing participants standing, watching, and then appearing apprehensive while attempting the movement. It is important for the GFI to repeat complex movements, demonstrate rehearsal moves, and offer modifications so that participants can find success.

Target a Variety of Muscle Groups

Instructors often have base moves (a series of movements that appear over and over again in a class) within the cardio-respiratory segment. These base moves often involve the use of the quadriceps and hip flexor muscle groups. Examples include marching in place, walking around the room, or performing high knees during a boot-camp class. Many participants use these muscle groups often during **activities of daily living (ADL)**; therefore, continuing to use the quadriceps and hip flexors repeatedly during exercise is unnecessary. Striving to balance daily flexion, which takes place in the **sagittal plane,** with movements in other planes (e.g., hip abduction and adduction in the **frontal plane**) is important.

Although it is impossible to individualize one's teaching within a group exercise set-

ting, understanding how the body functions in daily movement can help GFIs determine which muscles are generally stronger and which muscles need to be focused on during group exercise. For example, walking forward works the hip flexors. Focusing on movement selection that utilizes the gluteus maximus (the opposing muscle group to the hip flexors) would help with muscle balance. The hip abductors are important stabilizer muscles for standing balance, so incorporating some abductor moves within the cardiorespiratory segment is recommended. In aquatic exercise, muscle balance is automatically achieved since the effects of gravity have been eliminated. If the hip is flexed in water, which brings the leg toward the surface of the water, the iliopsoas and rectus femoris should perform the work, but buoyancy assists the movement. However, when the hip is extended in the water, the gluteus maximus performs the work. On land, returning the thigh from hip flexion toward hip extension would be an eccentric contraction of the hip flexors, but the resistance of the water causes the hip extensors to perform the movement. It is important to analyze what movements work which muscle groups and vary the selection to promote overall muscle balance. Most individuals have overly strong, tight muscles on the anterior side of the body and weak, overly stretched muscles on the posterior side. Therefore, functional movements that address these muscle imbalances should be incorporated into the class design. Functional movements, or movements that are similar to ADL, such as a squat with a forward reach, can be described as "reaching to get clothes from the dryer." Relating an exercise to a movement or activity that participants perform in life will make the exercise more purposeful.

Music

Most group exercise classes that contain a cardiorespiratory segment use music to motivate and inspire participants. It is best when the music selection matches the participants' interests. Older adults might enjoy big band, "oldies," and Broadway hits, whereas baby-boomers often select 60s music or classic rock. Asking participants about their preference for music is recommended. GFIs often make the mistake of choosing music they find motivating for their own workouts. Although it is important that music motivates the instructor, it is imperative that it motivate the participants. A student-centered instructor will make every effort to provide participants with the best service and an enjoyable experience. With the wide array of commercial music available, it is easy to find a variety to use in class (see the "Music Resources" list on page 83). GFIs can take formal and informal surveys of participants' preferences to get feedback on music. Soliciting for music suggestions and considering the group demographics will help GFIs select music and simplify what could be a time-consuming portion of class preparation. It is worth the time and effort to select good music, as music can make or break the experience for many participants. It is helpful for an instructor to use prearranged fitness-specific workout music for group exercise classes mixed in with other songs (see Chapter 11). Instructors may also create their own music progressions using software programs that allow users to develop their own unique beats and sounds.

Incorporate a Post-cardio Cooldown and Stretch Segment

The last few minutes of any group exercise session that contains cardiorespiratory work should be less intense to allow the cardiorespiratory system to recover. It is also important to cool down to prevent blood from pooling in the lower extremities and to allow the cardiorespiratory system time to make the transition to less-intense workloads. This is especially important if some type of muscle work will follow the cardiorespiratory segment. Encourage participants to relax, slow down, keep the arms below the level of the heart, and put less effort into the movements. Using less driving music, changing the tone of voice, and verbalizing the transition to the participants can create this atmosphere. Performing some static stretches at the end of this segment also works well. Participants often run off to their next commitment or go into the strength-and-conditioning area to perform resistance training, so they may risk missing the flexibility segment of the class if it is not included in this portion of the class format.

Muscular Strength and Endurance Segment

There are a few common principles for the muscular strength and endurance segment of most group exercise classes. It is suggested that a group fitness instructor:

- Promote muscular balance, functional fitness, and proper progression
- Maintain proper form, observe participants' form, and suggest modifications for injuries and special needs
- Give verbal, visual, and physical cues on posture/alignment and body mechanics
- Use equipment safely and effectively
- Create a motivational and instructional atmosphere

Encourage Muscle Balance, Functional Fitness, and Proper Progression

Meeting the muscular strength and endurance needs of participants in a one-on-one personal-training setting is relatively easy. The program can be tailored specifically to the individual, which gives personal trainers a distinct advantage. How, then, does a GFI determine which muscle groups to work and which movements are important during the muscular strength and endurance segment of the class? Knowing how the body functions in daily movement can guide appropriate exercise selection for muscle groups that are not normally used in the daily routine.

Think of the group exercise class as an opportunity to balance out work from daily living. Stretching and strengthening muscles that are not regularly used can help improve participants' overall muscle balance. This approach brings the GFI's role closer to that of a personal trainer (Kennedy & Yoke, 2009).

For a summary of what muscles generally need strengthening and stretching for improved health, refer to Table 3-5, which was created by analyzing the muscles most people use for routine living. For example, people normally pick up things using elbow flexion, which works the biceps concentrically (during the up phase). They then put down things working the biceps eccentrically (during the down phase) against gravity. Conversely, because of gravity, the triceps do not get worked often in daily living. In aquatic exercise, however, the same example would produce a concentric contraction of the biceps during elbow flexion and a concentric contraction of the triceps during elbow extension due to the relative absence of gravity in the water and the resistive properties of water. Keep in

Table 3-5
Key Muscles
Muscles that often need strengthening
Anterior tibialis
Hamstrings
Rhomboids/middle trapezius
Pectoralis minor/lower trapezius
Shoulder external rotators (teres minor and infraspinatus)
Triceps
Latissimus dorsi
Gluteals
Posterior deltoid
Posture/gait muscles that often need strengthening
Erector spinae
Abductors
Adductors
Abdominals
Muscles that often need stretching
Gastrocnemius
Quadriceps/iliopsoas
Upper trapezius
Pectoralis major
Hamstrings
Sternocleidomastoid
Anterior/medial deltoids

mind that the list in Table 3-5 is for functional daily living for participants who are exercising for health and fitness. This does not mean the stronger muscles should not be worked in a group exercise setting; however, the instructor's focus needs to be on achieving muscle balance and incorporating the use of weaker muscle groups as well as stronger muscle groups. For many group exercise participants, a strength class might be their only workout using body weight and strength devices.

Selecting exercises during the muscular strength and endurance segment can be a challenge. The wide variety of equipment and innovations available make it easy to get creative with exercise selection, but those choices must meet the needs of participants. For example, triceps dips on a stability ball would not be a good choice for a beginning strength class, as this is an advanced exercise that would not be appropriate for all participants. Many advanced exercises need to be reserved for one-on-one training. If a participant cannot perform an exercise properly, move closer and offer assistance, and always give options to modify or change the exercise. Select exercises that are more intermediate and then give options to make the work more or less difficult.

Teach Proper Technique

It is not uncommon for instructors to naturally have excellent form. However, "having" a skill and "teaching" a skill are two different things. Instructors who have good form may need instruction on effective cueing for the skills they naturally have, whereas those instructors who need help improving their form may more readily be able to cue what good form looks like. As an instructor, it is essential to have good alignment in all exercises demonstrated, especially for the benefit of the visual learners in the class. It is also essential that GFIs are able to understand participants' movements and find ways to help them achieve ideal form, technique, and posture. This skill is another "art" to group exercise leadership and will require instructors to think creatively to find ways to reach participants. A good GFI is able to be a teacher, a leader, and a coach. When asking participants to focus on technique and form, coaching skills are very useful. Thus, a group exercise "coach" will utilize various cues and demonstrations and provide feedback to help participants achieve optimal form.

Instructor Responsibilities

One of the most important differences between a teacher-centered instructor and a student-centered instructor is that a student-centered instructor can and will help participants with individual needs to make exercise safe and effective. To facilitate this, an instructor must know the problems and limitations of participants and observe what the participants are doing. Instructors must also be familiar with how a specific movement may affect a participant. For example, individuals often shrug their shoulders when performing upper-body exercises. Excessively contracted trapezius muscles tend to dominate movement, so instructing participants to pull the shoulder blades "inward and downward" helps establish correct shoulder alignment (Figure 3-2).

Figure 3-2
Correct shoulder alignment during a front raise

The point of this example is to encourage all GFIs to get out onto the floor to observe and assist, not just during the warm-up stretch segment, but throughout the workout. Demonstrate a move, perform a few repetitions, and then move around the room and observe participants' movements. Staying in one place only gives one frame of reference to participants. Plus, leadership involves "coaching" and requires more interaction with the participant. This technique also demonstrates to the participants that the GFI is concerned about their well-being and success in the class. If mirrors are available, this is a good opportunity to instruct participants to use the mirrors to watch their form and assist them in learning correct movement and developing proprioceptive awareness.

Verbal, Visual, and Physical Cues on Posture/Alignment

Poor posture and body mechanics are contributors to numerous chronic musculoskeletal conditions such as low-back pain. Eight out of 10 Americans will have back problems during their lifetimes; therefore, it is essential to give verbal cues on proper postural/spinal alignment as well as instruct correct body mechanics. Refer to Chapter 2 for guidelines for assessing a participant's standing posture. Helping participants gain **kinesthetic awareness** and improve how they interact with the working environment and perform ADL is essential. Incorporating alignment and mechanics cues into each segment of a group exercise class, and in every movement during the muscular strength and endurance segment, promotes fitness for health.

Giving appropriate verbal, visual, and physical cues is one of the most important aspects of leading the muscular strength and endurance segment. As a general rule, in most exercises, the stabilizers will be engaged. Give several postural cues (e.g., "ears over shoulders over hips," "reach the top of your head to the ceiling," or "brace your abdominals") before giving instruction on the specific muscle group to be worked. For example, if the instructor selects a standing overhead triceps strengthening exercise

using resistance tubing, he or she should cue participants to keep the "ears over shoulders over hips" to soften the knees, get a good base of support with the feet apart comfortably, and contract the abdominals while keeping the spine in a neutral position. Then the GFI can go on to cue the movement, maintaining awareness that tight shoulders will make this exercise difficult, and giving the option to perform a less challenging triceps exercise while still utilizing the resistance tubing.

A closer look at verbal, visual, and physical cues will reveal that there is more than one way to communicate and direct movement. Verbal cues include cueing movements with appropriate terminology and instruction. For example, when performing a standing side leg lift to strengthen the gluteus medius and core muscles, the following verbal cues are recommended:

- Ask participants to contract the stabilizer muscles.
- Give appropriate postural cues.
- Remind participants that the ROM of the movement is approximately 45 degrees, and suggest that they lead with the outside of the heel. If the toe leads the movement, hip flexion occurs, and the already strong quadriceps and hip flexor muscles do not need the work, whereas the weaker, gluteus medius does. It is important to key into the muscle being worked for maximum effectiveness.
- Keep the movements slow and controlled and alternate sides to promote participant comfort and enhance balance development.

Visual cues include the instructor's form. It is imperative that when the verbal cues are given the instructor also performs the movement effectively. For example, in the standing side leg lift, if the instructor is saying to keep the movement in a 45-degree ROM, but is lifting or abducting the leg more than that, it is confusing to the participants. Whatever instructions are given need to be mimicked in the movement example by the instructor. As with all skills, practice is needed to become good at being an effective visual demonstrator.

Physical cues are another way to give feedback to participants on their form. To give physical cues, it is important to walk around the room and actually observe participants. A good motivator/educator is rarely in a stationary position, but is instead moving around and observing participants from different angles. Most physical cues in group exercise classes are simply assigned to the entire class to perform simultaneously, as the instructor attends personally to all participants at one time. For example, when leading an abdominal plank exercise, it is important to cue "keep the neck in neutral spinal alignment, and don't drop your head toward the floor." A good instructor will walk around the room checking form and technique and correcting problems. Thus, a GFI should demonstrate a movement, then observe and coach form and technique. The instructor is not there for his or her own workout, but to ensure that the participants have the best experience possible.

These are just a few ways to give feedback to participants regarding proper form. It is important to note which style of learning works best for the participants—auditory (verbal/cueing), visual (demonstration), or kinesthetic (physical/feeling). Observing the group and being prepared to demonstrate alternative teaching techniques for different learning styles is an important skill for GFIs. Working on the learning style that

is most difficult for the participants will help the instructor improve. Giving and getting feedback is another important key to learning and growing. Fitness professionals who give a lot of feedback and ask participants for feedback on a regular basis are providing good customer service and learning how to make their classes better.

Utilize Equipment Safely and Effectively

Portable resistance-training equipment such as resistance tubing, stability balls, hand-held weights, and weighted bars are to group exercise what toys are to children. They make the class more fun and provide the ability to **overload** the muscles in a more effective, individualized way. Some instructors actually refer to them as "toys" and the group exercise experience as "play." The most important part of having equipment is to individualize exercises for various ability levels. Post information and be sure that participants work within their own capacity or skill levels. Also, stay informed about new equipment and training methods. Vendors often make claims that their product is the most effective or easiest device on the market, so instructors need to be in a position where they can make informed statements about these claims and determine when there is a need for new or additional equipment. Be sure to test all new equipment before introducing it to the class, and always exercise care when making any equipment-related recommendations or endorsements, as inappropriate advice can create liability concerns for the GFI. Keeping the muscular strength and endurance segment separate from the aerobic portion is also important, unless it is an interval- or circuit-style class. Research has shown that the addition of light hand-held weights to the aerobic segment of a traditional high/low (Yoke et al., 1988; Blessing et al., 1987) and a step class (Kravitz et al., 1997) does not significantly increase energy expenditure. Therefore, it is generally not recommended that instructors use, nor instruct others to use, hand-held weights

during the aerobic segment to enhance cardiorespiratory fitness.

Create an Effective Instructional Atmosphere

Using music and/or the music beat during the muscular strength and endurance segment is optional. For example, a musical tempo of 130 beats per minute (bpm) is too

Adding Weight to a Cardiovascular Workout

Adding extra weight in the form of hand or wrist weights increases the total mass that must be moved, so it seems logical that using extra weight would be beneficial in boosting the physiological demands of an activity. Research on the use of hand or wrist weights during a variety of different aerobic activities (e.g., walking, traditional aerobics, and step training) is very consistent and indicates that the use of 1- to 3-pound (450 to 1,350 g) weights can increase heart rate by five to 10 beats per minute and oxygen consumption (as well as caloric expenditure) by about 5 to 15% compared to performing the same activity without weights (Porcari, 1999). Weights greater than 3 pounds (1,350 g) are not generally recommended, because they may put undue stress on the arm and shoulder muscles and the wrist and elbow joints. In addition, wrist weights are preferred over hand weights because they do not have to be gripped, which can cause an exaggerated blood-pressure response in some people. It is important to keep in mind that according to some research, roughly two-thirds of the increase in oxygen uptake and caloric expenditure attributed to exercising with hand-held weights is simply the result of more active engagement of the upper extremities (Porcari, 1999). In other words, when individuals hold weights while performing cardiovascular exercise they tend to swing their arms to a greater degree. Thus, individuals can simply and safely increase exercise intensity by consciously swinging their arms more.

Other weight-related options for increasing the intensity of a cardiovascular workout include ankle weights and weighted vests. The beneficial effect of ankle weights is lower than that of either hand or wrist weights. Ankle weights ranging from 1 to 3 pounds (450 to 1,350 g) can increase HR by an average of three to five beats per minute and oxygen uptake by 5 to 10% over unweighted conditions (Porcari, 1999). A potential drawback to the use of ankle weights is that they may alter a person's walking or running mechanics, potentially leading to injury. As a consequence, ankle weights are not generally recommended for use during aerobic exercise activities. Wearing a weighted vest to increase exercise intensity appears to be an effective approach depending upon the magnitude of the load. The metabolic impact of wearing a weighted vest is greatest in activities requiring a significant component of vertical work (e.g., stepping exercise or inclined walking or running). Most experts recommend that individuals wear vests that do not exceed 5 to 10% of their body weight to help ensure safety and comfort.

fast for leading abdominal crunches. Slow down the rhythm to half tempo to gain control before going to the full musical tempo. Choose music that does not have excessive vocals so that cueing words can be clearly heard and understood. A tempo of <120 bpm will enhance safe and effective movement. Reduce the volume of the music and set a tone that is more focused than that of the aerobic segment. The following are some general cues for muscular strength/endurance exercises:

- Ask participants to perform each exercise slowly, smoothly, and with control.
- Have participants key into the muscle group being worked and try to relax or stabilize other body parts.
- Tell participants to stop when they feel tired or change to the other side or alternate sides as desired.
- Correct form is more important than the number of repetitions, keeping to the music tempo, or the amount of resistance used.
- Educate participants on breathing and cue them to exhale on the effort and inhale on the relaxation portion.

Flexibility Segment

It is important that GFIs lead the class through the stretching of the major muscle groups in a safe and effective manner. Relaxation and visualization techniques should conclude the flexibility segment.

Stretching

As mentioned earlier in this chapter, it is important to stretch the muscle groups that have been used in the group exercise activity as well as muscles that are commonly tight. For example, after an indoor cycling class, stretching the hip flexors, quadriceps, hamstrings, and calves makes sense because

they are major muscles used for cycling. In a kickboxing session it is important to stretch the muscles that surround the hip, as they are used in kicking movements. The stronger muscle groups people use all day for ADL (e.g., calves, hamstrings, pectorals, hip flexor, and anterior deltoids) also need to be lengthened with stretching.

ACSM (2014) guidelines suggest performing static stretches for 15 to 60 seconds, two to four repetitions per muscle group, a minimum of two to three days per week. It is not always possible to perform four repetitions. However, if leading a stretching-only class, this would be the ideal.

There are precautions for stretching. Ballistic (bouncing) stretching and passive overstretching are potentially dangerous. Although certain athletic populations may benefit from ballistic stretching, ballistic stretches have been shown by some researchers to be significantly less effective than other stretching methods (Wallin et al., 1985). Passive overstretching and ballistic stretching initiate a **stretch reflex.** Special receptors within the muscle fiber detect sudden stretches and excessive stretching (**muscle spindles** and **Golgi tendon organs,** respectively) of the muscle. There is a complicated and continual interplay between opposing muscle groups that leads to precision of control and coordinated movement. During this interplay, if a muscle is activated by a sudden stretch or if continued overlengthening of the muscle fiber occurs, the system stimulates the muscle to contract rather than lengthen and maintains the contraction to oppose the force of excessive lengthening. Simply put, if a person overstretches or bounces a stretch, then the muscle shortens to protect itself. Keep pulling on a shortened muscle and it will either cramp up or possibly tear—but it will not lengthen. This process is often referred to as the **myotatic stretch reflex.** Keep in mind that this is an involuntary reflex.

It is important that stretching be comfortable. Encourage proper form by using cues such as "move to the position where you can feel gentle tension, then hold; your muscles should not feel like a rubber band ready to snap; find a comfortable stretch and hold; if you are shaking, then back off the intensity of the stretch." Also, it is important for GFIs to model average flexibility so that participants do not imitate form they cannot match. As with any other activity, it is important to progress participants appropriately. Yoga is a good example of an activity that has many high-risk stretches. If they are taught progressively, the body adapts to them over time. Putting advanced yoga moves into a traditional group exercise class does not allow for proper progression.

Reminding participants of proper posture throughout stretching helps to promote overall body stability and balance, and enhances the effectiveness of the stretching experience. At least two to three verbal cues are needed on every stretch to make sure body positioning is effective. For example, when teaching a standing hamstring stretch, it is important to cue to tilt the pelvis anteriorly to lengthen the hamstring muscles and to straighten the knee as much as possible (Figure 3-3). Sullivan, Dejulia, and Worrell (1992) performed a study on anterior and posterior pelvic tilt positioning using two types of stretching techniques and found that the anterior pelvic position was the most important variable for enhancing hamstring flexibility.

Relaxation and Visualization

During a group exercise class, participants have been working hard and increasing the blood flow of nutrients and oxygen

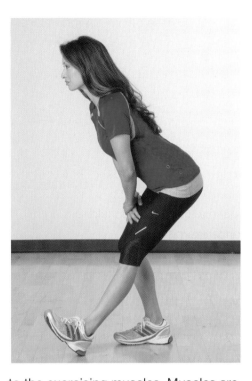

Figure 3-3

Hamstring stretch: Extend one leg and lean forward, using the hands for support.

to the exercising muscles. Muscles are now warmed and ready to be stretched to their full ROM. As each minute of the class passes, anxieties, worries, and stressors of the day are released. Participants have switched from logical and calculating cognition to functioning with more spontaneity and fluid thinking. Often, different thoughts or ideas stream in and out of consciousness, but no one idea of concern remains in focus as the class progresses. The hardest part for most participants is getting to an exercise class. When it is all over, they usually feel good about coming. It is this feeling that keeps them coming back. They have taken time to care for themselves and thereby taken another step toward healthier living. The relaxation and visualization segment is where the instructor can help participants complete their journeys. Take the last few minutes of class to let participants experience a few moments of increased relaxation or create an opportunity to reenergize before returning to their duties and commitments. These relaxation moments can be structured or free-flowing, philosophical or quiet.

Silence or quiet, slow, soothing music might be enough. Storytelling, guided imagery, or creative visualization might help deepen the sensation as the instructor describes quiet forests, gentle breezes, a warm fire, or a cozy room. Starbursts, bright, intense sunlight, or the power of a wave or waterfall might suggest the energy necessary to continue with the day's activities. While the participants are receptive, use the time to compliment them on their hard work and reinforce their positive choice to attend today's class. A GFI can let participants know that he or she looks forward to seeing them at the next class or even suggest they try another instructor's class. This helps advertise other instructors and classes, encourages participants to continue to find other opportunities for exercise, and reminds them that there is interest and support in their participation. An instructor can let the participants in on his or her life outside of class to create a cohesive, family-like atmosphere. Instructors can use these last few minutes to end the exercise experience on a high note, allowing participants to take their pos-

itive feelings with them to their next destination. These last few minutes just might be what helps them come back the next time.

Summary

Safe, effective, and purposeful group exercise class design requires knowledge of fitness to help participants achieve their desired gains as well as good psychosocial skills. Figure 3-4 presents a summary of the class format segments reviewed in this chapter. GFIs can use this checklist as a reminder, as well as a potential evaluation tool. Instructors will need to continually modify the different segments to keep up with changing trends in the fitness industry. It is important to know that group exercise carries with it considerable authority and influence. The instructor is in a position to ensure that participants feel welcome, learn effectively, improve physically, get to know each other, and feel their time spent was worthwhile. One of the biggest challenges of effective group exercise instruction is balancing all of these factors. It is important that instructors move beyond emphasizing the magnitude of fitness gains and future outcomes and understand that the real power of exercise lies in the experience itself.

Pre-class Preparation

The group fitness instructor:

☐ Knows participants' health histories and surveys new participants (see Chapter 2)

☐ Is available before class; orients new participants

☐ Discusses and models appropriate attire and footwear

☐ Has music cued and equipment ready before class begins

☐ Acknowledges the class and introduces him- or herself

☐ Previews class format and individual responsibilities

☐ Brings water to classes and encourages participants to do the same

Warm-up Segment

☐ Includes an appropriate amount of dynamic movement

☐ Focuses on rehearsal moves as a large part of the movement selection

☐ Stretches major muscle groups (if appropriate) after the dynamic warm-up and holds stretches briefly (five to 10 seconds)

☐ Offers clear verbal directions and ensures that the volume, tempo, and atmosphere created by the music are all appropriate (see Chapter 4)

Cardiorespiratory Segment

☐ Promotes independence and self-responsibility

☐ Gradually increases intensity

☐ Gives impact and/or intensity options

☐ Builds sequences logically and progressively

☐ Utilizes a variety of muscle groups

☐ Uses music to create a motivational atmosphere

☐ Monitors intensity using heart rate and/or ratings of perceived exertion

☐ Incorporates a post-cardio cool-down and stretch segment

Muscular Strength and Endurance Segment

☐ Encourages muscle balance and functional fitness

☐ Uses appropriate form, observes participants' form, and suggests adaptations for injuries and special needs

☐ Offers appropriate verbal, visual, and physical cues on posture, alignment, and body mechanics

☐ Utilizes equipment safely and effectively

☐ Creates a motivational and instructional atmosphere

Flexibility Segment

☐ Performs stretching of major muscle groups in a safe and effective manner

☐ Concludes with relaxation and visualization

Figure 3-4
Class format summary checklist

References

Alter, M. (2004). *Science of Flexibility* (3rd ed.). Champaign, Ill.: Human Kinetics.

American College of Sports Medicine (2014). *ACSM's Guidelines for Exercise Testing and Prescription* (9th ed.). Philadelphia: Wolters Kluwer/Lippincott Williams & Wilkins.

American Council on Exercise (2010). *ACE Personal Trainer Manual* (4th ed.). San Diego, Calif.: American Council on Exercise.

Anderson, P. (2000). The active range warm-up: Getting hotter with time. *IDEA Fitness Edge,* April 6–10.

Astrand, P. & Rodahl, K. (2003). *Textbook of Work Physiology* (4th ed.). New York: McGraw-Hill.

Bain, L., Wilson, T., & Chaikind, E. (1989). Participant perceptions of exercise programs for overweight women. *Research Quarterly,* 60, 2, 134–143.

Blahnik, J. & Anderson, P. (1996). Wake up your warm up. *IDEA Today,* June, 46–52.

Blessing, D. et al. (1987). The physiologic effects of eight weeks of aerobic dance with and without hand-held weights. *American Journal of Sports Medicine,* 15, 5, 508–510.

Boutcher, S. & Trenske, M. (1990). The effects of sensory deprivation and music on perceived exertion and affect during exercise. *Journal of Sport & Exercise Psychology,* 12, 167–176.

Crawford, S. & Eklund, R. (1994). Social physique anxiety, reasons for exercise, and attitudes toward exercise settings. *Journal of Sport & Exercise Psychology,* 16, 70–82.

Dishman, R. (2001). The problem of exercise adherence: Fighting sloth in nations with market economics. *Quest,* 53, 279–294.

Edmunds, J., Ntoumanis, N., & Duda, J.L. (2008). Testing a self-determined theory-based teaching style intervention in the exercise domain. *European Journal of Social Psychology,* 38, 375-388.

Ekkekakis, P. & Lind, E. (2006). Exercise does not feel the same when you are overweight: The impact of self-selected and imposed intensity on affect and exertion. *International Journal of Obesity,* 30, 652–660.

Evans, E. & Kennedy, C. (1993). The body image problem in the fitness industry. *IDEA Today,* May, 50–56.

Fox, L., Rejeski, J., & Gauvin, L. (2000). Effects of leadership style and group dynamics on enjoyment of physical activity. *American Journal of Health Promotion,* 15, 5, 277–283.

Gfeller, K. (1988). Musical components and styles preferred by young adults for aerobic fitness activities. *Journal of Music Therapy,* 25, 28–43.

Ginis, M., Jung, M., & Gauvin, L. (2003). To see or not to see: Effects of exercising in mirrored environments on sedentary women's feeling states and self-efficacy. *Health Psychology,* 22, 4, 354–361.

Goleman, D. (2006). The socially intelligent leader. *Educational Leadership,* 64, 1, 76–81.

Goleman, D. (2005). *Working with Emotional Intelligence* (10th ed.). New York: Bantam Books.

Goleman, D., Boyatzis, R.E., & McKee, A. (2004*). Primal Leadership: Learning to Lead with Emotional Intelligence.* Cambridge, Mass.: Harvard Business Press.

Handrakis, J.P. et al. (2010). Static stretching does not impair performance in active middle-age adults. *Journal of Strength and Conditioning Research,* 24, 9, 825–830.

Howley, E. & Franks, B. (2003). *Health Fitness Instructor's Handbook* (4th ed.). Champaign, Ill: Human Kinetics.

Kennedy, C. & Yoke, M. (2009). *Methods of Group Exercise Instruction* (2nd ed.). Champaign, Ill.: Human Kinetics.

Kravitz, L. (1994). The effects of music on exercise. *IDEA Today,* October, 56–61.

Kravitz, L. et al. (1997). Does step exercise with handweights enhance training effects? *Journal of Strength & Conditioning Research,* 11, 3, 194–199.

Martin, K. & Fox, L. (2001). Group and leadership effects on social anxiety experienced during an exercise class. *Journal of Applied Sport Psychology,* 31, 5, 1000–1016.

McArdle, W., Katch, F., & Katch, V. (2006). *Exercise Physiology* (6th ed.). Philadelphia: Lippincott Williams & Wilkins.

McNeill, L. et al. (2006). Individual, social, environmental, and physical environmental influences on physical activity among black and white adults: A structural equation analysis. *Annals of Behavioral Medicine,* 31, 1, 36–44.

Nardini, M., Raglin, J., & Kennedy, C. (1999). Body image disordered eating: Obligatory exercise and body composition among women fitness instructors. *Medicine & Science in Sports & Exercise,* May Supplement.

Neiman, D. (2003). *Exercise Testing and Prescription* (5th ed.). Mountain View, Calif.: Mayfield Publishing.

Porcari, J.P. (1999). Pump up your walk. *ACSM's Health & Fitness Journal,* 3, 1, 25–29.

Schroeder, J. & Dolan, S. (2010). 2010 IDEA fitness programs & equipment trends. *IDEA Fitness Journal,* 7, 7.

Seguin, R. et al. (2008). Factors related to leader

implementation of a nationally disseminated community-based exercise program: A cross-sectional study. *International Journal of Behavioral Nutrition and Physical Activity,* 5, 62.

Staum, M. (1983). Music and rhythmic stimuli in the rehabilitation of gait disorders. *Journal of Music Therapy,* 20, 69–87.

Strong, H. et al. (2006). Examining self-presentational exercise motives and social physique anxiety in men and women. *Journal of Applied Biobehavioral Research,* 11, 3–4, 209–225.

Sullivan, M., Dejulia, J., & Worrell, T. (1992). Effect of pelvic position and stretching method on hamstring muscle flexibility. *Medicine & Science in Sports & Exercise,* 24, 12, 1383–1389.

Sy, T. & Cote, S. (2005). The contagious leader: Impact of the leader's mood on the mood of the group members, group affective tone, and group process. *Journal of Applied Psychology,* 90, 2, 295–305.

Taylor, D. et al. (1990). Viscoelastic properties of muscle-tendon units: The biomechanical effects of stretching. *American Journal of Sports Medicine,* 18, 300–309.

U.S. Department of Health & Human Services (2008). *2008 Physical Activity Guidelines for Americans: Be Active, Healthy and Happy.* www.health.gov/paguidelines/pdf/paguide.pdf

Wallin, D. et al. (1985). Improvement of muscle flexibility: A comparison between two techniques. *American Journal of Sports Medicine,* 13, 4, 263–268.

Walter, J., Figoni, F., & Andres, F. (1995). Effect of stretching intensity and duration on hamstring flexibility. *Medicine & Science in Sports & Exercise,* 27, 5, Supplement S240.

Yoke, M. et al. (1988). The metabolic cost of two differing low impact aerobic dance exercise modes. *Medicine & Science in Sports & Exercise,* 20, 2 (Supplement) (Abstract #527).

Suggested Reading

American College of Sports Medicine (2014). *ACSM's Guidelines for Exercise Testing and Prescription* (9th ed.). Philadelphia: Wolters Kluwer/Lippincott Williams & Wilkins.

American Council on Exercise (2010). *Personal Trainer Manual* (4th ed.). San Diego, Calif.: American Council on Exercise.

Bryant, C.X., Franklin, B.A., & Merrill, S. (2007). *ACE's Guide to Exercise Testing and Program Design: A Fitness Professional's Handbook* (2nd ed.). Monterey, Calif.: Healthy Learning.

Jordan, P. (1997). *Fitness Theory and Practice.* Sherman Oaks, Calif.: Aerobics and Fitness Association of America.

Kennedy, C. & Yoke, M. (2009). *Methods of Group Exercise Instruction* (2nd ed.).Champaign, Ill.: Human Kinetics.

Yoke, M. & Kennedy, C. (2004). *Functional Exercise Progressions.* Monterey, Calif.: Healthy Learning.

Music Resources

Dynamix www.dynamixmusic.com 800-843-6499

Power Music www.powermusic.com 800-777-2328

Lawrence Biscontini, M.A., is a mindful movement specialist, author, and lecturer, and has received multiple industry fitness and spa recognition awards, including the ACE Group Instructor of the Year Award in 2002. He creates group-fitness and personal-training programming at facilities around the world, including Equinox®, 24 Hour Fitness®, Gold's Gym International®, Bally®, and Canyon Ranch® and Golden Door Spas®. Lawrence has been spa consultant and trainer for leading international spas in Europe, Asia, and the United States. He is a contributing author to several industry magazines and certification textbooks, works with many celebrity clients, and often appears on news and entertainment shows as a fitness expert.

ACE would like to acknowledge Lorna L. Francis, Ph.D., and Richard Seibert, M.A., M.Ed., who co-authored the previous edition of this chapter.

CHAPTER FOUR

Teaching a Group Exercise Class

By Lawrence Biscontini

For most health club or fitness facility members, the "movement studio," or group exercise room, represents the heart of the facility. While a wide variety of high-tech machines may populate gymnasium floors around the world, the true energy of any facility continues to be where the largest number of guests gather at any one time, which is in the studio. Some facilities use one movement studio to hold all of their group classes, while others have designated areas for such classes as indoor cycling, mixed-impact movement, kickboxing, **yoga, Pilates,** and many other forms of movement. Still other facilities include aquatics programming in pools. Regardless of the type of classes or the number of studios a club possesses, the common thread is the importance of the group fitness instructor (GFI) as a leader.

All successful GFIs embody strength in the two most important aspects of leadership: popularity and professionalism. Ask any committed group fitness participant why he or she continues to attend class on a regular basis, and the answer invariably includes not only a class's content, but also its leader. Leadership in the movement studio also requires polished teaching techniques, and it is those techniques that this chapter addresses.

While the most seasoned of instructors teach in such a way that everyone thinks the experience is serendipitous, truly professional instructors know the value of planning and practicing for as many aspects of the experience as possible. Research in education and learning sheds a great deal of light on how individuals learn. To provide GFIs with appropriate tools, this chapter includes learning techniques to facilitate teaching in the most effective way so that all individuals can effectively develop new skills. This chapter describes how individuals learn and, consequently, how GFIs can create classes that are both safe and effective.

Systematic Class Design

For group fitness classes to be safe and effective, instructors must understand the purpose of each class, as well as the types of participants who will most likely attend. Generally, instructors considering this information may wish to work backwards, first identifying the intended outcomes of a particular class and then designing an experience that makes those outcomes possible. After identifying the desired outcomes of a class, the next step in systematic class design is to consider what skills and teaching techniques are necessary to accomplish those objectives based on the specific participants who will attend any particular session.

Understanding Each Exercise Participant

When instructors greet participants entering class, they need to be able to ascertain immediately the group's abilities, strengths, and weaknesses. By the end of the warm-up, the instructor must decide which types of cues and what exercise intensity will prove most appropriate and effective for the individuals present. This section examines the learning process and describes strategies that will facilitate the teaching of **motor skills.**

Magill (2000) defines learning as an "internal change in the individual that is inferred from a relatively permanent improvement in performance of the individual as a result of practice." It is important that GFIs understand the difference between performing and teaching. When performing, a GFI leads participants through safe movement through mimicry and imitation; the participants follow the leader. In true teaching, the participants demonstrate the aforementioned "internal change" toward "permanent improvement" as they begin to learn and practice new behaviors and movement patterns that, over time, they can reproduce independently in life. GFIs who truly teach are able to get their participants to learn new things about their bodies and demonstrate movement patterns with less variability over time, thus indicating that the learning experience is taking place.

This learning takes place in three levels of human behavior: cognitive, affective, and motor. All of these prove important in the fitness field. The **cognitive domain** describes the brain's ability to gather and retain information and knowledge. This includes "left-brain" skills like counting out motor patterns as well as "right-brain" skills like remembering patterns of **choreography.** Education (i.e., training the cognitive domain) within an exercise program positively affects **motivation** and exercise compliance among participants, so GFIs should incorporate some elements of education into their classes (Casey, Benson, & MacDonald, 2004).

The **affective domain** describes emotional behaviors, beliefs, and attitudes. Overall feelings regarding health and motivational attitudes in general will shape a person's feelings about exercise. GFIs hold the potential to help participants develop positive attitudes about exercise. GFIs who are positive role models influence the affective domain of their participants.

Finally, the **motor domain** refers to those activities requiring movement. Learning new motor and breathing skills forms the basic foundation of exercise classes. While most instructors pay careful attention to the motor domain as they design classes, well-rounded, balanced instructors pay attention to all three of these domains in order to provide a more complete approach.

Stages of Learning

Understanding the three stages of learning helps GFIs gain an understanding for, and appreciation of, their participants in a deeper way. The traditional Fitts and Posner model (1967) explains the three stages of learning for motor skills: cognitive, associative, and autonomous. Within the **cognitive stage of learning,** movements are new to the participant, who acts as a novice; errors and imperfect form may be the norm. An example of this occurs the first time a group does **grapevines** together at a particular music speed. Many participants struggle with the skill itself, the

direction, and the coordination of the timing with the music.

The next stage, the **associative stage of learning,** includes improvements in the basic fundamentals of the skills. In this stage, the majority of participants are able to grapevine back and forth with the music and can concentrate on occasional cues from the instructor to improve performance.

During the **autonomous stage of learning,** the skill becomes automatic or habitual. Learners can perform without following a leader and can detect their own errors. In a group fitness setting, participants react automatically with music, direction, and movement upon hearing the instructor's cue: "Let's do eight grapevines."

GFIs who are aware of the different stages of learning, and can identify at which stage each participant is, can create a cohesive and positive experience for everyone. While novices concentrate on mastering gross movement patterns so that they can contribute to the overall cohesiveness of a class, they may forget to perform even the most basic tasks, like breathing appropriately or watching out for obstacles. Novices in the cognitive stage are just learning how to be participants in a group fitness class. Skilled GFIs try to find the right balance between over-cueing and under-cueing to the participants in this stage. Generally, just **cueing** the most important things first—safety, position, and breathing—produces enough confidence for the new participants to feel successful and move on to the associative stage. Instructors should not dwell on minor details with participants in the cognitive stage of learning.

Most classes have participants with various levels of ability, so instructors must be able to cue multilevel classes. Even though a class may be labeled "Yoga Level 3," for example, participants will often join particular classes not for specific levels or even disciplines, but based on the time of day, instructor, music, popularity, available parking and daycare, and countless other factors. To employ appropriate teaching strategies, then, instructors may wish to include the following techniques in teaching to a varied class: motivation, **progression** teaching, and cueing and correction.

Motivation

GFIs must take into consideration the learning stages of a class's participants in order to create the most successful experience possible. The more successful participants feel, the more motivated they become. Refer to Chapter 5 for detailed information on improving both motivation and **adherence.**

Progression Teaching

Instructors who teach by transitioning from simple movements to compound movements allow their participants to achieve more in their classes, as the participants can then reproduce both simple and compound movements successfully.

Cueing and Correction

GFIs who give individual **feedback** show that they care for the true progress of their participants. Wlodkowski (1998) defines feedback as information that learners receive about the quality of their performance on a given task. First, instructors should point out something positive the individual is doing. Second, they should mention the needed correction, known as the **performance standard** of the movement or exercise. Third, instructors should point out an additional positive feedback point, usually offering positive reinforcement on the immediate correction. For example, a GFI notices that a participant's shoulders are elevated during standing biceps

curls. A sample script could be, "Good job keeping your spine really tall and extended (positive point). You will get better results in the muscles we're working if you keep the shoulders down (performance standard). Yes, that's it! Notice how much less tension you now have in the shoulders (positive reinforcement)." More on the topic of cueing and correction appears later in this chapter.

Participant Needs

One of the most challenging aspects of the group experience is how varied the participants' motor skills and health and fitness levels can be among apparently healthy individuals, not to mention those with special needs, such as pregnant women, obese individuals, and those with other physical issues. Facilities should have all necessary paperwork on file, such as a **Physical Activity Readiness Questionnaire (PAR-Q),** for all registered group exercise participants. This serves as one means of communicating any special needs or requirements a participant may have to staff members, including personal trainers and GFIs. Be that as it may, individuals with special needs should make themselves known to instructors before class commences. Prudent instructors also make themselves available to their participants in their class introductions, usually stating something like, "If you have any special issues, please bring them to my attention now, or later when I walk around. I'm also available after class if you want to share anything with me in a more private setting." This type of statement allows any participant needing to acquaint the instructor with his or her health history to do so. Ultimately, an instructor who is trying to put together the most successful experience for each participant needs to learn how to be simultaneously cognizant of all of the group dynamics in a class. For more information on modifying exercise for special populations, see Chapter 6.

It is essential that GFIs refrain from diagnosing or attempting to treat any participant illnesses or injuries. Doing so would be an example of moving beyond one's **scope of practice** and would leave a GFI vulnerable to legal action if a participant experienced an exacerbation of his or her condition.

Program Implementation

Establishing Class Goals

Effective group leaders work backwards. Commencing with the behavioral objectives that they want their participants to achieve by the end of any session, they fill in the steps necessary to help everyone safely achieve those objectives. The effective use of this technique facilitates both the learning and performance of motor skills. Examples of common objectives include:

- *Sculpting class:* By the end of the session, participants will be able to execute squats and overhead presses in isolation, and then combine those moves.
- *Yoga class:* By the end of the hour, participants will be familiar with the basic **asana** postures in the **Sun Salutation.**
- *Cycling class:* Participants will learn how to harness their energy for an interval workout featuring six minutes of work and three minutes of active recovery.

Group Exercise Design

The difference between truly amazing classes and mediocre ones always returns to the topic of planning; the greatest experiences are well-planned to balance as many different variables as possible. To be sure, there are always some aspects of the group experience that cannot be controlled, like the expectations or energy levels of participants, electrical mishaps with equipment, and the tardiness of some individuals, but GFIs can control most aspects of group exercise design.

The newer the instructor, the more important it is that the group exercise design be written and practiced. Often seen as a "choreography cheat sheet," a class template helps the instructor prepare for, plan, and practice various components of the class (Figure 4-1). The list of considerations at the top of the chart will help the instructor create a successful experience for all by working out as many aspects of the experience as possible. For each of the three sections of class, instructors can plan the timeframe for the moves they wish to teach, being sure to create enough familiarity with these moves to be able to offer progressions and **regressions** of difficulty, intensity, and complexity. The final column, "functional purpose," helps instructors see their movements within the bigger picture of the class, transcending a focus on the muscles themselves to movements that enhance everyday life. A sculpting class, for example, should have movements that mimic strength-based **activities of daily living (ADL)**. Alternatively, the functional purpose of moves in a cardiorespiratory class should be to complement previously executed moves to create a multiplanar and balanced cardiorespiratory experience.

The group exercise planning sheet has three major class sections for "warm-up," "class body," and "cool-down." These three phases merit equal planning and preparation, with a focus on the "functional purpose" of each section to assist instructors in knowing why specific movements were chosen. In

Figure 4-1

Group
exercise
design
planning sheet

Class purpose and objectives: _____

Class duration: _____

Class participants: _____

Class theme: _____

Class equipment: _____

Choreography delivery method: _____

Music: _____

Dress: _____

Pre-class set-up: _____

Warm-up

Duration	Moves (with progressions/regressions)	Functional Purpose

Class Body

Duration	Moves (with progressions/regressions)	Functional Purpose

Cool-down

Duration	Moves (with progressions/regressions)	Functional Purpose

the choreography delivery method section, an instructor might write "freestyle technique using a **linear progression.**"

While "cool-down" is traditionally used to refer to the last section of a class, "transition" may more closely reflect what GFIs truly do in their classes, as they transition their participants from one mode of work (the class) to the lives to which they return after class (their jobs, errands, or homes).

Completing the items outlined in Figure 4-1 will help instructors prepare for the most positive experience possible. For example, for a class named "Dance and Define" that features a mixed-impact cardiorespiratory workout followed by strength training using stability balls, an instructor might fill out the sheet as presented in Figure 4-2.

Class Layout

First and foremost, group fitness classes should be arranged to ensure the safety of participants. This includes being able to hear the instructor over the music, not only for safety, but also for other factors including motivation and crowd control. Furthermore, GFIs should make choices regarding equipment in such a way that they avoid dangerous clutter. Class layout refers to the formations used by instructors to provide their participants with maximum opportunities for learning skills throughout class.

In the most typical group fitness class formation, the instructor stands at the front of the room either facing a mirror or the participants, and the participants face the teacher. An advantage to this approach is that participants quickly learn to choose spots in the room where they feel most comfortable. Usually the enthusiastic, experienced participants stand in the front of the room, while the less experienced exercisers stay in the back.

This advantage also can become a disadvantage; many times the instructors have the *least* visual access to the participants who need to be monitored the *most*. Instructors should therefore become accustomed to teaching to all sections of class at all times.

Any approach in the classroom has advantages and disadvantages. An advantage of facing the mirror is that this positioning gives the participants an easy understanding of movement orientations and directions; everyone follows the teacher exactly as he or she moves. A disadvantage to this approach is that the personal connection with each participant diminishes because instructors only make indirect eye contact through the reflection in the mirror. An advantage to standing in front of the class and facing the participants, is that instructors build camaraderie with their participants by making direct eye contact and allowing participants to see the front of the instructor's body directly with no reflection. A disadvantage to facing the class is that participants often have difficulty understanding how to follow an instructor cueing "raise your right arm," if the instructor is also raising his or her right arm. One solution to reducing this confusion is to use a technique called **mirroring.** An example of mirroring is when the GFI moves his or her left arm or leg while calling out to the participants to use their right arm or right leg. Thus, the participants see a mirror image of the move they are expected to follow. However, mirroring can be a difficult skill to learn and must be practiced before being used in class.

Whether facing the mirror or not, an instructor should not stand in the same place throughout a class. Instructors should get into the habit of making frequent walks through the class to observe all exercisers. An ideal time to do this is when a movement or

Figure 4-2

Sample group exercise design planning sheet

Dance and Define

Class purpose and objectives: Participants will improve or maintain cardiorespiratory fitness by performing mixed-impact cardiovascular movements for 15 to 30 minutes at 50 to 75% of heart-rate reserve.

Participants will learn six functional exercises to improve functional strength using the stability ball in both seated and supine bridge positions.

Participants will improve flexibility in the active and static stretching section of class.

Class duration: 45 minutes

Class participants: Mostly conditioned, seasoned participants; approximately 20% of participants remain from the previous yoga-sculpt class

Class theme: Combining visualization with breathwork to enhance effort, range of motion, and control

Class equipment: Appropriate footwear, small towel, exercise mat, and a stability ball

Choreography delivery method: Repetition-reduction choreography for the mixed-impact cardiovascular sections and freestyle with linear progression for the stability ball/strength section; 12 repetitions of all exercises

Music: Downloaded 130-bpm playlist from a professional fitness music site

Dress: Vibram® five-finger shoes, black Lycra® shorts (to prevent slipping on stability ball), cotton T-shirt, and headband wrap

Pre-class set-up: Stability balls and mats set up along the periphery of the room to leave the center area free for cardiovascular training

Warm-up

Duration	Moves (with progressions/regressions)	Functional Purpose
5–7 minutes	Alternating hamstring curls moving forward and alternating knee lifts moving backward (progression: add hops and hold the stability ball; regression: step-touches)	Movement rehearsal, balancing the anterior and posterior muscles of the legs, and choreography building with direction; ball familiarity
5 minutes	Rhythmic limbering and active stretching (hamstrings, hip flexors, quadriceps, and gastrocnemius) in all three planes of movement	To prepare muscles for cardiovascular and strength work

Figure 4-2
Sample
group
exercise
design
planning
sheet (cont.)

CHAPTER FOUR

Class Body

Duration	Moves (with progressions/regressions)	Functional Purpose
17 minutes	Choreography A: repetition-reduction of grapevines with hamstrings on the ends + marches reduced to a final repeated sequence of 1 grapevine + 4 marches Progression: add impact to the traveling grapevines and substitute 2 quick side squats for the 4 marches Choreography B: step-touches moving forward and back Progression: change step-touches to jump-rope running drills moving forward and back to increase impact and intensity	Balancing frontal plane cardiovascular movement with the sagittal plane movement rehearsed during the warm-up
12 minutes	6 stability ball functional exercises in 2 positions Seated: • Seated lumbar mobility • Seated walking down to incline position and return • Supine abdominal crunches Supine bridge position: • Supine bridge stability • Hip flexion and extension in supine bridge • Baseball rotations in seated bridge	Seated: lumbar warm-up and abdominal work in the sagittal plane for the anterior core Supine bridge: glute and hamstring work in the sagittal plane and posterior core work in the transverse plane

Cool-down

Duration	Moves (with progressions/regressions)	Functional Purpose
3 minutes	Static stretches for hamstrings, glutes, quadriceps, rectus abdominis, quadratus lumborum, and erector spinae using the stability ball	Active and static stretching of primary muscles used

Note: bpm = Beats per minute

movement series is bilateral. After teaching a side-squat and lunge sequence to the left, for example, the time will come to do the entire series to the right. This provides an ideal time to leave the front of the room and walk around to check on participants in less-visible areas of the room. Since the participants already have seen the movement series, they have acquired a kinesthetic familiarity and little is lost when the instructor leaves his or her position in the front of the room. Furthermore, the momentary absence of the teacher in the front of the room helps create **kinesthetic awareness** and independence, which returns to the definition of teaching as involving the internal changes that participants learn to reproduce movement independently in the autonomous stage of learning. When participants can reproduce movements without the instructor modeling them, the participants truly are learning.

Instructors may wish to experiment with other options of class layout. Group indoor cycling classes typically use a horseshoe pattern, with participants facing front. Some equipment-based classes, like step training and BOSU™ Balance Trainer classes, use a checkerboard layout with participants standing beside the equipment, with the instructor positioned in the front of the class. Aquatic exercise instructors typically stand on deck and face their participants, teaching with mirror-imaging from outside the pool. Instructors of yoga, **tai chi,** and other mind-body disciplines sometimes explore the option of classes in the round, in which the instructor leads from the center of the room, constantly shifting his or her position to face different participants. An apparent disadvantage to this technique is that participants may not have their usual visual access to mirrors to self-correct, but that in itself is a mind-body advantage, as the focus changes from external to internal kinesthetic awareness. Still other instructors try to keep their participants from becoming too adjusted to any one space or orientation and sometimes shift the class to face the back of the room as they teach a section or movement.

Facility and Equipment Considerations

Not all instructors can choose the facility in which they teach. Even fewer can choose the specifics to create an ideal work environment. Be that as it may, professional, safe movement studios offering freeform movement classes should feature the following:

- Good ventilation, with a temperature adjustable between 65 and 85° F (18 to 29° C)
- A wooden or synthetic flooring designed to absorb shock from movement and control undesirable medial-lateral motions of the foot
- Sufficient space for each participant to move comfortably as appropriate to the needs of the specific class
- Mirrors across both the front and sides of the room for participants to be able to observe their own exercise positions and postures. Ideally, mirrors can be covered by drapes at the instructor's discretion when mirrors prove inappropriate or a distraction.
- A raised platform for the instructor, particularly in large, "fish-bowl" style studios
- Controls for lighting, temperature, and sound connections (e.g., wireless microphone receivers and transmitters, CD player, and digital music player connection) all within easy access of the GFI's primary place of instruction
- Easy access to drinking water

- Easy and safe access to necessary cardiorespiratory and strength-training equipment for instructors to use in classes, as appropriate
- In aquatic fitness classes, water temperature must be appropriate for the discipline and usually ranges from 83 to 90° F (29 to 32° C). For traditional shallow- or deep-water strength and cardiorespiratory conditioning classes, the ideal water temperature is at the lower end of this spectrum; for mind-body aquatic classes (involving less dynamic movement and travel) and for classes for special populations (such as those for individuals with **arthritis**), ideal water temperature is at the higher end of this spectrum.
- In group indoor cycling classes, adjustable temperature ranging between 65 and 75° F (18 and 24° C)
- Easy access to first-aid equipment and an **automated external defibrillator (AED)**

Pre-class Leadership

Instructors should make a practice of arriving early to class for several reasons. First, they can check the availability and condition of equipment for a particular class. After connecting the musical equipment, instructors may also wish to check the pitch position, volume, treble, and bass controls of both the sound system and microphone to guarantee the most appropriate experience for all. Finally, they can establish a rapport with individuals even before the official class commences, welcoming new participants and welcoming back returning participants. This period can be used to investigate what participants like most and least about particular classes.

Volume

It is generally recommended that GFIs keep their music volume under 85 decibels (dB). By way of reference, normal conversations in quiet places range from 60 to 70 dB, an alarm clock ringing two feet away is about 80 dB, a chainsaw is 100 dB, and a jet plane takeoff is around 120 dB. The Occupational Safety and Health Administration (OSHA), which regulates noise standards for workers, states that ear protection must be provided for workers if noise level on the job averages 90 dB over an eight-hour period (Griest, Folmer, & Martin, 2007). Extended exposure to sound levels above 85 dB can impair and even damage a person's hearing. Instructors who use loud music are not only at risk of damaging their own hearing and that of their participants, but they are also much more likely to suffer from voice injury, as they find themselves having to shout over loud music, even when using a microphone. While determining decibel levels related to ambient sound was once a task reserved for the laboratory, many smartphone applications allow listeners to display the decibels of surrounding noise or music with surprising accuracy. When in doubt, a GFI should play the music at a volume at which participants can hear his or her voice clearly and easily at all times.

In addition to keeping the music volume at an appropriate level to protect the hearing of class participants, audiologists recommend that instructors turn up the bass and lower the treble, since high frequencies can be more damaging than low frequencies (Price, 1990). A higher bass setting can also be beneficial for class participants who have difficulty hearing the underlying **beat,** because they can feel the beat through the floor reverberations.

Technology

Many instructors choose to load their music onto computers and manage songs electronically. Features such as shuffle, repeat, continuous play, and even song editing allow instructors more control over their music than when using tapes or compact discs. For electronic playlists, setting the playlist to "continue" may help ensure continuous music during the class should the music end before the movement. For devices such as iPhones™ and iPods™, many applications, or "apps," exist to assist instructors. Currently, "apps" can perform such functions as determine the beats per minute (bpm) of a song, change the pitch control of all music loaded onto the device, determine the decibel level of any volume, and regulate treble and bass levels for desired effects.

Exercise Selection and Class Design

Learning how to choose the appropriate exercises is among the most important tasks performed by GFIs. Having both an understanding of exercise science and a framework within which to judge all exercis-

es proves valuable until this work becomes second nature. In addition, participants often ask instructors questions about exercises they may have seen others doing in the gym, on the Internet, or on television. Copeland (1991) outlines the three main factors for consideration for any exercise or movement pattern: physiological, biomechanical, and psychological factors. To this end, an **exercise evaluation** must be done for each movement in question to determine its effectiveness and safety (Figure 4-3).

The ability to evaluate the effectiveness and safety of exercises will improve as a GFI learns more about functional anatomy and the many factors that can affect efficient human movement. Using the exercise evaluation criteria helps instructors get into the habit of exploring their understanding of exercise specificity, joint actions and biomechanics, safety, and progressions/regressions. Working through the analysis requires thought, time, and practice at the onset.

Figure 4-3
Exercise evaluation criteria

Exercise evaluation criteria

1. What is the functional objective?

   • Is my purpose cardiovascular-, strength-, or flexibility-based, or a combination of two or more?

   • Am I trying to teach isolation or integration?

   • How does this skill contribute to, rather than detract from, the participants' ability to perform activities of daily living and overall functionality?

2. Which joint actions (and other movements) achieve that objective safely?

   • When using bodyweight as resistance, is the muscle action opposing gravity?

   • When using equipment, is the appropriate muscle being worked safely?

3. Does the exercise commence from a point of stability and add mobility as appropriate within a safe range of motion?

4. Who are my participants?

   • Am I prepared to offer progressions/regressions for the success of all participants?

Sample Exercise Evaluations

Example 1: An instructor wants to warm up with squats and lunges before commencing with choreography for a mixed-impact class that will include grapevines and step-touches.

1. What is the functional objective?
    *   A warm-up should be designed to warm up the body and rehearse future movement patterns; the squats and lunges would achieve only the first of these two purposes. Because of the principle of **specificity**, movements in the warm-up should be specific to the tasks at hand. Stationary squats and lunges intended for strength are different skills from movement-based grapevines and step-touches, which are intended for cardiorespiratory exercise. Simply put, cardiorespiratory exercises appropriately warm up participants for cardiorespiratory classes, while strength exercises should warm up participants for a strength-training class, though exercises like squats and lunges can be included in the warm-up if rehearsal moves are also introduced.

2. Which joint actions (and other movements) achieve that objective safely? When using bodyweight as resistance, is the muscle action opposing gravity? When using equipment, is the appropriate muscle being worked safely?
    *   The ankle, knee, and hip flexion involved in squats and lunges are appropriate for strength-training classes for the leg muscles. For a cardiorespiratory warm-up, rhythmic movements involving these muscles should be performed in all planes of movement to warm the body and create a rehearsal effect.

3. Does the exercise commence from a point of stability and add mobility as appropriate within a safe **range of motion**?
    *   Safe and effective squats and lunges do commence from strong stability points, but are not the most effective exercises to incorporate into a cardiorespiratory warm-up.

4. Who are my participants? Am I prepared to offer progressions/regressions for the success of all participants?
    *   If a class has participants with special needs that prevent them from executing grapevines and step-touches, marching in place or executing stationary knee lifts would prove more appropriate than stationary squats and lunges, because these movements would produce a more effective cardiorespiratory training effect.

Example 2: A participant asks the GFI about doing exercises for the rectus abdominis that involve lying supine with the hands behind the head, bringing straight legs (extended knees) up to a position perpendicular to the floor (i.e., 90 degrees of hip flexion) and down in a repeated fashion, keeping the upper torso stable on the floor.

1. What is the functional objective?
    *   The participant claims the exercise works the rectus abdominis muscles, which are in the front of the torso.

2. Which joint actions (and other movements) achieve that objective safely? When using bodyweight as resistance, is the muscle action opposing gravity? When using equipment, is the appropriate muscle being worked safely?
    *   The primary action of the rectus abdominis is spinal flexion. However, the exercise described here involves hip flexion, and no spinal flexion can take place with the torso stationary against the floor. This exercise, therefore, does not effectively engage the rectus abdominis as a prime mover.

3. Does the exercise commence from a point of stability and add mobility as appropriate within a safe range of motion?
    *   While the torso does seem to start from a point of stability for the spine, raising and lowering the legs with a long lever not only does not target the identified muscle (rectus abdominis), but also puts a great deal of shear force on the lumbar region of the spine with the full range of motion described (McGill, 2002).

4. Who are my participants? Am I prepared to offer progressions/regressions for the success of all participants?

- For most apparently healthy participants, keeping one or both feet anchored on the floor and engaging in spinal flexion would be appropriate. Raising both legs off of the floor is an appropriate progression for those with enough core strength to maintain a neutral spine for the duration of the movement. Regarding the arms, keeping the hands and elbows behind the head puts more weight away from the fulcrum (i.e., the thoracic and lumbar vertebrae) when flexing the spine and therefore represents a progression exercise. Instructors should also be able to offer regressions as appropriate for the individuals in class. In this case, offering participants the option of bringing their hands across the chest during spinal flexion (and/or keeping both feet on the floor) decreases the amount of load on the abdominals, thereby decreasing exercise intensity.

Example 3: A participant asks a GFI about the validity of the following "chest exercise": The exerciser is standing tall and holding hand weights. He flexes both shoulders so that the humerus bones are parallel to the floor, and then brings the elbows and wrists together and apart in front of the chest.

1. What is the functional objective?
- The participant claims the exercise works the chest muscles in a standing position.

2. Which joint actions (and other movements) achieve that objective safely? When using bodyweight as resistance, is the muscle action opposing gravity? When using equipment, is the appropriate muscle being worked safely?
- The primary chest muscle is the pectoralis major, which has a joint action of shoulder adduction. When standing and bringing the elbows together (with or without equipment), the chest is partially responsible for the move-

ment, but when a person is standing, these muscles are not in a position to work against gravity and therefore the pectoralis major is not sufficiently challenged to produce gains. The deltoids are working isometrically to stabilize the shoulders and hold up the arms, but the chest muscles are not working hard enough to produce strength gains. Possible solutions include changing the exercise entirely (e.g., do push-ups instead), performing the exercise described in a supine position, and changing from hand weights to elastic resistance, which does not need to be used against the pull of gravity to effectively work the targeted muscles.

3. Does the exercise commence from a point of stability and add mobility as appropriate within a safe range of motion?
- To effectively stabilize the pectoralis major using hand weights, the chest must be working against gravity. The position the participant described does not train the chest against gravity, since the standing position places the pectoralis major perpendicular to the force of gravity and requires the deltoid muscles to act as stabilizers.

4. Who are my participants? Am I prepared to offer progressions/regressions for the success of all participants?
- When deciding which supine position to use, knowing the participants' abilities helps. More novice exercisers will find success lying supine on a mat on the floor, while exercisers able to execute progressions would be challenged when doing this chest work while supine with hand weights on a bench or stability ball. Manipulating tempo, range of motion, and bilateral/unilateral arm movements should be considered when creating progressions and regressions for this exercise.

Selecting Effective Teaching Techniques

While the previous section will help GFIs decide *what* to teach (i.e., the appropriate exercises), this is only half of the challenge. GFIs must also explore *how* to teach each movement.

One of the most exciting aspects of group exercise instruction involves instructors who explore different teaching styles as they learn to settle on their own format. Mosston (2001) discusses five different teaching styles that are directly applicable to an exercise class: command, practice, reciprocal, self-check, and inclusion. Mosston discusses each style in terms of its practical application to group fitness instruction.

Command

An instructor using the **command style of teaching** makes all decisions about posture, rhythm, and duration, seeking mimicry and imitation by all participants. The effect created is one of uniformity. Advantages to this "follow-the-leader" style include:

- Immediate participant response
- Participant emulation of the instructor as a role model
- Movement control
- Safety control
- Didactic approach to cueing movement
- Efficient use of time
- Perpetuation of aesthetic standards

The command style has traditionally been the most commonly used style in group fitness classes. Some GFIs find this style particularly suited to warming up, cooling down, and learning new routines and exercises where the point is for everyone to follow uniformly. Effective leaders using the command style are able to follow the gist of a standardized script (such as those required of copyrighted, pre-choreographed classes) while still offering progressions and regressions to create a successful experience for all. The most successful GFIs are able to take inventory of their participants and weave in and out of these various styles and approaches as appropriate. For example, a GFI may begin the class in a command style with simpler moves that everyone can follow. Later, in a class involving a more complicated push-up sequence with rotation where progressions and regressions are required, the self-check system or reciprocal style (described in subsequent sections) may be a more inclusive way to create success for all of the different levels and abilities within one class.

Practice

The **practice style of teaching** provides opportunities for individualization and includes practice time and private instructor feedback for each participant. While all exercisers are working on the same task, instructors make it appropriate for participants to learn to choose their own intensity levels to guarantee their individual success. The effect created is one of nurturing all participants to discover what works best for them via practice. An advantage of this style is that it allows instructors to walk around and interact because they do not need to command from the front of the room as when using the command style.

Reciprocal

The **reciprocal style of teaching** involves the use of an observer or a partner to provide feedback to each participant. This style offers individual feedback to all participants, and works best for classes involving partner strength or flexibility work.

Self-check

The **self-check style of teaching** relies on participants to provide their own feedback. Participants perform a given task and then view or record the results, comparing their performance against given criteria or past performances. Instructors who emphasize **target heart rate** or **recovery heart rate** to their participants often incorporate this style into their classes. Participants can use these techniques both in class and outside of class. Many pieces of popular group exercise cardiorespiratory equipment, like rowers, treadmills, and indoor cycles, include electronic consoles that are invaluable for instructors who use the self-check style.

Inclusion

The **inclusion style of teaching** may be the most ubiquitous teaching style, largely because most group classes include many ability levels among the participants. The concept of this style is to make everyone feel included and successful by offering progressions and regressions for all base moves, whether in a cardiorespiratory, strength, flexibility, or fusion class.

Teaching Strategies

Slow-to-Fast or Half-time

When using the **slow-to-fast teaching technique,** instructors introduce movement patterns so that participants are first performing them more slowly than the desired speed. This often includes a rhythmic variation, as instructors use the **half-time** of the music. When introducing a grapevine to exercisers for the first time, a GFI may move slowly so that a grapevine that typically uses four counts of music uses eight counts. Because this strategy may reduce exercise intensity, GFIs should refrain from using it for extended periods of time during the peak of the aerobic segment of class.

Repetition Reduction

The **repetition reduction teaching strategy** involves reducing the number of repetitions that make up a movement sequence. An instructor may have participants execute four alternating grapevines followed by eight alternating hamstring curls. This could be reduced to two alternating grapevines and four alternating hamstring curls, eventually reduced to one grapevine and two alternating hamstring curls.

Spatial

The **spatial teaching strategy** helps instructors teach new body positions by referencing body parts in relation to other body parts or their surroundings. When standing, instructors usually begin by establishing stability with precise attention to the position of the feet, and then move upward, often using the metaphor of building a house with a firm foundation, and then adding stability floor by floor until reaching the top. In other positions, instructors may commence with other body parts. For example, in the quadruped position, an instructor may begin cueing to "come down to hands and knees to find a position where the spinal column is parallel to the floor." After this, the instructor may reference the direction the fingers should point and the stability of the ankles.

The spatial teaching strategy also helps with group dynamics and class set-up. Instructors may invite participants to find a position in the room where they can stand with arms outstretched "like an airplane" to be sure they will have enough room to execute movements during the class.

Part-to-Whole or Add-in

A GFI using the **part-to-whole teaching strategy** breaks down skills and teaches isolation before integration. Commencing with movements in their simplest form, the instructor teaches sections of a move, followed by the performance of an isolated movement. For example, an instructor teaching a squat and biceps curl combination may begin with either the arm or leg movements until he or she observes mastery by the majority of participants. Once participants have mastered each component, the instructor then demonstrates how to combine the movements to become more functional, teaching either the **concentric** or **eccentric** part of the elbow flexion with the downward or upward phase of the squat, as desired.

Simple-to-Complex or Layering

When using the **simple-to-complex teaching strategy**, which is an advanced teaching strategy, instead of separating movement patterns into sections, the instructor will reduce all complexity options to the least common denominator and engage the class in movement. Next, the instructor adds layers of complexity onto these movements. For example, consider the performance of a grapevine and two alternating step-touches for a total of eight counts. In this method, the instructor engages all participants in this pattern from the start. While engaging everyone in repetition for proficiency, the instructor offers additional options, which could include leaping to the side twice instead of the grapevine and a full 360-degree pivot with hamstring curls in place of the step-touches. Generally, the available variables for layering additional complexity involve changes in direction, rhythm, and lever length.

Integrating Music and Movement

Working in an environment that features music is one of the main draws of group exercise classes of all kinds. Instructors who practice a mastery of music understand the importance of coupling music with cueing skills.

Selecting Music

Music serves multiple purposes in group exercise classes. It provides motivation through its changing keys, lyrics, and instruments. It also can set the pace for a particular activity, such as pedaling in group cycling or moving around the room in a mixed-impact or dance class. Ultimately, all music chosen should contribute to, rather than detract from, the overall desired experience. To ensure the most professional experience, instructors should purchase legally licensed music specifically prepared for fitness professionals, because its phrases and beats are consistently developed according to industry-standardized beats-per-minute guidelines without the fluctuations and bridges that occur in music that one hears on the radio.

Understanding the components of music is essential for any GFI. The music beat is made up of the regular pulsations that usually have an even rhythm and occur in a continuous pattern of strong and weak pulsations. Strong pulsations collectively form the **downbeat,** while weaker pulsations form the **upbeat.** A series of beats forms the underlying rhythm of a song, which is the regular pattern of sound that is heard when listening to music. A **meter** organizes beats into musical patterns or **measures,** such as four beats per measure. A measure is a group of beats formed by the regular occurrence of a heavy **accent** on the first beat or downbeat of each group. Most group fitness routines use music with a meter of 4/4 time in which the first "4" indicates four beats per measure while the second "4" shows that the quarter note gets the beat.

When choosing music for a particular class, the first consideration is whether the music's role will be in the foreground or background. When music is in the foreground, instructors will incorporate its **tempo** (and sometimes its lyrics or general feeling) into the class. Examples of using music in the foreground include stepping to the downbeat of a musical compilation, doing dance-based movements, and performing choreographed formats. When music is in the background, instructors do not incorporate the tempo or volume as an integrated aspect of the experience. Music is often used in the background in yoga and some other mind-body disciplines, flexibility classes, and boot-camp classes where music is a motivator but not a key player in determining speed of movement. Not all classes delineate these two roles of music clearly. Classes like aquatic training and group indoor cycling, for example, generally include both foreground and background music. For example, during some songs, instructors ask participants to move at the rate of the music, while during others, the music is part of the background ambience.

The two main considerations when choosing music are purpose and participants. Understanding the music's purpose helps GFIs understand what types of music would be most appropriate for the objectives chosen. For example, if the purpose is **steady-state** cardiorespiratory training, such as in step training or aquatic conditioning, choosing music with a consistent tempo would be prudent. Alternatively, if

the purpose is to introduce mindfulness and introspection, such as in a stretching class, perhaps softer music with no beat would be appropriate. An awareness of the participants also helps guarantee a successful musical experience for everyone, as different populations and demographics will have preferences about both music type and volume.

Music tempo can determine the progression as well as the intensity of exercise. The tempo assists GFIs in determining a piece of music's appropriateness for a particular class. Most music specifically sold to GFIs lists the beats per minute for that release. Alternatively, the beats per minute for a song can be determined by counting the number of downbeats in 15 seconds and then multiplying by four.

Prudent instructors match music to movement, which means that they can depart from the general standards outlined in Table 4-1, which presents the industry guidelines for music tempo *when instructors use the music in the foreground and have their participants execute all movements on the downbeat*. It is essential that GFIs choose music that safely complements the purpose of any section or class.

As safety is the most important factor regardless of whether music is used in the foreground or background, instructors matching movements to music must consider the general level of participants, the range of motion required at the desired tempo, and even directional changes. For example, instructors need to be aware that participants with longer limbs need more time to cover distances. Similarly, walking is more economical than running at speeds less than 4.5 miles per hour (mph) [7.2 kilometers per hour (km/h)]. When people pass that speed, intensity increases considerably and running com-

Table 4-1	
Music Tempo for Common Group Fitness Modalities	
Tempo (beats per minute)	**Modalities**
<100	Most often used for background music or slower, mind-body classes like Pilates, yoga, or stretching classes
100–122	Beginner step-training classes, low end of low-impact aerobics, and hip-hop classes
	If cycling on the beat and using pedal stroke as a measure of beats per minute, this range represents the upper limit of music tempo
122–129	Muscle toning, advanced step-training classes, low-to-mid impact aerobics, some dance classes, aquatic exercise, and conditioning classes
130–160	Faster-paced movement classes, mid-to-high impact classes, some dance classes, trampoline jumping, and some martial-arts based classes

mences. On an average, the tempo of walking is about 3.0 mph (4.8 km/h), or about 80 steps per minute with each leg. When GFIs choose to work faster than a tempo of 80 beats per minute, they should be extra cautious, as such movements exceed the general speeds at which humans typically walk (Alexander, 1992).

When incorporating music into the foreground of a class, seasoned instructors demonstrate music mastery, which includes demonstrating an awareness of any chosen music's organization into **musical phrases.** According to Bricker (1991), "as letters of the alphabet combine to form sentences, so beats of music combine to form measures, and measures combine to form phrases. A phrase is composed of at least two measures of music. To learn to recognize musical phrases, imagine where you would pause for breath if you were singing a song." GFIs can think of music as being composed of sentences, each with eight beats. Combine four sentences and a musical phrase results, with a total of 32 counts.

Many GFIs add bilateral movement combinations to their routines, which are movement patterns that commence with one lead leg or arm to one particular side, which the instruc-

tor will also have participants perform to the other side to balance the body. Examples include a step routine that begins on the left leg, a mixed-impact routine that begins with a grapevine to the left, and a side-squat and left-lunge series that begins with the left leg moving left and back. If an instructor uses the typical 32 counts of music to one side, executing the series to the other side will take an additional 32 counts of music, for a total of 64 counts. For this reason, instructors typically execute bilateral movement combinations using 64 counts of music.

When creating music specifically for fitness instructors, most music companies make it easy for instructors to find the start of musical phrases. Adding special elements like drum rolls, vocal cues, and distinct chorus and verse sections of music all help the seasoned ear pick up the start of 32-count phrases. To guide participants in an effort to promote uniformity for direction and safety, professional instructors choosing to utilize music in the foreground should teach on the downbeat whenever appropriate. Furthermore, seasoned instructors are able to not only teach on the beat, but also to cue in advance of the start of each musical phrase so that their participants can begin 32-count combinations at the start, or "top," of the musical phrases.

Practicing Music Mastery

To practice music mastery, instructors should consider the following:

- Find the downbeat and march in place or tap the fingers. Next, find the separate music phrases and pinpoint the top of the musical phrases, which naturally introduce each new 32-count of music. At the top of each musical phrase, practice cueing "8-7-6-5-4-3-2-1" with the music.
- Practice cueing "8-7-6-5" for the first four counts of music and then substituting the four words "give (4)—them (3)—a (2)—command (1)" for the last four counts of music. When ready, practice cueing "8-7-

6-5" for the first four counts of music and then substituting specific verbal movement cues for the last four counts, such as "8-7-6-5, grapevine to the left." If participants are marching, for example, the total cue would be "8-7-6-5, grapevines left and right."

As GFIs become proficient at cueing movement skills at least four counts before the movement should initiate, they can then give meaningful cues in place of the four counts of "8-7-6-5." These cues could be for safety, alignment, numerical reference, direction, breathing, anatomical cues, reinforcement, or spatial awareness. An example of the total mastery in this case would be "shoulders back and down, grapevines left and right."

Cueing Sample—Warm-up

- *Step 1:* "Let's all march it out and get ready." The instructor makes sure that everyone finds the downbeat and chats with the class while waiting for the last few beats of a phrase, at which point he or she can start cueing the rest of the movements at the top of the phrase.
- *Step 2:* "8-7-6-5, alternating grapevines left and right" (for a total of eight counts of music)
- *Step 3:* "Shoulders back and down, two grapevines left and right" (for a total of eight counts of music)

The instructor should repeat cueing this movement until the majority of the class demonstrates mastery of the combination with minimal dependence on the cueing. When the instructor is ready to add more movement, such as step-touches, he or she could cue:

- *Step 4:* "8-7-6-5; step-touches left and right" (for a total of eight counts of music)

When the majority of the class demonstrates mastery of the new skill with minimal cueing dependence, the instructor might cue:

- *Step 5:* "8-7-6-5, four alternating knee lifts moving forward" (for a total of eight counts of music)

When the majority of the class demonstrates mastery of the new skill with minimal cueing dependence, the instructor might cue:

- *Step 6:* "8-7-6-5, hamstring curls moving backward, with single, single, double" (for a total of eight counts of music)

Notice how the script includes giving succinct verbal cues ("two grapevines left and right"), numerical cues (e.g., "four"), and directional cues (e.g., "moving forward"), but only in small pieces of movement, each taking up between four and eight counts of music. Understanding the finished product of that script means not only assigning a name to the combination, but understanding where individual movements fit in the entire combination, the moves themselves, the lead legs, and the number of counts involved for each skill. The resulting combination is presented in Table 4-2.

Table 4-2		
Warm-up Combination		
	Movement	**Counts**
A	LLL: Two alternating grapevines	1–8
B	LLL: Four alternating step-touches in place	9–16
C	LLL: Four alternating knee lifts moving forward	17–24
D	LLL: Hamstring curls moving back (single, single, double)	25–32
	Repeat the 32-count combination with a RLL	

Note: LLL= Left lead leg; RLL= Right lead leg

Assigning letters to different sections, or "blocks," of choreography is a practice in which instructors keep track of what sections of a combination they are teaching. Using Table 4-2 as an example, after teaching section "A" to participant mastery, an instructor may then teach "B." When participants demonstrate proficiency at "B," the instructor may then link "A" and "B" to create fluidity.

Two benefits of labeling blocks of choreography exist. First, notice how the letter "D" is the transition, which is made up of movements that change the lead leg. To be able to balance movement from a biomechanical perspective, GFIs may begin with the transition skills (in this case, "D") as the first movement in class because all subsequent movements will be balanced biomechanically. After teaching "A," "B," or "C," for example, the GFI can reintroduce transitional skill "D" at any time to biomechanically balance the class by ensuring that everyone is doing all movements to both sides.

Second, when instructors have labeled their skills, they can create variety in future classes just by mixing up the order of the skills instead of having to teach completely new movement skills to all participants each time. For example, the next week after the combination in Table 4-2 is used (i.e., A, B, C, D), a combination of D, C, B, A can be used in which participants execute the same skills in a different order. Being sure that the participants demonstrate movement mastery before layering or adding on is paramount to successful, effective group exercise instruction.

Whatever system instructors choose for writing down choreography, using these notation techniques will save time and effort when referencing movements later. Notice how the choreography notation accomplishes all of the following tasks:

- Names the combination for easier instructor recall
- Assigns a letter to each block
- Assigns a numerical count to movements
- Notes the lead leg responsible for initiating movement
- Names each skill
- Notes if the combination repeats to the other side

It is important to note that not all movements in group fitness classes must take up eight counts. When linked movements (which can be "blocks" of choreography) take more or less than eight counts, this is called a "**cross phrase**" or "**split phrase.**" An example of a split-phrased 32-count combination is presented in Table 4-3.

Table 4-3		
Sample Split-phrase Combination		
A	RLL: Walk up diagonal right; left knee up on 4	1–4
B	LLL: Grapevine left with a knee lift on the end; RLL: Grapevine right with a knee lift on the end	5–12
C	LLL: Four alternating skis in place	13–16
D	LLL: Three leaps to the left	17–22
E	LLL: Mambo–pivot	23–26
F	LLL: Begin two alternating step-touches moving backward	27–30
G	LLL: Two marches in place	31–32
Repeat combination with LLL on A		

Note: RLL = Right lead leg; LLL = Left lead leg

Notice how movements in this combination do not take up eight counts of music. Furthermore, notice how many more letters there are in the combination beyond the typical "A" through "D." Only instructors with a good deal of music mastery and experience should begin to integrate split-phrased movements into their combinations. While they work against the typical eight-count phrase, they offer variety and unique musical phrasing.

Safety in Choreography

Instructors have almost limitless combinations of safe movements available for designing strength, cardiorespiratory, and flexibility classes. That said, prudent instructors know that not any combination of movements will produce safe and effec-

tive gains for participants. Occasionally, candidates for ACE certification become preoccupied with the practical component of their certification and become overly focused on what movements to avoid putting into classes. The exercise evaluation criteria outlined in Figure 4-3 will assist GFIs in determining an exercise's appropriateness and efficacy.

GFIs should remember to use common sense when choosing exercises and movements. They should also maintain a focus on the class objectives and work backward, asking themselves if every movement chosen supports those objectives.

Common Group Fitness Safety Recommendations

Instructors should always rule in favor of the three S's: simplicity, safety, and stability. Generally, simple movements, even when biomechanically complex, prove easier for participants to master than complicated choreography that often results in frustration. Safety should never be compromised in favor of adding the latest move seen on the Internet or from the latest fitness craze or infomercial. Stability is the most important point of departure for all types of classes, and when adding mobility to the positions and postures of the body, instructors must do so with specific design integrity to promote benefits over any potential risks. Instructors should also consider:

- Keeping high-impact moves to a minimum
- Minimizing joint stress by limiting the number of consecutive hops on one leg to fewer than eight

- Being sure to lower the heels to the floor during most movements
- Staying within industry guidelines regarding music tempo
- Cycling below 110 revolutions per minute in cycling classes
- Paying careful attention to the position of the spine throughout any exercise movement
- Promoting muscular balance in cardiorespiratory strength, flexibility, and fusion classes
- Using anticipatory cues prior to movements

Control and balance are key in movement classes. GFIs should try to create classes in which all participants master kinesthetic awareness and physical control. Control and balance occur when instructors and participants:

- Move the arms and legs with conscious muscle activation instead of relying on momentum; control also includes avoiding raising the arms above the head for prolonged periods because of the **pressor response**
- Are able to balance opposing muscle groups within any class
- Find the prudent range of motion of joints while always avoiding **hyperflexion** and **hyperextension**
- Are conscious of all foot patterns, regardless of the floor surface, especially during lateral foot patterns
- Alternate lead leg and arm patterns to avoid overuse resulting from excessive, repeated movement; usually if a lead occurs more than eight times in a row on any one extremity, the risks begin to outweigh the benefits because of possible stress injury. If an instructor is repeating any movement or skill on one arm or leg

without interruption, not only could this induce stress, but it is also a likely indicator of a lack of creativity and variety in terms of choreography and/or programming design.
- Maintain spinal integrity at all times in all positions, including while hinging forward from the hips (not the waist) with active spinal extension; for most disciplines, this includes avoiding unsupported, uncontrolled spinal flexion, since it can stretch the longitudinal ligaments of the spine (McGill, 2002)
- Can change direction with control in a smooth manner instead of abruptly
- Facilitate the learning of improved kinesthetic awareness by incorporating balance into routines so that participants do the same number of repetitions on their right and left sides
- Stretch with an active/dynamic, static, or rhythmic approach that is not ballistic in nature, minimizing static stretching in the warm-up phase of class

Choreographic Delivery Methods

GFIs should prepare objectives for all classes, and then develop a plan to reach those goals. When instructors write out the program or conceptualize it in their minds, this planning of movements becomes choreography. Delivering choreography for any cardiorespiratory, strength, or flexibility class can take many forms, from **freestyle choreography** to various types of **repeating choreography.**

The freestyle method of choreography delivery occurs when an instructor teaches a movement or skill and then changes to a new movement or skill. Participants rarely return to previously taught movements to "add on" to them. If a class starts with squats, for example, after the participants finish the squats, the class is usually finished with this skill for that session. Advantages to the freestyle method include an always-changing environment that reduces boredom. A disadvantage of this method is that participants are unable to sequence combinations of movement and repeat them as their proficiency improves because they cannot predict upcoming movements.

To be sure, freestyle choreography does not always have to be a linear progression from skill to skill. If, for example, an instructor has repetition within a routine, this approach could be seen as freestyle, but it is not linear.

The structured method of repeating choreography has two forms: "scripted" and "planned." The strictest form is the pre-choreographed "scripted" form, and instructors subscribing to this format of delivery follow a written script with music, cues, and moves all outlined from start to finish. The intent is a "performance-like" consistency of delivery and product, discouraging variations among instructors. Examples of this format include Les Mills' BODY-PUMP® and Judi Sheppard Missett's Jazzercise®. An advantage from the perspective of participants includes the predictability of being able to gauge their intensity more effectively, since they know the general format and can measure their own improvements over time. A disadvantage of this style is that, because instructors must follow a script, there is often little room for customizing specific progressions and regressions as appropriate for the individuals in each class.

In "planned" choreographed formats, instructors receive guidelines and suggestions of what a class should include. As long as instructors follow these guidelines, they can make their own individual choices on such things as song selection and sequence of

moves as they plan for their classes, filling in a class template. Examples of this format include successful programs like Chalene Johnson's Pi-Yo® and Beto Perez's Zumba®. Note that even when instructors plan their own music, cues, and moves—instead of relying on a template—they still follow this "planned" choreographed method of instruction.

Advantages to the above pre-choreographed methods from an instructor's perspective include receiving a class "in a box" that almost guarantees success, complete with a support system from instructor networks that include sometimes thousands of instructors.

The freestyle method of delivery most often involves linear progression, in which an instructor lines up movements lacking combinations. Newer instructors often find the linear progression method easier because they only have to change one aspect of movement at a time, and never need to create repeating sequences or patterns. The method is simple: one skill at a time.

Linear Progression of Cardiorespiratory Choreography

- *Base movement:* Four alternating knee lifts in place (eight counts of music)
- *Add arms:* Four bilateral elbow flexions (eight counts of music)
- *Add direction:* Travel forward (eight counts of music); travel backward (eight counts of music)

Ready to move on? Change the skills:

- *Change the legs:* Eight alternating hamstring curls with same arm movements (16 counts of music)
- *Change the arms:* Clapping hands while moving front and back (16 counts of music)

Regardless which method an instructor chooses when developing choreography, Copeland (1991) recommends adding or changing one element at a time to keep the majority of participants in the learning curve. When deciding which elements to change, consider the acronym DRILL:

- D = Direction
- R = Rhythm
- I = Intensity
- LL = Lever length

Rhythm changes can add excitement to class by using familiar moves and making them seem unique by changing on which beats of music the movement occurs. Half-time may prove ideal for demonstrating complicated patterns slowly at first, before adding the challenge of **double-time. Syncopation** occurs in a grapevine when, instead of the normal four-count grapevine, instructors hold the first lead leg for two counts ("1, 2") and then rush the rest of the movement with counts ("and 3, 4"), in which case the travelling leg crosses behind the lead leg quickly (on count "and") and the movement returns to normal (on counts "3, 4").

When considering lever length, instructors should remember that moving shorter levers generally produce less intensity than moving longer levers.

Instructors choosing only the freestyle method may wish to bear in mind that Copeland (1991) further suggests considering at the very least a combination of freestyle and repeating choreography. "There are many advantages to using repeating patterns in your choreography. The human mind instinctively arranges events into patterns, which allow the mind to relax and easily anticipate what will happen next. This repetition allows participants to commit to the movement more fully and to maintain a steady-state workout."

Ultimately, all methods and teaching strategies are available to instructors when developing choreography. When putting the class together, GFIs can teach movement patterns using a combination of teaching strategies. Observant instructors continuously monitor their participants to see which techniques work best for which groups, and teach using the methods that guarantee the highest rate of success for all.

Cueing

In group fitness, cueing involves anything an instructor invokes to convey meaning, which can be in visual, verbal, or kinesthetic form. The overall purpose of cueing in group fitness classes is multifaceted; the acronym "STEMS" summarizes its uses: safety, timing, education, motivation, and structure (Biscontini, 2011).

- *Safety* involves anatomical, alignment, breathing, and equipment cues.
- *Timing* involves numerical, counting, tempo, and rhythm cues.
- *Education* involves general instruction, relevance, functional purpose, progressing and regressing exercises, and related cues.
- *Motivation* references encouraging, energetic, reinforcement, and even humorous cues.
- *Structure* involves most remaining types of cues that indicate movement, such as direction and spatial cues. It also may include cues about equipment usage during class.

To provide effective cues, GFIs should be aware that each of these types of cues should be delivered via a combination of verbal, visual, and kinesthetic methods to reach as many participants as possible since all learners, consciously or not, favor one of these three learning avenues (Ellerton, 2005).

Methods of Learning

The manner in which cues are delivered is based on the three types of ways people learn. All individuals fall into one of three categories of learners, though everyone uses all three techniques to varying degrees. While most participants can assimilate a range of different types of cues, most learners favor one particular method.

Verbal

A verbal learner needs to *hear* words and sound-specific cues. This learner most often waits until an instructor has finished explaining the exercise set-up before moving into a position to commence the exercise. To create the most successful learning experience possible for the verbal learners in the class, GFIs should get into the habit of:

- Imagining that at least one participant in class is blind and depends on specific words for instruction
- Using specific, succinct words that connote immediate movement, such as "four grapevines left lead" and using additional words for direction such as "toward the window, right" to assist those with right and left differentiation difficulty
- Avoiding non-specific cues that do not convey meaning, such as "let's do this now," "go this way," "if that's too hard, try this," "we're working this muscle"

Types of Effective Cues

Breathing (a component of safety): These cues indicate the best breathing technique to match the discipline, exercise, or movement series, and can indicate both *when* (e.g., on which phase of a movement to inhale or exhale) and *how* to breathe.

Alignment (a component of safety): These cues include exercise set-up, general posture, and awareness of body dynamics before and during a movement.

Anatomical (a component of safety): These cues reference the body to enhance kinesthetic awareness.

Numerical (a component of timing): These cues tell participants how many repetitions of an exercise or movement series will be performed in total or how many remain, and allow participants to gauge their intensity accordingly. This includes rhythm cueing.

Information (a component of education): These cues teach participants something new about the body, proper breathing, or the mind-body connection, such as which muscles are active during an exercise or movement pattern.

Reinforcement (a component of motivation): These cues are directed toward the group or individual exercisers to encourage positive reinforcement.

Directional (a component of structure): These cues tell participants where a movement will be taking place in relation to the classroom space and their own bodies.

Spatial (a component of structure): These cues reference areas of the body, equipment set-up around the body, and/or the body's orientation to the equipment and/or the classroom space.

- Counting down instead of up so that participants will be able to predict their intensity, as they will know how many movements remain before a change ensues. An exception to this rule is seen in dance classes, as dancers consistently cue upward: "5-6-7-8."
- Taking care of one's voice by doing the following:
  - ✔ Projecting from the diaphragm regardless of microphone usage, as MacLellan, Grapes, and Elster (1987) report that most vocal injuries result from a combination of overuse and raising and/or lowering one's pitch while screaming. They therefore recommend that instructors speak in a normal voice when using a microphone.
  - ✔ Avoiding frequent coughing, which stresses the voice box
  - ✔ Avoiding cueing at biomechanically inopportune times (e.g., in positions that inhibit abdominal breathing, such as during curl-ups, or constrict the vocal tract, such as when performing push-ups). It is preferable to give cues before the exercise is executed or to walk around during such verbal cueing.
  - ✔ Keeping sound/music at a decibel level that does not require the instructor to shout over the music
  - ✔ Taking frequent small sips of water to keep the vocal mechanism lubricated

Visual

A visual learner needs to *see* specific cues. This type of learner most often joins the instructor or other participants as soon as movement is observed. To create the most successful learning experience possible for the verbal learners in the class, instructors should get into the habit of:

- Imagining that at least one participant in class is deaf or does not speak the instructor's language and needs visual assistance
- Palpating the specific muscles or areas anytime they identify key muscles or body parts, such as saying "these spinal rotation exercises will really help you focus in on the obliques," while simultaneously running the fingers along the obliques
- Pointing to the direction that matches the cued words, so with the verbal cue "grapevine left," an instructor would always show an outstretched arm pointing to the left, and with "add direction to the front," an instructor will always wave his or her hands toward the front
- Holding up the specific number of fingers that represent the number of repetitions cued with words, so visual learners always can see how many repetitions remain
- Cueing the second series of a move, such as a squat–lunge sequence on one side that repeats to the other side, without words by incorporating Aerobic Q-signs (Webb, 1989), as presented in Figure 4-4. This not only prevents voice fatigue, but also enhances the visual learning curve for all participants.

Visual cueing not only assists visual learners and participants whose main language is different from the instructor's, but also helps create a successful experience for persons who are hearing impaired. Oliva (1988) promotes visual cues based on the principles of Visual-Gestural Communication and American Sign Language (Figure 4-5). Oliva maintains that visual cues must be "visually logical" and clearly visible to

Figure 4-4
Aerobic Q-signs

Source: Webb, T. (1989). Aerobic Q-signs. *IDEA Today,* 10, 30–31.

Watch me

Hold/stay

From the top

Forward/backward

Direction 2-4-8

Single/double

viewers. For example, GFIs can indicate lower-body moves by patting the lead leg. Differentiating between moves that travel and moves that simply change direction will prevent confusion. One of the most efficient ways to cue travel moves is for the GFI to demonstrate the desired travel while using outstretched arms to emphasize the direction. Alternatively, a GFI may wave his or her hands toward a desired location when signaling travel moves as if to say "come here" with body language. For lead leg changes without direction, simply patting the thigh of the leg that commences the new direction will suffice. An additional tip is to pat the side of the thigh when indicating a directional change in the frontal plane and the front of the thigh when indicating a directional change in the sagittal plane. Ultimately, the combination of visual cues with verbal and kinesthetic cues helps instructors reach the greatest number of participants.

Kinesthetic

A kinesthetic learner needs to *feel* specific cues. This type of learner most often will wait until others begin moving and then move with the majority of exercisers to feel comfortable with the crowd. This learner also relates well to using equipment because it

Left leg

Stay in place

Shift to face this direction

Figure 4-5
Visual cues for
exercise classes

Source: Oliva, G.A.
(1988). *Visual Cues
for Exercise Classes.*
Washington, D.C.:
Gallaudet University.

March in place

Hold this position and change
nothing

Or, which can be used to show
either a progression or a regression

Breathe exclusively
through the nose

Breathe through the
mouth on exhalation

"One thumb up" offers positive
reinforcement and praise

113

Figure 4-5
Visual cues
for exercise
classes
(continued)

Move it forward

Move it back

Contract the transverse
abdominis and brace the core

offers something specific and tactile to touch. More often than not, kinesthetic learners also do not mind a gentle touch from a passing instructor (*Note:* GFIs must always get permission before touching a class participant in any way). To make the most successful learning experience possible for the kinesthetic learners in the class, instructors should get into the habit of integrating the word "feeling" as often as possible when referencing the purpose of an exercise or movement pattern so that kinesthetic learners know not only *where* they should be feeling a movement, but also *how* it should be feel.

Analyzing Performance and Providing Feedback

When analyzing performance in a group setting, GFIs should always commence with an evaluation of the stability of their participants before introducing mobilization exercises. Establishing proper standing or floor-based postures is the key point to avoiding injury and promoting benefits. Ultimately, teaching techniques—including corrective teaching skills—help empower exercisers to improve in each class so that,

over time, their movement integrity improves independently.

When making corrections, the following tips will assist instructors in creating positive experiences for all participants (Biscontini, 2011):

- Instructors should cue to the solution, not to the problem. Instead of saying "don't let the knees lock out," for example, cueing to "keep a slight bend in the knees at all times while standing to stabilize the spine" offers a more positive approach. Eliminating the ubiquitous word "don't" from the GFI's vocabulary will help ensure a more positive experience for all participants, as Kaess and Zeaman (1960) demonstrated that positive feedback produces more favorable and immediate results.

- When making corrections, use the following three steps. First, cue verbally to the solution in a general sense. For example, "Be sure to keep that chest lifted in these spots, gang!" Second, if that does not resolve the issue, GFIs can gently call attention to the specific individual and concern if immediate safety is involved. For example, "Nancy, that's great form; be sure to keep the ribs lifted!" Third, if a kinesthetic intervention is needed because neither of the first two steps proved successful, GFIs should approach the exerciser, offering to place a palm at the specific place to where the exerciser should move—away from injury and toward correction. For example, consider a plank pose where the exerciser's cervical spine is in hyperextension, the elbows are asymmetrical and hyperextended, the hips are too low and out of alignment with the spine, and the knees are sagging. A GFI can approach the exerciser at his or her eye level and offer a palm. "Connie, I'm placing my palm under your chin. Bring your chin down to touch my palm. Now as I place my palms on either side of your elbows; gently guide your elbows toward my palms. Now my palm is above your hips; raise your hips until you feel my palm. Finally, my palm is behind your knees; raise the backs of your knees until you feel my palm. Excellent… now your entire spine is in alignment with your knees in the plank position." In this way, instructors avoid the issue of having to touch the exercisers because, in teaching kinesthetic awareness, exercisers take responsibility for positioning their body in space, and learn to move away from misalignment and toward solutions.

- When having to reorganize any particular movement to guarantee success for more participants, instead of using the word "modification" because it can be both nonspecific and negative, offer progressions and regressions. A regression offers an exerciser ways to decrease intensity or complexity, while a progression increases one or both. Offering "level 1" and "level 3" movements while teaching to the intermediate intensity of "level 2" for a majority of the time also offers positive

teaching techniques for all exercisers to feel successful. GFIs may want to avoid the terms "beginner," "intermediate," and "advanced," since these adjectives describe people and do not always appropriately identify difficulty.

- Offering specific and immediate feedback always takes a bit more thought and time, but signifies a seasoned instructor who is able to spot good form and verbalize it. Instead of cueing "Good job, Yury," for example, an instructor may cue specifically what is so good about what Yury is doing. Stating both what is good and why it merits mention constitutes effective and appropriate feedback. For example, saying "I really like the spinal integrity of both phases of the push-up (performance standard), and your lower back thanks you (rationale)" may take more time to say, but incorporates the components of effective cueing.

Analyzing Intensity

Both instructors and participants must monitor exercise intensity. Whether using target heart rate, **ratings of perceived exertion,** or another intensity-monitoring technique, GFIs should establish at the beginning of class which methods participants can use to gauge their intensity. Participants must also learn to take responsibility for monitoring their intensity via the formats that the GFI offers. Kinesthetic cues will tell their participants how a particular movement or training phase of class should feel. When offering intensity options, GFIs should try to create a non-competitive environment, reminding all exercisers to move at an intensity that is appropriate for them instead of comparing their workout to that of other people in class.

GFIs create experiences of empowerment every time they teach. To achieve this goal, they should evaluate the objectives of the class periodically to verify congruence between the class purpose and the participants. If a participant is not showing progress, an instructor can problem-solve to determine if unrealistic goals exist, or if another issue must be corrected. When instructors show that they care about each participant, this encourages long-term participation in group fitness.

Ultimately, GFIs must stay abreast of the changing standards, guidelines, and trends in an industry that changes quickly. Maintaining a familiarity with this information is key when dealing with the health and safety of so many participants at one time in each class.

Summary

When teaching group movement classes, GFIs should aim for creating an environment of both safety and success. To be sure, instructors need a carefully designed game plan for each class, but also should cultivate skills to be flexible enough to immediately "abandon the mission" and turn anything that does not create success into a positive experience for all. From incorporating the stages of learning to understanding the elements of effective cueing, a polished GFI has a finger on the pulse of education in an effort to truly teach in each class, which results in independent changes in behavior among the participants.

References

Alexander, R.M. (1992). *Exploring Biomechanics: Animals in Motion.* New York: Scientific American Library.

Biscontini, L. (2011). *Cream Rises: Excellence in Private and Group Fitness Education.* New York: FG2000.

Bricker, K. (1991). Music 101. *IDEA Today,* 3, 55–57.

Casey A., Benson, H., & MacDonald, A. (2004). *Mind Your Heart: A Mind/Body Approach to Stress Management Exercise and Nutrition for Heart Health.* New York: Free Press.

Copeland, C. (1991). Smooth moves. *IDEA Today,* 6, 34–38.

Ellerton, R. (2005). *Live Your Dreams Let Reality Catch Up: NLP and Common Sense for Coaches, Managers and You.* Ottawa, Canada: Trafford Publishing.

Fitts, P.M. & Posner, M.I. (1967). *Human Performance.* Belmont, Calif.: Brooks/Cole.

Griest, S.E., Folmer, R.L., & Martin, W.H. (2007). Effectiveness of dangerous decibels: A school-based hearing loss prevention program. *American Journal of Audiology,* 16, S165–S181.

Kaess, W. & Zeaman, D. (1960). Positive and negative knowledge of results on a Pressey-type punchboard. *Journal of Experimental Psychology,* 60, 12–17.

MacLellan, M.A., Grapes, D., & Elster, D. (1987). Voice injury. In: *Aerobic Dance-Exercise Instructor Manual.* San Diego, Calif.: International Dance-Exercise Association (IDEA) Foundation.

Magill, R.A. (2000). *Motor Learning* (6th ed.). New York: McGraw-Hill.

McGill, S. (2002). *Low Back Disorders: Evidence-Based Prevention and Rehabilitation* (2nd ed.). Champaign, Ill.: Human Kinetics.

Mosston, M. (2001). *Teaching Physical Education* (5th ed.). San Francisco: Benjamin Cummings.

Oliva, G.A. (1988). *Visual Cues for Exercise Classes.* Washington, D.C.: Gallaudet University.

Price, J. (1990). Hear today, gone tomorrow? *IDEA Today,* 5, 54–57.

Webb, T. (1989). Aerobic Q-signs. *IDEA Today,* 10, 30–31.

Wlodkowski, R.J. (1998). *Enhancing Adult Motivation to Learn.* San Francisco, Calif.: Jossey-Bass.

Suggested Reading

Aquatic Exercise Association (2010). *Aquatic Fitness Professional Manual* (6th ed.). Champaign, Ill.: Human Kinetics.

Astin, J.A. et al. (2003). Mind body medicine: State of the science, implications for practice. *The Journal of the American Board of Family Practice,* 16, 2, 131–147.

Benson, H. & Klipper, M.Z. (2000). *The Relaxation Response* (updated and expanded edition). New York: HarperTorch.

Bostic St. Clair, C. & Grinder, J. (2002). *Whispering in the Wind.* Scotts Valley, Calif.: J & C Enterprises.

Dishman, R.K. (1986). Exercise compliance: A new view for public health. *The Physician and Sportsmedicine,* 14, 127–143.

Fallon, D.J. & Kuchenmeister, S.A. (1977). *The Art of Ballroom Dance.* Minneapolis, Minn.: Burgess Publishing Company.

Faulkner, S. (1996). *NLP: The New Technology of Achievement.* New York: Harper Collins.

Franklin, B.A. (1986). Clinical components of a successful adult fitness program. *American Journal of Health Promotion,* 1, 6–13.

Griffith, B.R. (1992). *Dance for Fitness.* Minneapolis, Minn.: Burgess Publishing Company.

Harris, J.A., Pittman, A.M., & Waller, M.S. (1978). *Dance A While.* Minneapolis, Minn.: Burgess Publishing Company.

Institute for Aerobic Research (1988). Creative choreography with Candice Copeland. *Reebok Instructor News,* 6, 7.

Kravitz, L. (1994). *The effects of music on exercise.* IDEA Today, 12, 9, 56–61.

McGill, S. (2002). *Low Back Disorders: Evidence-Based Prevention and Rehabilitation* (2nd ed.). Champaign, Ill.: Human Kinetics.

Milgram, S. (1956). *Obedience to Authority: An Experimental View.* New York: Harper & Row.

Nieman, D.C. (1986). *The Sports Medicine Fitness Course.* Palo Alto, Calif.: Bull Publishing Company.

Rasch, P.J. (1989). *Kinesiology and Applied Anatomy.* Philadelphia: Lea & Febiger.

Rogers, C. (1995). *On Becoming a Person.* Boston, Mass.: Mariner Books.

Ryan, R.M. (1982). Control and information in the intrapersonal sphere: An extension of cognitive evaluation theory. *Journal of Personality and Social Psychology,* 43, 3, 450–461.

Shyba, L. (1990). Finding the elusive downbeat. *IDEA Today,* 6, 27–29.

Siedentop, D. (1983). *Developing Teaching Skills in Physical Education.* Palo Alto, Calif.: Mayfield Publishing Company.

Deborah Rohm Young, Ph.D., is an associate professor in the Department of Kinesiology, University of Maryland. Her research interests focus on physical-activity behavior and its association with cardiovascular-disease prevention. Dr. Young has a primary interest in developing and evaluating community-based physical-activity interventions, particularly in population subgroups that are known to be underactive. She also has expertise in evaluating determinants of physical activity and physical-activity assessment issues. Much of her research has focused on working with minority and female subgroups.

Abby C. King, Ph.D., professor of health research and policy and medicine at Stanford Medical School and senior scientist at the Stanford Prevention Research Center, is an expert on the behavioral determinants of physical activity. Dr. King's research interests include the applications of social cognitive theory and similar behavioral theories to achieve large-scale change in disease-prevention and health-promotion areas of relevance to adults, especially women, and mid-life and older adults; her focus has been on moving interventions that have proven effective in the laboratory to field settings.

Tracie Rogers, Ph.D., is a sport and exercise psychology specialist and an assistant professor in the Human Movement program at the Arizona School of Health Sciences at A.T. Still University. She is also the owner of the BAR Fitness Studio in Phoenix, Arizona. Dr. Rogers teaches, speaks, and writes on psychological constructs related to behavior change and physical-activity participation and adherence.

ACE would like to acknowledge the contributions to this chapter made by Barbara A. Brehm, Ed.D., professor of exercise science and sports studies at Smith College and fitness-industry author and educator.

CHAPTER FIVE

Principles of Adherence and Motivation

By Deborah Rohm Young, Abby C. King, & Tracie Rogers

With only about 45% of American adults engaging in physical activity at the minimum recommended levels [Centers for Disease Control and Prevention (CDC), 2005a], and with some reports indicating that levels of leisure-time physical activity have actually declined since 1994 (CDC, 2005b), it is clear that fitness professionals have a significant challenge in getting people motivated to start—and then stick with—an exercise program. From a fitness perspective, these are really two separate issues. There is a great difference between motivating someone to start a new program and motivating someone to stick with a program once he or she has begun.

For the purpose of this chapter, and to best address the issues that group fitness instructors (GFIs) face on a daily basis related to **adherence,** the focus will be on increasing the likelihood that people will adhere to a program once they have started. In other words, GFIs must learn to maximize the experiences of their current participants.

The issue of exercise adoption has received more research attention than exercise adherence and is based mainly around the concept of behavior change. Adopting any lifestyle-modification program, including exercise, requires an individual to break old habits and develop new ones. The **motivation** to start a new program can come from any source, such as concern over health, an upcoming event, wanting to look better, and peer pressure. The most important factor, however, in starting an exercise program is the individual. A person cannot be coerced into starting to work out, but he or she must be somewhat ready to make a change. This poses an ongoing challenge to all health professionals who spend their careers trying to get people to change. Understanding the **transtheoretical model of behavioral change (TTM)** and using interventions specific to an individual's stage of change will help increase the success of any health professional who is trying to help others adopt a new behavior.

It is important to note, however, that factors that may motivate an individual to start exercising are not the same factors that will keep him or her participating in an exercise program over the long haul. While getting people to start a new program can be challenging and frustrating, it is a mistake to think that this is the only battle that fitness professionals will face. The true challenge for the health and fitness industry is creating programming and exercise environments that maximize the likelihood that a person will stick with the program and adopt an active lifestyle.

Motivation is a complex construct that refers to the psychological drive that gives behavior direction and purpose. There is no simple answer or magic pill to create motivation, which requires the GFI to practice awareness, communication, and consistency. Once GFIs become proficient at helping to motivate others, they will understand the impact they have in changing lives and promoting life-long physical activity.

For the purposes of a fitness professional, exercise adherence refers to voluntary and active involvement in an exercise program. For the majority of participants, a moderate-intensity exercise program is appropriate, and according to the United States Department of Health & Human Services (2008), adults should engage in at least 2.5 hours of moderate-intensity aerobic physical activity each week. These guidelines are based on the substantial health benefits received from this amount of activity, but they also recognize that any activity is better than none. Additionally, it is recommended that adults engage in muscle-strengthening activities that are moderate or high intensity and involve all major muscle groups on two or more days a week, as these activities provide additional health benefits. For people who are physically active, reaching these recommended levels is typically not a problem, but they may seem intimidating for a new exerciser. Therefore, it is the GFI's responsibility to break these guidelines down into a manageable and achievable routine. Researchers have also suggested that following such guidelines too closely can prevent a GFI from creating an individualized exercise experience. Recommended activity guidelines should only guide a GFI in creating a class that meets the needs and preferences of each individual participant. Taking a "one size fits all" approach to class design is detrimental to long-term adherence. Instead, GFIs should be mindful of general guidelines while personalizing exercise classes that people actually enjoy (Morgan, 2001).

Most people know that being physically active has many health benefits and have even started an exercise program at some time in their lives. Yet, a well-known statistic states that more than 50% of people who start a new program will drop out within the first six months (Dishman, 1988), which demonstrates that existing programming models may not be effective for getting the majority of people to stick with a program. Unfortunately, the solution is not simple. There are many factors related to exercise that influence adherence and dropout (e.g., environment, support, leadership, and knowledge), and despite all of the knowledge and research about safe and effective exercise programming, not nearly enough is known about the specifics related to maintaining a regular exercise program (Dishman & Buckworth, 1997). In fact, much of the research has examined the people who quit, when it really may be much more relevant to understand the reasons why certain people stick with a program. Because there is no exact formula for helping people continue with a program, it is up to GFIs to combine all of their communication and class-design skills to create well-rounded exercise classes that not only get people fit and healthy, but that also create an exercise experience that is positive and worthwhile.

Transtheoretical Model of Behavioral Change

An important factor in the successful adoption of any exercise program is the individual's readiness to make a change. This individual readiness for change is the focus of a well-accepted theory examining health behaviors called the transtheoretical model of behavioral change (Prochaska & DiClemente, 1984). More commonly called the **stages-of-change model,** the TTM is important for GFIs to understand when promoting group fitness participation. Not everyone is necessarily ready to start a regular exercise program, and GFIs must stop using the "one-size-fits-all" approach to class design and implementation (Morgan, 2001; Marcus et al., 2000). Succeeding at making a behavioral change is not a simple task.

The TTM is made up of the five stages of behavior change. These stages can be related to any health behavior, but in the exercise context the stages are as follows:

- The first stage is the **precontemplation** stage, during which people are sedentary and are not even considering an activity program. These people do not see activity as relevant in their lives, and may even discount the importance or practicality of being physically active.

- The next stage is the **contemplation** stage. People in the contemplation stage are still sedentary. However, they are starting to consider activity as important and have begun to identify the implications of being inactive. Nevertheless, they are still not ready to commit to making a change.

- The **preparation** stage is marked by some physical activity, as individuals are mentally and physically preparing to adopt an activity program. Activity during the preparation stage may be a sporadic walk, or even a periodic visit to the gym, but it is inconsistent. People in the preparation stage are getting ready to adopt and live an active lifestyle.

- Next is the **action** stage. During this stage, people engage in regular physical activity, but have been doing so for less than six months.
- The final stage is the **maintenance** stage. This stage is marked by regular physical-activity participation for longer than six months.

Most of the time, GFIs will work with people who are at least in the preparation stage of change. People new to the GFI's group should be questioned to ascertain their background in the class material/type of activity. Those new to the activity may very well be in the preparation stage for that activity. The motivation of people in this stage may still be quite fragile, and their self-confidence may be low. People in preparation need plenty of support, as well as reassurance that they are doing the exercises or routines correctly.

When new class members have some experience, but have been participating in the class activity for less than six months, they are in the action stage. Many people in the action stage are still quite ambivalent about their participation and are likely to drop out in the next several weeks. The GFI should provide plenty of positive reinforcement and helpful feedback for these individuals, and not assume that just because they are exercising, they are committed.

Long-term exercisers joining the GFI's group are still at risk of dropout, even though they are in the maintenance stage. When a GFI thinks people are in the maintenance stage, it can be helpful to ask what keeps them going, how they are able to stick to their exercise programs so effectively, and how the GFI can help in the current group setting.

The GFI can benefit from knowing what new members are looking for from the group, and tailoring their teaching approach to the group's expectations, within reason.

Occasionally, the GFI will have people in earlier stages of change in class. A regular member may bring a friend along, who may not yet have decided to exercise. Rather than overwhelming people in the contemplation stage with too much feedback on their performance, the GFI should help them have fun, feel good about being part of the group, and assure them that in time, they will master the exercise skills being taught.

Table 5-1 presents the goal of each stage of change, as well as effective interventions that can be utilized to advance an individual to the next stage of change.

Factors Influencing Exercise Participation and Adherence

Much research has examined the factors related to physical-activity participation, creating a solid knowledge base for understanding the potential determinants for physical activity. In this context, determinants can be described as the factors that influence a person's decision to engage in exercise behavior. The potential determinants for physical activity can be broken down into three categories (Dishman & Buckworth, 1997):

- Personal attributes
- Environmental factors
- Physical-activity factors

Having a general understanding of these factors can help prepare GFIs for the various challenges that participants may face when trying to stick to an exercise program over the long haul.

Table 5-1		
Transtheoretical Model of Behavioral Change—Processes of Change		
Stage of Change	**Goal**	**Interventions**
Precontemplation	To make inactivity a relevant issue and to start thinking about being active	• Provide information about the risks of being inactive and the benefits of being active. • Provide information from multiple sources (e.g., news, posters, pamphlets, and general health-promotion material). Information is more effective from multimedia sources than from family and friends. • Make inactivity a relevant issue.
Contemplation	To get involved in some type of activity	• Provide opportunities to ask a lot of questions and to express apprehensions. • Provide information about exercise in general. • Provide information about different types of activity options, fitness facilities, programs, and classes. • Provide cues for actions, such as passes to nearby facilities and invitations to facility open houses, tours, or information sessions.
Preparation	Regular physical-activity participation	• Provide the opportunity to be active. • Provide a lot of support, feedback, and reinforcement. • Provide participants the opportunity to express their concerns and triumphs. • Introduce different types of exercise activities to find something they enjoy. • Help create support groups of similar people who are also adopting exercise programs.
Action	Maintain regular physical activity	• Provide continued support and feedback. • Identify things and events that are potential barriers to adherence. • Identify high-risk individuals and situations. • Educate participants about the likelihood of relapse and things that may trigger relapse. • Teach physical and psychological skills to deal with potential barriers. • Provide continuous opportunities to be active and a plan to maintain activity in the changing seasons, during vacations, and through schedule changes.
Maintenance	Prevent relapse and maintain continued activity	• Maintain social support from family and friends and from within the exercise environment. • Provide continued education about barrier identification. • Keep the exercise environment enjoyable and switch it up to fight boredom. • Create reward systems for continued adherence. • Identify early signs of staleness to prevent burnout.

Personal Attributes

Demographic Variables

Adherence to physical-activity programs has proven to be consistently related to education, income, age, and gender (CDC, 2005b; Morgan et al., 2003). Specifically, lower levels of activity are seen with increasing age, fewer years of education, and low income. Age, however, has been shown to be unrelated to adherence levels when examined in supervised exercise settings. Since GFIs are directly involved with supervised exercise classes, this is particularly relevant (Oldridge, 1982). Regarding gender, men demonstrate higher and more consistent activity adherence rates than women (CDC, 2005b, 2003; Dishman & Buckworth, 1997). Demographic variables always occur concurrently, so it can be difficult to understand the specific effects of one demographic variable versus another. Nevertheless, the general trends are apparent and consistent.

Biomedical Status

Biomedical status refers to health conditions, including obesity and cardiovascular disease, and is typically a weak predictor of exercise behavior. In general, research has shown that obese individuals are typically less active than normal-weight individuals, and are less likely to adhere to supervised exercise programs. Unfortunately, these relationships have not remained consistent, leaving experts a bit unsure about the exact relationship between obesity and physical-activity program adherence (Dishman & Buckworth, 1997). No consistent relationship between cardiovascular disease and activity adherence has been seen. It is likely that the relationship between these biomedical variables and behavior change is significantly related to the characteristics of the exercise program and the fitness industry itself.

Activity History

Activity history is arguably the most important and influential personal attribute variable. In supervised exercise programs, past program participation is the most reliable predictor of current participation. This relationship between past participation and current participation is consistent regardless of gender, obesity, and coronary heart disease status (Dishman & Buckworth, 1997). Therefore, it is important that GFIs gather activity history information from their participants. This information can help in the development of class design and long-term programming, as participant preferences should be considered, and it will also give the GFI a good idea of the challenges that the

participant may face in adhering to his or her current exercise program.

Psychological Traits

Psychological traits refer to general tendencies that people have in their personality or psychological makeup. Psychological traits account for individual differences among people and are often difficult to define and measure. However, the trait of self-motivation, which is reflective of one's ability to set goals, monitor progress, and self-reinforce, has been shown to have a positive relationship with physical-activity adherence (Dishman, 1982). Some research suggests that a feeling of self-worth enhances the likelihood that people will develop the self-regulatory skills necessary for regular exercise adherence, at least for women, but probably men as well (Huberty et al., 2008).

Knowledge, Attitudes, and Beliefs

Individuals have a wide variety of knowledge, attitudes, and beliefs about starting and sticking with an exercise program. Modifying the way an individual thinks and feels about exercise has been shown to influence his or her intentions regarding being active. Health perception, which is a knowledge, attitude, and belief variable, has been linked to adherence, such that those who perceive their health to be poor are unlikely to start or adhere to an activity program. Furthermore, if they do participate, it will likely be at an extremely low intensity and frequency (Dishman & Buckworth, 1997). **Locus of control** is another variable in this category, as a belief in personal control over health outcomes is a consistent predictor of unsupervised exercise activity among healthy adults. Finally, the variable of perceived barriers, such as lack of time, consistently demonstrates a negative relationship with physical-activity program adherence.

Environmental Factors

Access to Facilities

Access to facilities most frequently refers to facility location. When fitness facilities are conveniently located near a person's home or work, he or she is more likely to adhere to the program. Specifically, when facility access is measured objectively (i.e., true access and availability of a facility), it is a consistent predictor of physical-activity behavior, such that people with greater access are more likely to be physically active than people with less access (Dishman, 1994). GFIs should ask their participants about access issues and understand how convenient or inconvenient it is for each individual to reach the facility.

Time

A lack of time is the most common and arguably the longest held excuse for not exercising and for dropping out of an exercise program, as people perceive that they simply do not have time to be physically active (Oldridge, 1982). The perception of not having enough time to exercise is likely a reflection of not being interested in or enjoying the activity, or not being committed to the activity program. GFIs must teach their participants to change their perception of time availability through the use of goal setting, time management, and prioritizing. If an individual considers health and physical activity top priorities, he or she will find—or make—the time to be active.

Social Support

Social support from family and friends is an important predictor of physical-activity behavior (Duncan & McAuley, 1993). It is difficult for an individual to maintain an exercise program if he or she does not have support at home. When support is broken down into specific types, support from a spouse is shown to be an important and reliable predictor of program adherence. Social support is also a critical topic for GFIs and participants to discuss. If a participant is lacking support from family and friends, the GFI must be proactive in creating and establishing a support network for that individual.

Physical-activity Factors

Intensity

The drop-out rate in vigorous-intensity exercise programs is almost twice as high as in moderate-intensity activity programs. Additionally, when people are able to choose the type of activity they engage in, six times as many women and more than twice as many men choose to start moderate-intensity programs than vigorous-intensity programs. These results are true regardless of whether intensity is measured physiologically, such as by percentage of **heart-rate reserve,** or psychologically, such as by **ratings of perceived exertion (RPE)** (Sallis et al., 1986).

Injury

There is a reliable relationship between physical activity and injury, and it is estimated that as many as half of all people who engage in high-intensity activities (such as running or **plyometrics**) are injured each year (Macera et al., 1989). The red flag with this statistic is that injuries that occur as a result of program participation are directly related to program dropout. Research has also shown that injured exercisers are able to participate in modified exercise programs and often report engaging in significantly more walking than non-injured exercisers (Hofstetter et al., 1991).

Understanding Motivation

What is motivation and how does a person get it? The answer to this question is complex and multifaceted. It would be much easier to "build" motivation if it came from a single source and worked the same for all people. The reality is that motivation can be a lot of different things. It can come from within a person and is sometimes described as a personality trait. It can also come from other people's encouragement, guidance, and support. Motivation can even come from things, ideas, and events. Regardless of the source of motivation, even if it is external, the individual always plays an important role. Most fitness professionals will attest to the fact that it is nearly impossible to motivate someone who does not want to be motivated. The individual must buy into the process and into the motivators, whatever they may be. Because of the complexity of motivation, it is often a difficult topic for GFIs to handle. Some people are self-motivated, eager to be in the gym, and ready to get to work, while others make excuses, are inconsistent, and constantly complain. The natural tendency is for GFIs to describe an eager, hard-working participant as motivated and a difficult participant as unmotivated, and this is likely an accurate assessment. However, it is more important to evaluate how GFIs deal with each type of participant: Is it true that the eager individual may never need any motivational support from the GFI? Is the difficult individual a lost cause? The truth is that while the individual plays a critical role, his or her attitude toward exercise is not the only factor influencing motivation. Both of these individuals will need guidance and help in maintaining and building motivation for continued exercise participation (Duda & Treasure, 2005).

Because of the importance and complexity of motivation, numerous theoretical constructs have been proposed to explain motivation and its relationship with performance and achievement. Two commonly discussed approaches for evaluating motivation are **intrinsic** and **extrinsic motivation** and **self-efficacy.**

Intrinsic and Extrinsic Motivation

To be intrinsically motivated, in the exercise context, means that a person is engaged in exercise activity for the inherent pleasure and experience that comes from the engagement itself. For true intrinsic motivation to be in effect, no other factors (e.g., people or things) are instigating the participation (Vallerand & Losier, 1999). People who are intrinsically motivated report being physically active because they truly enjoy it. Such involvement in an activity is associated with positive attitudes and emotions (e.g., happiness, freedom, and relaxation), maximal effort, and persistence when faced with barriers. Consider an individual who is offered a "magic pill" that will make him or her lose weight, be healthy and fit, and look great without having to work out. An intrinsically motivated exerciser would still want to continue with the exercise program, regardless of the potential of the pill (Vallerand, 2001). While many people truly enjoy being physically active, very few (if any) adults are completely intrinsically motivated. The goal of GFIs should be to maximize enjoyment and engagement, but not expect that their participants will always demonstrate intrinsic motivation.

Many people who exercise regularly may be motivated by perceived exercise benefits, even though they may not actually enjoy the exercise itself. People who have internalized motivation for exercise benefits are said to have **integrated regulation** (Deci & Ryan, 2007).

The reality is that most adults depend on

some amount of extrinsic motivation. This type of motivation involves the engagement in exercise for any benefit other than for the joy of participation. They may exercise to earn a reward, such as a reduced insurance premium, praise from a friend, or a free water bottle.

The least effective type of motivation is a form of extrinsic motivation called **introjection** (Deci & Ryan, 2007). With introjection, people report being physically active because of some external factor suggested by someone else, and not accepted by themselves (e.g., to lose weight, to make my spouse happy, or to improve appearance) and are likely to experience feelings of being controlled, tension, guilt, or pressure related to their participation.

GFIs can help create optimal conditions for building the intrinsic motivation of participants by striving to enhance the feelings of enjoyment and accomplishment that come with participation. This can be done through creating mastery, providing consistent and clear **feedback,** including a participant in aspects of class design, and creating an environment that is aesthetically pleasing. These things will help increase the state of motivation during the actual workout. This is called situational motivation and refers to motivation as people are actually exercising. The second task of a GFI is to foster the development of motivation at the contextual level, which means how the participant generally views exercise and physical activity. The most important thing a GFI can do to help build this type of motivation is to empower each individual with the perception of control of his or her own participation and to actually give the individual control (Deci & Ryan, 2007). In general, GFIs must teach, not control. Trying to control or manipulate a participant

to act in a certain way will actually diminish intrinsic motivation. Instead, by encouraging participant ownership and involvement in the class and by teaching self-sufficiency and autonomy, GFIs can help facilitate the development of intrinsic motivation. Many fitness professionals are afraid to teach their clients or class participants to be independent because they fear that their services will no longer be needed. In reality, failing to build independence is related to less-motivated individuals who will ultimately be more likely to drop out. On the other hand, people who enjoy the experience are likely to continue coming to class and remain involved in an exercise program.

Self-efficacy

Self-efficacy is an important motivational concept for GFIs to clearly understand because it deals with positive thinking, which is an important precursor to motivation. Self-efficacy is particularly relevant in challenging situations in which people are trying to achieve a goal, as is the case with exercise adherence. In the exercise context, self-efficacy is defined as the belief in one's own capabilities to successfully engage in a physical-activity program. Self-efficacy beliefs influence thought patterns, emotional responses, and behavior (Bandura, 1986). Self-efficacy is positively related to motivation, because when people believe that they can effectively engage in exercise behavior, they do so with a positive attitude and more effort and persistence.

It is important that GFIs use communication and ongoing awareness to understand the self-efficacy levels of their participants. These levels can change quickly, so GFIs should be in touch with these thought patterns of their participants. GFIs can use self-efficacy to help influence ongoing adherence and motivation. This can be as simple as creating short-term success by designing a class that a participant will master and that will demonstrate growth and achievement. In fact, this should be the case for the program in general, as each class or series of classes should build on previous accomplishments.

Different participants will require different amounts of verbal encouragement and statements of belief. Being aware of how much feedback an individual needs and then providing that verbal support is an important motivational tool. Also, it is important to help participants reevaluate appraisals of their physiological states to create more positive interpretations. By teaching participants to appropriately identify muscle fatigue, soreness, and tiredness, as well as the implications of these states, GFIs can help participants view the "feelings" of working out in a more positive light. In general, by being aware of self-efficacy levels, GFIs will be better able to consistently motivate their participants and help them create positive self-belief.

Positive Emotions

Research suggests that people are more likely to be successful in changing their behavior when they attempt change from a position of optimistic strength and when change is done for positive reasons and associated with positive emotions (Fredrickson, 2009; Seligman, 2002). Many participants new to a group fitness class feel frustrated with the difficulty of the movements or the high intensity of the class. These people often leave the class because the class gives them negative emotions: frustration, anger, or disappointment. No wonder they never return. Some group fitness

classes seem as though the GFIs are giving a performance, showing off their skill and fitness, and almost pleased that they can perform better than the participants. While participants should enjoy watching the GFI, they should also feel good about their own performance and participation.

Positive emotions can be stimulated by fun activities, good music, friends in the group, and seeing progress toward fitness goals. Participants feel positive when they experience the sincere praise and appreciation of the GFI. Appropriate humor stimulates positive emotions as well.

Feedback

Providing participants with information about their progress and performance in an exercise class is one of the most important roles of a GFI. This information is called feedback. Learning is non-existent without feedback, because if participants do not know how they are doing, they do not have a reason to make adjustments and change their behaviors.

Feedback can be either intrinsic or extrinsic, and both are important for enhancing learning and building motivation. Extrinsic feedback is the reinforcement, error correction, and encouragement that GFIs give to their participants. Intrinsic feedback is information that the participants provide themselves based on their own sensory systems (i.e., what they feel, see, or hear). While extrinsic feedback is always important in the exercise environment, long-term program adherence is dependent on the participant's ability to provide his or her own feedback. It is important for GFIs to not give too much feedback. As participant motivation, efficacy, and ability develop, GFIs should allow their participants more opportunity to provide themselves feedback by tapering off the amount of external feedback provided.

Feedback serves an important role in motivation because it provides a guide to participants of how they are doing. The type of feedback that provides information on progress can be referred to as **knowledge of results** and without it, persistence suffers and people give up. General motivational comments during a class can keep participants on track. Feedback also helps in the goal-setting process. Both intrinsic and extrinsic feedback can contribute to knowledge of results and provide information about progress toward goal attainment. Whether a participant is achieving goals and experiencing success or is falling short of desired performance levels, it is up to the GFI to help the participant use the feedback information to adjust and reestablish goals for continued motivation and program participation (Coker, Fischman, & Oxendine, 2005).

Characteristics of an Ideal Group Fitness Instructor

A GFI's attitudes, personality, and professional conduct are among the strongest motivating factors cited for maintaining physical-activity adherence. Although GFIs are responsible for developing and administering a good exercise class, those factors alone will not guarantee optimal adherence. Personal attributes of the GFI can greatly augment his or her ability to effectively motivate participants. It is often thought that leadership is an innate trait, but leadership skills can be developed even by those not considered "born leaders." Some of the qualities of

an effective, adherence-producing GFI are presented in subsequent sections.

Punctuality and Dependability

GFIs must assure exercise participants that each exercise class will start and end on time. A class that starts late or does not end on schedule is disruptive. Participants also want to know that their regular instructor, not a parade of substitutes, will be there to greet them. Whenever possible, absences should be planned, meaning that substitutes have been scheduled in advance and participants have been informed.

Professionalism

All participants should be treated with respect. Gossiping about other class members or staff is inappropriate and should never occur. Professionalism extends to choice of exercise wear; although it is fine to be stylish, it is not professional to be dressed in a provocative manner (which can make participants feel uncomfortable).

Dedication

Part of being a professional is being dedicated to one's work. All GFIs should strive to obtain and maintain their certification. It shows dedication to the profession. Efforts should be made on a continual basis to keep exercise classes diverse, fun, and enjoyable for participants. This means going to workshops to keep up on the latest exercise trends and finding out answers to questions participants may have on health-related topics. It is imperative to stay abreast of the latest health news and be informed of the scientific basis for health claims. GFIs should be able to discern the credible Internet sites in this area and direct participants to those sites when appropriate. Acquiring certification for newer types of exercise programming keeps the GFI informed of the latest trends and can protect against professional **burnout.**

Good Communication Skills and Sensitivity to Participants' Needs

The ideal GFI recognizes that all participants are unique and come to exercise class for their own reasons. The purpose of class is not to treat all participants in the same way; instead, the GFI's responsibility is to work with the strengths of each individual participant to maximize his or her exercise session. Interacting with participants as individuals, treating them in an open, nonjudgmental manner, and expressing a willingness to listen are much appreciated.

Because the GFI usually has only fairly short conversations with individual group members, these conversations often can be fairly superficial. When the opportunity arises, and a participant approaches the GFI to share important information, it is appropriate for the GFI to take a few minutes to really focus on what the person is saying. Rather than interrupting after one or two sentences, the GFI should give the person full attention and listen carefully, in a nonjudgmental fashion, and with **empathy.** The GFI should tune in to both what the person is saying and to the person's facial expression and body language. The GFI should ask questions for clarification and to show understanding. Even just a few minutes of good listening can make a group participant feel understood and valued, rather than brushed off. In addition, the GFI may gather important information regarding the person's health concerns, goals, class participation, and so forth (Brehm, 2004).

Creating Compelling Experiences

Lawrence Biscontini (2010), internationally renowned group fitness expert, offers four tips for creating compelling experiences for group fitness participants.

Tip #1: Be both professional and popular

GFIs must educate and entertain simultaneously. Being a popular instructor is crucial if a GFI is going to maintain or improve class attendance numbers. Similarly, ACE-certified GFIs must uphold the certification's standards and code of ethics, while simultaneously designing safe and effective routines. To be truly successful, a GFI must continually work on the skills needed to be both professional and popular.

Tip #2: Set a theme

While an average instructor leads a class, an outstanding educator designs an experience. All aspects of a class come together to create a memorable experience, and it usually starts with a theme, or a central focus that ties the class together.

Tip #3: Utilize the five senses

Outstanding fitness professionals use the five senses to heighten an experience. Consider the following ways to use the senses when designing a class:

- *Hearing:* Biscontini recommends choosing music that complements the experience in a thematic way and using either silence or music so that it adds to, rather than detracts from, the overall experience.

- *Smell:* GFIs can use aromatherapy to complement a particular class. For example, lavender can be relaxing, while many people find sandalwood invigorating.
- *Taste:* Biscontini uses the sense of taste both literally and figuratively during a class. For a literal use, he recommends giving out a mint candy to help the participants focus on their breathing during a relaxation phase. The figurative interpretation involves creating experiences that are in good taste, featuring inclusive language and a lot of positive feedback.
- *Sight:* Successful GFIs use their attire and the class environment to create a pleasing aesthetic.
- *Touch:* GFIs can touch participants (with permission) to help them achieve a posture or movement. In another sense, personal anecdotes and success stories can be inspirational and "touch" participants.

Tip #4: Openings and closings

The beginning and ending of a class are absolutely crucial for success. Biscontini recommends a formal, memorized introduction and closing statement as a way to define the purpose of a class, set a professional tone, and bring a class to an inspirational conclusion.

Willingness to Plan Ahead

Participants appreciate when they are provided with advance notice of events that interfere with class, such as holiday closures, intersession breaks, or a planned vacation. They also are grateful when they are informed of upcoming events or fitness challenges that are offered in the community. If given enough advance notice, participants may want to train for a specific event. Helping participants set appropriate goals to prepare for these events and counseling them if a particular event is unrealistic demonstrates an interest in the participants and a high level of professionalism.

Recognition of the Signs of Instructor Burnout

Talking with other GFIs about how to prevent or work through burnout is invaluable. All exercise leaders will experience this phenomenon at some time or another, and getting another professional's advice will be useful. It is important to schedule regular vacations; it is amazing what a week or two away from work can do to improve one's attitude! Another strategy is to occasionally switch classes with another GFI for a time. Sometimes teaching a different class, using a different exercise format, or seeing different faces in the group can help alleviate burnout.

Willingness to Take Responsibility

Invariably, things will go wrong either with the exercise class itself or with the surroundings (e.g., broken air conditioning system). Taking responsibility for these problems and making sure that all efforts are made to correct the situation is appreciated by all. In addition, having backup plans available when such situations arise can prove to be very useful.

Strategies That Build Adherence

Motivation depends on a participant's personal resources, abilities, and strengths, as well as external factors and circumstances. By assuming otherwise—

that only innate personal factors influence adherence—a GFI may "write off" a participant rather than try to teach skills that will help the participant develop into a regular exerciser.

Rather than placing the blame for non-adherence on the participant, the GFI must view motivation as a joint responsibility shared with the participant. It is also helpful to view the process as a dynamic one; alternative strategies may be needed for different individuals at different stages in an exercise program.

Several strategies have proven successful in motivating participants to regularly attend exercise class. The following strategies can easily be integrated into any type of exercise class and will help motivate participants to become regular exercisers. (Some strategies, however, may not be applicable to a specific program, so the GFI must determine which strategies are appropriate for a given situation and subsequently apply them in an individualized manner.) After a particular strategic plan for adherence has been created, it should be reassessed often to determine its continued feasibility and effectiveness.

Formulate Reasonable Participant Expectations

Early on, determine each participant's expectations from the exercise class and help him or her formulate reasonable goals. Expectations must be realistic to avoid disappointment. Although regular physical activity provides many benefits, it is not a panacea, and the participant must be informed of what benefits can be expected from the type of exercise being performed in the class. For instance, if a participant expects dramatic weight loss as a result of attending an exercise class, he or she will be disappointed if this does not occur. It

is preferable to advise the participant that, without a concomitant decrease in caloric intake, actual loss of body fat from physical training is likely to be negligible.

More realistic expectations would be weight loss on the order of one-half pound per week (0.23 kg/week) *if typical caloric intake is reduced,* clothes fitting less snugly over time, new friends made in class, or an increased sense of well-being or energy after completing an exercise session.

Set Exercise Goals

When an individual joins an exercise class or program, it is important to take the time to develop realistic, flexible, and individualized short-term goals with that person. This can be accomplished by setting up a brief interview with a new participant shortly after he or she joins the class. Realistic goals are important to avoid injury and maintain interest.

Participants can be taught goal-setting strategies by applying **SMART goals.** This catchy acronym includes the key components for developing effective goals. Goals should be:

S = Specific: What will you do, when, where, and with whom? *Example:* Not "I will go to the gym for a workout," but "I will go to SportHealth gym with my wife for a cycling class on Monday, Wednesday, and Saturday at 6:30 p.m. after work."

M = Measurable: How will you know when you have reached your goals? *Example:* Not "I will exercise at a moderate intensity today," but "I will walk on the treadmill with my heart rate at 120 beats per minute for 2 miles." If heart rate and walking distance were achieved, then the goal was met.

A = Attainable: Can you really do this? Can you do it at this time? *Example:* Not "I will do 100 sit-ups without stopping Wednesday morning," but "I will do 25 sit-ups by Friday. I will work up to this by doing 16 sit-ups on Monday and 20 on Wednesday."

R = Relevant: Are your goals relevant to your particular interests, needs, and abilities? *Example:* Not "I will train to run a marathon in under three hours," but "I will increase the amount of physical activity I do by going to aerobics class twice this week."

T = Time-bound: How soon, how often, and for how long? *Example:* Not "I will lose at least 10% of my body weight in an effort to improve my appearance," but "I will lose 20 pounds in the four months between now and my high school reunion."

Although the GFI should help in the goal-setting process, the goals should be set, as much as possible, by the participant. Short-term goals determined for each exercise session in conjunction with longer-term monthly goals allow for flexibility on a daily basis without jeopardizing the longer-term goals.

Goals can be specific to the exercise process, such as attending a certain number of classes in the coming weeks, supplementing class exercise with physical activity at home, or reaching a predetermined **target heart rate** during class by a certain date. They also can be related to some benefits not normally associated with physical activity, such as making new friends or developing a new social network. It is useful to encourage goals related to enjoyment and pleasure from moving and being active rather than only physical goals such as weight loss. Participants should periodically be reminded about their goals, and those who meet goals should be publicly praised. If goals are listed and displayed on a chart or are in participant files, they can easily be reviewed and evaluated regularly (e.g., twice a month). When goals are met, it is the GFI's duty to

assist the participant in making new ones.

If it appears that the participant is unlikely to reach a specific goal, a more realistic goal should be encouraged. This will reduce the likelihood of disappointment or loss of interest associated with not meeting the goal, as well as the likelihood of physical injury that may occur when trying to "catch up" to reach a goal (such as performing too much exercise in too short a time). If a goal cannot be met, the GFI and participant can brainstorm reasons why the goal was not met and plan more realistic goals in the future. To avoid any potential embarrassment, this should not be done publicly, but rather by talking with the participant during the warm-up or cool-down phase of the exercise class. These periods can be used to talk individually with participants and provide personalized instructions.

Formalizing the commitment to exercise with participants through written or oral contracts is another effective motivational strategy. A contract is a written agreement signed by the participant and GFI (and others, if appropriate) that clearly itemizes the physical-activity goals and the rewards associated with achieving those goals. Contracts can increase a participant's commitment to the exercise program by defining the specific relationship between exercise goals and positive outcomes contingent on meeting those goals. They also involve each participant in planning the exercise program, thereby providing a sense of ownership of the program (Figure 5-1).

Physical-activity contracts should be jointly prepared by the GFI and the participant. This can be done during a brief meeting before or after class or as part of a discussion during a warm-up or cool-down period, as previously described. The responsibilities each person has in meeting the terms of the contract can

Figure 5-1

Sample exercise contract

This is an example of an exercise contract that can be used to formalize an individual's commitment to exercise. It specifies short-term goals, rewards to be received when goals are met, and promises of each party.

My Promises

1. To attend 10 out of 12 exercise classes during the next four weeks.

2. To exercise out of class for at least 30 minutes one time each week during the next four weeks

3. For any exercise class I have to miss due to illness or other unavoidable reasons, I will plan to make up the session by (specify):_____

4. To reward myself at the end of each week that I meet my exercise goals by (for example, going to the movies, meeting a friend to shop, buying a new CD) (specify)

_____

_____

My Group Fitness Instructor's Promises

1. To lead all classes, except when ill, unless advance notice is given

2. To give me individual feedback regarding my progress

3. To help me set new goals if the ones I set are unrealistic

This contract will be evaluated on: _____
                                                          Date

Participant Signature_____

Group Fitness Instructor Signature_____

---

be itemized at this time. Requirements for class attendance, additional home-exercise workouts, and completion of exercise logs are often specified in contracts. Make certain that the participant has the skills necessary to meet the terms of the contract; beginning with modest goals is one way to ensure this. Precautions should be written into the contract to ensure that the participant does not engage in unhealthy practices to meet contract requirements (e.g., extended exercising over several days to meet a time-based goal or starvation tactics to meet a weight-loss goal).

Give Regular, Positive Feedback

As often as possible, the GFI should provide participants with ample, ongoing, positive reinforcement and individual praise. Feedback that is specific and relevant to the participant is known to be a powerful reinforcer. Specific feedback can include information regarding the number of exercise sessions attended during the month, sessions during which target exercise heart rate or RPE was met, and progress made on becoming proficient in an aerobic exercise routine. Feedback also can be oriented toward the physical-activity behavior itself, as in routine logging. A log sheet can be developed and kept at the exercise facility, where participants can keep a record of resting heart rate, exercise heart rate, RPE, and feelings before and after the exercise session each time they attend class (Figure 5-2). Recording information only takes a few minutes and can be accomplished immediately after class. Reviewing log sheets at regular intervals (perhaps monthly) provides participants with important feedback (e.g., how resting heart

	Sunday	Monday	Tuesday	Wednesday	Thursday	Friday	Saturday
Date							
Type of exercise							
Number of minutes							
Resting heart rate							
Exercise heart rate							
Ratings of perceived exertion							
Feelings before class							
Feelings after class							

Figure 5-2

Sample exercise log

This is an example of an exercise log in which individuals record their daily exercise. This can be kept at the exercise facility for the individual to fill out before or after class, or can be given to class members to take home and complete. Examine these records on a regular basis (e.g., once a month) to check for progress.

rate has decreased over time, how many sessions were attended during the previous month, and improved sense of energy or well-being after exercise). Log sheets also provide participants with information about the intensity of their exercise sessions, letting them know if they are working too hard or need to pick up the intensity to obtain fitness benefits.

Inexpensive incentives, such as water bottles or key chains, can be provided to the participant when certain goals are met. Extrinsic rewards can be particularly important in the early stages of exercise adoption. Incentive-based goals should be set that can be realistically achieved by the majority of participants. Prizes based on attendance rather than large increases in performance are often preferred by participants and can motivate those experiencing less-than-optimal success in reaching physiological

goals. Fitness "challenges" can provide rewards for different levels of participation by offering alternative prizes for a variety of achievements. It is important to be creative to ensure that the challenges are attractive to both the beginner and the long-term exerciser.

Public monitoring of attendance as a means of providing feedback and distributing achievement awards can be useful for motivating participants. Posting attendance charts in the exercise room rewards the frequent attendee with a public display of adherence and may motivate the less-than-optimal adherer to attend class on a more regular basis. A chart with a group theme, such as "Exercise Around the World," can be devised in which daily attendance of each group member is worth a certain number of miles. When the group "reaches" predetermined countries, awards that are representative of that country can be given to all class participants. This strategy encourages group support and rewards the frequent attendee as well as the participant who attends class less often. It also may provide increased motivation to the wayward participant who receives a reward for being part of the group.

Make Exercise Sessions Interesting and Fun

As previously mentioned, aspects of the exercise session itself are related to adherence and motivational issues. The exercise routine should be easy to follow. One means of accomplishing this is to break up the routine into short segments so the participant can learn the routine and be successful.

Sure ways to guarantee dropout are to have an exercise routine that is so complicated that participants cannot follow it, or one so intense that participants are exhausted at the end of class. It is helpful to provide ample, positive reinforcement or support while participants are learning the routine. Varying the routine regularly and providing different types of music that suit the tastes of the class can be useful. Ask participants what type of music they prefer and prepare routines to match their interests.

Participants can be regularly polled to assess the enjoyment factor of the class, perhaps through the use of the RPE scale or a simple enjoyment-assessment scale. Participants should generally be exercising in an RPE range between 11 and 15 on the 6 to 20 scale or between 3 and 5 on the 0 to 10 scale (Table 5-2). If participants are working in an RPE range that is too high, they may not be enjoying the exercise; rather, they may be working hard just to keep up with the instructor.

Table 5-2	
Ratings of Perceived Exertion (RPE)	
RPE	**Category Ratio Scale**
6	0 Nothing at all
7 Very, very light	0.5 Very, very weak
8	1 Very weak
9 Very light	2 Weak
10	3 Moderate
11 Fairly light	4 Somewhat
12	strong
13 Somewhat hard	5 Strong
14	6
15 Hard	7 Very strong
16	8
17 Very hard	9
18	10 Very, very
19 Very, very hard	strong
20	* Maximal

Source: Adapted from American College of Sports Medicine (2014). *ACSM's Guidelines for Exercise Testing and Prescription* (9th ed.). Philadelphia: Wolters Kluwer/ Lippincott Williams & Wilkins.

Exercise enjoyment also can be assessed orally during the exercise session with a five-point rating scale, with one equaling "extremely unenjoyable" and five equaling "extremely enjoyable." The GFI can determine which parts of the exercise class are most favorable to participants by asking about their enjoyment level at different points during class. Another option is to develop a brief, anonymous written survey to assess the enjoyment level of the class and satisfaction with different aspects of the exercise program. Survey responses can be saved and used as documentation of exercise-leadership skills.

If it is evident that some participants are working excessively, the intensity of the routine can be lowered until the overworkers can "catch their breath" and get back into their exercise comfort zone. As previously mentioned, if the class is of varying abilities, visually provide both a lower-intensity and higher-intensity version of the routine.

Acknowledge Exercise Discomforts

Participants should be taught how to tell the difference between the transient discomforts associated with exercise and those discomforts that are potential signs of injury or more serious problems. Newcomers to exercise may not be accustomed to the feeling of increased breathing, heart rate, and sweating associated with exercise. They must be reassured that these are normal responses and should be expected.

Participants must be informed of potential injuries that may arise and be able to recognize a symptom that warrants attention. Any sudden, sharp pain that does not dissipate or muscle soreness that does not lessen after a few days may be a sign of injury and should be examined by a health professional. Similarly, participants must know the signs and symptoms of a heart attack, particularly when the exercisers are of middle and older ages. A dull, aching discomfort in the chest, neck, jaw, or arms associated with excessive sweating or clammy skin that is not relieved with rest may be signs of a heart attack; proper medical authorities should be contacted immediately (see Chapter 9).

It is helpful to ask participants individually how they are feeling and if they are experiencing any unusual discomforts. This information is often not offered voluntarily and potential injuries may not be discovered without prompting. After learning about minor injuries, the GFI can provide personal advice to take it easy for a class or two until the ache or pain lessens. Follow-up advice during successive classes lets the participant know that he or she is cared about and the GFI is looking out for the participant's best interests.

Use Exercise Reminders, Cues, and Prompts

Encourage participants to develop prompts or cues in their home or work environments that will promote regular class attendance, such as scheduling physical activity in a daily appointment book and laying out exercise gear the night before class.

Posters placed at participants' homes or work environments that depict individuals enjoying physical activity may encourage attendance. Newsletters can include clever flyers that remind participants of upcoming special events or fitness challenges. E-mail prompts or text messages are another avenue to cue participants. A variety of prompts at work, home, and the exercise location can help keep participants thinking about exercise.

Encourage an Extensive Social-support System

Develop a buddy system among participants so that they can call each other to make sure they attend class and have an additional support person to discuss progress and goals. Additional social support for exercise can be encouraged by having participants ask friends or relatives to pitch in by reminding them to attend their exercise classes. Ask participants to identify which types of support are helpful and motivating to them personally, and then ask them to identify individuals who can provide that specific type of support. Figure 5-3 lists different types of support and provides examples of how they can be used to encourage exercise attendance. Support does not have to be face-to-face; telephone, e-mail, and mail

Figure 5-3
Support for
exercise

Types of Support	Ways Support Can Be Received	Who can provide this type of support for me? (fill in)
Emotional providers	Sympathetic to struggles with starting to exercise	
Affection providers	Comfort and reassurance when goals are not met Reward-givers when goals are met	
Challengers	Challenge to make goals and achieve them	
Listeners	Sounding board for communicating experiences associated with exercise	
Appraisers	Feedback on goal achievements	
Role models/ partners	Exercise partner, set and work on goals together	
Experts	Information associated with exercise	

contacts are additional avenues of support that can be utilized. As previously described, newsletters are a useful means for keeping participants informed of class activities, and they add to a sense of belonging.

Telephone contacts initiated after one or two missed classes that let the lapsing participant know he or she was missed may encourage a return to class.

Develop Group Camaraderie

It is particularly important for class members to feel a sense of cohesiveness. Research shows that individuals who have strong beliefs about the cohesiveness of their class attend more exercise classes, are less likely to drop out, are more likely to enjoy physical activity, and have high self-efficacy toward physical activity (Estabrooks, 2000). Group cohesion starts when participants gather around a shared task. Learning a new routine as a group or working to meet group goals will enhance this type of group cohesion. As participants become satisfied with their accomplishments, social cohesion increases. Social cohesion can be enhanced by introducing new class members and encouraging participants to share information about themselves. Providing interesting, little-known facts about each participant in a newsletter also is beneficial. The social support and reinforcement for exercise developed through group membership is powerful and should not be overlooked. *Note:* GFIs must obtain written permission from participants before sharing any confidential information with others (see Chapter 11 and Appendix A).

By the same token, the GFI must be aware of individual behaviors that threaten to undermine positive group dynamics. Some groups have chronic complainers or generally disruptive individuals. These individuals must be dealt with early to avoid the tendency for them to take charge of the group or monopolize class time. When dealing with a chronic complainer, the GFI should listen attentively and acknowledge understanding of the participant's complaint, then agree on a solution and follow through to make any needed changes. The participant should be informed when the issue has been resolved.

The disruptive individual should not be given too much attention (since that may *encourage* the disruptive behaviors). If lack of attention does not change the individual's behavior, then the GFI should speak to the individual privately to discuss the interruptions and possible reasons for the disruptive behavior.

Emphasize the Positive Aspects of Exercise

Participants just starting to exercise should be encouraged to generally disregard minor exercise discomforts, recognize their own self-defeating thoughts, and counteract them with positive thoughts. Encourage participants to think "good thoughts," such as how refreshing it feels to move about freely, how encouraging other class members are, and so on, while performing the exercise routine. Comment on positive aspects of the routine throughout: "here comes the fun part," "looking great," and similar comments keep the participants focused on the positive. Martin et al. (1984) found that those who were told to attend to environmental surroundings and enjoy the outdoors during a class-based running program had greater attendance

and were more likely to continue exercising after the formal program ended compared to those who concentrated on increasing their performance during the exercise sessions. Pleasant thoughts that focus on enjoyment of movement and how accomplished the participants will feel when class is over will help the time move by quickly and enjoyably. The GFI can help participants who have been exercising regularly and have specific performance goals to visualize the sense of satisfaction they will get when those goals are met. This can serve as a positive motivator when the exercise intensity necessary to meet goals may be intense and somewhat uncomfortable for the participant.

Help Participants Develop Intrinsic Rewards

Once the exercise behavior has become part of the participant's routine, it is often useful to supplement class rewards and support with a natural reward system that is provided outside of exercise class. Positive feedback on exercise habits provided by family, friends, and coworkers transfers some of the positive feedback received during exercise class to other environments, as well as providing additional avenues of social support. Encourage the participant to develop a natural reward system that focuses on increased feelings of self-esteem, a sense of accomplishment, and increased energy levels instead of merely external rewards. Natural reinforcers add to a sense of personal identification as being an exerciser and will help participants continue to exercise even when they cannot make it to class.

Prepare Participants for Inevitable Missed Classes

It is important to realize that the participant will not be able to attend classes at some point in the program. Although the participant may be unable to make it to class during vacations, holidays, or times of increased work or family pressures, he or she may still be able to continue a home-based exercise program and should be encouraged to do so. Confidence about being physically active in different settings can be built by encouraging participants to add at least one day of physical activity outside of class time, preferably using a different mode of exercise (such as brisk walking, swimming, or any other type of exercise the participant enjoys). This will give participants experience with a beneficial alternative when they must miss a scheduled class. Ask participants about exercise performed outside of class and praise them when it has been accomplished. When a participant successfully exercises on his or her own, confidence for continuing exercise is being built.

Exercising with family or coworkers is ideal for out-of-class exercise sessions. If the participant cannot find someone to exercise with, encourage other class members to meet him or her in an alternative physical-activity setting. Not only does this provide an additional mode of social support for physical activity, it also provides participants with an opportunity to problem-solve any difficulties encountered with exercise. Additional days of exercise can be included in the exercise contract, and exercise logs of these sessions can be kept to document them. During times when participants are extremely busy, remind them that a shorter-than-normal workout is still beneficial and will keep them exercising regularly. Three 10-minute workouts performed throughout the day are just as effective in producing health-related

benefits and increasing fitness levels as a single 30-minute bout. Although the GFI's primary responsibility is to encourage class attendance, supporting the concept of at least one out-of-class exercise session per week will ultimately help participants' overall exercise achievement and long-term adherence.

Classes may not be offered in some instances. For example, if classes are provided as part of a university environment, there may be a break in classes due to semester breaks or holidays. By advising participants in advance, the GFI can prepare them for these breaks. It is also possible to make arrangements with other exercise classes at different locations in the community so participants can continue exercising in a similar format.

Prepare Participants for Changes in Instructors

A change in instructors is usually quite disruptive for participants. Unfortunately, typically little is done to prepare participants for this change. A planned change in leadership because of pregnancy leave, travel, or a permanent relocation can be smooth if participants are prepared for the change well ahead of time. If possible, introduce the new exercise instructor in advance. Having the regular and new instructor team-teach several exercise classes can help prevent fears of a change in format after the regular instructor departs. There will undoubtedly be times of illness, so substitutes should be planned for and arranged in advance. It would be a bonus if instructors could introduce the substitutes to the participants so that when they need to be used, participants are already familiar with them.

Train to Prevent Exercise Defeatism

Prepare participants for the eventual missed class. How slips are handled determines if they will be temporary or permanent. Let participants know that missing a class is a realistic probability. If participants can predict and prepare for lapses in their exercise programs, these occurrences will likely not be as disruptive. Certain issues make class attendance unlikely (e.g., family crises, holidays, illness, and extra pressure or deadlines at work). When these can be anticipated and seen as being temporary rather than as a breakdown in the success of the physical-activity program, adherence is more likely to be maintained. A lapse should be viewed as a challenge to overcome rather than as a failure.

Participants can be made aware of the defeatist attitude that accompanies the belief that once a physical-activity program is disrupted, total relapse or dropout is inevitable. Although breaking the adherence rule does place the participant at a higher risk for dropping out, it is not inevitable. If exercise is viewed by participants as a process during which there will undoubtedly be times that they will be less active than others, they will not consider themselves non-exercisers whenever a class is missed. Rather, they will catch the next available class or exercise on their own when time permits. Participants also can be encouraged to avoid "high-risk" situations (such as going to a "happy hour" before exercise class) that test their resolve to exercise. Encourage participants to surround themselves with cues that support the physical-activity behavior. A simple telephone call or e-mail message after one or two missed sessions may bring the participant back to class if he or she understands that missing class is not a sign of failure.

Emphasize an Overall Healthy Lifestyle

Physical activity is only one of a number of lifestyle-related activities that participants engage in throughout the week. It is often assumed that those who exercise regularly also practice other healthy behaviors. Unfortunately, this is often not the case. Diets of exercisers are generally not any different from the typical American diet. The GFI has an outstanding opportunity to provide accurate information and to encourage the development of additional healthy lifestyle behaviors. Questions regarding diet, weight control, and other behaviors will undoubtedly be asked. By being well-versed in these topics, the GFI can offer sound information with a scientific basis. Displaying posters that emphasize aspects of healthy lifestyles, such as the MyPlate Food Guidance System, can remind participants that physical activity is just one of many healthful behaviors.

Finally, the GFI is viewed as a model for a healthy lifestyle and should try to live up to the participants' expectations. Encourage by example. Do not smoke or abuse alcohol, and maintain a prudent, healthy diet and an appropriate **body composition.**

Exercise and Body Image

Cultural norms for attractiveness are often centered on "ideal body types." In the United States, this ideal body type has, in recent times, been associated with extreme thinness, particularly in women. While this body type may photograph well for fashion magazines, it is not ideal for most women and is most likely an unattainable and potentially unhealthy goal for many. When women perceive that their bodies are being compared to this unrealistic "ideal," many become dissatisfied with their body shape and fret over any extra pounds in undesirable places.

High levels of physical activity have been associated with a preoccupation with weight and body shape. These unhealthy attitudes may put some individuals, particularly teenage and young adult women, at risk for developing **eating disorders,** such as **anorexia nervosa** and **bulimia nervosa,** as well as **addictions** to exercise or overexercise, which is used as an additional method to lose weight or to "purge" calories that have recently been consumed (Brownell & Foreyt, 1986).

By being aware of this phenomenon, a GFI can encourage participants to accept their own body shapes. Remind participants that everyone has his or her own unique body shape and no amount of exercise is going to change that basic shape. Avoid pointing out specific exercises to "fix" certain body parts, which may lead to a preoccupation or dissatisfaction with that body part. It is better for participants to focus on the enjoyment of moving and the overall good feelings associated with exercise.

While the GFI wants to encourage regular exercise participation, a small number of individuals may take the exercise habit to the extreme and exhibit signs of **exercise dependence** or addiction. Exercise dependence has been defined in a variety of ways, though a good definition is when the commitment to exercise assumes a higher priority than commitments to family, work, or interpersonal relations (Morgan, 1979).

Signs of exercise dependence/addiction include continuing to exercise despite injuries or illness, extreme levels of thinness, and feelings of extreme guilt, irritability, or **depression** when unable to exercise. Typically, a GFI has limited interpersonal interaction with his or her exercise participants, which makes it difficult to get to know a participant well enough to recognize if feelings of guilt, irritability, or depression exist. In these situations, a GFI often has to rely on visual cues or observations of behavior to determine if a participant is suffering from a potential eating disorder or exercise addiction. Guidelines for spotting a potential problem include:

- Weight loss in a short period of time (often 10–15% of original bodyweight)
- Paleness
- Complaints of being cold
- Dressing in layers to hide weight loss or to keep warm
- Dizziness and fainting
- Hair loss
- Dry skin
- Compulsive exercise

Since any of these signs and symptoms may also be indicative of other health issues, it is important to *not* automatically assume a participant has an eating disorder or exercise addiction. However, if an individual displays several signs and symptoms and the GFI has witnessed these changes over time, it is certainly prudent to address these concerns with the participant.

If the GFI suspects a participant is exercising to excess or may have an eating disorder, the matter should be dealt with using forethought and sensitivity. Concern should be expressed over what has been observed and the participant should be asked directly about his or her exercise and eating habits. Chances are that if a disorder exists, the participant has already been confronted about the situation. Be sensitive and understanding, offering support as well as suggesting that professional guidance be sought. It is helpful if several names and telephone numbers of qualified professionals are available to the participant in need.

Finally, it is essential that GFIs provide accurate information about weight loss, body composition, and nutrition. GFIs should have a broad network of referrals (such as physicians and **registered dietitians**) who may be able to help educate individuals when appropriate.

Talking to a Participant About a Suspected Eating Disorder

If a GFI suspects that someone has an eating disorder, the GFI should consider using the "CONFRONT" approach advocated by the National Association of Anorexia Nervosa and Associated Disorders (ANAD) (www.anad.org):

C—Concern. Share that the reason you are approaching the individual is because you care about his or her mental, physical, and nutritional needs.

O—Organize. Prepare for the confrontation. Think about who will be involved, the best place to talk, why you are concerned, how you plan to talk to the person, and the most appropriate time.

N—Needs. What will the individual need after the confrontation? Have referrals to professional help and/or support groups available should the individual be ready to seek help.

F—Face the confrontation. Be empathetic but direct. Be persistent if the individual denies having a problem.

R—Respond by listening carefully.

O—Offer help and suggestions. Be available to talk and provide other assistance when needed.

N—Negotiate another time to talk and a time frame in which to seek professional help, preferably from a physician who specializes in eating disorders as well as an experienced psychologist.

T—Time. Keep in mind that the individual will not be "fixed" overnight. Recovery takes time and patience.

A GFI can play an important role in helping to identify individuals who may be suffering from an eating disorder and referring them to the appropriate trained professional. It is outside the scope of practice of a GFI to attempt to counsel or treat individuals with a suspected eating disorder.

Summary

Dropout rates for those beginning a group fitness program can reach 50% or more after only six months. Instead of placing the blame for non-adherence on the participant, the GFI must view motivation as a shared responsibility and work with the participant to develop a successful motivational strategy. Extra assistance should be provided to the participant who has been identified as at high risk for dropout.

Motivation is a dynamic process, and by applying a variety of strategies and reviewing and refining these strategies regularly, achievement of regular exercise can be attained by most participants. Motivational techniques include structuring appropriate expectations and goals, identifying short-term benefits, providing specific feedback, teaching problem-solving skills, serving as a positive role model, and training participants to manage their own reward systems.

Additionally, the convenience and attractiveness of the exercise setting, enjoyability of the exercise class, supportiveness of the exercise environment, as well as personal factors specific to both the GFI and the participant, are factored into the exercise-adherence equation. Understanding and applying the principles of adherence and motivation described in this chapter will help the GFI become a more effective teacher and health/fitness professional.

References

Bandura, A. (1986). *Social Foundations of Thought and Action: A Social Cognitive Theory*. Englewood Cliffs, N.J.: Prentice-Hall.

Biscontini, L. (2010). Creating compelling experiences. *IDEA Fitness Manager, 22*, 1.

Brehm, B.A. (2004). *Successful Fitness Motivation Strategies*. Champaign, Ill.: Human Kinetics.

Brownell, K.D. & Foreyt, J.P. (Eds.) (1986). *Handbook of Eating Disorders*. New York: Basic Books, Inc.

Centers for Disease Control and Prevention (2005a). Adult participation in recommended levels of physical activity: United States, 2001 and 2003. *Morbidity and Mortality Weekly Report, 54*, 47, 1208–1212.

Centers for Disease Control and Prevention (2005b). Trends in leisure-time physical inactivity by age, sex, and race/ethnicity: United States, 1994–2004. *Morbidity and Mortality Weekly Report, 54*, 39, 991–994.

Centers for Disease Control and Prevention (2003). Physical activity among adults: United States, 2000. *Advance Data, 333*.

Coker, C.A., Fischman, M.G., & Oxendine, J.B. (2005). Motor skill learning for effective coaching and performance. In: Williams, J.M. (Ed.) *Applied Sport Psychology: Personal Growth to Peak Performance*. New York: McGraw-Hill.

Deci, E.L. & Ryan, R.M. (2007). Facilitating optimal motivation and psychological well-being across life's domains. *Canadian Psychology, 49*, 1, 14–23.

Dishman, R.K. (1994). *Advances in Exercise Adherence*. Champaign, Ill.: Human Kinetics.

Dishman, R.K. (Ed.). (1988). *Exercise Adherence: Its Impact on Public Health*. Champaign, Ill.: Human Kinetics.

Dishman, R.K. (1982). Compliance/adherence in health-related exercise. *Health Psychology, 1*, 237–267.

Dishman, R.K. & Buckworth, J. (1997). Adherence to physical activity. In: Morgan, W.P. (Ed.) *Physical Activity & Mental Health* (pp. 63–80). Washington, D.C.: Taylor & Francis.

Duda, J.L. & Treasure, D.C. (2005). Toward optimal motivation in sport: Fostering athletes' competence and sense of control. In: Williams, J.M. (Ed.) *Applied Sport Psychology: Personal Growth to Peak Performance*. New York: McGraw-Hill.

Duncan, T. E. & McAuley, E. (1993). Social support and efficacy cognitions in exercise adherence: A latent growth curve analysis. *Journal of Behavioral Medicine, 16*, 199–218.

Estabrooks, P.A. (2000). Sustaining exercise participation through group cohesion. *Exercise and Sport Sciences Reviews, 28*, 63–67.

Fredrickson, B.L. (2009). *Positivity*. New York: Random House.

Hofstetter, D.R. et al. (1991). Illness, injury, and correlates of aerobic exercise and walking: A community study. *Research Quarterly for Exercise and Sport, 62*, 1–9.

Huberty, J.L. et al. (2008). Explaining long-term exercise adherence in women who complete a structured exercise program. *Research Quarterly for Exercise and Sport, 79*, 3, 374–384.

Macera, C.A. et al. (1989). Predicting lower-extremity injuries among habitual runners. *Archives of Internal Medicine, 149*, 2565–2568.

Marcus, B.H. et al. (2000). Physical activity behavior change: Issues in adoption and maintenance. *Health Psychology, 19*, 32–41.

Martin, J.E. et al. (1984). Behavioral control of exercise in sedentary adults: Studies 1 through 6. *Journal of Consulting & Clinical Psychology, 52*, 795–811.

Morgan, C.F. et al. (2003). Personal, social, and environmental correlates of physical activity in a bi-ethnic sample of adolescents. *Pediatric Exercise Science, 15*, 288–301.

Morgan, W.P. (2001). Prescription of physical activity: A paradigm shift. *Quest, 53*, 336–382.

Morgan, W.P. (1979). Negative addiction in runners. *Physician and Sportsmedicine, 7*, 57–70.

Oldridge, N.G. (1982).Compliance and exercise in primary and secondary prevention of coronary heart disease: A review. *Preventive Medicine, 11*, 56–70.

Prochaska, J.O. & DiClemente, C.C. (1984). *The Transtheoretical Approach: Crossing Traditional Boundaries of Therapy*. Homewood, Ill.: Dow Jones/Irwin.

Sallis, J.F. et al. (1986). Predictors of adoption and maintenance of physical activity in a community sample. *Preventive Medicine, 15*, 331–341.

Seligman, M.E.P. (2002). *Authentic Happiness: Using the New Positive Psychology to Realize Your Potential for Lasting Fulfillment*. New York: Simon & Schuster.

U.S. Department of Health & Human Services (2008). *2008 Physical Activity Guidelines for Americans: Be Active, Healthy and Happy*. www.health.gov/paguidelines/pdf/paguide.pdf.

Vallerand, R.J. (2001). A hierarchical model of intrinsic and extrinsic motivation in sport and exercise. In: Roberts, G. (Ed.) *Advances in Motivation in Sport and Exercise*. Champaign, Ill.: Human Kinetics.

Vallerand, R.J. & Losier, G.F. (1999). An integrative analysis of intrinsic and extrinsic motivation in sport. *Journal of Applied Sport Psychology, 11*, 142–169.

Suggested Reading

Bandura, A. (2001). Social cognitive theory: An agentive perspective. *Annual Review of Psychology, 52,* 1–26.

Bandura, A. (1997). *Self-efficacy: The Exercise of Control.* New York: Freeman.

Brehm, B.A. (2004). *Successful Fitness Motivation Strategies.* Champaign, Ill.: Human Kinetics.

Dishman, R.K. & Sallis, J. (1990). Determinants and interventions for physical activity and exercise. In: Bouchard, C. et al. (Eds.) *Exercise, Fitness, and Health.* Champaign, Ill.: Human Kinetics.

Fredrickson, B.L. (2009). *Positivity.* New York: Random House.

McAuley, E., Pena, M.M., & Jerome, G.J. (2001). Self-efficacy as a determinant and an outcome of exercise. In: Roberts, G.C. (Ed.) *Advances in Motivation in Sport and Exercise.* Champaign, Ill.: Human Kinetics.

Sallis, J.F. & Hovell, M.F. (1990). Determinants of exercise behavior. In: *Exercise and Sports Sciences Reviews,* 18. Baltimore: Williams & Wilkins, 307–330.

Seligman, M.E.P. (2002). *Authentic Happiness: Using the New Positive Psychology to Realize Your Potential for Lasting Fulfillment.* New York: Simon & Schuster.

U.S. Department of Health & Human Services (1996). *Physical Activity and Health: A Report of the Surgeon General.* Atlanta, Georgia: U.S. Department of Health & Human Services, Public Health Service, CDC, National Center for Chronic Disease Prevention and Health Promotion.

James H. Rimmer, Ph.D., is a professor in the Department of Disability and Human Development and adjunct professor in the Department of Kinesiology and Nutrition and the School of Public Health at the University of Illinois at Chicago. He also is an adjunct professor in the Department of Physical Medicine and Rehabilitation at Northwestern University, which is affiliated with the Rehabilitation Institute of Chicago. For the past 30 years, Dr. Rimmer has been developing and directing physical-activity and health-promotion programs for people with disabilities. He has published more than 100 peer-reviewed journal articles and book chapters on various topics related to physical activity, health promotion, secondary conditions, and disability. He is director of two federally funded centers, the National Center on Physical Activity and Disability (www.ncpad.org) and the Rehabilitation Engineering Research Center on Interactive Exercise Technologies and Exercise Physiology Benefiting People with Disabilities (www.rectech.org).

Exercise and Special Populations

By James H. Rimmer

Group Fitness Instructors (GFIs) frequently encounter participants with special needs and health concerns. While screening for these conditions is not typically the responsibility of a GFI, it is important to understand that they may significantly influence an individual's ability to perform physical activity. For example, intensity may need to be modified, and there may be specific movements or positions that are contraindicated. These types of guidelines and limitations will generally come from the individual's physician or physical therapist and must be adhered to by the GFI.

This chapter addresses basic guidelines for working with individuals with the following health conditions and/or special needs:

- Coronary heart disease
- Hypertension
- Obesity
- Diabetes
- Asthma
- Bronchitis
- Emphysema
- Arthritis
- Fibromyalgia
- Osteoporosis
- Low-back pain
- Multiple sclerosis

The following populations are discussed as well:

- Children
- Older adults

Cardiac Diseases

Coronary Heart Disease

Coronary heart disease (CHD) is the leading cause of death in the U.S. for both males and females, accounting for one of every five deaths in 2006 [American Heart Association (AHA), 2010]. CHD is a multifaceted disorder that varies greatly from person to person. Since the purpose of this chapter is to discuss conditions that GFIs will be exposed to in the workplace, patients with advanced CHD will not be discussed, as they would not be advised to exercise in these settings. It would be more appropriate to recommend an outpatient cardiac rehabilitation program for individuals with advanced CHD. General exercise guidelines for participants with known coronary heart disease are shown in Table 6-1.

Exercise and Coronary Heart Disease

If a participant has been approved by a physician to exercise in a less-supervised

Table 6-1
General Exercise Guidelines for Participants With Known Coronary Heart Disease
• Avoid extremes of heat and cold that can place a greater stress on the heart.
• Use heart-rate monitors to regulate exercise intensity, and avoid activities that cause large fluctuations in heart rate.
• Stay within the blood-pressure and target heart-rate zones established by the participant's physician.
• Report all symptoms, especially lightheadedness, chest pain, or dizziness, to the participant's physician.
• Make sure that heart rate and blood pressure return to resting levels before the participant leaves the exercise setting.
• If a participant complains of chest pain before, during, or after exercise, contact emergency medical services.

setting such as a fitness center, the major goal is to avoid high-intensity exercise that has a greater likelihood of precipitating a coronary event. The exercise program for persons with known CHD should include an extended warm-up that consists of low-intensity exercise such as light walking or riding a stationary bike with little or no resistance; several different stretching exercises, particularly in the chest region if a person has had open-heart surgery; and some mild breathing exercises that could be part of a **yoga** or postural relaxation class. An extended warm-up session may determine if any chest discomfort or dizziness is present before initiating higher-intensity exercise.

- Proper use of **ratings of perceived exertion (RPE)** should be taught to participants with known CHD. Some participants may have a pacemaker or be on **beta-adrenergic blocking agents** (commonly referred to as **beta blockers**), which blunt the heart-rate response and will not give an accurate indication of exercise intensity. Try to associate a certain RPE value with the person's **heart rate (HR).** Although the HR will be lower in persons who are on beta blockers, the RPE value should correlate fairly well with HR.

- Persons who have had a **stroke** or **cerebrovascular accident (CVA)** often suffer from CHD as well (Tamparo & Lewis, 2011). Strokes are caused by years of living with high blood pressure and high **cholesterol,** often precipitated by an unhealthy lifestyle (e.g., poor eating habits, lack of physical activity, or **obesity**). The term "brain attack" has been used to associate the circumstances of having a stroke with a heart attack.

- The two major types of stroke are hemorrhagic and ischemic. **Hemorrhagic strokes** (a ruptured blood vessel in the brain) are usually more life-threatening than **ischemic strokes.** Ischemic strokes are much more common and involve a reduced blood supply to the brain.

- Since stroke is sometimes accompanied by memory loss, it is important to make sure the participant has taken his or her medication before exercising. Participants should carry their medication with them at all times in case they forget to take it before leaving home. This will allow them to take their medicine while at the fitness center and not have to miss a day of exercise. Since many people with strokes have **hypertension,** exercise should be postponed until blood pressure is under control.

- As a precautionary measure, participants should complete a detailed evaluation before each exercise session. This includes whether they have taken their medication, generally feel good, have no signs of fatigue or chest discomfort, have had a good night's sleep, have eaten a light breakfast or meal earlier in the day, have a resting blood pressure within their normal range, and have consumed adequate amounts of fluid, especially participants who are taking **diuretics** to control blood pressure. If all of these responses are positive, a participant can begin the workout. At the end of the exercise session, each participant should have his or her blood pressure and HR checked before leaving the exercise setting to make sure that resting values have been restored.

Hypertension

Nearly 75 million Americans, or one in three adults, have high blood pressure (AHA, 2010). Hypertension is an important risk factor for cardiac insufficiency, **myocardial infarction,** stroke, and sudden death. For adults over age 50, **systolic blood pressure (SBP)** greater than 140 mmHg is a more important **cardiovascular disease (CVD)** risk factor than **diastolic blood pressure (DBP).** Specifically, beginning at 115/75 mmHg, CVD risk doubles for each increment of 20/10 mmHg, according to findings from *The Seventh Report of the Joint National Committee on Prevention, Detection, Evaluation, and Treatment of High Blood Pressure* (Chobanian et al., 2003) (Table 6-2).

Exercise and Hypertension

It is important to remember that exercise is only one component of hypertension management. Other healthy-lifestyle components for managing this disease include: (1) consuming a diet rich in fruits, vegetables, and low-fat dairy products; (2) reducing dietary sodium

Table 6-2			
Classification of Blood Pressure for Adults Age 18 and Older*			
Category	Systolic (mmHg)		Diastolic (mmHg)
Normal[†]	<120	and	<80
Prehypertension	120–139	or	80–89
Hypertension[‡] Stage 1 Stage 2	 140–159 ≥160	 or or	 90–99 ≥100

* Not taking antihypertensive drugs and not acutely ill. When systolic and diastolic blood pressures fall into different categories, the higher category should be selected to classify the individual's blood pressure status. For example, 140/82 mmHg should be classified as stage 1 hypertension, and 154/102 mmHg should be classified as stage 2 hypertension. In addition to classifying stages of hypertension on the basis of average blood pressure levels, clinicians should specify presence or absence of target organ disease and additional risk factors. This specificity is important for risk classification and treatment.

[†] Normal blood pressure with respect to cardiovascular risk is below 120/80 mmHg. However, unusually low readings should be evaluated for clinical significance.

[‡] Based on the average of two or more readings taken at each of two or more visits after an initial screening.

Chobanian, A.V. et al. (2003). *JNC 7 Express: The Seventh Report of the Joint National Committee on Prevention, Detection, Evaluation, and Treatment of High Blood Pressure.* NIH Publication No. 03-5233. Washington, D.C.: National Institutes of Health & National Heart, Lung, and Blood Institute.

to no more than 2.4 g daily; and (3) limiting alcohol consumption to no more than two drinks per day for males and one drink per day for women (AHA, 2010). In addition to these lifestyle recommendations, the AHA also recommends:

- Maintaining normal body weight [**body mass index (BMI)** of 18.5–24.9 kg/m^2]
- Engaging in regular aerobic activity such as brisk walking (at least 30 minutes per day, most days of the week)

Regular exercise for persons with hypertension can create a decrease in blood pressure that may last from four to 10 hours after exercise, with some reports indicating effects lasting up to 22 hours. These effects can translate into decreases of 15 mmHg and 4 mmHg of systolic and diastolic blood pressure, respectively (Pescatello et al., 2004). The American College of Sports Medicine (ACSM) offers the following exercise program recommendations for individuals with hypertension (ACSM, 2014):

- *Aerobic training:* Frequency of exercise should preferably be seven days per week for 30 to 60 minutes per session of continuous or intermittent moderate-intensity aerobic exercise [40% to <60% **V̇O$_2$reserve (V̇O$_2$R)**]. Suggested activities include walking, jogging, cycling, and swimming.
- *Strength training:* resistance training at 60 to 80% of **one-repetition maximum (1 RM)** for eight to 12 repetitions (minimum of one set)

Before placing a person with hypertension on an exercise program, it is important to note medications that may affect the response to exercise (Appendix C). Medications may include beta blockers, which can attenuate HR by approximately 30 beats per minute (bpm). **Alpha blockers, calcium channel blockers,** and **vasodilators** may cause postexertional **hypotension.** It is important not to have an individual exercise if his or her resting SBP is >200 mmHg or if his or her DBP is >110 mmHg. During exercise, maintain SBP ≤220 mmHg and/or DBP ≤110 mmHg.

Metabolic Disorders

Obesity

The most prevalent health disorder in American society is obesity, and the number of people affected by obesity has increased markedly in the past 20 years (Hedley et al., 2004). According to statistics from the National Center for Health Statistics of the Centers for

Disease Control and Prevention (CDC) that was gathered as part of the National Health and Nutrition Examination Survey (NHANES) from 2007 to 2008, 33.9% of adults over the age of 20 were obese. In addition, 16.3% of children and adolescents 2 to 19 years of age were found to be obese (at or above the 95th percentile) (Ogden et al., 2008).

Another study examining the prevalence of overweight, obesity, and extreme obesity in a predominantly minority group of adults with disabilities found that extreme obesity was approximately four times higher among people with disabilities than the general population (Rimmer & Wang, 2005).

In large-scale studies consisting of thousands of people, BMI is used to calculate the number of Americans who are **overweight** (see Table 2-7, page 49).

$$BMI = Weight~(kg)~/~Height^2~(m)$$

An adult who has a BMI between 25 and 29.9 is considered to be overweight, and an adult with a BMI of 30 or higher is considered to be obese. Obesity is associated with many other medical conditions, including hypertension, **type 2 diabetes, osteoarthritis,** heart disease, and **low-back pain** (Han et al., 1997; Rice et al., 1993). Excess weight is considered a major risk factor for premature mortality, cardiovascular disease, type 2 diabetes, osteoarthritis, certain cancers, and a multitude of other medical conditions (Ma, Ko, & Chan, 2009).

Exercise is one of the three major cornerstones of treatment for obesity. The other two components, which are not discussed in this chapter, are diet and behavior modification. Since diet alone results in a loss of lean muscle tissue, the only long-term mechanism for maintaining weight loss is to increase daily energy expenditure.

Exercise and Obesity

- A major strategy for getting persons who are excessively overweight to develop lifelong exercise habits is to make the activity as enjoyable and pain-free as possible. Exercising with an excess amount of **body fat** presents a major challenge because of the additional stress on joints and muscles, particularly in participants who are severely overweight. Additionally, these participants are often in extremely poor condition. The key to a successful program is to identify the right combination of activities that do not lead to pain or discomfort. Finding the appropriate comfort level must be done on an individual basis. GFIs should not assume that participants who come to them with suggested activities know what is best for their body types.

- The number-one priority with obese participants is to keep the activity at an intensity level that does not cause pain and soreness. Many persons who are severely overweight already have joint pain from simply performing daily activities. By using a variety of activities that involve the arms and legs together, the stress load on the joints will be displaced over four limbs as opposed to two. Do not place heavy emphasis on the intensity level of the activity. Instead, emphasize low-intensity, high-duration activities. It is more important for the participant to move more and enjoy the feeling of being physically active.

- Since weight maintenance is a lifelong process, participants should understand the caloric balance equation: energy input = energy output. If this balance tilts toward the energy-input side, there will be an excess of calories taken in and those not used will be stored as fat. Therefore, a daily dose of physical activity is needed to offset the calories being consumed. This does not necessarily mean that they have to go to the fitness center seven days a week, but it does suggest they should be physically active every day. A daily dose of physical activity can be performed at home or at work by using a variety of activities that can include housework and gardening.

- Since arthritis is a common condition among persons who are obese, protecting the joints is paramount. Cross-training programs should be employed that involve various types of exercise routines for 10 minutes or less. More and more products are coming on the market that place a lower load on the knee and hip joints. The elliptical trainer, stationary bike, and recumbent stepper (performed in a sitting position) are very popular among severely overweight participants. Some participants may perform 10-minute sessions on two or three different machines. Additionally, water-based activities are excellent options for obese participants who also have arthritis because of the reduced weightbearing effects of the water. Many participants, however, will not want to join an aquatics program because of their reluctance to wear a swimsuit.
- One of the areas often forgotten when developing exercise programs for individuals who are overweight is seat comfort. Many bicycle seats are too small or have too hard of a surface for obese participants. In some cases, it may be necessary to construct a special seat for severely overweight participants [300 lb (136 kg) or more]. It is

also important to make sure that the seat position is adjusted in such a way that a person's abdominal mass does not impair his or her ability to pedal the bike. Some overweight participants prefer to have their seat adjusted a little higher than normal to prevent their midsection from getting in the way of the pedaling motion. This position usually requires the knee to be in full extension to pedal without obstruction.

- Resistance training should be performed for 10 to 15 minutes a day, two to three days a week. This can be done with weights or elastic bands. Weight training improves body image and increases lean body mass, which makes this activity a nice complement to the cardiorespiratory-training component and adds variety to the program. Additionally, resistance training improves strength and makes **activities of daily living (ADL),** such as walking up a flight of steps, easier to manage.

Diabetes

Diabetes is one of the most debilitating conditions affecting the U.S. population and is often linked to a number of **chronic diseases** and disabilities, including heart disease, stroke, amputations, blindness, kidney failure, autonomic **neuropathy** (which affects HR), and peripheral neuropathy (which affects sensation in distal extremities) (National Institutes of Health, 2006). There are two principal types of diabetes: type 1 and type 2. **Type 1 diabetes** is caused by a destruction of the pancreatic cells that produce the body's **insulin** (Tsai et al., 2006). Type 2 diabetes results from **insulin resistance** combined with defective insulin secretion (Parchman, Romero, & Pugh, 2006).

Diabetes is a broadly applied term used to denote a complex group of syndromes that result in a disturbance in the utilization of **glucose.** Type 1 diabetes is a more serious condition and can result in death if not properly treated. A person with this condition must take regular amounts of insulin to sustain a safe amount of glucose in the blood. When insulin is not taken, blood glucose, which normally ranges between 80 and 120 mg/dL, can reach 1,000 mg/dL or higher, and cause the person to go into a diabetic coma.

Type 2 diabetes is the most common form of diabetes, affecting 90% of all individuals with diabetes. It typically occurs in adults who are overweight and is characterized by insulin resistance, a reduced sensitivity of insulin target cells to available insulin. Unfortunately, increasing numbers of children are being diagnosed with type 2 diabetes, making the term "adult-onset diabetes" inappropriate. Some people with type 2 diabetes never exhibit any of the classic symptoms of diabetes. Treatment usually includes diet modification, medication, and exercise.

Exercise can have a significant effect on lowering blood glucose and is an essential component of treatment for persons with type 1 and type 2 diabetes. However, because glucose is needed to perform exercise, persons with diabetes can easily run into trouble if their baseline blood glucose level is too high or too low.

Exercise and Diabetes

Important considerations when creating exercise programs for people with diabetes include (Hornsby & Albright, 2009):

- Knowledge of the type of medication they may be taking to lower blood glucose (insulin or oral hypoglycemic agents)
- Timing of medication administration
- Blood glucose level prior to exercise
- Timing, amount, and type of previous food intake
- Presence and severity of diabetic complications
- Use of other medication secondary to diabetic complications
- Intensity, duration, and type of exercise

People with type 2 diabetes can especially benefit from exercise in addition to medication and dietary factors that will work together to improve blood glucose control (Hornsby & Albright, 2009). Exercise can also be important in type 2 diabetes prevention. While individuals with type 1 diabetes may not encounter the same blood glucose–lowering advantages (Hornsby & Albright, 2009), people with type 1 and type 2 diabetes are encouraged to exercise to gain other benefits, such as reduction in body fat, cardiovascular improvement, and stress reduction, all of which improve overall health and well-being. The following are general exercise training guidelines for people with either type of diabetes.

- The most important aspects of the exercise program for persons with diabetes is maintaining the proper balance of food and insulin dosage and reducing heart-disease risk. If too many calories are ingested before exercise or too little insulin is taken, blood glucose can reach a high enough level where exercise will actually cause a further increase in blood glucose levels because of the breakdown of fatty acids and glycogen (the storage form of glucose).
- Physicians will usually instruct their patients to check their blood glucose level before and after exercise. If pre-exercise

blood glucose is below 100 mg/dL, advise the person to ingest 20 to 30 g of additional carbohydrates (ACSM, 2014). With additional carbohydrate consumption, exercise may be allowed to take place. Participants with diabetes should have specific guidelines to follow before starting an exercise program. These guidelines will depend upon a participant's clinical status and medical history with respect to blood glucose control.

- Persons with diabetes should carry a portable **glucometer** with them. This device is inexpensive and can be used to check blood glucose before and after exercise. Persons with diabetes should check their blood glucose level a few minutes before exercising and follow the guidelines regarding exercise.

- Another common problem in persons with diabetes is a condition known as **hypoglycemia,** which is defined as a blood glucose level lower than 70 mg/dL (ACSM, 2014) and occurs when there is not enough glucose in the bloodstream. Most experts agree that this is an even more dangerous situation than **hyperglycemia** (high blood glucose) because it can happen very quickly and can lead to an **insulin reaction.** This is often a greater problem in persons who have type 1 diabetes. If some form of food (preferably carbohydrate) is not ingested immediately, the person could go into **insulin shock** and die. Table 6-3 lists the early and late symptoms of an insulin reaction and details how to treat one if it does occur. GFIs should keep rapidly absorbed carbohydrates on site (e.g., orange juice or other fruit drinks) in case of an emergency.

Table 6-3

Insulin Reaction (Hypoglycemia)

Early Symptoms	Late Symptoms
Anxiety, uneasiness	Double vision
Irritability	Sweating, palpitations
Extreme hunger	Nausea
Confusion	Loss of motor coordination
Headaches	Pale, moist skin
Insomnia	Strong, rapid pulse
	Convulsions
	Loss of consciousness
	Coma

Helping a Participant Who Is Having an Insulin Reaction

- Stop the activity immediately.

- Have the person sit down and check his or her blood glucose level.

- Have the participant drink orange juice or some other rapidly absorbing carbohydrate.

- Allow the individual to sit quietly and wait for a response.

- When the participant feels better, check the blood glucose level again.

- If the blood glucose level is above 100 mg/dL and the participant feels better, resume activity.

- Check blood glucose level after 15 to 30 minutes to reassure that levels are within a safe range.

- Do not allow the participant to leave the facility until blood glucose levels are within a normal range.

- If the participant does not improve, seek medical attention immediately.

Rimmer, J.H. (1994). *Fitness and Rehabilitation Programs for Special Populations.* Dubuque, Iowa: WCB McGraw-Hill.

- Blood glucose should also be measured after exercise to make sure the participant does not become hypoglycemic. In persons with recently diagnosed diabetes, it will take a few sessions to learn how to maintain a normal balance of glucose and insulin before and after exercise.

- GFIs should know if participants with diabetes have secondary conditions that must be considered in the exercise program (e.g., foot ulcers, visual or kidney problems, and hypertension). For example, if a participant has a foot ulcer, high-impact or weightbearing exercise is contraindicated. If a person has diabetic retinopathy (damage to the retina) or hypertension, heavy resistance training is unsafe. It is important to know the complete medical history of the participant and develop the exercise program based on individual needs and limitations.

- Aerobic exercise that involves repetitive submaximal contractions of major muscle groups, such as swimming, cycling, and brisk walking, are recommended for individuals with diabetes. These activities are less jarring than jogging, racquet sports, basketball, and high-impact aerobics.

- The intensity, frequency, and duration of exercise should be based on the age, fitness level, medical status, and motivational level of the participant. For example, consider a participant with type 2 diabetes who wants to participate in a boot-camp class. In doing so, she elevates her HR to over 85% of her age-predicted **maximum heart rate (MHR).** Since she has other secondary conditions of concern (e.g., hyperten-

sion, retinopathy, and kidney complications), she is only permitted to exercise at 50 to 65% of her **target heart rate (THR)** as prescribed by her physician.

- Since it is difficult to maintain an optimal balance of glucose and insulin, exercise should be performed daily. This does not necessarily mean that the participant has to participate in group exercise classes on a daily basis. There are many other activities that can be done at home. Having the "best of both worlds" may involve a three-days-a-week structured program in the fitness center and a four-days-a-week program of general activity, including walking, gardening, or stationary cycling. The key is to get a regular "dose" of daily activity, preferably at the same time each day for better glycemic control.

- The duration of activity will also depend on the participant's comfort level, with a goal of 20 to 60 minutes. Individuals with a higher tolerance for exercise, and who are more motivated, will generally prefer to exercise for 45 to 60 minutes.

- Avoid exercise in the late evening. A person can have a nocturnal insulin reaction (i.e., an insulin reaction during sleep) if he or she exercises too close to bedtime and is low in carbohydrates. Since the person is unaware of the insulin reaction, he or she could go into a coma and die.

- People with diabetes need to take very good care of their feet, which should be regularly checked for any cuts, blisters, or signs of infection. Good quality exercise shoes also are very important.

- General guidelines and safety tips for persons with diabetes are listed in Table 6-4.

Table 6-4
General Guidelines and Safety Tips for Persons With Diabetes
• Regulating blood glucose levels requires optimal timing of exercise periods in relation to meals and insulin dosage.
• Aim to keep blood glucose levels between 100 and 200 mg/dL one to two hours after a meal.
• Exercise can have a significant effect on insulin reduction (American Diabetes Association, 2006). Some experts note that insulin may need to be reduced by 10 to 50% when starting an exercise program (Wallberg-Henriksson, 1992).*
• If blood glucose levels are lower than 100 mg/dL, have the person consume a rapidly absorbing carbohydrate to increase blood glucose.
• If blood glucose is greater than 300 mg/dL before exercise (some doctors may recommend that exercise not be initiated at blood glucose levels greater than 250 mg/dL), make sure that insulin or the oral hypoglycemic agent has been taken. In some circumstances, participants with a high blood glucose level (>300 mg/dL) may lower it to a safe enough level to exercise by drinking water.
• No participant should be allowed to exercise if his or her blood glucose level does not fall to a safe range before exercise.
• Teach participants to check their feet periodically to avoid foot ulcers. If an ulcer is found, have the person consult with his or her physician immediately for proper treatment. Foot ulcers can worsen and cause major problems if left untreated.
• Check blood glucose at the end of the exercise session to make sure that the person does not become hypoglycemic. This could happen very quickly, particularly after high-intensity or long-duration activities or when the person is not accustomed to understanding how the body reacts to exercise.
• Make sure the participant is well hydrated and drinking water frequently during the exercise class. Be especially cautious in hot environments, as blood glucose can be impacted by dehydration, and the sweating response of diabetics may be impaired, limiting their thermoregulatory abilities.

*A change in insulin or oral hypoglycemic medication should only be made on the recommendation of a participant's physician.

Respiratory and Pulmonary Disorders

Asthma

Chronic obstructive pulmonary disease (COPD) is the third leading cause of death in the United States (American Lung Association, 2011). The three major types of COPD are **asthma, chronic bronchitis,** and **emphysema.**

Asthma affects more than 20 million children and adults in the U.S. and is responsible for nearly 500,000 hospitalizations, 2 million emergency room visits, and 4,000 deaths in the U.S. each year (Moorman et al., 2007; National Asthma Education and Prevention Program, 2007). It is considered a multifactorial disease because it is linked to several potential causes, which include heredity, infections, allergies, socioeconomic status (incidence is higher in low-income groups), and psychosocial and environmental factors.

The majority of persons with asthma have a reduction in breathing capacity during and, more commonly, after exercise (Rimmer, 1994). This is called **exercise-induced asthma (EIA)**, which is characterized by transient airway obstruction usually five to 15 minutes following physical exertion (Clark & Cochrane, 2009). In addition to EIA, other conditions that may trigger an asthma attack are cold temperatures, stress, and air pollution (Blumenthal, 1996). Exercise is beneficial for persons with asthma, provided the program is tailored to the individual's needs (Emtner, Herala, & Stalenheim, 1996). Most doctors recommend exercise to child and adult asthma sufferers because of the physiological and psychological benefits derived from physical activity.

Exercise and Asthma

• It is important to make sure that the exercise program is coordinated with the timing of the asthma medication. Based on input from the participant's physician, the instructor must know when the medicine has to be taken to avoid an asthma episode during exercise. This will depend on the type of medication that is taken. Medicines used in inhalers work within a few minutes, while medicines taken in oral form may take up to 30 minutes to reach full capacity.

- Encourage the participant to use a **peak flow meter** to monitor the flow of air through the lungs. This simple plastic device can often determine if an asthma attack will occur or is occurring during or after exercise. The person simply blows into the meter and records the score. When peak flow drops more than 20% from normal values, activity should be reduced on that day. Peak flow meters can be purchased at any pharmacy for a relatively nominal cost. Steps for managing an asthma attack are shown in Table 6-5.

Table 6-5
Steps for Managing an Asthma Attack
The time to treat an asthma episode is when the symptoms (e.g., coughing, wheezing, chest tightness, and difficulty breathing) first appear.
Attack-management Steps
• Have the person rest and relax. • Have the person use medicines (inhaler) prescribed for an attack. • Have the person drink warm liquids.
Rest and Relax
• At the first sign of breathing difficulties, the person should STOP and rest for at least 10 minutes. • Make the person feel comfortable and relaxed.
Take Medication
• Make sure the prescribed medicine is available and that the person understands how to correctly take the medicine (inhalers require practice).
Drink Warm Liquid
• Have the person drink slowly. • Do not allow the person to ingest cold drinks.
Emergency Care
• If you have any doubts about the severity of the attack, get medical help immediately. • If the person's lips or fingernails are turning blue or if he or she exhibits shallow breathing and is focusing all attention on breathing, get medical help immediately.

- Light warm-ups may be very helpful in reducing the risk of an asthma attack. The participant should perform a light cardiovascular activity at 40 to 50% of THR for five to 10 minutes. This will help prepare the pulmonary system for more vigorous activity.

- Short bouts of exercise may reduce the incidence of an asthma attack in persons with severe asthma as noted by their physician. For example, three sets of four- to six-minute aerobic exercise routines with a five-minute rest interval between sets will allow the respiratory system to gradually adjust to the workload.

- Exercise intensity should lie within the participant's comfort zone. Young individuals with asthma may be able to exercise at very high intensity levels provided they take their medication before exercise. However, older individuals may have greater difficulty exercising at moderately high intensity levels (60 to 75% of target heart-rate range). This will depend on the participant's **functional capacity** and the severity of the asthma. Use RPE and peak flow readings along with HR to monitor the intensity of the exercise.

- Individuals with EIA should always carry their inhalers with them. If an asthma episode occurs, a **beta-adrenergic stimulating agent** (found in inhalers) is the only way to reverse the symptoms of a full-blown attack.

- Since cold air is a major trigger of asthma attacks, when exercising outdoors the participant may be advised to wear a scarf or surgical mask over the nose and mouth to warm the inspired air and reduce heat loss.

- After a cold or flu, individuals with asthma are more susceptible to breathing problems during exercise. The participant should be monitored closely after an illness and should be encouraged to return to physical activity very slowly by reducing the duration and intensity of the exercise.

Bronchitis and Emphysema

In the U.S., cigarette smoking is the primary risk factor for developing bronchitis and emphysema, which accounted for more than 120,000 adult deaths in 2006 (American Lung Association, 2010). Both conditions cause severe problems related to breathing capacity. Damaged lung tissue reduces the delivery of oxygen to working muscles. As pulmonary function declines, breathlessness and exercise intolerance become hallmark symptoms of these diseases.

Exercise is considered to be an essential component of treatment for individuals with bronchitis and emphysema. The primary aim of the exercise program is to reduce breathlessness and improve exercise tolerance. Exercise intensity should be based on RPE, which seems to be a more reliable indicator than HR in these participants (O'Donnell, Webb, & McGuire, 1993). Individuals who are in the advanced stages of the disease may require supplemental oxygen during exercise. If a GFI does not feel comfortable working with this population, a respiratory therapist or physical therapist should be consulted.

Exercise and Bronchitis and Emphysema

- The more impaired a participant with COPD is, the greater the emphasis on interval-training techniques. In some participants with very low exercise-tolerance levels, it may be necessary to exercise for 30 to 60 seconds and then rest for 30 to 60 seconds. As the person improves his or her fitness level, these numbers can be altered to accommodate a higher intensity level. For example, as the person's conditioning improves, the GFI might increase exercise time to two minutes with a 30-second rest interval.

- The exercise program should address the interest level and capabilities of the participant with prescribed endurance activities that vary little in oxygen cost. A relatively constant intensity may help prevent **dyspnea** (difficulty breathing), which is the number-one problem with exercise in this population.

- Examples of low-variability exercises include walking, recumbent stepping, and stationary cycling. High-variability exercises include walking up and down inclines, calisthenics, dancing, and sports such as basketball and racquet sports.

- Low-intensity weight training is relatively safe for individuals with COPD. A participant should feel comfortable lifting the weight and should not hyperventilate or become breathless. Avoid spikes in breathing rate by making sure that the weight is not too heavy and the person is not holding his or her breath.

- Although warm-up and cool-down activities are important components of an exercise program for all individuals, they are particularly important for persons with COPD. The goal of the exercise program is to gradually increase HR so that the lungs can slowly adjust to the increased workload. If strenuous exercise is started too quickly, there is a higher likelihood of respiratory distress. In addition, make sure the cool-down includes exercises of decreasing intensity (e.g., walking or cycling at a progressively slower rate).

- Teach participants to decrease their breathing frequency and to increase the amount of air they take into their lungs with each breath. Many participants with COPD take shallow breaths and do not get enough oxygen into the pulmonary system, which ultimately leads to dyspnea and fatigue. **Diaphragmatic breathing** and pursed-lip breathing can be used to help patients improve their breathing capacity. Table 6-6 explains how to teach and perform these two very important breathing techniques.

Table 6-6
Diaphragmatic and Pursed-lip Breathing Techniques
Diaphragmatic Breathing
• Have the participant lie down on his or her back.
• Have the participant place one hand on the abdomen and one hand on the chest.
• Teach the participant to inspire with maximal outward movement of the abdomen.
• Once the participant is comfortable in the supine position, he or she can perform the technique in sitting and standing positions.
Pursed-lip Breathing
• This can be performed separately or during diaphragmatic-breathing exercises.
• Teach the participant to slowly exhale against a slight resistance created by lightly pursing the lips. The resistance has the potential to increase oxygen saturation.

Joint and Bone Disorders

As the average lifespan approaches 80 years of age, joint and bone disorders will become pandemic in American society. Baby boomers that are starting to enter older adulthood will, in a few short years, dramatically increase the number of people who have arthritis and/or osteoporosis. GFIs and other fitness professionals will be involved in finding ways to develop exercise programs that will allow individuals with these conditions to continue to maintain an active lifestyle.

Arthritis

The two major types of arthritis are osteoarthritis and **rheumatoid arthritis.** Osteoarthritis is a degenerative joint disease characterized by cartilage deterioration that results in pain and loss of movement as bone surfaces interface [American Academy of Physical Medicine and Rehabilitation (AAPM&R), 2011a]. Rheumatoid arthritis is a systemic autoimmune disease in which membranes lining the joints become inflamed, causing pain, warmth, redness, and movement-limiting swelling (AAPM&R, 2011a). Both arthritis types have the same joint-destroying properties and similar treatment strategies, which include exercise.

One disease associated with arthritis because of primary associated arthritic symptoms is **systemic lupus erythematosus (SLE).** SLE is an autoimmune disease that affects connective tissues and results in painful joints and arthritis. Some sources state that SLE mimics RA, and in addition to the joint symptoms can include skin lesions, temporal-frontal hair loss, oral and nasal mucosal lesions, and in some cases there may be associated renal disease (Merck, 2008a). Severe cases can result in death, with nearly 1,500 fatalities per year attributed to this condition (CDC, 2002). For the purposes of providing general guidelines for exercise programs appropriate for people with arthritis, SLE will be included in this category.

Most persons with arthritis experience some degree of pain. While some participants will be able to tolerate high levels of pain, others will be unwilling to perform any exercise that causes discomfort. The exercise program must be tailored to the individual's pain threshold if he or she is likely to continue with the program.

Exercise and Arthritis

- Most persons with arthritis can benefit from an exercise program (Ettinger et al., 1997). The fitness program must not place excessive loads around damaged joints. For persons who have been **sedentary** for a long time, starting slowly is very important.

- The immediate goal of exercise is to increase muscle strength to maintain or improve joint stability. By strengthening muscles around damaged joints, there is a greater displacement of the stress load away from the joint and onto the surrounding muscles.

- Swimming is an ideal activity because of the lower stress loads on the joints due to the buoyancy of the water. However, many older adults are adverse to the time and energy that it takes to prepare for an aquatic exercise class, particularly if it is difficult to dress and undress because of joint stiffness and pain. Others may not know how to swim or may feel self-conscious in a swimsuit.

- The emphasis of the exercise program for individuals with arthritis is to mitigate pain during activity. Low-impact, non-weightbearing activities are recommended. The participant must understand that he or she will probably have to learn to tolerate some amount of pain or discomfort with any movement, but as long as the pain does not linger for longer than two hours after exercise or return 24 to 48 hours after exercise, it is considered an acceptable activity. Pain can be minimized in a number of ways, including using braces or straps, ice and/or heat before and after exercise, isolating the damaged joint during exer-cise, limiting movement to a pain-free **range of motion,** using water-based exercises, and not overusing the damaged joint. Consult with a physical therapist to learn more about pain management during activity.

- Exercise machines that allow the person to use all four limbs simultaneously seem to have the most benefit for persons with arthritis because the stress load is evenly distributed to all the limbs. Machines that require the use of all four limbs include some recumbent steppers and stationary bikes, which are utilized while sitting, and elliptical machines and cross-country ski machines, which are utilized while standing. *Note:* Mastering the complex motion involved in using a cross-country ski machine may require some practice.

- In circumstances where the participant is unable to use a certain leg or arm because of pain, the person can exercise with two or three limbs while resting the damaged joint. If both legs are affected, the person can use just the arms to perform a cardiovascular workout.

- One machine that may be too difficult to use or cause too much pain for some participants with arthritis is the stair-climber. This machine can place somewhat uncomfortable loads on the knees, hip joints, and spine and often results in pain in persons with arthritis. Other weightbearing activities that may cause pain include treadmill running and high-impact aerobics classes. Individuals with arthritis are advised to greatly limit or avoid these activities. General exercise guidelines for persons with arthritis are listed in Table 6-7.

Table 6-7

Exercise Guidelines for Persons With Arthritis

- Any exercise that causes pain during exercise, two hours after exercise, or 24 to 48 hours after exercise should be discontinued.

- Find alternative ways to exercise muscles around painful joints. For example, straight-leg exercises are a good way to strengthen the leg muscles around a painful knee.

- Warm-up and cool-down segments are essential components of most exercise programs, but are especially important for persons with arthritis due to joint stiffness.

- Resistance-training activities should be conducted, but exercises that cause pain to a particular joint should be replaced with isometric strength exercises.

- If conducting aquatic exercise, try to maintain a water temperature between 85° and 90° F (29° and 32° C).

- Use smooth, repetitive motions in all activities.

- Keep the exercise intensity level below the discomfort threshold.

- Be aware that acute flare-ups can occur in persons with rheumatoid arthritis. Exercise may not be advisable until the flare-up subsides.

- Participants with osteoarthritis often perform better in the morning, while participants with rheumatoid arthritis may be better off exercising several hours after waking.

Fibromyalgia

Fibromyalgia is defined as a group of common nonarticular disorders characterized by achy pain, tenderness, and stiffness of muscles, areas of tendon insertions, and adjacent soft-tissue structures (Merck, 2008b). This condition is thought to increase in severity when stress, poor sleep patterns, trauma, damp and cold conditions, or systemic infections are present (Merck, 2008b). Approximately 6 million people in the U.S. have been diagnosed with fibromyalgia,

80% of whom are females between the ages of 20 and 55 (Lemley & Meyer, 2009).

Exercise and Fibromyalgia

Potential benefits of exercise training for people with fibromyalgia include (Lemley & Meyer, 2009):

- Reduced number of tender points and decreased pain at tender points
- Decreased general pain
- Improved sleep and reduced fatigue
- Fewer feelings of helplessness and hopelessness
- More frequent and meaningful social interactions
- Lessened impact of the disease on daily activities

Generally recommended exercises for this population, provided there are no symptoms of pain or soreness 24 to 48 hours after exercise, are as follows:

- *Aerobic training:* Guidelines include achievement of 50 to 60% of MHR for 20 to 40 minutes, two to three days per week, favoring duration over intensity. Cycling may be appropriate (using a ramp or staged protocol, depending on the individual's tolerance level). Treadmill walking may be appropriate (increasing the incline and the duration from 15 to 20 minutes to 40 minutes, depending on the individual's tolerance level).

- *Flexibility training:* Controlled, dynamic movements through a pain-free range of motion may be used to increase joint flexibility, especially in the shoulders, hips, knees, and ankles, as well as decrease the risk of injury.

- *Functional training:* Exercises associated with household tasks may be appropriate, such as carrying laundry, vacuuming, and performing ADL.

Osteoporosis

It is estimated that 2.5 million people in the U.S. have been diagnosed with osteoporosis, which drains the bones of their mineral content and increases their susceptibility to fractures (AAPM&R, 2011b). In the later stages of the disease, bones often become brittle enough to fracture at the slightest tap of the wrist, or a rib could fracture from a cough or sneeze. In severe cases, the vertebra can become as thin as eggshells, leading to compression fractures and resulting in a stooped posture.

Osteoporosis is often referred to as the silent disease because in the majority of cases there are no signs of the disease until the person fractures a hip and complications ensue. However, as a person reaches his or her 60s and 70s, signs of osteoporosis may develop. As the bones in the spine lose their mineral content, the spine begins to curve forward at the top, which is referred to as **kyphosis** or **dowager's hump.** This is often accompanied by pain and psychological distress (Rimmer, 1999).

Reduced weightbearing due to disuse or immobilization leads to progressive thinning of the bone and eventual loss of bone mineral. Studies on astronauts found significant bone loss from being suspended in a gravity-free environment (Kaplan, 1995). Likewise, individuals who are confined to bed for several weeks at a time are also shown to have accelerated bone loss.

Exercise and Osteoporosis

- Before developing the exercise program, the GFI must know if any of the older male participants (over 65) or postmenopausal women have been diagnosed with osteoporosis. Since the vast majority of older individuals have never been tested for osteoporosis, it is important for the instructor to go through the following checklist to determine if a participant should be screened by his or her physician.
  - ✔ Is there a family history of osteoporosis?
  - ✔ Did the person go through early menopause?
  - ✔ Has the person had a hysterectomy?
  - ✔ Does he or she smoke or consume excessive amounts of alcohol?
  - ✔ Does he or she have a low calcium intake?
  - ✔ Are there any signs of osteoporosis (previous fracture, stooped posture)?
  - ✔ Does the person have a thin, small build?
  - ✔ Is he or she taking any medication that may increase bone loss (e.g., prednisone)?

  If the participant answers yes to any of these questions, it is suggested that he or she be screened by a physician for osteoporosis. By knowing that a participant may be at risk for osteoporosis, the GFI should ensure that the exercise program will be tailored to the individual's needs.

- For participants who have been diagnosed with osteoporosis and/or have signs of the disease, resistance exercises should be approved by a physician. For safety reasons, it is always best to progress slowly, using light weights for the first month of the program. As the participant's strength increases, he or she can progress to heavier weights if there is no pain in the area being strengthened. Begin with six to 12 repetitions and perform one to three sets, depending on the participant's comfort level. For participants with advanced osteoporosis (as noted by a physician), use elastic bands in the early stages of the program. After two to three months, progress to heavier bands or light weights. An individual with advanced osteoporosis will require more time to adapt to a resistance-training program and must progress at a much slower rate than a healthy older adult to avoid injury.

- Resistance exercises should be performed two to three days a week. Avoid exercises near or over the spine if pain is present. If pain is not present, target the muscles around the spine by performing shoulder-retraction exercises and shoulder raises. Make sure the movements are performed slowly and do not cause pain. These exercises will also help improve posture (many older adults become round-shouldered as they age), and will potentially "load" the vertebra enough to increase or maintain their density.

- In younger individuals (<50 years) who do not have advanced osteoporosis, it is acceptable to use **plyometric**-type exercises to improve bone density. This may be the most effective way to increase bone mass. Many experts have noted that bones must be stressed to a minimal threshold value to produce significant gains in bone mass (Frost, 1997). If the stress threshold is not high enough, the potential for bone development is greatly reduced. One study found that exercises such as step training and jumping down from a box or platform approximately 12 to 15 inches high significantly increased **bone mineral density (BMD)** in healthy sedentary women between the ages of 35 and 45 years (Heinonen, 1996). However, one very important caveat is that there is a higher risk of injury when performing these types of exercises. Older persons and postmenopausal women interested in participating in a high-impact group fitness class should ideally obtain medical

clearance, progress slowly, and be asked to sign a **waiver** that explains the risk of injury when performing these types of exercises.

- When developing plyometric step exercises, start with one step and gradually add steps as the person becomes more conditioned. Emphasize to the participants that they should limit these classes to two to three days a week because of their high stress load and potential for injury. Avoid performing these types of high-impact classes in consecutive workouts. Monitor participants very closely to make sure there is no soreness or pain after each class.

- Although most of the studies on exercise and osteoporosis have indicated that resistance training and plyometric-type exercises have achieved the greatest results in bone density, older persons with osteoporosis often become deconditioned from a lack of activity. This deconditioned state often leads to higher levels of inactivity and spirals the person into further disease and disability. If a person is in the advanced stages of osteoporosis (as noted by a physician), it is best to perform cardiovascular exercises from a seated position for part of the class time.

- Older persons with osteoporosis may have difficulty performing repetitive exercises that use the same muscle groups for extended periods of time. Therefore, circuit-training programs that require short periods of work using various muscle groups are recommended.

- In addition to circuit-training programs, interval-training activities that require brief periods of work followed by a rest interval may also be beneficial for deconditioned participants with advanced osteoporosis.

For example, riding a stationary bike for one minute followed by a 30-second rest interval may delay fatigue and allow the person to sustain longer periods of activity. Other cardiovascular activities can be used to improve functional performance, provided that they do not incur pain or result in premature fatigue. Although swimming and aquatic exercises are excellent modalities for improving cardiorespiratory endurance, they are not recommended for improving bone density. Water is a nongravity environment and does not seem to place enough of a stress load on bone tissue to increase its mass (Bravo et al., 1997). General safety guidelines for developing an exercise program for persons with osteoporosis are shown in Table 6-8.

Table 6-8

Safety Concerns When Developing an Exercise Program for Persons With Osteoporosis

- Always obtain physician consent before developing the exercise program.

- Screen the participant before developing the program. Consult with his or her physician on developing resistance exercises at the site where a fracture may have occurred.

- Avoid jarring or high-load exercises in persons with advanced osteoporosis.

- Avoid back exercises in participants who have localized pain in this region and show signs of kyphosis.

- When performing standing exercises with older participants who have a high risk of injury from a fall or fracture, or who have fallen previously, make sure there is something to hold onto at all times (e.g., ballet barre, parallel bars, or chair).

- Reevaluate the program if there are any signs of pain or fatigue during or after an exercise session in the osteoporosis zones (hip, back, and wrist).

Low-back Pain

Exercise is one of the cornerstones of both the prevention and treatment of low-back pain. In fact, many physicians feel that the major cause of low-back pain is physical deconditioning, especially in large muscle groups such as the back extensors (Dugan, 2006). Aerobic training and exercises for the lower back should be performed on a regular basis and proper technique for each exercise should be taught and practiced. Maintaining and improving muscular balance across the joints is particularly important for people with skeletal irregularities.

Exercise and Low-back Pain

The GFI should share the following guidelines with participants with low-back pain:

- Individuals with low-back pain, or a history of low-back pain, should consult with a physician and get specific recommendations for exercise. Participants with low-back pain who have not had a course of physical therapy should be encouraged to ask their physicians about a referral.

- Adequately warm up and cool down before and after each workout session or class.

- Always be aware of proper form and alignment.

- Do not try to work through pain.

- Always maintain neutral pelvic alignment and an erect torso during any exercise movements.

- Avoid forward-head positions in which the chin is tilted up.

- When leaning forward or lifting or lowering an object, always bend the knees. Do not lift objects that are too heavy, do not twist when lifting, and keep objects close to the body.

- Avoid hyperextending the spine in an unsupported position.

Medications and modalities used to treat low-back pain vary from **nonsteroidal anti-inflammatory drugs (NSAIDs)** such as aspirin, ibuprofen, indomethacin, and nabumetone to non-narcotic analgesics such as acetaminophen (Simmonds & Derghazanian, 2009). Ice or heat applied to the area are standard modalities shown to be effective in treating low-back pain. Other modalities known to be effective for some individuals include ultrasound and electrical stimulation. It should be noted that these treatments can only be administered by a properly licensed professional.

Daily Routine for Enhancing Low-back Health

Because of the high prevalence of low-back pain, GFIs should consider incorporating the following movements as part of a core conditioning class or during the cool-down segment of other group fitness classes. The following exercises will spare the spine, enhance the muscle challenge, and enhance the motor control system to ensure that spine stability is maintained in all other activities. Keep in mind that these are only examples of well-designed exercises and may not be for everyone—the initial challenge may or may not be appropriate for every individual, nor will the graded progression be the same for all participants. These are simply examples to challenge the muscles of the torso (McGill, 2007).

Cat-Camel

The routine should begin with the cat-camel motion exercise (spine flexion-extension cycles) to reduce spine viscosity (internal resistance and friction) and "floss" the nerve roots as they outlet at each lumbar level. Note that the cat-camel is intended as a motion exercise—not a stretch—so the emphasis is on motion rather than "pushing" at the end ranges of flexion and extension. Five to eight cycles have shown to be sufficient to reduce most viscous-frictional stresses.

Cat position

Camel position

Birddog

The extensor program consists of leg extensions and the "birddog." In general, these isometric holds should last no longer than seven to eight seconds given evidence from near infrared spectroscopy indicating rapid loss of available oxygen in the torso muscles when contracting at these levels; short relaxation of the muscle restores oxygen. The evidence supports building endurance with increased repetitions rather than extending "hold time."

Modified Curl-up

The cat-camel motion exercise is followed by anterior abdominal exercises, in this case the curl-up. The hands or a rolled towel are placed under the lumbar spine to preserve a neutral spine posture. Do not allow the participant to flatten the back to the floor, as doing so flexes the lumbar spine, violates the neutral spine principle, and increases the loads on the discs and ligaments. One knee is flexed but the other leg is straight to lock the pelvis–lumbar spine and minimize the loss of a neutral lumbar posture. Have participants alternate the bent leg (right to left) midway through the repetitions.

Side Bridge

The lateral muscles of the torso (i.e., quadratus lumborum and abdominal obliques) are important for optimal stability, and are targeted with the side

bridge exercise. The beginner level of this exercise involves bridging the torso between the elbow and the knees. Once this is mastered and well-tolerated, the challenge is increased by bridging using the elbow and the feet. It is important when performing the side bridge exercise to maintain a neutral neck and spine position and not let the hips rotate forward.

Human Development and Aging

Children

This section identifies exercise guidelines and considerations for children, whose needs differ from adults in that their growth status is an indicator of health. For children with disabilities who may be restricted by exacerbations of illness, exercise may be difficult at certain stages in life. Although children without disabilities may not have the periods of restriction imposed by a chronic condition or illness, lack of regular exercise could impact functional development and skeletal and muscular growth. In addition, inactive lifestyles could lead to obesity, which has become an epidemic among today's youth (Riner & Sabath, 2009). A report to the President of the United States from the Secretary of Health and Human Services and the Secretary of Education stated that "Our nation's young people are, in large measure, inactive, unfit, and increasingly overweight" (CDC, 2000). Sadly, this trend has only worsened in the years since this report, increasing the importance of the role of health and fitness professionals in designing and implementing effective exercise and activity programs for youth.

General Exercise Recommendations for Children

Recommendations to increase physical activity and fitness for youth include the following (CDC, 2000):

- Promoting physical activity within families who model and support participation in enjoyable physical activity
- Engaging children in physical education, health education, recess, and extracurricular activities in the context of school programs that promote these behaviors

- Involving children in youth sports and recreation programs for developmentally appropriate activities that are accessible to all children
- Involving children in community activities such as riding bicycles and walking to physical-activity facilities
- Physical-activity promotion for children can have lasting effects on the performance of healthy lifestyle behaviors for their entire lives. For example, physical-activity programs for children can (1) help strengthen and maintain healthy joints, muscles, and bones; (2) control weight, build lean muscle, and reduce fat; (3) prevent or delay high blood pressure or reduce hypertension in youth; (4) prevent the development of type 2 diabetes; and (5) reduce feelings of **depression** and **anxiety.**

General exercise recommendations for children include the following:

- Children and adolescents should participate in at least 60 minutes and up to several hours of moderate-intensity physical activity most days of the week, preferably daily (U.S. Department of Health & Human Services, 2008; CDC, 2000). This activity should include aerobic activities as well as age-appropriate muscle- and bone-strengthening exercises.
- Some of the exercise should occur in several bouts of moderate to vigorous physical activity lasting 10 to 15 minutes or longer each day (CDC, 2000).
- Children should start out slowly with an exercise program that is interesting and fun to them. By beginning a program gradually, children can decrease the risk of injury and lowered self-esteem that could result from unrealistic goals.

- Be aware that children sweat less than adults during heat-related exercise and therefore have a more difficult time acclimating to exercising in the heat. Take special precautions to gradually expose children to exercising in high-heat conditions and encourage them to drink fluids every 15 to 20 minutes.
- For children, MHR is much higher than in the adult population, and is generally 200 to 205 bpm (Riner & Sabath, 2009).
- Resting breathing rate also differs between children and adults. As children age, their resting breathing rate decreases progressively, as does maximal breathing frequency (Riner & Sabath, 2009).
- Blood pressure responses during exercise are similar among children and adults, although SBP changes during exercise tend to be lower in children. For young children, a 2 to 3 mmHg rise may occur per **metabolic equivalent (MET),** while adolescents may experience a 4 to 6 mmHg per MET increase in exercise intensity (Riner & Sabath, 2009).
- RPE may be a way to measure exercise intensity for children over age eight, but young children may not have the cognitive skills to use the RPE scale accurately and consistently.
- For children, muscle-mass increases occurring during growth lead to increased muscular strength. There are marked differences among males and females during this growth process, particularly in terms of upper-body strength. Before the onset of puberty, muscular strength can be improved similarly in both males and females through the performance of resistance training, whereas during the onset of puberty, maturation and **testosterone** levels increase muscle

size and strength more significantly among males (Riner & Sabath, 2009).

Older Adults

Older adults face many debilitating health problems that affect them physically, psychologically, and socially. A GFI can motivate older adults to perform exercises as a way of improving function, but also as a means of improving the ability to live an emotionally satisfying life.

Among the health problems associated with aging are cardiovascular disorders such as heart disease, coronary artery disease, and hypertension; respiratory disorders such as asthma, bronchitis, and emphysema; and the two primary types of arthritis (osteoarthritis and rheumatoid arthritis).

When recommending exercise programs for older adult populations, consider their medical history, and also observe their fitness level, mobility limitations, motivation to participate, **self-efficacy,** willingness to commit time to a program, and their goals and interests. By incorporating all of these variables into a program, a GFI will be able to identify the best approach for maximizing participants' ability and willingness to commit to a long-term exercise program.

General Exercise Recommendations for Older Adults

General exercise recommendations for older adult populations include the following:

- Design interventions that participants can replicate on their own at home or elsewhere once formal training ends.
- Tailor the intervention to participants' perceived performance needs and goals, as well as their health and cognitive conditions.

169

- Provide systematic reinforcement regarding participants' ability to improve their exercise performance over time.
- Key components of physical-activity programs for older adults include endurance, strength, flexibility, and **balance** activities.
  - ✔ Endurance activities include physical activity with continuous movement that involves large muscle groups and is sustained for a minimum of 10 minutes. Examples include biking, swimming, and walking.
  - ✔ Strength activities increase muscle strength by moving or lifting some type of resistance such as weights or elastic bands at a level requiring physical effort. Examples include biceps curls, triceps extensions, hip abduction or adduction against the resistance of an elastic band, and squats while holding hand weights.
  - ✔ Flexibility activities facilitate greater range of motion around the joint. They should be performed a minimum of two days per week (preferably all days per week) in addition to a formal physical-activity program. Examples include arm circles or pendulum exercises that involve suspending the arms while flexed at the hips and performing circles with gravity eliminated.
  - ✔ Balance activities promote the ability to maintain control of the body over its base of support. Static-balance activities include performing standing exercises while decreasing the base of support and progressing to single-leg support. Dynamic-balance activities involve movement, and examples include decreasing the base of support while walking or altering a normal walking pattern around set obstacles such as cones or blocks laid out on the gym floor.

Autoimmune Diseases

Common autoimmune disorders include RA (see page 161), fibromyalgia (see page 163), and **multiple sclerosis (MS)**. Because RA and fibromyalgia are often thought of as bone and joint disorders, they are classified as arthritic conditions. However, these painful diseases are actually thought to result from a dysfunction of the immune system and are considered autoimmune disorders.

Multiple Sclerosis

MS is one of the most common neuromuscular disorders, affecting approximately 400,000 people in the U.S. (National Multiple Sclerosis Society, 2011). Diagnosed more often in Caucasians and women, MS is classified as a progressive disease, which means that the symptoms have a tendency to worsen as the person ages. A wide variety of complications can occur from MS, including gait disturbances and bladder and bowel problems. The disease often consists of flare-ups (exacerbations) and periods of stability (remission). In the usual course of the disease, exacerbations occur every few years. The progression of the disease varies from person to person.

Exercise and Multiple Sclerosis

- Be aware that the symptoms of MS may get progressively worse over time. The treatment strategy aims to slow the progression of the disease. People with MS should make exercise an integral part of their daily regimen. As long as activities are not too strenuous, exercise should not be harmful.

- Balance is often compromised in persons with MS. Take every precaution to make the exercise setting as safe as possible to minimize the risk of falling. Provide chairs or a portable ballet barre that the person can hold onto for stability while performing exercises in the standing position.

- As balance worsens, the risk of falls increases. When and if balance worsens, develop activities that can be performed in a sitting position. Change from free weights to machines to eliminate the risk of a weight being dropped on a participant's foot. Stationary bikes, recumbent steppers, and upper-arm ergometers can be used to enhance cardiovascular fitness in a seated position. When balance is very poor, use a recumbent bike for further stability.

- Because participants with MS often experience a great deal of **spasticity** (tightness) as their condition progresses, make sure that flexibility exercises are a major component of the program.

- Because participants with MS often have difficulty initiating a movement in the advanced stages of the disease, allow them the extra time to begin and complete each movement.

- Swimming is one of the best activities for participants with MS, provided the water temperature remains below 80° F (27° C).

Warm water will cause premature fatigue in this population.

- Since overheating can cause a temporary loss of function, make sure the facility is well-ventilated and the room temperature is at a comfortable level. Exercise should be discouraged in warm, humid environments.

- Individuals with MS often lose control of their bladder in the later stages of certain forms of the disease. The bladder should be voided before and after exercise. A GFI should be prepared for possible accidents by having the appropriate cleaning materials available (e.g., bleach), and making sure that the participant understands that he or she is aware that a possible accident can occur.

Summary

Trends show that Americans continue to be sedentary and gain weight, resulting in numerous chronic health conditions. GFIs may lead classes with individuals from various special populations, from middle-aged adults with diabetes to young athletes recovering from injury. Therefore, it is essential that GFIs have a basic understanding of how to appropriately modify movements to meet the unique needs of individual participants while still providing an effective workout for the class as a whole.

References

American Academy of Physical Medicine and Rehabilitation (2011a). *Arthritis.* http://www.aapmr.org/condtreat/pain/arthritis.htm

American Academy of Physical Medicine and Rehabilitation (2011b). *Are You at Risk for Osteoporosis?* http://www.aapmr.org/condtreat/other/osteorisk.htm

American College of Sports Medicine (2014). *ACSM's Guidelines for Exercise Testing and Prescription* (9th ed.). Philadelphia: Wolters Kluwer/Lippincott Williams & Wilkins.

American Diabetes Association (2006). *Complete Guide to Diabetes* (4th ed.). New York: Bantam Press.

American Heart Association (2010). *Heart Disease and Stroke Statistics—2010 Update.* Dallas, Tex.: American Heart Association.

American Lung Association (2011). *Chronic Obstructive Pulmonary Disease (COPD) Fact Sheet.* Washington, D.C.: American Lung Association.

American Lung Association (2010). *Trends in COPD: Morbidity & Mortality.* Washington, D.C.: American Lung Association.

Blumenthal, M.N. (1996). Sports-aggravated allergies: How to treat and prevent the symptoms. *The Physician & Sportsmedicine,* 18, 12, 52–66.

Bravo, G. et al. (1997). A weight-bearing, water-based exercise program for osteopenic women: Its impact on bone, functional fitness, and well-being. *Archives of Physical Medicine & Rehabilitation,* 78, 1375–1380.

Centers for Disease Control and Prevention (2002). Trends in deaths from systemic lupus erythematosus—United States, 1979–1998. *Morbidity and Mortality Weekly Report,* 17, 371–373.

Centers for Disease Control and Prevention (2000). *A Report to the President from the Secretary of Health and Human Services and the Secretary of Education.* Atlanta, Ga.: Centers for Disease Control and Prevention.

Chobanian, A.V. et al. (2003). *JNC 7 Express: The Seventh Report of the Joint National Committee on Prevention, Detection, Evaluation, and Treatment of High Blood Pressure.* NIH Publication No. 03-5233. Washington, D.C.: National Institutes of Health & National Heart, Lung, and Blood Institute.

Clark, C.J. & Cochrane, L.M. (2009). Asthma. In Durstine, J.L. et al. (Eds.) *ACSM's Exercise Management for Persons with Chronic Diseases and Disabilities* (3rd ed.). Champaign, Ill.: Human Kinetics.

Dugan, S.A. (2006). Role of exercise in prevention and management of acute low back pain. *Clinics in Occupational and Environmental Medicine,* 5, 3, 615–632.

Emtner, M., Herala, M., & Stalenheim, G. (1996). High-intensity physical training in adults with asthma. A 10-week rehabilitation program. *Chest,* 109, 323–330.

Ettinger, W.H. et al. (1997). A randomized trial comparing aerobic exercise and resistance exercise with a health education program in older adults with knee osteoarthritis. *Journal of the American Medical Association,* 277, 1, 25–31.

Frost, H.M. (1997). Why do marathon runners have less bone than weight lifters? A vital biomechanical view and explanation. *Bone,* 20, 183–189.

Han, T.S. et al. (1997). The prevalence of low back pain and associations with body fatness, fat distribution and height. *International Journal of Obesity,* 21, 600–607.

Hedley, A.A. et al. (2004). Prevalence of overweight and obesity among US children, adolescents, and adults, 1999–2002. *Journal of the American Medical Association,* 23, 2847–2850.

Heinonen, A. (1996). Randomised controlled trial of effect of high-impact exercise on selected risk factors for osteoporotic fractures. *Lancet,* 348, 1343–1347.

Hornsby, W.G. & Albright, A.L. (2009). Diabetes. In Durstine, J.L. et al. (Eds.). *ACSM's Exercise Management for Persons with Chronic Diseases and Disabilities* (3rd ed.). Champaign, Ill.: Human Kinetics.

Kaplan, F.S. (1995). Prevention and management of osteoporosis. *Clinical Symposia,* 47, 1–32.

Lemley, K. & Meyer, B. (2009). Fibromyalgia. In Durstine, J.L. et al. (Eds.) *ACSM's Exercise Management for Persons with Chronic Diseases and Disabilities* (3rd ed.). Champaign, Ill.: Human Kinetics.

Ma, R.C.W., Ko, G.T.C., & Chan, J.C.N. (2009). Health hazards of obesity: An overview (pp. 213–234). In: Williams, G. & Fruhbeck, G. (Eds.). *Obesity: Science to Practice.* Hoboken, N.J.: Wiley-Blackwell.

McGill, S.M. (2007). *Low Back Disorders* (2nd ed.) Champaign, Ill.: Human Kinetics.

Merck (2008a). *Merck Manual: Rheumatoid Arthritis.* www.merckmanuals.com

Merck (2008b). *Merck Manual: Fibromyalgia.* www.merckmanuals.com

Moorman, J.E. et al. (2007). National surveillance for asthma—United States 1980–2004. *Morbidity and Mortality Weekly Report Surveillance Summary,* 56 (SS08), 1–14, 18–54.

National Asthma Education and Prevention Program (2007). *Expert Panel Report 3: Guidelines for the Diagnosis and Management of Asthma.* Bethesda, Md.: U.S. Department of Health and Human Services, Public Health Service, National Institutes of Health, National Heart, Lung, and Blood Institute; NIH publication number 08-4051.

National Institutes of Health (2006). National

diabetes statistics; National Diabetes Information Clearinghouse. National Institute of Diabetes and Digestive and Kidney Diseases (NIDDK), http://diabetes.niddk.nih.gov/dm/pubs/statistics/index.htm

National Multiple Sclerosis Society (2011). *Epidemiology of MS.* www.nationalmssociety.org

O'Donnell, D.E., Webb, K.A., & McGuire, M.A. (1993). Older patients with COPD: Benefits of exercise training. *Geriatrics,* 48, 1, 59–66.

Ogden, C.L. et al. (2008). Prevalence and trends in overweight among US children and adolescents, 1999–2000. *Journal of the American Medical Association,* 299, 2401–2405.

Parchman, M.L., Romero, R.L., & Pugh, J.A. (2006). Encounters by patients with type 2 diabetes—complex and demanding: An observational study. *Annals of Family Medicine,* 4, 40–45.

Pescatello, L.S. et al. (2004). American College of Sports Medicine position stand: Exercise and hypertension. *Medicine and Science in Sports and Exercise,* 36, 3, 533–553.

Rice, T. et al. (1993). Segregation analysis of fat mass and other body composition measures derived from underwater weighing. *American Journal of Human Genetics,* 52, 967–973.

Rimmer, J.H. (1999). Programming for participants with osteoporosis. *IDEA Health and Fitness Source,* 17, 6, 46–55.

Rimmer, J.H. (1994). *Fitness and Rehabilitation Programs for Special Populations.* Dubuque, Iowa: WCB McGraw-Hill.

Rimmer, J.H. & Wang, E.W. (2005). Obesity prevalence among a group of Chicago residents with disabilities. *Archives of Physical Medicine and Rehabilitation,* 86, 1461–1464.

Riner, W.F. & Sabath, R.J. (2009). Physical activity for children and youth. In Durstine, J.L. et al. (Eds.). *ACSM's Exercise Management for Persons with Chronic Diseases and Disabilities* (3rd ed.). Champaign, Ill.: Human Kinetics.

Simmonds, M.J. & Derghazanian, T. (2009). Lower back pain syndrome. In Durstine, J.L. et al. (Eds.). *ACSM's Exercise Management for Persons with Chronic Diseases and Disabilities* (3rd ed.). Champaign, Ill.: Human Kinetics.

Tamparo, C. & Lewis, M.A. (2011). *Diseases of the Human Body* (5th ed.). Philadelphia: F.A. Davis.

Tsai, E.B. et al. (2006). The rise and fall of insulin secretion in type 1 diabetes mellitus. *Diabetologia,* 49, 261–270.

U.S. Department of Health & Human Services (2008). *2008 Physical Activity Guidelines for Americans: Be Active, Healthy and Happy.* www.health.gov/paguidelines/pdf/paguide.pdf

Wallberg-Henriksson, H. (1992). Exercise and diabetes mellitus. In: Holloszy, J.O. (Ed.) *Exercise and Sport Sciences Reviews*, Vol. 20, 339–368. Baltimore, Md.: Williams & Wilkins.

Suggested Reading

Bryant, C.X., Franklin, B.A., & Merrill, S. (2007). *ACE's Guide to Exercise Testing and Program Design: A Fitness Professional's Handbook* (2nd ed.). Monterey, Calif.: Healthy Learning.

Durstine, J.L. et al. (Eds.) (2009). *ACSM's Exercise Management for Persons with Chronic Diseases and Disabilities* (3rd ed.). Champaign, Ill.: Human Kinetics.

Franklin, B.A., Gordon, S., & Timmis, G.C. (1989). *Exercise in Modern Medicine.* Baltimore, Md.: Williams & Wilkins.

Kavanagh, T. (1994). Cardiac rehabilitation. In Goldberg, L. & Elliot, D.L. (Eds.). *Exercise for Prevention and Treatment of Illness* (pp. 41–79). Philadelphia: F.A. Davis.

Miller, P.D. (1995). *Fitness Programming and Physical Disability.* Champaign, Ill.: Human Kinetics.

Rimmer, J.H. (2005). Common health challenges faced by older adults. In: *Exercise for Older Adults: ACE's Guide for Fitness Professionals.* San Diego, Calif.: American Council on Exercise.

Rimmer, J.H. (1999). Health promotion for persons with disabilities: The emerging paradigm shift from disability prevention to prevention of secondary conditions in persons with disabilities. *Physical Therapy,* 79, 5, 495–502.

Rimmer, J.H. (1997). Programming for participants with disabilities: Exercise guidelines for special medical populations. *IDEA Today,* 15, 5, 26–35.

U.S. Census Bureau (2008). *Americans With Disabilities: 2005.* Washington, D.C.: U.S. Department of Commerce/Economics and Statistics Administration/U.S. Census Bureau.

Lenita Anthony, M.A., is a clinical exercise physiologist and exercise specialist with 25 years of experience in group exercise and personal training. She is a former Reebok Master Trainer and Program Development team member for Reebok University, and former Program Director for the Professional Certificate in Exercise Science at University of California, San Diego. Anthony is a respected fitness presenter, author, and trainer of trainers who has developed well-known prenatal exercise programs and worked extensively with this population.

Camilla Callaway, M.Ed., owns and operates a personal-training facility in Columbus, Georgia. Working with Denver's Swedish Medical Center and Katie Beck's "Mothers in Motion," Callaway has trained instructors, taught prenatal classes, educated moms-to-be throughout the Colorado region, and facilitated classes at the IDEA International Convention. She has been a volunteer on various committees with the American Council on Exercise and serves as an ACE media spokesperson.

Exercise and Pregnancy

By Lenita Anthony & Camilla Callaway

The number of women who exercise during pregnancy has increased steadily in recent years. A study on physical-activity patterns during pregnancy revealed a prevalence of activity between 3% and 38%, depending on the type of activity and measurement of intensity (Borodulin et al., 2008). The American College of Obstetricians and Gynecologists (ACOG) recommends that pregnant women engage in moderate-intensity exercise for at least 30 minutes on most, if not all, days of the week (ACOG, 2002). The Centers for Disease Control and Prevention (CDC) recommend that healthy pregnant women get at least 150 minutes per week of moderate-intensity aerobic exercise (U.S. Department of Health and Human Services, 2008).

When low- to moderate-intensity physical activity (such as brisk walking) is included in the definition of exercise, pregnant women show a higher prevalence of participation than when vigorous-intensity exercise is included (Borodulin et al., 2008).

An increased focus on health during pregnancy means that more pregnant women will be seeking the instruction of knowledgeable fitness professionals. These women will need sound information and guidance regarding exercise, and group fitness instructors (GFIs) need to be aware of the unique physical and physiological changes that occur during pregnancy.

These adaptations require continual exercise modifications to ensure exercise effectiveness and safety. Each woman enters pregnancy with different abilities and different goals and attitudes toward exercise. While broad, general guidelines apply to the pregnant population as a whole, they do not take into account the specific needs of every individual.

The "right" exercise program for a pregnant woman should be based on many factors, pregnancy being only one of them. Equally important are the pregnant exerciser's goals, experience, state of training, apprehensions, expectations, and motivation. In other words, "one size" will not "fit all" when it comes to prenatal exercise programs.

The objective of the American Council on Exercise is for GFIs to be knowledgeable about the special needs of pregnant women and to provide classes that are well-designed, effective, challenging, and, above all, safe. Accordingly, the main purposes of this chapter are to enable GFIs to develop such exercise programs for pregnant participants and to educate GFIs on important issues regarding exercise and prenatal conditions.

Benefits and Risks of Exercise During Pregnancy

The ACOG Guidelines: Clearing Up the Confusion

ACOG first published recommendations on exercise and pregnancy in 1985. This information was widely disseminated to physicians, fitness professionals, and concerned women, who were eager to hear the long-awaited answers to their questions. Due to the limited scientific evidence and lack of outcome data on the topic at that time, the 1985 guidelines were written from a perspective of "first do no harm" and thus were extremely conservative. Specifically, restrictions were placed on the type of exercises performed, duration, and intensity.

However, the guidelines were soon challenged by individuals in the exercise science and fitness communities, as well as by women who had continued to exercise vigorously through their pregnancies with no ill effects. A number of research studies using human subjects were published over the ensuing years, leading to the need for substantial revisions to the original document. In 1994, ACOG published a second set of guidelines. The specific application of these guidelines for prenatal exercise, as well as of the 2002 ACOG guidelines, is discussed later in this chapter.

Although most of the restrictions outlined in the 1985 ACOG guidelines became "outdated" with the publication of the 1994 guidelines, the use of the earlier document is still widespread among physicians and fitness professionals. GFIs must understand the differences that exist among the three sets of recommendations and the confusion surrounding them. It is likely that, in some cases, pregnant women will have been given information based on the original guidelines published in 1985 that is outdated and unnecessarily restrictive.

While much more research is available on the effects of exercise and pregnancy than existed in 1985, there are still areas in which the literature is limited. For example, most of the current research involves the effects of cardiovascular exercise, with less data on the effects of strength training during pregnancy. It is important that fitness professionals working with this population keep an eye toward ongoing research developments and how this information applies to pregnant exercisers.

Benefits of Prenatal Exercise

Benefits During Pregnancy

The potential benefits of a well-designed prenatal exercise program are numerous. Pregnant women who exercise can maintain or even increase their cardiovascular fitness, muscular strength, and flexibility. Investigative studies have suggested that women who exercise during pregnancy experience fewer common prenatal discomforts such as constipation, swollen extremities, leg cramps, nausea, varicose veins, insomnia, fatigue, back pain, and other orthopedic conditions (Clapp & Little, 1995; Artal, 1992). Exercise can assist in controlling **gestational diabetes** and help prevent urinary **incontinence,** pregnancy-induced **hypertension, diastasis recti,** and **deep vein thrombosis** (Hall & Brody, 2005; Yeo et al., 2000). Additionally, exercise can improve posture and body mechanics, facilitate circulation, reduce pelvic and rectal pressure, and increase energy levels (Sternfeld, Sidney, & Eskenazi, 1992). While even very fit women will experience fatigue at some point during pregnancy, their energy reserve and

fatigue "threshold" remain consistently higher than in unfit women. Fit pregnant women also retain a lower **resting heart rate,** a higher **stroke volume,** and higher $\dot{V}O_2$**max** throughout pregnancy and during the **postpartum** period.

Pregnant women who exercise have a lower incidence of excessive weight gain and are more likely to stay within the range recommended by ACOG. Exercise also helps to stabilize mood states during pregnancy. Active women have been shown to experience fewer feelings of stress, **anxiety,** insomnia, and **depression**—negative emotions that are commonly experienced during pregnancy [American College of Sports Medicine (ACSM), 2014; Goodwin, Astbury, & McKeeken, 2000]. In general, exercise appears to enhance women's psychological well-being, increase confidence in their changing body image, and decrease feelings of apprehension about labor and delivery.

Pregnancy is one of the critical "windows" of time in the female lifespan during which positive health-behavior changes are more readily accepted. During pregnancy, many women sense an increased responsibility toward their personal health as they become aware of how their behaviors and actions impact the health and well-being of their unborn child. There is frequently an increased motivation to eat more healthfully, stop smoking, and become more physically active. By seizing this opportunity to help pregnant women acquire an exercise "habit," and to realize the benefits this provides, GFIs can set the stage for their activity patterns for the rest of their lives.

Benefits During Labor and Delivery

There are mixed reports on the effects of exercise during pregnancy on the course or outcome of labor and delivery. Some studies show exercise has no effect, yet others show exercise causes either shorter or longer labors. These variances may have been due to differences in exercise programs, data collection, or other methodological discrepancies. A study conducted by Clapp (1998) compared the labors of women who continued performing vigorous, weightbearing exercise throughout pregnancy to "physically active" controls who did not perform structured exercise but occasionally engaged in activities such as gardening, tennis, and walking. The women who continued weightbearing exercise throughout gestation experienced less problematic deliveries, including a 75% decrease in the need for forceps or Caesarean section, a 75% decrease in maternal exhaustion, a 50% decrease in the need for oxytocin (Pitocin—a labor-inducing drug), and a 50% decrease in the need to intervene due to fetal heart-rate abnormalities. Clapp also found that exercising women had a significantly higher rate of uncomplicated, spontaneous deliveries and an active labor that was 30% shorter than the controls (Figure 7-1). However, the women who discontinued exercise midpregnancy did not experience these benefits and did not differ significantly from the controls. Another study on exercise and the

type of delivery found non-exercising women to be four-and-a-half times more likely to have Caesarean section (Bungum et al., 2000). It appears that for labor and delivery benefits, it is important to encourage pregnant women to continue exercising regularly until they are as near term as possible (barring any medical reasons to the contrary).

Benefits During Recovery

Exercise during pregnancy appears to promote a faster recovery from labor. Women who exercise throughout their pregnancies return to activities of normal daily life 40% faster than less-active controls (Clapp, 1998). It stands to reason that women with higher **functional capacities** going into the marathon of labor and delivery would be taxed to a lesser degree than women with low functional capacities. Fit women recover faster than unfit women because of their greater energy reserves. Others have reported that exercisers retain less weight and score higher on measures of maternal adaptation (Sampselle & Seng, 1999). Exercising women also experience fewer incidences of postpartum depression. Additionally, women who have made exercise part of their lifestyle during pregnancy are more likely to continue exercising after the baby is born than those who did not (Devine, Bov, & Olson, 2000).

Ultimately, a healthy **placenta** that can adequately support the needs of the growing **fetus** is perhaps the most critical determinant of the advisability and benefits of exercise. Emphasis should be placed on early prenatal care, healthy lifestyle habits, and optimal prenatal nutrition to help ensure the growth of a healthy placenta. If the placenta is not functioning optimally, the potential exists for exercise to place excess and even unhealthy stress on maternal and fetal systems.

Figure 7-1
Regular exercise shortens labor by approximately one-third on average.

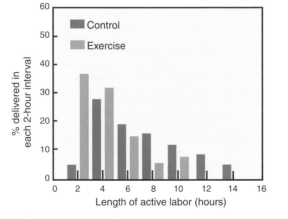

J.F. Clapp III, 1998, *Exercising through Your Pregnancy*, page 94, figure 6.6. © 1998 by James F. Clapp III. Reprinted with permission from Human Kinetics (Champaign, IL).

Contraindications and Risk Factors

Healthy women with uncomplicated pregnancies tend to not need to limit their exercise for fear of adverse effects. Studies focusing on both aerobic and strength-training regimens in pregnancy have shown no increase in early pregnancy loss, late pregnancy complications, abnormal fetal growth, or adverse neonatal outcomes (Davies et al., 2003). Indeed, pregnant women and their healthcare providers should seriously consider the potential risks of *not* participating in exercise activities during pregnancy; these include not only a loss of fitness and possible excess weight gain, but also increased risk of pregnancy-induced hypertension, gestational diabetes, varicose veins, deep vein thrombosis, low-back pain, and other physical complaints (Davies et al., 2003). Conversely, "extreme" training such as that involved with marathons, triathlons, adventure racing, and competitive athletics is not encouraged. While no known adverse effects have been documented in pregnant women participating in competitive athletics, potential risks of fatigue, **dehydration,** and under-nutrition may, theoretically, make them poor candidates for such vigorous activity.

It is important to recognize that ACOG has established that there are some women for whom exercise during pregnancy is absolutely contraindicated, and others for whom the potential benefits associated with exercising may outweigh the risks (ACOG, 2002). It is outside the **scope of practice** of a GFI to attempt to diagnose any of the **contraindications** outlined by ACOG (Tables 7-1 and 7-2). Therefore, it is imperative that a GFI is certain that a routine health screening has been performed on all participants (either by the facility if working as a staff instructor, or by the GFI if working independently) and that

Table 7-1
Absolute Contraindications to Aerobic Exercise During Pregnancy
• Hemodynamically significant heart disease
• Restrictive lung disease
• Incompetent cervix/cerclage
• Multiple gestation at risk for premature labor
• Persistent second- or third-trimester bleeding
• Placenta previa after 26 weeks of gestation
• Premature labor during the current pregnancy
• Ruptured membranes
• Preeclampsia/pregnancy-induced hypertension

Exercise during pregnancy and the postpartum period. ACOG Committee Opinion No. 267. American College of Obstetricians and Gynecologists. *Obstetrics and Gynecology,* 2002; 99, 171–173.

Table 7-2
Relative Contraindications to Aerobic Exercise During Pregnancy
• Severe anemia
• Unevaluated maternal cardiac arrhythmia
• Chronic bronchitis
• Poorly controlled type 1 diabetes
• Extreme morbid obesity
• Extreme underweight (body mass index <12)
• History of extremely sedentary lifestyle
• Intrauterine growth restriction in current pregnancy
• Poorly controlled hypertension
• Orthopedic limitations
• Poorly controlled seizure disorder
• Poorly controlled hyperthyroidism
• Heavy smoker

Exercise during pregnancy and the postpartum period. ACOG Committee Opinion No. 267. American College of Obstetricians and Gynecologists. *Obstetrics and Gynecology,* 2002; 99, 171–173.

a GFI asks if there are any special considerations or problems. Additionally, a GFI should require a physician's clearance before any pregnant or postpartum woman begins an exercise program. ACSM recommends the use of a screening tool called the PARmed-X for Pregnancy for the health screening of pregnant women before their participation in exercise programs (Figure 7-2).

Should a GFI become aware of any of the conditions listed in Tables 7-1 or 7-2, exercise should be stopped immediately until the postpartum period, unless the participant obtains written permission from a physician to resume.

Figure 7-2
PARmed-X for
Pregnancy

PARmed-X for PREGNANCY PHYSICAL ACTIVITY READINESS MEDICAL EXAMINATION

PARmed-X for PREGNANCY is a guideline for health screening prior to participation in a prenatal fitness class or other exercise.

Healthy women with uncomplicated pregnancies can integrate physical activity into their daily living and can participate without significant risks either to themselves or to their unborn child. Postulated benefits of such programs include improved aerobic and muscular fitness, promotion of appropriate weight gain, and facilitation of labour. Regular exercise may also help to prevent gestational glucose intolerance and pregnancy-induced hypertension.

The safety of prenatal exercise programs depends on an adequate level of maternal-fetal physiological reserve. PARmed-X for PREGNANCY is a convenient checklist and prescription for use by health care providers to evaluate pregnant patients who want to enter a prenatal fitness program and for ongoing medical surveillance of exercising pregnant patients.

Instructions for use of the 4-page PARmed-X for PREGNANCY are the following:

1. The patient should fill out the section on PATIENT INFORMATION and the PRE-EXERCISE HEALTH CHECKLIST (PART 1, 2, 3, and 4 on p. 1) and give the form to the health care provider monitoring her pregnancy.

2. The health care provider should check the information provided by the patient for accuracy and fill out SECTION C on CONTRAINDICATIONS (p. 2) based on current medical information.

3. If no exercise contraindications exist, the HEALTH EVALUATION FORM (p. 3) should be completed, signed by the health care provider, and given by the patient to her prenatal fitness professional.

In addition to prudent medical care, participation in appropriate types, intensities and amounts of exercise is recommended to increase the likelihood of a beneficial pregnancy outcome. PARmed-X for PREGNANCY provides recommendations for individualized exercise prescription (p. 3) and program safety (p. 4).

NOTE: Sections A and B should be completed by the patient before the appointment with the health care provider.

A PATIENT INFORMATION

NAME _____

ADDRESS _____

TELEPHONE _____ BIRTHDATE _____ HEALTH INSURANCE No. _____

NAME OF
PRENATAL FITNESS PROFESSIONAL _____

PRENATAL FITNESS
PROFESSIONAL'S PHONE NUMBER _____

B PRE-EXERCISE HEALTH CHECKLIST

PART 1: GENERAL HEALTH STATUS

In the past, have you experienced (check YES or NO):

	YES	NO
1. Miscarriage in an earlier pregnancy?	❏	❏
2. Other pregnancy complications?	❏	❏
3. I have completed a PAR-Q within the last 30 days.	❏	❏

If you answered YES to question 1 or 2, please explain:

_____

Number of previous pregnancies? _____

PART 2: STATUS OF CURRENT PREGNANCY

Due Date: _____

During this pregnancy, have you experienced:

	YES	NO
1. Marked fatigue?	❏	❏
2. Bleeding from the vagina ("spotting")?	❏	❏
3. Unexplained faintness or dizziness?	❏	❏
4. Unexplained abdominal pain?	❏	❏
5. Sudden swelling of ankles, hands or face?	❏	❏
6. Persistent headaches or problems with headaches?	❏	❏
7. Swelling, pain or redness in the calf of one leg?	❏	❏
8. Absence of fetal movement after 6th month?	❏	❏
9. Failure to gain weight after 5th month?	❏	❏

If you answered YES to any of the above questions, please explain:

PART 3: ACTIVITY HABITS DURING THE PAST MONTH

1. List only regular fitness/recreational activities:

_____

_____

INTENSITY	FREQUENCY (times/week)			TIME (minutes/day)		
	1-2	2-4	4+	<20	20-40	40+
Heavy	___	___	___	___	___	___
Medium	___	___	___	___	___	___
Light	___	___	___	___	___	___

2. Does your regular occupation (job/home) activity involve:

	YES	NO
Heavy Lifting?	❏	❏
Frequent walking/stair climbing?	❏	❏
Occasional walking (>once/hr)?	❏	❏
Prolonged standing?	❏	❏
Mainly sitting?	❏	❏
Normal daily activity?	❏	❏
3. Do you currently smoke tobacco?*	❏	❏
4. Do you consume alcohol?*	❏	❏

PART 4: PHYSICAL ACTIVITY INTENTIONS

What physical activity do you intend to do?

_____

Is this a change from what you currently do?　❏ YES　　❏ NO

*NOTE: PREGNANT WOMEN ARE STRONGLY ADVISED NOT TO SMOKE OR CONSUME ALCOHOL DURING PREGNANCY AND DURING LACTATION.

© Canadian Society for Exercise Physiology
Société canadienne de physiologie de l'exercice

Supported by: Health Canada / Santé Canada

Physical Activity Readiness Medical Examination for Pregnancy (2002)

Figure 7-2
PARmed-X for Pregnancy (continued)

PARmed-X for PREGNANCY PHYSICAL ACTIVITY READINESS MEDICAL EXAMINATION

C CONTRAINDICATIONS TO EXERCISE: to be completed by your health care provider

Absolute Contraindications

Does the patient have:

	YES	NO
1. Ruptured membranes, premature labour?	❑	❑
2. Persistent second or third trimester bleeding/placenta previa?	❑	❑
3. Pregnancy-induced hypertension or pre-eclampsia?	❑	❑
4. Incompetent cervix?	❑	❑
5. Evidence of intrauterine growth restriction?	❑	❑
6. High-order pregnancy (e.g., triplets)?	❑	❑
7. Uncontrolled Type I diabetes, hypertension or thyroid disease, other serious cardiovascular, respiratory or systemic disorder?	❑	❑

Relative Contraindications

Does the patient have:

	YES	NO
1. History of spontaneous abortion or premature labour in previous pregnancies?	❑	❑
2. Mild/moderate cardiovascular or respiratory disease (e.g., chronic hypertension, asthma)?	❑	❑
3. Anemia or iron deficiency? (Hb < 100 g/L)?	❑	❑
4. Malnutrition or eating disorder (anorexia, bulimia)?	❑	❑
5. Twin pregnancy after 28th week?	❑	❑
6. Other significant medical condition?	❑	❑

Please specify: ______________________

NOTE: Risk may exceed benefits of regular physical activity. The decision to be physically active or not should be made with qualified medical advice.

PHYSICAL ACTIVITY RECOMMENDATION: ❑ Recommended/Approved ❑ Contraindicated

Prescription for Aerobic Activity

RATE OF PROGRESSION: The best time to progress is during the second trimester since risks and discomforts of pregnancy are lowest at that time. Aerobic exercise should be increased gradually during the second trimester from a minimum of 15 minutes per session, 3 times per week (at the appropriate target heart rate or RPE to a maximum of approximately 30 minutes per session, 4 times per week (at the appropriate target heart rate or RPE).

WARM-UP/COOL-DOWN: Aerobic activity should be preceded by a brief (10-15 min.) warm-up and followed by a short (10-15 min.) cool-down. Low intensity calesthenics, stretching and relaxation exercises should be included in the warm-up/cool-down.

F	I	T	T
FREQUENCY	**INTENSITY**	**TIME**	**TYPE**
Begin at 3 times per week and progress to four times per week	Exercise within an appropriate RPE range and/or target heart rate zone	Attempt 15 minutes, even if it means reducing the intensity. Rest intervals may be helpful	Non weight-bearing or low-impact endurance exercise using large muscle groups (e.g., walking, stationary cycling, swimming, aquatic exercises, low impact aerobics)

"TALK TEST"- A final check to avoid overexertion is to use the "talk test". The exercise intensity is excessive if you cannot carry on a verbal conversation while exercising.

PRESCRIPTION/MONITORING OF INTENSITY: The best way to prescribe and monitor exercise is by combining the heart rate and rating of perceived exertion (RPE) methods.

TARGET HEART RATE ZONES

The heart rate zones shown below are appropriate for most pregnant women. Work during the lower end of the HR range at the start of a new exercise program and in late pregnancy.

Age	Heart Rate Range
< 20	140-155
20-29	135-150
30-39	130-145

RATING OF PERCEIVED EXERTION (RPE)

Check the accuracy of your heart rate target zone by comparing it to the scale below. A range of about 12-14 (somewhat hard) is appropriate for most pregnant women.

6	
7	Very, very light
8	
9	Somewhat light
10	
11	Fairly light
12	
13	Somewhat hard
14	
15	Hard
16	
17	Very hard
18	
19	Very, very hard
20	

The original PARmed-X for PREGNANCY was developed by L.A. Wolfe, Ph.D., Queen's University. The muscular conditioning component was developed by M.F. Mottola, Ph.D., University of Western Ontario. The document has been revised based on advice from an Expert Advisory Committee of the Canadian Society for Exercise Physiology chaired by Dr. N. Gledhill, with additonal input from Drs. Wolfe and Mottola, and Gregory A.L. Davies, M.D.,FRCS(C) Department of Obstetrics and Gynaecology, Queen's University, 2002.

No changes permitted. Translation and reproduction in its entirety is encouraged.

Disponible en français sous le titre «Examination medicale sur l'aptitude à l'activité physique pour les femmes enceintes (X-AAP pour les femmes enceintes)»

Additional copies of the PARmed-X for PREGNANCY, the PARmed-X and/or the PAR-Q can be downloaded from: http://www.csep.ca/forms.asp.
For more information contact the:

Canadian Society for Exercise Physiology
185 Somerset St. West, Suite 202, Ottawa, Ontario CANADA K2P 0J2
tel.: 1-877-651-3755 FAX (613) 234-3565 www.csep.ca

Figure 7-2
PARmed-X
for Pregnancy
(continued)

Physical Activity Readiness
Medical Examination for
Pregnancy (2002)

PARmed-X for PREGNANCY PHYSICAL ACTIVITY READINESS MEDICAL EXAMINATION

Prescription for Muscular Conditioning

It is important to condition all major muscle groups during both prenatal and postnatal periods.

WARM-UPS & COOL DOWN:
Range of Motion: neck, shoulder girdle, back, arms, hips, knees, ankles, etc.

Static Stretching: all major muscle groups

(DO NOT OVER STRETCH!)

EXAMPLES OF MUSCULAR STRENGTHENING EXERCISES

CATEGORY	PURPOSE	EXAMPLE
Upper back	Promotion of good posture	Shoulder shrugs, shoulder blade pinch
Lower back	Promotion of good posture	Modified standing opposite leg & arm lifts
Abdomen	Promotion of good posture, prevent low-back pain, prevent diastasis recti, strengthen muscles of labour	Abdominal tightening, abdominal curl-ups, head raises lying on side or standing position
Pelvic floor ("Kegels")	Promotion of good bladder control, prevention of urinary incontinence	"Wave", "elevator"
Upper body	Improve muscular support for breasts	Shoulder rotations, modified push-ups against a wall
Buttocks, lower limbs	Facilitation of weight-bearing, prevention of varicose veins	Buttocks squeeze, standing leg lifts, heel raises

PRECAUTIONS FOR MUSCULAR CONDITIONING DURING PREGNANCY

VARIABLE	EFFECTS OF PREGNANCY	EXERCISE MODIFICATIONS
Body Position	• in the supine position (lying on the back), the enlarged uterus may either decrease the flow of blood returning from the lower half of the body as it presses on a major vein (inferior vena cava) or it may decrease flow to a major artery (abdominal aorta)	• past 4 months of gestation, exercises normally done in the supine position should be altered • such exercises should be done side lying or standing
Joint Laxity	• ligaments become relaxed due to increasing hormone levels • joints may be prone to injury	• avoid rapid changes in direction and bouncing during exercises • stretching should be performed with controlled movements
Abdominal Muscles	• presence of a rippling (bulging) of connective tissue along the midline of the pregnant abdomen (diastasis recti) may be seen during abdominal exercise	• abdominal exercises are not recommended if diastasis recti develops
Posture	• increasing weight of enlarged breasts and uterus may cause a forward shift in the centre of gravity and may increase the arch in the lower back • this may also cause shoulders to slump forward	• emphasis on correct posture and neutral pelvic alignment. Neutral pelvic alignment is found by bending the knees, feet shoulder width apart, and aligning the pelvis between accentuated lordosis and the posterior pelvic tilt position.
Precautions for Resistance Exercise	• emphasis must be placed on continuous breathing throughout exercise • exhale on exertion, inhale on relaxation using high repetitions and low weights • Valsalva Manoevre (holding breath while working against a resistance) causes a change in blood pressure and therefore should be avoided • avoid exercise in supine position past 4 months gestation	

✂ ···

PARmed-X for Pregnancy - Health Evaluation Form

(to be completed by patient and given to the prenatal fitness professional after obtaining medical clearance to exercise)

I, _____ PLEASE PRINT (patient's name), have discussed my plans to participate in physical activity during my current pregnancy with my health care provider and I have obtained his/her approval to begin participation.

Signed: _____
(patient's signature)

Date: _____

HEALTH CARE PROVIDER'S COMMENTS:

Name of health care provider: _____

_____

Address: _____

_____

_____

Telephone: _____

_____

(health care provider's signature)

Physical Activity Readiness
Medical Examination for
Pregnancy (2002)

Figure 7-2
PARmed-X
for Pregnancy
(continued)

Advice for Active Living During Pregnancy

Pregnancy is a time when women can make beneficial changes in their health habits to protect and promote the healthy development of their unborn babies. These changes include adopting improved eating habits, abstinence from smoking and alcohol intake, and participating in regular moderate physical activity. Since all of these changes can be carried over into the postnatal period and beyond, pregnancy is a very good time to adopt healthy lifestyle habits that are permanent by integrating physical activity with enjoyable healthy eating and a positive self and body image.

Active Living:

➤ see your doctor before increasing your activity level during pregnancy

➤ exercise regularly but don't overexert

➤ exercise with a pregnant friend or join a prenatal exercise program

➤ follow FITT principles modified for pregnant women

➤ know safety considerations for exercise in pregnancy

Healthy Eating:

➤ the need for calories is higher (about 300 more per day) than before pregnancy

➤ follow Canada's Food Guide to Healthy Eating and choose healthy foods from the following groups: whole grain or enriched bread or cereal, fruits and vegetables, milk and milk products, meat, fish, poultry and alternatives

➤ drink 6-8 glasses of fluid, including water, each day

➤ salt intake should not be restricted

➤ limit caffeine intake i.e., coffee, tea, chocolate, and cola drinks

➤ dieting to lose weight is not recommended during pregnancy

Positive Self and Body Image:

➤ remember that it is normal to gain weight during pregnancy

➤ accept that your body shape will change during pregnancy

➤ enjoy your pregnancy as a unique and meaningful experience

For more detailed information and advice about pre- and postnatal exercise, you may wish to obtain a copy of a booklet entitled *Active Living During Pregnancy: Physical Activity Guidelines for Mother and Baby* © 1999. Available from the Canadian Society for Exercise Physiology, 185 Somerset St. West, Suite 202, Ottawa, Ontario Canada K2P 0J2 Tel. 1-877-651-3755 Fax: (613) 234-3565 Email: info@csep.ca (online: www.csep.ca). Cost: $11.95

For more detailed information about the safety of exercise in pregnancy you may wish to obtain a copy of the Clinical Practice Guidelines of the Society of Obstetricians and Gynaecologists of Canada and Canadian Society for Exercise Physiology entitled *Exercise in Pregnancy and Postpartum* © 2003. Available from the Society of Obstetricians and Gynaecologists of Canada online at www.sogc.org

For more detailed information about pregnancy and childbirth you may wish to obtain a copy of *Healthy Beginnings: Your Handbook for Pregnancy and Birth* © 1998. Available from the Society of Obstetricians and Gynaecologists of Canada at 1-877-519-7999 (also available online at www.sogc.org) Cost $12.95.

For more detailed information on healthy eating during pregnancy, you may wish to obtain a copy of *Nutrition for a Healthy Pregnancy: National Guidelines for the Childbearing Years* © 1999. Available from Health Canada, Minister of Public Works and Government Services, Ottawa, Ontario Canada (also available online at www.hc-sc.gc.ca).

SAFETY CONSIDERATIONS

◆ Avoid exercise in warm/humid environments, especially during the 1st trimester

◆ Avoid isometric exercise or straining while holding your breath

◆ Maintain adequate nutrition and hydration — drink liquids before and after exercise

◆ Avoid exercise while lying on your back past the 4th month of pregnancy

◆ Avoid activities which involve physical contact or danger of falling

◆ Know your limits — pregnancy is not a good time to train for athletic competition

◆ Know the reasons to stop exercise and consult a qualified health care provider immediately if they occur

REASONS TO STOP EXERCISE AND CONSULT YOUR HEALTH CARE PROVIDER

◆ Excessive shortness of breath

◆ Chest pain

◆ Painful uterine contractions (more than 6-8 per hour)

◆ Vaginal bleeding

◆ Any "gush" of fluid from vagina (suggesting premature rupture of the membranes)

◆ Dizziness or faintness

Additionally, it is recommended that GFIs secure an informed consent or waiver of liability prior to participation (see Chapter 11).

Encourage participants to give regular feedback on how they are feeling during and after exercise, and remind them to alert the instructor to the presence of any unusual symptoms. GFIs should familiarize themselves and their participants with specific signs or symptoms that may indicate a problem, including the items listed in Tables 7-3 and 7-4. Refer women with any of these complaints to their physicians for evaluation before continuing any exercise program.

Table 7-3
Reasons to Discontinue Exercise and Seek Medical Advice
• Any sign of bloody discharge from the vagina • Any "gush" of fluid from the vagina (premature rupture of membranes) • Sudden swelling of the ankles, hands, or face (possible preeclampsia) • Persistent, severe headaches and/or visual disturbances (possible hypertension) • Unexplained spell of faintness or dizziness • Swelling, pain, and redness in the calf of one leg (possible phlebitis) • Elevation of pulse rate or blood pressure that persists after exercise • Excessive fatigue, palpitations, or chest pain • Persistent contractions (more than six to eight per hour) that may suggest onset of premature labor • Unexplained abdominal pain • Insufficient weight gain [less than 1 kg/month (2.2 lb/month) during last two trimesters]

Exercise during pregnancy and the postpartum period. ACOG Committee Opinion No. 267. American College of Obstetricians and Gynecologists. *Obstetrics and Gynecology,* 2002; 99, 171–173.

Table 7-4
Warning Signs to Cease Exercise While Pregnant
• Vaginal bleeding • Dyspnea prior to exertion • Dizziness • Headache • Chest pain • Muscle weakness • Calf pain or swelling (need to rule out thrombophlebitis) • Preterm labor • Decreased fetal movement • Amniotic fluid leakage

Exercise during pregnancy and the postpartum period. ACOG Committee Opinion No. 267. American College of Obstetricians and Gynecologists. *Obstetrics and Gynecology,* 2002; 99, 171–173.

High-risk Exercise

Women can continue most activities during their pregnancy by using common sense and making appropriate modifications. However, they should avoid any activity that has a potential for impact that may cause abdominal trauma. Additionally, exercises involving a high degree of **balance** or agility (e.g., gymnastics, rock climbing, and downhill skiing) are not recommended during pregnancy (Table 7-5). This is particularly important in the latter trimesters, when changes in a woman's **center of gravity (COG)** put her at increased risk of falling. Women who are not accustomed to exercising at high altitude (e.g., cross-country skiing and hiking) should use caution and exercise at lower-than-normal intensities, to ensure adequate oxygenation and to avoid undue complications.

Table 7-5
High-risk Exercises
• Snow- and waterskiing • Rock climbing • Snowboarding • Diving • Scuba diving • Bungee jumping • Horseback riding • Ice skating/hockey • Road or mountain cycling • Vigorous exercise at altitude (nonacclimated women)

Note: Risk of activities requiring balance is relative to maternal weight gain and morphologic changes; some activities may be acceptable early in pregnancy but risky later on.

Physiological Adaptations to Pregnancy

Of the myriad physiological changes that occur during pregnancy, perhaps those that have the most impact on exercise-program design are those related to the cardiovascular, respiratory, and musculoskeletal systems. While the adaptations listed in the following sections are by no means the only ones, a GFI who understands them will have a foundation of knowledge that allows safer and more effective work with this special group.

Cardiovascular System

When GFIs prepare beginning participants for group fitness classes, they often inform them of the short-term effects of exercise. They discuss how the body will heat up, that their breathing rates will increase because they are using more oxygen, and that their heart rates will rise to help move the much-needed oxygen and nutrients to the working muscles via the blood or circulatory system. This simplistic statement could also describe the body's response to pregnancy; pregnancy and exercise elicit many similar physiological responses. During an exercise session, heart rate, respiratory rate, oxygen consumption, metabolic rate, **cardiac output,** stroke volume, and body temperature all increase; pregnancy mimics these responses. A pregnant woman's body is in a constant state of work; the acute physiological responses of a low level of exercise are constantly present. It is not an exaggeration to say that a pregnant woman is performing a certain amount of exercise, even when she is at rest.

The cardiovascular, respiratory, and musculoskeletal systems must each adapt to the level of function required to grow a new life in 40 weeks. These adaptations include a gradual climb in resting heart rate, which reaches a peak of 15 beats per minute (bpm) over prepregnancy rates near the third trimester. Left ventricular volume and stroke volume increase by 40%. Resting cardiac output and blood volume are 40% higher by the third trimester (Clapp, 1998; Artal, 1992). Resting oxygen consumption also climbs

and reaches a level near term approximately 20 to 30% above prepregnancy levels (Artal, 1992; Wolfe et al., 1989).

These physiological changes have implications for the exercise program. Because the heart is already working at a higher capacity to pump the increased blood volume throughout the body, there is a decrease in **cardiac reserve.** The oxygen cost of weightbearing activity is also greater, due to increases in body weight. All of these factors combine to decrease maximum work capacity as pregnancy advances. Prenatal exercisers should gradually yet progressively reduce the volume of work done during exercise so as to complement the increased workload under which their body is functioning as they advance through pregnancy.

Respiratory System

Pregnant women ventilate 50% more air per minute than nonpregnant women. This occurs through a 40 to 50% increase in tidal volume, or the amount of air in each breath. Although many pregnant women feel that it is difficult to get a deep breath, maximum breathing capacity is actually maintained or increased over prepregnancy values. Respiratory rate does not change significantly. As the baby grows, the uterus pushes the diaphragm farther up into the chest cavity. The pregnant woman has to use more oxygen during **inspiration** as the diaphragm contracts to push the uterus downward. This increase in the oxygen cost of breathing also means less oxygen is available to the working muscles. The ribcage often flares and widens to help compensate for the decrease in lung space caused by the growing fetus.

Musculoskeletal System

To facilitate the expansion of the uterine cavity, increased amounts of the **hormones**

relaxin and **progesterone** are released during the first trimester. These hormones act to soften the ligaments surrounding the joints of the pelvis (hips and lumbosacral spine), thereby increasing mobility and joint laxity. A gentle but effective expansion occurs, providing the necessary space. This effect continues through the postpartum lactating period, when relaxin levels have been reduced.

The by-product of this hormonally induced joint laxity is a decrease in joint stability, which may leave the affected joints more susceptible to injury. Whether or not joint laxity occurs in the neck, shoulders, and peripheral joints is still controversial. If it does, the pregnant woman may have a greater chance of injuries resulting from overstretching, ligamentous tears, or sprains. However, research studies have not demonstrated an increased incidence of exercise-related joint injury among pregnant women (Clapp, 1998; Schauberger et al., 1996; Karzel & Friedman, 1991).

Researchers speculate that this is because pregnant women take greater precautions and are more careful during exercise. Whether or not relaxin has any effect on joints like the knees, common sense indicates that the increased mechanical stress of a 25- to 40-pound (11- to 18-kg) weight gain is cause to use caution with high-impact activities.

As weight is gained and hormonal influences on the hips and low back increase, postural alignment is altered. The pelvis tilts anteriorly, changing the COG and increasing the **lordotic** curve of the lumbar spine. The upper back is also realigned due to the increased weight of the breast tissue. The chest and shoulders are pulled forward and inward, increasing the kyphotic curve of the thoracic spine. A forward-head position often accompanies these postural deviations and an extreme exaggeration of the vertebral column's normal "S" curve results. This is known as a kyphotic-lordotic postural alignment (Jacobson, 1991; Artal et al., 1990). Postural realignments induced by the anterior weight gain of pregnancy, and the attendant muscular imbalances created, could predispose women to upper- or lower-back pain. These conditions are addressed more fully later in this chapter.

Additional Concerns

Blood returning to the heart from the body is known as **venous return.** Due to the increase in blood volume and sensitivities to postural positions, venous return may be impaired or disturbed during pregnancy. **Supine hypotension** is an example of such a disturbance. In the **supine** position (lying on the back), the weight of the uterus presses against blood vessels, especially the inferior vena cava. This pressure occludes the vessels, causing a restriction in blood flow, which may, in turn, cause a reduction in cardiac output, blood pressure, and blood flow to the fetus. If the fetus is subjected to repeated periods of **hypoxia** due to prolonged and/or repetitive supine exercise, there is the potential for developmental disorders to occur. Participants should be advised to avoid exercise in the supine position after the first trimester (ACOG, 2002; 1994).

GFIs often have to remind pregnant women that they are supposed to gain weight during pregnancy. Exercise should not be used as a means to prevent a healthy, normal weight gain during pregnancy. Average pregnancy weight gains are between approximately 27 and 34 pounds (12 and 15 kg); body fat increases by an average of 4 to 5% (Artal, 1992; Clark, 1992). Prevention of normal weight gain may be detrimental since weight gains are predictive of fetal birth weight. Nutritional diets should be encouraged to provide for the baby's growth and development and appropriate weight gains. The Institute of Medicine recommendations for a single pregnancy are presented in Table 7-6.

Table 7-6		
Weight Gain Recommendations During Pregnancy		
Prepregnancy Body Mass Index (kg/m²)	**Category**	**Recommended Weight Gain**
<18.5	Underweight	28 to 40 lb (12.5 to 18.0 kg)
18.5–24.9	Normal weight	25 to 35 lb (11.5 to 16.0 kg)
25.0 to 29.9	Overweight	15 to 25 lb (7.0 to 11.5 kg)
>30.0	Obese	11 to 20 lb (5.0 to 9.0 kg)

Source: Institute of Medicine (2009). *Weight Gain During Pregnancy: Reexamining the Guidelines.* http://iom.edu/Reports/2009/Weight-Gain-During-Pregnancy-Reexamining-the-Guidelines.aspx

Fetal Risks Associated With Exercise

Available research includes no evidence to show that regular exercise during a normal, healthy pregnancy is associated with any adverse fetal outcomes. However, there are several areas of theoretical concern of which GFIs should be aware. These include the effects of exercise on uterine-placental blood flow, **carbohydrate** utilization, and **thermoregulation**. This section addresses the basis for these concerns and the practical application for the group exercise setting.

The first concern is the potential conflict between the circulatory demands of exercise and those of pregnancy. During exercise, the oxygen-transport system analyzes the actions taking place and reacts to provide for the higher level of activity. Blood flow is preferentially redistributed to the heart, skin, and working muscles and shunted away from the renal, gastrointestinal, and reproductive organs. The

concern is that this may result in a decreased oxygen supply (i.e., hypoxia) and/or decreased nutrient supply to the fetus. If the fetus is subjected to repetitive, sustained bouts of hypoxia brought on by exercise, developmental abnormalities could occur.

In general, it appears that the fetus can adjust safely to reductions of blood flow resulting from moderate exercise bouts (ACSM, 2000; Uzendoski et al., 1989). Several adaptations have been identified that protect the fetus and compensate for the decrease in visceral blood flow during exercise. These adaptations include a significant increase in maternal **hematocrit,** which occurs with exercise. This adjustment decreases plasma volume and increases the oxygen-carrying capacity of the blood. Also, cardiac output in the fetus is redistributed to favor vital organs such as the heart, brain, and adrenal gland. Women who exercise regularly in early to mid-pregnancy experience a more rapid growth of the placenta and have improved placental function. At any rate of uterine blood flow, oxygen and nutrient delivery to the baby will be higher in a woman who exercises than in one who does not (Clapp, 1998; Wolfe, Brenner, & Mottola, 1994). And finally, an inverse relationship exists between blood flow and oxygen extraction in which the **arterial-mixed venous oxygen difference (a-$\bar{v}O_2$ difference)** increases as flow decreases. This means that as the rate of blood flow decreases, a greater percentage of the oxygen in that blood will be taken out and used to meet the needs of the uterus and fetus. As a result of these compensatory adjustments, oxygen delivery to the fetus does not appear to be compromised during maternal exercise (Sternfeld, 1997).

The second area of concern is that of carbohydrate utilization. Maternal blood **glucose** is the fetus' primary energy source. Several studies have shown maternal blood glucose to drop significantly following vigorous exercise in late gestation (Clapp & Capeless, 1990). This has been cause for concern, since low maternal blood glucose could compromise fetal energy supply. If this scenario were repeated regularly (as with physical conditioning), intrauterine growth retardation, lower birth weight, or other developmental problems might result. Several studies have also reported lower birth weights in women who continued heavy exercise throughout pregnancy. This weight discrepancy was primarily attributed to a decrease in subcutaneous fat in the newborn (Clapp & Capeless, 1990). Intrauterine growth retardation, or other short- or long-term effects on newborns of this decreased fat, has not been documented (ACOG, 2002; 1994; Clapp, Lopez, & Harcar-Sevcik, 1999).

Other studies have found no difference in birth weight among exercising mothers, particularly when the mothers received nutritional counseling. Clapp and Rizk (1992) studied placental weight in recreational athletes and found that it was significantly greater than the controls at 16, 20, and 24 weeks. The athletes who remained active but decreased or modified their activities in late pregnancy had the highest birth weight and placental weight, while the athletes who maintained or increased their exercise in late pregnancy had birth weights lower than the controls. This study suggests that exercise through midpregnancy may stimulate placental growth, allowing for better delivery of oxygen and nutrients to the baby. However, high-volume exercise in late pregnancy, when fetal and maternal energy requirements are high, may reduce fetal and placental weight (Clapp et al., 1992).

A GFI working with prenatal exercisers should be aware of the nutritional demands of pregnancy and reinforce good dietary habits. The metabolic needs of pregnancy add approximately 300 kcal/day. The energy requirements of exercise must be factored in as well. Pregnant women have lower fasting blood glucose levels than nonpregnant women and also utilize carbohydrate during exercise at a greater rate (ACOG, 2002; 1994). They are therefore more likely to become **hypoglycemic**, both during exercise and at rest. Pregnant women should be reminded to have a pre-exercise snack and to eat frequent small meals throughout the day. Help pregnant participants recognize the signs of hypoglycemia, such as weakness, dizziness, fatigue, and nausea. Suggest to those performing high levels of exercise that their exercise volume should start to taper from mid- to late-pregnancy. Finally, maternal weight gain and fetal growth (measured by a doctor at regular prenatal visits) should be within normal limits.

Glucose intolerance, another type of carbohydrate utilization dysfunction, can also be a problem in pregnancy. Glucose intolerance that is first recognized or diagnosed during pregnancy is called gestational diabetes. Maternal muscular **insulin resistance** during mid-pregnancy is a normal response to hormonal adaptations that occur to ensure adequate glucose regulation for fetal growth and development. In women with gestational diabetes, this insulin resistance is exacerbated, resulting in maternal hyperglycemia.

Women with gestational diabetes are more likely to have complications such as a difficult labor and delivery, as well as delivery by Caesarean section. Risk factors for gestational diabetes include a family history of diabetes, previous diagnosis of gestational diabetes, belonging to a high-risk ethnic group (Aboriginal, Hispanic, South Asian, Asian, or African descent), age ≥35 years, overweight [**body mass index (BMI)** ≥25]), obesity (BMI ≥30), or a history of insulin resistance (ACOG, 2001).

Once diagnosed, women with gestational diabetes are primarily treated through nutritional management by a **registered dietician (R.D.).** Exercise is considered an adjunct therapy. Preliminary studies have found that women who participated in any type of recreational activity within the first 20 weeks of gestation decreased their risk of gestational diabetes by almost half (Dempsey et al., 2004). Another study has shown that even mild exercise (30% of $\dot{V}O_2$max, regardless of modality) combined with nutritional control can help prevent gestational diabetes and excessive weight gain during pregnancy (Batada et al., 2003). It has also been shown that physical activity, especially vigorous-intensity activity, before pregnancy and at least light-to-moderate intensity activity during pregnancy, may reduce the risk for abnormal glucose tolerance and gestational diabetes (Oken et al., 2006). GFIs who work with women with gestational diabetes should be certain that the pregnant participant understands her nutritional needs and how they are influenced by physical activity as explained by her personal physician and/or R.D.

The third area of concern is that of fetal **hyperthermia,** which is known to be **teratogenic** (i.e., capable of causing birth defects) (McMurray & Katz, 1990). Febrile illness in the first trimester has been associated with neural tube defects. Retrospective studies searching for a common factor in neural development defects found that heat (such as would be seen in fetal hyperthermia) was a major cause. However, there is no demonstrated increase in neural tube defects or other birth defects in women who participate in even vigorous exercise during early pregnancy (ACOG, 2002; 1994; Clapp & Little, 1995).

Normal fetal temperature is slightly higher than that of the mother. Fetal temperature is contingent on maternal temperature, fetal metabolic rate, and uterine blood flow, with the greatest effect stemming from maternal temperature. Fetal thermoregulation depends on the mother's ability to cool herself. Very high-intensity exercise, or exercise in a hot, humid environment, has the potential to raise maternal core temperature above the baby's and reverse the temperature gradient. This could cause the baby to take on heat from the mother.

Maternal resting core temperatures are slightly higher than prepregnancy levels, but exercise temperatures in pregnant women do not mirror this increase. Peak rectal temperature in pregnant women after exercise at 64% of $\dot{V}O_2$max has been shown to decrease by 0.3° C by eight weeks and continues to drop at a rate of 0.1° C per month through the 37th week (ACOG, 2002; 1994; Clapp, 1991).

It appears that pregnant women have physiological adaptations that enhance thermoregulation during exercise. These adaptations include a downward shift in the sweating threshold (allowing evaporative heat loss at a lower body temperature), better skin-to-environment heat transfer due to increased skin blood flow during pregnancy, and increased heat loss through the respiratory tract due to increased ventilation in pregnancy.

While these compensatory mechanisms serve to protect the fetus from heat stress, caution should nevertheless be taken to avoid overheating when working with this population. Remember that early pregnancy (the first trimester) is the most critical phase regarding heat sensitivity and fetal development. Participants should be advised to (1) exercise in a cool, well-ventilated, low-humidity environment, (2) drink plenty of cool water to avoid dehydration, and (3) avoid very high-intensity activities.

Musculoskeletal System Imbalances and Dysfunctions

An understanding of alterations to the musculoskeletal system will enable GFIs to wisely choose and modify various exercises for the benefit of their pregnant participants. The following are some of the most commonly encountered complaints among prenatal exercisers.

Muscle Imbalances

When posture is not in the ideal alignment, muscle imbalances are likely to arise. The common muscle imbalances identified in pregnancy are either "tight" (scapula protractors, levator scapulae, hip flexors, tensor fascia latae, piriformis, hamstrings, adductors, and calves) or "weak" (scapula retractors, low lumbar paravertebral muscles, gluteus maximus and medius, abdominals, and quadriceps) (Wilder, 1988).

Muscle imbalances must be considered when an instructor is choosing exercises for class. Prenatal classes should be designed to reduce these muscle imbalances. The reduction will, in turn, help reduce the postural deviations. When dealing with muscle imbalances, it is more effective to first relax the tightened muscles through stretches and mobility exercises and then follow with strengthening exercises for the weaker muscle groups.

When participants are unable to perform certain exercises because of discomfort or irritation, the GFI should react to the short-term situation by modifying exercises to reduce such difficulties. When discomfort or irritations persist, the participant must realize that she may need to cease the activity to rest the area and prevent further aggravation. In all cases, the participant should communicate concerns to her physician. In severe cases in which discomfort becomes chronic, consulting a physical therapist specializing in prenatal care should be considered.

Dysfunctions and Irritations

This section provides a summary of common dysfunctions and irritations, including backache, **pelvic floor** weakness, diastasis recti, ligament strain, pubic pain, sacroiliac joint dysfunction, **sciatica,** nerve compression syndromes, overuse syndromes, and muscle cramps. While suggestions for exercise modifications are touched on in this section, detailed exercise modifications are found later in this chapter.

Backache

The most frequent complaint during pregnancy is backache. About half of all pregnant women develop pain in the low-back area. Proper body mechanics, exercise, massage, relaxation, and physical therapy can help reduce and, in some cases, prevent low-back pain.

As noted previously, postural realignments during pregnancy contribute heavily to the incidence of backache. An exaggerated lumbar **lordosis,** rounded upper back, and a forward-head position characterize the typical posture of a pregnant woman.

Exercises appropriate for this situation should focus on reducing the improper alignment. Mobility and stretching exercises should emphasize relaxing and lengthening the back extensors, hip flexors, shoulder protractors, shoulder internal rotators, and neck flexors. Strengthening exercises focused on the abdominals (which can be modified after the first trimester), gluteals, and scapula retractors will reinforce their ability to support proper alignment.

Gentle reminders to participants are helpful in maintaining proper alignment throughout each section of class. To practice maintaining a neutral pelvis, participants can strengthen the muscles that tilt the pelvis posteriorly (i.e., the abdominal and gluteal muscle groups). The gluteal muscles should be pulled downward and together with an upward pull of the abdominals. This motion should reduce the anterior pelvic tilt position.

Various cues, such as "heads up," "shoulders back," "buttocks tight," "belly buttons up," or "abdominals hugging the baby," may communicate alignment to participants. Even a simple question such as, "How does that low back feel?" may stimulate better posture. Posture breaks during class for pelvic tilts and other back exercises can increase comfort.

Aside from postural alterations that bring on back pain, other factors that may contribute to the condition are increases in relaxin, hypermobility of the sacroiliac joint, improper body mechanics, **edema** due to water retention that places excess pressure on spinal nerves (a possible cause of nighttime back pain), and psychosocial stress (Hummel-Berry, 1990).

Pelvic Floor Weakness

The five layers of muscle and **fascia** attached to the bony ring of the pelvis are commonly referred to as the pelvic floor. From superficial to deep layers, they are as follows: the superficial outlet muscles, urogenital triangle, pelvic diaphragm or levator ani muscles, smooth muscle diaphragm, and endopelvic diaphragm. They support the pelvic organs like a sling to withstand all the increases in pressure that occur in the abdominal and pelvic cavity and provide **sphincter** control for the three **perineal** openings (Noble, 1995).

There are fascial connections between the levator ani muscles, the sacroiliac ligaments, the hip rotator muscles, and the hamstrings. These connections allow weaknesses of the pelvic floor muscles to refer stress to these areas. Pelvic floor weaknesses can cause the pelvic alignment to falter and thus irritate the sacroiliac joint and the hip joint (Wilder, 1988). It is crucial that these muscles function competently. In addition, prolapse of the bladder, uterus, or rectum may develop if muscles become too weak to support the pelvic organs. Finally, urinary stress incontinence can often be initiated during pregnancy because of pelvic floor weakness.

Kegel exercises are designed to strengthen the pelvic floor and ensure its proficient function. The benefits of strengthening the pelvic floor include providing support for the heavy pelvic organs; preventing prolapse of the bladder, uterus, and rectum; supporting pelvic alignment; reinforcing sphincter control; enhancing circulation through a congested area of the vascular system; and providing a healthy environment for the healing process after labor and delivery (Dunbar, 1992).

Diastasis Recti

Diastasis recti is the partial or complete separation of the rectus abdominis muscle and occurs as the linea alba widens and finally gives way to the mechanical stress of an advancing pregnancy (Wilder, 1988). The linea alba, a tendinous fiber that merges the abdominal muscles with the fascia, extends from the xiphoid process to the **symphysis pubis.** Some separation is a normal part of every pregnancy.

Proficient prenatal instructors may test for diastasis recti (Figure 7-3). The most common test is performed by placing two fingers horizontally on the suspected location of the diastasis recti while the participant lies in a supine or semirecumbent position with knees bent. Have her perform a curl-up. If the fingers are able to penetrate at the location, there is probably a split. The abdominal muscles can be felt to the side of the split. The degree of separation is measured according to the number of finger-widths of the split. One to two finger-widths is considered normal. If the separation is greater than three finger-widths, avoid exercises that place direct stress on this area (Noble, 1995). Focus on abdominal compression exercises and using the abdominals to help maintain neutral spinal alignment with all activities.

Figure 7-3
Testing for diastasis recti

Diastasis recti is most common during the third trimester and immediately postpartum and is attributed to the following influences:

- *Maternal hormones:* Relaxin, **estrogen,** and progesterone encourage the connective tissue to become less supportive. There is a loosening effect on the abdominal fascia and a reduction of the cohesion between the collagen fibers.

- *Mechanical stress within the abdominal cavity:* This varies according to fetus size and number, placental size, the amount of amniotic fluid, the number of previous pregnancies, and the amount of weight gain. The abdominal musculature is designed to shorten and lengthen in a vertical direction, but pregnancy demands that the abdominal wall expand horizontally, and it is not normally elastic in the transverse direction. This situation causes mechanical stress that can end in functional failure for the abdominal wall. After a slow deformation of the soft tissue, the separation is often caused by a sudden action made with improper body mechanics.

- *Weak abdominal muscles:* A correlation exists between diastasis recti and weak abdominal muscles. Women with strong abdominal musculature are considered more prepared to resist this condition (Boissonnault & Blaschak, 1988). Other predisposing factors include heredity, obesity, multiple-birth pregnancy, a large baby, excess uterine fluid, and a lax abdominal wall from previous pregnancies.

Abdominal exercises that may introduce susceptibility in people prone to diastasis are those that put direct pressure on the linea alba from within due to uterine resistance, and from without due to gravitational resistance.

Round, Inguinal, and Broad Ligament Irritations

The **round, inguinal,** and **broad ligaments** are the ligaments most commonly irritated or strained during pregnancy. The inguinal ligament is formed as the fascia of the internal oblique, the external oblique, and transverse abdominis muscles blend together at their lower margin. It runs between the pubic tubercle and the anterior superior iliac spine. As the abdominal wall expands, the inguinal ligament is also stretched. It continues to be stretched throughout the pregnancy, slowly adapting with the abdominal wall expansion. This constant state of tension can easily cause the muscles of the abdominal wall to spasm with an increase in abdominal pressure such as that which results from a cough, sneeze, or laugh.

Workouts must be attuned to the current state of ligamentous tension. On days when the participant feels vulnerable, the intensity of the workout and strain put on the ligament should be reduced. Sensitivity is common with abdominal exercises and inner- and outer-thigh exercises. When performing abdominal exercises, pregnant participants can try to relieve the tension by keeping the knee and hip joints bent and the curling height low. With hip **abduction** and **adduction,** the knee and hip joints should again be slightly bent. This places the inguinal ligament in a more relaxed position and reduces the leverage of the leg. Avoid quick shifts of body position, especially changing from right to left side-lying positions. Prepare the body to change positions by warming joints with pelvic tilts, maintaining proper alignment, and using the arms to help lift the body from the floor.

The round and broad ligaments directly support the uterus within the pelvic cavity. The round ligament connects to both sides of the uterine fundus and extends forward through the inguinal canal and terminates in the labia majora (Figure 7-4). The round ligament may be irritated with extreme stretches above the head, rapid twisting movements, or jackknifing off the floor or bed. The use of proper mechanics for lying down and rising will also prevent strain on the round ligament (Figure 7-5). In the exercise arena, women may experience discomfort when the round ligament is jostled from jogging or jumping. A unilateral, standing hip hike held for five seconds and repeated for several repetitions can decrease the discomfort of, or even prevent, round ligament pain (Figure 7-6). To perform this exercise, have the participant elevate one iliac crest by shifting the weight to one leg, thereby unloading the other leg and lifting it slightly off the floor. The knee should be straight. Adequate warm-up for the inguinal ligament, the round ligament, and the abdominal wall may also include torso **range of motion (ROM)** activities, pelvic tilts, and

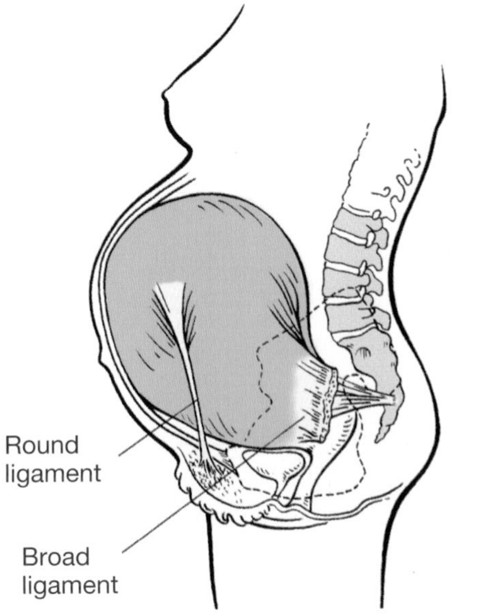

Figure 7-4
Round and broad ligaments

Round ligament

Broad ligament

Figure 7-5
Proper body mechanics for rising from the side-lying position to the standing position

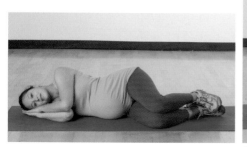

a.

b.

c.

d.

e.

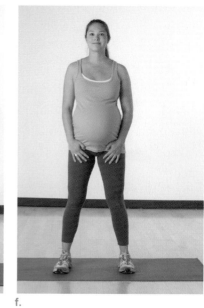

f.

Figure 7-6
Unilateral standing hip hike

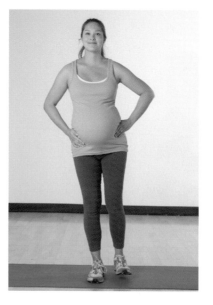

an effleurage massage. (An effleurage massage is a very light, stroking movement, done in this case by placing the fingertips on the pubis and sliding them upward along the linea alba, then sliding them down both sides of the abdominal wall near the round ligament, gently rubbing along the inguinal ligament, and meeting at the pubis to begin the circular motion again.)

The largest ligament supporting the ovaries, as well as the uterine tubes, uterus, and vagina, is the broad ligament (see Figure 7-4). It connects the lateral margins of the uterus to the posterior pelvic walls. The pull it receives from the enlarged uterus can cause a severely arched and aching low back. Relaxation of this ligament can be aided with performance of pelvic tilts, the cat stretch, trunk **flexion** exercises, self-massage of the low back, and torso ROM movements, all of which help to relieve tension in the broad ligament as well as in the extensor muscles of the back. Encourage participants to avoid exaggerating the arch of the low back, maintain good postural alignment, and use good body mechanics.

Pubic Pain

As the growth of the fetus demands more space, the pelvis accommodates by expanding. The loosened ligaments that allow this necessary expansion also allow increased motion. The irritation of the pubic symphysis caused by the increased motion at the joint is called **symphysitis** (Wilder, 1988). This irritation may be worsened by exercise. Ice may be used to relieve immediate irritation (see Chapter 8 for **RICE** guidelines). A physician consultation is advised and physical therapy may be ordered. Pelvic belts, which compress the pelvis and minimize motion in the symphysis pubis and sacroiliac joint, may be pre-

scribed. Partial symphyseal separations and complete dislocations are possible during pregnancy, as are pubic stress fractures. They usually result from delivery and, therefore, are a greater concern for postnatal participants.

When pubic pain occurs, efforts to alleviate irritation will determine the choice of activity and exercise. Exercises using hip adduction and abduction and, to a lesser extent, hip **extension** can cause further irritation of the pubis. The relationship of the tendons to the hip joints during hip abduction, adduction, and extension may cause excessive movement of the pubis, which intensifies the pain. Appropriate modifications include reducing hip joint exercises to a level of tolerance or to avoid pain completely. Participants can also perform standing hip abduction and extension exercises to reduce symphysis pubis irritation. GFIs should reduce the impact and weightbearing aspects of aerobic activities and suggest aqua aerobics, swimming, or stationary biking as alternative exercises. Shoe quality is important to mention to these participants (see page 225), as walking or jogging in worn-out shoes can worsen joint irritations.

Sacroiliac Joint Dysfunction

According to Hummel-Berry (1990), 50% of all back pain is related to lumbosacral pain. During pregnancy, the sacroiliac joint functions to resist the anterior pelvic tilt that is accentuated by the increase in lumbar lordosis caused by the uterine growth and weight gain. To facilitate the passage of the fetus through the pelvis, relaxin is released and softens the normally rigid ligaments of the sacroiliac joint and symphysis pubis. Postural adjustments, which pull the pelvis anteriorly, in conjunction with the hormonal relaxation effect, ultimately combine to force the sacroiliac ligaments to give, stretch, and, possibly become hypermobile (Daly et al., 1991).

Symptoms of sacroiliac dysfunction include pain during the following activities: prolonged sitting, standing, or walking; climbing stairs; standing with weight on one leg; and twisting (Lile & Hagar, 1991). The pain is usually unilateral (on one side) and in some cases radiates to the buttocks, lower abdomen, anterior medial thigh, groin, or posterior thigh (Daly et al., 1991). Participants may complain of having pain in the sacroiliac area when they stand up out of a chair or when they get out of bed. The pain is felt at the sacroiliac joint and radiates into the buttocks, but it does not radiate down the leg, as is characteristic of sciatica.

Exercises should be chosen to add strength and support to the sacroiliac area and to facilitate pelvic stability. If the lumbosacral angle (the angle between the lumbar vertebrae and the sacrum) is reduced, pain will usually be reduced. The gluteal muscles add the most direct support, but endurance exercises for the abdominals are also helpful. Abdominal endurance assists in preventing the anterior pelvic tilt that is straining the sacroiliac joint and ligament. Suggestions for class include accentuating proper postural alignment, using abdominal compression exercises throughout class, and using standing hip extension and abduction exercises. All of the preceding actions should incorporate pelvic stability (refer to the hip exercises in the "Strength Training" section that begins on page 201). Participants with severe cases of sacroiliac dysfunction should be advised to see their physician.

Sciatica

Pressure placed on the sciatic nerve due to the position of the fetus or postural structures can produce nerve irritation that is extremely painful. A woman experiencing pain that radiates from her buttocks down to her legs is possibly experiencing sciatic nerve irritation. Exercise can do little to relieve this situation. Participants should be advised to note the activities that preceded the irritation and either avoid those activities in the future or review the body mechanics used during the aggravating activity. Pelvic tilts may offer some immediate relief by shifting the irritating pressure away from the nerve. After experiencing a sciatic nerve irritation, the gluteal muscles and hamstrings will respond by tightening. Gently stretching these muscles can help to relax them out of this protective response.

Nerve Compression Syndromes

Most pregnant women have some degree of swelling during their pregnancy. Soft-tissue swelling may decrease the available space in relatively constrained anatomical areas. The result of this constriction and fluid retention can be nerve compression syndromes or, less commonly, compartment syndromes.

The most prevalent nerve problem during pregnancy is **carpal tunnel syndrome,** which results from compression of the median nerve within the wrist. Complaints of numbness and tingling sensations in the thumb and index and middle fingers are characteristic. Participants with carpal tunnel syndrome should avoid loading the wrists in **hyperextension,** grasping objects tightly, and performing repetitive flexion/extension of the wrist. Keep the wrist joint in its neutral position as much as possible.

A related nerve compression syndrome, **tarsal tunnel syndrome,** involves compression of the posterior tibial nerve at the ankle. The characteristic complaints are pain, burning, tingling, and/or a pins and needles sensation on the sole of the foot.

Thoracic outlet syndrome is an uncommon syndrome that usually begins with pain down the inner aspect of the arm and forearm, accompanied by paresthesias (tingling and pins and needles sensations) extending into the medial aspect of the palm as well as the ring and little fingers. These symptoms can occur as a result of compression of the brachial plexus. Postural deviations with internally rotated shoulders can aggravate the situation. Exercises to encourage external **rotation** of the shoulder and stretches to reduce internal rotation of the shoulder should be added to the workout regimen to balance the muscles. A bra that supports the weight of the breast tissue may help to reduce upper-back strain.

Encourage participants to avoid long periods of standing and sitting throughout the day. Taking short breaks at work to walk around and sitting with the feet elevated can help to improve circulation and reduce swelling. Prolonged standing should be avoided, as it can cause significant reductions in venous return and cardiac output. Advise participants to lie whenever possible on their left side with the feet slightly elevated. An example of this position involves side-lying on a sofa with the feet elevated on the sofa arm. This position is the most efficient at facilitating venous return and reducing fluid retention. Drinking plenty of water and reducing salt intake may also prevent excessive fluid retention. Severe swelling and fluid retention can indicate other medical conditions related to pregnancy, in addition to contributing to nerve compression, and should be reported immediately to the primary physician.

Overuse Syndromes

Weight gain, postural changes, and hormonal influences create a perfect environment for producing overuse syndromes. Many common overuse syndromes associated with exercise are intensified by these adaptations of pregnancy. Patellofemoral syndrome (knee pain) is often brought on or worsened by the changes that accompany pregnancy. This condition may worsen to cause a gradual degeneration of the articular cartilage that lines the back surface of the patella (**chondromalacia**), potentially becoming more irritated and inflamed due to the stress placed on the knee joint due to poor alignment. Pain can become incapacitating. Classes should include strengthening exercises for the quadriceps muscles to add support to the knee joints, and extra attention should be given to maintaining proper knee alignment during these exercises. **Hyperflexion** of the knee when bearing weight can accentuate the aggravation. Alignment is an especially important issue in stepping activities because the repetitive motion can easily result in improper alignment as the participant becomes fatigued.

The feet often become flatter and more pronated during pregnancy due to weight gain. When the feet are not striking properly, further alignment deviations in the hips and knees can result. **Plantar fasciitis,** which is an inflammation of the plantar fascia, the broad band of connective tissue running along the sole of the foot, may result from improper foot placement. Advise participants to avoid wearing worn or unsupportive shoes.

Muscle Cramps

Awakening abruptly to a muscle cramp can be very painful and frustrating. This is not an uncommon experience for pregnant women, who often do not know how to relieve cramps. Advise participants to avoid extreme pointing of the toes (**plantarflexion**) and wearing high heels and tight shoes, as these actions may stimulate muscle cramping. To relieve a muscle cramp, put the muscle in a stretched position and hold it there until the sensation subsides. For example, straighten the knee to alleviate a hamstring cramp, straighten the knee and **dorsiflex** the foot to relieve a calf cramp, and dorsiflex the foot and spread the toes to relieve a foot cramp.

Cardiovascular Exercise Classes and Programs for Pregnant Women

Research on pregnancy and exercise has advanced significantly since ACOG published the first guidelines on the topic in 1985. At that time, most of the research was limited to animal subjects. The initial guidelines were justifiably conservative, reflecting the lack of information available at that time. Since 1985, studies involving the use of human subjects have provided much more information on the physiological responses (both maternal and fetal) to exercise during pregnancy. Both the 2002 and 1994 ACOG guidelines reflect this increase in the body of scientific knowledge and include significant changes from the original recommendations. Notably, the recommendation to use heart rate as a means of monitoring exercise intensity has been removed (the original ACOG recommendation in 1985 was to limit heart rate to 140 bpm or less). The heart-rate response to exercise among pregnant women is variable throughout pregnancy, and from one individual to another. Blunted, exaggerated, and normal linear responses may all be seen at different stages during the same pregnancy. It is important to realize that often these changes are not due to exercise itself but rather to the other physiological influences

of pregnancy. There is an increase of 10 to 15 bpm in resting heart rate in pregnancy; however, at maximal exercise levels there is a blunted heart-rate response compared to the non-pregnant state (Davies et al., 2003).

Monitoring Exercise Intensity

ACSM recommends moderate-intensity aerobic exercise (40–60% of $\dot{V}O_2max$) for pregnant women on at least three—but preferably all—days of the week (ACSM, 2014). There are several suggested ways to monitor and regulate exercise intensity during pregnancy, each of which carries its own pros and cons.

Ratings of perceived exertion (RPE) has been shown to correlate more closely than heart rate to actual measured oxygen consumption during exercise in pregnancy, making it a simple yet effective way to cue intensity. Since it is a subjective rating, it allows for the large variances in exercise capacity that exist in a typical class setting. The RPE scale (6–20) or the "category-ratio" scale (0–10) may be used (Table 7-7). The numbers corresponding to "fairly light" to "somewhat hard" are the recommended range during pregnancy (Clapp, Lopez, & Harcar-Sevcik 1999; Pivarnik et al., 1991).

The **talk test** is another simple, yet effective way to cue and monitor exercise intensity during pregnancy (ACSM, 2014). When a participant can speak a short sentence and hold a reasonable conversation during exercise without obvious gasps for breath, she is working at an intensity at or below the recommended 40–60% of $\dot{V}O_2max$.

Lastly, if heart-rate monitoring is used to monitor exercise intensity in a pregnant participant, standard calculations of heart-rate ranges should not be utilized due to the reduction in maximal heart-rate reserve. Table 7-8 provides modified heart rate train-

Table 7-7	
Ratings of Perceived Exertion (RPE)	
RPE	**Category Ratio Scale**
6	0 Nothing at all
7 Very, very light	0.5 Very, very weak
8	1 Very weak
9 Very light	2 Weak
10	3 Moderate
11 Fairly light	4 Somewhat strong
12	5 Strong
13 Somewhat hard	6
14	7 Very strong
15 Hard	8
16	9
17 Very hard	10 Very, very strong
18	* Maximal
19 Very, very hard	
20	

Source: Adapted from American College of Sports Medicine (2014). *ACSM's Guidelines for Exercise Testing and Prescription* (9th ed.). Philadelphia: Wolters Kluwer/Lippincott Williams & Wilkins.

Table 7-8	
Heart-rate Ranges Corresponding to Moderate-intensity Exercise	
Age (Years)	**Heart-rate Range (bpm)**
<20	140–155
20–29	135–150
30–39	130–145
>40	125–140

Note: bpm = Beats per minute
Source: American College of Sports Medicine (2014). *ACSM's Guidelines for Exercise Testing and Prescription* (9th ed.). Philadelphia: Wolters Kluwer/Lippincott Williams & Wilkins.

ing zones that have been developed for various age groups during pregnancy (ACSM, 2014; Davies et al., 2003).

The 1994 ACOG guidelines state: "There are no data to indicate that pregnant women should limit exercise intensity and lower target heart rates because of potential adverse effects." However, GFIs must keep in mind that there may be other reasons to limit exercise intensity. The 1994 ACOG recommendations also removed specific limitations on exercise duration, reflecting the tremendous individual differences that exist in pregnant women's abilities. ACOG recommends "mild to moderate" exercise, but adds that highly trained women may be able to maintain higher intensities in the earlier part of pregnancy. ACOG further states that consistent exercise (three days per week or more) is preferable

to intermittent activity. It is essential that the GFI knows the participants and their exercise histories and cues pregnant women regarding the effort appropriate for the individual. The exercise intensity and duration selected should not result in fatigue or exhaustion. Maternal symptoms are the basis for changes and modifications to the program (ACOG, 2002; 1994). ACOG's recommendations are the **standard of care** for exercise during pregnancy. It takes a thoughtful and purposeful plan to teach an effective fitness class. The challenge is to design and choose exercises that will allow success, comfort, and safety for the pregnant participant.

Whether a pregnant exercise participant wishes to be integrated into an exercise class of nonpregnant women—perhaps a class she has already been in—or joins a prenatal class, it is the GFI's responsibility to be aware of any pregnant woman's new physical status and to make appropriate individualized adjustments for that participant.

For GFIs with large classes, the greatest challenge may be knowing who, if anyone, is pregnant in the class. Many women well into their second trimester may not "show." While pre-exercise screening will identify the newcomer to exercise, it does not help the

GFI identify a new pregnancy in a regular class participant. Therefore, unless the GFI actually mentions to the class from time to time the need to know about pregnancies, he or she may not find out about pregnancies for quite a while.

Specialized classes for pregnant women have several benefits over integrated classes. Individual participants can be better monitored for such things as strain, discomfort, and fatigue. In addition, the prenatal exercise class forms a natural support group, with discussions of many pregnancy-related issues and help in maintaining stress control, self-esteem, and body confidence.

However, the experienced or highly fit pregnant woman may wish to continue to exercise in a nonspecialized group fitness environment, especially when her favorite exercise mode is not taught specifically for pregnant women. This situation may arise in early pregnancy or if it is not the participant's first baby. While this should not be discouraged, the GFI will need to give additional attention and guidance to the pregnant participant in an integrated class.

In both specialized and integrated classes, there should be communication between the GFI and pregnant participants on a range of subjects, including sufficiency of warm-up time, needed modifications of exercises, intensity of movements, perceived exertion, weight gain, and comfort and pain levels.

Always be mindful of conditions such as hyperthermia, hypoxia, hypoglycemia, and musculoskeletal injuries. An exercise activity should be stopped and alternatives immediately given if the participant finds it awkward to perform or if it causes discomfort, pain, or embarrassment.

The aerobic exercise warm-up should gradually increase muscle temperature through general body movement and joint ROM activity. Give special emphasis to stimulating those areas under mechanical stress from pregnancy—the abdomen, pelvis, back, and hips.

Aquatic Exercise

The favorite exercise modality for many pregnant women is water-based activity. In the water, body temperatures appear to rise less and dissipate sooner, which can help minimize the risk of hyperthermia (McMurray & Katz, 1990). However, water temperatures should feel cool or these benefits may be negated. If the water feels like bath water, it is probably too warm (Karsenec & Grimes, 1984). Because of the hydrostatic effects of water, submaximal exercise in water is associated with a smaller plasma volume decrease than exercise on land, which may result in better maintenance of uterine and placental blood flow (Watson et al., 1991).

The pressure of water appears to lessen fluid retention and swelling, two common discomforts of pregnancy. The prone position in swimming actually facilitates optimum blood flow to the uterus by redistributing the weight of the uterus away from the inferior vena cava and the aorta. Another positive attribute of water classes is the buoyant effect of water, which increases comfort by supporting body weight and eliminating trouble with balance. This wonderful weightless feeling can be a major relief to a pregnant woman. Water exercises are easy on the musculoskeletal system due to the reduced stress placed on the weightbearing joints and ligaments. This non-weightbearing position gives relief to those muscles bearing extra mechanical stress and pressure from the pregnancy.

Pregnant swimmers should use caution with forceful frog or whip kicks, as they may place undue stress on the unstable pubic joint. Additionally, traditional use of a kickboard may amplify the exaggerated lumbar lordosis of pregnancy and should therefore be used judiciously.

Indoor Cycling

Because cycling is non-weightbearing, many women find it a comfortable activity even in the later trimesters, when activities like walking can become awkward and difficult. As with other forms of exercise, there are some modifications and precautions that should be kept in mind when pregnant women participate in group cycling classes. Crosscurrent convective cooling (i.e., fans) and adequate hydration are musts, as the potential to overheat or dehydrate is great. Fluids should be taken frequently, with a goal of drinking 7–10 ounces for every 10–20 minutes of exercise. Workload (cadence, resistance, or both) should be decreased to achieve the same relative cardiovascular **overload** as pregnancy progresses. The tendency to overexert in these classes may be high, and, therefore, specific, individualized instruction should be given to the pregnant rider. Morphologic changes will affect cycling mechanics; the hips gradually externally rotate to accommodate the enlarging uterus. Increased weight on the saddle may necessitate wider, padded saddles or seat covers, in addition to padded shorts. The anterior weight gain of pregnancy, coupled with the laws of gravity, makes maintaining neutral lumbar alignment while hinging at the hip to reach the handlebars difficult and fatiguing; adjust the handlebars to the most upright position and give pregnant riders frequent postural breaks. Be aware that toward the later trimesters, anterior weight gain will tend to pull a pregnant rider further forward over the pedals during out-of-the-saddle drills, putting the knees in a position susceptible

to injury. Edema (swelling) in the feet can make tight toe straps uncomfortable; cleated shoes eliminate this problem.

Mind-Body Classes

GFIs teaching classes like **tai chi, yoga, and Pilates,** among others, are seeing more pregnant participants as well. While the outcomes of these classes have not been studied extensively in the pregnant population, the mind-body orientation they employ is known to facilitate relaxation and reduce stress. Most women feel that although pregnancy is a happy, exciting time for them, it is also a stressful time. Any major change in one's life, good or bad, can create stress—and a new baby certainly changes one's life. Classes such as these can be a great opportunity for effective management of stress. Other relaxation techniques, such as progressive relaxation, visualization, and breathing techniques, can easily be incorporated into the cool-down/stretch portion of any group exercise class, and will especially benefit the pre- or postnatal woman. Participants should be cautioned to stretch or perform exercise movements in an average to normal ROM to protect potentially hypermobile joints. Additionally, the GFI can reassure the pregnant participant that the stress or anxiety she feels is a normal part of pregnancy, and help equip her with tools she can use once the baby arrives.

Strength Training

Strength training is a beneficial and safe activity during a normal, uncomplicated pregnancy if the standard safety rules of resistance exercise training are adhered to. Safety suggestions include staying in control of the resistance, moving through a functional ROM, using slow, appropriate speeds for the exercise, and avoiding the **Valsalva maneuver** and the supine position (Sinclair, 1992; Work, 1989). Problems could arise if the participant tends to jerk, swing, perform the exercise too quickly, or use poor control when she is lifting. Functional ROM should match (not exceed) the prepregnancy range to protect the joints from injury. Exercises done in the supine position should be modified after the first trimester; a semirecumbent position (wherein the participant is propped up on pillows or an incline platform with the back supported) is often an acceptable modification. Overhead lifting should be avoided to prevent irritation or injury to the low back due to the decreased ability of the weakened abdominals to stabilize the torso against the pull of the belly (Artal, 1992).

Functional strength training is recommended for pregnant participants. Exercises should be selected based on the physical demands a new mom will face. Extended periods of time spent carrying, lifting, nursing, and holding an infant place the postpartum participant at risk for upper- and lower-back strain and injury. The emphasis during prenatal training is to develop the muscular strength and endurance necessary to ward off the chronic aches and pains common in new moms. Regular strength training will also help to reduce the time needed to resume normal **activities of daily living (ADL)** without undue fatigue.

A general guideline for strength training in pregnancy put forth by ACSM recommends a program that incorporates all major muscle groups with a resistance that can be performed to the point of moderate fatigue with 12 to 15 repetitions (ACSM, 2014). However, specific repetition and load recommendations should be determined based on a partici-

pant's exercise history, state of pregnancy, motivation, and other variables. Repetitions in the range of 10 to 15 would be appropriate for the pregnant woman who is new to strength training, while a woman who has been lifting regularly and is in the early prenatal stages may safely perform eight to 12 repetitions and make very few changes, if any, to her current program. GFIs teaching group strength training classes will need to pay close and constant attention to the pregnant participants' technique, biomechanics, and exercise choice, giving modifications as necessary.

All exercises should be performed with smooth and controlled speed and a ROM that allows the exerciser to maintain proper alignment and comfort. If any exercise stimulates discomfort it should be immediately discontinued. Special attention should be given to teaching proper body mechanics when moving to a seated position or rising from the floor (see Figure 7-5).

Neck

Neck ROM activities help to reduce tension. After muscles are warmed, stretch the sternocleidomastoid, levator scapulae, and upper trapezius to further relieve tension and reduce the forward-head position associated with poor postural alignment. Complete the neck stretches with an examination of proper head and neck alignment.

Shoulder Girdle

To correct suspected muscle imbalances, begin with a warm-up and stretch of the scapula levators, scapula protractors, and shoulder internal rotators. Balance this with scapular retraction exercises of the rhomboids, middle trapezius, and lower trapezius. Correct body placement during scapular retraction exercises can reduce the chance of low-back extension; a slight lunge such as that used when stretching the calf muscles is a perfect adjustment. The abdominals and gluteals function as pelvic stabilizers and need to be incorporated into this workout to prevent hyperextension of the lower back. Shoulder external rotation exercises improve postural alignment by widening and opening the chest area. They also reduce constriction of the brachial plexus, a negative element that could be associated with thoracic outlet syndrome.

Shoulder and Elbow Joints

The workout of the anterior, middle, and posterior deltoids, the pectoralis major, and the latissimus dorsi may proceed as usual. Work on the biceps and triceps also does not need extensive modification. Maintaining functional ranges of motion during exercises, especially when weights are being used, will help prevent over-lengthening muscles, tendons, and ligaments associated with vulnerably loose joints. The body placement and positioning chosen for various exercises should facilitate circulation and promote proper alignment. Many arm exercises can be performed in combination with other exercises, such as standing legwork or stretches. If exercises are performed in a sitting position, back alignment may be facilitated by placing a towel roll just under the tailbone, which will tilt the pelvis slightly anteriorly and adjust for the rounded back (Figure 7-7). Sitting on the edge of a bench may be another comfortable sitting position when working on the shoulder and elbow joint muscles.

Wrist Joint

A small amount of time should be allocated to wrist ROM to promote circulation in a tight compartment area. Finger motion may also be performed to reduce swelling of this stagnant peripheral circulatory area. These movements can be used during arm exercises or choreographed into the aerobic segment.

Figure 7-7
Back alignment may be facilitated by placing a towel roll just under the tailbone to slightly tilt the pelvis anteriorly.

Low Back

These muscles are often tight and strained from the weight of the uterus pulling the abdominal wall and pelvis forward, resulting in the exaggerated lumbar lordosis posture. The class goal for this area is to relax these muscles to improve posture and decrease possible back pain. ROM exercises may be used to warm these muscles, followed by stretches to encourage them to lengthen and relax. Back ROM consists of flexion, extension, **lateral flexion,** and rotation. The many possible exercises and stretches for the low back include side bends, twists, standing back rolls, pelvic tilts, pelvic rotations, pelvic side lifts, cat and camel stretches (Figure 7-8), lateral rolls, tail wags, modified press-ups, cross backs, knee-to-chest stretches, and knee rolls. Please refer to ACE's *Pre- and Post-Natal Fitness* for a more complete collection of photo illustrations of various exercises and stretches.

Figure 7-8
The cat stretch

Figure 7-9
The side-lying position easily replaces the supine position for many abdominal exercises.

Abdominal Wall

The abdominal wall seems to be of particular concern to GFIs. The concern is probably derived from attempting to maintain abdominal strength while avoiding supine hypotension and diastasis recti. Concern is definitely warranted, since most abdominal workouts are performed in the supine position. Exercising in the supine position may induce supine hypotension syndrome and place excessive mechanical stress on the abdominal wall along the linea alba, especially in mid- to late-pregnancy. Positioning participants in a semirecumbent position removes the constricting uterine pressure from the inferior vena cava and aorta and reduces the direct gravitational strain on the linea alba. Many conventional abdominal exercises may be easily modified for the side-lying position (Figure 7-9). For additional support to the linea alba, the abdominal wall may be splinted with crossed arms and hands (Noble, 1995). Stress to the inguinal ligament is reduced when the hip and knee joints remain flexed and rolled

to the side, as in the side-lying position. Besides the usual curl-up abdominal exercises, experiment with various pelvic tilt and abdominal compression exercises. This group of exercises is essential for maintaining postural alignment and pelvic stability. They may be performed in a variety of positions, from standing to the all-fours position. Abdominal compression should be combined with other exercises throughout class to help maintain proper pelvic alignment.

Pelvic Floor

The introduction of Kegel exercises is essential. There are numerous routines for performing Kegel exercises. For example, GFIs can have participants begin with an **isometric** contraction of the pelvic floor, feel the muscles lift and tighten, hold for a slow count of 10, then relax the muscles for another count of 10 and repeat. Most participants will have difficulty identifying and isolating these muscles if they have not performed Kegels before. Since it is impossible for a GFI to know if participants are performing them correctly, effective cues are essential. Asking participants to contract the muscles they would use to stop urinary flow improves awareness and control of these muscles (Noble, 1995). Another technique is to imagine an elevator going up and down as the pelvic floor is lifted. Stopping the elevator on each floor is a variation that requires more muscle control (Noble, 1995).

Kegel exercises can be integrated in a class along with abdominal and gluteal exercises. For example, initiate a semirecumbent curl-up, lift for two counts, hold for two counts, incorporate a Kegel during the hold for two counts, then lower for two counts and repeat the sequence again. Suggest that each participant choose a cue to remind herself to Kegel outside of class; when they brush their teeth, talk on the phone, cough, sneeze, or laugh, they can be cued to Kegel. A suggested workout program includes four daily sets of 10 initially, working up to four daily sets of 25.

Hip Flexors

The hip flexor muscles are often tight as a result of the prenatal posture. The fact that people tend to spend a large part of their day sitting causes them to shorten. Therefore, the emphasis in class is to stretch and relax them. Care should be taken not to hyperextend the low back when performing hip flexor stretches in the standing, kneeling, or side-lying positions.

Hip Extensors

The role of the hip extensors is to oppose the hip flexors' pull of the pelvis anteriorly and to assist the abdominals in their role of tilting the pelvis posteriorly. When assisting with the posterior pelvic tilt, the hip extensors also help alleviate the strain placed on the sacroiliac joint. Standing may be a more comfortable position for gluteus maximus workouts, since it seems to place less stress on vulnerable areas. The common all-fours and side-lying positions often place strain on the symphysis pubis, inguinal ligament, sacroiliac joint, and the lumbar spine and, therefore, may be replaced with the standing position. To facilitate support for the sacroiliac joint, hip

extension exercises are used to strengthen the gluteal muscles. To recruit more muscle fibers from the gluteal muscle group, perform hip extensions while the hip joint is abducted and externally rotated (Figure 7-10). Abdominal compression should be included in the exercises to assist in maintaining pelvic stability.

Figure 7-10
Standing hip exercises should be performed in conjunction with a posterior tilt of the pelvis triggered by abdominal and gluteal contractions.

Hip Abductors

To promote more fiber recruitment of the gluteal muscles, perform hip abduction while the hip is extended and/or externally rotated, in addition to in the neutral position. Participants should be encouraged to perform this exercise in a standing position, as with the hip extensors. This is another exercise that offers indirect muscle support to the sacroiliac joint. Incorporating abdominal compression will assist in maintaining a stable pelvis. A towel roll or the participant's arm may be used to support the neck and the abdominal wall, and thus maintain body alignment when lying sideways (Figure 7-11). If the inguinal ligament or the symphysis pubis is sensitive, the hip and knee joints should be

Figure 7-11
A towel roll or the exerciser's arm may be used to support the neck and facilitate proper alignment.

Figure 7-12
Hip adduction is performed with both the knee and hip joints bent to reduce the leverage of the leg.
Note: A towel roll can be used to support the abdominal wall.

flexed during hip abduction. This repositioning reduces the leverage weight and puts the inguinal ligament in a more relaxed position. If irritation still occurs, then the exercise should be deleted from the workout.

Hip Adductors

Because of the anterior tilt position of the pelvis, the tendons of the hip joint muscles are pulled slightly forward. The hip adductors may become tensed and strained in this new alignment. During hip adduction exercises, strain may occur in nearby vulnerable areas, such as the symphysis pubis, the groin area, or the inguinal ligament. If exercises cause a significant amount of stress on these areas, the participant may complain of discomfort during or after class. Modifications for hip adductor work may relieve the stress. Side-lying hip adductor exercises may be conducted with minute variations, such as use of a towel roll to promote body alignment (Figure 7-12). In addition, bending the hip and knee joints

reduces the amount of stress placed on the inguinal ligament, symphysis pubis, and hip joint because the leverage of the leg is reduced in this more relaxed position (Figure 7-13). If irritation becomes chronic or if the exercise feels uncomfortable, then adductor exercises should be deleted from the workout. Lateral movement such as side lunges in the frontal plane is best avoided because of the decreased stability of the pelvis during pregnancy.

Figure 7-13
The butterfly sitting position for hip adduction

Quadriceps/Knee Extensors

An important muscle group to strengthen is the quadriceps. Strength in this muscle group better equips the participant for the squatting and bending necessary in her daily activities. Activities such as getting out of a chair take on new dimensions with the pregnant body. The abdominal wall may limit the ability to lean forward and stand, and so the legs and arms must assist more in rising. Exercises that incorporate daily activities are most helpful. They not only train the muscles, but also educate participants on proper body mechanics when performing simple activities with a sometimes awkward pregnant body. Pretending to pick up a two-year-old child, take groceries out of the car, open lower drawers, vacuum, or any other daily scenario may be utilized. Safety for the knee joint is the same as with all populations, but remember that a greater weight is being carried. Deep knee bends or squats past 90 degrees of flexion should be avoided. Participants should remain around a comfortable 45 degrees of flexion. Avoid hyperflexion of the knee while bearing weight because of the extreme pressure this action places on the knee joint.

Hamstrings/Hip Extensors and Knee Flexors

The hamstrings may be tighter during pregnancy due to postural adaptations, such as the anteriorly tilted pelvis. ROM activities and stretches may be implemented to reduce tightness. The common supine hamstring stretch may be replaced with a standing or side-lying hamstring stretch to avoid discomfort and supine hypotension.

Ankle Joint

The main goals for this joint are to facilitate circulation and maintain flexibility. Warm-ups should include stimulation of the calf muscles and the anterior lower-leg muscles. Ankle ROM activities may help reduce swelling in the ankles by promoting venous return. Avoid extreme plantarflexion or pointing of the toes during all exercises, as this can easily initiate a calf muscle cramp, which may be relieved by dorsiflexing the ankle to stretch the calf muscles. A pleasant activity for cool-down or relaxation is a self–foot massage. Pregnant women's feet are overloaded with natural weight gain, and a massage can be very soothing.

Programming Suggestions and Modifications

The following suggestions and modifications may be implemented as needed to further individualize programming for the prenatal exerciser:

- Design longer warm-ups to soothe vulnerable areas, such as the inguinal, round, and broad ligaments.
- Demonstrate and emphasize proper alignment to be used throughout class.
- Keep legs moving while standing to stimulate sluggish venous return.
- Choose positions to give the participant the best workout within her comfort zone while maintaining proper body alignment.
- Replace supine positions with semirecumbent and side-lying positions, and replace prone positions with an all-fours position or an elbows-and-knees position.

Many positions may be easier with the use of towel rolls or pillows to help maintain body alignment. Changing positions often in class may facilitate circulation, but be aware that simply moving from the left side to the right side can be a strain if good body mechanics are not used. There are an infinite number of exercises for each muscle of the body. Use creativity to discover exercises to train muscles without causing discomfort for the pregnant participant. Experiment with methods to challenge participants appropriately.

The prenatal exerciser presents many interesting challenges to a GFI. From the initial warm-up through the final cool-down, numerous factors must be considered to make an exercise program both safe and effective for the pregnant exerciser. Table 7-9 summarizes an entire prenatal class format.

Table 7-9

Prenatal Class Format

Carefully observe each individual for signs of stress, strain, discomfort, and/or fatigue. Always be prepared to show modifications of exercises to meet each participant's personal needs.

Warm-up		General movements to increase muscle temperature Normal joint range of motion (ROM): Neck, shoulders, wrist, pelvis, hips, knees, and ankles Emphasis on back, pelvis, and hip joints Stimulate postural alignment Keep movements slow, controlled, and comfortable Gradually increase ROM
Nonimpact Aerobics	Intensity	Perceived exertion, fairly light to somewhat hard Breathing rate, conversational
	Duration	Depends on each participant's fitness level and state of pregnancy
	Mode	Nonbouncy, nonjerky, and rhythmical Contract–relax, smooth, and flowing Large, controlled ROM of arms and legs Maximize traveling; minimize standing in place Avoid quick changes of direction
Cool-down I		Easy, pumping leg movement to facilitate circulation (ankle ROM, anterior lower leg stimulated) Stretches—easy positions, not to maximum ROM or tension
Body Work (Muscular strength, endurance, and flexibility)	Positions	Varied to promote circulation (standing, sitting, or side-lying)
	Upper body	Deltoids, triceps, pectorals, biceps, middle and lower trapezius (stimulate scapular retraction and posture here and throughout class)
	Lower body	Quadriceps, hips (extension, abduction, and adduction in controlled repetitions; keep knees and hips slightly bent to eliminate strain to commonly irritated areas)
	Abdominals	Avoid or limit time in the supine position in those past the first trimester
		Slow repetitions, smaller ROM, low lift, knees and hips bent, predominantly from side
		Alternative: use stability ball as an incline
		Abdominal compression exercises
		Pelvic tilts and pelvic stabilization exercises
		Attention to posture with all standing activity
	Additional	Exhale during contraction; inhale as relaxing
		Remember modifications for those with diastasis recti
		Pelvic tilts as well as back ROM exercise (e.g., cat-camel stretch*) are welcomed throughout class whether standing, sitting, or lying
Cool-down II		Final stretching; low-back stretch Relaxation, visualizations, and deep breathing Neck ROM and stretches Normalize circulation for standing

* The "camel" portion of this exercise can help alleviate low-back pain for some women, especially early in pregnancy. However, for some women in the later stages of pregnancy, with larger and heavier bellies and weakened abdominal muscles, this position puts a direct gravitational pull on those muscles. Some women may not have the strength to counter these forces effectively. In these instances, it is potentially uncomfortable for the low back and it may also add to the risk of diastasis recti.

Postnatal Exercise

Returning to exercise after delivery is like going backward through pregnancy. The situation is similar to the relationship between a warm-up and cool-down; they mirror each other, but in reverse. All of the things a woman does to prepare for and endure pregnancy continue to be done in the postpartum period to slowly return to prepregnancy status.

The first priority after delivery is to bond with one's baby. The second priority is to resume Kegel exercises as soon as possible. The pelvic floor has been traumatized during delivery by severe stretching and possibly episiotomy or tears. Kegels after delivery may be a little scary, since the incision may be felt. The GFI should encourage postnatal participants to perform Kegels because these actions can help the healing process of the pelvic floor. Before intense abdominal exercises can be considered, the pelvic floor should be rehabilitated.

Postpartum Return to Exercise

The suggested time for returning to group exercise activities is after the participant's postpartum doctor appointment, or six weeks after delivery. Factors that may determine postpartum return include complications of labor and delivery, uterine involution, pelvic floor healing, prepregnancy fitness levels, and self-motivation. Before this appointment, gentle walking can be resumed and gradually progressed if the participant desires.

Walking will help tone and strengthen the muscles of the lower body and, to some extent, the torso. During labor and delivery, the muscles of the pelvic floor undergo considerable stress and become relaxed and weakened. Temporary urinary stress incontinence is a common problem and may make exercise like running or aerobics difficult. The low-impact nature of walking helps to minimize this problem. Additionally, it has been shown that women who exercise during pregnancy and in the early postpartum months have a shorter duration of urinary stress incontinence than those who do not (Clapp, 1998). Focusing on good spinal alignment and form while walking will allow the body to strengthen important postural muscles in the torso that have become weakened by the shift in COG created by the increased size of the uterus during pregnancy.

When a participant returns to group exercise classes, advise her to gradually build back up to prepregnancy exercise levels. Remind her to listen to her body, exercise comfortably hard, but not to overdo it. Goals at this time are often unrealistic. A return to prepregnancy body weight and composition will take six months to one year in most cases. An instructor can help set realistic goals and create an environment that discourages weight loss as the sole reason to exercise.

As the postpartum participant rejoins the group exercise class, remember that caring for an infant is a 24-hours-a-day, seven-days-a-week commitment. Personal time often disappears, sleep is diminished, and a feeling of being overwhelmed coupled with fatigue may cause increased tension and anxiety. This can affect not only the new mom's health and well-being, but also her relationship to the baby and other family members. One out of four first-time moms experience these feelings to such a degree that postpartum depression occurs. Help new moms learn to recognize this "overwhelmed" feeling in the early stages and encourage them to create some time for self-care. This time can help them develop the necessary coping skills. Exercise has been shown to help reduce stress and create significant gains in general psychological well-being. Studies have indicated that women who engage in regular exercise programs before, during, and after pregnancy have higher levels of self-esteem, which has been linked to a reduction in symptoms of postpartum depression (Artal, 1992).

Postpartum Musculoskeletal Conditions

Many women find that the back pain they experienced during pregnancy is relieved once the baby is born. However, attention should still be placed on low-back health. The weight of the uterus is no longer pressing against the abdominal wall, but the abdominal wall is now loose and nonsupportive to the low back. The use of good body mechanics is crucial during this hectic, new period. Poor body mechanics and postural adjustments, in combination with the fatigue experienced by a new mother, can easily predispose her to back pain unless these muscles are retrained and are again able to effectively stabilize the spine.

Breast weight is increased for lactation, which pulls the shoulders and scapulae forward, exaggerating the thoracic kyphotic ("cuddling") posture. Prior to delivery, participants should be instructed on shoulder external rotation and scapular retraction exercises for the postpartum period. If a participant plans to push a stroller while walking, she should make sure the handles are high or use handle extenders; handles that are too low will exacerbate thoracic kyphosis and make good spinal alignment impossible. If the handles are raised, she can focus on scapular retraction and maintenance of a neutral head and pelvis while she walks. Good breast support during postpartum exercise is essential, especially for the nursing mother. Bras that compress the breasts against the chest are preferable

to those that lift, but they should be changed immediately after exercise to avoid discomfort or inhibition of milk production. Some women find layering two sports bras gives them better support during exercise.

Diastasis recti is of less concern after delivery than during pregnancy due to the fact that the internal mechanical stress on the abdominals (i.e., the baby) is no longer exerting force against them. However, participants should still be advised to evaluate their abdominal wall for the extent of separation that exists. All participants will have some separation; one to two fingers is considered normal. Although research has not shown abdominal hernias to result from postpartum crunches (Clapp, 1998), if the gap is three fingers or wider, special care and attention to strengthening is warranted. An intelligent progression from early isometric abdominal exercises to pelvic tilts and pelvic stabilization exercises to head raises and partial crunches will rapidly improve abdominal tone and facilitate closure of this gap. For participants with wide separations, it is prudent to avoid abdominal exercises that involve spinal rotation. The other abdominal muscles that are indirectly attached to the rectus abdominis can exert a pull that may widen the gap as they shorten. Noble's splinting abdominal exercise is a cautious first choice for early abdominal curl-up exercises (Noble, 1995) (Figure 7-14). To do this exercise, the participant lays supine over a towel that is placed under the middle and lower back. With knees bent and hands holding the opposite ends of the towel, the participant assists in pulling the area of the muscle that is separated together (toward the midline of the body) while slowly raising the head to chest level. This motion should continue until just before the bulging begins, while exhaling. While inhaling, the participant then slowly lowers the head

Figure 7-14
Splinting
abdominal
exercise

back down to the floor. Remind participants that they should focus on using their abdominals throughout the day. Abdominal compression (i.e., pulling the navel toward the spine while slowly and forcibly exhaling) can be done whenever they think of it to help strengthen the transverse abdominals and improve **kinesthetic awareness.** To balance the abdominal workout, they should perform back extension and scapular retraction exercises as well.

Resuming Exercise After Caesarean Delivery

Caesarean section, also called C-section, is a major abdominal surgery and, as such, results in pain and tenderness in the abdomen for some time, as well as considerable fatigue. Most Caesarean incisions do not actually cut the abdominal muscles; the incision is made through the skin and the doctor pushes aside the muscles to open the uterus and deliver the baby. Due to the advances in surgical procedures, many women who have undergone C-section are ready to resume intermittent walking or other gentle forms of exercise by two weeks postpartum. During this time, the degree of discomfort, fatigue, and motivation will determine activity levels. Vigorous exercise is to be avoided; the goal is to encourage the

healing process by performing rehabilitative exercises and getting adequate rest for the recovery process. Postpone re-entry into a structured exercise program until a doctor's clearance has been obtained after the six-week check-up. Women who have had C-sections may then participate in the same postpartum exercise programs as women who have had vaginal births, with similar guidelines. Any activity causing pain should be avoided. While most incisions from C-section heal without complications, some may develop scar tissue or adhesions that cause discomfort months after the surgery. Massage can sometimes be of help in these cases.

Breastfeeding and Exercise

New mothers are often concerned that exercise may affect the quality or quantity of breast milk. Research has shown that regular, sustained, moderate- to high-intensity exercise does not impair the quality or quantity of breast milk (Dewey, 1998). However, in a minority of women, exercise that is **anaerobic** in nature (e.g., high-intensity interval training) may increase lactic acid levels in breast milk enough to cause a sour taste and decrease infant suckling (Wallace, Inbar, & Ernsthausen,1992). Only minor changes in the lactic acid content of breast milk appear after more typical workouts, and these small amounts do not affect infant suckling behavior (Wallace, Inbar, & Ernsthausen, 1994). If a GFI encounters a participant whose baby rejects post-exercise breast milk, he or she can offer the participant several solutions: decrease exercise intensity to prevent accumulation of lactic acid, nurse the baby before exercising, collect pre-exercise breast milk for later consumption (lactic acid will clear the breast milk 30 minutes to one hour after exercise), or pump and discard the breast milk produced during the first 30 minutes after exercise (Wallace, 1993). In sum, this is an infrequent problem that should not prevent any lactating woman who wishes to exercise from doing so.

Summary

Attitudes about exercise during pregnancy have changed dramatically over the past two decades. The stereotype of pregnancy being a time of "fragility" and "weakness" that necessitates near inactivity has long been discarded. This is largely due to the increasing body of scientific information regarding the safety and numerous benefits of maternal exercise, as well as anecdotal reports by thousands of active women.

Armed with the knowledge regarding the efficacy and safety of prenatal exercise, GFIs have a unique opportunity to help pregnant women acquire an exercise "habit," and to realize the benefits this provides. However, ACOG has established that there are some women for whom exercise during pregnancy is absolutely contraindicated, and others for whom the potential benefits associated with exercising may outweigh the risks (ACOG, 2002). It is outside the scope of practice of a GFI to attempt to diagnose any of these contraindications (see Tables 7-1 and 7-2). It is, therefore, essential that all pregnant or postpartum women obtain a physician's clearance before beginning an exercise program.

For more detailed information on exercise and pregnancy, refer to *Pre- and Post-Natal Fitness: A Guide for Fitness Professionals* from the American Council on Exercise, available at www.acefitness.org.

References

American College of Obstetricians and Gynecologists (2002). *ACOG Committee Opinion #267: Exercise During Pregnancy and the Postpartum Period.* Washington, D.C.: American College of Obstetricians and Gynecologists.

American College of Obstetricians and Gynecologists (2001). Clinical management guidelines for obstetrician-gynecologists: Gestational diabetes. *Obstetrics and Gynecology*, 98, 525–538.

American College of Obstetricians and Gynecologists (1994). *ACOG Technical Bulletin #194.* Washington, D.C.: American College of Obstetricians and Gynecologists.

American College of Sports Medicine (2014). *ACSM's Guidelines for Exercise Testing and Prescription* (9th ed.). Philadelphia: Wolters Kluwer/Lippincott Williams & Wilkins.

American College of Sports Medicine (2000). *Current Comment: Exercise During Pregnancy.* Indianapolis: American College of Sports Medicine.

Artal, R. (1992). Exercise and pregnancy. *Clinics in Sports Medicine,* 11, 2.

Artal, R. et al. (1990). Orthopedic problems in pregnancy. *The Physician and Sportsmedicine,* 18, 9.

Batada, A. et al. (2003). Effects of a nutrition, exercise and lifestyle intervention program (NELIP) on women at risk for gestational diabetes (GDM). *Canadian Journal of Applied Physiology*, 28, S29.

Boissonnault, J.S. & Blaschak, M.J. (1988). Incidence of diastasis recti abdominis during the childbearing year. *Physical Therapy,* 68, 7.

Borodulin, K.M. et al. (2008). Physical activity patterns during pregnancy. *Medicine & Science in Sports & Exercise*, 40, 11.

Bungum, T.J. et al. (2000). Exercise during pregnancy and type of delivery in nulliparae. *Journal of Obstetrics, Gynecology and Neonatal Nursing,* 29, 3, 258–264.

Clapp, J.F., III. (1998). *Exercising Through Your Pregnancy.* Champaign, Ill.: Human Kinetics.

Clapp, J.F., III. (1991). The changing thermal response to endurance exercise during pregnancy. *American Journal of Obstetrics & Gynecology,* 178, 3, 594–599.

Clapp, J.F., III & Capeless, E.L. (1990). Neonatal morphometrics after endurance exercise during pregnancy. *American Journal of Obstetrics & Gynecology,* 163, 6, 1805–1811.

Clapp, J.F., III & Little, K.D. (1995). Effect of recreational exercise on pregnancy weight gain and subcutaneous fat deposition. *Medicine & Science in Sport & Exercise,* 27, 2, 170–177.

Clapp, J.F., III, Lopez, B., & Harcar-Sevcik, R. (1999). Neonatal behavioral profile of the offspring of women who continued to exercise regularly throughout pregnancy. *American Journal of Obstetrics & Gynecology,* 180, 91–94.

Clapp, J.F., III & Rizk, K.H. (1992). Effect of recreational exercise on midtrimester placental growth. *American Journal of Obstetrics & Gynecology,* 167, 1518–1521.

Clapp, J.F., III et al. (1992). Exercise in pregnancy (S294-S300). *Medicine & Science in Sports & Exercise,* 24–6.

Clark, N. (1992). Shower your baby with good nutrition. *The Physician & Sportsmedicine,* 20, 5.

Daly, J.M. et al. (1991). Sacroiliac subluxation: A common, treatable cause of low-back pain in pregnancy. *Family Practice Research Journal,* 11, 2.

Davies, G.A.L. et al. (2003). Joint SOGC/CSEP Clinical Practice Guideline: Exercise in pregnancy and the postpartum period. *Canadian Journal of Applied Physiology,* 28, 3, 329–341.

Dempsey, J.C. et al. (2004). A case-control study of maternal recreational physical activity and risk of gestational diabetes mellitus. *Diabetes Research and Clinical Practice,* 66, 203–215.

Devine, C.M., Bov, C.F., & Olson, C.M. (2000). Continuity and change in women's weight orientations and lifestyle through pregnancy and the postpartum period: The influence of life trajectories and transitional events. *Social Science and Medicine,* 50, 4, 567–582.

Dewey, K.G. (1998). Effects of maternal caloric restriction and exercise during lactation. *Journal of Nutrition,* 128, 2 Suppl, 3865–3895.

Dunbar, A. (1992). Why Jane stopped running. *The Journal of Obstetric and Gynecologic Physical Therapy,* 16, 3.

Goodwin, A., Astbury, J., & McKeeken, J. (2000). Body image and psychological well being in pregnancy: A comparison of exercisers and non-exercisers. *Australia and New Zealand Journal of Obstetrics and Gynecology,* 40, 4, 442–447.

Hall, C. & Brody, L. (2005). *Therapeutic Exercise: Moving Toward Function* (2nd ed.). Philadelphia: Lippincott Williams & Wilkins.

Hummel-Berry, K. (1990). Obstetric low back pain: Part I and Part II. *The Journal of Obstetric & Gynecologic Physical Therapy,* 14, 1, 10–13 & 14, 2, 9–11.

Institute of Medicine (2009). *Weight Gain During Pregnancy: Reexamining the Guidelines.* www.iom.edu/Reports/2009/Weight-Gain-During-Pregnancy-Reexamining-the-Guidelines.aspx

Jacobson, H. (1991). Protecting the back during pregnancy. *American Association of Occupational Health Nurses Journal,* 39, 6.

Karsenec, J. & Grimes, D. (1984). *HydroRobics* (2nd ed.). West Point, N.Y.: Leisure Press.

Karzel, R.P. & Friedman, M.C. (1991). Orthopedic injuries in pregnancy. In: Artal, R., Wiswell, R.A., & Drinkwater, B.L. (Eds.). *Exercise in Pregnancy.* Baltimore: Williams & Wilkins.

Lile, A. & Hagar, T. (1991). Survey of current physical therapy treatment for the pregnant client with lumbopelvic dysfunction. *Journal of Obstetric and Gynecologic Physical Therapy,* 15, 4.

McMurray, R.G. & Katz, V.L. (1990). Thermoregulation in pregnancy, implications for exercise. *Sports Medicine,* 10, 3.

Noble, E. (1995). *Essential Exercises for the Childbearing Year* (4th ed.). Boston: Houghton Mifflin Company.

Oken, E. et al. (2006). Associations of physical activity and inactivity before and during pregnancy with glucose tolerance. *Obstetrics and Gynecology,* 108, 5.

Pivarnik, J.M. et al. (1991). Physiological and perceptual responses to cycle and treadmill exercise during pregnancy. *Medicine & Science in Sports & Exercise,* 23, 4.

Sampselle, C.M. & Seng, J. (1999). Physical activity and postpartum well-being. *Journal of Obstetrics, Gynecology, and Neonatal Nursing,* 28, 1, 41–49.

Schauberger, C.W. et al. (1996). Peripheral joint laxity increases in pregnancy but does not correlate with serum relaxin levels. *American Journal of Obstetrics & Gynecology,* 174, 667–671.

Sinclair, M. (1992). In training for motherhood? Effects of exercise for pregnant women. *Professional Nurse.* May.

Sternfeld, B. (1997). Physical activity and pregnancy outcome: Review and recommendations. *Sports Medicine,* 23, 33–47.

Sternfeld, B., Sidney, S., & Eskenazi, B. (1992). Patterns of exercise during pregnancy and effects on pregnancy outcome. *Medicine & Science in Sports & Exercise,* 24, S170.

United States Department of Health and Human Services (2008). *Physical Activity Guidelines for Americans.* http://www.www.health.gov/paguidelines/guidelines/default.aspx

Uzendoski, A.M. et al. (1989). Short review: Maternal and fetal responses to prenatal exercise. *Journal of Applied Sport Science Research,* 3, 4.

Wallace, J.P. (1993). Breast milk and exercise studies, *ACE Insider,* 3, 6–8.

Wallace J.P., Inbar, G., & Ernsthausen, K. (1994). Lactate concentrations in breast milk following maximal exercise and a typical workout. *Journal of Women's Health,* 3, 91–96.

Wallace, J.P., Inbar, G., & Ernsthausen, K. (1992). Infant acceptance of post-exercise breast milk. *Pediatrics,* 89, 1245–1247.

Watson, W.J. et al. (1991). Fetal responses to maximal swimming and cycling exercise during pregnancy. *Obstetrics & Gynecology,* 77, 3.

Wilder, E. (1988). *Obstetric and Gynecologic Physical Therapy.* Edinburgh: Churchill Livingstone.

Wolfe, L.A., Brenner, I., & Mottola, M. (1994). Maternal exercise, fetal well-being, and pregnancy outcome in exercise and sports science reviews. *American College of Sports Medicine,* 22, 145–194.

Wolfe, L.A. et al. (1989). Physiological interactions between pregnancy and aerobic exercise. *Medicine & Science in Sports & Exercise.* Supplement.

Work, J.A. (1989). Is weight training safe during pregnancy? *The Physician & Sportsmedicine,* 17, 3.

Yeo, S. et al. (2000). Effect of exercise on blood pressure in pregnant women with a history of gestational hypertensive disorders. *Journal of Reproductive Medicine,* 45, 4, 293–298.

Suggested Reading

Anthony, L. (2006). *Pre- and Post-Natal Fitness.* Monterey Calif.: Healthy Learning.

Artal, R., Wiswell, R.A., & Drinkwater, B.L. (1991). *Exercise in Pregnancy.* Baltimore: Williams and Wilkins.

Bursch, G.S. (1987). Interrater reliability of diastasis recti abdominis measurement. *Polyform Products Inc.,* 67, 7.

Clapp, J.F. et al. (1998). The one-year morphometric and neurodevelopment outcome of the offspring of women who continued to exercise regularly throughout pregnancy. *American Journal of Obstetrics and Gynecology,* 178, 3, 594–599.

Huch, R. & Erkkola, R. (1990). Pregnancy and exercise—exercise and pregnancy. A short review. *British Journal of Obstetrics and Gynecology,* 97.

Jones, R. et al. (1985). Thermoregulation during aerobic exercise in pregnancy. *Obstetrics & Gynecology,* 65, 340.

McMurray, R.G. et al. (1991). The thermoregulation of pregnant women during aerobic exercise in the water: A longitudinal approach. *European Journal of Applied Physiology,* 61.

Prentice, A. (1994) Should lactating women exercise? *Nutrition Reviews.* 52, 10, 358–360.

Schelkun, P.H. (1991). Exercise and breast-feeding mothers. *The Physician & Sportsmedicine,* 19, 4.

Scott Cheatham, DPT, OCS, ATC, CSCS, PES, is owner of Bodymechanix Sports Medicine & PT. He previously taught at Chapman University and is currently a national presenter. He has authored various manuscripts and has served on the exam committee for the National Physical Therapy Board Exam and the National Athletic Training Certification Exam. Dr. Cheatham is currently a reviewer for the *Journal of Athletic Training* and *NSCA Strength & Conditioning Journal,* and is on the editorial board for *NSCA's Performance Training Journal.*

Christine "CC" Cunningham, M.S., ATC, LAT, CSCS, owns Chicago-based performENHANCE, which helps adventure travelers physically prepare for their trips, in addition to training athletes and traditional fitness clients. Cunningham has more than 15 years of experience working with clients and athletes at all levels—professional, division I college, high school, and youth—and has been endorsed by NIKE, Inc.™ for her expertise in performance training. She is working on her Ph.D. in movement science at the University of Illinois at Chicago. Cunningham has served on many industry boards, including at the American Council on Exercise, the American College of Sports Medicine, Life Fitness Academy, and the Chicago Mayor's Fitness Council. She has authored many articles and book chapters on training and is a frequent industry lecturer.

CHAPTER EIGHT

The Prevention and Management of Common Injuries

By Scott Cheatham & Christine Cunningham

Musculoskeletal injuries present complicated challenges for group fitness instructors (GFIs). They are experienced by participants as well as instructors and can interfere with an individual's ability to participate. It is a difficult task to create an environment in which participants can achieve their varied fitness goals, while also addressing each of the participant's individual needs to ensure everyone's safety. Doing so requires knowledge of the factors associated with injuries, methods for prevention, and appropriate modifications for specific injuries.

The injury-related responsibilities of GFIs are to (1) prevent injury by carefully planning and executing every exercise class, (2) provide modifications for participants with injury limitations, and (3) properly handle injuries that may occur during a class (see Chapter 9). Execution of these responsibilities is challenging because participants attending a group exercise class have a wide variety of exercise goals, backgrounds, and physical strengths or limitations. It is the job of a GFI to encourage participants to work within their own individual limits and to inform them that they ultimately have control over their workout intensity. The instructor is there for the participants' workout, not his or her own, and should appropriately set the intensity of the class by example. It is important to remember that the risk of a musculoskeletal injury occurring or being aggravated is always present. Therefore, a primary objective for a GFI is to provide a safe environment for all participants.

New class formats are constantly being introduced into group exercise schedules. They range from **yoga** and martial arts to group strength training and indoor cycling. Classes are even leaving the aerobics studio and moving outdoors. Equipment ranges from traditional steps and microhurdles to indoor cycles and treadmills. Unfortunately, there are many new risks and potential injuries emerging with each new format. GFIs must be able to manage the risks and provide modifications for participants with injury limitations. Success is dependent on understanding musculoskeletal injuries, their causes, and **contraindications** for participation.

General Musculoskeletal Injuries

The following sections describe a few general types of musculoskeletal injuries. Specific injuries are discussed later in the chapter. As a GFI, it is important to be familiar with these injuries and know enough about them to prevent their onset and provide appropriate modifications during an exercise class. The suggestions given in this chapter should only be used as guidelines for exercise modification. Diagnosis and treatment of musculoskeletal injuries is the domain of the appropriately credentialed healthcare professional, not the fitness professional. Refer all participants with complaints of injury symptoms to their healthcare providers.

Sprain

A **sprain** refers to an **acute** injury to a **ligament** caused by sudden trauma to the joint. Sprains can occur at any joint, but are most common at the ankle and knee. Damage can vary from stretched ligaments to complete tears. Sprains are rated in degrees: 1st degree (mild), 2nd degree (moderate), and 3rd degree (severe). Symptoms of sprains include pain, localized swelling, discoloration, loss of motion, loss of use, and joint instability. A medical evaluation is recommended for sprains to rule out tears or associated **fractures.** Treatment for sprains by a healthcare professional ranges from conservative, using ice and rest, to surgery. Ligaments can heal, but the healing is dependent on the degree of injury and the blood supply to the damaged ligaments. It is these factors that determine the chosen course of treatment.

Sprains: Considerations for Group Exercise

- Choose exercise that does not involve the injured joint until the symptoms of sprain are minimal or no longer present.
- Gradually reintroduce activity involving the joint, since exercise introduced too early or too aggressively can increase the amount of damage.
- Avoid movement in the end ranges of motion. The instability of the joint caused by the damage to the ligament makes it more susceptible to further and recurrent injury.
- Monitor the participant for a return of symptoms or an increase in their severity resulting from the activity.

Strains: Considerations for Group Exercise

- Avoid introducing strenuous or ballistic exercise after a participant experiences a muscle strain until the symptoms are minimal or no longer present.
- Gradually increase the intensity of activity.
- Incorporate additional gentle stretching of the muscle before and after exercise.
- Confine movement to the pain-free **range of motion (ROM).**
- Monitor the participant for a return of symptoms or an increase in their severity resulting from the activity.

Strain

A **strain,** often called a muscle "pull," is an injury to a muscle, usually caused by overexertion.

Strains can be acute, occurring suddenly during activity, or can gradually develop from repeated overuse. Symptoms of a muscle strain are pain, loss of motion, and reduced strength. Swelling and discoloration are often difficult to see, depending on the location of the injury or how deep within the muscle the injury occurred. Bruising may be found below the actual injury site, where fluids can pool close to the surface of the skin. A healthcare professional may treat a muscle strain using ice, gentle stretching, and exercise. Gentle muscle activity promotes healing by assisting with circulation and reducing deep swelling.

Overuse Conditions

When the body is put through excessive demands during activity, it often results in overuse conditions such as **tendinitis, bursitis,** and **fasciitis.** Tendinitis (i.e., inflammation of the **tendon** or tendon–muscle junction) is commonly diagnosed in the shoulders, elbows, knees, and ankles. Typically, participants begin new activities or exercise programs too quickly and the tendon cannot handle this new level of demand, resulting in an irritation that triggers an inflammatory response. Tendinitis is a classic overuse injury caused by repeated stress without adequate recovery time. Symptoms of tendinitis include pain, swelling, and loss of function. High-repetition lifting or jumping, poor lifting technique, and repeated movement throughout the same ROM can cause this condition.

Bursitis is an inflammation of the bursa sac that surrounds certain joints. Acute trauma, repetitive stress, muscle imbalance, or muscle

219

tightness on top of the **bursa** can all contribute to this condition. Bursitis commonly affects the shoulders, hips, and knees.

Lastly, fasciitis is inflammation of the connective tissue called **fascia** (Anderson, Hall, & Martin, 2008). It most commonly occurs as **plantar fasciitis** (i.e., inflammation in the bottom of the foot toward the heel) and has been linked to various intrinsic and extrinsic factors such as poor gait mechanics and improper footwear, respectively.

Overuse Conditions: Considerations for Group Exercise

- Avoid high-repetition activity or heavy loading at the site of inflammation.
- For lower-extremity inflammation, assess the appropriateness of jumping, especially box jumps and other plyometric-type techniques with high loads.
- Use caution when incorporating ballistic movements, such as kicking and punching, that place high eccentric loads on the joints and that may put connective tissues at risk.
- Check equipment for proper fit. Repetitive movements, like cycling, can cause inflammation of the soft tissues if the equipment is improperly fit to the exerciser.
- Allow adequate recovery between sessions.
- Avoid very high repetitions or moderate to heavy loads in strength training and always focus on proper technique.
- Monitor the participant for a return of symptoms or an increase in their severity resulting from the activity.

Cartilage Damage

Cartilage is a dense, protective connective tissue. A specific type of cartilage, called hyaline cartilage, covers the ends of bones and facilitates the gliding of two bones against each other. While cartilage is found at various sites throughout the body, injuries to the cartilage of the knee are common among regular exercisers. Damage to the joint surface of the knee often involves damage to both the hyaline cartilage and the menisci cartilage (which act as shock absorbers).

The most commonly reported knee injury is damage to the menisci. The menisci have an important role within the knee due to their multiple functions—shock absorption, **stability,** joint congruency, lubrication, and **proprioception** (see Figure 8-7 on page 233) (Manske, 2006). Meniscal injuries predominantly occur from trauma or degeneration. When meniscal injuries are the result of trauma, they are usually associated with a combination of loading and twisting of the joint or occur in conjunction with traumatic injuries such as anterior cruciate ligament (ACL) tears (i.e., lateral meniscus) or medial collateral ligament (MCL) injuries (i.e., medial meniscus) (Manske, 2006). Older individuals with degenerative joints are more predisposed to meniscal tears (Goldstein & Zuckerman, 2000).

When a participant has a meniscal tear, he or she may complain of signs such as stiffness, clicking or popping with weightbearing activities, giving way, catching, and locking (in more severe tears). Symptoms may include joint pain, swelling, and muscle weakness (e.g., in the quadriceps) (Manske, 2006).

The cartilage under the patella (the kneecap) can also become damaged, resulting in **chondromalacia.** Chondromalacia is a softening or wearing away of the cartilage behind the patella, resulting in inflammation and pain. This is caused by the posterior surface of the patella not properly tracking in the femoral groove. Chondromalacia is commonly associated with improper training methods (e.g., overtraining or poor running style), sudden changes in training surface (e.g., from grass to concrete), lower-extremity muscle weakness and/or tightness, and even foot overpronation (i.e., flat feet). The affected knee may appear swollen and warm, and pain often occurs behind the patella during activity (Anderson, Hall, & Martin, 2008).

Cartilage Damage: Considerations for Group Exercise

- Avoid high-repetition activity or heavy loading of the lower extremity.
- Avoid introducing deep squats, cutting, pivoting, or twisting for as long as symptoms are present.
- Closed-chain activities, such as squats and lunges, can be performed initially from 0 to 45 degrees and progressed to 90 degrees.
- Open-chain activities, such as the straight-leg raise, side-lying abduction, and side-lying adduction, can be included at any time. However, knee extensions should be kept within a limited range from 90 to 60 degrees until the participant is cleared by a physician.
- Monitor the participant for a return of symptoms or an increase in their severity resulting from the activity.

Bone Fractures

The causes of bone fractures are classified as either low or high impact. Low-impact trauma, such as a short fall on a level surface or repeated microtrauma to a bone region, can result in a minor fracture or a **stress fracture,** respectively. Stress fractures often occur in distance runners, track athletes, and court sport athletes (e.g., volleyball and basketball) (Figure 8-1). It is important not to confuse stress fractures with **shin splints** (refer to "Shin Splints" on page 231). Stress fractures have the following specific signs and symptoms (Cosca & Navazio, 2007):

- Progressive pain that is worse with weightbearing activity
- Focal pain
- Pain at rest in some cases
- Local swelling

High-impact trauma often occurs in motor vehicle accidents or during high-impact sports such as football. These injuries are often disabling and require immediate medical attention. Other medical conditions

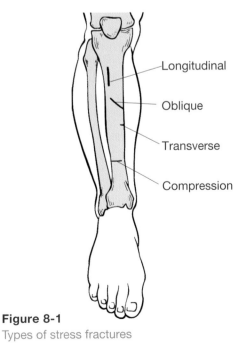

Longitudinal

Oblique

Transverse

Compression

Figure 8-1
Types of stress fractures

such as infection, cancer, or **osteoporosis** can weaken bone and increase the risks for fracture (Cosca & Navazio, 2007). Such fractures are commonly called pathological fractures given their association with disease.

Bone Fractures: Considerations for Group Exercise

- Since treatment for a bone fracture typically includes immobilization of the area (e.g., casting), participants returning to group exercise after healing will have strength and proprioception deficits in their affected limb.

- A gradual return to exercise is recommended with low-impact activities and low-loading strength exercises that prevent excessive stress.

- Easy balance and functional exercises are an appropriate class component to introduce to participants returning after healing from a fracture.

- Monitor the participant for a return of, or an increase in, pain and swelling resulting from the activity.

Tissue Reaction to Healing

When an injury occurs, the healing process begins immediately. The body goes through a systematic progression with three distinct phases. These phases must be understood if a GFI is going to be able to design safe exercise classes for his or her participants following injury.

The first phase is the inflammatory phase, which can typically last for up to six days, depending on the severity of the injury. The focus of this phase is to immobilize the injured area and begin the healing process. Increased blood flow occurs to

bring in oxygen and nutrients to rebuild the damaged tissue.

The second phase is the fibroblastic/proliferation phase, which begins approximately at day 3 and lasts approximately until day 21. This phase begins with the wound filling with **collagen** and other cells, which will eventually form a scar. Within two to three weeks, the wound can resist normal stresses, but wound strength continues to build for several months (Anderson, Hall, & Martin, 2008).

The third phase, the maturation/remodeling phase, begins approximately at day 21, and can last for up to two years. This phase begins the remodeling of the scar, rebuilding of bone, and/or restrengthening of tissue into a more organized structure (Anderson, Hall, & Martin, 2008). Exercise progression must always be conservative when working with individuals recovering from a musculoskeletal injury.

Signs and Symptoms of Inflammation

When the tissues of the body (e.g., muscles, tendons, and ligaments) become inflamed, they will elicit specific signs and symptoms of which the GFI needs to be aware. This is particularly important for participants who are post-injury or post-surgery. The goal is to give these individuals a challenging exercise routine that will not cause further damage to the injured area. The signs and symptoms of tissue inflammation are as follows (Magee, 2007):

- Pain
- Redness
- Swelling
- Warmth
- Loss of function

Managing Musculoskeletal Injuries

Pre-existing Injuries

If a participant suffers from a pre-existing injury, proper management is essential. People will often approach a fitness professional seeking advice for present or past injuries. A GFI must respect the defined **scope of practice** and refrain from diagnosing the injury. A thorough medical history and assessment will help a GFI make appropriate decisions regarding exercise programming. It is important to be able to answer the most important question: "Is this individual appropriate for exercise or should he or she be cleared by a medical professional?" This will ensure participant safety and provide the GFI with guidelines to follow. However, with local injuries (e.g., ankle sprains), the participant may be able to participate in a modified exercise class or a different group class using the non-injured parts of the body. For example, a participant with an ankle injury who is used to working out in a functional/core training class can engage in a **Pilates** mat class or yoga class and still work the whole body with exercises that do not load the ankle. After obtaining medical clearance and guidelines, the GFI can proceed with a program that incorporates the injured region.

Exercise Modifications

If a participant has a pre-existing condition, the GFI may need to provide modifications to certain movements during class. The participant should be monitored for any changes in symptoms, including pain. The following are some commonly reported symptoms of post-injury/post-surgery overtraining (Brotzman & Wilk, 2003):

- Soreness that lasts for more than 24 hours
- Pain when sleeping or increased pain when sleeping
- Soreness or pain that occurs earlier in a workout or is increased from the prior session
- Increased stiffness or decreased ROM over several sessions
- Swelling, redness, or warmth in healing tissue
- Progressive weakness over several sessions
- Decreased functional usage

Acute Injury Management

Acute injuries need to be handled quickly, but with caution. Participant safety is paramount. A GFI needs to refer the participant to an appropriate medical professional when an injury is serious enough (e.g., an individual who is unable to walk after twisting an ankle during agility exercises or who feels sudden shoulder pain and weakness after swinging a kettlebell). If an acute injury occurs, early intervention often includes medical management. The acronym P.R.I.C.E. (protection, rest or restricted activity, ice, compression, and elevation) describes a safe early-intervention strategy for an acute injury. In the following example, an ankle injury has taken place.

- *Protection* includes protecting the injured ankle with the use of crutches and appropriate ankle bracing.
- *Rest or restricted activity,* especially weightbearing activity, is advised until cleared by the physician.
- *Ice* should be applied every hour for 10 to 20 minutes until the tendency for swelling has passed.

- *Compression* involves placing a compression wrap on the area to minimize local swelling.
- *Elevation* of the ankle 6 to 10 inches above the level of the heart will also help control swelling. This is done to reduce hemorrhage, inflammation, swelling, and pain (Anderson, Hall, & Martin, 2008).

Flexibility and Musculoskeletal Injuries

Decreased flexibility has been associated with various musculoskeletal injuries, including the muscle strains and the overuse conditions described previously. When a muscle becomes shortened and inflexible, it cannot lengthen appropriately or generate adequate force. This inflexible and weakened state often leads to injury. To address this inflexibility and help prevent further injury, GFIs commonly include a stretching segment for their participants at the conclusion of class.

The following are **relative contraindications** to stretching that need to be considered to prevent injury (Kisner & Colby, 2007):

- Pain in the affected area
- Restrictions from the participant's doctor
- Prolonged immobilization of muscles and connective tissue
- Joint swelling (**effusion**) from trauma or disease
- Presence of osteoporosis or **rheumatoid arthritis**
- A history of prolonged **corticosteroid** use

There are also **absolute contraindications** to stretching (Kisner & Colby, 2007):

- A fracture site that is healing
- Acute soft-tissue injury
- Post-surgical conditions
- Joint hypermobility
- An area of infection

If a participant presents with any type of contraindication, the GFI should get further clearance from a medical professional prior to beginning a stretching routine.

Factors Associated With Injury

There are many factors that can lead to an injury, including flooring, footwear, equipment, movement execution, and class intensity. Other factors such as teaching technique, warm-up, and cool-down are discussed in other chapters. Be aware of all of these factors and assess each new class format for additional factors that may lead to participant or instructor injury.

Flooring/Exercise Surface

Flooring needs to absorb shock to reduce the negative effects on the bones and joints. Repeated jarring can result in stress fractures and tendinitis. Hardwood flooring should be suspended to provide additional shock absorption and reduce injury risk. In addition, hardwood flooring offers good traction for dynamic movements and allows for lateral movement and pivoting. Concrete is not recommended as a surface for group exercise. It absorbs little shock and can be quite dangerous in the event of a fall. Carpeting reduces the stress on the bones and joints, but can catch the edge of shoes during dynamic lateral movements or pivoting, resulting in ankle sprains or knee injuries. Carpeting is appropriate for floorwork-based classes such as yoga or stretching.

Outdoor classes take exercise onto grass, sand, and hiking trails. Each surface causes concerns for participant safety.

In general, natural surfaces offer good shock absorption, but may vary in terrain predictability and traction. Be aware of potential risks and choose the appropriate surface for the class format.

Is Softer Always Safer?

A common misconception is that softer running surfaces are gentler on the lower extremities and therefore safer. While it is true that running on soft surfaces can be easy on the joints of the lower body because of a dampening of the ground-reaction forces, running on too soft of a surface (e.g., sand or plush grass) can introduce a level of instability that may actually increase injury potential. These uneven surfaces appear to place an excessive challenge on the foot and ankle to maintain whole-body balance while running. Some research has shown an increased risk of Achilles tendon issues when running on sand surfaces compared to running on asphalt, which was deemed safer (Knobloch, Yoon, & Vogt, 2008). The following tips can help protect participants' lower extremities when they run on soft, uneven surfaces:

- Wear an athletic shoe with good motion control.
- Supplement running workouts with exercises that dynamically strengthen the foot and ankle joints (e.g., calf raises performed on a wobble board or a BOSU™).
- Avoid soft/uneven surfaces if participants have a history of lower-extremity problems, especially involving the ankle joint.

Footwear

Proper footwear will provide good cushioning, support, and flexibility. Many group exercise formats, including step training, kickboxing, and sport-conditioning classes, require that the ball of the foot absorb repetitive impact during the landing and pushing-off of dynamic movements. Footwear must provide cushion under the forefoot in addition to heel cushioning to reduce the possibility of injury to the foot from the repeated impact. Lateral movement demands support on the lateral aspect of the shoe to keep the foot from rolling over the base of support and causing an ankle sprain. Running shoes are designed for forward-movement efficiency and are not appropriate for classes with lateral or pivoting movements or repeated impact on the forefoot.

Various sole designs allow for good forefoot flexibility without sacrificing traction. They provide freedom of movement without slipping during cutting, stopping, or rapid changes of direction. Forefoot flexibility is also necessary for many flexibility-based classes in which full ROM is desired.

Surface, equipment, intensity, and quality of movement determine the requirements of appropriate footwear. Be sure to evaluate the class content and adhere to any footwear guidelines indicated for different formats.

Educating Participants on Proper Footwear

Proper footwear is mentioned several times in this chapter as a point of emphasis when working with individuals following lower-extremity injuries. GFIs can offer some basic guidelines to help their participants purchase appropriate footwear for their activities. When shopping for athletic shoes, the first step is deciding what type is needed. If a participant engages in a specific activity two or three times each week, such as running, walking, tennis, basketball, or aerobics, he or she will want a shoe designed specifically for that sport. Multipurpose shoes such as cross trainers may be a good alternative for individuals who participate in several sports or activities, such as cardiovascular and weight training, in a single workout. Ideally, they should look for a specialty athletic shoe store with a good reputation in the community. Their sales staffs are more likely to be knowledgeable about selecting appropriate shoes for the individual, considering his or her activity level and specific foot type. General recommendations include the following:

- Get fitted for footwear toward the end of the day. It is not unusual for an individual's foot to increase by half a shoe size during the course of a single day. However, if an individual plans to exercise consistently at a specific time, he or she should consider getting fitted at that exact time.
- Allow a space up to the width of the index finger between the end of the longest toe and the end of the shoe. This space will accommodate foot size increases, a variety of socks, and foot movement within the shoe without hurting the toes.
- The ball of the foot should match the widest part of the shoe, and the participant should have plenty of room for the toes to wiggle without experiencing slippage in the heel.
- Shoes should not rub or pinch any area of the foot or ankle. The individual should rotate the ankles when trying on shoes, and pay attention to the sides of the feet and the top of the toes, common areas for blisters.
- The participant should wear the same weight of socks that he or she intends to use during activity. Participants should look for socks that are made with synthetic fibers such as acrylic, polyester, or Coolmax® for better blister prevention.

It is also important to understand the factors that determine when shoes need to be replaced. If they are no longer absorbing the pounding and jarring action, the person is more likely to sustain ankle, shin, and knee injuries. Athletic shoes will lose their cushioning after three to six months of regular use [or 350 to 500 miles (~560 to 800 km) of running]. However, participants should look at the wear patterns as a good indicator for replacement. Any time the shoe appears to be wearing down unevenly, especially at the heel, it is time to replace the shoes. Additionally, if the traction on the soles of the shoes is worn flat, it is time for new shoes.

Equipment

Improper equipment set-up, fit, or use can cause injury. Class formats have adopted the use of a wide variety of equipment, from steps and tubing to bikes, hurdles, and treadmills. Each piece of equipment has specific set-up and fit requirements. Adhere to these requirements at all times to minimize the risk of injury. Check equipment regularly for wear and tear and replace items when necessary. If equipment is manufactured in various sizes, have all sizes available to accommodate all participants.

Misuse of equipment can also cause injury. Use caution when incorporating new equipment and/or movements into a group situation for the first time. Be sure to learn the intended use, limitations, and safety precautions for all equipment. Apply these to the development of the class format and specific movements. Instructor creativity without adequate consideration for safety may lead to unintentionally dangerous situations for participants.

Movement Execution

Improper execution creates the greatest risk for injury in a group exercise class. Large participant-to-instructor ratios make individual attention difficult and participants can often repeat movements incorrectly numerous times without correction, leading to injury. The best defense against movement error is to use teaching progressions, provide modifications, and explain methods for self-evaluation.

Progressions should gradually build complicated movements in a step-by-step fashion. Along the way, participants should be instructed on modifications for ROM, strength, and impact. Include tips for participants to use to determine if they are ready to safely go on with the next progression.

When incorporating movements from other disciplines, such as elite sport training or martial arts, be sure to learn what progressions and evaluations are used in the traditional settings to safely teach the movements. Incorporate these techniques into the class format to reduce the risk of poor execution and the resulting injury.

Class Intensity and Frequency of Participation

Class intensity needs vary from participant to participant. Training effects are achieved at individually relative exercise intensities, not absolute exercise intensities. In other words, maximum intensity for each participant occurs at a different rate of work, such that one intensity may be too easy for one participant and too hard for another. Intensity applies to heart rate, loading, speed of movement, and impact. A common teaching error is to assume that the intensity needed for a good workout for the instructor is the same intensity needed for all participants. A fit and experienced instructor may direct the class at exercise intensities that are too high for the less

fit or inexperienced participants. This practice can result in participant fatigue and overexertion, increasing the risk of injury. When appropriate and feasible, an instructor can avoid this problem by assessing the participants prior to each class. Always gear the intensity of the class to the participants.

Frequency of participation is a factor because individuals sometimes attend class too often without allowing for adequate recovery between sessions. Inform participants of the appropriate frequency of participation before each class session. Promote cross-training by suggesting alternative classes that use different muscle groups or are nonimpact for days when participants should be recovering.

Overtraining is also a concern. GFIs are especially at risk for overtraining. Teaching numerous classes a day without enough recovery can lead to sleep loss, elevations in resting heart rate, and injury. Apply the alternative class approach to teaching as well.

Pre-class Evaluation

The group exercise environment makes individual participant evaluation difficult. Because instructors usually do not know who will attend class on any given day, using a health and exercise history questionnaire to screen participants is not always realistic. With experience, an instructor can become very proficient at using on-the-spot indicators to assess the class prior to each session (see Chapter 2). Whenever possible, however, utilize a preparticipation screening to assess individual needs and limitations.

There are three on-the-spot indicators that can be used to gauge potential participants' limitations and alert the instructor to the type of exercise modifications he or she may need to provide during the class. These indicators are:

- *Age*—Participants may have age-associated limitations that require the GFI to offer appropriate modification of the class content. Be sure to monitor these participants and evaluate if they are in need of modifications throughout the class.
- *Posture*—Poor posture is associated with some muscles being short and tight and others being long and weak. This results in ROM being limited by the short muscles and strength or endurance being affected by the weak muscles. This imbalance makes proper movement execution increasingly difficult and increases the importance of providing modifications.
- *New participation*—New participants always make teaching more difficult. The more frequently an individual attends class, the less instruction he or she needs to modify movements and perform them safely. New participants require increased attention and should be watched during the class.

If possible, use the warm-up to incorporate movements that could indicate which participants need modifications or increased attention. Watch for ROM or strength limitations and coordination or balance problems. As the class progresses, incorporate modifications for these individuals to ensure safety and participation success.

Specific Musculoskeletal Injuries

The following sections cover some of the most frequently seen musculoskeletal injures, though there are many other injuries that GFIs may encounter. Use these guidelines to understand prevention and modifications for activity. Do not attempt to diagnose an injury based on the symptoms given. Many injuries have similar symptoms, but very different treatments and modifications for exercise. Always refer an injured participant to his or her healthcare provider. In the event that the guidelines provided here are different than those provided by a physician or physical therapist, follow the guidelines provided by the healthcare professional. The description of each specific musculoskeletal injury presents the anatomy involved, the common treatment used by healthcare professionals during rehabilitation, and the **prognosis** for recovery. Considerations for the GFI include suggestions for modifying class content for participants who have had previous injuries and methods for preventing injury when designing a class session. It is beyond the scope of practice of the GFI to diagnose an injury or prescribe rehabilitative exercise.

Plantar Fasciitis

Plantar fasciitis is microtearing of the fascia at or near its attachment to the calcaneus bone (heel) and is thought to be caused by repetitive overloading of the tissue at its calcaneal attachment (Kibler, Goldberg, & Chandler, 1991). Common treatment for plantar fasciitis is rest, ice massage, stretching, modifications in training intensity, and strengthening of the muscles of the foot and ankle. Orthotics to correct abnormal foot mechanics and surgery are used in some cases of plantar fasciitis. Evaluation of exercise footwear to ensure proper fit and support is also recommended. Full return to pre-injury ROM, strength, and function, including athletic participation, is expected in most cases of plantar fasciitis. However, the condition may recur in some individuals.

Plantar Fasciitis: Considerations for Group Exercise

- Encourage an extended warm-up prior to class.
- Incorporate additional stretching of the gastrocnemius, soleus, and plantar fascia.
- Avoid sudden increases in training intensity or frequency.
- Do not introduce plyometric exercises such as jumping or high-force loading of the foot until full strength and ROM have returned.
- Monitor the progression in the increase of the impact of the given activity.
- Suggest strengthening the muscles of the lower leg and foot to reduce the chance of recurrence of plantar fasciitis.
- Double-check that participants are wearing footwear appropriate for the class.
- Monitor the participant for a return of symptoms or an increase in their severity resulting from the activity.

Achilles Tendinitis

Injury to the Achilles tendon is common in athletes as well as the active population. The condition is most common in runners, gymnasts, and dancers. Other sports where it is common include track and field, volleyball, and soccer. Typically, older individuals are more affected by **Achilles tendinitis** than teens or children (Mazzone, 2002). This condition can eventually lead to a partial tear or complete tear (i.e., rupture) of the Achilles tendon if not addressed appropriately.

Individuals often complain about pain that is 2 to 6 cm (0.8 to 2.3 inches) above the tendon insertion into the calcaneus (the heel bone). The typical pattern is initial morning pain that is "sharp" or "burning" and increases with more vigorous activity. Rest will often alleviate the pain, but as the condition worsens the pain becomes more constant and begins to interfere with **activities of daily living (ADL)** (Mazzone, 2002).

Management includes controlling pain and inflammation by using modalities (e.g., ice), rest, and oral anti-inflammatory medication (Mazzone, 2002). Proper training techniques, losing weight, proper footwear, orthotics, strengthening, and stretching can help alleviate pain and prevent progression of the condition (Paavola et al., 2002; Mazzone, 2002). It is important for the GFI to monitor a participant's symptoms as he or she returns to activity. It is common for participants to exercise in the presence of discomfort and put themselves at risk for an Achilles tendon rupture. Individuals aged 45 and older are at higher risk for Achilles ruptures (Kettunen et al., 2006). GFIs must inform these individuals that Achilles tendinitis can progress to a rupture if not managed properly.

Achilles Tendinitis: Considerations for Group Exercise

- A gradual, pain-free return to activity is indicated for this condition.
- Overstretching of the Achilles tendon can cause irritation and should be avoided. Thus, the participant should be cautioned to stretch to tolerance and avoid overexertion.
- Progressively loading the Achilles tendon carefully with eccentric activity (such as performing heel raises on the edge of a step platform) can be beneficial to the participant.
- Regaining calf flexibility is a key component of managing this problem.

• The participant should be taught to properly position the back foot to point straight ahead, which will ensure that the target muscle will be stretched (Figure 8-2). Figure 8-3 shows alternative stretches for the calf.

Figure 8-2
Standing calf stretches

Gastrocnemius stretch   Soleus stretch

Figure 8-3
Calf stretch modifications

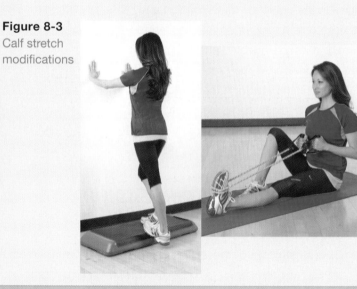

Lateral Ankle Sprain

A lateral ankle sprain occurs when the foot is inverted forcefully during weightbearing activity (Figure 8-4). Damage to the anterior talofibular ligament is most common; however, the calcaneofibular ligament can also be involved. Sprains range in severity from slight tears or stretching of the ligament

to complete ruptures of one or more of the lateral ligaments (Malone & Hardaker, 1990). Lateral ankle sprains are commonly treated with **RICE** (rest or restricted activity, ice, compression, and elevation) and progressive exercise to regain normal function. Surgical intervention is less common but may be used to correct chronic instability. The prognosis for a lateral ankle sprain is very positive and most individuals recover full ROM, strength, and function to pre-injury levels.

Lateral Ankle Sprains: Considerations for Group Exercise

• Limit motion to a pain-free range and intensity.
• Remind participants to resume activity only when released by a physician or when all symptoms of the injury are gone.
• Avoid incorporating cutting, jumping, and lateral movements until full strength and proprioception of the ankle have returned.
• Encourage workouts that are predominantly nonimpact to minimize ankle discomfort until the ankle has fully healed.
• Load closed-chain strengthening of the lower extremity, such as squats and lunges, according to the tolerance of the ankle joint.
• Double-check that participants are wearing footwear appropriate for the class. Ankle sprains frequently occur when participants wear running shoes in classes that involve dynamic lateral movement.
• Use lateral movement cautiously on carpet or uneven surfaces.

- Monitor the participant for for a return of symptoms or an increase in their severity resulting from the activity.

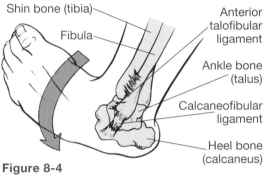

Figure 8-4
Lateral ankle sprain

Shin Splints

Shin splints are also known as **tibial stress syndrome.** The exact pathology involved in shin splints is not known. It is theorized that shin splints are a microtearing of the attachment of the muscles of the lower leg on the tibia (Figure 8-5). Pain is the major symptom associated with shin splints. The anterior tibialis is frequently involved, but all of the muscles that attach below the knee on the anterior tibia may be affected. Shin splints are an overuse injury caused by repetitive loading of the lower leg accompanied by weak musculature. Runners frequently experience shin splints from the repetitive impact. An inability of the foot to absorb shock due to weak arches can contribute to the onset of the condition. Lack of flexibility of the posterior muscles can also overload the anterior musculature, causing the microtearing. Footwear and exercise surface are major factors in the onset of shin splints. Treatment for shin splints includes ice, rest, stretching, and strengthening of the muscles of the foot and

lower leg. Footwear should be evaluated and orthotics may be prescribed. With treatment and rehabilitation, shin splints can be managed to allow full return to activity.

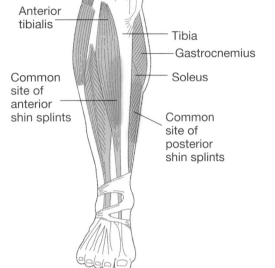

Figure 8-5
Site of pain for anterior and posterior shin splints

Shin Splints: Considerations for Group Exercise

- Avoid repetitive impact on hard surfaces.
- Do not drastically change the amount of impact in a class format, as this can lead to shin splints.
- Use shock-absorbing surfaces for all class formats involving impact.
- Encourage additional stretching of the anterior and posterior muscles of the lower leg.
- Incorporate additional warm-up time before class.
- Double-check that participants are wearing footwear with adequate support and cushioning in both the forefoot and heel.
- Watch indoor cyclists who do not regularly participate in weightbearing/impact class formats for signs of shin splints when taking a class with impact.
- Monitor participants for a return of symptoms or an increase in their severity resulting from the activity.

Patellofemoral Pain Disorders

The **patellofemoral pain disorders (PFPD)** may involve the patella, the femoral condyles, the quadriceps muscles, and/or patellar tendon (Figure 8-6). Together, these components are referred to as the extensor mechanism. Numerous conditions affect the extensor mechanism, including chondromalacia, patellar tendinitis, anterior knee pain, and patellofemoral malalignment (Shelton & Thigpen, 1991).

Figure 8-6
Components typically involved in patellofemoral pain disorders

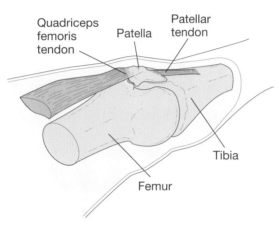

Quadriceps femoris tendon · Patella · Patellar tendon · Tibia · Femur

The majority of PFPD are considered overuse syndromes and, thus, are associated with overload or repetitive microtrauma to the knee. Training errors, improper footwear, anatomical abnormalities, and postsurgical complications all contribute to PFPD (Rintala, 1990). There are many similarities among the conditions, which allow the exercise guidelines to be generalized.

It should be noted, however, that each specific condition requires modifications that should be determined by a healthcare professional to ensure appropriateness.

Conservative treatment of PFPD is highly effective and generally used prior to surgical treatment. If nonoperative treatment fails, surgical management may be used. Rest, ice, lower-extremity strengthening emphasizing the quadriceps, lower-extremity stretching, and gradual functional progressions are all

used in conservative management of PFPD. **Nonsteroidal anti-inflammatory drugs (NSAIDs)** and bracing or taping may also be included. Prognosis for recovery depends on the specific cause of PFPD.

Patellofemoral Pain Disorders: Considerations for Group Exercise

- Avoid full squats or excessive knee **flexion.**
- Use strengthening within a range of eight to 20 repetitions, since most PFPD are sensitive to overuse.
- Encourage additional stretching of the lower extremity, as full ROM is essential for extensor-mechanism function and the reduction of PFPD (Hertling & Kessler, 1996; Shelton & Thigpen, 1991; Woodall & Welsh, 1990).
- With indoor cycling, elevate the seat as high as possible without causing the pelvis to rock. This reduces the amount of knee flexion at the top of the pedal stroke.
- Avoid repeated jumping or **plyometrics.**
- Monitor participants for a return of symptoms or an increase in their severity resulting from the activity.

Infrapatellar Tendinitis

Infrapatellar tendinitis or "jumper's knee," is an overuse syndrome characterized by inflammation of the patellar tendon at the insertion into the distal part of the patella and the proximal tibia. This injury is common in sports such as basketball, volleyball, and track and field due to the jumping aspects producing significant strain in the tendinous tissues in this area. Potential causes include improper training methods (e.g., poor running style, overtraining), sudden change in training surface, lower-extremity inflexibility, and muscle imbalance (Brotzman & Wilk, 2003).

Commonly reported symptoms include pain at the distal kneecap into the infrapatellar tendon. Pain has also been reported with running, walking stairs, squatting, or prolonged sitting (i.e., "theater sign") (Anderson, Hall, & Martin, 2008).

Management of infrapatellar tendinitis includes the following (Anderson, Hall, & Martin, 2008; Dixit et al., 2007):

- Avoiding aggravating activities (e.g., plyometrics, prolonged sitting, deep squats, and running)
- Modifying training variables (e.g., frequency, intensity, and duration)
- Proper footwear
- Physical therapy
- Patellar taping
- Knee bracing
- Arch supports
- Foot orthotics
- Participant education
- Oral anti-inflammatory medication
- Modalities (e.g., ice and heat)

Infrapatellar Tendinitis: Considerations for Group Exercise

- The focus of exercise should be to restore proper flexibility and strength in the lower extremity.
- Stretching and self–myofascial release of the quadriceps, **iliotibial (IT) band**, hamstrings, and calves will help restore muscle-length balance across the knee joint.

- Functional movement exercise that restores strength throughout the hip, knee, and ankle should be included to return the knee to proper function.
- Initially, high-impact activities should be avoided, as a slow return to loading activity is recommended to further reduce the chances of re-injury.

Anterior Cruciate Ligament Tear and Reconstruction

The anterior cruciate ligament (ACL) lies within the joint capsule of the knee (Figure 8-7). It attaches superiorly on the femur and inferiorly on the tibia. The ACL is instrumental in preventing the tibia from shifting forward on the femur, especially during forceful quadriceps contraction. Injuries to the ACL are commonly caused by rapid deceleration, such as a basketball player stopping suddenly, or by a direct blow to the knee that causes the knee to hyperextend (Roy & Irvin, 1983).

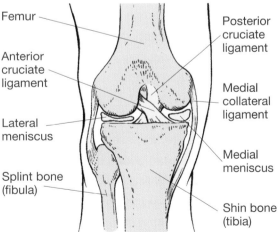

Figure 8-7
Knee joint anatomy depicting the anterior cruciate ligament (ACL), the medial collateral ligament (MCL), the posterior cruciate ligament, and the medial and lateral menisci

Instability of the knee, or the tendency for the tibia to shift during quadriceps contraction or weightbearing, is a concern when the integrity of the ACL is disrupted. This shifting can cause additional damage to the structures of the knee, such as the menisci. The amount of instability is related to the extent of the damage to the ACL. ACL injuries range from a partial tear to a complete rupture of the ligament. Partial tears are frequently treated with RICE and an extensive rehabilitation program to return the knee to full ROM and strength. Throughout rehabilitation, and all activity thereafter, the ACL is protected to prevent additional damage to the ligament, which may result in increased instability. Reconstructive surgery is often encouraged after large tears and complete ruptures to restore the stability of the knee and avoid further damage.

The most common procedure for ACL reconstruction involves taking out a portion of the patellar tendon and using it as a graft to replace the torn ligament. The lengthy rehabilitation after an ACL reconstruction is a careful progression to return full ROM, strength, proprioception, and function to the knee without damaging the graft. Range-of-motion limitations are used to avoid premature stress on the graft. A person's ability to contract the quadriceps reflects the state of tissue healing and the integrity of the graft during each phase of rehabilitation (Wilk & Andrews, 1992). All exercise involving the knee should be directed by a physician or therapist to avoid complications. Successful ACL reconstruction and rehabilitation results in the return to full activity, including participation in athletic competition.

ACL Tear and Reconstruction: Considerations for Group Exercise

- Do not allow participation in group exercise until the participant is released by a physician or physical therapist.
- The participant should adhere closely to all limitations in ROM and loading provided by the physician or physical therapist.
- Avoid cutting, jumping, sprinting, kicking, and pivoting unless specifically approved by a physician or physical therapist.
- Watch for difficulty with balance and movement execution caused by the loss of strength and proprioception after the injury. Provide safe modifications for these activities.
- Encourage participation in cycling or aquatic exercise classes after an ACL injury if directed by a physician or physical therapist.
- Incorporate additional stretching of the lower-extremity muscles before and after class.
- Monitor the participant for a return of symptoms or an increase in their severity resulting from the activity.

Greater Trochanteric Bursitis

Greater trochanteric bursitis is characterized by painful inflammation of the greater trochanteric bursa between the greater trochanter of the femur and the gluteus medius tendon/proximal IT band complex (Bierma-Zeinstra et al., 1999). This condition is more common in female runners, cross-country skiers, and ballet dancers (Anderson, Hall, & Martin, 2008;

Lievense, Bierma-Zeinstra, & Schouten, 2005). Inflammation of the bursa may be due to an acute incident or repetitive (cumulative) trauma to the area. Acute incidents may include trauma from falls, contact sports (e.g., football), and other sources of impact. Repetitive trauma may be due to excessive friction from prolonged running, cycling, or even kickboxing, or increases or changes in activity (Foye & Stitik, 2006).

Trochanteric pain and/or parasthesias (i.e., tingling, prickling, and numbness) often radiate from the greater trochanter to the posterior lateral hip, down the iliotibial tract, to the lateral knee (Little, 1979). Symptoms are most often related to an increase in activity or repetitive overuse, which irritates the bursa and causes irritation. The individual may walk with a limp (e.g., **Trendelenberg gait**) due to pain and weakness. This often results in decreased muscle length (e.g., quadriceps and hamstrings), myofascial tightness (e.g., in the iliotibial band complex), and decreased muscular strength.

When the participant is ready to return to gym activity, a written clearance from his or her physician may be necessary. He or she should slowly return to activity with an emphasis on proper training techniques, proper equipment (e.g., footwear), and early injury recognition.

Greater Trochanteric Bursitis: Considerations for Group Exercise

- Focus on regaining flexibility and strength at the hip.
- Stretching of the IT band complex, hamstrings, and quadriceps should be the focus to ensure proper lower-extremity mobility.

- Strengthening the gluteals and deeper hip rotator muscles is important to maintain adequate strength.
- Proper gait techniques in walking and running should be a priority.
- Avoid side-lying positions that compress the lateral hip, as the participant may still have tenderness over the affected area.
- Higher-loading activities such as squats or lunges may not be immediately tolerated.
- These individuals may benefit from aquatic exercise because the buoyancy of the water can unload the hips and help provide a gradual return to land-based exercises.

Iliotibial Band Syndrome

Iliotibial band syndrome (ITBS) is a repetitive overuse condition that occurs when the distal portion of the iliotibial band rubs against the lateral femoral epicondyle (Anderson, Hall, & Martin, 2008; Brotzman & Wilk, 2003). ITBS is common among active individuals 15 to 50 years of age and is primarily caused by training errors in runners, cyclists, volleyball players, and weight lifters (Anderson, Hall, & Martin, 2008; Martinez & Honsik, 2006). Risk factors may include the following (Anderson, Hall, & Martin, 2008; Martinez & Honsik, 2006):

- Overtraining (e.g., increased speed, distance, or frequency)
- Improper footwear or equipment use
- Changes in running surface
- Muscle imbalance (e.g., weakness or tightness)
- Structural abnormalities (**pes planus,** knee **valgus,** and leg-length discrepancy)

• Failure to stretch correctly

Participants often report a gradual onset of tightness, burning, or pain at the lateral aspect of the knee during activity. The pain may be localized, but generally radiates to the outside of the knee and/or up the outside of the thigh. The pain may appear as a sharp "stabbing" pain along the lower outside of the knee. Snapping, popping, or pain may be felt at the lateral knee when it is flexed and extended (Anderson, Hall, & Martin, 2008; Martinez & Honsik, 2006; Brotzman & Wilk, 2003). Aggravating factors may include any repetitive activity such as running (especially downhill) or cycling. Symptoms are often resolved with rest, but can increase in intensity and frequency if not properly treated.

The participant may present with weakness in the hip abductors, IT band shortening, and tenderness throughout the IT band complex (Martinez & Honsik, 2006; Brotzman & Wilk, 2003). As in trochanteric bursitis, this can cause a limp due to pain. A slow return to activity is recommended, with an emphasis on proper training techniques, proper equipment (e.g., shoe wear), and early injury recognition.

Iliotibial Band Syndrome: Considerations for Group Exercise

• The exercises used in class should focus on regaining flexibility (Figure 8-8) and strength at the hip and lateral thigh.
• Individuals with ITBS may not tolerate higher-loading activities such as lunges or squats. These activities should be introduced at a slower pace.

• Lunges and squats limited to 45 degrees of knee flexion can be introduced with a progression to 90 degrees and beyond, if tolerated.
• Aquatic exercise may also be beneficial if these individuals have pain with activity.

Figure 8-8
Iliotibial band range-of-motion exercises

Low-back Pain

Low-back pain is one of the most difficult conditions to understand. Low-back pain itself is a symptom that can be caused by a number of underlying conditions, including genetic abnormalities, muscle strains, sprains, disc herniations, and bony abnormalities. In general, symptoms of low-back pain include loss of motion, loss of strength, and reduced function. Each condition has contraindications and modifications specific to the injury. It is far beyond the scope of the GFI to try to determine the cause of a participant's low-back pain. Refer all complaints of low-back pain to a healthcare provider. The following guidelines can be used to provide modifications for movement and create a safe environment for exercise.

- *Avoid motion that causes an increase in pain.* It is not always true that back **extension** is bad. In some cases, trunk extension is preferred over flexion. In other cases, this is reversed. For example, spinal stenosis, a narrowing of the spinal canal due to aging, is a contraindication for lumbar extension. It is therefore always a good rule to offer a modification for any activity that requires the trunk to move into extremes of flexion or extension. This is necessary for loaded and unloaded (stretching) movements. **Rotation** of the lumbar spine may also be contraindicated, especially with herniated discs. Disc compression is greatest in the seated position, so seated rotation can be a risk. Modify the movement by using a standing or **supine** position.

- *Always engage the abdominal muscles for protection of the lumbar spine during motion.* The abdominal and back muscles work in concert to support and move the trunk without overloading the spine. Abdominal strength and endurance is essential and should be trained in the supine, prone, and standing positions. When standing, training involves the functional incorporation of abdominal contraction into movement so that the pelvis is stabilized throughout the movement. Always cue participants to remember to actively contract the abdominals for lumbar support. Modify movements that place high demand on abdominal support to accommodate participants who do not have the strength or coordination. Loaded squats, ballistic kicks, and end-range trunk motion are examples of high-demand activity. Failure to provide modifications can result in injury to the low back.

- *Emphasize the maintenance of good posture.* Poor posture can cause low-back strains and sprains, as well as potentially damage the discs and bony structures. Good postural alignment means that the head is aligned so that the ears are over the shoulders. The shoulders should be pulled back to align with the hips. The back is slightly curved forward at the lumbar region, with the top of the pelvis parallel to the ground. Excessive lumbar or thoracic curvature indicates poor posture and high risk of low-back problems. Cueing for correct posture is essential and participants with poor posture may require movement modifications to reduce the risk of injury. Avoid loading of the spine with increased curvatures (e.g., **lordosis** or **kyphosis**) or poor posture.

- *Encourage stretching of the trunk and lower extremities to maintain full ROM.* Limited ROM, especially in the hamstrings, has been associated with the onset of low-back pain. It is theorized that the hamstring tension reduces the ability of the pelvis to move properly, placing more mobility demands on the intervertebral joints. This can cause sprains and strains of the low back, especially with ballistic movements. Tight hip flexors can also alter pelvic mobility and cause lumbar lordosis (i.e., an increase in the lumbar curve). Flexibility is essential for proper execution of many group exercise movements. Participants without the necessary flexibility may stress their backs when trying to execute certain movements. Offer modifications for movements such as kicks, leg lifts, and advanced stretching.

Shoulder Instability

Anterior Shoulder Instability

Anterior shoulder instability is a weakness in the anterior wall musculature (subscapularis, pectoralis major, latissimus dorsi, and teres major) and/or stretching of the anterior capsule and ligaments that allows the humeral head to subluxate or dislocate anteriorly (Jobe & Pink, 1993). This condition can be caused acutely by a fall or blow to the shoulder. Chronic instability is a gradual onset of muscle weakness and progressive damage of the anterior structures.

Anterior shoulder instability is treated conservatively with rest, stretching, and gradual strengthening of weak muscles. Significant anatomical damage to the anterior structures is repaired surgically. If conservative treatment is appropriate and started early, there is a high rate of return to full activity. Postsurgical prognosis is dependent upon the surgical procedure used and the adherence to rehabilitation guidelines (Jobe & Pink, 1993). Different surgical procedures result in varying losses in ROM and function and, therefore, an exercise that is allowed after one type of repair may not be allowed after another. Always follow the guidelines for exercise provided by the healthcare provider.

Anterior Shoulder Instability: Considerations for Group Exercise

- Limit motion to avoid humeral abduction with external rotation or horizontal extension. An unstable shoulder can dislocate or subluxate if put in these positions.
- Be very cautious during all movements that place the shoulder in an externally rotated position, even with stretching.
- Avoid military shoulder presses behind the neck, pec flys, lat pull-downs behind the neck, and full-range or wide-grip chest presses because of the stress they place on the anterior shoulder (Litchfield et al., 1993).
- Encourage stretching of the posterior cuff.
- Discourage stretching of the anterior shoulder.
- Monitor the participant for a return of symptoms or an increase in their severity resulting from the activity.

Posterior Shoulder Instability

Posterior shoulder instability is less common, but it does occur. Posterior dislocations are rare. The mechanism of injury is usually a fall on an outstretched hand in a position of shoulder flexion, adduction, and internal rotation. More common are subluxations related to overhead activities such as throwing a ball or the serving motion in tennis. Individuals with posterior shoulder instability will often complain of pain when following through after throwing or swinging motions. Also, repetitive activities such as bench pressing or push-ups can stretch the posterior shoulder capsule, thus promoting instability.

A participant with posterior shoulder instability should avoid or minimize positions of shoulder flexion, internal rotation, and horizontal adduction. Contrary to anterior instability, closed-chain or weightbearing activities must be minimized or modified to avoid excessive stretch to the posterior capsule. Furthermore, any exercises that may force the humeral head posteriorly should be performed with posterior support or in the plane of the scapula to avoid excessive stretching of the capsule.

Posterior Shoulder Instability: Considerations for Group Exercise

- Positions of shoulder flexion, internal rotation, and horizontal adduction should be minimized or avoided.
- When restoring strength, the posterior shoulder musculature should be emphasized to provide secondary restraints to the posterior stabilizers of the shoulder.
- Rowing with scapular retraction, external rotation, shoulder extension, and horizontal abduction are important exercises with posterior instability.
- Activities such as push-ups, which drive the humeral head posteriorly, are often contraindicated. Bench pressing is often contraindicated. However, participants who want to continue performing this exercise should use a wider grip and avoid full elbow extension. This will limit the amount of horizontal adduction and decrease stress on the posterior capsule.
- Discourage stretching of the posterior shoulder.
- Monitor the participant for a return of symptoms or an increase in their severity resulting from the activity.

Shoulder Strain/Sprain

Shoulder strain/sprain occurs when the soft-tissue structures (e.g., bursa and rotator cuff tendons) get abnormally stretched or compressed. Strains most often involve a tendon, while sprains usually involve a ligament. Additionally, shoulder strains/sprains can result from an impingement secondary to the compression and end up as tendinitis. These injuries can eventually lead to rotator cuff tears if they are not managed properly (Anderson, Hall, & Martin, 2008). Impingement is particularly common in young individuals who participate in overhead activities such as tennis, baseball, and swimming. Middle-aged adults can also be at risk from doing repetitive overhead activities such as painting or lifting objects (Anderson, Hall, & Martin, 2008). In general, strains/sprains are common in the shoulder as a result of this joint's significant mobility and its sacrifice of stability to achieve it.

Participants who suffer from shoulder strains/sprains often complain of local pain at the shoulder that radiates down the arm. Aggravating activities may include lifting objects and reaching overhead or across the body or any movements that stretch the strained/sprained tissues. There may be swelling and tenderness in the shoulder that causes pain and stiffness with movement (Anderson, Hall, & Martin, 2008).

Shoulder Strain/Sprain: Considerations for Group Exercise

- Avoid overhead and across-the-body movements, as well as any movements that involve placing the hand behind the back.
- Educate participants on avoiding aggravating activities and improving posture and body positioning.

- Strengthen the scapular stabilizers (e.g., rhomboids, middle trapezius, and serratus anterior) and rotator cuff muscles to help restore proper scapulohumeral motion.
- Focus on stretching the major muscle groups around the shoulder to restore proper length to these muscles.
- Teach overhead-activity modifications, such as avoiding full extension of the arms and positioning the shoulders more toward the front of the body (i.e., in the **scapular plane,** where the shoulder is positioned between the **sagittal plane** and the **frontal plane**, approximately 30 degrees anterior to the frontal plane (Figure 8-9)

Figure 8-9
Shoulder press in the scapular plane

Rotator Cuff Strain

A rotator cuff strain is the overstretching, overexertion, or overuse of the musculo-tendinous unit of one or more of the rotator cuff muscles (Kisner & Colby, 2007). Symptoms of a rotator cuff strain include pain and loss of motion, strength, and function. Rotator cuff strains can be acute or chronic. Rest, stretching, and progressive strengthening exercises are used to return the shoulder to pre-injury function. The prognosis for return to full ROM, strength, and **functional capacity** is good following a rotator cuff strain.

Rotator Cuff Strain: Considerations for Group Exercise

- Avoid loading the shoulder joint in excess of the tolerance of the rotator cuff. Overloading might occur in the dumbbell press or pec flys, where the rotator cuff is too weak to stabilize the shoulder against the load needed to effectively stimulate the chest muscles.
- Watch for complaints of pain and altered mechanics that indicate that the load is too much for the shoulder.
- Do not fatigue the rotator cuff muscles with isolated exercise prior to executing movements that require their activity for stabilization. These movements include punches, medicine ball throws, and pressing or pushing exercise movements.
- Monitor the participant for a return of symptoms or an increase in their severity resulting from the activity.

Rotator Cuff Impingement

Rotator cuff impingement is a common overuse syndrome of the shoulder in athletes who participate in overhead sports (e.g., swimming, baseball, and volleyball) or individuals who perform repetitive overhead work (e.g., carpenters and painters). It is characterized as a pinching of the rotator cuff tendon under the coracoacromial arch when the arm is abducted (Roy & Irvin, 1983) (Figure 8-10). Rotator cuff impingement is treated conservatively with rest, stretching, and gradual strengthening exercises. Other treatments for impingement include various surgical techniques and anti-inflammatory injections. Each treatment is different in its approach to relieving the disorder and in the exercise guidelines. Impingement syndrome treated early, before anatomical damage has occurred, will likely return to full functional capacity, including participation in athletic competition (Jobe & Pink, 1993).

- Minimize the repetition of abduction or overhead motion, including lifts and arm swings.
- Do not have participants perform military presses, triceps pull-overs, lat pull-downs, or pull-ups behind the neck, as they are likely to exacerbate shoulder impingement (Litchfield et al., 1993).
- Monitor the participant for a return of symptoms or an increase in their severity resulting from the activity.

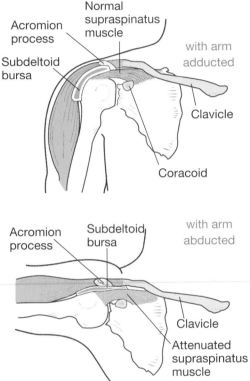

Figure 8-10
Impingement of bursa and supraspinatus under the coracoacromial arch with abduction movement

Rotator Cuff Impingement: Considerations for Group Exercise

- Encourage additional stretching of the posterior cuff.
- Discourage stretching of the anterior shoulder.
- Avoid active abduction and overhead arm movements unless pain-free.

Lateral Epicondylitis (Tennis Elbow) and Medial Epicondylitis (Golfer's Elbow)

Lateral epicondylitis, or **tennis elbow,** is an overuse injury affecting the musculotendinous junction of the wrist extensor muscles at the lateral epicondyle of the humerus (Figure 8-11). Repetitive activities involving the wrist, such as playing tennis, carpentry, or pruning shrubs, result in microdamage to the tissue.

Medial epicondylitis, or **golfer's elbow,** is an overuse injury affecting the musculotendinous junction of the wrist flexor muscle at the medial epicondyle of the humerus. Repetitive activities involving the wrist, such as throwing, striking a golf ball, or carrying a heavy suitcase, result in microdamage to the tissue.

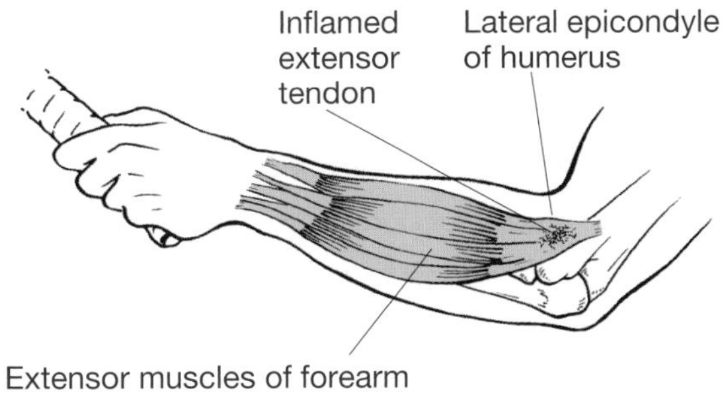

Figure 8-11
Lateral epicondylitis, or "tennis elbow"

These elbow injuries are associated with inadequate strength, power, endurance, and flexibility in the wrist extensors or flexors. The onset for both conditions is usually gradual. Conservative treatment consists of rest, ice, gradual stretching, and strengthening of the wrist extensors or flexors. Cortisone injections and surgery are used when conservative management is not successful. A return to full activity is expected.

Lateral and Medial Epicondylitis: Considerations for Group Exercise

- Encourage stretching for all motions of the wrist, including flexion, extension, radial/ulnar deviation, and **pronation/supination.**
- Perform wrist flexion and/or extension stretching before all activities that involve the wrist (e.g., punching, push-ups, and jumping rope).
- Use lighter loads for the wrist during repetitive motion to avoid overloading the tissue and causing pain during or after the exercise.
- Do not include high repetitions of wrist exercises.
- Avoid having participants hold hand positions for a prolonged period of time during cycling. Encourage frequent changes of position to avoid irritation.
- Monitor the participant for a return of symptoms or an increase in their severity resulting from the activity.

Carpal Tunnel Syndrome

Carpal tunnel syndrome is the most frequently occurring compression syndrome of the wrist. Repetitive wrist and finger flexion when the flexor tendons are strained results in a narrowing of the carpal tunnel due to inflammation, which eventually compresses the median nerve (Figure 8-12). Women are three times more likely than men to develop the syndrome and the dominant hand is usually affected first (Prentice, 1994; Calliet, 1978). Anything that narrows the carpal tunnel can result in this syndrome.

Carpal tunnel syndrome usually starts gradually with pain, weakness, or numbness in the radial side of the hand and the palmar

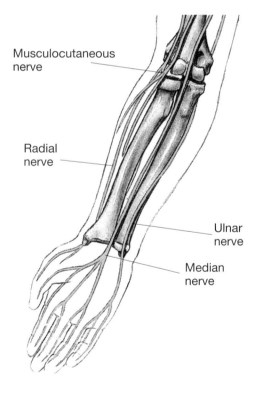

Musculocutaneous nerve

Radial nerve

Ulnar nerve

Median nerve

Figure 8-12
The nerves of the wrist

Source: Human Anatomy, 3rd ed., by Martini, F.H., Timmons, M.J., & McKinley, M.P. Copyright 2008. Reprinted by permission of Pearson Education.

aspect of the thumb. As the condition progresses, more specific symptoms begin to appear (Prentice, 1994; Calliet, 1978):

- Night or early-morning pain or burning
- Loss of grip strength and dropping of objects
- Numbness or tingling in the palm, thumb, index, and middle fingers
- Long-standing affects may include **atrophy** of the thumb side of the hand, loss of sensations, and **paresthesias.**

Carpal Tunnel Syndrome: Considerations for Group Exercise

- Participants may be prescribed wrist splints to wear during activity.
- Provide education on avoiding aggravating activities and improving posture and body positioning.
- Emphasize regaining strength and flexibility of the elbow, wrist, and finger flexors and extensors.
- Avoid movements that involve full wrist flexion or extension. These end-range positions can further compress the carpal tunnel, which can increase symptoms. Exercise should focus on the mid-range of these motions.

Record Keeping and Confidentiality

If a participant experiences any of the previously mentioned injuries or any other emergency-related event during the course of class, it the responsibility of the GFI to keep a record of the occurrence (see Chapter 11). After an incident, complete documentation of the event should be done by the staff member who was the most directly involved. Each facility may have its own type of medical emergency response report, but all should include the name of the victim, the date and time of the incident, what happened, and what was done to care for the victim and by whom. The names, addresses, and phone numbers of witnesses should also be documented.

This form should be filled out immediately after the event with as much detail as possible and kept on file for several years, depending on company policy and state law. If no form exists, the GFI should write down everything exactly as it occurred and keep that on record. If the victim or the victim's family decides to take legal action, this report is vital to the facility's defense, as well as that of the rescuer.

Other than sharing the incident report with the medical director and/or facility general manager, rescuers need to keep the information about the incident and the victim confidential. The **Health Insurance Portability and Accountability Act (HIPAA)** of 1996 is a federal law that ensures the victim's privacy by putting him or her in control of who has access to personal health information. This means that the event should not be discussed with anyone who has not received appropriate permission to view such information. The records of the event should be stored in a locked file drawer or cabinet or a secure, password-protected electronic file.

Summary

GFIs have several responsibilities regarding musculoskeletal injuries. They must (1) prevent injury by carefully reviewing the class environment and equipment and by thoughtfully preparing and executing every exercise class, (2) provide modifications for participants with injury limitations, and (3) properly handle injuries that may occur during a class. Success is dependent on knowing the factors associated with injuries, methods for prevention, and contraindications and appropriate modifications for specific injuries.

Symptoms of many musculoskeletal injuries include pain, swelling, loss of motion and strength, and reduced functional capacity. These symptoms are present in various degrees and combinations in most injuries. Acute injuries are the result of an immediate trauma. Chronic injuries are developed gradually from repeated stress over time. Both types of injuries can be caused by any number of factors, including footwear, flooring or exercise surface, equipment, movement execution, class intensity, and frequency of participation.

Other factors, such as teaching techniques and the inclusion of a proper warm-up and cool-down, are discussed in other chapters.

Specific musculoskeletal injuries can be described based on the structures involved and their symptoms. Every injury has different recommendations for modifying movements or class formats to avoid exacerbating the condition. Diagnosis and treatment of musculoskeletal injuries is the responsibility of a physician or other healthcare professional and is not within the scope of practice for a GFI.

Continuously changing class formats introduces new potential for injuries in every class. GFIs cannot forget their responsibility for preventing injury through proper design and execution of the class. Providing modifications for all participants based on their needs is difficult but essential to ensure an outstanding group exercise experience for everyone.

References

Anderson, M.K., Hall, S.J., & Martin, M. (2008). *Foundations of Athletic Training: Prevention, Assessment, and Management* (4th ed.). Baltimore, Md.: Lippincott Williams & Wilkins.

Bierma-Zeinstra, S. et al. (1999). Validity of American College of Rheumatology criteria for diagnosing hip osteoarthritis in primary care research. *Journal of Rheumatology, 26,* 1129–1133.

Brotzman, B. & Wilk, K. (2003). *Clinical Orthopedic Rehabilitation* (2nd ed.). St. Louis, Mo.: Mosby.

Calliet, R. (1978). *Rehabilitation of the Hand.* St. Louis, Mo.: Mosby.

Cosca, D. & Navazio, F. (2007). Common problems in endurance athletes: Meniscal tears. *American Family Physician, 76,* 2, 237–244.

Dixit, S. et al. (2007). Management of patellofemoral pain syndrome. *American Family Physician, 75,* 194–204.

Foye, P.M. & Stitik, T.P. (2006). Trochantaric bursitis. *E-Medicine Online Journal* (Web MD), Dec 21, 1–14.

Goldstein, J. & Zuckerman, J.D. (2000). Selected orthopedic problems in the elderly. *Rheumatic Disease Clinics of North America, 26,* 3, 593–616.

Hertling, D. & Kessler, R.M. (1996). *Management of Common Musculoskeletal Disorders* (3rd ed.). Philadelphia: Lippincott Williams & Wilkins.

Jobe, F.W. & Pink, M. (1993). Classification and treatment of shoulder dysfunction in the overhead athlete. *Journal of Orthopaedic and Sports Physical Therapy, 18,* 2, 427–432.

Kettunen, J.A. et al. (2006). Health of master track and field athletes: A 16-year follow-up study. *Clinical Journal of Sports Medicine, 16,* 2, 142–148.

Kibler, W.B., Goldberg, C., & Chandler, T.J. (1991). Functional biomechanical deficits in running athletes with plantar fasciitis. *American Journal of Sports Medicine, 19,* 1, 66–71.

Kisner, C. & Colby, L. (2007). *Therapeutic Exercise: Foundations and Techniques* (5th ed.). Philadelphia, Pa.: F.A. Davis Company.

Knobloch, K., Yoon, U., & Vogt, P.M. (2008). Acute and overuse injuries correlated to hours of training in master running athletes. *Foot & Ankle International, 29,* 7, 671–676.

Lievense, A., Bierma-Zeinstra, S., & Schouten, B. (2005). Prognosis of trochantaric pain in primary care. *British Journal of General Practice, 55,* 512, 199–204.

Litchfield, R. et al. (1993). Rehabilitation for the overhead athlete. *Journal of Orthopedic and Sports Physical Therapy, 18,* 2, 433–441.

Little, H. (1979). Trochanteric bursitis: A common cause of pelvic girdle pain. *Canadian Medical Association Journal, 120,* 456–458.

Magee, D.J. (2007). *Orthopedic Physical Assessment* (5th ed.). Philadelphia: WB Saunders.

Malone, T.R. & Hardaker, W.T. (1990). Rehabilitation of foot and ankle injuries in ballet dancers. *Journal of Orthopaedic and Sports Physical Therapy, 11,* 8, 355–361.

Manske, R.C. (2006). *Postsurgical Orthopedic Sports Rehabilitation: Knee and Shoulder.* St. Louis, Mo.: Mosby.

Martinez, J.M. & Honsik, K. (2006). Iliotibial band syndrome. *E-Medicine Online Journal* (Web MD). Dec 6, 1–14.

Mazzone, M. (2002). Common conditions of the Achilles tendon. *American Family Physician, 65,* 1805–1810.

Paavola, M. et al. (2002). Current concepts review: Achilles tendinopathy. *Journal of Bone & Joint Surgery, 84-A,* 11, 2062–2076.

Prentice, W. (1994). *Rehabilitation Techniques in Sports Medicine* (3rd ed.). St. Louis, Mo.: Mosby.

Rintala, P. (1990). Patellofemoral pain syndrome and its treatment in runners. *Journal of Athletic Training, 25,* 2, 107–110.

Roy, S. & Irvin, R. (1983). *Sports Medicine: Prevention, Evaluation, Management, and Rehabilitation.* Englewood Cliffs, N.J.: Prentice-Hall.

Shelton, G.L. & Thigpen, L.K. (1991). Rehabilitation of patellofemoral dysfunction: A review of literature. *Journal of Orthopedic and Sports Physical Therapy, 14,* 6, 243–249.

Wilk, K.E. & Andrews, J.R. (1992). Current concepts in the rehabilitation of the athletic shoulder. *Journal of Orthopedic and Sports Physical Therapy, 15,* 6, 279–289.

Woodall, W. & Welsh, J. (1990). A biomechanical basis for rehabilitation programs involving the patellofemoral joint. *Journal of Orthopaedic and Sports Physical Therapy, 11,* 11, 535–542.

Suggested Reading

American Council on Exercise (2015). *ACE Medical Exercise Specialist Manual.* San Diego, Calif.: American Council on Exercise.

Anderson, M.K., Hall, S.J., & Martin, M. (2008). *Foundations of Athletic Training: Prevention, Assessment, and Management* (4th ed.). Baltimore, Md.: Lippincott Williams & Wilkins.

Bahr, R. & Maehlum, S. (2004). *Clinical Guide to Sports Injuries,* Champaign, Ill.: Human Kinetics.

Brotzman, B. & Wilk, K. (2003). *Clinical Orthopedic Rehabilitation* (2nd ed.). St Louis Mo.: Mosby.

Kisner, C. & Colby, L. (2007). *Therapeutic Exercise: Foundations and Techniques* (5th ed.). Philadelphia, Pa.: F.A. Davis Company.

Julia Valentour, M.S., EMT-B, is the program coordinator for live workshops for the American Council on Exercise, an American Heart Association (AHA) Training Center Coordinator, and an instructor for Basic Life Support and Heartsaver courses. She is an ACE-certified Personal Trainer and holds a health and fitness specialist certification from the American College of Sports Medicine. Valentour has developed content for ACE webinars and has contributed material for the AHA's Start! Walking Program. She has served as an assistant professor of kinesiology for California State University San Marcos. Valentour spent several years working for the U.S. Navy, where she served as the Afloat Fitness Director aboard the aircraft carrier USS NIMITZ (CVN-68), including an eight-month deployment to the Persian Gulf in 2003 for Operation Iraqi Freedom.

CHAPTER NINE

Emergency Procedures

Julia Valentour

Over the long term, exercise can greatly improve health and wellness and play an important role in enhancing overall public health. However, there are inherent risks involved with exercise due to the physical demands placed on the body. During exercise, the risk of heart attack and sudden death are increased, even in athletic individuals. The likelihood of injuries also increases. Therefore, fitness professionals work in an environment where they might be called upon to react to an emergency as a first responder.

Handling emergency situations requires quick, decisive action. The person who takes charge should be capable of assessing the victim and managing the scene. Because this person's demeanor will affect how others react, it is important for him or her to stay in control and remain calm.

Emergencies can vary widely, including such minor incidents as when an exerciser sprains an ankle during a step-training class or scrapes his or her shin on the pedal during a group indoor cycling class. Although rare, some situations are much more serious, and can involve a person who is bleeding heavily or who is unconscious with impaired breathing or circulation. Having a systematic approach for handling any of these situations, no matter how severe, requires training and practice.

Personal Protective Equipment

Dealing with emergencies begins with protecting one's own safety as well as the safety of others and the victim. When administering first aid, a GFI should start by wearing personal protective equipment (PPE). Gloves are a universal standard and should be worn in all cases, but other equipment, such as eye protection and a mask, may also be necessary to avoid the possible transfer of **pathogens** (microorganisms that cause disease) (Mistovich & Karren, 2008). **Human immunodeficiency virus (HIV)** and **hepatitis** are the bloodborne diseases of most concern to a GFI. Universal precautions state that everyone is to be treated as if he or she is infected, and first responders should always avoid contact with a victim's bodily fluids [American Heart Association (AHA), 2006] (see "Universal Precautions and Protection Against Bloodborne Pathogens" on page 270 for more information).

Scene Safety

Scene safety requires knowing when it is safe to approach a victim and when it is not. For example, people are sometimes struck and killed on the road while trying to help at the scene of an accident. Other dangerous situations might involve a smoke-filled building, downed power lines, hazardous materials, a crime in progress, or unstable surfaces such as a car on its side. If in doubt, a potential rescuer should wait for trained help to arrive, as he or she can make the situation much worse by becoming another victim. For GFIs, scene safety requires situational awareness, whether leading a class in the fitness facility or outdoors (Mistovich & Karren, 2008). What are the potential hazards? Is there a first-aid kit or an **automated external defibrillator (AED)** on the premises? Where is the nearest phone, or is there cell phone coverage in the area? Where is the nearest hospital? Are there others nearby who can help in case of an emergency?

Maintaining a First-aid Kit

A first-aid kit should be systematically maintained and stocked with the following supplies:

For airway management:
- CPR microshield or pocket mask with one-way valve for protected mouth-to-mouth ventilations (Figure 9-1)

For assessing circulation:
- Sphygmomanometer (blood pressure cuff)
- Stethoscope
- Penlight or flashlight

For general wound management:
- Personal protective equipment, including latex gloves, mask, and eye protection
- Sterile gauze dressings (medium and larger sizes)
- Adhesive tape (1- and 2-inch sizes)
- Bandage scissors

- Liquid soap or hand sanitizer (if soap is unavailable in the workplace)

For suspected sprains or fractures:

- Splinting materials
- Chemical cold pack, or ice and plastic bag
- Compression wrap

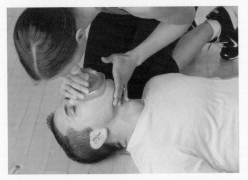

Figure 9-1

Mouth-to-mask ventilations: A mask with a one-way valve prevents contact with a victim's mouth and face during mouth-to-mouth resuscitation. Small pocket masks are also effective, inexpensive, and convenient.

Emergency Policies and Procedures for Fitness Facilities

While some emergency situations are unavoidable, the best approach is to be prepared. The AHA and American College of Sports Medicine (ACSM) published guidelines for fitness facilities in 1998 that involve pre-screening members, having adequate staffing, and establishing emergency policies. A fitness facility can take the following steps to minimize the risk of injuries (Balady et al., 1998):

- All employees should be trained in first aid, **cardiopulmonary resuscitation (CPR),** and AED usage. CPR and AED training is required by ACE. Also, many states now have laws that require health clubs to have at least one AED on the premises, as well as staff members who are trained to use them.

- Fitness staff should hold current accredited certifications in their specialty areas (e.g., personal training, group fitness instruction, or lifeguarding). If a staff member works with a special population such as seniors, youth, or pre- or postnatal women, additional training for working safely and effectively with that population is recommended (Canadian Fitness Matters, 2004).

Facilities should screen new members to identify those at high risk for cardiovascular events by using a simple screening questionnaire such as the **Physical Activity Readiness Questionnaire (PAR-Q)** (see Chapter 2). People with cardiac disease are 10 times more likely to have a cardiovascular event during exercise than those who are apparently healthy. The PAR-Q can help to identify high-risk individuals who need medical referral or require modifications to their exercise programs. This tool can also help identify the need for additional qualified staff members if there are a number of high-risk participants (Canadian Fitness Matters, 2004; Balady et al., 1998).

Fitness facilities should establish a method of notifying participants about the risk of injury with exercise, such as having new members sign **informed consent** forms. Additionally, fitness facilities should have participants complete medical screening forms and obtain medical clearance when necessary, as determined by the participant's risk stratification (Canadian Fitness Matters, 2004; Balady et al., 1998).

The club should take responsibility for minimizing any additional risks by ensuring the following (Canadian Fitness Matters, 2004; Balady et al., 1998):

- Adequate staffing and supervision
- Cleanliness and clear walkways
- Adequate lighting
- Nonslip surfaces around showers and pools
- Caution signs for wet floors and other hazards (for example, "No Diving" signs at the shallow end of the pool)
- Regular maintenance and repair of equipment
- A clean drinking water supply
- Fire/smoke alarms installed
- Limiting the number of people in the building and in group fitness classes to avoid overcrowding
- First-aid kits that are kept in convenient locations and assigned to someone to restock on a regular basis
- Phones that can be easily accessed with emergency numbers posted nearby

Having the right equipment available is not enough—training and practice are also vital to effectively handle emergencies. Each club should have an emergency action plan taught to all employees and practiced quarterly. Documentation should be kept, noting when this training took place and who was involved. The plan should include instructions on how to handle the types of emergencies that are more likely to occur when people are exercising, such as hypoglycemic events, cardiac events, **strokes,** heat illnesses, and orthopedic injuries. Handling other events such as fires should also be rehearsed. The personnel involved should understand the roles of first, second, and third responders. Staff members (including GFIs) should know the location of emergency equipment, such as first-aid kits, AEDs, phones, emergency exits, and the most accessible route for emergency personnel.

Someone at the club should be identified as the facility's coordinator for ensuring the facility is capable of handling an emergency. Local medical professionals can help the facility's management team create this emergency response plan (ACSM, 2007).

For emergencies with a single victim, staff members should *not* move a victim with head or neck injuries unless there is danger of further injury if the victim is not moved. When trained help is needed, one staff member should stay with the victim while another goes to call and wait outside for **emergency medical services (EMS)**. This person can guide rescuers by using the shortest route available to the scene of the incident. A third staff member (if available) can get a first-aid kit and AED. When rescuers arrive, staff members should be ready to assist as needed.

Emergency Assessment

Primary Assessment

Some emergencies are easily recognizable as life-threatening, while others may not be. To make that determination, first check to see if the victim is conscious and able to speak. Tap the victim's shoulder and ask "Are you okay?" With a conscious victim, the rescuer should introduce him- or herself, ask what the problem is, and ask if he or she can provide any help. (Consent to receive help must be given verbally if the victim is conscious and alert.) If the victim is able to speak, that means there is a patent (open) airway and the person is breathing, conscious, and has a pulse. This quick assessment is valuable in determining the cause of the emergency (Mistovich & Karren, 2008). If there is no reply, the GFI should call EMS or, preferably, stay with the victim and send another person to call. In situations where the victim is unresponsive or disoriented, implied consent can be assumed (meaning that the victim agrees to treatment). If there is no sign of trauma to the spine, perform a head tilt–chin lift (a technique for opening the airway) (Figure 9-2). This will remove the tongue from resting on the back of the throat, which could block the airway. If there is evidence of a fall or other signs of trauma to the face, neck, or head, open the airway by the jaw thrust method instead (Figure 9-3). (These techniques are learned and practiced in a CPR/AED course.)

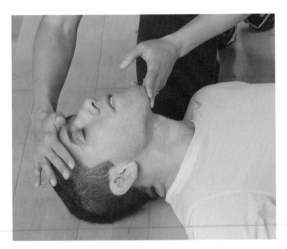

Figure 9-2
The head tilt–chin lift maneuver: Tilt the head back and lift the chin to move the tongue away from the back of the throat.

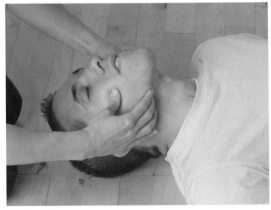

Figure 9-3
The jaw thrust method: Place the fingers on the angles of the jaw, and lift the jaw to move it forward. This moves the tongue away from the back of the throat and opens the airway.

To assess respirations (breathing), the rescuer should observe the victim for breathing that is absent or not normal. It is no longer recommended to "look, listen, and feel for breathing" to aid in the assessment of whether or not a victim is breathing (Travers et al., 2010). If no breath is recognized, or if breaths are gasping or irregular, the rescuer should start chest compressions. If blood loss is apparent, and if others are available to help, it may be necessary to simultaneously control severe bleeding with gauze pads and direct pressure. This is secondary to performing CPR and is not urgent unless there is major blood loss, making the situation life-threatening.

Secondary Assessment

Once a person is conscious and speaking, or unconscious but with a stable airway and is breathing, a **secondary assessment** can be completed to address any issues that are not immediately life-threatening.

If the cause of injury is not known, there could be something life-threatening that is not being recognized and treated, such as internal bleeding, heat stress, and shock. For a victim of trauma or someone who is unconscious, a head-to-toe assessment might be done to look for additional injuries, such as deformities, abrasions, tenderness, or swelling. This is also a good time to check for medical alert jewelry. Vital signs should be taken, such as pulse and **blood pressure,** and it is important to check skin color and temperature. Skin color can provide information about a person's general health. Skin that is warm and has a pinkish tone indicates adequate blood flow and oxygenation, whereas grayish, pale skin may indicate poor circulation (American Academy of Orthopedic Surgeons, 2006). A conscious victim might also be asked about his or her signs and symptoms, any known allergies, what medications he or she has been taking, pertinent medical history, the type and location of the pain, and any events that led up to the incident. The victim should be monitored closely, and if the person can talk, the rescuer should keep the conversation going to reassure him or her, let the person know what is happening, and keep monitoring the airway (Mistovich & Karren, 2008; Anderson, Hall, & Martin, 2000).

Activating EMS

Determining the likely cause of the emergency helps the 9-1-1 dispatcher know what agency to call for help and what the responders should be prepared to handle.

When to Call 9-1-1

It is appropriate to call EMS when there is a life-threatening situation or anything that requires immediate medical attention, such as a person who is not breathing, has an open wound to the chest, or is bleeding profusely (Mistovich & Karren, 2008).

A GFI should phone the facility's emergency response number (or 9-1-1) whenever someone is seriously ill or when unsure of what to do. For example, a GFI should call EMS when a victim (AHA, 2006):

- Does not respond to voice or touch
- Has chest pain or chest discomfort
- Has signs of stroke (e.g., slurred speech, facial drooping, loss of balance, vision problems, and severe headache)
- Has a problem breathing
- Has a severe injury or burn
- Has a seizure
- Suddenly cannot move a part of the body
- Has received an electric shock
- Has been exposed to a poison
- Tries to commit suicide or is assaulted, regardless of the victim's condition

Other situations that require EMS include:

- Crimes in progress
- First witnesses of a fire, traffic accident, or chemical spill
- When fire, smoke, or carbon monoxide alarms sound in a building
- Electrical hazards, such as sparking of a power line

It is appropriate for a GFI to call in any other emergency if he or she is unsure. However, a GFI should not call if there is *not* a true emergency, as doing so can delay response time to true emergencies. For non-emergencies, call the appropriate agency. For example, call the emergency contact listed in the participant's file or another individual as requested by the participant if he or she trips and appears to have a broken bone. While a broken bone requires immediate attention from a healthcare professional, it typically does not require the activation of EMS. Also, people should not call to inquire about the status of an emergency or fire. Instead, call 2-1-1 or listen to local news (San Diego Fire-Rescue Department, 2008).

Land Lines vs. Cell Phones

If the GFI has a choice, it is always better to call EMS from a land line than from a cellular phone. A call from a cell phone may have to be routed to different places depending on whether it is a police, fire, or medical emergency. Unlike with a land line, it is difficult to determine the caller's exact location when using a cell phone (depending on the technology in the phone and at the dispatch center), and even if a location is found it may be an area as large as three football fields. The caller may also need to provide the phone number, which would not be necessary if calling from a land line. Having to provide the additional information such as the address and phone number takes precious time away from responders.

Emergency Call Centers

Public Safety Answering Points (PSAPs) are the dispatch centers that receive 9-1-1 calls. They do not have the same technology as the callers. For example, they do not receive text messages—which may be a more desirable means of communication during times of disaster when the system is overloaded. A bill passed by Congress (The NET 911 Improvement Act of 2008) calls for the creation of a plan that will improve the 9-1-1 system from analog to digital to match newer technology, primarily by incorporating Internet protocol (IP) network technology into the emergency system. This will allow better connections and faster communication between PSAPs, responders, and emergency warning systems. Video, text, and data transmission could be used for calls, in addition to voice. This would help service those who are deaf and hearing impaired, although the 9-1-1 centers currently can take calls from TTYs (text telephones used by the deaf, hard of hearing, and speech impaired). This new directive would also help pinpoint the location where the call was made, which currently is more difficult for those in high-rise buildings or rural areas. While some states have begun to implement these changes, how and when the process will be complete has not yet been determined (Moore, 2008).

When calling 9-1-1, it is important to stay calm and try to give the dispatcher the exact location of the emergency. Stay on the line—the dispatcher will ask questions regarding the emergency to make sure rescuers are ready to respond to the exact situation when they arrive. Callers should give the number of victims in case it is necessary for the dispatcher to send multiple units to the scene. The dispatcher may give directions on providing immediate care for the victim, such as performing CPR and controlling bleeding. It is essential to have someone wait outside for EMS to direct rescuers to the exact location as quickly as possible. Remember, there may be locked doors or access codes to gated communities, and addresses may not be clearly marked. Also, it is important to secure any pets that may endanger the safety of rescuers.

Calling 9-1-1

When a person phones the company's emergency response number (or 9-1-1), he or she should be prepared to answer some questions about the emergency. An emergency dispatcher might ask some or all of the following questions:

"What is the emergency?"

"Where is your emergency and what number are you calling from?"

"What is your name?"

"Is the victim conscious?"

"Is the victim breathing normally?"

"Are you able to assist with CPR?"

"Do you have access to an AED?"

It is essential that the caller not hang up until the dispatcher tells him or her to do so (AHA, 2006).

Initial Response

It takes EMS an average of seven to 10 minutes to reach a victim, but brain death can occur in only four to six minutes (Gonzales & Lino, 2008). What can be done to improve a victim's chances of survival?

Cardiopulmonary Resuscitation

Sudden cardiac arrest (death from sudden cardiac arrest is called **sudden cardiac death**) is a leading cause of death in the United States, accounting for an estimated 350,000 deaths each year (Travers et al., 2010). Most of these deaths occur outside of hospitals, so it is important to be trained and ready to respond whenever this situation might occur. Cardiac arrest is the cessation of heart function, when the person loses consciousness, has no pulse, and stops breathing. The person may be gasping, snorting, or gurgling, but this is not breathing and should not deter someone from starting CPR. In this circumstance, the chance of survival is remote without an intervention. To educate the public about what to do, the American Heart Association has developed the Chain of Survival, which includes four steps or "links" to increase the likelihood of survival (Travers et al., 2010):

- Immediate recognition of cardiac arrest and activation of EMS
- Early CPR (with an emphasis on chest compressions)
- Rapid defibrillation
- Integrated post–cardiac arrest care

A fitness professional could potentially be actively involved with the first three links in the Chain of Survival. Immediate recognition of cardiac arrest involves early recognition of the emergency and immediate activation of EMS. The second step, early CPR, is important to help the body maintain **perfusion** (blood flow and oxygen delivery to body tissues). Research on the effectiveness of CPR on survival rates of victims has revealed that rescuers have a wide variety of training, experience, and skills. Also, the cardiac arrest victim's status and response to CPR maneuvers are factors that influence the success rates of resuscitation (Travers et al., 2010). To encourage successful CPR for as many victims as possible, chest compressions should be given to all victims of cardiac arrest. Chest compressions are the foundation for CPR and can be performed by all rescuers, regardless of the extent of their training. Rescuers who are able should also provide ventilation in combina-

tion with chest compressions at a ratio of 30 compressions to two ventilations (30:2) (Figure 9-4). CPR, compressions only or a combination of breaths and compressions for a person who is in a state of cardiac arrest, should ideally begin within two minutes of the onset of cardiac arrest (Mistovich & Karren, 2008). Without treatment, the person's chance of survival declines by about 10% every minute.

Because EMS takes an average of seven to 10 minutes to arrive, CPR should be started by a bystander—a friend, family member, employee, or stranger (Mistovich & Karren, 2008). However, most victims of out-of-hospital cardiac arrest do not receive treatment. In fact, only 27% of out-of-hospital victims receive bystander CPR (Nichol et al., 1999), despite the fact that bystander CPR can more than double the chance of survival (Herlitz et al., 2005).

Saving More Lives: Hands-only CPR

Interviews with people who witnessed a cardiac arrest have found that the major reason bystanders do not attempt to perform CPR is because they panic. Although more than half of the interviewees had CPR training at some time in their lives, many reported that they were afraid to cause harm or afraid they would not perform well. The fear of disease was not a factor because most were family members of the victim (Swor et al., 2006). In 2007, several AHA studies found that in some instances, CPR could be simplified to performing chest compressions only, which is referred to as "hands-only CPR" (Nagao et al., 2007; Bohm et al., 2007; Iwami et al., 2007). In this type of CPR, a bystander only needs

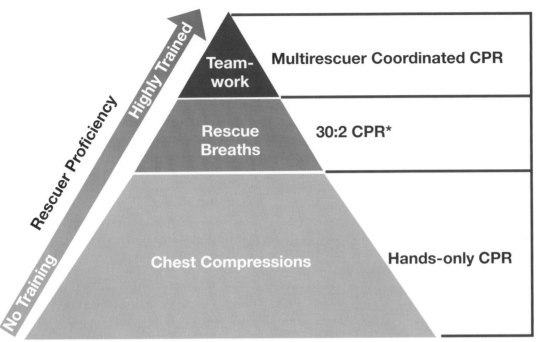

Figure 9-4
Buidling blocks
of cardiopulmonary
resuscitation (CPR)

Travers, A.H.
et al. (2010).
Cardiopulmonary
resuscitation
and emergency
cardiovascular
care. *Circulation*,
122, S676–S684.
Reprinted with
permission.

*Refers to CPR performed with a ratio of 30 chest compressions to 2 ventilations

to remember to push hard and fast on the center of the victim's chest until trained help arrives. This is effective for victims who are adults and who have been witnessed going into cardiac arrest. When the collapse is witnessed and CPR begins immediately, the victim's blood still contains oxygen, and oxygen remains in the lungs. By pumping the chest, this oxygenated blood can be distributed to the body. Because of its simplicity, hands-only CPR will hopefully encourage bystanders to do *something*—and any CPR is better than none for a victim of cardiac arrest (Sayre et al., 2008).

Although it is just as effective in some circumstances, hands-only CPR does not replace traditional CPR in situations where oxygen is needed. When an adult is found unconscious (and when the blood is no longer oxygenated), and in emergencies involving infants

or children, drug overdoses, drowning victims, or any adult who collapses due to a respiratory problem, a combination of breaths and compressions is needed. It is absolutely essential that fitness professionals keep their CPR provider cards current (Sayre et al., 2008). *Note:* Current CPR certification is required for all ACE-certified Fitness Professionals.

Automated External Defibrillation

While CPR alone cannot change an abnormal heart rhythm, it is important to buy time before defibrillation. During cardiac arrest, the heart is beating erratically and ineffectively. The most common rhythm during cardiac arrest is **ventricular fibrillation (VF),** which is a spasmodic quivering of the heart that is too fast to allow the heart chambers to adequately fill and empty, so little or no blood is pushed out to the body or lungs. An AED is used to convert VF back to a normal rhythm by delivering an electric shock to the heart through two adhesive electrode pads placed on the person's chest. By keeping the tissues perfused with oxygenated blood, CPR preserves the heart and brain and can prevent VF from deteriorating into an unshockable rhythm while waiting for an AED to arrive.

The AED should be used as soon as it becomes available, ideally within the first three to five minutes. Compressions should be continued and only interrupted when the shock is given. When a shock is provided within the first minute of cardiac arrest, victims with VF have survival rates as high as 90%. The number of AEDs in a fitness facility should depend on the size of the building and the time it takes to get the AED to any location in the facility. If a building has multiple floors, having one per floor is recommended. Defibrillation cannot treat all heart rhythms, and an AED will not shock a victim when a normal heart rhythm is found. The machine will first analyze the victim's heart rhythm to determine if a shock is appropriate. When a shock is delivered, the heart's pacemaker (i.e., the **sinoatrial node**) may be able to restart.

When an AED is used on a child between one and eight years old, a child key or switch—or a smaller set of electrode pads that delivers a lower shock dose—should be used. If the child pads are not available, use adult pads for a child from age one to eight and give an adult shock dose. Always use the adult pads and adult shock dose for a child eight and older. An AED should not be used on an infant under one year old—there is not yet conclusive data for using an AED in this situation, as most infant cardiac arrests are due to a respiratory problem. An AED must never be used on a person who is conscious, breathing, or has a pulse (Mistovich & Karren, 2008).

Many states, including Arkansas, California, Illinois, Indiana, Louisiana, Massachusetts, Michigan, New Jersey, New York, Oregon, and Rhode Island, as well as the District of Columbia, have passed laws that require at least one AED in health clubs, and several other states are considering adopting this legislation. Good Samaritan laws exist in most states that offer liability protection to the person who administers the AED. The federal government also passed the Cardiac Arrest Survival Act in 2000, which granted Good Samaritan protection for anyone in the U.S. who acquired an AED or who uses an AED in a medical emergency, except in cases of wanton misconduct or recklessness. This federal law does not override state policies, but fills in the gaps for those states without these laws. This legal protection should allay any fears of liability for those organizations that want to offer a public-access defibrillation program, as well as the first responders who use them.

Common Medical Emergencies and Injuries

The following sections present common medical emergencies and injuries, the signs and symptoms of each, and recommended treatments. It is essential for a GFI to have a general knowledge about these situations in case they occur sometime during his or her career.

It should be noted that many of the diseases and disorders covered in Chapter 6 can cause in-class emergencies that require a quick response from the GFI. For example, if a participant is known to have diabetes, the GFI should be alert for signs of an insulin or hypoglycemic reaction (Table 9-1). Similarly, if a GFI works with individuals who have had a stroke or heart attack, have **asthma** (Table 9-2), or are coping with any other disease or injury,

Table 9-1

Insulin Reaction (Hypoglycemia)

Early Symptoms	Late Symptoms
Anxiety, uneasiness	Double vision
Irritability	Sweating, palpitations
Extreme hunger	Nausea
Confusion	Loss of motor coordination
Headaches	Pale, moist skin
Insomnia	Strong, rapid pulse
	Convulsions
	Loss of consciousness
	Coma

Helping a Participant Who Is Having an Insulin Reaction

- Stop the activity immediately.
- Have the person sit down and check his or her blood glucose level.
- Have the participant drink orange juice or some other rapidly absorbing carbohydrate.
- Allow the participant to sit quietly and wait for a response.
- When the participant feels better, check the blood glucose level again.
- If the blood glucose level is above 100 mg/dL and the participant feels better, resume activity.
- Check the blood glucose level after 15 to 30 minutes to reassure that it is within a safe range.
- Do not allow the participant to leave the facility until the blood glucose level is within a normal range.
- If the participant does not improve, seek medical attention immediately.

Rimmer, J.H. (1994). *Fitness and Rehabilitation Programs for Special Populations*. Dubuque, Iowa: WCB McGraw-Hill.

Table 9-2

Steps for Managing an Asthma Attack

The time to treat an asthma episode is when the symptoms (e.g., coughing, wheezing, chest tightness, and difficulty breathing) first appear.

Attack-management Steps

- Have the person rest and relax.
- Have the person use medicines (inhaler) prescribed for an attack.
- Have the person drink warm liquids.

Rest and Relax

- At the first sign of breathing difficulties, the person should STOP and rest for at least 10 minutes.
- Make the person feel comfortable and relaxed.

Take Medication

- Make sure the prescribed medicine is available and that the person understands how to correctly take the medicine (inhalers require practice).

Drink Warm Liquid

- Have the person drink slowly.
- Do not allow the person to ingest cold drinks.

Emergency Care

- If you have any doubts about the severity of the attack, get medical help immediately.
- If the person's lips or fingernails are turning blue or if he or she exhibits shallow breathing and is focusing all attention on breathing, get medical help immediately.

the GFI should be aware of the ways in which those ailments can manifest in a group setting and know the appropriate response.

Another concern for GFIs is cold- or heat-related illness, particularly if they are leading outdoor classes in extreme conditions. It is essential that GFIs are aware of the heat index during the summer months and the windchill index during the winter. These topics are covered in *ACE's Essentials of Exercise Science for Fitness Professionals.*

Dyspnea

Dyspnea (difficult and labored breathing) can be a common occurrence, such as when an unconditioned person attempts to exercise vigorously. In some cases, however, dyspnea can come on suddenly and be a very uncomfortable and distressing situation for the participant, and it can even become life-threatening. A trauma such as a blow to the chest in boxing or a barbell dropped on the chest during a bench press could cause air to escape the lungs and move into the pleural space. The high pressure this causes outside of the lungs reduces lung volume and the person can experience severe difficulty breathing (Mistovich & Karren, 2008). Other causes of dyspnea include emotional stress, asthma, and airway obstruction. Heart problems can also cause dyspnea when the heart is not pumping enough blood to properly oxygenate the tissues. How the GFI should react to the situation is determined by the severity of the breathing difficulty, the cause, and how suddenly the onset occurred.

Breathing adequately involves both an appropriate rate and depth of inhalation. The respiratory rate for adults averages between 12 and 20 breaths per minute. A rate that is too fast may be just as bad as one that is too slow. When breathing is too fast, such as during **anxiety** or panic attacks, the lungs do not have time to fill between breaths, so oxygen exchange is insufficient. Inappropriate depth (i.e., shallow breathing) indicates an inadequate **tidal volume,** or too little air inhaled with each breath. This can be due to many causes depending on whether the onset was sudden or it is a chronic problem.

The outward signs of respiratory distress are poor movement of the chest wall, flaring of the nostrils, straining of the neck muscles, and poor air exchange from the mouth and nose. Pale, diaphoretic (sweaty) skin can be an early sign of respiratory distress. **Cyanosis,** a bluish color, can develop around the lips, nose, fingernails, and inner lining of the eyes as a late sign of respiratory distress. Because the brain is not receiving enough oxygen, the person can become restless, agitated, confused, or unresponsive.

To assess breathing in an unconscious person, a GFI can feel for air flow on his or her own cheek while looking for the chest to rise and fall, although the chest rising and falling alone may not mean that the air flow is adequate. It is also important to listen for unusual sounds that may indicate a partial airway blockage such as snoring, gurgling, or high pitched "crowing" sounds caused by swelling of the larynx. If there is no chest movement or no sounds indicating air movement around the mouth and nose, the GFI should give breaths. If there is no pulse, CPR should be initiated.

Dyspnea Scale

The dyspnea scale is a subjective score that reflects the relative difficulty of breathing as perceived by the participant during physical activity.

+1 Mild, noticeable to the exerciser, but not to an observer

+2 Mild, some difficulty that is noticeable to an observer

+3 Moderate difficulty, participant can continue to exercise

+4 Severe difficulty, participant must stop exercising

A participant with a severe breathing difficulty or who is not breathing (**apneic**) is considered a priority for EMS rescuers, so it is important to call for help and convey that information. Ambulances are equipped with tanks of 100% pure oxygen to use in a wide variety of situations (Mistovich & Karren, 2008). A conscious person should be placed in a position of comfort to wait for emergency personnel to arrive. In many cases, this may mean sitting up or a "tripod" position (i.e., sitting up, leaning forward, and using the hands for support). Lying down may increase the difficulty of breathing (Schenck, 2005).

Choking

A person who is choking will have a blocked airway, and this can be mild or severe. If the blockage is mild, the airway is not completely blocked, allowing some air to get through. An individual with a mild airway blockage can still cough or make sounds. No assistance is necessary in this situation unless the object cannot be dislodged and the person becomes **hypoxic** (oxygen deficient). The GFI (or someone else nearby) should call EMS immediately if this happens.

If the person cannot breathe, make sounds, or has a very quiet cough, or if a child cannot cry, the blockage is severe. A person in this situation may make the universal choking sign (holding the neck with one or both hands). The rescuer should stand behind the victim with both arms wrapped around the victim's waist, make a fist with one hand, and put the thumb side just above the victim's belly button. The other hand should grab the fist, and several upward thrusts should be done to compress the diaphragm and force the object out of the victim's airway. If the victim is much smaller than the rescuer, the rescuer can kneel. If the victim is larger, the rescuer can ask the victim

to kneel. If the victim is very large or in the late stages of pregnancy, the rescuer can wrap his or her arms around the victim's breastbone instead of the abdomen. If the thrusts (i.e., the **Heimlich maneuver**) do not succeed in dislodging the object, the victim may become unconscious. If this occurs, the GFI should have someone call for help and start the steps of CPR (AHA, 2006).

Syncope

Syncope, or fainting, is a temporary loss of consciousness due to insufficient blood flow and oxygen to the brain. There are many different causes, including emotional stress, severe pain, **dehydration**/heavy sweating, overheating, and exhaustion. Syncope may also be caused by sudden postural changes after blood has pooled in the legs, such as squatting for a period of time and then standing up. Violent coughing spells, especially in men, may cause syncope due to a rapid change in blood pressure. Abnormal heart rhythms (too fast or too slow) can cause syncope. Neurologic, metabolic, or psychiatric disorders can also cause syncope, as well as problems with the heart and lungs. Syncope is also a side effect of some medications. Although syncope is usually benign, some cases may signal life-threatening situations. Syncope is considered to be serious when it occurs with exercise, is associated with palpitations or an irregular heartbeat, or there is a family history of syncope associated with sudden cardiac death. A careful physical examination can determine whether or not a person is at risk.

Before a person faints, he or she may feel a warm sensation, nausea, or lightheadedness. Sweaty palms and a visual "grayout" may also occur. When these warning signs happen, have the person sit with the head lowered or lie down. To avoid fainting, the person should drink plenty of fluids to keep blood volume at adequate levels. Some people may need to be treated with medication.

Seizures

A seizure occurs when there is abnormal and excessive electrical activity in the brain. While 10% of the population may have a seizure at some point in their lives, only 1% of all seizures occur due to epilepsy (Schenck, 2005). Age-adjusted prevalence of epilepsy ranges from four to eight per 1,000 people. There are numerous causes of seizures, including metabolic abnormalities (such as low blood sugar), drugs, vascular disease (such as strokes), **central nervous system** tumors or infections, toxins, degenerative diseases, and genetic predisposition (Corey-Bloom & David, 2009).

Seizures are either generalized or partial. The most common and well-known type of generalized seizure is the **tonic clonic seizure** or **grand mal seizure.** It may start with an "aura"—the person experiences a smell or sound that indicates a seizure is about to occur. When the seizure starts, the victim experiences a loss of consciousness and whole-body jerking movements (i.e., tonic clonic movements), where the muscles contract and relax, the jaw is clenched, and bowel or bladder control might be lost. This could last one or more minutes, and is followed by a state of exhaustion called the **postictal state.** The victim may still be unconscious in this state for 10 to 30 minutes (Schenck, 2005).

The emergency procedures for a generalized tonic clonic (grand mal) seizure are as follows (AHA, 2006):
- Clear the area so the victim will not hit his or her head on nearby furniture or objects.
- Place a towel under the victim's head to help protect it from injury.
- Turn the person onto his or her side
- Never restrain the victim or place anything in the victim's mouth.
- Have someone phone EMS.

After the seizure, check to make sure the victim is breathing, and if not, start CPR. With a victim who is not suspected of having a head, neck, or spinal injury, roll him or her into the recovery position (on his or her side) to prevent vomit or mucus from obstructing the airway. The victim may be confused and very tired after a seizure, so it is important to stay nearby and reassure him or her upon awakening.

During a generalized tonic clonic seizure, the person stops breathing. However, **hypoxia** is rarely a problem unless the seizure is prolonged—normal breathing resumes in the postictal state. It is important to make sure the airway is clear. If the seizure lasts more than five minutes, or multiple seizures occur without the person regaining consciousness in between, the body may develop a severe lack of oxygen. The GFI should call EMS immediately (Rubin et al., 2009).

Epilepsy is a **chronic disease** that requires treatment with antiepileptic drugs and is characterized by recurrent seizures due to an underlying brain abnormality (Corey-Bloom & David, 2009). They are actually less likely to occur during exercise than during rest, and exercise may be helpful in controlling them. If seizures are associated with exercise, they occur during prolonged exercise such as triathlons or marathons, when other metabolic states might act as contributing factors (such as **hyponatremia,** a sodium deficiency). Contact sports, even those involving head trauma, have not been shown to increase the prevalence of seizures (Mellion et al., 2003).

Soft-tissue Injuries

Because the skin is the outer covering of the body, it is frequently injured. Blisters are caused by **shear force** in one or more directions, which causes fluid to go to the injury site and settle between the dermis and epidermis of the skin. Bruises occur when a compressive blow to the skin damages **capillaries** below the surface. The area fills with blood to cause bruising (**ecchymosis**). **Contusions** are similar to bruises in that they are caused by blunt trauma that does not break the surface of the skin, but contusions also feature swelling and the formation of a **hematoma,** a hard, localized mass of blood and dead tissue that could restrict movement or cause pain or even temporary paralysis due to nerve compression (Anderson, Hall, & Martin, 2000).

There are several types of breaks that can occur in the skin (Anderson, Hall, & Martin, 2000):

- **Abrasion**—A scraping of tissue from a fall against a rough surface, usually in one direction
- **Incision**—A clean cut to the skin from a tensile force, likely from a sharp edge
- **Laceration**—A jagged tear of the skin caused by both shear and tensile forces
- **Avulsion**—A severe laceration, with skin torn away from the tissue below
- **Puncture**—A penetration of the skin by an object

Treatment for these injuries is to clean the area thoroughly and irrigate with plenty of water, and then apply a dry dressing. Applying direct pressure over the injury site can help control bleeding (Figure 9-5). If the gauze gets soaked through, the GFI can apply more gauze pads without removing the first ones so as not to rip off any scab that starts to form. It is necessary to seek medical attention for large wounds where bleeding cannot be controlled,

Figure 9-5
Direct pressure for hemorrhage control

or if the person begins to feel dizzy, confused, or agitated, and is pale, cold, and clammy— these may be signs of shock (Mellion et al., 2003). For any broken skin, the individual may be required to update his or her tetanus shot (Lillegard, Butcher, & Rucker, 1999). See "Universal Precautions and Protection Against Bloodborne Pathogens" on page 270 for more information on handling situations in which a GFI may come in contact with a participant's blood or other bodily fluid.

Tendons and ligaments are formed primarily from collagen tissue. Collagen is a **protein** with fibers arranged in a wavy pattern, giving it a slight amount of stretch when under tension. However, injuries occur when tendons and ligaments are overstretched. A sprain is an acute trauma to a ligament, which connects bone to bone. Sprains are classified as first, second, or third degree, depending on the number of fibers torn and the amount of joint instability. Ligaments tear when bones become displaced, such as with an ankle sprain or shoulder dislocation. Although immediate stabilization and immobilization are necessary, healthcare professionals may not immobilize the joint for long, as doing so may cause atrophy and strength loss. Ligaments and tendons grow stronger as controlled stress is placed on them, so long periods of immobilization are detrimental to healing. Decreased blood flow in tendons and ligaments means slow healing times, even up to one year (Anderson, Hall, & Martin, 2000).

A strain involves injury to a tendon, which connects muscle to bone. Since tendons are stronger than the muscles they attach to, most strains are actually an injury to the muscle fibers and are commonly called pulled muscles. Strains can also be first, second, or third degree, depending on the number of muscle fibers involved and the ability to contract the injured muscle (Mellion et al., 2003). The tendon structure itself typically does not tear (Anderson, Hall, & Martin, 2000).

General primary treatment for soft-tissue injuries is **RICE** (rest or restricted activity, ice, compression, and elevation) or PRICES, which also includes protection and support. Rest or restricted activity is necessary to allow the body to heal. Ice should be applied for approximately 20 minutes to relieve swelling and pain. Although different theories exist, ice (not heat) is usually used in the first 24 hours. Ice massage is also a technique used to decrease pain and swelling. For example, water can be frozen in a Styrofoam™ or paper cup, which is torn back about an inch from the top so that the ice can be rubbed on the injured area. Do this for approximately 20 minutes, depending on the type of cold pack applied, the area of injury, and sensitivity of the person (Holcomb, 2005). Ice gets colder than gel packs, so if the ice pack is held stationary on the skin, the GFI may want to place a towel under the ice pack so the tissue does not sustain damage. Compression bandages help prevent swelling and should be applied distally and wrapped proximally. Elevating the

injury above the level of the heart can help further reduce swelling (Mellion et al., 2003).

Secondary treatment involves medical care and may include corticosteroid shots, physical therapy, something to brace the area, such as a cast or splint, and **nonsteroidal anti-inflammatory drugs (NSAIDs)**, such as aspirin, ibuprofen, or naproxen, which relieve pain, fever, and inflammation. Heat is used to increase blood flow to muscle tissue to increase temperature, elasticity, and healing. Superficial heat, such as hot packs or hot whirlpools, is used to relieve muscle spasms and stiffness and to reduce pain (Mellion et al., 2003).

Ultrasound is a deep heating modality used in athletic training and physical therapy settings to increase circulation to an area and decrease inflammation. Ultrasound delivers heat to tissues below the surface by using high- or low-frequency sound waves.

Remember that the diagnosis and treatment of injuries is outside the **scope of practice** of a GFI. If a participant asks about an injury, the GFI should refer him or her to an appropriate healthcare provider and contact the provider to obtain guidelines and contraindications related to fitness training and the injured area.

Fractures

A fracture is a disruption or break in bone continuity. The type of fracture depends on bone health, age, and the stress that caused it (Anderson, Hall, & Martin, 2000). The term "closed fracture" is used to describe a fracture where there is no break in the surface of the skin. With "open fractures," there is an open wound that may or may not have the end of the broken bone protruding through it. A GFI should suspect a broken bone when any of the following are present (Mistovich & Karren, 2008):

- Deformity or angulation—a difference in size or abnormal position
- Pain and tenderness
- Grating, **crepitus** with associated pain or discomfort
- Swelling
- Disfigurement
- Severe weakness and loss of function
- Bruising
- Exposed bone ends
- A joint locked in position
- Audible snap at the time of injury
- Inability to bear weight on the limb (stand or walk)

A fracture is a serious injury not only because the bone is broken, but also because of the potential injury to the surrounding soft tissue. Tendons, ligaments, muscles, nerves, and blood vessels may be damaged, with a threat of permanent disability. Fractures may result from a direct blow or more indirect cause, such as a fall.

Immediate care for a victim with a suspected fracture involves controlling hemorrhage, preventing further injury to the bone and soft tissue, and providing first aid for shock, if necessary. If a GFI suspects a fracture, he or she should take the following steps:

- Keep the victim as still as possible; do not allow him or her to move the injured part or attempt to put weight on it.
- Remove or cut away clothing that covers the injury. This step allows more thorough assessment and prevents contamination of an open fracture.
- Cover an open fracture with a sterile gauze dressing or clean cloth to prevent further contamination. Activate the EMS system immediately and keep the victim lying down if there is significant bleeding

to improve circulation to the heart and brain until help arrives. Apply gentle pressure to slow or stop the bleeding, using care not to disturb the fractured site.
- Leave the protruding ends of bone where they are. Attempting to push them back in place will increase the risk of infection and further injury to soft tissues.
- If the victim must be transported, splint the limb to immobilize it. However, if the extremity is grossly deformed and splinting may be difficult, merely prevent the injured limb from moving until medical help arrives. An untrained person's attempt to move a fractured limb can convert a closed fracture into an open one, or cause nerve and vascular injury in an uncomplicated fracture.

Splinting or immobilizing a fractured limb protects it against further injury during transportation, reduces pain, and prevents bone fragments from injuring arteries or other tissues. Many household objects or pieces of equipment in a health club may be converted to emergency splints—any object that provides support or prevents movement can serve this purpose. Some examples include heavy cardboard, newspapers, rolled blankets or towels, exercise mats, and straight sticks. The splint should simply be long enough to extend past the joints above and below the suspected fracture and should be padded to prevent pressure injuries due to contact with hard surfaces or sharp edges. A first-aid course will provide guidance in how to splint an extremity.

Figures 9-6 and 9-7 illustrate properly applied splints of the forearm and ankle, using materials commonly found in a home or fitness facility.

Stress injuries occur where there is an imbalance in **bone formation** and **bone**

Figure 9-6

Splinting the forearm: The bone has been immobilized by newspaper that has been rolled up, padded with a towel, and tied with strips of material to hold the splint in place. Using a sling in combination with the splint will immobilize the joints below the fracture (wrist) and above the fracture (elbow). The sling also elevates the hand slightly above the elbow to minimize swelling.

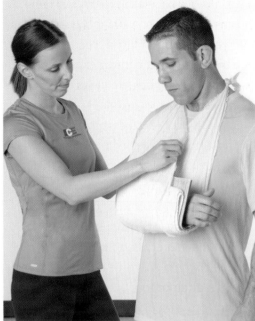

Figure 9-7

Splinting the ankle: Check circulation and sensation. Splint the ankle using a rolled blanket, towel, or exercise mat, applying it around the ankle and sole of the foot and tying it into place with cloth strips.

resorption. Stress fractures often occur in the tibia when abnormal stress is placed on the bone. The primary symptom is usually pain when bearing weight on that limb. Active individuals who are susceptible to stress fractures are typically those participating in high-repetition, high-intensity, or high-impact activities (e.g., endurance running, jumping, and sprinting). An adequate intake of calcium and vitamin D is essential for optimal bone health, as are sufficient estrogen levels for women. Proper progression in an exercise program and supportive footwear can also help prevent stress fractures. Management involves resting the

injured area and exercising only at levels that do not cause symptoms. Nonweightbearing exercises such as swimming or stationary biking are recommended during the healing process (Mellion et al., 2003).

Head Injuries

The head has a natural protection from injury—the skull—which forms a bony covering around the brain and contains many cranial and facial bones. Three layers of protective covering called the **meninges** lie beneath the surface of the skull. Besides offering protection to the brain and spinal cord, the meninges also allow venous drainage through vessels that flow between them and through the middle layer of the three meninges, the arachnoid mater—so named because of the spider-like web of vessels it contains. Just below the arachnoid mater is a space that contains cerebrospinal fluid that cushions the brain by distributing blunt forces over a larger area. When the skull is fractured, this clear fluid may be seen on bandages forming a "halo" or ring of clear wet liquid around the blood. It may also leak from ear canals due to a fracture at the base of the skull or through the nose if the fracture was in the anterior cranial area (Schenck, 2005).

The term "concussion" describes an injury to the brain resulting from an impact to the head associated with a change in mental status. By definition, a concussion is not immediately life-threatening, but can cause both short- and long-term problems. Concussions can occur during contact sports, as the result of falls or blows to the head (such as in football or martial arts training). There may be an accompanying temporary loss of consciousness. The first signs of a concussion are often confusion and disorientation. The person may not be able to explain what happened and may experience memory loss that causes him or her to ask the same question repeatedly. Speech may be slow or slurred, and the person may be uncoordinated and have a headache or nausea. Following a concussion, the brain cells are in a vulnerable state and a second injury could be debilitating, so rest is absolutely necessary.

It is sometimes difficult to recognize a concussion, as the initial signs can be subtle. GFIs should be aware of the following warning signs:

- Amnesia
- Confusion
- Memory loss
- Headache
- Drowsiness
- Loss of consciousness
- Impaired speech
- **Tinnitus**
- Unequal pupil size
- Nausea
- Vomiting
- Balance problems or dizziness
- Blurry or double vision
- Sensitivity to light or noise
- Any change in the individual's behavior, thinking, or physical functioning

A common and sometimes dangerous misconception exists that a loss of consciousness always accompanies a concussion. It is important that GFIs diligently watch for other symptoms after a possible brain injury, such as a vacant stare, delayed verbal or motor responses, increased sensitivity to light or sound, irritability, **depression,** poor coordination, fatigue, sleep disturbances, and loss of sense of taste or smell. Another disturbing misconception is the notion that if loss of consciousness does not occur, the concussion is minor and the athlete or participant can safely return to the activity. It is essential that GFIs understand that no concussion is ever minor.

For days or months after a concussion, there might be a number of symptoms still present, such as a headache and the inability to focus or concentrate (Mellion et al., 2003). Individuals who experience any post-concussion symptoms should be kept from activity until given permission to return by a healthcare professional with experience in evaluating for concussion. A repeat concussion that occurs before the brain recovers from the first can slow recovery or increase the likelihood of long-term problems.

For any head trauma, the GFI should initiate CPR, if necessary. It is always prudent to assume there is a spinal injury until it can be ruled out, so the GFI must try not to move the victim. If the person can talk, check his or her level of consciousness by asking questions such as the victim's name, where he or she is, and what happened. Look for unequal pupil size, as that might indicate a serious head trauma.

Depending on how the head trauma occurred, individuals who suffer concussions may need to get additional medical attention for other possible injuries (Lillegard, Butcher, & Rucker, 1999):

- For any injury close to the eye area, it is essential that the victim get an evaluation from an ophthalmologist.
- For nasal injuries, the victim should be checked for damage to the nasal septum.
- If a tooth becomes avulsed (i.e., knocked out), the GFI should keep it clean and place it in milk or salt water, or have the victim keep the tooth in the cheek area and see a dentist immediately to re-implant it. A root canal might be required two to three weeks afterward.

Neck and Back Injuries

The most common neck injuries are cervical strains and sprains. A cervical strain is due to overstretching of the neck musculature, such as the paraspinals, upper trapezius, and sternocleidomastoids. Similarly, cervical sprains can happen when ligaments are stretched beyond their capacities (Lillegard, Butcher, & Rucker, 1999). Although they may be more severe than strains, sprains have similar causes and symptoms (Anderson, Hall, & Martin, 2000). They can range from grade I (mild) to grade III (severe), depending on ligament laxity. Pain and stiffness are the usual symptoms, along with a decreased ROM. To relieve spasm, ice massage for eight to 10 minutes is recommended. Symptoms may take a few days or months to disappear. For these injuries, exercise is not recommended unless there is a pain-free ROM and clearance to exercise has been provided by a doctor. Medical treatment might require the person to wear a cervical collar for six to 12 weeks if necessary (Lillegard, Butcher, & Rucker, 1999).

A "stinger" is a sharp burning pain down the arm after a head or shoulder injury. Short-term loss of arm function might accompany this injury. Symptoms usually last for five to 15 minutes. If they last any longer, medical treatment is recommended (Vaccaro, 2003).

Spine Injuries

The uppermost part of the spinal column, the cervical spine, is located in the neck and made up of seven cervical vertebrae (Figure 9-8). This part of the spinal column is the most mobile and delicate. Some situations where a neck injury might occur are when a person falls from a height or sustains trauma to the face or head, such as in a diving or sports-related accident (Mistovich & Karren, 2008).

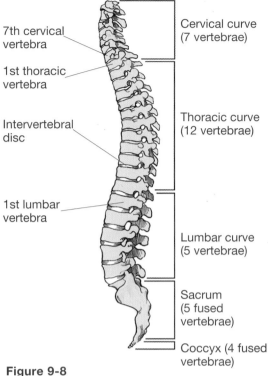

7th cervical vertebra

1st thoracic vertebra

Intervertebral disc

1st lumbar vertebra

Cervical curve (7 vertebrae)

Thoracic curve (12 vertebrae)

Lumbar curve (5 vertebrae)

Sacrum (5 fused vertebrae)

Coccyx (4 fused vertebrae)

Figure 9-8
Vertebral column (lateral view)

When a neck injury is suspected, it is important that further damage is prevented. The victim should not be moved and the head must be immobilized until EMS professionals arrive. The GFI can check to see if the victim is breathing. In an unconscious victim, open the airway with the jaw thrust method instead of the head tilt–chin lift (see Figures 9-2 and 9-3). If the person can talk, the GFI should instruct him or her to look straight ahead and *not* try to follow the GFI with his or her eyes when talking to keep the head as still as possible (Vaccaro, 2003). Damage to the spinal cord may interfere with the phrenic nerve's signals to the diaphragm, which interferes with breathing, so the GFI must be aware of possible respiratory distress or failure. Manual in-line stabilization (holding the head still as shown in Figure 9-9) should be done until EMS rescuers can strap the person to a backboard (Mistovich & Karren, 2008). The

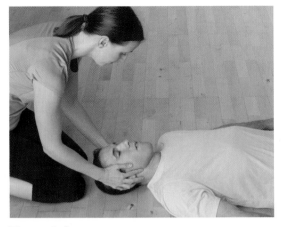

Figure 9-9
Immobilization of the head and neck: Kneel at the victim's head, place the hands on either side of the head and neck, and hold them firmly in place. Keep the victim quiet and prevent movement of the head. Do not try to reposition the victim.

GFI should continue monitoring the victim until help arrives.

The middle part of the spinal column, the thoracic spine, is made up of 12 vertebrae of the upper and mid-back that allow flexion, extension, and rotation (see Figure 9-8). There are four normal curves of the spine (cervical, thoracic, lumbar, and sacral). The curve of the thoracic spine is **kyphotic,** which means that it curves posteriorly as a rounding of the upper back. An increase of this curvature has been called "swimmer's back" because swimming (especially the butterfly stroke) can cause this curve to become exaggerated due to the development of tight pectoral muscles. Similarly, weight trainers who overtrain the pectorals and do not adequately train the back muscles can develop this postural deviation (Anderson, Hall, & Martin, 2000). An increase in kyphosis also accompanies osteoporosis or weak back musculature in older adults. Compression fractures can occur in this area, as well as the low back, in association with osteoporosis. While unlikely to cause spinal cord injury, they can occur acutely, producing

severe pain. If there is any indication of neurologic compromise, emergency medical treatment is required.

The lower back, or lumbar spine, is made up of five vertebrae that allow flexion, extension, and side bending (see Figure 9-8). The **lordotic** curve of the lumbar spine curves anteriorly, making the low back curve into **hyperextension.** An example of an exaggerated lumbar curve can be seen in many gymnasts, for whom movements often require hyperextension of the back. Weak abdominal muscles, high amounts of body fat in the abdominal region, and poor posture can also contribute to this excessive curvature, as does as an anterior pelvic tilt. Altering any of these natural curves of the spine can interfere with load transfer between the upper and lower extremities and cause injury or low-back pain. A herniated or prolapsed disc, bony encroachment, or inflammation can cause burning or shooting pain, weakness, numbness, and tingling due to nerve compression. These commonly occur in the lumbar spine, most often between the fourth and fifth lumbar vertebrae (L4 and L5) or the fifth lumbar and first sacral vertebrae (L5 and S1). Any of the aforementioned acute signs or symptoms of back injury should be addressed immediately by the participant's healthcare provider. Treatment is determined by the severity of the injury (Anderson, Hall, & Martin, 2000; Lillegard, Butcher, & Rucker, 1999).

Low-back pain is estimated to affect 80% of the adult population at some point in their lives and is one of the leading causes of disability and missed work time (Lillegard, Butcher, & Rucker, 1999). Runners are likely to suffer from low-back pain because of their tendency to have tight hip flexors and hamstrings. These both act to tilt the pelvis anteriorly and to increase the lordotic curve of the lumbar

269

spine. To reduce the likelihood of low-back pain, runners should be sure to include flexibility exercises for the hip flexors and hamstrings and be conservative when increasing distance and speed. Tension develops in the muscles surrounding the lumbar spine to counteract the body's tendency to lean forward, especially when running. Runners also may experience another type of lumbar injury—low-back muscle strain. This injury can occur when the runner overstrides, making this area susceptible to hyperextension (Lillegard, Butcher, & Rucker, 1999).

GFIs should teach their participants proper lifting technique to avoid low-back strains: keeping objects close to the body, bending at the knees while keeping the back straight, and contracting the abdominal and leg muscles to assist with the lift. It is a good idea to avoid simultaneous bending and twisting movements while lifting heavy weight and to exhale during the lift. Lifting weights with a slow, controlled motion is best to lower the compression and shear force on the spine and decrease the tension in the paraspinal muscles. Finally, good posture should be maintained when doing all ADL, including sitting, standing, and walking, to avoid chronic strains or sprains (Anderson, Hall, & Martin, 2000).

Shock

Shock, also known as **hypoperfusion,** occurs when blood is not adequately distributed in the body and tissues do not receive the oxygen and nutrients needed for proper function and survival. There are four major types of shock: hypovolemic, obstructive, distributive, and cardiogenic.

Hypovolemic shock occurs when fluid, such as blood, is lost as a result of severe dehydration or from severe internal or external bleeding. This should be suspected in any trauma victim who may be internally bleeding or when a person has lost a lot of blood from an open wound. Obstructive shock occurs when a blood clot or other mechanical obstruction does not allow blood to reach the heart. Distributive shock occurs when vessels are dilated and not allowing normal blood distribution. This can be due to a spinal or head injury, an allergy such as a bee sting or food allergy, or toxins from a severe infection. Cardiogenic shock is caused by the failure of the heart to pump effectively. It can be due to damage to the heart muscle, most often from a major heart attack. Other causes include abnormal heart rhythms, **cardiomyopathy** (disease or disorder of cardiac muscle), and cardiac valve problems (Brandler & Sinert, 2010; Mistovich & Karren, 2008).

The signs and symptoms of shock are restlessness; anxiety; altered mental status; pale, cool, and clammy skin; fast and weak pulse; irregular breathing; nausea; and thirst. Shock is a serious condition that requires immediate medical attention. The GFI should initiate CPR and control severe bleeding. If there is no trauma to the lower body, it is important to elevate the victim's legs 8 to 12 inches (20 to 30 cm). It is also a good idea to cover the victim with a blanket, because shock decreases the ability to regulate body temperature, and the person may feel cold (Mistovich & Karren, 2008).

Universal Precautions and Protection Against Bloodborne Pathogens

Due to the threat of communicable disease, it is necessary to take universal precautions when dealing with another other person's blood or body fluids. The bloodborne pathogens of the most concern are **hepatitis B** and HIV. Rescuers should wear gloves, use a protective barrier device when performing CPR, and, if there is potential for blood to splash on the rescuer, a gown and eye protection should also be worn. To dispose of anything that touched blood or body fluid, use biohazard bags if they are available and be sure to properly seal them. If they are not available, use a sealable plastic bag. Do not toss these bags in the trash. Instead, dispose of them according to company policy or give them to trained emergency personnel. Make sure that all first-aid kits include latex gloves. All rescuers should wash their hands with soap and warm water for at least 10 to 15 seconds afterward, whether or not gloves were worn. Hand washing is the best way to prevent the spread of disease (AHA, 2006).

Hepatitis B and C are transmitted more easily than HIV. Hepatitis can be transmitted by drug injection, contact with mucous membranes or broken (non-intact) areas of skin, or possibly by casual contact such as living in close quarters with someone who is a hepatitis B carrier (Mellion et al., 2003).

Summary

Fitness facilities can better serve their members and avoid possible emergency situations by having a risk-management plan and maintaining a well-stocked first-aid kit. Although the diagnosis and treatment of injuries is outside the scope of practice for GFIs, all fitness professionals should have a knowledge and understanding of possible medical emergencies that can arise during the course of a career in the fitness industry. GFIs should learn to recognize medical emergencies and know when it is necessary to activate EMS.

HIV Infection and Exercise

Those infected with HIV are encouraged to be active and even participate in sports. There is very low risk to the other participants. As long as the infected person is healthy and asymptomatic, the disease can be managed better when he or she stays active, and the individual will have better overall health and quality of life. Some research has even found that exercise can slow the progression of the disease (Mustafa et al., 1999). Infected individuals should not exercise to a point of exhaustion and should discontinue competition when CD4 counts are below 500. CD4 cells, also known as T4 or T-Helper cells, are a type of white blood cell that fight infection. Normal ranges for healthy individuals are usually 500 to 1500. As HIV progresses, CD4 counts decrease, and with treatment the number increases. At a CD4 count of less than 200, a person infected with HIV is considered to have **acquired immunodeficiency syndrome (AIDS)** (American Association of Clinical Chemistry, 2005). When AIDS is diagnosed, the person can continue to stay active, but should exercise only as symptoms allow (Mellion et al., 2003).

According to the Centers for Disease Control and Prevention (CDC), there are no documented cases of HIV being transmitted during participation in sports. The very low risk of transmission during sports participation would involve sports with direct body contact in which bleeding might be expected to occur. Because most transmissions occur with deep hollow-bore needle sticks, transmission is very unlikely to occur during exercise (Mellion et al., 2003) and sweat has not been found to contain HIV (CDC, 2007). Universal precautions do not apply to sweat, tears, saliva, urine, nasal discharge, and sputum unless blood is visible (CDC, 1996). If someone is bleeding, his or her participation in the sport should be interrupted until the wound stops bleeding and is both antiseptically cleaned and securely bandaged.

References

American Academy of Orthopedic Surgeons (2006). *First Aid and CPR* (5th ed.). Sudbury, Mass.: Jones and Bartlett.

American Association of Clinical Chemistry (2005). *CD4 Count.* www.labtestsonline.org/understanding/analytes/cd4/sample.html

American College of Sports Medicine (2007). *ACSM's Health/Fitness Facility Standards and Guidelines* (3rd ed.). Champaign, Ill.: Human Kinetics.

American Heart Association (2006). *Heartsaver First Aid with CPR and AED Student Workbook.* Dallas, Tex.: American Heart Association.

Anderson, M., Hall, S.J., & Martin, M. (2000). *Sports Injury Management* (2nd ed.). Media, Pa.: Williams & Wilkins.

Balady, G.J. et al. (1998). AHA/ACSM Scientific Statement: Recommendations for cardiovascular screening, staffing, and emergency policies at health/fitness facilities: A Joint Position Statement by the American College of Sports Medicine and the American Heart Association. *Circulation,* 97, 2283–2293.

Bohm K. et al. (2007). Survival is similar after standard treatment and chest compression only in out-of-hospital bystander cardiopulmonary resuscitation. *Circulation,* 116, 25, 2908–2912.

Brandler, E.S. & Sinert, R.S. (2010). *Cardiogenic Shock.* www.emedicine.medscape.com/article/759992

Canadian Fitness Matters (2004). *Canadian Fitness Safety Standards.* www.canadianfitnessmatters.ca/cf_standards.aro

Centers for Disease Control and Prevention (2007). *HIV and Its Transmission.* www.cdc.gov/hiv/resources/factsheets/transmission.htm

Centers for Disease Control and Prevention (1996). *Universal Precautions for Prevention of Transmission of HIV and Other Bloodborne Infections.* www.cdc.gov/ncidod/dhqp/bp_universal_precautions.html

Corey-Bloom, J. & David, R.B. (Eds.) (2009). *Clinical Adult Neurology* (3rd ed.). New York: Demos Medical Publishing.

Gonzales, L. & Lino, K. (2008). Workplace teamwork saves lives. *Currents in Cardiovascular Care,* Winter, 3.

Herlitz, J. et al. (2005). Efficacy of bystander CPR: Intervention by lay people and health care professionals. *Resuscitation,* 66, 3, 291–295.

Holcomb, W.R. (2005). Duration of cryotherapy application. *Athletic Therapy Today,* 10, 1, 60–62.

Iwami T. et al. (2007). Effectiveness of bystander-initiated cardiac-only resuscitation for patients with out-of-hospital cardiac arrest. *Circulation,* 116, 25, 2900–2907.

Lillegard, W.A., Butcher, J.D., & Rucker, K.S. (1999). *Handbook of Sports Medicine: A Symptom-Oriented Approach.* Stoneham, Ma.: Butterworth-Heinemann.

Mellion, M.B. et al. (2003). *Sports Medicine Secrets* (3rd ed.). Philadelphia, Pa.: Hanley and Belfus.

Mistovich, J.J. & Karren, K.J. (2008). *Prehospital Emergency Care* (8th ed.). Upper Saddle River, N.J.: Pearson Education.

Moore, L.K. (2008). *Emergency Communications: The Future of 911.* CRS Report for Congress.

Mustafa, T. et al. (1999). Association between exercise and HIV disease progression in a cohort of homosexual men. *Annals of Epidemiology,* 9, 2, 127–131.

Nagao K. et al. (2007). Cardiopulmonary resuscitation by bystanders with chest compression only (SOS-KANTO): An observational study. *Lancet,* 369, 920–926.

Nichol, G. et al. (1999). A cumulative meta-analysis of the effectiveness of defibrillator-capable emergency medical services for victims of out-of-hospital cardiac arrest. *Annals of Emergency Medicine,* 34, 517–525.

Rimmer, J.H. (1994). *Fitness and Rehabilitation Programs for Special Populations.* Dubuque, Iowa: WCB McGraw-Hill.

Rubin, D.H. et al. (2009). Neurologic disorders. In: Marx, J.A. (Ed.) *Rosen's Emergency Medicine: Concepts and Clinical Practice* (7th ed.). Philadelphia, Pa.: Mosby Elsevier.

San Diego Fire-Rescue Department (2008). *What is 9-1-1?* The City of San Diego. www.sandiego.gov/fireandems/911/whatis911.shtml

Sayre, M.R. et al. (2008). Hands-only (compression-only) cardiopulmonary resuscitation: A call to action for bystander response to adults who experience out-of-hospital sudden cardiac arrest: A science advisory for the public from the American Heart Association Emergency Cardiovascular Care Committee. *Circulation,* 117, 2162–2167.

Schenck, R.C. (Ed.). (2005). *Athletic Training and Sports Medicine* (4th ed.). Rosemont, Ill.: American Academy of Orthopedic Surgeons.

Swor, R. et al. (2006). CPR training and CPR performance: Do CPR-trained bystanders perform CPR? *Academy of Emergency Medicine,* 13, 6, 596–601.

Travers, A.H. et al. (2010). Cardiopulmonary resuscitation and emergency cardiovascular care. *Circulation,* 122, S676–S684.

Vaccaro, A.R. (2003). Acute cervical spine injuries in the athlete: Diagnosis, management, and return-to-play. *International Sports Medicine Journal,* 4, 1, 1–9.

Suggested Reading

American Academy of Orthopedic Surgeons (2009). *Sports First Aid and Injury Prevention*. Sudbury, Mass.: Jones and Bartlett.

American Council on Exercise (2010). *ACE's Essentials of Exercise Science for fitness Professionals*. San Diego, Calif.: American Council on Exercise.

American Council on Exercise (2015). *ACE Medical Exercise Specialist Manual.* San Diego, Calif.: American Council on Exercise.

Carline, J.D. et al. (2004). *Mountaineering First Aid: A Guide to Accident Response and First Aid Care.* Seattle, Wash.: The Mountaineers Books.

Epilepsy Foundation (2009). *About Epilepsy.* www.epilepsyfoundation.org/about/firstaid/

Flegel, M.J. (1997). *Sport First Aid.* Champaign Ill.: Human Kinetics.

Kulund, D. (1988). *The Injured Athlete* (2nd ed.). Philadelphia, Pa.: Lippincott Williams & Wilkins.

Travers, A.H. et al. (2010). Cardiopulmonary resuscitation and emergency cardiovascular care. *Circulation,* 122, S676–S684.

Shannon Fable, the 2006 ACE Group Fitness Instructor of the Year and a Top 3 Finalist for 2009 IDEA Instructor of the Year, is the founder and CEO of Sunshine Fitness Resources, a fitness consulting firm that provides services for instructors, aspiring presenters, fitness manufacturers, and managers. She is also the owner of Balletone® and creator of GroupEx PRO™. Fable, a Power Bar®–sponsored athlete, is an international presenter for several well-known companies, including Schwinn®, BOSU®, and Power Systems®. As a program developer, educator, and freelance writer for the past 15 years, Fable was recently added to the American Council on Exercise's Industry Advisory Panel.

CHAPTER TEN

The Business of Group Fitness

By Shannon Fable

The role of the group fitness instructor (GFI) has certainly changed over the past two decades. Not only have the clothes improved and the formats expanded, but the potential impact an instructor can have on the bottom line of a fitness facility has greatly increased as well. Unfortunately, it is common for facilities to have trouble harnessing a GFI's contributions or coordinating individual talent to better serve the members and ultimately enhance the facility's earning potential. The recipe is a delicate one, requiring constant adjustments, communication, nurturing, and a high level of involvement from management. With limited budgets allocated to non-revenue-producing departments, the resources needed to continue moving the GFI forward are constantly being evaluated.

Which side will give first? Will owners and managers begin to connect the dots on the accounting side to match the GFI's monetary contributions to the facility beyond revenue programs and then be able to increase pay and resources so that GFIs are more inclined to focus on the business side of the club? Or will GFIs grasp the magnitude of their role and realize they have a direct line to dues, and then increase their focus on the business in hopes that owners and general managers will see the impact a GFI team can have and allocate additional resources? Either way, the more the GFI understands what he or she can do that ultimately leads to member retention, increased new business, and customer satisfaction, the better. Stated simply, a GFI should learn as much as possible about the business of group fitness.

GFIs are the ultimate ambassadors for a fitness facility. Responsibilities include creating relationships among members, disseminating important club information, bringing in new members to try classes, providing safe and effective programming, encouraging and motivating members and non-members alike, and much more. Many of the things GFIs must do involve the "art" of fitness and cannot be measured directly by totaling membership sales, participant weight loss, the purchasing of packages, or other hard numbers found on accounting spreadsheets. Therefore, it is important to develop a metric to help create objectivity in the GFI's subjective world.

To date, **class count, cost per head,** and **penetration** have been the only means to determine if a GFI was doing a "good job." And, with the number of participants in a given class considered the ultimate factor for determining a GFI's worth, many of the other responsibilities that affect the facility as a whole can often take a back seat. A true

measurement of a GFI's contributions must encompass so much more than how many bodies are in the classroom.

A GFI's ability to positively impact the bottom line at a fitness facility hinges on three key areas, which together form the "group fitness trifecta":
- Education
- Teamwork
- Class value

Understanding the group fitness trifecta will help GFIs better connect their efforts with the ultimate success of the facility, while maintaining professional standards and adherence with the ACE Code of Ethics (see Appendix A). GFIs should concentrate equally on what happens on stage (teaching classes and interacting with members) and "backstage" (the preparation that goes into creating class plans) in all three of these areas to be most effective. A GFI's "worth" can easily be calculated when each area is assessed. Managers can develop objective assessments of a GFI's performance to better assist in career development and growth based on the three areas. A GFI can also create his or her own action plan around the three areas to ward off burnout, complacency, and boredom, which often result in decreased satisfaction for both the GFI and his or her class participants.

GFIs instructing classes outside the traditional health club model will still find the trifecta applicable. All GFIs in the industry work to motivate people to be healthier through safe and effective programming. And, even if they are small business owners or entrepreneurs working outside the health club, individual GFIs should still strive to continually increase their value by judging performance based on the group fitness trifecta metric. Striving for excellence in education, teamwork (on a more global scale), and class value will greatly increase the level of professionalism in the industry and continue to change the perception of the GFI from entertainer to fitness leader.

Education

Earning the ACE Group Fitness Instructor Certification is the first step toward beginning a career as a GFI. However, this is only the beginning. While ACE's certification exam tests a candidate's theoretical understanding of fitness principles and group fitness techniques, learning to effectively use music, equipment, choreography, communication, and cueing techniques at the same time requires study and practice. It is critical to gain additional knowledge and hands-on experience through specialty trainings, workshops, and conferences that may be one- to four-hours long or may even span several days. This in-person experience may be equipment-based in nature (e.g., stability balls or kettlebells) or focus on a specific format (e.g., indoor cycling or **Pilates** mat training). Beyond the additional education in the basics of leading group fitness classes, it is also important to take advantage of the mentoring opportunities to become a successful GFI.

Group Fitness Specialization

The landscape of group fitness has changed and "group fitness instructor" is now a generic term used to encompass all instructors that lead a wide variety of class formats for participants covering a broad spectrum of interests and ability levels. From indoor cycling and step training to dance-based classes and **yoga** fusion, the directions a GFI can go during a career in teaching are diverse. And, while most formats are based on the initial education received in a base certification, more in-depth training is necessary before teaching many of the formats available in fitness facilities today.

Fitness formats fall under three broad categories (or combinations thereof):
- *Cardio:* The focus is on conditioning the cardiovascular system with drills (non-choreographed) or combinations/patterns (choreographed).
- *Strength training:* The focus is on strengthening the muscles using a variety of equipment and exercises.
- *Mind/body:* The focus is on flexibility, strength, balance, and core training, sometimes combined with relaxation and focusing techniques.

Within these categories, several class types and formats exist. It is important for a GFI to choose a small number of formats to focus on initially, and then work toward building a larger repertoire over time. Resources, both written and live, exist to help GFIs create classes within each of the categories. More in-depth education is available through specialty trainings or workshops and is sometimes required to teach formats involving new equipment or class concepts. Fitness industry trend surveys and the GFI's personal interests and skill sets should help determine a specialization path. Refer to Appendix D for more information on various group fitness modalities and Chapter 6 for a discussion of special populations.

Personal Training and Small-group Training

Many GFIs enter the fitness industry part-time and later decide they would like to take their careers a bit further. Unfortunately, the body can only handle so many classes per week and at some point the potential for increased income is limited. A natural evolution for many GFIs is to transition into personal training or small-group personal training. As a successful GFI, building a base of clientele should be easy because there is a room full of potential clients in each class the instructor leads. However, additional training in both fitness and business are highly suggested and, in most cases, required before a GFI can legitimately pursue a personal-training career.

Moving Beyond Fitness

A GFI might also explore career paths inside and outside of the health club. Inside the health club, GFIs might be drawn toward becoming a group fitness manager/coordinator/supervisor. GFIs should keep in mind that the management side of the department is quite different than the front lines. A desire to staff, budget, create schedules, evaluate, mentor, and partake in ongoing customer service is essential for a group fitness manager. Once one becomes a group fitness manager, the role of instructor will begin to take a backseat to the business side of the department. Additional education or study should be devoted to leadership, communication, customer service, accounting, general business, and computer skills to make a smooth transition to management.

Outside of the club, GFIs could explore moving into the consumer side of the fitness industry. Community involvement could be rewarding for the GFI. Creating educational presentations or seminars for local businesses, clubs, or schools is a way for a GFI to share his or her knowledge outside of the fitness facility. GFIs can use this involvement in the community as an extension of his or her work for the fitness facility by using these opportunities as membership drives or marketing sessions. Reaching out to local television stations or other journalistic outlets could provide a platform for promoting a GFI's business or that of the club where he or she

works. In addition, creating websites, social media sites, blogs, podcasts, or videos based on a particular skill set or niche knowledge could potentially lead to increased income and be a way to share a GFI's passion for fitness with a much larger audience. As always, checking with current employers to be sure additional streams do not present a conflict of interest is important. Many DVD and TV celebrities, as well as fitness writers, got their start as GFIs looking for increased exposure and income via community outreach.

Beyond the community, the GFI could potentially explore becoming an educator for other fitness professionals. Whether locally, nationally, or internationally, becoming an expert in a specific field (e.g., a particular type of class, piece of equipment, or technique) can provide exciting opportunities for a GFI. Providing continuing education workshops, writing for industry publications, or creating educational DVDs are just a few options that exist for breaking into the educational arena.

Whether a GFI is interested in increasing revenue potential, looking for professional growth, or searching for a wider audience, many opportunities exist beyond teaching. Specializing in formats to create marketability, crossing over into personal training or small-group training, and even exploring options inside and outside of the club for advancement can help keep a GFI active in the industry. Continuing to specialize and enhance one's education is the secret to the success for any GFI. Remember, the base-level GFI certification is merely the beginning, and a GFI's learning should not end when he or she closes this manual and takes the exam. Education is the number-one ingredient in the group fitness trifecta and will directly influence an instructor's overall success.

Teamwork

Group fitness, regardless of the size or type of health club or fitness facility, has often been seen as an individual endeavor. Multiple instructors may work for the same company and instruct many of the same members, but the degree to which they interact is not always the main objective of a club's management. Typically, instructors are hired to fill a specific need (i.e., teach a specific class at a specific time on a certain day in a specific format) based on his or her experience and expertise. And while how that class coordinates with others is taken into consideration when management is making decisions about appropriate hiring and scheduling, a GFI's ability to understand how his or her individual actions can affect all other aspects of the facility—including other classes, programs, instructors, personal training, and membership sales—is often last on the list for discussion.

A GFI, as mentioned earlier, has a direct line to dues and can cause ripple effects that are felt throughout an entire organization. The GFI is often one of the few individuals a club member will interact with on an ongoing basis. Therefore, his or her ability to speak the mission and vision of a club; understand and direct new initiatives, events, and protocols; and positively influence members to participate in many areas of the club can have a profound impact on the business. Superb customer service to all members, both inside and outside of the GFI's class, is extremely important to the overall success of the club.

Teamwork involves GFIs being on the same page with fundamental fitness education and programming concepts. GFIs should have an understanding of a facility's mission and vision. In addition, a team of GFIs should know how their collective actions help support

and drive that mission and vision. The group fitness department as a whole should understand how working from the same playbook can increase a facility's earning potential, both through new members and member retention. A GFI embracing the teamwork aspect of his or her position is the second secret to success in the group fitness business.

A team is created with the blending of individual talents and the coordination of various strengths to create something greater than the sum of its parts. Teamwork is a constant process and requires hard work from all members involved, but the rewards for the facility, staff, and individual are well worth the effort. Teamwork does not thrive in an organization because talent and ambition are present, nor can it be summed up as cooperation. A group fitness manager (or the supervisor of the GFIs) should ultimately be responsible for creating a system to promote and advocate teamwork beyond the individual success of the instructor. But each GFI can benefit from understanding how adopting a more team-centric attitude as an employee can positively affect an organization.

Teamwork in a group fitness department can achieve the following:

- Increased professionalism
- Increased class participation and success
- Member retention and new business
- Cohesiveness and community
- A more engaged employee, thus enhanced employee retention
- A more enjoyable place to work

Increased Professionalism

GFIs who combine to create a staff often come from different backgrounds, have wide-ranging experiences in the industry, and are on unique paths in their fitness careers. Public perception of the group fitness instructor varies from community to community and individual to individual, and is often based on interactions inside and outside of the club environment. If a consumer is faced with conflicting information from GFIs within a club or bases a global opinion on one bad experience, the GFI's ability to make a great impact on the health and wellness of that individual and others is threatened. There are two ways that teamwork can help ensure that the perception of the staff is the best it can be: speaking from the same playbook and supporting one another.

If a member comes to a cycling class on Monday and is told that standing up is the most effective and efficient way to burn calories by one instructor, comes to cycling class on Wednesday and is told that standing up is *less* effective and efficient, and then comes on Friday and hears that it does not matter, what conclusion will the member draw? Chances are, the member will be confused and make up his or her own mind about the validity of the GFIs' statements, begin seeking the opinion of third parties (Internet, other fitness professionals, friends), or simply side with the instructor he or she likes best. The important thing is that this individual's perception of the group as a whole is damaged, in which case everyone stands to lose, particularly since multiple participants will undoubtedly be having this same negative experience.

GFIs should possess individual talent and personality and have the ability to make a class uniquely their own, but the fundamentals learned through the GFI certification and specialized training should be standardized within a facility to be certain that members are receiving the most up-to-date, appropriate education possible. Of course, the entertainment value of a class is important as well; the energy in a group fitness class keeps people

engaged, motivated, and coming back for more, but the education or content must be present first. When the education and entertainment can come from the same individuals, the group fitness program will thrive.

GFIs can do their part by making sure their education is up to date and continually enhanced. Subscribing to industry publications and attending continuing education classes will allow a GFI to be on the cutting edge while utilizing the most current information to design and deliver classes. Sharing this information with other instructors and checking in with the group fitness supervisor to be sure his or her ideas are in line with the overall program is a start. Choosing to work for facilities that promote and create this type of consistency, or suggesting a process for implementing such a plan, could help a GFI become more successful.

Being able to speak intelligently about one's teammates—listing similar formats that are offered at other times during the week, knowing about the instructors who teach those formats, confidently introducing a substitute instructor who will be teaching for a week, knowing how to answer questions regarding policy or schedule changes, and feeling empowered to answer questions on behalf of the group fitness program and facility—can greatly enhance the perception of the staff while providing outstanding customer service for the member. Being seen as a trusted voice regarding health and wellness, as well as club business, will indirectly influence class size, member retention, and the creation of new business.

Increased Class Participation and Success

A GFI is often judged based on the number of participants in a class. Therefore, GFIs are expected to do what they can to create a positive experience for anyone who may walk through the doors in order to drive the numbers up and keep costs down. When a GFI views this responsibility as an individual, he or she has to rely on personality, communication, entertainment, and education value and constantly strive to improve his or her performance from week to week in the effort to gain numbers. While ongoing self-evaluation is a great course of action, it can be tough to constantly outdo oneself week after week, keep the momentum going when out of town and using a substitute instructor, or when switching formats or time slots.

When GFIs interact and form relationships with other members of the team, the potential for numbers to increase across the board exists regardless of class time or format. When a group of GFIs are viewed as a team as opposed to competing individuals, members can develop trust in the program as a whole and will choose to attend classes more often and from a wider variety of instructors. For example, when an instructor can announce on Monday that Wednesday's class with a fellow instructor will be a great complement to what was just done in his or her class, and follow that up with real-life examples from having communicated with the other instructor about what he or she will be focused on that week, members know that the two are on the same page and can trust in the recommendation. Similarly, when participants witness GFIs taking one another's classes, trust in both instructors is heightened. The GFI who is teaching receives a boost, as the members think, "If this instructor would take her class, then I must be in the right place!" The GFI attending the class also receives a boost, as the members think "If this instruc-

tor will learn from my favorite instructor, her class must be good, too!"

Member Retention and New Business

Creating a community where instructors are bonded to one another and members bond to more than one instructor—as well as to other members—can increase member retention and create new business.

Special events are a big part of increasing perceived value for a member and can be used by the membership/sales department to court new business. Special events might include a team-taught New Year's Day class to kick off the New Year or the GFI team hosting a "smoothie happy hour" in the café immediately following a class where members can ask questions about classes, exercises, or the instructors' credentials. A six-week cycling program that culminates with a four-hour "century" ride to benefit a charitable organization is another great example. Events such as these create connections between members and GFIs, as well as among the members themselves. The more bonds that are created in the club setting, the more likely a member will stay at the facility. Special events provide more opportunities for these bonds to be formed.

The success of special events typically hinges on teamwork within the group fitness department. GFIs who jump in to support an event by agreeing to teach, market, greet, clean up, and so on will elevate their personal stock with management, as well as with other teammates and members. A successful event also provides members with another way to connect, and new members can see something special that might shift their decision to participate in group fitness classes.

Teamwork and Progressive Class Design

Hopefully, a facility's management will be establishing the means for teamwork to flourish among the members of the group fitness staff. But if a GFI finds him- or herself in a position where individual instructors within a facility are competing against one another, it is possible for the GFI to help start the shift.

Attending fellow instructors' classes is a great way to begin. A team that plays together succeeds together. Not only will GFIs receive new ideas for their own classes and a great workout, it is extremely helpful to be a participant every once and a while. Keeping a beginner's frame of mind, while becoming more of an expert in leading fitness classes, keeps the GFI grounded and open to exploring new ideas for communicating and delivering information to all participants. In addition, when GFIs frequent one another's classes, the perception of the staff is elevated.

Progressive class design is challenging when members come and go due to work, home, and leisure schedules. Unless a GFI is leading a scheduled program that has a registration process or clearly defined start and finish date, the chances of being able to loosely periodize for optimal results is diminished. However, a "training variety plan" is possible with group fitness staffs that work as a team. In some clubs, the managers will help coordinate instructors to allow members optimal cross-training and effective training programs. For example, a manager may schedule a high-intensity cardio class on Monday and Fridays at 9:00 a.m., a strength class on Tuesday and Thursday at 9:00 a.m., and a mind-body or flexibility class on Wednesdays at 9:00 a.m., thereby allowing participants to maintain a balanced training program by attending at the same time each day. The group fitness manager could also talk to the instructors in each of these formats and make sure their weekly class designs are varied enough to ensure a full-body workout that is consistent (e.g., equipment used, level of the class, or focus of the class) for the participants. GFIs should inquire to find out if this is how the schedule was developed in order to properly educate members.

If a GFI works for a club that does not yet program in this manner, he or she can begin the process by reaching out to instructors who teach in the same time slots and/or in the same format to coordinate efforts. For example, if a GFI teaches cycling on Mondays at 5:30 p.m., she could reach out to the other 5:30 p.m. cycling instructors at the facility and coordinate a weekly plan to ensure that members do not end up doing intervals every night that week. Similarly, an instructor who teaches a strength-training class on Monday at noon could reach out to the Wednesday noon instructor to let her know what type of equipment she used and what the focus of her class happened to be. Then, when the Wednesday instructor plans her class around the information and announces to members, "I know what you did Monday, so here's what I have in store today to complement that workout," the members gain confidence in the program as a whole, as well as in the two instructors specifically. Above all, the members receive more effective workouts because of the coordination, which will allow them to achieve results faster.

Communication is key for any staff. In a typical facility, the group fitness department will see roughly 15% of the members that visit the gym on any given day. Besides the front desk staff—who should see 100% of the members walking through the door—no other department makes as much contact with membership as the group fitness staff. Therefore, club-wide initiatives, as well as those programs running in specific departments, can gain greater traction if GFIs are all properly informed. GFIs can remain aware of facility events by staying in direct communication with the group fitness supervisor, connecting with teammates via email and by attending classes, participating as an active member of the facility, and asking questions and seeking out other employees as needed. For all GFIs, being an effective employee requires two-way communication for everyone to be successful.

Cohesiveness and Community

Community is created through connections. When people feel connected to a facility, they show up more frequently. When people show up, they utilize more services and become further connected inside of a club. The sense of community is a unique selling point that cannot be trumped by new equipment or cheaper pricing from a club down the street. Teamwork in a group fitness staff begins the process.

A staff that communicates and works together produces a great environment and a feeling of community. When instructors are taking other classes, participating in club events, and positively commenting on the contributions of their teammates, members notice. A club becomes a place of connection when members do not feel like they are being competed for by GFIs for class numbers. When the focus is turned to members having positive experiences and becoming

more active and healthier regardless of how they do it (step class, cycling class, personal training, spa, treadmill, or the pool), opportunities for relationships emerge. GFIs should encourage members to cross train, take other classes, and engage in other activities within and beyond the club. The members' health and well-being are the top priority and a GFI should help members find the appropriate path that will work for them (even if it means recommending someone or something else).

Community affects the bottom line of a facility. The owners and managers of fitness facilities are striving to do two things: gain members and retain members. The sales side can be done through pricing strategies, marketing campaigns, and special offers and events. Member retention is achieved through safe, effective programming in all arenas and services that increase the perceived value of a membership.

Both sales and retention are greatly enhanced by feelings of community. GFIs have the opportunity every day to make connections that can help build community. Arriving early to a class will allow the GFI time to welcome regulars, introduce him- or herself to new participants, and invite other people exercising in the facility to join the class. This time can also be used to forge connections among members. During class, making eye contact, providing personal attention when appropriate, and designing classes where each participant (regardless of ability level) feels successful and part of the group also creates strong connections. Then, following classes, GFIs can take time to thank participants and congratulate them on a job well done by making as many personal connections as possible while members are putting away equipment or exiting the classroom. Creating opportunities for socializing following classes, whether in the café or

lobby, can provide time for quality interaction outside of class, which can prove very valuable in opening the lines of communication and creating a community.

A group fitness staff that is empowered to answer questions and serve the members beyond the classes they teach will help with retention of current members, as well as get the current members to talk to their friends and family about what a different "feel" there is at this fitness facility. GFIs should strive to know as much information about the club's mission, vision, and overall procedures to act as this liaison between the facility and class participants. A common complaint with many organizations' customer service is the inability to receive answers promptly and having to deal with employees who do not know what is going on, how to find the answers, or how to be proactive in solving an issue. A GFI should get to know the organizations he or she works for and be sure that his or her individual mission and vision align with that of each facility. It is much easier to help create a community when everyone involved has shared values.

Teamwork is the second area where a GFI should spend energy to increase longevity in the industry and, more importantly, to improve the lives of those that he or she currently reaches or has the potential to reach in the community. A narrowly focused instructor who is motivated solely by the participants that frequent his or her classes and forgets to check in with the bigger picture of promoting health and wellness to the entire club while carrying out the company's mission and vision will be more limited in the success he or she can find as a GFI. GFIs who reach out to fellow instructors within a facility and make decisions based on the good of the employer, as well as the needs of the members, will master the business of group exercise.

Class Value

Class value is the final aspect of the group fitness trifecta. Understanding the objective data that classes are often judged by from a business perspective can help a GFI. Each class on a facility's schedule can be thought of as very expensive real estate. When calculating the "investment" involved to make space available for the hour that a GFI leads a class (e.g., square footage, electricity, sound system, equipment, and personnel, including the GFI and support staff), it is easy to see why so much emphasis is placed on the bottom-line value of a class. Management and owners compare class value to create the most economical, diverse, and appealing group fitness schedule for the membership base. A GFI should develop a firm understanding of the metrics by which he or she will be judged to develop strategies for increasing participation while remaining team-focused and ethical.

Group fitness class value is calculated in a few different ways:
- Class counts
- Cost per head
- Penetration

Each club will have a different system for assigning value and setting targets in the class-value categories. GFIs should always have a clear understanding of which values are held in highest esteem for a particular facility and how individuals are judged or compared based on the metrics. Developing a clear understanding of the three measurements and keeping track of each independently will help a GFI stay on track.

Class Counts

Class counts are the basis of the other two class-value indicators. GFIs are typically responsible for recording the number of participants in each class, whether electronically or simply in a notebook. At some facilities, a manager on duty or the front desk staff is asked to record the class count, which should be taken toward the middle of the class to account for any latecomers or those that have to leave class early. Of course, it is important to take note of the difference between the starting numbers of a class and the final numbers of the class. It is common (though certainly not recommended) for participants to leave prior to the final cool-down or stretch (or somewhere in the middle of the final stretch), but if a large number of participants leave prior to the cool-down or in the middle of the workout, the GFI should assess if something could have prevented their early departure. Causes may be external, such as a schedule that is not convenient for a majority of participants, or internal, such as posted class descriptions that do not match what actually happens in class, or a class design that is too difficult to follow.

Many clubs set target numbers for class counts based on member usage during a particular time slot and/or the square footage of the room. Others set the minimum number of participants a class should be averaging and keep an eye on the classes that seem to be underperforming. When schedule changes come around, these classes may be up for a modification in terms of format, time, or instructor to remedy the situation. In some clubs, numbers are simply compared and monitored to see trends that help determine future schedule shifts, additions, and deletions.

Class numbers alone may not tell the whole story. For example, a 2:00 p.m. class designed for pre- and postnatal fitness will have a much harder time attracting a large crowd. Specialty classes or classes in less desirable time slots will not look successful when measured using raw class counts. That said, such a class is important nonetheless. The same holds true for popular time slots. For example, 30 people attending a strength-training class mid-morning in a suburban facility is not all that uncommon, regardless of class quality. While the numbers may look impressive on paper, members could be attending because it is at the right time in the right place. A GFI should never assume that low numbers in specialty classes or off-peak hours mean that he or she is doing a bad job, nor should he or she believe that high attendance numbers when teaching in a popular time slot mean that the GFI is doing all he or she can to make the member experience the best it can be. Basing all opinions regarding the success of the class on raw numbers may lead a GFI astray. Regardless of numbers, GFIs should continually seek feedback from peers, participants, and managers to be certain they are doing all they can to provide the best experience possible. Continuing to raise the bar will ensure success.

Cost Per Head

Cost per head (CPH) takes class numbers and GFIs' salaries into consideration to determine the value of the class. By dividing the instructor's rate for teaching the class by the number of participants in a class, the cost per head reveals how much money it is taking to serve each participant. For example, if a 60-minute class has 20 attendees and the GFI's salary is $25/hour, the CPH would be $1.25 ($25 divided by 20 attendees), meaning that each participant is essentially paying $1.25 of his or her membership fee to attend class for that one hour.

Establishing a standard desirable CPH is difficult, as not all clubs and programs are created equal. A general rule of thumb when judging a class's CPH is to consider anything above $2.50 "in the red" or up for review, anything between $1.50 and $2.50 should be monitored or be deemed "in the yellow," while anything under $1.50 gets a "green light." Some clubs recommend striving to have the same number of people in a class as the GFI's hourly rate, which would result in $1.00 CPH (e.g., 25 people for a GFI that makes $25 per class).

CPH is limited by two factors that might make following either of these recommendations impossible. First, the number of people a room or available equipment can accommodate must be considered. For example, if an indoor cycling room only has 15 bikes and the instructor makes $25, the lowest CPH possible will be $1.67. Therefore, this CPH should be considered excellent, since it cannot be improved upon. The salary of an instructor can be the second limiting factor. If an instructor commands $50 an hour because of a specialty he or she possesses and the class he or she teaches is a niche program that is presented in off-peak times and draws 10 people on average, the CPH would be $5.00. Servicing the special needs of a specific group of members may prove more valuable and trump any concerns regarding CPH.

As of 2010, the average salary of a GFI per class was $23.50/hour for full-time instructors and $24.49/hour for part-time instructors (American Council on Exercise, 2010). Therefore, one can assume that classes should have between 20 and 30 participants to keep CPH in the average to above-average range. GFIs should discuss CPH averages with facility management to find out what the trends are in that specific facility. Aiming to fall in line with average CPHs at a club is the first step in using CPH as a metric. Reviewing CPH for a specific time slot

will provide an even more realistic picture. It is always important to inquire about the limits of class size (square footage or equipment) to gain a better understanding of what is possible for a particular modality.

Penetration

One additional metric for determining class value is penetration, which takes into account facility usage and class counts to determine if a class is serving an appropriate percentage of the members. Penetration divides the number of participants in group fitness classes by the number of "swipes," or the number of people that access the club during a specified time period, to arrive at a percentage of the members that are utilizing group fitness. Penetration can be determined for the day, hour, or specific class duration.

Most clubs determine daily penetration to be certain that group fitness schedules are reaching an appropriate number of participants. An average number for daily penetration is 15%, meaning that 15% of the members that use the club on any given day are participating in a group fitness class. Management strives to have the penetration number high, because when members are exercising in groups, especially during peak times, equipment and space in the rest of the facility is freed up for other paying members. The higher the penetration at a health club, the better the opportunity for communication and connection with the members. Everyone wins when a high percentage of members are engaged with live human beings rather than machines!

GFIs should talk to management about penetration for specific time slots. Knowing the usage pattern of the club allows the GFI to know if he or she is providing a product that is welcoming to the right number of people during that time. For example, if a GFI finds out that 200 people are in the club between 9:00 and 10:00 a.m. and the average penetration during that hour is 15%, it is safe to assume that all classes during that hour should combine for 30 participants. If the GFI is the only one teaching during that hour, his or her class should have 30 participants. If there is a cycling class and a step class during that time slot, the two classes should combine to have 30 participants.

Penetration helps put everything in perspective with regards to CPH and class counts. A GFI may have a higher CPH and lower class count for a specific class. But, when looking at the average number of swipes during the class time, it may become obvious that the participation is right on target with usage. For example, recall the example about the $50 instructor that had 10 people in a specialty class. If the class was held between 1:00 and 2:00 p.m. on Tuesdays and the usage during that time was only 50 people, the penetration is actually 20%, which is considered above average. If a manager or a GFI only reviewed the CPH, the class might be in jeopardy, but the penetration numbers reveal a different story.

GFIs should keep an eye on all three of the class value metrics. Understanding what class counts do and do not reveal, comparing the raw numbers with the expense of the class by studying CPH and, finally, viewing the big picture in terms of penetration (both daily and hourly) will help the GFI see the financial picture of what he or she brings to the table. These numbers can also be used as benchmarks for personal growth. Lastly, being able to approach the manager of a department proactively, armed with statistics based on the three value derivatives, will increase a GFI's professionalism. The numbers may lead a GFI to ask for help from the manager or fellow instructors in similar time slots to improve

class performance or provide the GFI with backing when requesting a raise in pay. Striving to increase class counts, decrease cost per head, and strategize with teammates to enhance overall penetration helps provide a clear performance improvement plan for a GFI.

Strategies for Increasing Class Value

Increasing class value begins with teamwork and education. When a GFI is working with other GFIs to ensure members are taken care of, and continuously updating and specializing his or her education, the quality of classes is sure to improve. Beyond these two global strategies for increasing class value, there are a few areas where a GFI can focus to find additional participants and turn them into class regulars.

Music

Music motivates people to move. In 2010, ACE sponsored a research review exploring the effects of music on exercise intensity (Foster, Porcari, & Anders, 2010). In that article, Costas Karageorghis, Ph.D, explained that music "can reduce the perception of effort significantly and increase endurance by as much as 15%."

Continually updating the music and carefully selecting playlists for classes are two easy ways to increase the participants' enjoyment. Consider having music cued up as members enter the class to set the mood, select music for the body of class that builds as the routine does, and then have music ready for the final stretching segment to leave members relaxed as they exit. Exit or "outro" music is another nice touch as people are putting away equipment and leaving the classroom. Today, with the addition of the digital music players to the GFI's arsenal, music has never been easier to customize to fit the mood of each section of class perfectly. Taking time to prepare music in this way adds a special touch. It is essential that GFIs comply with copyright law and legal responsibilities associated with the use of music (see Chapter 11).

Choreography/Exercise Selection

Continuing to update and refine choreography and exercise selection is a great way to increase class value. Participating in other GFIs' classes, attending continuing education workshops, purchasing or downloading DVDs, and utilizing online or print choreography resources are perfect ways to increase the number of items in one's teaching toolbox. Organizing choreography exchanges or sharing class plans with fellow instructors will both increase teamwork and provide new ideas for GFIs.

Changes to choreography and exercises should always have a purpose and fit within the context of the overall class goal, as well as have the ability to be progressed and regressed to meet the needs of a wide audience. When considering new choreography and exercises, the success of the participants should be the number-one priority. The best way to increase class value is to provide classes that leave everyone feeling successful.

Equipment

Incorporating new equipment options is an easy way to spruce up a class. For example, if a GFI has always used hand weights and weighted bars in strength-training class but rarely uses tubing, taking a weekend to review the best way to incorporate tubing into the class could reinvigorate the workout. As with new choreography and exercise ideas, equipment should not be added simply to make exercises more complex or different. The

product should match the overall goal of the class and be suitable for the audience.

One consideration with regards to equipment is the number of pieces a GFI uses in one class. With the countless "toys" that are available today, many classes have become a playground. Limiting classes to one or two pieces of resistance equipment and one prop is a great recommendation for strength classes. Of course, cardio classes are typically dependent on one piece of equipment, but adding a second may be appropriate in some cases. Keep in mind that fitness equipment is not always as exciting for new members as it is for the experienced participant and GFI. For some, equipment can be intimidating, and new participants may become overwhelmed at the site of equipment scattered about the room.

Member Interaction

The more members feel attached to one another, the more they tend to participate, and more participation equals increased class value. Making it a point to capitalize on any opportunity for member interaction and social camaraderie will increase class numbers and enhance loyalty to both the class and the club in general.

Being completely prepared for class will allow a GFI time to have quality interactions with members prior to class. Having music ready to go and choreography prepared, and arriving at the club early will provide five to 10 minutes of concentrated effort spent meeting and greeting and helping members make connections with each other. A GFI should also plan to arrive in time to turn on the stereo, set up equipment, and prepare the microphone. Greeting members at the door or near the equipment they will use is a great way to make connections. A GFI should avoid talking only to the members who are already frequenting the class, but target new faces and introduce them to regulars (much like a host or hostess does at a party). Help participants select the proper equipment and provide a rundown of the day's class. Explain the overall goal, highlight the hard parts, and give simple suggestions for having the best experience possible.

During class, the GFI should focus on eye contact, personal recognition, and delicate feedback to ensure quality member interactions. Regardless of the complexity of the class, there should be points where the movements will be easy to follow with the GFI facing the class, such as the warm-up, cool-down, or core section. At times, the GFI should walk through the class or assist with form. Getting down off the stage or away from the front of the room is a way to create a different, more welcoming dynamic in the classroom. Personal recognition via names and warm body language will help validate the participants' efforts. Learning as many names as possible and using them often will prove beneficial. Smile and make eye contact with as many people as possible. Lastly, **feedback** is a delicate subject in group fitness. Group participants like the camaraderie and energy of the group, but few like to be "called out" in front of the group. When providing feedback, it is always best to try to provide general feedback and get the point across as a group. More importantly, to avoid the need for direct feedback, it is critical to program classes in which all people can be successful and provide as many options as possible for participants to figure it out for themselves. While direct feedback cannot be completely eliminated, take care in delivering it as delicately as possible and be sure to follow up with anyone who has received direct feedback when the class is over.

After class is the best opportunity for soliciting feedback from members and providing reasons to return. A GFI should strive to finish on time (respecting the schedules of members) and then position him- or herself near the door or where the equipment is being returned. A personal thank you and an invitation to return goes a long way in member interactions. GFIs will receive solid feedback from members if they ask the right questions following class: "What were your favorite parts?" "How did you like the new CD?" "What would you like to focus on next week?" If classes are scheduled back to back, a simple announcement of where the GFI can be found directly following class would be helpful (e.g., "I'll be right outside the doors if you have any questions").

Before and after classes, GFIs can help with facility-wide customer service. As mentioned previously, a GFI may be the only person that a particular member feels comfortable enough with to ask questions, though it is often the case that GFIs do not have the information to help answer certain questions (e.g., billing concerns or locker room issues). However, the more the GFI becomes integrated into a facility, the easier this becomes. In some cases, the best customer service response might be, "I'm not sure, but I'm happy to find out for you. Can I get your information and get back to you or tell you before our next class?" This type of response is far better than, "I'm not sure… ask at the front desk" or "I'm not sure… Why don't you fill out a comment card?" Becoming a trusted resource for information is a wonderful way to increase class value and help the club's mission of serving members in the best way possible. The GFI should always have the club's best interest in mind when relaying information to members, regardless of the subject. At times, it may be difficult to act as an employee as opposed to as a friend of the member, but a GFI should learn ways to be helpful yet professional in these instances.

GFIs can also strive to interact with members at club events. Attending special holiday parties, café happy hours, and other instructors' classes are perfect ways to get to know members outside of the class setting. Being engaged in as many facets of the club as possible will help increase a GFI's reach and provide an ideal setting to promote classes and participation.

Outside of the club, in the larger community, is another place to interact with members or potential members. Carrying a business card for the club, a personal business card, or class schedules to the hairdresser, grocery store, or doctor's office might provide a great opportunity to promote the club or specific classes and make connections with members and potential members. Once a GFI is viewed as a walking, talking, breathing human being, **rapport** is enhanced. Creating common ground with members at church, school, and sports leagues can be the catalyst to increasing class value. GFIs should discuss with the manager how outside "advertising" on behalf of the club should be handled to avoid any misunderstandings. Many clubs have specific policies in place that will help the GFI make the biggest impact possible.

Ongoing Evaluation

A GFI's development in the industry is, in many ways, self-driven. GFI certifications require continuing education every two years, and some clubs may provide additional benchmarks for professional development. That said, the path that a GFI takes in terms of ongoing specialization and increased knowledge, customer service, and teamwork skills is often left for the GFI to develop and track. GFIs should insist on continued evaluation.

Whether the evaluations are formal (with the manager they report to), informal (soliciting comments from members and peers), or private (self-reviews), a GFI should be reviewed a minimum of four times a year (i.e., quarterly). If at all possible, a formal yearly review by the group fitness manager should be requested.

Formal Reviews

In most clubs, managers perform formal reviews at least once a year. It is often tough to be certain that a GFI is reviewed in *all* of the formats he or she teaches. However, the GFI should always request this from management. While reviewing one class for each GFI will help provide feedback on overall teaching ability, being reviewed in specific formats will help address class design, exercise selection and progression, as well as customer service for the specific crowd. At times, a GFI may choose to solicit feedback from a mentor or an expert on a specific format (e.g., yoga or group cycling).

Informal Reviews

Some clubs arrange a process for informal reviews, as the value they provide is tremendous. While a manager or an expert on specific formats can provide a GFI with his or her opinion of how the GFI is doing, seeing the class through a peer's eyes or, even better, through a member's eyes is uniquely helpful.

With peer reviews, it is important to establish ground rules. If a GFI asks another instructor for feedback, he or she should be certain to demand candor. Reviews are not meant to be an ego boost, but should instead help GFIs increase their proficiency. If all that comes from a peer review is how great the class was with no constructive criticism to consider for future use, time may have been wasted. GFIs should ask reviewers to list at least two things that they can improve in a class.

Participant reviews or secret shoppers are possibly the most valuable of any of the reviews. While a fitness professional has a specific filter through which he or she views a class, the participant is providing information on the real "buying decision." The aspects of a class that a participant values are often worlds apart from what a fitness professional may focus on. A participant looks at the total package, the energy, and the way he or she feels at the finish, all of which are extremely important when trying to increase the value of a class. While it may be frustrating to receive confusing or seemingly off-topic feedback from members who often cannot articulate the technical aspects that would make a difference or the precise points they consider negatives, it is important to remember that the participants are the customers, and they are the ones instructors need to please—and this sometimes requires that GFIs have "thick skin" when receiving or reviewing participant feedback. Comment cards and unsolicited feedback are often communicated with upper management and group fitness managers. GFIs should always take comments with a grain of salt, especially if they are personal in nature. However, there is typically something to be gleaned from a directed comment card. GFIs should take any issues to the group fitness manager and solicit professional feedback if he or she is unsure of how to correct the problem. At times, simply having the information brought to the surface will provide enough forethought to alleviate the problem in the future.

Self-review

Taking the time to deconstruct a class and reflect on the best parts, as well as what could have been improved upon, is an important process for the GFI. Rethinking the preparation process (How much time was allowed to prepare and what resources were used in preparing?), considering class construct (Was there an overall goal, how did each part support that goal, and was the goal achieved during class?) and connection (Was there enough time to greet participants, were the new participants identified prior to class, were connections made between participants, were connections made between the GFI and participants, and was time allowed for interaction at the end of class?) will help the GFI make adjustments for future classes. This process can be formal (writing out thoughts on the class plan) or informal (simply taking the time to reflect after class). Regardless of how in-depth or formal the process, constantly assessing performance and thinking about how class participants can better be served is a must in the group fitness profession. Consider filming or audiotaping a class for a self-review. Receiving a real-time capture of teaching style, communication, and choreography can provide valuable feedback for continued improvement.

While feedback is often hard to listen to, it is an extremely valuable resource for improving classes and increasing participation. It may be true that a GFI often knows if something went wrong and probably knows the areas in need of improvement, but receiving an objective third-party review, as well as contemplating his or her own performance a bit more deeply, can go a long way. GFIs can be swept away by large class numbers and positive reviews from members and falsely assume that everything is good or that what they are doing is enough. While the numbers and great reviews are positive and should be celebrated, it is also important to remember that increasing class value means reaching beyond the walls and the members already being reached. To put it in perspective, if a GFI has 50 people in his or her class at a club that has 5,000 members, there are still 4,950 people who are not taking the class. While 100% penetration is an impossibility, looking at the actual numbers helps keep things in perspective and reminds every GFI that constant evaluation is important. Continuing to improve is the quickest way to increase class value.

Summary

The GFI's role has become much more than showing up and leading a memorable class experience. Not only must the GFI prepare safe and effective classes and deliver the workouts with impeccable cueing and motivation, but he or she must also see how group fitness impacts the facility as a whole and work toward weaving the club's mission and vision into his or her actions. A strong GFI will develop a better understanding of a facility's business and always remember that he or she has a direct line to dues; membership can grow and members can be retained as a result of his or her efforts.

When a GFI understands the group fitness trifecta—education, teamwork, and class value—directing efforts in the facility will become easier. Remembering to focus "on stage" (teaching classes and interacting with members) and "backstage" (the preparation that goes into creating class plans) in all three of these areas will ensure success for the GFI. Using the trifecta to create an action plan will keep a GFI growing and thriving in the fitness industry for years to come.

References

American Council on Exercise (2010). *2010 ACE Fitness Salary Survey.* www.acefitness.org

Foster, C., Porcari, J., & Anders, M. (2010). ACE-sponsored research: Exploring the effects of music on exercise technique. *ACE Certified News,* September. www.acefitness.org/certifiednewsarticle/805/ace-sponsored-research-exploring-the-effects-of/

Suggested Reading

Carnegie, D. (2010). *How to Win Friends and Influence People.* New York: Simon & Schuster.

Collins, J. (2002). *Good to Great.* New York: Harper Business.

Covey, S.R. (2004). *The 7 Habits of Highly Effective People.* New York: Free Press.

DiJulius III, J.R. (2008). *What's the Secret? To Providing a World-Class Customer Experience.* Hoboken, N.J.: Wiley.

DiJulius III, J.R. (2003). *Secret Service: Hidden Systems that Deliver Unforgettable Customer Service.* New York: AMACOM.

Maxwell, J.C. (2010). *Everyone Communicates, Few Connect: What the Most Effective People Do Differently.* Nashville, Tenn.: Thomas Nelson.

Maxwell, J.C. (2006). *Developing the Leader Within You.* Nashville, Tenn.: Thomas Nelson.

Schroeder, J. & Dolan, S. (2010). 2010 IDEA fitness programs & equipment trends. *IDEA Fitness Journal,* 7, 7.

David K. Stotlar, Ed.D., is a professor and Director of the School of Kinesiology and Physical Education at the University of Northern Colorado, where he teaches sport marketing and sport management. He has served as a consultant to sports professionals, attorneys, and international sports administrators, and has been published extensively on sports law issues.

Mark S. Nagel, Ed.D., is an associate professor in the Sport and Entertainment Management Department at the University of South Carolina. Dr. Nagel has published extensively in a variety of areas of sport management, including law, finance, and marketing. Prior to becoming a professor, Dr. Nagel worked in campus recreation and intercollegiate athletics.

CHAPTER ELEVEN

Legal and Professional Responsibilities

By David K. Stotlar & Mark S. Nagel

Most people who teach or administer group fitness programs have received some form of training in exercise instruction and supervision. Often their experience with the law, if any, has been limited to cases involving common sports injuries. However, the rapid expansion of the fitness industry has created new forms of legal **liability.** The purpose of this chapter is to explain basic legal concepts that concern group fitness instructors (GFIs) and to show how these concepts can be applied to reduce injuries to program participants. Taking proper action can reduce the likelihood that a lawsuit will be filed, and can mitigate potential damages.

Liability and Negligence

The term liability refers to responsibility. Legal liability concerns the responsibilities recognized by a court of law. Every instructor or exercise leader who stands in front of a class faces the responsibilities of knowing the capacities of, and setting limitations on, participants before they begin an exercise program. Studio owners and managers have the added responsibility of ensuring that the facilities and equipment are appropriate and safe. Fitness professionals cannot avoid liability any more than they can avoid assuming the responsibilities inherent in their positions. However, those liabilities may be reduced through adherence to the appropriate **standard of care** and the implementation of certain risk-management principles.

The responsibilities arising from the relationship between the GFI and the participant produce a legal expectation, commonly referred to as the standard of care. This means that the quality of services provided in a fitness setting is commensurate with current professional standards. In the case of a lawsuit alleging **negligence,** the court would ask the question, "What would a reasonable, competent, and prudent GFI do in a similar situation?" An instructor or facility owner who failed to meet that standard could be found negligent by a court of law.

Negligence is usually defined as "failure to act as a reasonable and prudent person would act under a similar circumstance." For the GFI, this definition has two important components. The first deals specifically with actions: "Failure to act" refers to acts of omission as well as acts of commission. In other words, a GFI can be sued for not doing something that should have been done, as well as for doing something that should not have been done. The second part of the definition of negligence pertains to the appropriateness of the action in light of the standard of care, or a "reasonable and prudent" professional standard. If other qualified instructors would have acted similarly under the same circumstances, a court would probably not find an instructor's action negligent.

To legally substantiate a charge of negligence, four elements must be shown to exist. As stated by Wong (2010), they are: (1) that the **defendant** (person being sued) had a duty to protect the **plaintiff** (person filing the suit) from injury; (2) that the defendant failed to exercise the standard of care necessary to perform that duty; (3) that such failure was the proximate cause of an injury; and (4) that the injury caused damage to occur to the plaintiff.

Consider this situation as an example: A GFI is leading a group fitness class in which a participant badly sprains her ankle while following instructions for a low-impact aerobics routine. According to the plaintiff, the movement that directly led to the injury consisted of prolonged and excessive hopping on one foot. If the participant sues the instructor for negligence, the following questions and answers would likely be discussed in court:

- Was it the instructor's duty to provide proper instruction? Yes, instructors of aerobics classes have a duty to their participants.
- Was that duty satisfactorily performed? A continual one-footed hopping routine is not usually advocated by aerobics instructors, indicating that the standard of care was likely violated.
- Was the instructor's failure to provide safe instruction the direct cause of the injury? The plaintiff will likely successfully argue

that the injury was directly caused by the improper movement.

- Did actual damages occur? The plaintiff's doctor will certainly testify that an injury occurred and, at a minimum, damages involving medical care will be sought.

Areas of Responsibility

The duties assigned to fitness professionals vary from one position to another and from organization to organization. Seven major areas of responsibility are presented in this chapter: **health screening,** testing and programming, instruction, supervision, facilities, equipment, and **risk management.** Each area poses unique questions that are important even to the beginning instructor. ACE's Code of Ethics is quite helpful in guiding the actions of fitness professionals (see Appendix A).

Health Screening

A fitness professional's responsibility begins when a new participant walks in the door. Most prospective participants will be healthy people with a goal of improving their personal health and fitness levels. Others, however, may have not exercised for years or may have various health/medical conditions. Therefore, it is imperative that facilities conduct a preparticipation screening for each participant to document any existing conditions that might affect safe performance in an exercise program (see Chapter 2). The screening procedure should be valid, simple, cost- and time-efficient, and, most importantly, appropriate for the target population.

The screening questionnaires should ideally be interpreted and documented by qualified staff to limit the number of unnecessary medical referrals and avoid barriers to participation. For an explanation of the components of a quality pre-participation screening, refer to Chapter 2.

An instructor's responsibility does not end with collecting information. The health-history form and other collected data must be examined closely for information that affects programming decisions. Instructors have been charged with negligence for not accurately assessing available information that could have prevented an injury. Every club or studio needs to establish policies and procedures to ensure that each participant's personal history and medical information are taken into account when designing an exercise program.

Health Screening Guidelines

Each participant beginning a fitness program should receive a thorough evaluation. Specific risk-management criteria may include the following:

- Evaluation is conducted prior to participating in exercise.
- Screening methods concur with national guidelines (such as those recommended by the American Council on Exercise, American College of Sports Medicine, and American Heart Association).

Fitness Testing and Exercise Programming

Many states require "medical prescriptions" to be developed by licensed medical doctors. Once the medical prescription is developed, a physical therapist is legally allowed to administer and supervise its implementation. The purpose of an exercise "prescription" is to induce a physiological response that will result in a clinical change in a given condition. As a result, fitness professionals are usually limited to providing exercise programs, not exercise prescriptions, which may be construed as medical prescriptions under these circumstances. Although the difference between the terms "program" and "prescription" may seem like a technicality, it could be important in a court of law.

Fitness testing presents similar issues. The health and fitness level of the participant, the purpose of the test, and the testing methods should all be defined before test administration. The use of relatively simple tests, such as body-composition estimation by the skinfold method, would not normally pose significant legal problems. On the other hand, the use of a maximal **graded exercise test** on a treadmill with a multiple-lead **electrocardiogram (ECG)** could expose an unqualified GFI to a charge of practicing medicine without a license. Therefore, it is important that the test be recognized by a professional organization as appropriate for the intended use, be within the qualifications and training of the instructor, and that an accepted protocol (testing procedure) be followed as designed.

Exercise Programming Guidelines

The primary responsibilities of all GFIs include program design and exercise selection. Specific risk-management criteria may include the following:

- Health-history data is used appropriately in program design.
- Programs and tests selected are recognized by a professional organization as appropriate for the intended use.
- Programs and tests are within the qualifications and training of the GFI.
- Accepted protocols are followed exactly in all programs and procedures.

Instruction

To conduct a safe and effective exercise program, fitness professionals are expected to provide instruction that is both adequate and proper. Adequate instruction refers to the amount of direction given to participants before and during their exercise activity. For example, an instructor who asks a class to perform an exercise without first demonstrating how to do it properly could be found negligent if a participant performs the exercise incorrectly and is injured as a result. Proper instruction is factually correct. In other words, an instructor may be liable for a participant's injury resulting from an exercise that was not demonstrated or was demonstrated improperly, or from an unsafe exercise that should not have been included in a group fitness routine.

In the courtroom, the correctness of instruction is usually assessed by an expert witness who describes the proper procedures for conducting the activity in question. Therefore, the instructional techniques used by a GFI should be consistent with professionally recognized standards. Proper certification from a nationally recognized professional organization, as well as appropriate documentation of training (e.g., degrees and continuing education) can enhance a GFI's competence in the eyes of a court, should he or she ever be charged with negligence.

In addition to providing adequate and proper instruction, fitness professionals should also be careful not to diagnose or suggest treatment for injuries. This includes not only injuries sustained in the instructor's exercise class, but also those injuries acquired through other activities.

When participants ask for medical advice regarding injuries, it is best to suggest they call their doctor. In general, only physicians and certain other healthcare providers are allowed to diagnose, prescribe treatment, and treat injuries.

Even providing advice that may seem like "common sense" to the GFI can result in potential legal problems, especially when the participant is not familiar with typical injury rehabilitation. For example, consider the following situation: When a participant sprained her ankle during a fitness routine, the instructor told her to go home and ice the ankle to reduce the swelling. Because the ice made the injury feel much better, the participant kept her foot in ice water for two to three hours. As a consequence, several of her toes later had to be amputated because of frostbite.

This example may be extreme, but it serves as a valuable warning. There are several ways the instructor could have avoided this unfortunate situation. First, the instructor could have advised the participant to see a physician. While this approach protects the instructor, it would be costly if every participant who suffered a sprained ankle had to see a doctor. Second, the instructor could have provided a more precise description of the first-aid ice treatment. The third and best approach would be a combination of the first two; the instructor would provide specific instructions (both written and verbal) on the first-aid procedures recommended by the American Heart Association or the American Red Cross and suggest that if the injury did not respond well, then the participant should seek the advice of a physician.

Instruction Guidelines

A fitness professional must provide instruction that is both "adequate and proper." To fulfill this standard, the following criteria would apply to instruction:

- Instructions or directions provided to participants prior to, and during, activity are sufficient and understandable.
- The GFI conforms to the standard of care (what a reasonable and prudent instructor would provide in the same situation).

Supervision

The GFI is responsible for supervising all aspects of a class. The standards that apply to supervision are the same as those for instruction: adequate and proper. A prerequisite to determining adequate supervision is the ratio of participants to instructors and supervisors. A prudent instructor should allow a class to be only as large as can be competently monitored. The participant/instructor ratio will, of course, vary with activity, facility, and type of participant. An exercise class of 30 may be appropriate in a large gymnasium, but too big for an aquatic exercise class. Adequate and proper supervision may be different for a class of fit 20-year-olds than for a class of 55-year-old beginning exercisers.

General, or non-individualized, supervision can be used when the activity can be monitored from a position in general proximity to the participants. For example, in an aerobics class a conscientious GFI can give enough attention to all participants to keep them relatively safe through general but systematic observation. On the other hand, a series of fitness tests administered to a participant before an exercise program calls for specific, or individualized, supervision. The person qualified to administer the testing must provide continuous attention in immediate proximity to the participant to ensure safety. Whether general or specific, required supervision should be based on one's own judgment of the nature of the activity and the participants involved, compared with what other prudent professionals would do under the same circumstances.

Supervision Guidelines

GFIs must perform their supervisory duties in accordance with the following professionally devised and established guidelines:

- Continuous supervision is provided in immediate proximity to the participant to ensure safety.
- Larger groups are supervised from the perimeter of the exercise area to ensure all participants are in full view of the instructor.
- Specific supervision is employed when the activity merits close attention to an individual participant.

Facilities

Safety is the basic issue for a fitness facility. Instructors should continually inspect the environment and ensure that it is free from unreasonable hazards, and that all areas of the facility are appropriate for the specific type of activity to be conducted in that area. For example, aerobic dance and martial arts require a floor surface that will cushion

the feet, knees, and legs from inordinate amounts of stress. Similarly, workout areas or stations of a circuit-training class should have adequate free space surrounding them to ensure that observers will not be struck by an exercising participant.

Some facilities provide locker room and shower facilities. These areas must be sanitary, the floors must be textured to reduce accidental slipping, and areas near water must be protected from electrical shock. Although GFIs may not be responsible for designing and maintaining the exercise facility, any potential problem should be detected, reported, and corrected as soon as possible. Until then, appropriate signs should be clearly posted to warn participants of the unsafe conditions and access to the area should be restricted.

In some cases, a GFI may be assigned to teach in an area that is unsafe or inappropriate for the activity. Under these circumstances, a prudent instructor would refuse to teach and would document that decision in writing to the club or studio management so that constructive action may be taken.

Facilities Guidelines

The basic issue regarding facilities centers on the safety of the premises (Table 11-1). The central focus is whether the environment is free from unreasonable hazards. Examples of risk-management criteria include the following:

- The floor surface is appropriate for each activity.
- Lighting is adequate for performance of the skill and for supervision.
- Entrances and exits are well marked.

Table 11-1

Standards for Health/Fitness Facilities

- All facilities offering exercise equipment or services must offer a general pre-activity cardiovascular risk screening (e.g., PAR-Q) and/or a specific pre-activity screening tool (e.g., HRA, MHQ) to all new members and prospective users. (Chapter 2)

- All specific pre-activity screening tools (e.g., HRA, MHQ) must be interpreted by qualified staff and the results of the screening must be documented. (Chapter 2)

- If a facility becomes aware that a member/user has a known cardiovascular, metabolic, or pulmonary disease, or two or more major cardiovascular risk factors, or any other major self-disclosed medical concern, that person must be advised to consult with a qualified healthcare provider before beginning a moderate-to-vigorous physical-activity program. (Chapter 2)

- All facilities with qualified staff must offer each new member a general orientation to the facility, including identification of resources available for personal assistance with developing a suitable physical-activity program and the proper use of any exercise equipment to be used in that program. (Chapter 3)

- Facilities must have in place a written system for sharing information with users and employees/independent contractors regarding the handling of potentially hazardous materials, including the handling of bodily fluids by the facility staff in accordance with the Occupational Safety and Health Administration (OSHA). (Chapter 4)

- Facilities must have written emergency-response system policies and procedures that must be reviewed and rehearsed regularly. These policies must be capable of handling basic first-aid situations and emergency cardiac events. (Chapter 4)

- Facilities must have as part of their written emergency response system a public access defibrillation (PAD) program. (Chapter 4)

- he fitness and healthcare professionals who have supervisory responsibility for the physical-activity programs (supervise and oversee members, users, staff and/or independent contractors) of the facility must demonstrate the appropriate professional education, certification, and/or experience. (Chapter 5)

- The fitness and healthcare professionals who serve in counseling, instructional, and physical-activity supervision roles for the facility must demonstrate the appropriate professional education, certification, and/or experience. (Chapter 5)

- Fitness and healthcare professionals engaged in pre-activity screening, instructing, monitoring, or supervising physical-activity programs for facility members/users must have current AED/CPR (automated external defibrillator and cardiopulmonary resuscitation) certification from an organization qualified to provide such certification. (Chapter 5)

- Facilities, to the extent required by law, must adhere to the building design standards that relate to the designing, building, expanding, or renovating of space as presented by the Americans with Disabilities Act (ADA). (Chapter 6)

- Facilities must be in compliance with all federal, state, and local building codes. (Chapter 6)

- The aquatic and pool facilities must provide the proper safety equipment and signage, per state and local codes and regulations. (Chapter 7)

- Facilities must have a system in operation that monitors the entry to, and usage of, the facility by all individuals, including members and users. (Chapter 8)

- Facilities that offer a sauna, steam room, or whirlpool must make sure that these areas are maintained at the proper temperature and that the appropriate warning systems are in place to notify members/users of any unwarranted changes in temperature. (Chapter 8)

- Facilities that offer members/users access to a pool or whirlpool must make sure that the pool-water chemistry is maintained in accordance with state and local codes. (Chapter 8)

- A facility that offers youth services or programs must provide appropriate supervision. (Chapter 8)

- Facilities must post the appropriate caution, danger, and warning signage in conspicuous locations where existing conditions and situations warrant such signage. (Chapter 9)

- Facilities must post the appropriate emergency and safety signage pertaining to fire and related emergency situations, as required by federal, state, and local codes. (Chapter 9)

- Facilities must post all required ADA and Occupational Safety and Health Administration (OSHA) signage. (Chapter 9)

- All cautionary, danger, and warning signage must have the required signal icon, signal word, signal color, and layout, as specified by the American National Standards Institute (ANSI) and reflected in the American Society of Testing and Materials (ASTM) standards for fitness equipment and fitness facility safety signage and labels. (Chapter 9)

Note: Chapters in parentheses refer to *ACSM's Health/Fitness Facility Standards and Guidelines* (3rd ed.); PAR-Q = Physical Activity Readiness Questionnaire; HRA = Health-risk assessment; MHQ = Medical health questionnaire

American College of Sports Medicine, *ACSM's Health/Fitness Facility Standards and Guidelines* (3rd ed.). pages 1–2, table 1.1. © 2007 by American College of Sports Medicine. Adapted with permission from Human Kinetics (Champaign, Ill.).

Equipment

For a program that uses exercise equipment, the legal concerns center primarily on selection, installation, maintenance, and repair. Equipment should meet all appropriate safety and design standards in the industry. If the equipment has been recently purchased from a competent manufacturer, these standards will probably be met. However, some organizations may try to save money by using homemade or extremely old, inexpensive equipment. If an injury is caused by a piece of equipment that fails to perform as expected, and the injured party can show that the equipment failed to meet basic safety and design standards, the club or studio would be exposed to increased liability.

It is also important that trained technicians assemble and install all equipment. Having untrained people assemble some types of machinery may void the manufacturer's warranty and expose the program to additional risks and liability. A schedule of regular service and repair should also be established and documented to show that the management has acted responsibly. Defective or worn parts should be replaced immediately, and equipment that is in need of repair should be removed for service.

Instructors and supervisors should instruct each participant regarding equipment safety. In addition, each instructor and participant should be required to examine the equipment before each use and report any problems to the person in charge.

Several states have begun to require that **automated external defibrillators (AEDs)** be available in spas and health and fitness clubs. This means that GFIs must be competent in using AEDs should a critical incident arise. In 2010, the American Heart Association (AHA) published a paper recommending a change in the basic life support (BLS) sequence (Travers et al., 2010). The recommendation involved moving away from the traditional "A-B-C" (airway, breathing, chest compressions) to a new sequence: "C-A-B" (chest compressions, airway, breathing) (see Chapter 9). Professionals in the medical community still believe that CPR is the best treatment for cardiac arrest until the arrival of an AED and advanced cardiac life support care.

Another equipment-related situation arises when participants ask their instructor about which shoes to wear or what exercise equipment to purchase for home use. An exercise professional should be extremely cautious when giving such recommendations. Before an instructor is qualified to provide advice, he or she must have a thorough knowledge of the product lines available and the particular characteristics of each product. If this condition cannot be met, the GFI should refer the participant to a retail sporting-goods outlet. Otherwise, the GFI could be held liable for a negligent recommendation. An instructor who makes a recommendation based solely on personal experience should clearly state that it is a personal, and not a professional, recommendation. Instructors who are receiving money for endorsing a particular product must be especially careful not to portray themselves as experts providing professional advice.

Equipment Guidelines

In the equipment area, the legal concerns center primarily on selection, maintenance, and repair of the equipment. A risk-management plan should examine the following points:
- Equipment selected meets all safety and design standards within the industry.

- Assembly of equipment follows manufacturers' guidelines.
- A schedule of regular service and repair is established and documented.
- Caution is exercised in relation to recommending equipment.
- Homemade equipment is avoided if at all possible.

Accident Reporting

Regardless of the safety measures provided, some injuries are going to occur in the conduct of fitness activities. When someone is injured, it is necessary for the GFI to file an accident report, which should include the following information:

- Name, address, and phone number of the injured person
- Time, date, and place of the accident
- A brief description of the part of the body affected and the nature of the injury (e.g., "cut on the right hand")
- A description and model number of any equipment involved
- A reference to any instruction given and the type of supervision in force at the time of the injury
- A brief, factual description of how the injury occurred (no opinions as to cause or fault)
- Names, addresses, and phone numbers of any witnesses
- A brief statement of actions taken at the time of the injury (e.g., first aid given, physician referral, or ambulance called)
- Signatures of the supervisor and the injured person

Accident reports should be kept for several years, depending on each state's **statute of limitations.** If the person was injured in a

formal class setting, it may also be helpful to file a class outline or lesson plan with the accident report. In addition, a yearly review of injuries can be helpful in reducing accidents causing injuries to participants.

Common Approaches for Managing Risks

One of the duties of professionals in the fitness industry is to effectively manage risk. The process of risk management is more than just avoiding accidents; it encompasses a total examination of risk areas for the fitness professional. Each of the responsibilities identified in this chapter presents various levels of risk that should be assessed. The steps involved in a comprehensive risk-management review include the following:

- Identification of risk areas
- Evaluation of specific risks in each area
- Selection of appropriate treatment for each risk
- Implementation of a risk-management system
- Evaluation of success

Risk management is an important professional duty. Too often, it is considered merely a process by which to avoid lawsuits. Professionals in the fitness industry should approach risk management as a way to provide better service to their participants. With this philosophy, risk management can become a method of properly conducting activities, not just a way to avoid potential legal trouble. The end goal is to create a safe, enjoyable experience for participants. The most common approaches for the management of potential risks are: avoidance, reduction, retention, and transfer.

Avoidance—This simply means that the activity is judged to be too hazardous to justify its use. Some examples may include high-risk exercises such as explosive full squats and straight-leg sit-ups.

Reduction—Many fitness activities pose various levels of risk because of where and how they are implemented. Instructors should continue to compare their instruction, facilities, equipment, and procedures to national standards. Implementing changes that make activities safer constitutes reduction.

Retention—The nature of physical activity involves some risks of injury. Certainly, the risks that are retained should be ones that result in minimal potential damage. In some instances, instructors will simply want to budget for these situations.

Transfer—The risk of participation in some activities may be transferred to other parties. For example, the facility may transfer the risk to the participant through an assumption of risk or **waiver** document. Another common transfer mechanism is insurance. Fitness personnel and clubs should have adequate insurance coverage that will pay the cost of legal defense and any potential claims awarded. It is critical to read the provided coverage carefully, because policies can vary considerably. The general types of coverage that should be obtained include the following:

- **General liability insurance** covers basic trip-and-fall-type injuries.
- **Professional liability insurance** covers claims of negligence based on professional duties.
- **Disability insurance** provides income protection in the event of an injury to the instructor.
- **Individual medical insurance** provides hospitalization and major medical coverage.

- An **umbrella liability policy** provides the insured with "additional" coverage across all insurance categories.

Every GFI will want to assess his or her liability insurance needs. A GFI employed at a club should inquire about the general liability policy and any other liability insurance the owner might have. **Independent contractors** may not be covered by a club's general policy and, if not, should ask the club if they can be added by special endorsement. If they are covered by the club's general policy, all aspects of coverage should be included in the written agreements for services. Regardless of the coverage an individual or facility retains, it is wise for GFIs to secure an umbrella liability policy, as these are typically inexpensive and provide additional coverage for extreme situations where standard insurance reimbursement is exhausted.

Many nonprofit groups, such as churches and recreation centers, may not have coverage that includes their contract instructors. The instructors at these venues should have their own general liability coverage, which would not only cover them for claims of improper instruction, but would also cover an accident resulting from the facility's negligence, such as a participant tripping over a loose floorboard and getting injured.

GFIs seeking affordable liability policies should check with their certifying agency or discuss their needs with insurance agents who may suggest liability coverage be added onto the GFI's residence insurance as a "business pursuits rider." ACE-certified GFIs can obtain more information regarding professional liability insurance at www.aceiftness.org/insurancecenter/default.aspx.

Safety Guidelines

An important aspect of risk management is

anticipating and preparing for emergencies. Since injuries are more likely to occur if proper instruction is not followed, fitness instructors should provide clearly written safety guidelines for each type of activity. These guidelines should be posted in appropriate areas of the facility and rigidly enforced by the supervisor to prevent unwarranted injuries. Unfortunately, there are often situations, such as a fire, earthquake, or other natural disaster, during which an emergency may occur despite the proper behavior of fitness professionals and participants. Regardless of the situation, every employee should be thoroughly familiar with the facility's emergency plan for various situations and should have actual practice in executing its steps. For example, every club or studio should conduct a "heart attack drill," requiring all staff to execute emergency plans and procedures such as those recommended by the American Heart Association. The program manager should maintain records of these simulations.

Many GFIs and supervisors are needlessly exposed to liability because they permit indiscriminate use of the facility. Supervisory personnel should restrict the facility to people who have a legitimate entitlement. Each staff member should have a list of the people scheduled to use the equipment and facilities during specific time periods, and the supervisor should allow access only to those people. This policy should be enforced with the same vigor as the safety procedures.

Implementation of a Risk-management System

I t is critical that management implement the risk-management system. For a complete review of considerations regarding the creation and implementation

of policy and staffing concerns, consult the *AHA/ACSM Scientific Statement: Recommendations for Cardiovascular Screening, Staffing, and Emergency Policies at Health/Fitness Facilities* (Balady et al., 1998). Attention must be given to all subject areas identified in this chapter. This process is normally called a safety audit and should be conducted regularly (certainly once a year, but ideally every six months). Many professionals in the field develop safety checklists, while clubs often have professional consultants conduct safety audits. Regardless, a systematic evaluation of the risks in group fitness activities is essential for safe program operation.

Waivers and Informed Consent

The staff members of many facilities attempt to absolve themselves of liability by having all participants sign a liability waiver to release the instructor and fitness center from all liability associated with the conduct of an exercise program and any resulting injuries. In some cases, these documents have been of little value because the courts have enforced the specific wording of the waiver and not its intent. In other words, if negligence was found to be the cause of injury, and negligence of the instructor or fitness center was not specifically waived, then the waiver would not be effective. Therefore, waivers must be clearly written and include statements to the effect that the participant waives all claims to damages, even those caused by the negligence of the instructor or fitness center.

Some fitness centers use an **informed consent** form. While this document may look similar to a waiver, its purpose is different. The informed consent form is used to make the dangers of a program or test procedure known to the participant

Legal and Professional Responsibilities

and thereby provide an additional measure of defense against lawsuits.

Obtaining informed consent is very important. It should be an automatic procedure for every person who enters the program, and it should be done before every fitness test. The American Council on Exercise suggests the following procedures:

- Inform the participant of the exercise program or testing procedure, and explain the purpose of each. This explanation should be thorough and unbiased.
- Inform the participant of the risks involved in the testing procedure or program, along with the possible discomforts.
- Inform the participant of the benefits expected from the testing procedure or program.
- Inform the participant of any alternative programs or tests that may be more advantageous to him or her.
- Solicit questions regarding the testing procedure or exercise program, and give unbiased answers to these inquiries.
- Inform the participant that he or she is free, at any time, to withdraw consent and discontinue participation.
- Obtain the written consent of each participant.

Figure 11-1

Sample agreement to participate

I, _____, have enrolled in a program of strenuous physical activity including, but not limited to, traditional aerobics and other group fitness activities, weight training, stationary bicycling, and the use of various aerobic-conditioning machinery offered by [name of fitness professional and/or business]. I am aware that participating in these types of activities, even when completed properly, can be dangerous. I agree to follow the verbal instructions issued by the fitness professional. I am aware that potential risks associated with these types of activities include, but are not limited to, death, serious neck and spinal injuries that may result in complete or partial paralysis or brain damage, serious injury to virtually all bones, joints, ligaments, muscles, tendons, and other aspects of the musculoskeletal system, and serious injury or impairment to other aspects of my body, general health, and well-being.

Because of the dangers of participating, I recognize the importance of following the fitness professional's instructions regarding proper techniques and training, as well as other organization rules.

I am in good health and have provided verification from a licensed physician that I am able to undertake a general fitness-training program. I hereby consent to first aid, emergency medical care, and admission to an accredited hospital or an emergency care center when necessary for executing such care and for treatment of injuries that I may sustain while participating in a fitness-training program.

I understand that I am responsible for my own medical insurance and will maintain that insurance throughout my entire period of participation with [name of fitness professional and/or business]. I will assume any additional expenses incurred that go beyond my health coverage. I will notify [name of fitness professional and/or business] of any significant injury that requires medical attention (such as emergency care and hospitalization).

Signed_____

Printed Name_____ Phone Number_____

Address_____

Emergency Contact_____ Contact Phone Number_____

Insurance Company_____

Policy #_____ Effective Date _____

Name of Policy Holder_____

Note: This document has been prepared to serve as a guide to improve understanding. Group fitness instructors should not assume that this form will provide adequate protection in the event of a lawsuit. Please see an attorney before creating, distributing, and collecting any agreements to participate, informed consent forms, or waivers.

Figure 11-1 provides an example of an agreement to participate form designed to protect the GFI from a participant claiming to be unaware of the potential risks of physical activity. An agreement to participate is not typically considered a formal **contract,** but rather serves to demonstrate that the participant was made aware of the "normal" outcomes of certain types of physical activity and willingly assumed the risks of participation. Typically, the agreement to participate is utilized for "class" settings. The agreement to participate form should detail the nature of the activity, the potential risks to be encountered, and the expected behaviors of the participant (Cotten & Cotten, 2004). This last consideration is important, as the participant recognizes that he or she may need to follow instructions while participating.

Every fitness professional should consult with an attorney who has experience and expertise in local laws regarding fitness participation. For extensive guidance on many of these issues, consult *IHRSA's Guide to Club Membership and Conduct* (International Health, Racquet, and Sportsclub Association, 2005), which provides specific standards, sample forms, and suggested policies and procedures that could be used in risk-management implementation.

Basic Defenses Against Negligence Claims

It is important for GFIs to know and understand that they are not without protection under the law if they are accused of negligence. Several defenses are available for use by fitness professionals as defendants in litigation in fitness-related personal-injury cases.

Assumption of Risk

This defense is used to show that the participant voluntarily accepted dangers known to exist with participation in the activity. The two most important aspects of this definition are "voluntary" and "known danger." If the participant does not voluntarily engage in a program or test, this defense cannot normally be utilized. Also, if the participant was not informed of the specific risks associated with the program or test, then he or she cannot be held to have assumed them. The best way to prove that a participant was knowledgeable of the risks involved is to utilize the assumption-of-risk documents (e.g., informed consent and waivers) described earlier.

Contributory Negligence

A **contributory negligence** defense means that the plaintiff played some role in his or her own injury. Although this legal doctrine is viable in only a few states (check applicable state law), it provides a total bar to recovery for any damages. An example might consist of a participant exceeding the designated maximum heart rate in an exercise program. A salient factor would also be whether an instructor was there to monitor the participant, or if the participant was exercising alone and following program guidelines.

Comparative Negligence

In a **comparative negligence** defense, the relative fault of both the plaintiff and the defendant are measured to see who was most at fault for the injury. The result is an apportionment of guilt and any subsequent award for damages. The court (or jury) determines the percentage of responsibility of each party and then prorates the award. This can be useful if a participant is somewhat to blame for his or her own injury.

Act of God

Although this defense is not often used in fitness and sport law cases, it may be of interest. It involves injury caused by unforeseeable acts of nature. The foreseeability aspect is the most crucial. If, during an exercise session, an earthquake opened sections of the floor and a participant was injured, it may be applicable.

Other Legal Considerations

GFIs are providers of a special service. As a result, they must be familiar with the special aspects of the law that are most frequently encountered in the conduct of their business.

Contracts

Fitness personnel must have an adequate knowledge of legal contracts to perform their tasks, get paid, and avoid costly legal battles with participants and/or clubs. Some GFIs will want to work as individuals not affiliated with one particular club, while others may want to be employed by a club or fitness center.

Whatever the nature of the work arrangement, a GFI must be aware of the essentials of contract law. Basic contract law indicates that the following elements are necessary to form a binding contract:

- *An offer and acceptance:* Mutual agreement to terms
- *Consideration:* An exchange of items of value
- *Legality:* Acceptable form and subject under the law
- *Capacity:* Such as majority age and mental competency

The general considerations that should be addressed in contracts for use with participants, as well as contracts between exercise professionals and clubs for which they intend to work, should include the following:

- Identification of the parties (GFI and participant/club)
- Description of the services to be performed (group fitness instruction and consultation)
- Compensation ($X.00 per hour, day, month, or class, and payment method)
- Confidential relationship (agreement by each party not to divulge personal or business information gained through the relationship)
- Business status (confirmation of employment status)
- Term and termination (express definition of the length of the contract and the conditions under which termination is allowed by either party)

Employment Status

As noted above, another prominent concern for many fitness professionals deals with employment status: independent contractor versus **employee.** Both of these terms can apply to those who work in a fitness center. However, only the independent contractor status applies to self-employed GFIs working independently from a club. However, most clubs still require independent contractors hired by the club to follow club rules.

Clients or participants who hire a fitness professional do not intend, for the most part, to hire that person as an employee, but prefer to lease their services for a brief period of time. Hence, most self-employed fitness professionals are independent contractors and not employees of their clients or class participants.

In some instances, owners of fitness centers or clubs have used the term independent contractor for employees. Club owners are often motivated to hire independent contractors in place of regular employees because the company does not have to train them, provide medical or other benefits, arrange for social security withholding, or pay into worker's compensation or unemployment funds for independent contractors. Club owners also find an advantage in having independent contractors because it is more complicated, from a legal standpoint, to fire existing employees than it is to simply not renew contracts with independent contractors.

A legal dichotomy exists between regular employees and independent contractors. Most commonly, the courts have considered 10 "tests" to determine if the business relationship in question between a club and a fitness professional is that of a regular employee or an independent contractor. These tests are:

- *The extent of control that, by agreement, the employer can exercise over the details of the work.* The existence of a right to control is indicative of an employer–employee relationship.

- *The method of payment, whether by time or by the job.* Generally, those persons scheduled to be paid on a regular basis at an hourly or weekly rate have been considered employees. Conversely, those paid in a single payment for services rendered have more easily qualified as independent contractors.

- *The length of time for which the person is employed.* Individuals hired for short periods of time (a few days or weeks) have more often been seen as independent contractors, whereas employment periods that extended upward of a full year have been ruled

as establishing an employer–employee relationship.

- *The skill required for the provision of services.* When the worker needs no training because of the specialized or technical skills that the employer intends to utilize, the independent contractor status has prevailed. On the other hand, if an employer provides training to a recently hired individual, that person will more than likely be judged to be an employee.

- *Whether the person employed is in a distinct business or occupation.* If a worker offers services to other employers or clients, a status of independent contractor would probably be found. If, however, the worker only intended to provide services for one employer, and failed to offer the services to others as an independent business, the employee status could be found.

- *Whether the employer or the worker provides the equipment.* If independent contractor status is desired, GFIs will have a better chance of getting it if they provide their own equipment.

- *Whether the work is a part of the normal business of the employer.* Court rulings have favored classifying individuals as regular employees when services rendered are integral to the business of the employer. Supplemental, special, or one-time services are more likely to be provided by independent contractors.

- *Whether the work is traditionally performed by a specialist in similar businesses.* Employers and employees must examine their field of business to gain an understanding of current practices and align themselves with the prevailing trends.

- *The intent of the parties involved in the arrangement.* The courts will attempt to enforce intent of the parties at the time the agreement was executed. If a professional thought that he or she was hired as an independent contractor, as did the club, it would influence the court's determination. Therefore, a clear understanding of the arrangement is critical.

- *Whether the employer is engaged in a business.* The intent here is to protect clients or participants from being construed as employers when a fitness professional is hired to perform work of a "private" nature. This is most common when fitness professionals sell their services to private citizens rather than to clubs or corporations.

The process of determining employment status is marked by careful analysis of the facts and the weighing of interpretations on both sides of the issue. All of the issues addressed above have been used in court cases dealing with this matter, each with varying degrees of authority. It is, therefore, imperative that all fitness professionals and club owners understand and examine these factors when initiating agreements.

For more specific information on the legal aspects surrounding the independent contractor versus employee issue, consult the guidelines published by the Internal Revenue Service (www.irs.gov).

Copyright Law

One of a GFI's major legal responsibilities is compliance with **copyright** law. All forms of commercially produced creative expression are protected by copyright law, but music is the area most pertinent to exercise instructors. This has become an extremely important issue with the availability of downloadable music. Simply stated, almost all musical compositions that one can hear on the radio or television or buy from music outlets are owned by artists and studios and are protected by federal copyright law. Whether an instructor burns a CD or creates a playlist from various songs on the radio or from media he or she has purchased does not matter; the instructor who uses that music in a for-profit exercise class—legally speaking, a **public performance**—is in violation of copyright law.

Performance Licenses

To be able to use copyrighted music in an exercise class, one must obtain a performance license from one of the major **performing rights societies**, the **American Society of Composers, Authors and Publishers (ASCAP), Broadcast Music, Inc. (BMI),** or the **Society of European Stage Authors and Composers (SESAC).** These organizations vigorously enforce copyright law for their memberships and will not hesitate to sue a health club, studio, or freelance instructor who plays copyrighted music without a license.

Accordingly, most clubs and studios obtain a **blanket license** for their instructors. The license fees for the clubs are determined by the number of participants who attend classes each week, by the number of speakers used in the club, or by whether the club has a single- or multifloor layout.

GFIs who teach as independent contractors at several locations may have to obtain their own licenses. They should check with the clubs where they teach to see if each club's blanket license covers their classes. If freelance instructors teach at several different locations with their own music, they will have to obtain their own performance licenses.

Given that the fees for either getting licenses or paying damages for copyright infringement may be prohibitive, independent instructors in particular may want to consider other options. One is to create rhythm CDs or digital recordings of their own using a drum machine, an electronic instrument that can range in sophistication from toy to professional recording device. A professional model is not needed, however, to make an appealing rhythm CD or digital recording. A local music store owner or salesperson could probably steer the instructor to someone who could help create such a CD or recording.

Other options include buying licensed music expressly made for fitness and aerobic exercise classes, where the copyright holder expressly permits the original music to be used in a class, or asking exercise class participants to bring their own recordings for the workouts, in effect using them for the participants' own noncommercial use. Another trend is for clubs to buy "packaged" group fitness programs where all of the advertising, music, and instructor training are provided and the fitness center is allowed to use the name brand of the program in its advertising.

Professional liability insurance will usually not cover an instructor for copyright infringement claims or offer protection in suits involving libel, slander, invasion of privacy, or defamation of character. These sorts of actions may be considered intentional torts and are not typically covered.

Obtaining Copyright Protection

Some GFIs may want to obtain copyright protection for certain aspects of their work, including the following:

- *Pantomimes and choreographic work*—If an instructor creates more than a simple routine, and publicly distributes (through a dance notation system), performs, or displays the choreography, it can be copyrighted.
- *Books, videos, and films*—If a choreographed work by an instructor is sold to a **publisher,** video distributor, or movie studio, that business entity will own the copyright for the material and the instructor will be compensated with either an advance or a certain portion of the proceeds (royalties), or both. Through negotiation with the producing or distributing company, the instructor may be able to retain certain rights to the material.
- *Compilations of exercise routines*—If an instructor makes an original sequence of routines, it may be protected by copyright and licensed to others for a book, video, film, or other presentation form.
- *Graphic materials*—If an instructor creates pictures, charts, diagrams, informational handouts, or other graphic materials for instructional aides or promotional material, these too may be copyrighted.

For copyright information or applications, write to:
Register of Copyrights
United States Copyright Office
Library of Congress
Washington, D.C. 20559
www.copyright.gov

Americans With Disabilities Act

Fitness professionals can be affected by a variety of legislative mandates. One of the laws that affect the profession is the **Americans With Disabilities Act,** which became law in 1992. Modeled after the Civil Rights Act, it prohibits discrimination on the basis of disability. The law provides for equal treatment and equal access to programs for disabled

Americans. The act extends provisions to all areas of public accommodation, including businesses such that all participants, regardless of disability, are guaranteed access to all programs and spaces within the facility. Therefore, it is essential that GFIs make sure that their buildings, equipment, and programs are available to persons with disabilities. Employers must also provide reasonable accommodations for employees with disabilities, including adjusted work stations and equipment as necessary. Therefore, whether a person with a disability is an employee or a participant, steps must be taken to ensure that the professional and business environment is one that respects the dignity, skills, and contributions of that individual.

Scope of Practice in the Profession

GFIs are generally in the business of providing exercise leadership and exercise-related advice. They are not normally physicians, physical therapists, or dietitians (although some may be certified or licensed in these areas).

The primary area in which the **scope of practice** comes into question is generally the health-history or wellness-history form. As described earlier, this form is used as a general screening document prior to the participant's entry into a fitness program. Fitness law expert David Herbert says that "wellness-assessment documents should be utilized for...determination of an individual's level of fitness...*never* for the purpose of providing or recommending *treatment* of any condition." Use of such a form in recommending treatment could constitute the practice of medicine without a license.

Another area of interaction between GFIs

and participants that can cause issues related to the scope of certain professional practices is in dietary and nutritional counseling. With the tremendous growth in the nutritional supplements market, this is an issue that affects many professionals in the industry. According to the American Dietetic Association, most states have statutes that regulate or license nutritionists. In the other states, anyone is able to claim to be a nutritionist. Laws in each state should be examined to ensure that healthcare-practice statutes are not violated by fitness professionals who may be surpassing their training and expertise. If a participant has complex dietary questions, referral should be made to a **registered dietitian (R.D.)** or other qualified healthcare professional. Refer to Appendix E for ACE's Position Statement on Nutrition Scope of Practice for Fitness Professionals.

Similarly, GFIs are not psychologists or marriage counselors and therefore should not provide advice or counseling on issues related to a participant's emotional and/or psychological status. Participants should always be referred to licensed practitioners in these and other related areas.

Summary

No fitness program, regardless of how well it is designed and operated, can completely avoid all participant injuries. In an attempt to reduce injuries to participants and the accompanying legal complications, a GFI would be wise to adhere to the following guidelines:

- Obtain professional education, guided practical training under a qualified exercise professional, and current certification from an established professional organization.

- Design and conduct classes that reflect current professional standards.
- Formulate and enforce policies and guidelines for the conduct of the program in accordance with professional recommendations.
- Establish and implement adequate and proper procedures for supervision in all phases of the program.
- Establish and implement adequate and proper methods of instruction in all phases of the program.
- Post safety regulations in the facility and ensure that they are rigidly enforced by supervisory personnel.
- Keep the facility free from hazards and maintain adequate free space for each activity.
- Establish and document inspection and repair schedules for all equipment and facilities.
- Formulate policies and guidelines for emergency situations, rehearse the pro-

cedures, and require all instructors to have current first-aid, **cardiopulmonary resuscitation (CPR),** and AED training and certification.

By applying these recommendations, GFIs can help reduce the probability of injury to participants. Should legal action result from an injury, the facts of the case would be examined to determine whether negligence was the cause. A properly trained, competent, and certified GFI conducting a program that was in accordance with current professional standards would probably prevail.

All GFIs should remember that professional standards in the exercise field are continually changing. It is the responsibility of the fitness professional to remain aware of all legal developments in the industry, just as they would remain appraised of emerging exercise techniques. By understanding legal responsibilities, exercise programs can be implemented that permit participant enjoyment and limit instructor liability.

Legal and Professional Responsibilities

References

American College of Sports Medicine (2007). *ACSM's Health/Fitness Facility Standards and Guidelines* (3rd ed.). Champaign, Ill.: Human Kinetics.

Balady, G.J. et al. (1998). AHA/ACSM Scientific Statement: Recommendations for cardiovascular screening, staffing, and emergency policies at health/ fitness facilities: A Joint Position Statement by the American College of Sports Medicine and the American Heart Association. *Circulation, 97,* 2283–2293.

Cotten, D.J. & Cotten, M.B. (2004). *Waivers & Releases of Liability.* Statesboro, Ga.: Sport Risk Consulting.

International Health, Racquet, and Sportsclub Association (2005). *IHRSA's Guide to Club Membership and Conduct* (3rd ed.). http://download. ihrsa.org/pubs/club_membership_conduct.pdf

Travers, A.H. et al. (2010). Cardiopulmonary resuscitation and emergency cardiovascular care. *Circulation, 122,* S676–S684.

Wong, G. (2010). *Essentials of Sports Law* (4th ed.). Santa Barbara, Calif.: ABC-CLIO.

Suggested Reading

Broadcast Music, Inc. (2009). *Business Using Music: Fitness Clubs.* www.bmi.com/licensing/entry/C1299/ pdf533620_1/

Carpenter, L.J. (2009). *Legal Concepts in Sport: A Primer* (3rd ed.). Champaign, Ill.: Sagamore Publishing.

Herbert, D.L. & Herbert, W.G. (2002). *Legal Aspects of Preventive and Rehabilitative Exercise Programs* (4th ed.). Canton, Ohio: PRC Publishing.

National Conference of State Legislatures (2008). *State Laws on Heart Attacks, Cardiac Arrest & Defibrillators.* www.ncsl.org/programs/health/aed.htm

Reents, S. (2007). *Personal Trainers Should not Offer Nutritional Advice.* www.athleteinme.com/articleview. aspx?id=264

APPENDICES

Appendix A
ACE Code of Ethics

Appendix B
Group Fitness Instructor Certification
Exam Content Outline

Appendix C
Effects of Medications on
Heart-rate Response

Appendix D
Group Fitness Specialties

Appendix E
ACE Position Statement on Nutrition
Scope of Practice for Fitness Professionals

ACE Code of Ethics

ACE-certified Professionals are guided by the following principles of conduct as they interact with clients/participants, the public, and other health and fitness professionals.

ACE-certified Professionals will endeavor to:

✔ Provide safe and effective instruction

✔ Provide equal and fair treatment to all clients/participants

✔ Stay up-to-date on the latest health and fitness research and understand its practical application

✔ Maintain current CPR certification and knowledge of first-aid services

✔ Comply with all applicable business, employment, and intellectual property laws

✔ Maintain the confidentiality of all client/participant information

✔ Refer clients/participants to more qualified health or medical professionals when appropriate

✔ Uphold and enhance public appreciation and trust for the health and fitness industry

✔ Establish and maintain clear professional boundaries

Provide Safe and Effective Instruction

Providing safe and effective instruction involves a variety of responsibilities for ACE-certified Professionals. Safe means that the instruction will not result in physical, mental, or financial harm to the client/participant. Effective means that the instruction has a purposeful, intended, and desired effect toward the client's/participant's goal. Great effort and care must be taken in carrying out the responsibilities that are essential in creating a positive exercise experience for all clients/participants.

Screening

ACE-certified Professionals should have all potential clients/participants complete an industry-recognized health-screening tool to ensure safe exercise participation. If significant risk factors or signs and symptoms suggestive of chronic disease are identified, refer the client/participant to a physician or primary healthcare practitioner for medical clearance and guidance regarding which types of assessments, activities, or exercises are indicated, contraindicated, or deemed high risk. If an individual does not want to obtain medical clearance, have that individual sign a legally prepared document that releases you and the facility in which you work from any liability related to any injury that may result from exercise participation or assessment. Once the client/participant has been cleared for exercise and you have a full understanding of the client's/participant's health status and medical history, including his or her current use of medications, a formal risk-management plan for potential emergencies must be prepared and reviewed periodically.

Assessment

The main objective of a health assessment is to establish the client's/participant's baseline fitness level in order to design an appropriate exercise program. Explain the risks and benefits of each assessment and provide the client/participant with any pertinent instructions. Prior to performing any type of assessment, the client/participant must be given an opportunity to ask questions and read and sign an informed consent. The types and order of assessments are dictated by the client's/participant's health status, fitness level, symptoms, and/or use of medications. Remember that each assessment has specific protocols and only those within your scope of practice should be administered. Once the assessments are completed, evaluate and discuss the results objectively as they relate to the client's/participant's health condition and goals. Educate the client/participant and emphasize how an exercise program will benefit the client/participant.

Program Design

You must not prescribe exercise, diet, or treatment, as doing so is outside your scope of practice and implies ordering or advising a medicine or treatment. Instead, it is appropriate for you to design exercise programs that improve components of physical fitness and wellness while adhering to the limitations of a previous injury or condition as determined by a certified, registered, or licensed allied health professional. Because nutritional laws and the practice of dietetics vary in each state, province, and country, understand what type of basic nutritional information is appropriate and legal for you to disseminate to your client/participant. The client's/participant's preferences, and short- and long-term goals as well as current industry standards and guidelines must be taken into consideration as you develop a formal yet realistic exercise and weight-management program. Provide as much detail for all exercise parameters such as mode, intensity, type of exercise, duration, progression, and termination points.

Program Implementation

Do not underestimate your ability to influence the client/participant to become active for a lifetime. Be sure that each class or session is well-planned, sequential, and documented. Instruct the client/participant how to safely and properly perform the appropriate exercises and communicate this in a manner that the client/participant will understand and retain. Each client/participant has a different learning curve that will require different levels of attention, learning aids, and repetition. Supervise the client/participant closely, especially when spotting or cueing is needed. If supervising a group of two or more, ensure that you can supervise and provide the appropriate amount of attention to each individual at all times. Ideally, the group will have similar goals and will be performing similar exercises or activities. Position yourself so that you do not have to turn your back to any client/participant performing an exercise.

Facilities

Although the condition of a facility may not always be within your control, you are still obligated to ensure a hazard-free environment to maximize safety. If you notice potential hazards in the health club, communicate these hazards to the client and the facility management. For example, if you notice that the clamps that keep the weights on the barbells are getting rusty and loose, it would be prudent of you to remove them from the

training area and alert the facility that immediate repair is required.

Equipment

Obtain equipment that meets or exceeds industry standards and utilize the equipment only for its intended use. Arrange exercise equipment and stations so that adequate space exists between equipment, participants, and foot traffic. Schedule regular maintenance and inspect equipment prior to use to ensure it is in proper working condition. Avoid the use of homemade equipment, as your liability is greater if it causes injury to a person exercising under your supervision.

Provide Equal and Fair Treatment to All Clients/ Participants

ACE-certified Professionals are obligated to provide fair and equal treatment for each client/participant without bias, preference, or discrimination against gender, ethnic background, age, national origin, basis of religion, or physical disability.

The Americans with Disabilities Act protects individuals with disabilities against any type of unlawful discrimination. A disability can be either physical or mental, such as epilepsy, paralysis, HIV infection, AIDS, a significant hearing or visual impairment, mental retardation, or a specific learning disability. ACE-certified Professionals should, at a minimum, provide reasonable accommodations to each individual with a disability. Reasonable simply means that you are able to provide accommodations that do not cause you any undue hardship that requires additional or significant expense or difficulty. Making an existing facility accessible by modifying equipment or devices, assessments, or training materials are a few examples of providing reasonable accommodations. However, providing the use of personal items or providing items at your own expense may not be considered reasonable.

This ethical consideration of providing fair and equal treatment is not limited to behavioral interactions with clients/participants, but also extends to exercise programming and other business-related services such as communication, scheduling, billing, cancellation policies, and dispute resolution.

Stay Up-to-Date on the Latest Health and Fitness Research and Understand Its Practical Application

Obtaining ACE-certification required you to have broad-based knowledge of many disciplines; however, this credential should not be viewed as the end of your professional development and education. Instead, it should be viewed as the beginning or foundation. The dynamic nature of the health and fitness industry requires you to maintain an understanding of the latest research and professional standards and guidelines, and of their impact on the design and implementation of exercise programming. To stay informed, make time to review a variety of industry resources such as professional journals, position statements, trade and lay periodicals, and correspondence courses, as well as to attend professional meetings, conferences, and educational workshops.

An additional benefit of staying up-to-date is that it also fulfills your certification renewal requirements for continuing education credit (CEC). To maintain your ACE-certification status, you must obtain an established amount of CECs every two years. CECs are granted for structured learning that takes place within the educational portion of a course related to the profession and presented by a qualified health and fitness professional.

Maintain Current CPR Certification and Knowledge of First-aid Services

ACE-certified Professionals must be prepared to recognize and respond to heart attacks and other life-threatening emergencies. Emergency response is enhanced by training and maintaining skills in CPR, first aid, and using automated external defibrillators (AEDs), which have become more widely available. An AED is a portable electronic device used to restore normal heart rhythm in a person experiencing a cardiac arrest and can reduce the time to defibrillation before EMS personnel arrive. For each minute that defibrillation is delayed, the victim's chance of survival is reduced by 7 to 10%. Thus, survival from cardiac arrest is improved dramatically when CPR and defibrillation are started early.

Comply With All Applicable Business, Employment, and Intellectual Property Laws

As an ACE-certified Professional, you are expected to maintain a high level of integrity by complying with all applicable business, employment, and copyright laws. Be truthful and forthcoming with communication to clients/participants, coworkers, and other health and fitness professionals in advertising, marketing, and business practices. Do not create false or misleading impressions of credentials, claims, or sponsorships, or perform services outside of your scope of practice that are illegal, deceptive, or fraudulent.

All information regarding your business must be clear, accurate, and easy to understand for all potential clients/participants. Provide disclosure about the name of your business, physical address, and contact information, and maintain a working phone number and email address. So that clients/participants can make an informed choice about paying for your services, provide detailed information regarding schedules, prices, payment terms, time limits, and conditions. Cancellation, refund, and rescheduling information must also be clearly stated and easy to understand. Allow the client/participant an opportunity to ask questions and review this information before formally agreeing to your services and terms.

Because employment laws vary in each city, state, province, and country, familiarize yourself with the applicable employment regulations and standards to which your business must conform. Examples of this may include conforming to specific building codes and zoning ordinances or making sure that your place of business is accessible to individuals with a disability.

The understanding of intellectual property law and the proper use of copyrighted materials is an important legal issue for all ACE-certified Professionals. Intellectual property laws protect the creations of authors, artists, software programmers, and others with copyrighted materials. The most common infringement of intellectual property law in the fitness industry is the use of music in an exercise class. When

commercial music is played in a for-profit exercise class, without a performance or blanket license, it is considered a public performance and a violation of intellectual property law. Therefore, make sure that any music, handouts, or educational materials are either exempt from intellectual property law or permissible under laws by reason of fair use, or obtain express written consent from the copyright holder for distribution, adaptation, or use. When in doubt, obtain permission first or consult with a qualified legal professional who has intellectual property law expertise.

Maintain the Confidentiality of All Client/Participant Information

Every client/participant has the right to expect that all personal data and discussions with an ACE-certified Professional will be safeguarded and not disclosed without the client's/participant's express written consent or acknowledgement. Therefore, protect the confidentiality of all client/participant information such as contact data, medical records, health history, progress notes, and meeting details. Even when confidentiality is not required by law, continue to preserve the confidentiality of such information.

Any breach of confidentiality, intentional or unintentional, potentially harms the productivity and trust of your client/participant and undermines your effectiveness as a fitness professional. This also puts you at risk for potential litigation and puts your client/participant at risk for public embarrassment and fraudulent activity such as identity theft.

Most breaches of confidentiality are unintentional and occur because of carelessness and lack of awareness. The most common breach of confidentiality is exposing or storing personal data in a location that is not secure. This occurs when a client's/participant's file or information is left on a desk, or filed in a cabinet that has no lock or is accessible to others. Breaches of confidentiality may also occur when you have conversations regarding a client's/participant's performance or medical/health history with staff or others and the client's/participant's first name or other identifying details are used.

Post and adhere to a privacy policy that communicates how client/participant information will be used and secured and how a client's/participant's preference regarding unsolicited mail and email will be respected. When a client/participant provides you with any personal data, new or updated, make it a habit to immediately secure this information and ensure that only you and/or the appropriate individuals have access to it. Also, the client's/participant's files must only be accessed and used for purposes related to health and fitness services. If client/participant information is stored on a personal computer, restrict access by using a protected password. Should you receive any inquiries from family members or other individuals regarding the progress of a client/participant or other personal information, state that you cannot provide any information without the client's/participant's permission. If and when a client/participant permits you to release confidential information to an authorized individual or party, utilize secure methods of communication such as certified mail, sending and receiving information on a dedicated private fax line, or email with encryption.

Refer Clients/Participants to More Qualified Health or Medical Professionals When Appropriate

A fitness certification is not a professional license. Therefore, it is vitally important that ACE-certified Professionals who do not also have a professional license (i.e., physician, physical therapist, dietitian, psychologist, and attorney) refer their clients/participants to a more qualified professional when warranted. Doing so not only benefits your clients/participants by making sure that they receive the appropriate attention and care, but also enhances your credibility and reduces liability by defining your scope of practice and clarifying what services you can and cannot reasonably provide.

Knowing when to refer a client/participant is, however, as important as choosing to which professional to refer. For instance, just because a client/participant complains of symptoms of muscle soreness or discomfort or exhibits signs of fatigue or lack of energy is not an absolute indication to refer your client/participant to a physician. Because continual referrals such as this are not practical, familiarize and educate yourself on expected signs and symptoms, taking into consideration the client's/participant's fitness level, health status, chronic disease, disability, and/or background as he or she is screened and then begins and progresses with an exercise program. This helps you better discern between emergent and non-emergent situations and know when to refuse to offer your services, continue to monitor, and/or make an immediate referral.

It is important that you know the scope of practice for various health professionals and which types of referrals are appropriate. For example, some states require that a referring physician first approve visits to a physical therapist, while other states allow individuals to see a physical therapist directly. Only registered or licensed dietitians or physicians may provide specific dietary recommendations or diet plans; however, a client/participant who is suspected of an eating disorder should be referred to an eating disorders specialist. Refer clients/participants to a clinical psychologist if they wish to discuss family or marital problems or exhibit addictive behaviors such as substance abuse.

Network and develop rapport with potential allied health professionals in your area before you refer clients/participants to them. This demonstrates good will and respect for their expertise and will most likely result in reciprocal referrals for your services and fitness expertise.

Uphold and Enhance Public Appreciation and Trust for the Health and Fitness Industry

The best way for ACE-certified Professionals to uphold and enhance public appreciation and trust for the health and fitness industry is to represent themselves in a dignified and professional manner. As the public is inundated with misinformation and false claims about fitness products and services, your expertise must be utilized to dispel myths and half-truths about current trends and fads that are potentially harmful to the public.

When appropriate, mentor and dispense knowledge and training to less-experienced fitness professionals. Novice fitness professionals can benefit from your experience and skill as you assist them in establish-

ing a foundation based on exercise science, from both theoretical and practical standpoints. Therefore, it is a disservice if you fail to provide helpful or corrective information—especially when an individual, the public, or other fitness professionals are at risk for injury or increased liability. For example, if you observe an individual using momentum to perform a strength-training exercise, the prudent course of action would be to suggest a modification. Likewise, if you observe a fitness professional in your workplace consistently failing to obtain informed consents before clients/participants undergo fitness testing or begin an exercise program, recommend that he or she consider implementing these forms to minimize liability.

Finally, do not represent yourself in an overly commercial or misleading manner. Consider the fitness professional who places an advertisement in a local newspaper stating: Lose 10 pounds in 10 days or your money back! It is inappropriate to lend credibility to or endorse a product, service, or program founded upon unsubstantiated or misleading claims; thus a solicitation such as this must be avoided, as it undermines the public's trust of health and fitness professionals.

Establish and Maintain Clear Professional Boundaries

Working in the fitness profession requires you to come in contact with many different people. It is imperative that a professional distance be maintained in relationships with all clients/participants. Fitness professionals are responsible for setting and monitoring the boundaries between a working relationship

ACE Code of Ethics

and friendship with their clients/participants. To that end, ACE-certified Professionals should:

- Never initiate or encourage discussion of a sexual nature
- Avoid touching clients/participants unless it is essential to instruction
- Inform clients/participants about the purpose of touching and find an alternative if the client/participant objects
- Discontinue all touching if it appears to make the client/participant uncomfortable
- Take all reasonable steps to ensure that any personal and social contacts between themselves and their clients/participants do not have an adverse impact on the trainer–client or instructor–participant relationship.

If you find yourself unable to maintain appropriate professional boundaries with a client/participant (whether due to your attitudes and actions or those of the client/participant), the prudent course of action is to terminate the relationship and, perhaps, refer the client/participant to another professional. Keep in mind that charges of sexual harassment or assault, even if groundless, can have disastrous effects on your career.

For the most up-to-date version of
the Exam Content Outline, please go to
www.acefitness.org/GFIexamcontent
and download a free PDF.

Group Fitness Instructor Certification Exam Content Outline

The Exam Content Outline is essentially a blueprint for the exam. As you prepare for the exam, it is important to remember that all exam questions are based on this outline.

Target Audience Statement

The certified Group Fitness Instructor is responsible for planning and leading group exercise sessions to enhance the general well-being (e.g., fitness and health) and exercise skills of participants. The certified Group Fitness Instructor is at least 18 years of age and possesses current valid cardiopulmonary resuscitation (CPR) and automated external defibrillator (AED) certificates.

Domains, Tasks, and Knowledge and Skill Statements

A Role Delineation Study, or job analysis, was conducted by the American Council on Exercise and Castle Worldwide, Inc., for the ACE Group Fitness Instructor certification. The first step in this process was completed by a panel of subject matter experts in the various disciplines within group exercise. The primary goal of the panel was to identify the primary tasks performed by group fitness instructors in designing and delivering safe and effective exercise classes. The panel first identified the major categories of responsibility for a professional. These categories are defined as "Domains" and it was determined that the profession of group fitness instruction could be divided into four Performance Domains, or major areas of responsibility.

These Performance Domains are listed below with the percentage indicating the portion of the exam devoted to each domain:

- Domain I: Exercise Programming and Class Design – 19%
- Domain II: Group Instructional Methods – 37%
- Domain III: Group Leadership and Class Management – 29%
- Domain IV: Professional Responsibilities – 15%

Each Domain is composed of Task Statements, which detail the job-related functions under that particular Domain. Each Task Statement is further divided into Knowledge and Skill Statements that detail the scope of information required to perform each Task and how that information is applied in a practical setting.

The Performance Domains, Task Statements, and Knowledge and Skill Statements identified by the panel of subject matter experts were then validated by a sample of currently practicing ACE-certified Group Fitness Instructors. This completed the Role Delineation Study, with the outcome of this study being the ACE Group Fitness Instructor exam content outline detailed below. Please note that not all Knowledge and Skill Statements listed in the exam content outline will be addressed on each exam administration.

DOMAIN I: EXERCISE PROGRAMMING AND CLASS DESIGN   19%

Task 1

Select appropriate music and/or equipment based on an understanding of the objectives of the type of class for a varied group of participants to create a safe and effective class design.

Knowledge of:

1. Applicable music licensing laws, decibels, and lyrics/content
2. Basic components of a class (e.g., warm-up, conditioning, cool-down, flexibility)
3. Music styles and tempos appropriate for each class format or class component
4. Various group fitness–related equipment and their appropriate uses (steps, indoor cycles, free weights, elastic resistance, medicine balls, stability balls, balance-related tools, etc.)
5. Varied class formats (traditional high-impact/low-impact, step, kickboxing, indoor cycling, water exercise, interval, circuit, muscular conditioning, sports

conditioning, flexibility, mind-body, pre-choreographed, etc.)

6. A/V equipment capabilities and use
7. Safe use of the equipment

Skill in:

1. Assessing music for bpm, structure, etc.
2. Applying awareness of cultural sensitivity to music and equipment selection
3. Analyzing equipment in relation to class design and location

Task 2

Create a class plan of safe and effective exercise movements using general fitness principles in order to achieve individual health, fitness, and wellness goals, reduce potential injury, promote adherence, and enhance the experience for a varied group of participants.

Knowledge of:

1. Skill-related components (balance, agility, speed, power, coordination, reaction time)
2. Principles of training (overload, specificity, reversibility, progression, adaptation)
3. Basic components of a class (e.g., warm-up, conditioning, cool-down, flexibility)
4. Applied kinesiology, exercise physiology, biomechanics, and anatomy
5. Major fitness-related components (cardio-respiratory endurance, muscular strength and endurance, flexibility, and body composition)
6. Current and established guidelines for improving and maintaining cardiorespiratory endurance, muscular strength and endurance, flexibility, and body composition, with reference to appropriate frequency, intensity, time, and type (FITT)
7. Current research on safe and effective exercise and movement

8. Training guidelines for health, fitness, and athletic performance
9. Choreography and sequencing

Skill in:

1. Incorporating fitness components and training principles
2. Adjusting training and skill-related principles to reach desired results
3. Selecting different methods to teach correct exercise and movement for desired results
4. Identifying the safe and effective exercise and/or movements for the desired results
5. Designing choreography, including sequencing, transition, and flow

Task 3

Integrate variety into class design by changing class elements (e.g., exercises, sequencing, equipment, music) for the participants in order to achieve individual health, fitness, and wellness goals, reduce potential injury, promote adherence, and enhance the experience.

Knowledge of:

1. Class components such as movement, instruction, format, and equipment
2. Overload, metabolic pathways, progression, etc.
3. Music styles and tempos appropriate for each class format or class component
4. Use and application of various group fitness–related equipment (e.g., steps, indoor cycles, free weights, elastic resistance, medicine balls, stability balls, balance-related tools)
5. Functional training principles to improve the quality of life

6. Exercises to develop skill-related fitness components including balance, agility, speed, power, coordination, and reaction time
7. Teaching styles (e.g., command, practice, reciprocal, self-check, inclusion) appropriate for a group fitness class
8. Choreographic methods (e.g., freestyle vs. structured)
9. Verbal and non-verbal communication skills

Skill in:

1. Lesson planning
2. Integrating functional-training principles into a group fitness class setting
3. Incorporating the skill-related fitness components where appropriate
4. Manipulating various exercises, equipment, and music within any class format
5. Varying the class in accordance with fitness principles and established guidelines (frequency, intensity, duration, mode, sets, repetitions)
6. Recognizing the need for, and implementing, progression
7. Using appropriate communication and teaching styles
8. Selecting appropriate motivational techniques for desired outcomes

DOMAIN II: GROUP INSTRUCTIONAL METHODS 37%

Task 1

Lead a class using appropriate and effective instructional techniques (i.e., teaching methods) to accommodate cultural and demographic differences of class participants in order to achieve individual health, fitness, and wellness goals, reduce potential injury, promote adherence, and enhance the experience.

Knowledge of:

1. Teaching styles (e.g., command, practice, reciprocal, self-check, inclusion) appropriate for a group fitness class
2. Teaching strategies (e.g., slow-to-fast, repetition reduction, spatial, part-to-whole, simple-to-complex) used to facilitate participant learning
3. Choreographic methods (e.g., freestyle vs. structured)
4. Domains and stages of learning
5. Various communication and learning styles (e.g., visual, auditory, kinesthetic)
6. Precautions when using touch to correct improper form
7. Motivational strategies that engage participants with various skills, limitations, preferences, and expectations

Skill in:

1. Using teaching styles (e.g., command, practice, reciprocal, self-check, inclusion) appropriate for a group fitness class
2. Selecting appropriate teaching strategies (e.g., slow-to-fast, repetition reduction, spatial, part-to-whole, simple-to-complex) to accommodate participant fitness and skill levels and class modality
3. Applying appropriate feedback based on participant skill, fitness level, and/or cultural background
4. Recognizing and interpreting participant nonverbal communication
5. Recognizing the cultural and demographic requirements of participants
6. Selecting appropriate motivational technique for desired outcomes
7. Selecting appropriate communication styles

Task 2

Lead a class using appropriate and effective instructional techniques in order to accommodate participants' various learning styles and motor development for optimal participant physical performance and to achieve individual health, fitness, and wellness goals, reduce potential injury, promote adherence, and enhance the experience.

Knowledge of:

1. Teaching styles (e.g., command, practice, reciprocal, self-check, inclusion) appropriate for a group fitness class
2. Teaching strategies (e.g., slow-to-fast, repetition reduction, spatial, part-to-whole, simple-to-complex) used to facilitate participant learning
3. Various communication and learning styles
4. Strategies for identifying participants with poor kinesthetic awareness
5. Principles of learning theory with respect to effective teaching in a group exercise setting
6. Stages of learning

Skill in:

1. Using teaching styles (e.g., command, practice, reciprocal, self-check, inclusion) appropriate for a group fitness class
2. Selecting appropriate teaching strategies (e.g., slow-to-fast, repetition reduction, spatial, part-to-whole, simple-to-complex) to accommodate participant fitness and skill levels and class modality
3. Accommodating participants in the various stages of learning
4. Identifying stages of learning (e.g., cognitive, associative, autonomous)

Task 3

Educate participants on how to monitor their own intensities using a variety of methods to enable them to exercise at the most appropriate level to achieve individual health, fitness, and wellness goals, reduce potential injury, promote adherence, and enhance the experience.

Knowledge of:

1. Reasons for monitoring exercise intensity
2. Methods for monitoring exercise intensity: heart rate, talk test, Borg's ratings of perceived exertion (RPE), dyspnea scale, metabolic equivalents (METs), and zone training, and their use, precautions, and limitations (e.g., abnormal heart-rate responses, effect of medications, pregnancy, other special populations)
3. Heart-rate response to various class components (warm-up, cardiovascular phase, muscular conditioning, and cool-down)
4. Applications and limitations in the calculations of target heart rate: percent of heart-rate reserve, age-predicted maximum heart rate, and measured maximum heart rate

Skill in:

1. Using and explaining the talk test, RPE, and dyspnea scales as methods for monitoring exercise intensity
2. Modifying exercise intensity
3. Identifying signs and symptoms of over- and under-exertion, and making appropriate modifications
4. Selecting an appropriate intensity-monitoring method to accommodate special populations (e.g., pregnancy) and/or the effects of medications on heart-rate response

Task 4

Observe class participants' exercise and movement techniques and exertion levels and provide feedback and/or corrections using appropriate strategies in order to prevent injury and improve exercise performance.

Knowledge of:

1. Appropriate body alignment and posture (e.g., neutral spine) during proper execution of exercises
2. Correct mechanics for each exercise, movement, and balance (static and dynamic)
3. How to apply effective instructional methods for correcting exercise techniques, balance, and movement
4. Physical signs and symptoms of over- and under-exertion, fatigue, and dehydration
5. Verbal and non-verbal (e.g., demonstrations and hands-on) communication strategies

Skill in:

1. Teaching correct mechanics for each exercise, movement, and balance
2. Recognizing incorrect exercise form and techniques
3. Providing effective feedback to the class to help participants improve exercise form without negatively impacting self-efficacy and/or adherence
4. Providing individualized correction using appropriate strategies when necessary, while maintaining class control

Task 5

Instruct and educate participants using clear, concise, and timely cues during the class in order to facilitate safe and effective movement execution and transitions.

Knowledge of:

1. Appropriate musical application for the class format (e.g., beats per minute)
2. Verbal and non-verbal (visual) cueing techniques
3. Timing and strategies for effective cueing exercise
4. Teaching styles (e.g., command, practice, reciprocal, self-check, inclusion) appropriate for a group fitness class
5. Teaching strategies (e.g., slow-to-fast, repetition reduction, spatial, part-to-whole, simple-to-complex) used to facilitate participant learning
6. Learning stages (e.g., cognitive, associative, autonomous)
7. Various learning styles (e.g., visual, auditory, kinesthetic)
8. Appropriate techniques and situations for cueing movements via touch
9. Components of effective feedback (e.g., informational rather than controlling, based on performance standards, specific and immediate) and the types of feedback (e.g., corrective, value, and neutral statements)
10. Strategies for effective verbal cueing and prevention of vocal stress

Skill in:

1. Teaching using various styles (e.g., command, practice, reciprocal, self-check, inclusion) appropriate for a group fitness class
2. Implementing appropriate teaching strategies (e.g., slow-to-fast, repetition reduction, spatial, part-to-whole, simple-to-complex) to accommodate participant

fitness, skill levels, cultural background, and class modality

3. Effective timing and use of verbal and visual (non-verbal) cueing methods and techniques (e.g., 32-count phrase when applicable)
4. Using verbal cueing methods that effectively prevent vocal stress
5. Teaching and executing exercises with proper form and technique
6. Leading exercise through mirroring and matching techniques

Task 6

Motivate and educate a varied group of participants, using academically sound resources as well as appropriate strategies and techniques within the GFI scope of practice, to set realistic goals and take ownership of the exercise experience.

Knowledge of:

1. How to identify and access credible re-sources for academically sound information
2. Methods of learning (verbal, visual, kinesthetic)
3. Effective motivational techniques
4. Scope of practice for ACE-certified Group Fitness Instructors

Skill in:

1. Identifying credible resources
2. Determining pertinent information to disseminate to class participants based on level of interest and information complexity
3. Teaching groups and individuals about exercise science–related topics at a level appropriate for non-fitness professionals
4. Determining appropriate action within the GFI Scope of Practice

DOMAIN III: GROUP LEADERSHIP AND CLASS MANAGEMENT   29%

Task 1

Lead classes that are safe and effective by accommodating for the needs of the multiple fitness levels of participants, by offering exercise and movement modifications, progressions, and regressions to achieve individual health, fitness, and wellness goals, reduce potential injury, promote adherence, and enhance the experience.

Knowledge of:

1. Concepts of variety and progression as they relate to the prevention of injury and boredom
2. Teaching strategies (e.g., slow-to-fast, repetition reduction, spatial, part-to-whole, simple-to-complex) used to facilitate participant learning
3. Methods used to accommodate various fitness levels
4. Strategies for identifying areas of weakness and designing exercises and movements, and providing feedback to encourage improvement
5. Basic flexibility, exercise, movement, and balance progressions, regressions, and modifications

Skill in:

1. Adapting the fitness components to accommodate various fitness levels within the class
2. Manipulating various exercises, equipment, music, and teaching styles within any class format
3. Recognizing the need for progression, regression, and modification

4. Implementing appropriate progression rates
5. Teaching multiple options for flexibility, exercise, movement, and balance to accommodate various fitness levels

Task 2

Lead classes that are safe and effective by accommodating for the needs of participants from various special population groups by offering exercise and movement modifications and variations to achieve individual health, fitness, and wellness goals, reduce potential injury, promote adherence, and enhance the experience.

Knowledge of:
1. General medical conditions and common physical disabilities of special populations
2. Varied ability and capabilities within each special population group
3. What constitutes a special population and their particular needs
4. Exercise guidelines for different special population groups (youth, older adults, pre/post-natal, people with medical conditions, diseases, disorders, and disabilities)

Skill in:
1. Identifying participants who may need options to either decrease or increase intensity
2. Integrating and modifying programs to meet the needs of a special population
3. Recognizing health issues that interfere with participant ability to exercise safely within a specific class format
4. Recognizing the needs and capabilities of different special population groups

5. Designing safe and effective classes that address the specific needs of a special population

Task 3

Conduct pre-class and ongoing assessments of the space, environment, and participants in order to identify potential hazards and undertake necessary modifications to ensure a safe setting for a varied group of participants.

Knowledge of:
1. Applicable laws, regulations, and insurance needs for outdoor/public spaces
2. Specific environmental factors as they relate to the safety of the class participants (cold, heat, humidity, altitude, acoustics, exercise surface, exercise area)
3. Physiological responses and adaptations that result from variations in environmental conditions
4. Recommendations and precautions, including industry guidelines, for exercising in heat, cold, humidity, altitude, and pollution
5. Space risk management and emergency protocols, including EMS activations
6. Space evacuation procedures
7. Risk management implementation protocols, including assumption of risk, risk assessment, waivers, informed consent, professional liability insurance, and general liability insurance
8. Recommended hydration guidelines
9. Environmental factors that influence adherence

Skill in:
1. Adapting class content and/or programming based on specific environmental conditions

2. Identifying signs and symptoms of over-exertion, overexposure, and dehydration

3. Determining the need for evacuation processes of class participants in accordance with facility evacuation procedures

Task 4

Foster a comfortable exercise environment by utilizing effective communication skills with groups and individuals to establish and enhance rapport, develop relationships, and build community in order to improve class adherence.

Knowledge of:

1. Methods for developing and enhancing rapport

2. Appropriate use of feedback (e.g., corrective, value, and neutral statements)

3. Effective group and interpersonal communication techniques that enhance rapport (e.g., active listening, open-ended questioning, acknowledgement, use of empathy and compassion)

4. Participant-centered teaching approaches

5. Methods for improving adherence

Skill in:

1. Developing rapport with and among class participants

2. Fostering a sense of community among class participants

3. Leading a group of individuals with different goals through a set class with modifications as needed (e.g., addressing individual needs and concerns, alleviating conflicts)

4. Listening effectively (e.g., use of minimal encouragement, reflecting, summarizing)

5. Establishing rapport (e.g., learning participant names, being accessible and approachable, using culturally appropriate non-verbal techniques such as eye contact)

Task 5

Create a positive participant experience by utilizing customer service and skills required to be professional with groups and individuals in order to enhance class adherence.

Knowledge of:

1. Factors that create a positive experience for class participants

2. Strategies and methods for providing effective customer service

3. Participant-centered teaching approaches

4. Strategies to facilitate conflict resolution

5. Factors that facilitate adherence

6. Fair and equal treatment for all participants

Skill in:

1. Providing quality customer service to a group and one-on-one

2. Establishing an atmosphere of trust

3. Establishing rapport (e.g., learning participant names, being accessible and approachable, using culturally appropriate non-verbal techniques such as eye contact)

4. Building group camaraderie

5. Addressing and alleviating class conflicts

6. Observing and interpreting nonverbal communication

7. Listening effectively (e.g., use of minimal encouragement, reflecting, summarizing)

DOMAIN IV: PROFESSIONAL RESPONSIBILITIES 15%

Task 1

Prepare for, practice, and respond to, facility emergencies, acute medical conditions, and injuries, by following established protocols and documentation requirements in order to maximize participants' safety and manage risk.

Knowledge of:

1. Industry guidelines, appropriate laws, and facility procedures relating to safety, risk management, emergencies, and injuries in fitness facilities and/or group exercise classes (indoor and outdoor)
2. Physiological responses to, and recommendations for, exercising in various environmental conditions (e.g., heat, cold, humidity, altitude, pollution)
3. Basic procedures for injury management and emergency response within the GFI Scope of Practice (e.g., CPR, AED, basic first aid, RICE)
4. Medical conditions that affect a participant's ability to exercise safely in class (e.g., diabetes, hypertension, heart disease, arthritis, osteoporosis)
5. Procedures for documenting accidents, injuries, and incident reports, while safeguarding participant confidentiality
6. Appropriate insurance protections (e.g., professional liability insurance, general liability insurance, workers' compensation insurance, health and disability insurance) for fitness professionals working in a variety of settings
7. Scope of practice for ACE-certified Group Fitness Instructors

Skill in:

1. Adapting class content, format, and/or programming based on specific environmental conditions in order to maximize participants' safety (e.g., adequate warm-up and cool-down, recognizing potential hazards, providing proper instruction)
2. Utilizing various methods for monitoring intensity (e.g., RPE, heart rate, dyspnea) to prevent overexertion in regular class and adverse environmental conditions
3. Identifying signs and symptoms of overexertion and making appropriate modifications
4. Administering basic injury-management procedures and completing appropriate reports (e.g., incident reports)
5. Safeguarding confidential information
6. Carrying out facility evacuation procedures in the event of an emergency

Task 2

Assess, document, and maintain requirements for certification and liability insurance in order to help minimize risk for the class participants, organizations, and the ACE-certified Group Fitness Instructor.

Knowledge of:

1. Various insurance policies and coverage (e.g., professional liability insurance, general liability insurance, workers' compensation insurance, health and disability insurance) for classes taught in a variety of settings (e.g., indoors, pool, outdoors)
2. American Council on Exercise Professional Practices and Disciplinary Procedure
3. Standards, laws, and regulations governing confidentiality
4. Scope of practice for the ACE-certified Group Fitness Instructor

Skill in:

1. Following industry guidelines to minimize risk for the GFI and class participants (e.g., adequate warm-up and cool-down, recognizing potential hazards, providing proper instruction)
2. Completing requirements to maintain certification
3. Determining appropriate insurance and levels of coverage necessary for the GFI based on the teaching facility and class logistics
4. Referring participants to more qualified fitness, medical, or health professionals when appropriate

Effects of Medication on Heart-rate (HR) Response

Table C-1

Effects of Medication on Heart-rate (HR) Response

Medications	Resting HR	Exercising HR	Maximal Exercising HR	Comments
Beta-adrenergic blocking agents	↓	↓	↓	Dose-related response
Diuretics	←→	←→	←→	
Other antihypertensives	↑, ←→ or ↓	↑, ←→ or ↓	Usually ←→	Many antihypertensive medications are used. Some may decrease, a few may increase, and others do not affect heart rates. Some exhibit dose-related response.
Calcium channel blockers	↑, ←→ or ↓	↑, ←→ or ↓	Usually ←→	Variable and dose-related responses
Antihistamines	←→	←→	←→	
Cold medications: without sympathomimetic activity (SA)	←→	←→	←→	
with SA	←→ or ↑	←→ or ↑	←→	
Tranquilizers	←→, or if anxiety reducing may ↓	←→	←→	
Antidepressants and some antipsychotic medications	←→ or ↑	←→	←→	
Alcohol	←→ or ↑	←→ or ↑	←→	Exercise prohibited while under the influence; effects of alcohol on coordination increase possibility of injuries
Diet pills: with SA	↑ or ←→	↑ or ←→	←→	Discourage as a poor approach to weight loss; acceptable only with physician's written approval
containing amphetamines	↑	↑	←→	
without SA or amphetamine	←→	←→	←→	
Caffeine	←→ or ↑	←→ or ↑	←→	
Nicotine	←→ or ↑	←→ or ↑	←→	Discourage smoking; suggest lower target heart rate and exercise intensity for smokers

↑ = increase   ←→ = no significant change   ↓ = decrease

Note: Many medications are prescribed for conditions that do not require clearance. Do not forget other indicators of exercise intensity (e.g., participant's appearance and ratings of perceived exertion).

Sabrena Merrill, M.S., has been actively involved in the fitness industry since 1987, successfully operating her own personal-training business and teaching group exercise classes. Merrill is a former full-time faculty member in the Kinesiology and Physical Education Department at California State University, Long Beach. She has a bachelor's degree in exercise science as well as a master's degree in physical education/biomechanics from the University of Kansas. Merrill, an ACE-certified Personal Trainer and Group Fitness Instructor, is an author, educator, and fitness consultant who remains very active within the industry.

Group Fitness Specialties

By Sabrena Merrill

The introduction of the ACE Integrated Fitness Training™ (ACE IFT™) Model has provided fitness professionals, including GFIs, a comprehensive training model for health, fitness, and performance that can be implemented with all apparently healthy individuals (see page 59). Thus, a GFI can use the ACE IFT Model to guide group fitness participants into the appropriate type and level of exercise class. In general, most group exercise classes can be appropriate for individuals with various fitness skills and abilities, as long as the GFI is capable of student-centered instruction wherein exercise modifications are shown frequently throughout the workout session.

Of course, certain group exercise classes, such as those promoting skill-specific conditioning like plyometric training, should be attended by participants who are indeed ready for that kind of high-intensity training. A class that is suitable for only a narrow portion of the population should be named accordingly. For example, a plyometric training class might be named "Sports and Jump Training EXTREME!" It would be hard to imagine a deconditioned participant who would read the name of that class and think that he or she could realistically participate.

While it is given that each group exercise class is unique, Table D-1 provides general information on how common group fitness classes could fit into the ACE IFT Model. Keep in mind that the complexity and intensity level of any genre of class can be altered to make it more appropriate for a broader or narrower range of the population.

Table D-1

Integrating Group Fitness Classes Into the ACE IFT Model

	Phase 1	Phase 2	Phase 3	Phase 4
Functional Movement & Resistance Training	**Stability & Mobility Training**	**Movement Training**	**Load Training**	**Performance Training**
Group Fitness Classes	*Pilates (mat & reformer); stability ball training*	*Pilates (mat & reformer); fitness yoga*	*Aquatic resistance exercise; group strength training*	*Fitness boot camp; sports conditioning*
Cardiorespiratory Training	**Aerobic-base Training**	**Aerobic-efficiency Training**	**Anaerobic-endurance Training**	**Anaerobic-power Training**
Group Fitness Classes	*Aquatic aerobic exercise*	*Traditional aerobics; step training*	*Group indoor cycling; kickboxing fitness*	*Sports conditioning*

Traditional Aerobics

Following the publication of Dr. Kenneth Cooper's book *Aerobics* in 1968, movement forms reflecting a shared cultural value of health and fitness proliferated. Traditional aerobics was among these, tracing its early lineage to such pioneers as Jacki Sorensen, founder of Aerobic Dancing, Inc., and Judi Sheppard Missett, president of Jazzercise, Inc. These women and others adapted Dr. Cooper's concept of aerobic exercise to exercise classes with music, creating what became known as aerobic dance-exercise or, simply, aerobics. With the release of "Jane Fonda's Workout" video in 1982, the dissemination of traditional aerobics to a mass market via electronic media forever changed the fitness culture worldwide.

Traditional aerobics continues to provide the form, methodology, and objectives upon which subsequent group fitness forms have been modeled. While the three primary types of traditional aerobics—high-impact, combination high-low impact, and low-impact—continue to appear on group fitness class schedules, many of these classes have taken on new forms to appeal to a wide range of participants. Hip hop and African dance classes, for example, are variations on a traditional aerobics class. Creative fitness professionals continue to come up with new ways to keep participants engaged in group exercise classes.

Benefits

The main benefits of traditional aerobics are improved cardiorespiratory endurance and body composition. In addition, the social interaction and sense of community that develops from frequent participation in a group exercise program promotes adherence and motivation.

The potential for freedom of movement is greater in traditional aerobics than many other modes of aerobic training. Only the anatomical limits of the body and the boundaries of the room dictate the form of the movement. Because traditional aerobics is a weightbearing activity, it has important implications for postural balance and bone mineral density. Individuals who participate in a high- or low-impact aerobics class are required to move quickly in many directions while keeping their balance intact. This promotes dynamic stability as the muscles work to stabilize the joints during movement in various planes, and has a high carryover to the activities of daily living. Bone mass is also positively affected by weightbearing exercise. The consistent performance of land-based, standing exercise increases participants' bone mineral density in the lumbar and hip regions. This benefit is increased significantly when exercisers add impact (e.g., hopping and jumping) to their programs. Furthermore, older adults who regularly participate in aerobic weightbearing exercise programs are less likely to fall due to loss of balance, thereby potentially reducing their risk of fractures.

Participant Suitability

Traditional aerobics classes are well-suited for individuals who enjoy choreography-based exercise and are fond of pacing their movements to rhythms in music. Historically, more women than men have participated in aerobics classes, possibly due to the classes' dance-like characteristics. However, both men and women can benefit from the cardiorespiratory-endurance and balance-training opportunities provided by this type of weightbearing, land-based exercise.

Individuals who are new to exercise, are overweight or obese, or who have certain joint injuries or chronic diseases may find an entire traditional aerobics class too difficult. Furthermore, individuals who are at risk for falling (e.g., seniors with osteoporosis and late-term pregnant women) should consult with their physicians prior to engaging in this type of activity. Individuals with health risks may find that modifying the choreography to include only low-impact moves allows them to safely enjoy a traditional aerobics class.

Step Training

Introduced in the late 1980s, step training has become a staple in group exercise programming. Also called bench aerobics, step/bench training, and aerobic stepping, step training is a relatively low-impact exercise program that utilizes a platform ranging from 4 to 12 inches in height. Participants step up and down while performing a variety of movement skills and sequences to music and utilizing large muscle groups to tax the cardiovascular, respiratory, and muscular systems.

The physiological response to stepping up and down off a bench has been known for decades. Exercise physiologists in the early 20th century developed fitness tests based on the heart-rate response to repetitive stepping, such as the Harvard Step Test. Further step-test protocols have been developed and validated in major universities for estimating physical work capacity and aerobic fitness. For example, Fred Kasch, Ph.D., of San Diego State University developed the Three-Minute Step Test, which is currently used by YMCAs for mass testing of participants. Stepping is also used in sports medicine rehabilitation, most specifically as a standard form of knee rehabilitation exercise. Stepping emphasizes conditioning the quadriceps muscles, which are important for knee stability, provides low injury potential to the recovering knee due to its low-impact nature, and is an ideal progressive exercise for knee rehabilitation because of its adjustability and control. It was the use of stepping in knee rehabilitation that ultimately led to its application in the fitness industry.

Step exercise evolved primarily out of a need for another type of challenging, interesting, and effective cardiovascular activity. Despite the advent of complex choreography and power step training, which utilizes hops and jumps to increase intensity, it is the relatively low-impact nature of the exercise that has largely contributed to the popularity of step training.

Benefits

Step training is a moderate- to high-intensity aerobic activity that effectively challenges the cardiorespiratory system. In a study at San Diego State University, testing on an 8-inch platform revealed that a class utilizing non-propulsive step patterns and arm movements averaged 7.7 METs, a value comparable to traditional high/low aerobic dance (Francis et al., 1992). Woodby-Brown, Berg, and Latin (1993) studied the oxygen cost of aerobic dance bench stepping and found that step has oxygen requirements similar to other forms of aerobic dance, providing appropriate intensity challenges for improving aerobic fitness. Stanforth, Stanforth, and Velasquez (1993) and Williford et al. (1998) also found step training to significantly improve aerobic capacity.

Several studies have evaluated the energy expenditure of step training to determine its usefulness in weight control. Scharff-Olson et al. (1991) studied step exercise and energy expenditure. It was determined that

for participants desiring weight or fat loss, step exercise must be performed for longer than 30 minutes to expend a minimum 300 calories per session, which is considered helpful for weight management. Combining all factors, including step height, step rate, body weight, and step patterns, makes it difficult to determine the precise number of calories expended in a step-training session (Scharff-Olson & Williford, 1998).

Balance has also been studied by researchers as it relates to outcome measures after participation in a step-training program. Clary et al. (2006) compared the static and dynamic balance of women aged 50 to 75 years before and after participation in a step training class that met for one hour per day, three days per week for 13 weeks. The results were compared against other subjects in the study who performed the same volume and frequency of exercise in other training modalities—a walking program and a Ballates class (i.e., a fusion class of stability ball training and Pilates principles). The results showed that the step-training and walking programs improved measures of both static and dynamic balance, whereas the Ballates program was effective for improving dynamic balance only.

Participant Suitability

Similar to traditional aerobics, step training provides a choreography-based workout to music where the music sets the pace or stepping cadence for the class. Therefore, step training typically appeals to participants who enjoy following combinations and routines set to musical rhythms.

One of the greatest appeals of step training is its appropriateness for a variety of fitness levels. Many studies have demonstrated that step is easily modified according to fitness needs by adjusting step height (Stanforth, Stanforth, & Velasquez, 1993; Scharff-Olson et al., 1991). Participants at a beginning level can use the 4-inch step height. As they become familiar with stepping techniques and their fitness level improves, the height of the platform can be increased, demanding greater intensity. If step height adjustments are not appropriate, step cadence can be increased to achieve greater intensity (Darby, Browder, & Reeves, 1995; Goss et al., 1989).

According to Reebok Step Training Guidelines, beginners are easily and appropriately challenged at music speeds of 118 to 122 bpm. Safe cadences of 122 to 128 bpm are acceptable for participants at intermediate to advanced fitness levels seeking greater aerobic challenges.

Although step training may be performed safely with low levels of impact, individuals with health risks, such as obesity, low-back pain, or arthritis of the hips and knees, may find a step training class too difficult. Similar to traditional aerobics classes, individuals who are at risk for falling should consult with their physicians prior to engaging in this type of activity. Modifications to the choreography that allow all of the step movements to be performed on the floor without using the step may be an option for participants with health risks to be able to safely enjoy a step-training class.

References

Clary, S. et. al. (2006). Effects of Ballates, step aerobics, and walking on balance in women aged 50–75 years. *Journal of Sports Science and Medicine*, 5, 390–399.

Darby, L., Browder, K., & Reeves, B. (1995). The effects of cadence, impact, and step on physiological responses to aerobic dance exercise. *Research Quarterly for Exercise and Sport,* 66, 231–238.

Francis, P. et al. (1992). Effects of choreography, step height, fatigue and gender on metabolic cost of step training (Abstract). *Medicine & Science in Sports & Exercise,* 23 (S839).

Goss, F. et al. (1989). Energy cost of bench stepping and pumping light handweights in trained subjects. *Research Quarterly for Exercise and Sport,* 60, 369–372.

Scharff-Olson, M. & Williford, H. (1998). Step aerobics fulfills its promise. *ACSM's Health and Fitness Journal,* 2, 32–37.

Scharff-Olson, M. et al. (1991). The cardiovascular and metabolic effects of bench stepping exercise in females. *Medicine & Science in Sports & Exercise,* 23, 1311–1316.

Stanforth, D., Stanforth, P., & Velasquez, K. (1993). Aerobic requirement of bench stepping. *International Journal of Sports Medicine,* 14, 129–133.

Williford, H. et al. (1998). Bench stepping and running in women. *The Journal of Sports Medicine and Physical Fitness,* 38, 221–226.

Woodby-Brown, S., Berg, K., & Latin, W. (1993). Oxygen cost of aerobic dance bench stepping at three heights. *Journal of Strength and Conditioning Research,* 7, 163–167.

Kickboxing Fitness

Kickboxing is a cardiovascular workout that uses the hands, feet, knees, and elbows, and mimics kickboxing training to obtain health and fitness benefits. Workouts based on boxing and kickboxing entered the mainstream in the late 1990s and appeal equally to men and women. Today, most health clubs and martial arts schools offer some type of boxing or kickboxing classes.

Equipment-based Workouts

Equipment-based workouts are designed to allow participants to spend a defined amount of time performing kickboxing skills using the heavy bag, punching mitts, kicking pads, speed bags, and/or jump rope, and may be made up of several components. Following a general warm-up, for instance, a group fitness instructor (GFI) may spend 10 to 15 minutes leading participants through basic footwork, punches, kicks, and combinations before moving to performance drills using equipment. The participants may then work together performing the drills for two or three work periods and then be assigned another skill.

It is expected that participants in equipment-based workouts will naturally experience accidental contact. For example, when teaching defensive drills, a GFI may assign participants to work in pairs, with one throwing slow-speed punches while the other practices slipping. Participants may react slowly or move in the wrong direction and occasionally be tapped with a glove on the chin or forehead. Although contact may be slow and controlled, a GFI must still supervise these types of exercises. Participants should never be allowed to perform any sparring. It increases the liability of risk and is clearly outside the scope of practice for a fitness professional.

Workouts may also be structured as circuits, where stations are set up in a circle or row and participants rotate between pieces of equipment. Stations may include exercises for strength, flexibility, and conditioning. If equipment is limited, arrange for participants to alternate between equipment stations and non-equipment stations or work in pairs.

Non-equipment-based Workouts

Non-equipment-based workouts mirror a traditional aerobics class in that the instructor leads participants through a warm-up and specific boxing and/or kickboxing skills designed to elicit a certain intensity. Movements and combinations are typically based on 32-count phrasing. One punch is typically performed every two counts and a kick is usually performed every two or four counts. Higher-intensity combinations may be performed at a faster tempo of one count (punches) or two

counts (punches and/or kicks) for brief work periods.

Benefits

Research continues to support the efficacy of martial arts and kickboxing training as means of improving fitness and health. A 1997 study (Bellinger et al.) found that a 60-minute boxing training session (without kicking) was equivalent in energy expenditure to running about 5.6 mph (9 kph) for 60 minutes on the treadmill. In 1999, the American Council on Exercise (ACE) investigated the physiological effects and benefits of kickboxing (ACE, 1999). The researchers found that the activity provides a workout sufficient to improve and maintain cardiovascular fitness, and noted some additional benefits, such as increased strength and flexibility, improved coordination, and sharper reflexes.

Jumping rope may also be an integral part of kickboxing training, as it helps to develop neuromuscular skills, muscular strength, and cardiovascular endurance, and thus is an excellent complement to kickboxing training. Furthermore, regular participation in weightbearing activities that provide impact, such as jumping rope and some of the movements performed in kickboxing, can have a positive impact on bone mineral density.

Participant Suitability

Kickboxing fitness classes are enjoyed by various types of individuals for different reasons. Typically, kickboxing fitness classes are performed to music. However, the pacing of the movements may or may not be influenced by the beats and rhythms of the music. For example, a non-equipment-based workout may resemble a traditional aerobics class with choreography matched to the music, whereas an equipment-based workout may consist of participants moving through circuit-training stations with music being played in the background for enjoyment. This range in styles of kickboxing workouts ensures that most exercise participants can find a class that suits their needs. That is, participants who enjoy structured choreography programmed to music may enjoy the non-equipment-based workout and individuals who prefer a more athletic, non-choreographed routine may feel more comfortable in an equipment-based class.

Individuals with health risks, such as obesity, low-back pain, or arthritis, may find kickboxing fitness classes too difficult. Similar to traditional aerobics classes, individuals who are at risk for falling should consult with their physicians prior to engaging in this type of activity. Modifications to the exercises that limit the impact and speed of the movements may be appropriate for some special populations. In addition, participants who are inflexible may need to limit the range of motion of certain kickboxing moves (e.g., front kick, side kick, and roundhouse kick).

References

American Council on Exercise (1999). Cardio kickboxing packs a punch. *ACE FitnessMatters,* 5, 4, 4–5.

Bellinger, B. et al. (1997). Energy expenditure of a noncontact boxing training session compared with submaximal treadmill running. *Medicine & Science in Sports & Exercise,* 29, 12, 1653–1656.

Group Indoor Cycling

Group indoor cycling has evolved into a fitness phenomenon. In the mid-1980s, Johnny Goldberg, who is better known as Johnny G, partnered with Schwinn® to create Spinning® and develop a bike specifically for the program. This program was introduced to the fitness industry in 1995 and focuses on visualizing an outdoor ride, complete with wind, hills, and butterflies. The primary goal of Johnny G's program is empowerment. One year later, both Keiser and Reebok developed their own programs.

Both outdoor and indoor cycling activity has increased dramatically in recent years. More and more participants are training indoors with a commitment to stay in shape and perfect their cycling techniques. In addition, there are individuals who prefer to train aerobically without adding stress to their joints, and indoor cycling fits this need. Indoor cycling programs can be adapted for a variety of populations and are currently being used successfully for individuals with spinal cord injuries, arthritis, and cerebral palsy, and as rehabilitation following surgery.

Benefits

Cycling is an excellent cardiorespiratory activity and a good alternative for those who do not like to jog or run, or who have orthopedic limitations to weightbearing exercise.

The many physical benefits of indoor cycling include improved cardiorespiratory endurance, an increase in muscular strength and endurance, and a decrease of body fat and increase of lean body mass. It is also a great weight-management tool when used in conjunction with a well-balanced diet. Psychological benefits include stress relief, an increase in beta-endorphins, and the enjoyment drawn from participating in a fun, social activity.

In addition to convenience, another advantage of indoor cycling is its relative safety, which can lead to a more intense workout. Distractions are minimized, allowing participants to focus on maximizing or maintaining heart rate for the session without worrying about cars, potholes, and other road hazards. The workout can also be more precise, since participants can lend more focus to the program.

There are a number of additional benefits to the indoor cycling format. Participants improve pedal stroke action by focusing on a smooth and complete pedal cycle on each leg independently.

Also, participants achieve personalized workouts within a group setting by modifying resistance, cadence, and body position. Indoor cycling may also be used for recovery. By working at a lower intensity, riders enhance venous return and speed up lactic acid clearance from the muscle and diminish post-training stiffness and soreness.

Participant Suitability

Group cycling classes are generally suitable for participants of varying fitness levels and for those with health risks because this format is nonimpact, nonweightbearing, and the participants have complete control over the amount of resistance, and thus intensity, used during the workout. As with any mode of exercise, an extended warm-up and cool-down and intensity modification may be necessary for participants with special needs.

Participants who have some experience training on a cycle (indoor or outdoor) usually have an easier transition into a group indoor cycling class. Experienced cyclists are accustomed to the flexed-forward spinal posture and hand-gripping techniques used in most indoor cycling classes. Individuals who are new to cycle exercise, however, may need to incorporate several modifications to the riding technique until they become more

comfortable on the bike. For example, it is recommended that novice riders adjust the handlebars so that they are slightly higher than the seat, take frequent postural breaks (i.e., sit upright in the saddle during class), and use a preferred cycling cadence instead of focusing on pedaling as fast as possible.

While not an absolute necessity, participants often choose to invest in specialized shoes that attach to the pedals to enhance their in-class cycling experience. Most cyclists use clipless pedals that allow the foot to "float" a few degrees inward or outward on the pedal as it moves through the pedal cycle. Research has shown that these pedal systems put less strain on the knees and allow a more natural pedaling motion. The floating-pedal systems allow the tibia to move in and rotate as riders push down on the pedal. In a fixed-pedal system, the knee and its ligaments absorb much of this rotation, which can potentially cause knee pain or other problems (Burke, 1995). In addition, cycling shorts and/or seat pads may be purchased to decrease the discomfort often experienced by participants new to training on a cycle. Participants who see the value in purchasing the accessories that accompany training on an indoor cycle may be more likely to adhere to the program.

Reference

Burke, E. (1995). *Serious Cycling*. Champaign, Ill.: Human Kinetics.

Aquatic Exercise

Aquatic exercise is one of the most adaptable and versatile exercise training modalities. Water's natural resistance allows for a healthy, balanced workout with little risk of injury, while its buoyancy allows for minimal impact on joints. Because of water's myriad other properties, the aquatic environment provides a unique opportunity for participants to develop both physical and motor fitness, along with a variety of skills that aid movement on land. It is not surprising, then, that aquatic exercise participation is at an all-time high for both trained and untrained exercisers.

Aquatic fitness instructors have a multitude of options when it comes to teaching methods and formats and choosing equipment for their participants. Instructors may choose to teach from the deck, in the water, or a combination of both. Several different aquatic exercise formats have been successfully established (e.g., circuit, interval, aquatic step, and water tai chi). A variety of aquatic exercise equipment makes the possibility of exercise progression in the water a more realistic task. For example, instructors can choose from different pieces of equipment that provide balance, resistance, traction, safety, comfort, warmth, buoyancy, drag, cardiovascular work, sports training, and functional training.

Benefits

Aquatic exercise is unique in that it can provide training effects in all of the recommended fitness components (cardiorespiratory conditioning, muscular strength and endurance, and flexibility) with minimal risk of injury for exercisers of all ages and fitness levels. Because of water's versatility and safety, due mostly to its physical properties, water provides an ideal training medium for healthy fitness enthusiasts, competitive athletes, older adults, sedentary individuals, prenatal women, people recovering from injury or surgery, or those with chronic medical conditions such as arthritis or low-back pain.

One of the key benefits of water is injury prevention. Depending on water depth, the body is significantly less weightbearing in water than on land. Bearing less weight reduces joint stress and allows for full range of motion, while also allowing for greater overall intensity because of the water's resistance. Additionally, since buoyancy offsets the effects of gravity, participants can move unrestrained without fear of falling. Athletes can continue training in the cushioning environment of the water and maintain performance, while reducing the risk of injury from impact forces.

Another key benefit to aquatic exercise is progression. Properly using the properties of water (e.g., buoyancy, surface area, and drag) allows exercisers to cater their workouts to their individual needs. Aquatic exercise involves progressive resistance by allowing for training in multiple ranges of motion and with uninterrupted overload. Because of water's properties, an exerciser can instantly alter a movement, such as increasing or decreasing movement speed, to adjust intensity.

Aquatic exercise provides a wide variety of additional benefits. It promotes postural stability and enhances balance, due to the effects of water currents on trunk musculature. Performing exercise in heart-to-neck-level water strengthens respiratory musculature, due to the effects of hydrostatic pressure on the lungs. Water also provides a somewhat private, less-intimidating exercise environment for certain special populations, as being submerged allows them to feel comfortable while exercising, rather than feeling as though they are on display. Lastly, regular participation in an aquatic exercise has been shown to be an effective part of a systematic weight-loss program (Krist, 2007).

Participant Suitability

During the past two decades, numerous

research studies have confirmed the value and versatility of aquatic fitness as an exercise modality. Its widespread and growing popularity among exercisers of all levels, ages, and abilities helps to validate these research outcomes.

The benefits of water therapy for rehabilitation have long been known (Koury, 1996). The properties of water, such as buoyancy, help prevent injuries because of reduced impact (Sanders, 1999). Further, hydrostatic pressure reduces tissue swelling and blood pooling in the extremities during exercise, and increases metabolic waste excretion (Becker & Cole, 1997).

Training in the water has also been shown to improve performance of activities of daily living (ADL) for a variety of populations. Tsourlou et al. (2006) found that a properly designed water exercise program that includes a combination of aerobic work and resistance training results in increases in both isometric and dynamic muscular strength, flexibility, and functional mobility in healthy women over the age of 60. Sufferers of chronic back pain who undergo therapeutic aquatic exercise programs experience reduced pain and improved ADL performance (Landgridge & Phillips, 1988). Studies that looked at joint motion and ADL performance for persons with arthritis and rheumatic diseases also reported decreased pain and increased range of motion after water-therapy exercise programs. For example, subjects with fibromyalgia who were followed for one year during an aquatic exercise therapy study showed improvement in physical function, mood, and self-efficacy measures for pain (Gowens et al., 2004).

Results have been just as positive in healthy (nondiseased or injured) older adults who gained functional postural mobility through aquatic exercise. An aquatic exercise study conducted through the Sanford Center on Aging at the University of Nevada, Reno evaluated ADL performance in older adults (Sanders, Constantino, & Rippee, 1997). The authors found that water training significantly improved functional abilities, increased muscle strength and flexibility, decreased body fat, and improved self-esteem.

References

Becker, B. & Cole, A.J. (1997). *Comprehensive Aquatic Therapy.* Boston, Mass.: Butterworth-Heinemann.

Gowens, S.E. et al. (2004). Six-month and one-year follow-up of 23 weeks of aerobic exercise for individuals with fibromyalgia. *Arthritis & Rheumatism (Arthritis Care & Research),* 51, 6, 890–898.

Koury, J. (1996). *Aquatic Therapy Programming Guidelines for Orthopedic Rehabilitation.* Champaign, Ill.: Human Kinetics.

Krist, P.S. (2007). Water exercise: You can melt away pounds. *AKWA The Official Publication of the Aquatic Exercise Association: Research Reviews.* February/March, 40–41.

Landgridge, J. & Phillips, D. (1988). Group hydrotherapy exercises for chronic back pain sufferers. *Physiotherapy,* 74, 269–273.

Sanders, M.E. (1999). Cross over to the water. *IDEA Health & Fitness Source,* March, 53–58.

Sanders, M., Constantino, N., & Rippee, N. (1997). A comparison of results of functional water training on field and laboratory measures in older women. *Medicine & Science in Sports & Exercise,* 29, ixx.

Tsourlou, T. et al. (2006). The effects of a twenty-four-week aquatic training program on muscular strength performance in healthy elderly women. *Journal of Strength and Conditioning Research,* 20, 4.

Fitness Yoga

Yoga as an exercise activity has become a permanent fixture in the fitness arena. Long recognized as an effective stress-management technique and a great way to improve flexibility, yoga has more recently become known for what it can do for building strength and stamina. In fact, a large body of research continues to point toward yoga's positive health effects. Guarracino, Savino, and Edelstein (2006) showed that in women and men aged 18 years or older, improved measures of obesity prevention, hypertension control, and quality of life were experienced in individuals who participated in a hatha relaxation yoga program for one to four years. While most yoga programs do not appear to significantly increase physical-fitness outcomes, they have been shown to improve stress and anxiety for regular participants. A research review that looked at studies comparing the effects of yoga and other forms of exercise seemed to indicate that, in both healthy and diseased populations, yoga may be as effective as, or better than, traditional forms of exercise at improving a variety of health-related outcome measures other than those involving physical fitness (Ross & Thomas, 2010). The authors went on to state that further research is needed to determine the differences between other exercise modalities and yoga, as well as the differences between different types of yoga, on health and fitness outcome measures.

Yoga, however, is much more than another form of exercise. It is part of an extensive ancient Eastern philosophical tradition. What is referred to as "yoga"—the exercise activity—is really hatha yoga, the physical aspect of this philosophy. There are many different ways in which hatha yoga may be practiced. Guidelines govern the practice and reflect the basic principles of yoga, regardless of style. It takes education, maturity, and experience to teach yoga safely and effectively.

Hatha yoga, initially created to prepare the body for meditation, includes exercises designed to strengthen the body and nervous system, thereby creating the appropriate psychophysiological state for a higher level of consciousness. The repertoire consists of postures, movements, breathing, and relaxation techniques that affect every system of the body, bringing about an optimal state of health and well-being. GFIs will undoubtedly encounter questions regarding yoga's religious and spiritual components. In response, GFIs should stress that yoga is not a religion. However, its philosophy has been embraced by religious traditions in India and elsewhere.

Yoga's current status reflects the growing interest in the mind-body connection. In both the medical and fitness communities, the importance of the mind in promoting wellness, reducing stress, and combating disease is becoming more prevalent. Yoga techniques provide both a blueprint for stress management and a system for physical fitness. There is also a therapeutic aspect to the practice of yoga. This area deals with specific breathing techniques, poses, and meditations to remedy various structural, physiological, and psychological conditions.

Whereas fitness experts once paid little attention to what yoga had to offer, leaders in the field now recognize its value as a viable fitness choice. While not all styles of hatha yoga cover all the essential facets of a fitness regimen—aerobic, strength, and flexibility training—many do. At the very least, hatha yoga can provide a balanced strength and flexibility workout that can be supplemented with a cardiovascular routine.

Styles of Hatha Yoga

As indicated earlier, there are many different

353

styles, or systems, of hatha yoga practice. Some are vigorous and intense while others are gentle and more meditative. While yoga itself is a very ancient practice, most of the hatha yoga systems practiced today have been refined and developed in the twentieth century. GFIs should be aware of newly emerging hybrids of these systems, developed by teachers interested in creating their own variations on these traditional forms. Many yoga instructors teach eclectic styles, having been influenced by a number of methods.

Hatha yoga has proven to be a practice that continues to change and evolve with the times, while remaining true to the essential principles of the philosophy. Physical health and fitness level and personal goals will determine which style is best for the individual. The following list describes the styles most commonly practiced today.

Ananda: This gentle and meditative approach developed by Swami Kriyananda places emphasis on deeply relaxing into the poses along with the use of affirmations, with the view that hatha yoga's ultimate purpose is to heighten self-awareness.

Ashtanga: This is an intense and vigorous system developed by K. Pattabhi Jois that is characterized by equal emphasis on strength, flexibility, balance, and stamina. A modified version of this system is taught and often called "power yoga."

Bikram: Developed by Bikram Choudhury, this intense routine consists of 26 postures, including many standing single-leg balances, and begins and ends with a pranayama, or breath awareness, technique. The focus of this style is to detoxify the system and to warm up the muscles, allowing for maximum mastery of the poses. Therefore, teachers often use a humidifier and set the thermostat at 90° F (27° C) or higher for this practice.

Integral: This system was developed by Swami Satchidananda and reflects the teachings of Swami Sivananda. This method promotes the integration of yoga principles into lifestyle and thought, with the advice to be "easeful, peaceful, and useful."

Iyengar: A precise and detailed system developed by B.K.S. Iyengar, this style emphasizes correct postural alignment and proper body mechanics. The use of props and therapeutic applications are also characteristic of this style.

Kripalu: An internally directed approach developed by Yogi Amrit Desai, Kripalu is characterized by focusing on the breath and monitoring of the physical, mental, and emotional effects of the practice. Intensity ranges from gentle to vigorous.

Kundalini: A moderate-to-intense practice developed by Yogi Bhajan, this style focuses on the activation of the kundalini (serpent power) energy, believed to be stored at the base of the spine. Many breathing techniques are employed, along with poses and meditation, to facilitate the release of this energy.

Sivananda: This is a five-point method of practice that includes proper exercise, breathing, deep relaxation, vegetarian diet, and positive thinking through meditation. Swami Sivananda's system was popularized by Swami Vishnu-devananda and follows a standard format that includes breathing techniques, Sun Salutations, 12 yoga postures, relaxation, and chanting and prayers at the beginning and end of each class.

Viniyoga: Developed by T.K.V. Desikachar, this style employs a step-by-step approach (vinyasa krama) and emphasizes the use of the breath during asana practice. Another characteristic of this technique is the focus on tailoring the practice to the individual.

Teachers of this system often design therapeutic applications.

Benefits

Yoga offers many benefits. While the ultimate goal of this age-old philosophy is to realize one's divine nature, the positive effects on physical health and mental well-being are impressive. Hatha yoga's methodology dictates a balance between effort and relaxation and positively influences every system of the body. The repertoire includes poses for strength, flexibility, and balance. Some styles even include a cardiovascular component. The breathing techniques in yoga improve respiration while producing a cognitive quiescence, or "mental stillness," and an associated decrease in central nervous system activity. In fact, the breathing and meditative techniques of yoga, long known as effective stress- and pain-management tools, have been employed by Western physicians and therapists for a good portion of the 20th century. Many modern-day methods such as biofeedback and Dr. Herbert Benson's Relaxation Response (Benson, 1976) are patterned after these techniques. In addition to promoting strength and flexibility, it is believed that yoga can promote healing if practiced under supervision in a controlled fashion.

Participant Suitability

As noted previously, the health and fitness benefits of yoga are well established, making this mode of exercise appealing to individuals of various fitness levels and abilities. Background music and dim lighting may be used to create an atmosphere of peace and mind-body-connection enhancement. Specific poses and breathing techniques are thought to prevent or even remedy many physical and mental conditions. Similarly, there are poses and techniques that are contraindicated for specific health issues. The following are the most common contraindications:

Menstruation

Back bends, certain standing postures, and inverted postures, such as head, hand, and shoulder stands, are discouraged for women during menstruation. However, for women with menstrual discomfort, forward bends and relaxation techniques may be effective at thwarting symptoms.

Pregnancy

Pregnant women should avoid inverted postures, extreme ranges of motion, and holding of the breath during yoga practice. Additionally, abdominal contractions, such as the stomach lift, are prohibited for a woman during pregnancy. After obtaining the appropriate training and experience, many yoga instructors specialize in prenatal yoga instruction.

Sciatica

Extreme flexion and intense hamstring-stretching poses should be avoided by individuals with sciatica. Back-extension poses, such as the cobra, may be more suitable for participants diagnosed with sciatica or who have sciatica-type symptoms.

Hypertension, Glaucoma, Eye Problems, and Ear Congestion

Holding of the breath, inverted poses, or prolonged standing forward bends should be avoided by individuals with these conditions. A practice that promotes relaxation is more appropriate for participants with these health limitations.

High-risk Postures

Controversial poses, such as the shoulder stand, plow, headstand, and back bend, should be taught only by an experienced instructor who understands the precise biomechanical benefits and limitations of each posture. Generally, instructors who teach fitness-based yoga should stick to modifications of these postures to ensure the safety of their participants and reduce their risk of liability.

References

Benson, H. (1976). *The Relaxation Response.* New York: Avon Books.

Guarracino, J.A., Savino S., & Edelstein, S. (2006). Yoga participation is beneficial to obesity prevention, hypertension control, and positive quality of life. *Topics in Clinical Nutrition*, 21, 2, 108–113.

Ross, A. & Thomas, S. (2010). The health benefits of yoga and exercise: A review of comparison studies. *Journal of Alternative and Complementary Medicine*, 16, 1, 3–12.

Pilates

Joseph Hubertus Pilates created the Pilates method of exercise at the beginning of the 20th century. Born in 1880 near Düsseldorf, Germany, Pilates suffered a sickly childhood with asthma, rickets, and rheumatic fever. To improve his health as a youth, he turned to physical training and pursued diving, skiing, gymnastics, boxing, and bodybuilding. By age 14, his physique was so well developed that he worked as a model for anatomical charts. He pursued a varied career as a boxer, fitness trainer, and circus performer, among other activities.

In 1912, Pilates moved to England, where he had many jobs, including self-defense instructor to detectives at Scotland Yard. When World War I erupted, the British government labeled Pilates as an enemy alien and placed him in an internment camp. While imprisoned, he provided exercise training to other internees and worked in a hospital to help bedridden patients. He used his time to develop physical-conditioning methods to rehabilitate these patients and created training equipment from hospital beds, using springs to facilitate exercise. These inventions formed the basis for the now popular reformer, which still resembles a cot, and for the trapeze table, sometimes called the "Cadillac," which looks like a table with hanging springs and bars. In 1926, Pilates immigrated to New York and opened a training studio with his wife, Clara, whom he met on the ship as he traveled to America. The Pilates' clientele included many prominent ballet and modern dancers of the era. Today, Pilates exercises remain a staple of dance conditioning.

In 2001, the Pilates Method Alliance (PMA) was founded by Kevin A. Bowen and Colleen Glenn as a nonprofit, unbiased information resource dedicated to the teachings of Joseph H. and Clara Pilates. Unlike other organizations that offer instructor training and certification programs, the PMA is a separate body with an organizational mission to protect the public by establishing certification and continuing education standards for Pilates professionals. The PMA has created a national certification test for the Pilates method.

The many variations of Pilates are united by their common foundation and adherence to the basic principles of Pilates. Due to similarities between Pilates and yoga, fusion-styled classes that blend Pilates exercises with hatha yoga postures are becoming increasingly popular. While these two disciplines are distinct, both yoga and Pilates have much to offer consumers on both a physical and mental level, because they not only offer physical-conditioning benefits, but also require mental concentration that enhances the mind-body connection.

The two most common types of Pilates

programs offered in the group-fitness setting are mat classes and reformer classes. Mat classes are pervasive in fitness clubs because the equipment is common to other class modalities (e.g., mats, yoga blocks, stability balls, and elastic resistance bands) and the required instructor training is less extensive than it is for other equipment-based Pilates formats. Pilates mat routines primarily use body weight as resistance as the exercisers move through a series of spinal flexion, rotation, lateral flexion, and extension movements.

The Pilates reformer is a resistance machine made up of a rolling platform (called a carriage) attached to springs, which provide the resistance. The carriage moves when the exerciser pulls on straps that are placed through pulleys and attached to the carriage. Reformer exercises can be done lying down, sitting, kneeling, or standing on the carriage. Reformer classes are becoming more common in group-fitness settings as Pilates equipment manufacturers have begun offering light-weight, portable reformers for commercial club use. In fact, some reformer models are stackable so their footprint in the group exercise room is minimized when they are not in use.

Benefits

The regular practice of Pilates exercise offers the following benefits for apparently healthy participants, in addition to improvements in overall strength, flexibility, stability, and mobility:

- Improved posture
- Stronger abdominal and back muscles
- Stronger pelvic and shoulder stabilizer muscles
- Balanced muscle development
- Improved breathing

- Better coordination and balance
- Reduced likelihood of back pain or injury
- Enhanced confidence and self-esteem
- Enhanced mind-body connection
- Enhanced athletic performance

Practicing Pilates provides these benefits because the exercises combine the use of the core musculature to stabilize the torso with rhythmic, coordinated movements accompanied by deep breathing. Precise attention to detail and form creates a stronger core and more efficient movement habits. This translates into better posture and more effective movement mechanics in both functional activities and in sports. In addition, imbalances in muscular development immediately become apparent and can be addressed by performing the exercises regularly and by progressing the level of difficulty over time.

Participant Suitability

The various difficulty levels and class formats available to consumers make Pilates classes an appropriate mode of exercise for any individual who is comfortable in a group fitness setting. Class size is typically limited so that participants can receive focused attention from the instructor. In addition, knowledgeable and experienced instructors can provide modifications to the exercises to accommodate participants with special needs or health limitations.

With Pilates exercises, as with any exercise program, there is always a risk of injury. For this reason, it is important that fitness professionals ensure that adequate prescreening has been conducted in accordance with industry standards and guidelines and that medical clearances are obtained as necessary. In particular, because Pilates exercises involve spinal flexion, rotation, and extension, there is a higher risk of injury for individuals with orthopedic problems. In addition, certain Pilates exercises include high-risk hatha yoga poses such as the plow and the shoulder stand that should not be taught unless the instructor is highly experienced and trained and the participants are ready and individually supervised.

Although Pilates is widely accepted in rehabilitation, GFIs should not provide any training services beyond the appropriate scope of practice as defined by their specific training, certification, or licensure. As with all forms of exercise, GFIs should always consider the safety of the participant first, and only offer instructional services that are based on solid and in-depth training. GFIs should not teach any movements without a complete understanding of the benefits and risks and of the necessary modifications for people with different body types and needs.

Stability Ball Training

Known by many names, from Swiss Ball to Gymnastic Ball to Physioball, the "stability ball" is a large, inflated vinyl rubber ball that comes in a variety of sizes, colors, and even shapes. Its most common use is, not surprisingly, in the area of balance training, with advocates continually promoting core musculature stabilization. In addition, the stability ball is a valuable exercise tool that offers cardiovascular, muscle strength, muscle endurance, and flexibility training for the entire body. Most importantly, this is an exercise prop that is both challenging and fun, offering options to exercisers of virtually all skill and ability levels.

Contrary to what many fitness professionals might think, the stability ball is not a new invention. In fact, use of the ball began in the physical therapy arena more than 100 years ago. The stability ball was first used by Dr. Susanne Klein-Vogelbach in Switzerland in 1909, where it came to be known as the Swiss Ball. Dr. Klein-Vogelbach introduced the Swiss Ball in her physical therapy work with children with cerebral palsy, helping them to maintain reflex response as well as improve their balance. Recognizing the value of the ball, the physical therapy community used it in the treatment of various neurological and orthopedic disorders as well as spinal injuries. The ball made its appearance in the United States in the late 1970s and early 1980s, where it continued to be used as an exercise, balance, and therapy aid in the medical rehabilitation arena, primarily by physical therapists. It is only in the past 15 to 20 years that the stability ball made the transition to the fitness industry.

In 1992, Mike and Stephanie Morris developed a total-body fitness-training program around the ball and are credited by many as having led the way for use of the stability ball in both the group exercise and personal training fields. Their Resist-A-Ball® program introduced this unique piece of exercise equipment, along with an extensive educational program, to the mainstream health and fitness market. Since then, the stability ball has become a staple in fitness facilities across the country and, indeed, around the world. In fact, teachers of different disciplines, such as Pilates and yoga, frequently incorporate the use of stability balls into their exercise programming. A variety of different resources, including books, videos, and fitness professional training programs and seminars, have been developed. Since that time, many other fitness professionals have been instrumental in bringing stability ball exercise into the traditional fitness and performance-training arenas.

Benefits

The stability ball is perhaps the most versatile piece of equipment currently available, as it utilizes the neuromuscular system in a way that most other exercise equipment does not, requiring the integrated involvement of strength, flexibility, and balance. Ball exercises are designed primarily to enhance the exerciser's ability to move the body without restrictions and to perform functional movements necessary to meet the needs and challenges of daily life. Regular use of the stability ball can give users an improved quality of life as they develop the strength, flexibility, and balance to work and play without movement limitations.

One of the greatest benefits of stability ball usage is improved balance. The ball challenges the individual to develop the ability to continually balance and focuses effort on the core stabilizer muscles (i.e., muscles of the trunk and hips), regardless of the movement being performed. To train on the ball requires balance and motor control, both of which will improve through regular use of the ball. Exercises can be designed to work solely on balance, while other exercises can work on strengthening and/ or stretching practically any muscle group in the body. The best feature of the ball is that while strength or flexibility work is being performed, balance work is taking place simultaneously. No muscle or muscle group can be targeted in isolation to the exclusion

of the stabilizing muscles that balance the body. This time-efficient training feature makes stability ball exercises challenging and beneficial to users of all skill and ability levels.

Probably the most publicized and well-known benefit of stability ball training is that the balls allow exercisers to train and develop strength and tone of the trunk musculature, particularly the abdominals. A study conducted by researchers at San Diego State University used electromyography (EMG) equipment to examine muscle activity in 13 common abdominal exercises. Crunches on the stability ball ranked third overall in abdominal muscle activity (ACE, 2001).

However, there was less activity in the hip flexor muscles during ball crunches than the bicycle maneuver and the Captain's Chair exercise, which were ranked number one and two in the study, respectively. As hip flexion during abdominal work indicates that the exercise does not isolate the abdominals preferentially, researchers concluded that crunches on the stability ball arguably are the most effective abdominal exercise overall (ACE, 2001). It is no wonder then that stability balls are a top pick for home exercise equipment, due to their low cost, high level of effectiveness, and versatility.

Another benefit of the ball is its demand for any movement to be performed with correct posture. Proper posture with neutral spinal alignment is a necessity as the stabilizer muscles of the core work to balance the body on the ball. Regular use of the stability ball improves spinal stability as the core stabilizer muscles become stronger at adapting to an unstable base of support. Chronically bad posture is one of the main causes of muscle imbalance that leads to low-back pain, which is statistically likely to be experienced by approximately 80% of the adult population at some point in their lives (Darragh, 1999). Improved posture through stability ball training can be a very effective way of preventing or relieving low-back pain. One of the greatest benefits of regular stability ball training is its effect on everyday life, yielding improved quality of life with better functioning, decreased risk of injury, and improved posture and balance. Much of traditional fitness training, while certainly effective at improving cardiorespiratory function, muscle strength, and flexibility, involves movement in a stable environment. Stability balls challenge the body to react and learn to move efficiently in an unstable environment. As so much of real-life motion involves adapting to changing conditions, such as when playing soccer, gardening, or carrying groceries upstairs, ball work is quite effective at improving functional abilities.

Participant Suitability

Because stability ball training has been shown to have positive results for people with a wide variety of diagnosed medical conditions, there are very few special populations for which the ball is inappropriate. Use of the ball for strength or stretch work can be safe and effective for just about any condition, provided the exercises are carefully chosen. It is critical that GFIs are familiar with the variety of common conditions and injuries and know what types of movements are most suitable to each population.

From the exerciser's perspective, the ball is lightweight, fun, and low-tech. The stability ball is large and colorful and has a comforting shape, which promotes a sense of play that makes exercise fun and interesting. Laughter is often one of the first responses from novice stability ball users, before they realize how challenging exercise on the ball can be. The endless variety of exercises possible on the ball also helps counteract boredom. Many fitness enthusiasts find themselves intimidated by complex exercises and awkward equipment. The ball is extremely user-friendly, as it supports and eases the body into proper posture and exercise positions. It is also simple to vary the resistance and/or balance challenge within each exercise by simply changing body position on the ball. Stability balls also are extremely durable and adaptable for use with just about any population.

References

American Council on Exercise (2001). Strong abs, strong core. *ACE Certified News, 7,* 4, 7–9.

Darragh, A. (1999). Training clients in back and spinal post-rehab. *IDEA Personal Trainer,* May, 43–51.

Group Strength Training

The development of group strength training has undergone four distinct phases. Group strength training initially began as group calisthenics. Exercises were simple and equipment was scarce. Classes were offered as part of sports team training or physical education. A typical class included sit-ups, push-ups, and squats. Exercises were selected with little attention to safety, and modifications were rarely offered.

During the next phase, group strength training developed in health clubs as group exercise classes. The emphasis of the classes was on high repetitions and "feeling the burn." Participants were attracted to the misconception that high-repetition exercises burned fat, spot reduced, or somehow slimmed the body. Exercise selection was diverse and, although attention was paid to form, safety and effectiveness were lacking.

During the third phase of group strength training, more attention was paid to safety and effectiveness. Traditional exercises (e.g., full sit-ups) were excluded and limits were placed on controversial movements such as forward flexion and deep knee flexion. A greater variety of exercise equipment became available, creating program diversity. The number of repetitions was reduced as the emphasis shifted from endurance training to strength training.

In the most recent phase, classes emphasize functional strength training along with a greater diversity of exercises, formats, and equipment. Also, classes have begun to shift from muscle-isolation exercises to multijoint, functional exercises that are sport-specific and may improve participants' abilities to perform activities of daily living.

Benefits

Some potential participants may avoid group strength training due to misconceptions about the effects of regular strength training. They may not understand the important role strength training plays in losing or maintaining body weight. Also, in some cases, women may mistakenly believe that strength training will create bulky muscles. To keep exercise motivation high, communicate the benefits with participants before, during, and after class. For example, explain that strength training improves physical working capacity and appearance, metabolic function, and injury risk. Use positive statements to sell the benefits of strength training.

An effective strength-training program will provide the following physiological, physical,

and performance improvements:

- Increased muscle fiber size
- Increased muscle contractile strength
- Increased tendon tensile strength
- Increased bone strength
- Increased ligament tensile strength
- Reduced injury risk
- Increased functional capacity
- Improved body composition

Participant Suitability

Group strength classes are ideal for participants who enjoy exercising to music and following a structured set of exercises emphasizing muscular fitness. Typically, a variety of resistance-training equipment (e.g., hand weights, barbells, resistance tubing, and medicine balls) is utilized, allowing an efficient whole-body workout during class time. Individuals interested in increasing muscular strength, endurance, and functionality may be well-suited for participation in a group strength class.

Because group strength classes typically call for multiple repetitions of various exercises with added load or resistance, instructors should carefully screen participants prior to class. Musculoskeletal conditions, such as low-back pain, tendinitis, and arthritis, may be aggravated by certain resistance-training exercises. Instructors should be knowledgeable and experienced in providing modifications to all the exercises presented in class to accommodate all participants.

Fitness Boot Camp and Sports Conditioning

Participants in fitness boot camp and sports conditioning classes typically are of the mindset that challenging the body through intense exercise is a time-efficient and effective way to increase

Group Fitness Specialties

fitness. Many of these types of programs are held outdoors and incorporate the use of environmental features such as stairs, railings, water, and sand. In areas where seasonal climates prevent outdoor exercise, fitness boot camp and sports conditioning classes are held in group-fitness rooms or in dedicated areas of a fitness facility's main floor. Indoor programs also make use of the environment, as they acquire usable space, equipment, and structural features (such as stairs, ledges, and ramps) to give participants a variety of workout options.

While the name "boot camp" is inspired by military training, successful instructors avoid using intimidation tactics in their classes, and instead rely on encouragement and proper exercise progression. Often, fitness boot camps are centered on a common goal of losing weight and increasing overall physical fitness. Some are promoted to specific population groups (e.g., children, older adults, brides-to-be, and new moms), with the underlying theme of getting in better shape while working alongside like-minded individuals. Similar to fitness boot camps, sports conditioning classes offer a variety of challenging exercises to individuals with a common goal of preparing for the demands of a particular sport or recreation. For example, a ski-conditioning program might be offered in the weeks prior to peak ski season to prepare the participants for an upcoming winter vacation. It is common for sports conditioning and seasonal boot-camp classes to be offered as limited-engagement programs lasting only six to eight weeks.

Benefits

Aside from the benefits of increased cardiorespiratory fitness and muscular conditioning, fitness boot camp and sports conditioning classes provide a "team" environment, which fosters camaraderie and group support that may be lacking in more traditional group fitness classes. Friendly relationships often develop between participants who encourage and cheer for each other as they are grouped together for drills or tasks. These programs also offer the benefit of featuring variety and an element of fun, ultimately motivating the participant to adhere to the class schedule.

Participant Suitability

Most individuals attending these types of programs have worked up to a base level of conditioning prior to engaging in the class and can handle the rigors of plyometrics, calisthenics, and sports-skills training that they offer. For already established boot camps or sports conditioning classes, an individual with a competitive personality and a fair amount of exercise self-efficacy might fare better than a person new to exercise whose abilities are still being developed. However, beginner boot-camp classes are also successful, especially in areas or clubs where this class format is still relatively new. As with any other group fitness–related activity, the instructor's capacity for leadership and knowledge of exercise modifications ultimately determines the safety and effectiveness of the program.

For additional instructor resources and educational opportunities related to these and other group fitness specialties, visit the education center of the ACE website at

www.acefitness.org.

ACE Position Statement on Nutrition Scope of Practice for Fitness Professionals

I t is the position of the American Council on Exercise (ACE) that fitness professionals not only can but should share general nonmedical nutrition information with their clients.

In the current climate of an epidemic of obesity, poor nutrition, and physical inactivity paired with a multibillion dollar diet industry and a strong interest among the general public in improving eating habits and increasing physical activity, fitness professionals are on the front lines in helping the public to achieve healthier lifestyles. Fitness professionals provide an essential service to their clients, the industry, and the community at large when they are able to offer credible, practical, and relevant nutrition information to clients while staying within their professional scope of practice.

Ultimately, an individual fitness professional's scope of practice as it relates to nutrition is determined by state policies and regulations, education and experience, and competencies and skills. While this implies that the nutrition-related scope of practice may vary among fitness professionals, there are certain actions that are within the scope of practice of all fitness professionals.

For example, it is within the scope of practice of all fitness professionals to share dietary advice endorsed or developed by the federal government, especially the Dietary Guidelines for Americans (www.dietaryguidelines.gov) and the MyPlate recommendations (www.ChooseMyPlate.gov).

Fitness professionals who have passed National Commission for Certifying Agencies (NCCA)– or American National Standards Institute (ANSI)– accredited certification programs that provide basic nutrition information, such as those provided by ACE, and those who have undertaken nutrition continuing education, should also be prepared to discuss:

- Principles of healthy nutrition and food preparation
- Food to be included in the balanced daily diet
- Essential nutrients needed by the body
- Actions of nutrients on the body
- Effects of deficiencies or excesses of nutrients
- How nutrient requirements vary through the lifecycle
- Information about nutrients contained in foods or supplements

Fitness professionals may share this information through a variety of venues, including cooking demonstrations, recipe exchanges, development of handouts and informational packets, individual or group classes and seminars, or one-on-one encounters.

Fitness professionals who do not feel comfortable sharing this information are strongly encouraged to undergo continuing education to further develop nutrition competency and skills and to develop relationships with registered dietitians or other qualified health professionals who can provide this information. It is within the fitness professional's scope of practice to distribute and disseminate information or programs that have been developed by a registered dietitian or medical doctor.

The actions that are outside the scope of practice of fitness professionals include, but may not be limited to, the following:

- Individualized nutrition recommendations or meal planning other than that which is available through government guidelines and recommendations, or has been developed and endorsed by a registered dietitian or physician
- Nutritional assessment to determine nutritional needs and nutritional status, and to recommend nutritional intake
- Specific recommendations or programming for nutrient or nutritional intake, caloric intake, or specialty diets
- Nutritional counseling, education, or advice aimed to prevent, treat, or cure a disease or condition, or other acts that may be perceived as medical nutrition therapy
- Development, administration, evaluation, and consultation regarding nutritional care standards or the nutrition care process
- Recommending, prescribing, selling, or supplying nutritional supplements to clients

- Promotion or identification of oneself as a "nutritionist" or "dietitian"

Engaging in these activities can place a client's health and safety at risk and possibly expose the fitness professional to disciplinary action and litigation. To ensure maximal client safety and compliance with state policies and laws, it is essential that the fitness professional recognize when it is appropriate to refer to a registered dietitian or physician. ACE recognizes that some fitness and health clubs encourage or require their employees to sell nutritional supplements. If this is a condition of employment, ACE suggests that fitness professionals:

- Obtain complete scientific understanding regarding the safety and efficacy of the supplement from qualified healthcare professionals and/ or credible resources. Note: Generally, the Office of Dietary Supplements (ods.od.nih.gov), the National Center for Complementary and Alternative Medicine (nccam.nih.gov), and the Food and Drug Administration (FDA.gov) are reliable places to go to examine the validity of the claims as well as risks and benefits associated with taking a particular supplement. Since the sites are from trusted resources and in the public domain, fitness professionals can freely distribute and share the information contained on these sites.
- Stay up-to-date on the legal and/or regulatory issues related to the use of the supplement and its individual ingredients
- Obtain adequate insurance coverage should a problem arise

Abduction Movement away from the midline of the body.

Abrasion A scraping away of a portion of the skin or mucous membrane.

Absolute contraindication A situation that makes a particular treatment or procedure absolutely inadvisable.

Accent Emphasis on a given beat.

Achilles tendinitis A painful and often debilitating inflammation of the Achilles tendon.

Acquired immunodeficiency syndrome (AIDS) A syndrome of the immune system caused by the human immunodeficiency virus (type HIV-1 or HIV-2) and characterized by opportunistic infection and disease.

Action The stage of the transtheoretical model of behavioral change during which the individual started a new behavior less than six months ago.

Activities of daily living (ADL) Activities normally performed for hygiene, bathing, household chores, walking, shopping, and similar activities.

Acute Descriptive of a condition that usually has a rapid onset and a relatively short and severe course; opposite of chronic.

Addiction The devotion or surrendering of oneself to something habitually or obsessively.

Adduction Movement toward the midline of the body.

Adherence The extent to which people stick to their plans or treatment recommendations. Exercise adherence is the extent to which people follow, or stick to, an exercise program.

Aerobic In the presence of oxygen.

Affective domain One of the three domains of learning; involves the learning of emotional behaviors.

Alpha blocker A type of antihypertension medication that ultimately relaxes the blood vessels and leads to an increase in blood flow and a lower blood pressure. Also called an adrenergic blocker.

American Society of Composers, Artists and Publishers (ASCAP) One of two performing rights societies in the United States that represent music publishers in negotiating and collecting fees for the nondramatic performance of music.

Americans with Disabilities Act Civil rights legislation designed to improve access to jobs, work places, and commercial spaces for people with disabilities.

Anaerobic Without the presence of oxygen.

Anaerobic threshold The point during high-intensity activity when the body can no longer meet its demand for oxygen and anaerobic metabolism predominates. Also called the lactate threshold.

Anorexia nervosa An eating disorder characterized by refusal to maintain body weight of at least 85% of expected weight; intense fear of gaining weight or becoming fat; body-image disturbances, including a disproportionate influence of body weight on self-evaluation; and, in women, the absence of at least three consecutive menstrual periods.

Anthropometric assessment The measurement of the human body and its parts, most commonly performed using skinfolds, girth measurements, and body weight.

Anthropometry   The measurement of the size and proportions of the human body.

Anxiety   A state of uneasiness and apprehension; occurs in some mental disorders.

Apnea   A temporary absence or cessation of breathing; when this condition occurs during sleep it is called sleep apnea.

Arterial-mixed venous oxygen difference (a-$\overline{v}$ O$_2$ difference)   The difference in oxygen content between arterial and mixed venous blood, which reflects the amount of oxygen removed by the whole body.

Arthritis   Inflammation of a joint; a state characterized by the inflammation of joints.

Asana   A posture or manner of sitting, as in the practice of yoga.

Associative stage of learning   The second stage of learning a motor skill, when performers have mastered the fundamentals and can concentrate on skill refinement.

Asthma   A chronic inflammatory disorder of the airways that affects genetically susceptible individuals in response to various environmental triggers such as allergens, viral infection, exercise, cold, and stress.

Athletic trainer   A healthcare professional who collaborates with physicians and specializes in providing immediate intervention when injuries occur and helping athletes and clients in the prevention, assessment, treatment, and rehabilitation of emergency, acute, and chronic medical conditions involving injury, impairment, functional limitations, and disabilities. Must have a bachelor's or master's degree from an athletic training program accredited by the Commission on Accreditation of Athletic Training Education (CAATE), pass the Board of Certification, Inc. (BOC), athletic training certification exam, and meet all state requirements for practicing as a Certified Athletic Trainer (A.T.C.).

Atrophy   A reduction in muscle size (muscle wasting) due to inactivity or immobilization.

Automated external defibrillator (AED)   A portable electronic device used to restore normal heart rhythms in victims of sudden cardiac arrest.

Autonomous stage of learning   The third stage of learning a motor skill, when the skill has become habitual or automatic for the performer.

Avulsion   A wound involving forcible separation or tearing of tissue from the body.

Balance   The ability to maintain the body's position over its base of support within stability limits, both statically and dynamically.

Beats   Regular pulsations that have an even rhythm and occur in a continuous pattern of strong and weak pulsations.

Beta-adrenergic blocking agents   Medications used for cardiovascular and other medical conditions that "block" or limit sympathetic nervous system stimulation; commonly called "beta blockers." They act to slow the heart rate and decrease maximum heart rate.

Beta-adrenergic stimulating agents   A class of drugs that stimulate the sympathetic nervous system and are commonly prescribed for the treatment and management of respiratory disorders such as asthma and COPD. They increase heart rate, breathing rate, sweat rate, and other stress-related bodily functions. Ultimately results in a lowering of heart rate during stress, thus reducing the workload of the heart.

Beta blockers   *See* Beta-adrenergic blocking agents.

Bioelectrical impedance analysis (BIA) A body-composition assessment technique that measures the amount of impedance, or resistance, to electric current flow as it passes through the body. Impedance is greatest in fat tissue, while fat-free mass, which contains 70–75% water, allows the electrical current to pass much more easily.

Blanket license A certificate or document granting permission that varies and applies to a number of situations.

Blood pressure (BP) The pressure exerted by the blood on the walls of the arteries; measured in millimeters of mercury (mmHg) with a sphygmomanometer.

Body composition The makeup of the body in terms of the relative percentage of fat-free mass and body fat.

Body fat A component of the body, the primary role of which is to store energy for later use.

Body mass index (BMI) A relative measure of body height to body weight used to determine levels of weight, from underweight to extreme obesity.

Bone formation The processes resulting in the formation of normal, healthy bone tissue, including remodeling and resorption.

Bone mineral density (BMD) A measure of the amount of minerals (mainly calcium) contained in a certain volume of bone.

Bone resorption The breaking down of bone by osteoclasts.

Broad ligament The ligament that extends from the lateral side of the uterus to the pelvic wall; keeps the uterus centrally placed while providing stability within the pelvic cavity.

Broadcast Music, Inc. (BMI) One of two performing rights societies in the U.S. that represent music publishers in negotiating and collecting fees for the nondramatic performance of music.

Bulimia nervosa (BN) An eating disorder characterized by recurrent episodes of uncontrolled binge eating; recurrent inappropriate compensatory behavior such as self-induced vomiting, laxative misuse, diuretics, or enemas (purging type), or fasting and/or excessive exercise (non-purging type); episodes of binge eating and compensatory behaviors occur at least twice per week for three months; self-evaluation is heavily influenced by body shape and weight; and the episodes do not occur exclusively with episodes of anorexia.

Burnout A state of emotional exhaustion caused by stress from work or responsibilities.

Bursa A sac of fluid that is present in areas of the body that are potential sites of friction.

Bursitis Swelling and inflammation in the bursa that results from overuse.

Calcium channel blockers A class of blood pressure medications that relax and widen the blood vessels.

Capillaries The smallest blood vessels that supply blood to the tissues, and the site of all gas and nutrient exchange in the cardiovascular system. They connect the arterial and venous systems.

Carbohydrate The body's preferred energy source. Dietary sources include sugars (simple) and grains, rice, potatoes, and beans (complex). Carbohydrate is stored as glycogen in the muscles and liver and is transported in the blood as glucose.

Cardiac output   The amount of blood pumped by the heart per minute; usually expressed in liters of blood per minute.

Cardiac reserve   The work that the heart is able to perform beyond that required of it under ordinary circumstances.

Cardiomyopathy   Disease of the myocardium.

Cardiopulmonary resuscitation (CPR)   A procedure to support and maintain breathing and circulation for a person who has stopped breathing (respiratory arrest) and/or whose heart has stopped (cardiac arrest).

Cardiorespiratory fitness (CRF)   The ability to perform large muscle movement over a sustained period; related to the capacity of the heart-lung system to deliver oxygen for sustained energy production. Also called cardiorespiratory endurance or aerobic fitness.

Cardiorespiratory segment   The portion of a group exercise class designed for improving cardiorespiratory fitness and body composition and keeping the heart rate elevated for a sustained time period.

Cardiovascular disease (CVD)   A general term for any disease of the heart, blood vessels, or circulation.

Carpal tunnel syndrome   A pathology of the wrist and hand that occurs when the median nerve, which extends from the forearm into the hand, becomes compressed at the wrist.

Center of gravity (COG)   The point around which all weight is evenly distributed; also called center of mass.

Central nervous system (CNS)   The brain and spinal cord.

Cerebrovascular accident (CVA)   Damage to the brain, often resulting in a loss of function, from impaired blood supply to part of the brain; more commonly known as a stroke.

Cholesterol   A fatlike substance found in the blood and body tissues and in certain foods. Can accumulate in the arteries and lead to a narrowing of the vessels (atherosclerosis).

Chondromalacia   A gradual softening and degeneration of the articular cartilage, usually involving the back surface of the patella (kneecap). This condition may produce pain and swelling or a grinding sound or sensation when the knee is flexed and extended.

Choreography   The art of designing sequences of movements.

Chronic bronchitis   Characterized by increased mucus secretion and a productive cough lasting several months to several years.

Chronic disease   Any disease state that persists over an extended period of time.

Chronic obstructive pulmonary disease (COPD)   A condition, such as asthma, bronchitis, or emphysema, in which there is chronic obstruction of air flow.

Class count   A simple count of participants in a group fitness class, which is used as the basis for determining class value; often used in conjunction with "cost per head" and "penetration."

Claudication   Cramplike pains in the calves caused by poor circulation of blood to the leg muscles; frequently associated with peripheral vascular disease.

Cognitive domain   One of the three domains of learning; describes intellectual activities and involves the learning of knowledge.

Cognitive stage of learning   The first stage of learning a motor skill when performers make many gross errors and have extremely variable performances.

Collagen   The main constituent of connective tissue, such as ligaments, tendons, and muscles.

Combinations   Two or more movement patterns combined and repeated in sequence several times in a row.

Command style of teaching   A teaching style in which the instructor makes all decisions about rhythm, posture, and duration while participants follow the instructor's directions and movements.

Comparative negligence   A system used in legal defenses to distribute fault between an injured party and any defendant.

Compilations   Original, copyrightable sequences or a program of dance steps or exercise routines that may or may not be copyrightable individually.

Concentric   A type of isotonic muscle contraction in which the muscle develops tension and shortens when stimulated.

Contemplation   The stage of the transtheoretical model of behavioral change during which the individual is weighing the pros and cons of behavior change.

Contract   A binding agreement between two or more persons that is enforceable by law composed of an offer, acceptance, and consideration (or what each party puts forth to make the agreement worthwhile).

Contraindication   Any condition that renders some particular movement, activity, or treatment improper or undesirable.

Contributory negligence   A legal defense used in claims or suits when the plaintiff's negligence contributed to the act in dispute.

Contusion   A wound, such as a bruise, in which the skin is not broken; often resulting in broken blood vessels and discoloration.

Copyright   The exclusive right, for a certain number of years, to perform, make, and distribute copies and otherwise use an artistic, musical, or literary work.

Coronary artery disease (CAD)   *See* Coronary heart disease (CHD).

Coronary heart disease (CHD)   The major form of cardiovascular disease; results when the coronary arteries are narrowed or occluded, most commonly by atherosclerotic deposits of fibrous and fatty tissue; also called coronary artery disease (CAD).

Corticosteroid   One of two main hormones released by the adrenal cortex; plays a major role in maintaining blood glucose during prolonged exercise by promoting protein and triglyceride breakdown.

Cost per head   A number calculated by dividing an instructor's hourly salary by the number of participants in a one-hour class; used as one determinant of class value.

Crepitus   A crackling sound produced by air moving in the joint space; also called crepitation.

Cross phrase   A type of choreography in which a series of linked movements take more or less than the standard eight counts of music. Also called a split phrase.

Cueing   Visual or verbal techniques, using hand signals or minimal words, to inform participants of upcoming movements.

Cyanosis   A bluish discoloration, especially of the skin and mucous membranes, due to reduced hemoglobin in the blood.

Deep vein thrombosis   A blood clot in a major vein, usually in the legs and/or pelvis.

Defendant   The party in a lawsuit who is being sued or accused.

Dehydration   The process of losing body water; when severe can cause serious, life-threatening consequences.

Depression   1. The action of lowering a muscle or bone or movement in an inferior or downward direction. 2. A condition of general emotional dejection and withdrawal; sadness greater and more prolonged than that warranted by any objective reason.

Diabetes   A disease of carbohydrate metabolism in which an absolute or relative deficiency of insulin results in an inability to metabolize carbohydrates normally.

Diaphragmatic breathing   A deep, relaxing breathing technique that helps chronic obstructive pulmonary disorder (COPD) patients improve their breathing capacity.

Diastasis recti   A separation of the recti abdominal muscles along the midline of the body.

Diastolic blood pressure (DBP)   The pressure in the arteries during the relaxation phase (diastole) of the cardiac cycle; indicative of total peripheral resistance.

Disability insurance   Insurance that provides income protection in the event of an injury to the instructor.

Diuretic   Medication that produces an increase in urine volume and sodium excretion.

Dorsiflexion   Movement of the foot up toward the shin.

Double-time   A means of adding challenge to a choreographed workout routine that involves the performance of movement twice as fast as in an earlier section.

Dowager's hump   An exaggerated outward curve of the thoracic spine, often associated with vertebral fractures and osteoporosis.

Downbeat   The regular strong pulsation in music occurring in a continuous pattern at an even rhythm.

Dynamic balance   The act of maintaining postural control while moving.

Dyspnea   Shortness of breath; a subjective difficulty or distress in breathing.

Dyspnea scale   A subjective four-point scale that reflects an individual's perception of the difficulty of breathing during physical activity, with 1 reflecting mild difficulty that is noticeable to the exerciser but not an observer, and 4 reflecting severe difficulty that forces the individual to stop exercising.

Eating disorders   Disturbed eating behaviors that jeopardize a person's physical or psychological health.

Eccentric   A type of isotonic muscle contraction in which the muscle lengthens against a resistance when it is stimulated; sometimes called "negative work" or "negative reps."

Ecchymosis   The escape of blood into the tissues from ruptured blood vessels marked by a black-and-blue or purple discolored area.

Edema   Swelling resulting from an excessive accumulation of fluid in the tissues of the body.

Effusion   The escape of a fluid from anatomical vessels by rupture or exudation.

Electrocardiogram (ECG) A recording of the electrical activity of the heart.

Emergency medical services (EMS) A local system for obtaining emergency assistance from the police, fire department, or ambulance. In the United States, most cities have a 911 telephone number that will automatically set the EMS system in motion.

Empathy Understanding what another person is experiencing from his or her perspective.

Emphysema An obstructive pulmonary disease characterized by the gradual destruction of lung alveoli and the surrounding connective tissue, in addition to airway inflammation, leading to reduced ability to effectively inhale and exhale.

Employee A person who works for another person in exchange for financial compensation. An employee complies with the instructions and directions of his or her employer and reports to them on a regular basis.

Endorphin Natural opiate produced in the brain that functions to reduce pain and improve mood.

Estrogen Generic term for estrus-producing steroid compounds produced primarily in the ovaries; the female sex hormones.

Exercise dependence A state in which physical activity is extreme in frequency and duration, relatively resistant to change, and is associated with an irresistible impulse to continue exercise despite injury, illness, or fatigue.

Exercise evaluation A process of evaluating an exercise based on its effectiveness and safety.

Exercise-induced asthma (EIA) Transient and reversible airway narrowing triggered by vigorous exercise; also called exercise-induced bronchospasm (EIB).

Extension The act of straightening or extending a joint, usually applied to the muscular movement of a limb.

Extrinsic motivation Motivation that comes from external (outside of the self) rewards, such as material or social rewards.

Fartlek training A form of training during which the exerciser randomly changes the aerobic intensity based on how he or she is feeling. Also called speed play.

Fascia Strong connective tissues that perform a number of functions, including developing and isolating the muscles of the body and providing structural support and protection. Plural = fasciae.

Fasciitis An inflammation of the fascia.

Feedback An internal response within a learner; during information processing, it is the correctness or incorrectness of a response that is stored in memory to be used for future reference. Also, verbal or nonverbal information about current behavior that can be used to improve future performance.

Fetus The developed embryo and growing human in the uterus, from usually three months after conception to birth.

First ventilatory threshold (VT1) Intensity of aerobic exercise at which ventilation starts to increase in a non-linear fashion in response to an accumulation of metabolic by-products in the blood.

Flexibility The ability to move joints through their normal full ranges of motion.

Flexion The act of moving a joint so that the two bones forming it are brought closer together.

Fracture Any break in the continuity of a bone, ranging from a simple crack to a severe shatter of the bone with multiple fracture fragments.

Freestyle choreography   A way of designing the cardiovascular segment of a class that uses movements randomly chosen by the instructor.

Frontal plane   A longitudinal section that runs at a right angle to the sagittal plane, dividing the body into anterior and posterior portions.

Functional capacity   The maximum physical performance represented by maximal oxygen consumption.

General liability insurance   Insurance for bodily injury or property damage resulting from general negligence such as wet flooring, an icy sidewalk, or poorly maintained equipment.

Gestational diabetes   An inability to maintain normal glucose, or any degree of glucose intolerance, during pregnancy, despite being treated with either diet or insulin.

Glucometer   A device used by diabetics to check blood sugar.

Glucose   A simple sugar; the form in which all carbohydrates are used as the body's principal energy source.

Golfer's elbow   Pain on the inner side of the elbow at the attachment of the forearm muscles; medial epicondylitis.

Golgi tendon organ (GTO)   A sensory organ within a tendon that, when stimulated, causes an inhibition of the entire muscle group to protect against too much force.

Graded exercise test   A test that evaluates an individual's physiological response to exercise, the intensity of which is increased in stages.

Grand mal seizure   A major motor seizure characterized by violent and uncontrollable muscle contractions.

Grapevine   A common dance move used in group fitness choreography wherein the exerciser steps to the side, then crosses the other foot behind the support foot, and then performs another side step. The sequence is then continued or repeated on the other side.

Greater trochanteric bursitis   An inflammation of the bursa sac that lies over the greater trochanter of the femur. Often due to acute trauma, repetitive stress, muscle imbalance, or muscle tightness.

Half-time   A means of reducing the challenge of a portion of choreography that involves performing a movement at half of the usual speed; often used when teaching new movements.

Health Insurance Portability and Accountability Act (HIPAA)   Enacted by the U.S. Congress in 1996, HIPAA requires the U.S. Department of Health and Human Services (HHS) to establish national standards for electronic health care information to facilitate efficient and secure exchange of private health data. The Standards for Privacy of Individually Identifiable Health Information ("Privacy Rule"), issued by the HHS, addresses the use and disclosure of individuals' health information—called "protected health information"—by providing federal protections and giving patients an array of rights with respect to personal health information while permitting the disclosure of information needed for patient care and other important purposes.

Health screening   A vital process that identifies individuals at high risk for exercise-induced heart problems that need to be referred to appropriate medical care as needed.

Heart rate (HR)   The number of heart beats per minute.

Heart-rate reserve (HRR)   The reserve capacity of the heart; the difference between maximal heart rate and resting heart rate. It reflects the heart's ability to increase the rate of beating and cardiac output above a resting level to maximal intensity.

Heimlich maneuver   First aid for choking, involving the application of sudden, upward pressure on the upper abdomen to force a foreign object from the windpipe.

Hematocrit   A measure of the number of red cells found in the blood, stated as a percentage of the total blood volume. The normal range is 43–49% in men and 37–43% in women.

Hematoma   A large bruise or collection of blood under the skin, producing discoloration and swelling in the area; usually caused by trauma.

Hemorrhagic stroke   Disruption of blood flow to the brain caused by the presence of a blood clot or hematoma.

Hepatitis   Inflammation of the liver, often due to viral infection.

Hepatitis B   A potentially life-threatening bloodborne disease of the liver, which is transmitted primarily by sexual activity or exposure to blood.

High-density lipoprotein (HDL)   A lipoprotein that carries excess cholesterol from the arteries to the liver.

Hormones   A chemical substance produced and released by an endocrine gland and transported through the blood to a target organ.

Human immunodeficiency virus (HIV)   A retrovirus (family Retroviridae, subfamily Lentvirinae) that is about 100 nm in diameter and is the etiologic agent of AIDS.

Hydrostatic weighing   Weighing a person fully submerged in water. The difference between the person's mass in air and in water is used to calculate body density, which can be used to estimate the proportion of fat in the body.

Hyperextension   Extension of an articulation beyond anatomical position.

Hyperflexion   Flexion of an articulation beyond anatomical position.

Hyperglycemia   An abnormally high content of glucose (sugar) in the blood (above 100 mg/dL).

Hypertension   High blood pressure, or the elevation of resting blood pressure above 140/90 mmHg.

Hyperthermia   Abnormally high body temperature.

Hypoglycemia   A deficiency of glucose in the blood commonly caused by too much insulin, too little glucose, or too much exercise. Most commonly found in the insulin-dependent diabetic and characterized by symptoms such as fatigue, dizziness, confusion, headache, nausea, or anxiety.

Hyponatremia   Abnormally low levels of sodium ions circulating in the blood; severe hyponatremia can lead to brain swelling and death.

Hypoperfusion   A diminished blood supply to the tissues.

Hypotension   Low blood pressure.

Hypoxia A condition in which there is an inadequate supply of oxygen to tissues.

Iliotibial (IT) band A band of connective tissue that extends from the iliac crest to the knee and links the gluteus maximus to the tibia.

Iliotibial band syndrome (ITBS) A repetitive overuse condition that occurs when the distal portion of the iliotibial band rubs against the lateral femoral epicondyle.

Incision A cut in the skin, frequently from a sharp object.

Inclusion style of teaching A teaching style that enables multiple levels of performance to be taught within the same activity.

Incontinence The loss of sphincter control that results in the inability to retain urine, semen, or feces.

Independent contractor A person who conducts business on his or her own on a contract basis and is not an employee of an organization.

Individual medical insurance Insurance that provides hospitalization and major medical coverage.

Informed consent A written statement signed by a participant prior to testing that informs him or her of testing purposes, processes, and all potential risks and discomforts.

Infrapatellar tendinitis Inflammation of the patellar tendon at the insertion into the proximal tibia.

Inguinal ligament The ligament that extends from the anterior, superior iliac spine to the pubic tubercle.

Inspiration The drawing of air into the lungs; inhalation.

Insulin A hormone released from the pancreas that allows cells to take up glucose.

Insulin reaction The result of hypoglycemia, not enough sugar in the blood, in which diabetics experience symptoms such as anxiety, confusion, headache, and irritability; if unchecked may lead to insulin shock.

Insulin resistance An inability of muscle tissue to effectively use insulin, where the action of insulin is "resisted" by insulin-sensitive tissues.

Insulin shock Severe hypoglycemia associated with the presence of excessive insulin in the body; if left untreated, can result in convulsions and coma.

Integrated regulation A psychological characteristic that describes the act of achieving goals for reasons extrinsic to the self, rather than the inherent enjoyment or interest in the task. People who have internalized motivation for exercise benefits are said to have integrated regulation.

Interval training Short, high-intensity exercise periods alternated with periods of rest (e.g., 100-yard run, one-minute rest, repeated eight times).

Intrinsic motivation Motivation that comes from internal states, such as enjoyment or personal satisfaction.

Introjection A form of extrinsic motivation that involves an individual being physically active because of an external factor suggested by someone else, and not accepted by him- or herself; often leads to feelings of guilt, tension, and being controlled.

Ischemic stroke A sudden disruption of cerebral circulation in which blood supply to the brain is either interrupted or diminished.

Isometric A type of muscular contraction in which the muscle is stimulated to generate tension but little or no joint movement occurs.

Kegel exercise Controlled isometric contraction and relaxation of the muscles surrounding the vagina to strengthen and gain control of the pelvic floor muscles.

Kinesthetic awareness (kinethesis) The perception of body position and movement in space.

Knowledge of results The motivational impact of feedback provided to a person learning a new task or behavior indicating the outcomes of performance.

Kyphosis A type of curve of the spine; concave anteriorly and convex posteriorly.

Kyphotic *See* Kyphosis.

Laceration A jagged, irregular cut or tear in the soft tissues, usually caused by a blow. Because of extensive tissue destruction, there is a great potential for contamination and infection.

Lactate threshold (LT) The point during exercise of increasing intensity at which blood lactate begins to accumulate above resting levels, where lactate clearance is no longer able to keep up with lactate production.

Lactic acid A metabolic by-product of anaerobic glycolysis; when it accumulates it increases blood pH, which slows down enzyme activity and ultimately causes fatigue.

Lateral epicondylitis An injury resulting from the repetitive tension overloading of the wrist and finger extensors that originate at the lateral epicondyle; often referred to as tennis elbow.

Lateral flexion Bending of the vertebral column to the side.

Liability Legal responsibility.

Ligament A strong, fibrous tissue that connects one bone to another.

Linear progression Consists of one movement that transitions into another without cycling sequences.

Locus of control The degree to which people attribute outcomes to internal factors, such as effort and ability, as opposed to external factors, such as luck or the actions of others. People who tend to attribute events and outcomes to internal factors are said to have an internal locus of control, while those who generally attribute outcomes to external factors are said to have an external locus of control.

Lordosis Excessive anterior curvature of the spine that typically occurs at the low back (may also occur at the neck).

Lordotic *See* Lordosis.

Low-back pain (LBP) A general term to describe a multitude of back conditions, including muscular and ligament strains, sprains, and injuries. The cause of LBP is often elusive; most LBP is probably caused by muscle weakness and imbalance.

Low-density lipoprotein (LDL) A lipoprotein that transports cholesterol and triglycerides from the liver and small intestine to cells and tissues; high levels may cause atherosclerosis.

Maintenance The stage of the transtheoretical model of behavioral change during which the individual is incorporating the new behavior into his or her lifestyle.

Maximal oxygen consumption ($\dot{V}O_2max$) The maximum capacity for the body to take in, transport, and use oxygen during exercise; a common indicator of physical fitness.

Maximal oxygen uptake   *See* Maximal oxygen consumption ($\dot{V}O_2$max).

Maximum heart rate (MHR)   The highest heart rate a person can attain. Sometimes abbreviated as HRmax.

Measure   One group of beats in a musical composition marked by the regular occurrence of the heavy accent.

Medial epicondylitis   An injury that results from an overload of the wrist flexors and forearm pronators; often referred to as golfer's elbow.

Meninges   The three-layer system of membranes that envelops the brain and spinal cord.

Metabolic equivalents (METs)   A simplified system for classifying physical activities where 1 MET is equal to the resting oxygen consumption, which is approximately 3.5 milliliters of oxygen per kilogram of body weight per minute (3.5 mL/kg/min).

Meter   The organization of beats into musical patterns or measures.

Minute ventilation ($\dot{V}_E$)   A measure of the amount of air that passes through the lungs in one minute; calculated as the tidal volume multiplied by the ventilatory rate.

Mirroring   In group fitness classes, the practice of an instructor facing the class while teaching movements so that the participants can make direct eye contact with the instructor and see a "mirror image," rather than looking at the instructor's back.

Motivation   The psychological drive that gives purpose and direction to behavior.

Motor domain   One of the three domains of learning; involves the learning of motor skills.

Motor skill   The degree to which movements using agility, balance, and coordination are executed.

Motor unit   A motor nerve and all of the muscle fibers it stimulates.

Multiple sclerosis (M.S.)   A common neuromuscular disorder involving the progressive degeneration of muscle function, including increased muscle spasticity.

Muscle spindle   The sensory organ within a muscle that is sensitive to stretch and thus protects the muscle against too much stretch.

Muscular endurance   The ability of a muscle or muscle group to exert force against a resistance over a sustained period of time.

Muscular strength   The maximal force a muscle or muscle group can exert during contraction.

Musical phrase   A short musical passage; used as a means of choreographing movement to a piece of music.

Myocardial infarction (MI)   An episode in which some of the heart's blood supply is severely cut off or restricted, causing the heart muscle to suffer and die from lack of oxygen. Commonly known as a heart attack.

Myotatic stretch reflex   Muscular reflex created by excessive muscle spindle stimulation to prevent potential tissue damage.

National Commission of Certifying Agencies (NCCA)   An organization created to help ensure the health, welfare, and safety of the public through the accreditation of a variety of certification programs/organizations that assess professional competence; part of the Institute for Credentialing Excellence (ICE).

Negligence Failure of a person to perform as a reasonable and prudent professional would perform under similar circumstances.

Neuropathy Any disease affecting a peripheral nerve. It may manifest as loss of nerve function, burning pain, or numbness and tingling.

Nonsteroidal anti-inflammatory drug (NSAID) A drug with analgesic, antipyretic, and anti-inflammatory effects. The term "nonsteroidal" is used to distinguish these drugs from steroids, which have similar actions.

Obesity An excessive accumulation of body fat. Usually defined as more than 20% above ideal weight, or over 25% body fat for men and over 32% body fat for women; also can be defined as a body mass index of >30 kg/m^2 or a waist girth of $\geq$40 inches (102 cm) in men and $\geq$35 inches (89 cm) in women.

Occupational therapist A rehabilitation expert specializing in treatments that help people who suffer from mentally, physically, developmentally, or emotionally disabling conditions to develop, recover, or maintain daily living and work skills that include improving basic motor functions and reasoning abilities.

One-repetition maximum (1 RM) The amount of resistance that can be moved through the range of motion one time before the muscle is temporarily fatigued.

Onset of blood lactate accumulation (OBLA) The point during high-intensity exercise at which the production of lactic acid exceeds the body's capacity to eliminate it; after this point, oxygen is insufficient at meeting the body's demands for energy.

Osteoarthritis A degenerative disease involving a wearing away of joint cartilage.

This degenerative joint disease occurs chiefly in older persons.

Osteoporosis A disorder, primarily affecting postmenopausal women, in which bone density decreases and susceptibility to fractures increases.

Overload The principle stating that a physiological system subjected to above-normal stress will respond by increasing in strength or function accordingly.

Overweight A term to describe an excessive amount of weight for a given height, using height-to-weight ratios.

Parasthesia An abnormal sensation such as numbness, prickling, or tingling.

Part-to-whole teaching strategy A teaching strategy involving breaking a skill down into its component parts and practicing each skill in its simplest form before placing several skills in a sequence.

Patellofemoral pain syndrome (PFPS) A degenerative condition of the posterior surface of the patella, which may result from acute injury to the patella or from chronic friction between the patella and the groove in the femur through which it passes during motion of the knee.

Pathogen Any virus, microorganism, or other substance capable of causing disease.

Peak flow meter A device used to measure the flow of air through the lungs; useful for chronic obstructive pulmonary disorder (COPD) patients to aid in activity selection.

Pelvic floor The muscles and tissues that act as a support or reinforcement to the lower border of the pelvis.

Penetration A number, calculated by dividing the number of participants in a class by the number of people who access the facility during the duration of the class, that is used as one determinant of class value.

Performance standard   A level of expectation concerning the performance of a task achieved by an individual, group, or organization according to pre-established requirements and/or specifications.

Performing rights society   An organization to which the copyright or publisher assigns the nondramatic performing rights in a musical composition.

Perfusion   The passage of fluid through a tissue, such as the transport of blood through vessels from the heart to internal organs and other tissues.

Perineal   The region of the body between the anus and the genital organs, including the underlying structures.

Pes planus   Flat feet.

Physical Activity Readiness Question-naire (PAR-Q)   A brief, self-administered medical questionnaire recognized as a safe pre-exercise screening measure for low-to-moderate (but not vigorous) exercise training.

Physical therapist   A rehabilitation expert specializing in treatments that help restore function, improve mobility, relieve pain, and prevent or limit permanent physical disabilities in patients of all ages suffering from medical problems, injuries, diseases, disabilities, or other health-related conditions.

Pilates   A method of mind-body conditioning that combines stretching and strengthening exercises; developed by Joseph Pilates in the 1920s.

Placenta   The vascular organ in mammals that unites the fetus to the maternal uterus and mediates its metabolic exchanges.

Plaintiff   A party who brings a suit against another party in a court of law.

Plantar fasciitis   Inflammation of the plantar fascia, a broad band of connective tissue running along the sole of the foot; caused by stretching or tearing the tissue, usually near the attachment at the heel.

Plantarflexion   Distal movement of the plantar surface of the foot; opposite of dorsiflexion.

Plyometrics   High-intensity movements, such as jumping, involving high-force loading of body weight during the landing phase of the movement.

Postictal state   The altered state of consciousness that a person enters after experiencing an epileptic seizure.

Postpartum   The period of time after childbirth.

Posture   The arrangement of the body and its limbs.

Practice style of teaching   A teaching style that provides opportunities for individualization and includes practice time and individualized instructor feedback.

Pre-class preparation   Methods or principles for successful group exercise instruction, including professional attributes such as knowing participants' health histories, being available to orient new participants before class, and having music/equipment cued and ready to go before class begins.

Precontemplation   The stage of the transtheoretical model of behavioral change during which the individual is not yet thinking about changing.

Preparation   The stage of the transtheoretical model of behavioral change during which the individual is getting ready to make a change.

Pressor response   A disproportionate rise in heart rate during resistance training resulting from autonomic nervous system reflex activity.

Professional liability insurance   Insurance to protect an instructor against professional negligence or failure to perform as a competent and prudent professional would under similar circumstances.

Progesterone   Female sex hormone secreted by the ovaries that affects many aspects of female physiology, including menstrual cycles and pregnancy.

Prognosis   Assessment of progress toward recovery from an accident or condition.

Progression   The systematic process of applying overload. For example, in resistance training, more resistance is added to progress the training stimulus.

Pronation   Internal rotation of the forearm causing the radius to cross diagonally over the ulna and the palm to face posteriorly.

Proprioception   Sensation and awareness of body position and movements.

Proprioceptive   *See* Proprioception.

Protein   A compound composed of a combination 20 amino acids that is the major structural component of all body tissue.

Public performance   Playing a recording of a copyrighted musical composition at a place where a substantial number of persons outside of a normal circle of a family and its social acquaintances are gathered.

Publisher   The entity to which the owner of a copyrighted artistic, musical, or literary work assigns such copyright for licensing and income-collection purposes.

Pulse rate   The wave of pressure in the arteries that occurs each time the heart beats.

Puncture   A piercing wound from a sharp object that makes a small hole in the skin.

Qigong   A wide variety of traditional cultivation practices that involve methods of accumulating, circulating, and working with *qi,* breathing or energy within the body. Qigong is practiced for health maintenance purposes, as a therapeutic intervention, as a medical profession, as a spiritual path, and/or as a component of Chinese martial arts.

Range of motion (ROM)   The number of degrees through which an articulation will allow one of its segments to move.

Rapport   A relationship marked by mutual understanding and trust.

Rate coding   The frequency of impulses sent to a muscle. Increased force can be generated through an increase in either the number of muscle fibers recruited or the rate at which the impulses are sent.

Ratings of perceived exertion (RPE)   A scale, originally developed by noted Swedish psychologist Gunnar Borg, that provides a standard means for evaluating a participant's perception of exercise effort. The original scale ranged from 6 to 20; a revised category ratio scale ranges from 0 to 10.

Reciprocal style of teaching   Teaching style that involves using an observer or partner to provide feedback to the performer.

Recovery heart rate   The number of heartbeats per minute following the cessation of vigorous physical activity. As cardiorespiratory fitness improves, the heart rate returns to resting levels more quickly.

Registered dietitian (R.D.) A food and nutrition expert that has met the following criteria: completed a minimum of a bachelor's degree at a U.S. accredited university, or other college coursework approved by the Commission on Accreditation for Dietetics Education (CADE); completed a CADE-accredited supervised practice program; passed a national examination; and completed continuing education requirements to maintain registration.

Regression Offering participants ways or modifications to decrease the intensity or complexity of an exercise or movement.

Relative contraindication A condition that makes a particular treatment or procedure somewhat inadvisable but does not completely rule it out.

Relaxin A hormone of pregnancy that relaxes the pelvic ligaments and other connective tissue in the body.

Repeating choreography A structured method of choreographing movement that creates consistency of delivery; two forms are "scripted" and "planned."

Repetition reduction teaching strategy Teaching strategy involving reducing the number of repetitions that make up a movement sequence.

Resting heart rate (RHR) The number of heartbeats per minute when the body is at complete rest; usually counted first thing in the morning before any physical activity takes place.

Rheumatoid arthritis (RA) An autoimmune disease that causes inflammation of connective tissues and joints.

RICE An immediate treatment for injury: rest or restricted activity, ice, compression, and elevation.

Risk management Minimizing the risks of potential legal liability.

Rotation Movement in the transverse plane about a longitudinal axis; can be "internal" or "external."

Round ligament Ligament found on the side of the uterus near the fallopian tube insertion to help the broad ligament keep the uterus in place.

Sagittal plane The longitudinal plane that divides the body into right and left portions.

Scapular plane A shoulder angle about halfway between the sagittal plane and the frontal plane, which represents approximately 30–45 degrees of shoulder flexion. This angle is in line with the orientation of the scapula as it rests naturally against the ribcage and helps protect the shoulder joint during overhead movements.

Sciatica Pain radiating down the leg caused by compression of the sciatic nerve; frequently the result of lumbar disc herniation.

Scope of practice The range and limit of responsibilities normally associated with a specific job or profession.

Second ventilatory threshold (VT2) A metabolic marker that represents the point at which high-intensity exercise can no longer be sustained due to an accumulation of lactate.

Secondary assessment After immediate life- or limb-threatening injuries/illnesses have been identified, this more thorough evaluation is performed to identify more subtle, yet still important, injuries.

Sedentary Doing or requiring much sitting; minimal activity.

Self-check style of teaching A teaching style that relies on individual performers to provide their own feedback.

Self-efficacy One's perception of his or her ability to change or to perform specific behaviors (e.g., exercise).

Shear force Any force that causes slippage between a pair of contiguous joints or tissues in a direction that parallels the plane in which they contact.

Shin splints A general term for any pain or discomfort on the front or side of the lower leg in the region of the shin bone (tibia).

Simple-to-complex teaching strategy Advanced teaching strategy that treats a sequence of movement patterns as a whole, teaching small changes (adding small amounts of complexity) to progressively challenge the exercise participant.

Sinoatrial node (SA node) A group of specialized myocardial cells, located in the wall of the right atrium, that control the heart's rate of contraction; the "pacemaker" of the heart.

Slow-to-fast teaching strategy Teaching strategy used to allow participants to learn complex movement at a slower pace, emphasizing proper placement or configuration of a movement pattern (e.g., teaching a movement at half-tempo).

SMART goals A properly designed goal; SMART stands for specific, measurable, attainable, relevant, and time-bound.

Social support The perceived comfort, caring, esteem, or help an individual receives from other people.

Society of European Stage Authors and Composers (SESAC) A performing rights organization designed to represent songwriters and publishers and their right to be compensated for having their music performed in public.

Spasticity Increased tone or resistance of muscle causing stiff, awkward movements.

Spatial teaching strategy Teaching strategy used when introducing participants to a new body position, involving describing the position of different portions of the body.

Specificity Exercise training principle explaining that specific exercise demands made on the body produce specific responses by the body; also called exercise specificity.

Sphincter A circular muscle, the function of which is constricting an opening.

Split phrase *See* Cross phrase.

Sprain A traumatic joint twist that results in stretching or tearing of the stabilizing connective tissues; mainly involves ligaments or joint capsules, and causes discoloration, swelling, and pain.

Stability Characteristic of the body's joints or posture that represents resistance to change of position.

Stages-of-change model A lifestyle-modification model that suggests that people go through distinct, predictable stages when making lifestyle changes: precontemplation, contemplation, preparation, action, and maintenance. The process is not always linear.

Standard of care Appropriateness of an exercise professional's actions in light of current professional standards and based on the age, condition, and knowledge of the participant.

Static balance The ability to maintain the body's center of mass (COM) within its base of support (BOS).

Statute of limitations A formal regulation limiting the period within which a specific legal action may be taken.

Steady state Constant submaximal exercise below the lactate threshold where the oxygen consumption is meeting the energy requirements of the activity.

Step test (submaximal) A test for cardiovascular fitness that requires the subject to step up and down from a bench at a prescribed rate for a given period.

Strain A stretch, tear, or rip in the muscle or adjacent tissue such as the fascia or tendon.

Stress fracture An incomplete fracture caused by excessive stress (overuse) to a bone. Most common in the foot (metatarsal bones) and lower leg (tibia).

Stretch reflex An involuntary motor response that, when stimulated, causes a suddenly stretched muscle to respond with a corresponding contraction.

Stroke A sudden and often severe attack due to blockage of an artery into the brain.

Stroke volume The amount of blood pumped from the left ventricle of the heart with each beat.

Sudden cardiac death Immediate death resulting from a sudden change in the rhythm of the heart usually caused by heart rhythms that are too fast. This condition is also called cardiac arrest.

Sun Salutation A 12-step yoga sequence that coordinates breath with movement and aims to improve posture by stretching the spine and strengthening the muscle groups that surround it.

Supination External rotation of the forearm (radioulnar joint) that causes the palm to face anteriorly.

Supine Lying face up (on the back).

Supine hypotension An abnormal reduction in blood pressure related to position (lying on the back).

Symphysis pubis The fibrocartilaginous joint between the pelvic bones in the midline of the body.

Symphysitis Irritation of the pubic symphysis caused by increased motion at the joint.

Syncopation A rhythmic device that temporarily shifts the normal pattern of stressed to unstressed beats or parts of beats.

Syncope A transient state of unconsciousness during which a person collapses to the floor as a result of lack of oxygen to the brain; commonly known as fainting.

Systemic lupus erythematosus (SLE) An autoimmune disease that affects connective tissues and results in painful joints and arthritis.

Systolic blood pressure (SBP) The pressure exerted by the blood on the vessel walls during ventricular contraction.

Tachycardia Elevated heart rate over 100 beats per minute.

Tai chi A Chinese system of slow meditative physical exercise designed for relaxation, balance, and health.

Talk test A method for measuring exercise intensity using observation of respiration effort and the ability to talk while exercising.

Target heart rate (THR) Number of heartbeats per minute that indicate appropriate exercise intensity levels for each individual; also called training heart rate.

Tarsal tunnel syndrome A syndrome characterized by pain and numbness in the sole of the foot caused by entrapment of the posterior tibial nerve.

Telemetry The process by which measured quantities from a remote site are transmitted to a data collection point for recording and processing, such as what occurs during an electrocardiogram.

Tempo The rate of speed of music, usually expressed in beats per minute.

Tendinitis Inflammation of a tendon.

Tendon A band of fibrous tissue forming the termination of a muscle and attaching the muscle to a bone.

Tennis elbow Pain on the outside of the elbow at the attachment of the forearm muscles; lateral epicondylitis.

Teratogenic Nongenetic factors that can cause birth defects in the fetus.

Testosterone In males, the steroid hormone produced in the testes; involved in growth and development of reproductive tissues, sperm, and secondary male sex characteristics.

Thermoregulation Regulation of the body's temperature.

Tibial stress syndrome *See* Shin splints.

Tidal volume The volume of air inspired per breath.

Tinnitus The perception of noise, such as a ringing or beating sound, which has no external source.

Tonic clonic seizure The classic type of epileptic seizure consisting of two phases: the tonic phase, in which the body becomes rigid, and the clonic phase, in which there is uncontrolled jerking. Also known as a grand mal seizure.

Transtheoretical model of behavioral change (TTM) A theory of behavior that examines one's readiness to change and identifies five stages: precontemplation, contemplation, preparation, action, and maintenance. Also called the stages-of-change model.

Transverse plane Anatomical term for the imaginary line that divides the body, or any of its parts, into upper (superior) and lower (inferior) parts. Also called the horizontal plane.

Trendelenburg gait A drop of the pelvis on the side opposite the stance leg, indicating weakness of the hip abductors and gluteus medius and minimus on the side of the stance leg.

Type 1 diabetes Form of diabetes caused by the destruction of the insulin-producing beta cells in the pancreas, which leads to little or no insulin secretion; generally develops in childhood and requires regular insulin injections; formerly known as insulin-dependent diabetes mellitus (IDDM) and childhood-onset diabetes.

Type 2 diabetes Most common form of diabetes; typically develops in adulthood and is characterized by a reduced sensitivity of the insulin target cells to available insulin; usually associated with obesity; formerly known as non-insulin-dependent diabetes mellitus (NIDDM) and adult-onset diabetes.

Umbrella liability policy Insurance that provides additional coverage beyond other insurance such as professional liability, home, automobile, etc.

Upbeat The deemphasized beat in a piece of music.

Valgus   Characterized by an abnormal outward turning of a bone, especially of the hip, knee, or foot.

Valsalva maneuver   A strong exhaling effort against a closed glottis, which builds pressure in the chest cavity that interferes with the return of the blood to the heart; may deprive the brain of blood and cause light-headedness or fainting.

Vasodilator   Any drug that causes dilation of blood vessels; typically prescribed for the treatment of hypertension.

Venous return   Return to the heart of the circulatory fluids by way of the veins.

Ventilatory threshold   Point of transition between predominately aerobic energy production to anaerobic energy production; involves recruitment of fast-twitch muscle fibers and identified via gas exchange during exercise testing.

Ventricular fibrillation (VF)   An irregular heartbeat characterized by uncoordinated contractions of the ventricle.

$\dot{V}O_2$max   *See* Maximal oxygen consumption ($\dot{V}O_2$max).

$\dot{V}O_2$reserve ($\dot{V}O_2$R)   The difference between $\dot{V}O_2$max and $\dot{V}O_2$ at rest; used for programming aerobic exercise intensity.

Waiver   Voluntary abandonment of a right to file suit; not always legally binding.

Yoga   Indian word for "union." A combination of breathing exercises, physical postures, and meditation that has been practiced for more than 5,000 years.

INDEX

as cue, 110b

giving cues on, 75–76

Allied healthcare continuum, 4–5, 5f

Alpha blockers, 152

American College of Sports Medicine (ACSM)

AHA/ACSM Health/Fitness Facility
Preparticipation Screening
Questionnaire of, 22, 24f

exercise programming guidelines of, 56–57

health/fitness facility standards and
guidelines of, 13–14

American Congress of Obstetricians and
Gynecologists (ACOG) guidelines, on
exercise in pregnancy, 176–177, 199

Americans with Disabilities Act, 311–312,
321–322

Anaerobic threshold, 40, 40f

Ananda yoga, 354

Anatomical cue, 110b

Ankle joint strength training, in pregnancy, 207

Ankle sprain, lateral, 230–231, 231f

Ankle weights, 77b

Anorexia nervosa, 142–143

Anterior cruciate ligament (ACL)

anatomy of, 233, 233f

reconstruction of, 234

tear of, 220, 233–234, 233f

Anthropometric assessments, 47

Anthropometry, 47

Antidepressants, 341t

Antihistamines, 341t

Antihypertensives, 341t

Antipsychotics, 341t

Apnea, 260–261

Aquatic exercise

in pregnancy, 200–201

specialty of, 350–352

thermoregulation in, 64

Arachnoid mater, 266

Arterial-mixed venous oxygen difference, in
pregnancy, 187

Arthritis, 161–162

exercise with, 162, 163t

in obese, 154

Ashtanga yoga, 354

Assessment, anthropometric, 47

Assessment, emergency, 252–254

primary, 252–253, 253f

secondary, 253–254

Assessment, observational, 43–45

of exercise tolerance and fatigue, 45

of form and technique, 44–45

of posture and movement, 43–44, 44f

Assessment, physical-fitness, 46–50

ACE Code of Ethics on, 319

administration of, 46–47

challenges in, 46

health-related components of, 47–50

body composition, 47–49, 48f, 48t, 49t

cardiorespiratory endurance, 49

flexibility, 50

muscular strength and endurance,
49–50

neuromuscular efficiency, 50

short-term programs and, 46

sporadic attendance on, 46

value of, 46

Associative stage of learning, 87

Assumption of risk, 307

Disability insurance, 304

Disciplinary procedures, 9–10

Discomforts, acknowledging exercise, 137

Disease risk stratification, 25–28, 25t, 27f

Dispatch centers, 9-1-1, 255

Disruptive individuals, 139

Distributive shock, 270

Diuretics, 151, 341t

Dowager's hump, 164

Downbeat, 101

DRILL, 109

Dropout rates, 120. *See also* Adherence;
    Motivation

Duration, recommendations for, 57–58, 57t

Dynamic movement, in warm-up, 65–66

Dyspnea, 41, 69

    with bronchitis and emphysema, 160

    emergency procedures for, 260–261

Dyspnea scale, 35, 41, 260

E

Eating disorders, 142–143

Ecchymosis, 263

Edema, in pregnancy, 201

Education, 277–278

    for ACE GFI certification, 8

    continuing, 10, 15–17

        ACE Code of Ethics on, 322

        specialty certificates from, 16

    for group fitness specialization, 277

    for non–health club careers, 278

    for personal training and small-group
        training, 277–278

Efficiency, neuromuscular, 50

Effleurage massage, 195

Elbow joint strength training, in pregnancy, 203

Elderly

    exercise for, 169–170

    injury prevention in, 228

Electrocardiogram (ECG), 37b, 298

Electronic heart-rate monitors, 38b

Emergency action plan, 252

Emergency assessment, 252–254

    primary, 252–253, 253f

    secondary, 253–254

Emergency medical services (EMS), calling
    and waiting for, 252

Emergency procedures, 249–271

    assessment in, 252–254, 253f

    bloodborne pathogen precautions, 270–
        271

    common medical emergencies and injuries

        asthma attack, 258, 259t

        choking, 261

        cold-related illness, 260

        dyspnea, 260–261

        fractures, 264–266, 266f

        general points on, 258

        head injuries, 266–267

        heat-related illness, 260

        insulin reaction (hypoglycemia), 258,
            259t

        low-back injuries, 268f, 269–270

        lumbar spine injuries, 268f, 269

        neck injuries, 268–269, 269f

        seizures, 262

        shock, 270

        soft-tissue injuries, 263–264, 263f

N

T